PRAISE FOR *EDWARD SAID: EMANCIPA*

M000217831

"The very distinguished and diverse group of scholars
explore and illuminate the intellectual and political dimensions, and profound impact, of
Edward W. Said's life and work. Their original and lively essays enrich our understanding
of Said's writings, and the book as a whole is both testimony and tribute to the continuing
importance, vitality, and productivity of Said's legacy as a scholar, public intellectual, cultural
critic, and political activist."

Zachary Lockman, author of *Contending Visions of the Middle East: The History and Politics
of Orientalism*

"In this remarkable and important book, the authors interact with Edward Said in so many
different ways that the reader is both amazed and out of breath. This book makes one think."

Immanuel Wallerstein, Yale University

"These fine essays bring sympathetic yet critical attention to Said's remarkable range of contributions to politics and to the study of literature and culture. Reading them, one gets a vivid
sense not merely of his ideas and his arguments but his vast yet unsentimental humanity."

Akeel Bilgrami, Director, Heyman Center for the Humanities, Columbia University

"This timely volume takes seriously the vast and challenging writings of Edward Said as they
traverse the praxis of humanism, the literary contours of orientalism, and the intransigent
and persistent critical of colonial power and the Palestinian struggle for freedom. A wide range
of authors contest the proper stance and trajectory of Said's work, the ramifications of his work
for literary studies, aesthetics, politics, the status of humanism, and secular criticism. They
converge, however, in appreciating the passionate critique of colonial occupation and dispossession from the perspective of the displaced and the refugee. Taken together, these essays show
how academic reflection can and must enter the public world at precisely those junctures that
the border patrols of thought would shut down. They show that the critical responsibility of
intellectuals consists in marshalling media for articulating loss and hope, insisting on a presence
for those whose lives are threatened time and again with erasure. This is an important and rich
volume that continues the critical task of Said in a plurivocal mode, establishing the unceasing
intellectual force and fecundity of Said's work."

Judith Butler, University of California at Berkeley

Edward Said

Edward Said

A Legacy of Emancipation and Representation

———

Edited by

Adel Iskandar and Hakem Rustom

UNIVERSITY OF CALIFORNIA PRESS

Berkeley   Los Angeles   London

University of California Press, one of the most distinguished university presses in the United States, enriches lives around the world by advancing scholarship in the humanities, social sciences, and natural sciences. Its activities are supported by the UC Press Foundation and by philanthropic contributions from individuals and institutions. For more information, visit www.ucpress.edu.

University of California Press
Berkeley and Los Angeles, California

University of California Press, Ltd.
London, England

Library of Congress Cataloging-in-Publication Data

Edward Said : a legacy of emancipation and representation / edited by Adel Iskandar and Hakem Rustom.
    p.   cm.
  Includes bibliographical references and index.
  ISBN 978-0-520-24546-4 (cloth : alk. paper)
  ISBN 978-0-520-25890-7 (pbk. : alk. paper)
  1. Said, Edward W.   2. Orientalism.   3. Imperialism.
4. Arab-Israeli conflict.   5. Postcolonialism.   I. Iskandar, Adel.
II. Rustom, Hakem.
CB18.S25E39   2010
306.092—dc22   2009050627

Manufactured in the United States of America

19 18 17 16 15 14 13 12 11 10
10 9 8 7 6 5 4 3 2 1

This book is printed on Cascades Enviro 100, a 100% postconsumer waste, recycled, de-inked fiber. FSC recycled certified and processed chlorine free. It is acid free, Ecologo certified, and manufactured by BioGas energy.

To the nomads whose morality, in Adorno's words,
is to "not be at home in one's home."

CONTENTS

ACKNOWLEDGMENTS

During the compilation and preparation of this book, we were the fortunate recipients of much encouragement and support from a large number of people, from close friends to enthusiastic colleagues. We can but mention them here as a modicum of acknowledgment for their contribution to this volume. Alas, so many people have supported this work that we regret this list cannot be as exhaustive as it should be. First and foremost, to the authors whose intellectually stimulating work compose this book, we applaud their illuminating, provocative, and contemplative contributions.

We could not have wished for a more dedicated, thoughtful, and supportive publisher than the team at the University of California Press. As to the executive editor Naomi Schneider, we are very fortunate to have her faith in this volume from the earliest days shortly after Said's passing and appreciate her ceaseless support and patience throughout. We are grateful to our project editor, Suzanne Knott, who navigated the work steadily toward the finish line and our extraordinarily meticulous and indefatigable copyeditor, Adrienne Harris, who read revision after revision of this voluminous manuscript while maintaining a most positive disposition. We extend our gratitude to the anonymous reviewers whose persuasive comments about the essays were instrumental in refining the work.

Joseph Massad has been an adamant supporter and advocate of this volume from its inception to its final publication. Our lengthy deliberations were always accented by his incisive comments, glaring honesty, and sharp wit. We also had the pleasure of meeting the gentle Mariam C. Said, whose encouragement and patience saw this volume to fruition. We are appreciative of the time she volunteered on numerous occasions and for her toleration of our all-too-frequent inquiries.

We are thankful to the organizers and participants of several conferences on Edward Said at the University of Sussex, University of Chicago, Bibliothèque Nationale de France, School of Oriental and African Studies, and Edward Said Symposium in Berlin, where some of this volume's chapters were working papers. We are also indebted to Daniel Barenboim, Noam Chomsky, and Gayatri Chakravorty Spivak—all interviewed for this book—for their accommodation and receptiveness. To Antje Werkmeister and Tabaré Perlas at the Berlin Staatsoper and to Beverly Stohl at Noam Chomsky's office, we offer thanks for their assistance in making the interviews possible. Rashid Khalidi, the editor of the *Journal of Palestine Studies,* and W. J. T. Mitchell, the editor of *Critical Inquiry,* provided valuable assistance and support. To the encyclopedic and imaginative mind of Dr. Talaat I. Farag we owe many epiphanous moments in the book's evolution. Our sincere appreciation goes to Layal Al-Rustom, Sinem Adar, and Magi Abdul-Masih for their editorial input and patience during the lengthy discussions at the many stages of this project.

We are deeply grateful to Egypt's literary colossus, Khairy Shalaby, who shared his meditations on Edward Said. Thanks also to Michael Wood, Immanuel Wallerstein, and Marc Ellis for their candid conversations and frequent correspondence. To Albert Aghazarian, the Armenian Palestinian who is both the bulwark and raconteur of Jerusalem's cosmopolitanism, and to Mathieu Courville, we are thankful for their passionate and incisive reflections about Said.

We thank the faculty and staff at the Center for Contemporary Arab Studies at Georgetown University for their support throughout and for providing Adel with a vibrant enclave as a visiting scholar to complete this manuscript. Special commendations go to Michael C. Hudson, Rochelle Davis, and the many stellar students who shared their ruminations about Said.

To the colleagues and faculty of the Department of Anthropology at the London School of Economics, who have furnished Hakem with a stimulating intellectual forum, we express our thanks, especially to Martha Mundy and Peter Loizos at the school and to Yael Navaro-Yashin at the University of Cambridge.

For his always prompt replies to our queries on all matters poetic during the preparation of the book, we express our thanks to Jahan Ramazani. Several close friends and colleagues allowed us to explore the book's ideas with them and provided valuable input at various points in the manuscript preparation: Nick Mulhern at the Association of Commonwealth Universities, Andrew Babson, Greg Houle, Rajesh Gaur, Amanda Farnham, Lindsay Nielsen, Farid Farid, Najib Coutya, and Lina Wardani.

To the scholars who imparted their knowledge and expertise to us, we are infinitely grateful: Pauline Gardiner Barber, Jerome Barkow, Douglas A. Boyd, Tom Faulkner, Sherif Hetata, Yahya R. Kamalipour, Aram Kerovpyan, Victor and Tania Li, Thomas R. Lindlof, Barbara Petzen, Ravi Ravindra, and Nawal El-Saadawy.

Discussions on decolonization, philosophy, Middle Eastern politics, and other musings with the following friends and colleagues from the Halifax days piqued our curiosity about Said and in some measure informed this book: Ardi Imseis, Dr. Ismail Zayid, Ehab Shanti, Rema Jamous, Fadi Masoud, Ayat El-Dewary, Reham Amin, Mohamed Sabe, the members of Radio Egypt and the Dalhousie Arabic Society, Said and Sharon Awad, Hassan Felfel, and Maximos Saikali.

Our families have supported us generously and stood by us with great compassion during the gestation. We extend our heartfelt gratitude to Amer, Marianne, and Bassel Al-Rustom, and to Essam and Meriam Farag, for without them this project would not have been possible.

And finally to the countless Saidians who have prodded us along the way and to whom this volume is ultimately dedicated, we respectfully offer this work as a collective homage to an exemplary life lived in the cause of humanism.

Introduction

Emancipation and Representation

Adel Iskandar and Hakem Rustom

CAIRENE MEMORIES

Tucked away in a poorly lit crevice of downtown Cairo and in the shadow of a small alley mosque, Le Grillon, a late-night bar and restaurant that has hosted the city's writers and political adversaries for decades, is in a part of the city from which Edward W. Said often felt estranged. A repository of the city's unpreserved yet vibrant collage of discordant memories of its many identities and histories, the eatery that was once frequented by foreigners, Levantine merchants, and Egyptian aristocrats is now almost exclusively local. Its secluded location and unassuming appearance once attracting the region's oppositional voices, Le Grillon now houses a dusty bookshelf lined with progovernment propaganda. Ignored and unattended to, the shelf is easily overlooked by the café's oldest commoners, there to relive the city's cultural and political heyday, if only for a few hours. On a warm July night in 2005, a small group of writers, poets, physicians, aging revolutionaries, and intellectuals convened to honor Khairy Shalaby, one of Egypt's most prolific contemporary authors, who had only days earlier received the country's highest literary accolade.[1] The gathering was a mosaic of starkly contrasting personalities, accented by such animated characters as political cartoonist Ahmed Toughan, an anticolonial Arab nationalist in his eighties and a compatriot of Frantz Fanon's in Algeria.

The evening began with a poetry recital by Shalaby—interspersed with glimpses of his literary life spent mostly in Cairo's graveyards and impoverished *'Ashwa'eyat,* or shantytowns—but soon turned to ruminations about the city's old days.[2] Striking a contrast with his own Cairene experiences, Shalaby described a cosmopolitan and opulent side of the city inhabited by the teenage Edward Said as both unrelenting in its mosaicism and unrepentant for its contradictions. Chewing on a stubborn filet for what seemed like an eternity, Shalaby shifted smoothly and seam-lessly between thoughts, memories, and fantasies.

We had sought the company of seventy-year-olds in our role as the editors of this volume on Edward Said, a still-nascent project that Shalaby greeted with sur-prise and exhilaration. He expressed his enthusiastic appreciation of the late intel-lectual. "If a book needed to be written about anyone, it would be Edward Said," he exclaimed, admitting that he owned copies of both Arabic translations of *Orientalism*. In poetically extemporaneous classical Arabic, Shalaby shared his admira-tion for Said's memoir *Out of Place*, in which he narrates his upbringing in Cairo, taking particular interest in retelling his angst-ridden adolescence and recounting his temptation for belly dancing's most prominent icon and eccentric temptress, Tahia Carioca.[3]

Said's first exposure to the sensual performer of pre- and postrevolutionary Egypt was as a teenager discreetly escaping his restrained, disciplined, and sexually re-pressed urban elite social setting. Belly dancing and Carioca would have been seen as oversexed, lustful, and tastelessly suggestive, a prohibition that aroused fourteen-year-old Said. Yet Said's fascination with Carioca extended far beyond her dancing. He marveled at her unresolved persona—the eclectic and inharmonious juxtapo-sition of her roles as eroticized spectacle, political militant, and symbol of national culture.[4] Shalaby's musings on Said's Carioca highlighted the porous boundaries be-tween the colony and the postcolony and between historical eras, political realities, and spatial landscapes—boundaries Said spent much of his intellectual career per-meating, forcibly and willfully. With Cairo and Carioca, we arrive at the confluence of Said's unstable mélange of identity, politics, resistance, and art.

BEGINNINGS WITH SAID

The paths to Edward Said's work are varied, whether via a Cairo pub, antiwar ac-tivist circles on university campuses, or his numerous interviews with Charlie Rose on YouTube. We came across Said in the mid-1990s during our undergraduate stud-ies at Dalhousie University in Halifax, Canada. This frequently cited, sharply opin-ionated, and eloquent intellectual with a peculiar hybrid name caught our atten-tion and curiosity. As inquisitive undergraduates toiling our way through the liberal arts, we scoured the literature on the Middle East in an attempt to both overcome the emotional strain of our own migration and fulfill our desire for self-exploration. One book was impossible to miss on all Middle Eastern history bookshelves, par-ticularly because it stood in stark contrast to the Islamophobic literature that dom-inated the canon. With Jean-Leon Gerome's *The Snake Charmer* adorning the front of Said's *Orientalism*, the striking cover invited further investigation, conveying both curious familiarity and fetishized exoticism.

This period coincided with the deplorable 1997 brutal attacks on tourists in

Luxor, Egypt. To counteract the seemingly ceaseless denigration of the region and Islam in the Canadian press in the wake of the attacks, we produced a fourteen-hour feature radio program titled *Through Arab Eyes* on the local campus and community radio station, CKDU-FM. The special broadcast sought to offer a corrective debate on the histories, politics, cultures, and religions of the region. The intervention was an effort to overcome the deep void, invisibility, and perhaps violation caused by the incessant, alienating public discourse about the region and its peoples. *Orientalism* became an indispensable resource, a primer that helped us decipher and grapple with these issues, catalyzing our understanding of how and why negative discursive constructions dominated mainstream depictions of the region. Through its meticulous documentation and historicization of such narratives, the book was a guide to navigating cautiously through the prickly terrain of representation. Beyond *Orientalism*, Said's reflections on the relationship of intellectuals to power and their responsibilities within academia and beyond resonated with scholars who sought a humanist method and purpose to their work.

Over three decades, Said's political writings provided a stubborn and unwavering source of enlightenment that aided in the interpretation of current events and exposed gross failures by the political and media establishments to deal contextually with the Middle East. Said offered a sober and sobering utterance amid a cacophony of voices in and on the wider Arab, Muslim, and Middle Eastern societies. Through these interjections, Said exercised a form of criticism based on media literacy that enabled him to disambiguate vernaculars and expose ideologies. His essays amalgamated politics and aesthetics, addressing culture and society as a whole without erecting rigid fences between them, inspiring cultural critics, activists, and human rights advocates.

Said's death in 2003 was abrupt. When he died, his disappearance from the public arena left a gaping hole in the understanding of contemporary international politics in the region. It happened at a point in Middle East politics that was perilous for Arabs and Muslims. The region that occupied Said's imagination, scholarship, and activism continues to be viewed monolithically as a security threat to the governments of the United States and other "Western" countries. Indeed, since *Orientalism*'s first publication in 1978, the problems that characterize the international political arena have been exacerbated. For this reason, we wanted to ensure that Said's criticism continues to inform on the most pressing issues of the day and to interrupt the dehumanizing representations of the region and their underlying policies. The invasion and destruction of Iraq, the constant accelerating degradation of Palestinian life under Israeli occupation, and the United States' continued support for undemocratic and unpopular regimes and repressive dictators are but a few of the acts of physical and emotional violence experienced by the peoples of the region. On Arab and Muslim societies, Said unrelentingly assailed the rise of intolerant religious fundamentalism, sectarianism in daily life, corruption among the ruling classes, misguided intelligentsias, deteriorating economic conditions, and the suppression of all democratic alternatives to the presiding regimes.

The idea for this book emerged mere days after Said's death, originally as a means of channeling the loss of Said the public intellectual and eventually to create a space for scholars to move beyond eulogization and engage critically with his work. Yet any examination of Said's work must be situated within a biographical chronology, one that historicizes his writings. In a review of his memoir, *Out of Place*, Ahdaf Soueif described the year 1991 as a critical historical juncture in Said's life, both personally and intellectually. It was a violation to Said—a physical violation in the discovery of mortality following his diagnosis with leukemia and a political violation in the signing of the Oslo Accords. Not long after, Said would go on his first visits to Palestine and Cairo since his departure, in 1992 and 1993, respectively. He would also give the Reith Lectures on the responsibilities of intellectuals in 1993 and begin writing his memoir in 1994. In his introduction to Said's posthumously published *On Late Style*, Michael Wood wrote that Said's lateness is a result of his facing death, both the passing of his mother in 1990 of the same illness and his own impending finitude.[5] These cataclysmic events became the impetus for *Musical Elaborations,* which he dedicated to the memory of his mother, *Out of Place*, and several urgent manuscripts on the Palestine he saw vanishing swiftly before his eyes.[6]

Our affiliation with Edward Said stemmed from our need for change and from our desire to find an alternative to the polarized political, social, intellectual, and cultural orders. Said carved a space where we could be more than an inaudible minority on the margins, where we could join a movement that is dynamic, self-representing, and heard. Asserting the responsibility of the intellectual to be politically engaged, Said himself produced "worldly" ideas that traversed academic, political, geographic, and artistic realms. He has inspired a new generation of intellectuals to embrace a sense of purpose, a commitment to critical action, and a faith in dignity as vehicles of self-representation in the Saidian style.[7]

THE SAIDIAN

The Secular Exile

Born in Jerusalem, raised in Cairo, living most of his life in New York, and buried on Mount Lebanon, Edward Said was always itinerant and eternally uprooted. During his early days, moving between pre-1948 Palestine, Egypt, Lebanon, and the United States, he experienced the anguish of psychic and actualized exile and displacement. His urban aristocratic upbringing allowed him to relate to the colonizers through Western pedagogy anchored in the canonical classics. Despite this, as he explained in his memoir, *Out of Place*, he was made to feel continually delinquent and insufficient while attending colonial schools in Cairo, despite his façade of confidence. He described his estrangement and his longing to return "home" when he first moved to the United States as a student, which had him stare end-lessly at photos and set his clock to Cairo time.[8] Even during those early days, he was acutely aware of the abstract nature of "home," a place that cannot be arrived at or even imagined.

In "The Rootless Cosmopolitan," Tony Judt explained that Said "lived all his life at a tangent to the various causes with which he was associated."[9] Said used the term *apogee* to elaborate his position in society; he described the height of a civilization's enlightenment and achievement but more importantly referring to the farthest point from the point of origin.[10] Said saw the spirit of apogee as a dissociated fringe position—the most distant point from the center of an issue, apart from any site of grounding, attachment, lineage, or origin.[11] This distance guarantees that one is away from both home and origin, in the spirit expressed by twelfth-century Saxon monk Hugo of St. Victor: "He is perfect to whom the entire world is a foreign land."[12] Throughout his life, Said orbited around these origins, exposing issues of emanci-pation and oscillating between perigee (point of proximity and intimacy) and apogee (distance and elevation) with seamless ease and shrewd decisiveness. When ad-dressing colonial and postcolonial subjectivity, being in apogee afforded him both an appreciation of the colonial classics in literature and music and the ability to in-terrogate their subjugating elements.

The "untidiness" of exile presented Said with a desituated posture that informed much of his criticism.[13] If the Saidian exilic state were to "house" anything, it would do so as a refuge for emancipatory action.[14] This explains his affinity for Deleuze and Guattari's notion of the "nomadic" as not simply one of lived experience and personal affliction but as a discursive apparatus for the reconfiguration of master narratives.[15] Itself a source of liberation, an alternative theology, a site of contra-diction, and a terrain of shifting contours, Said's nomadism was theoretically un-housed, methodologically untidy, and spatially fluid.[16] At once inhabitable and un-inhabitable, Said's critical nomadism was intrinsically veracious. Theoretically, it resisted any master paradigm, contested all-encompassing theorization, and ques-tioned the predictability of dominant knowledge systems.[17] Said's emphasis on the informal and the disaggregated reflected his nomadism, embedding it in an "epis-temology of displacement" that searched beyond the "rituals and performances of conventional metropolitan intellectuals."[18] This view of unsettledness extends to Said's overarching critical project, which he acknowledged was unfinished, a con-dition he showed little interest in rectifying. Indeed, Said resisted all forms of at-tributive delineation, scorned intellectual specialization, admonished the assured conviction of policymaking, disavowed academic self-aggrandizement, and rejected the containment of disciplinary accolades.

Said expanded his critique into the realm of familiarity, predictability, control, and status (being known) to deconstruct filial connection.[19] Said's "home" obviated filiation, walling no one and nothing in or out; it was a permeable space with no distinct boundaries. Hence one could not speak of the other. By deterritorializing the home, Said "de-othered the other," making "otherness" obsolete. This act also dispelled the myth of arrival. The constant pilgrimage negates the existence of a destination, a Holy Land. Said described a deeply unrestful state, suggesting that in exile one never arrives at a destination, thereby rendering the nomadic ontological.[20]

As a nomadic cosmopolitan, Said associated with the motif and the experience of the Judaic exile.[21] In an interview with the Israeli daily *Ha'aretz,* he described himself as "the last Jewish intellectual." While expressing his hopes for the future of Palestine/Israel, Said endorsed a one-state solution, causing discomfort for many Israelis and Palestinians. "I want a rich fabric of some sort, which no one can fully comprehend, and no one can fully own," Said affirmed.[22] Such a vision encapsulated his persona: he was the intellectual of the unresolved, intent on overcoming the appeal of purity, tidiness, and homogeneity. In this idea of a desituated home, political, ethnic, and religious boundaries are suspended by exiles who "cross borders, break barriers of thought and experience."[23] In his especially expressive interview, Said made a compelling case for his binational vision for Palestine/Israel by leveling a compassionate critique at the Zionist obsession with the notions of "state" and "home." When the interviewer observed that Said "sounds very Jewish" in his commentary, Said responded, "Of course. I'm the last Jewish intellectual. You don't know anyone else. All your other Jewish intellectuals are now suburban squires. From Amos Oz to all these people here in America. So I'm the last one. The only true follower of Adorno. Let me put it this way: I'm a Jewish-Palestinian."[24]

In this statement, Said embodied the exile in his ability, affinity, and desire to destigmatize and congeal into the "other." The forced seamlessness of his Palestinianness and Jewishness expressed the underlying exilic nature of these identities. Through this exclamation, Said defined himself as asymmetrical and irreconciled in his political vision. He harmonized the contradictory, demonstrating counterpoint to undermine the exclusivity of nationalism. He shattered the boundary of the label and aligned himself with a long tradition of Jewish intellectualism, which for him implied the wanderer prophet-intellectual described by Noam Chomsky— one who chooses exile and refuses the comfort of serving and legitimizing power agendas and who eschews the possibility of gaining rewards for such allegiances.[25] By describing himself as a Jewish-Palestinian, Said reduced the difference between the two identities to a hyphen and emphasized their roving exile.

In the physical sense, exile is often a result of oppression and is rarely a choice, yet metaphorically it is an expression of dissidence. For Said, exile, whether physical or metaphorical or both, is an alternative state, apart from the domination of mass institutions and distant from the gravitational center of the status quo, despite his personal geographic proximity to these.[26]

This view of exile perhaps explains why Said's loyalties were not static, instead shifting constantly in relation to power. To emancipate the individual by overcoming allegiance to tradition, Said was committed to justice over identity and "never solidarity before criticism."[27] For him, allegiance to a group or a nation, whose nationalism "affirms the home created by a community of language, culture, and customs" was counter to the estrangement of exile.[28] Said was therefore echoing Adorno's well-known statement "It is part of morality not to be at home in one's home," making exile obligatory, both morally and practically, for any emancipatory project.[29] Hence, Said's exile was the interstitial borderland where Jewish and Palestinian morality rendezvoused. He saw greater possibility for confluence in the exilic than in the rooted: "Better our wanderings, I sometimes think, than the horrid clanging shutters of their return."[30]

While refusing to have his experience viewed as mere signification, especially in his posture on Palestine, Said inhabited the crossroads and interstitial spaces, thereby transforming the unsituated orphanhood of exile into a respectable state. He was able to convert the unpredictable, unresolved, dissociated, and unrestful space of in-betweenness into habitable terrain, turning exile into a tolerated state shared by the like-minded—a locale distant from the gravity of power, comfortable in its discomfort, situated yet in persistent motion, and wandering while grounded.

Nevertheless, the violence of exile took its toll on Said in the intellectual, figurative, and practical senses. With the deterioration of Palestinian livelihood and in the aftermath of the September 11, 2001, attacks, he felt a "general sense of curtailment" and refrained from giving media interviews as he witnessed how nothing remained of his homelands.[31] He also found it increasingly difficult to recover and memorialize these lost lands. In his last interview, he said that his leukemia accentuated the eternity of his exile, leaving him neither dead nor recovered and in a state of "in-betweenness." Said—who had spent his intellectual life vacillating between geographies, identities, historical junctures, and literacies—found himself agonizingly suspended between life and death, constantly unresolved and interminably dislocated up to his final moments. And in his death, his intellectual legacy, while astoundingly comprehensive, is largely beyond cartographic delineation. In a sense, Said was the philosopher of nomadism.[32]

This pedagogy of nomadism that Said elucidated in his writings and considered a responsibility of the intellectual was rooted in an "irremediably secular and unbearably historical" exile that exposed the intersections of power and knowledge.[33] Said's "exile knows that in a secular and contingent world, homes are always provisional. . . . Exiles cross borders, break barriers of thought and experience."[34] His unabashed attempt to disrupt the silence of consent, demystify the instruments of control, and stimulate voices of dissent came at the expense of orthodoxy. Said used the religious lexicon to describe civil and secular establishments, thereby drawing comparisons between the institutional dogmatic hierarchy of religious and other authorities that command obedient consent, loyalty, conformity, and unwavering allegiance from an "unknowing" public.

For Said, exile and nationalism are dialectical in the Hegelian sense, at once contesting and justifying one another. Nationalism that serves as an impetus for liberation and expresses an emancipatory function develops as a reaction to estrangement.[35] Alternatively, Said regarded nationalism as an allegiance akin to that of religious institutions, because both have "founding fathers . . . quasi-religious texts, their rhetoric of belonging . . . [and] official enemies and heroes."[36] Therefore, for Said, exile itself is necessarily secular. This secularity is exilic in that it interrogates the status quo and remains permanently "on the other side of power."[37] Not only does it free the individual from the authority of religious institutions, in the usual sense of the term, but it also liberates from the sentimental attachments to and the apologetic worship of any form of ideology or belonging. Hence, secularity is the state of being untamed by power, the foremost role for the intellectual.[38] Said often quoted a line by the English poet Gerard Manley Hopkins to describe this posture, capturing his perpetual state of criticism: "all things counter, original, spare, strange."[39]

Consequently, Vico's secular criticism became a hallmark of Said's philosophy. By highlighting the centrality of human agency in making and interpreting history, Said distinguished between beginnings and origins—the former being historical, dynamic, and secular and the latter being ahistoric, latent, and divine.[40] Beginnings invited critique and engagement, whereas origins drew preconditional passivity and compliance. Yet for Said, neither was beyond criticism. Belonging and affiliation did not overrule the ability to deconstruct, which explains his desire to witness a Palestinian state in order to critique it.[41]

The Saidian secular critic sees action as a dialectical negotiation, fluctuating and swaying to and fro in a gradual process of development and knowledge acquisition. His is not a systematized body of theory and method. This view gives rise to contradictions and inconsistencies. As Aamir Mufti has written, "Secular criticism does not imply the rejection of universalism per se. It implies a scrupulous recognition that all claims of a universal nature are particular claims."[42] While Said neither privileged nor attacked the culture or tradition of any society, his intonations remind us that tradition can be repressive.[43] When one focuses on praising and demeaning, one loses the space to read histories critically within their social, political, and economic contexts. Nationalism, dogmatism, and universalism all simplify historic narratives by sacrificing context, manipulating experience, drawing borders, normalizing distinctions, and erecting fences between "civilizations," creating apartheids and interventionist politics. The issues that Said raised about narration remain urgent, offering a self-challenge to pose queries that strip the shroud off power: Who writes? Why? For whom? And in what circumstances?[44]

In his criticisms, Said did not silence or censor but rather disrupted the order that empires build to legitimize their domination and unsettled their sphere of comfort. Simplification commodifies the self and the other, through lax dehistoricization and social decontextualization, by venerating classic texts and creating sim-

ple formulas for mass consumption.[45] Those formulas of domination, a symptom
of imperial endeavors, coercively dissipate people's right to agency and their will
to change and re-create their histories as continuous, democratic, and secular processes. The colossal task of reversing power's erosion of collective memory and simplification of histories and peoples (as "authors" of history) remains the prime duty
of both the intellectual and the humanist. Stathis Gourgouris goes as far as to assert that by exposing power, Said's urgent intellectual legacy is the "resistance to
amnesia."[46]

Secular criticism is not a procedural trait but a permanent mode defined by
action. Said's is a space of considerable loneliness and solitude, a perpetual state of
criticism that is interminably in exile.

The Amateur Humanist

Alongside Gayatri Chakravorty Spivak and Homi Bhabha, Said is widely credited
with infusing epistemic purpose and discursive coherence into postcolonial studies. Although *Orientalism* was its founding text, Said maintained a distance from
the label of "postcolonial" and indeed defied it, as he did all categorical identifications that he viewed as theoretically limiting and intellectually confining.[47] By
discarding all labels and transcending academic disciplinism, he spoke against
professionalism and expertise, encouraging a rebuke of the canonical coziness of
specialization.[48] Across his oeuvre runs a counternarrative that contests simplified
taxonomies, convenient identification, and the theoretical predictability of dogmatism. This resistance is a condition of the Saidian approach and explains his
affinity for and commitment to divergent conceptual modalities, literary traditions,
intellectual camps, and philosophical schools, none of which he sought to inhabit
or defined as a home. By resisting labels, the strict Saidian constantly vacillates between modernism and postmodernism, between Conrad and Mahfouz, Yeats and
Darwish, Chomsky and Foucault, Wagner and Umm Kulthum, and between public activism and the meditative and idiomatic abstraction of academia. Said gently
carved out a space at the locale of confluence, the realm of the hybrid, and the state
of in-betweenness.

Said argued that the critic should separate the work being examined from the
personal conviction of its creator. This separation allows one to appreciate, understand, and learn from a person who might disagree with one's moral, ideological,
or personal grounds. He exemplified this commitment when he supported Israeli
maestro Daniel Barenboim's appreciation of Wagner.[49] Moreover, he felt compelled
to acknowledge and appreciate style and aesthetics, as he did in his writings on
Joseph Conrad and Jane Austen.[50] Said's appreciation for literature did not extend
to romanticizing it, which would have called for denying the political realities of
empire at the time of a work's composition. One of the axioms of what he called his
"contemporary reality" was the blurring of distinctions between "pure and politi-

cal knowledge."[51] Through this hermeneutics of literature, critics need to place works of fiction in historical context. By extension, they have a duty to express narratives representing subaltern cultures and histories while preserving the ability to critique them as works of literature: he maintained that "no one has ever devised a method for detaching the scholar from . . . his involvement . . . with a class, a set of beliefs, a social position . . . or of being a member of a society."[52]

Over time, as Said committed his voice in the arena of cultural politics, he gravitated away from the type of professionalism that automatizes and impoverishes criticism. Having pioneered the critique of identity discourses in colonial enterprises generally and their Orientalist varieties specifically, Said later decried the tendency of discourse analysis to shun humanism.[53] He described his intellectual stance as a "perpetual state of beginning" that at its core is amateurish—where the intellectual endeavor is "fuelled by care and affection rather than by profit and selfish narrow specialization."[54] This amateurism is also exilic as it is apart from the professional cults that are exploitable by the establishment. For one whose writings shifted disciplines and inspired others, Said's relationship to intellectual authority was that of an "unrewarded, amateurish conscience" rather than that of a "professional supplicant."[55]

Said's hermaneutic method is dialectical yet holistic in its critique: the aesthetic and the political are not separated but can be viewed both in unison and in contrast. The contrapuntal reading of colonial literature abounds in Said's work. Achebe asserted that one should not read Conrad's *Heart of Darkness* because it dehumanizes Africans.[56] Although Said agreed with Achebe's characterization of dehumanization, he argued that a critic can historicize the text only through engagement with it, thereby acknowledging both its intention and its aesthetic.[57]

To Said, the aesthetics of a work can be both contradictory and complementary, allowing the juxtaposition of oppositional narratives. Perhaps Said's fascination with the European classical musical tradition and the centrality of polyphony and counterpoint in his vernacular informed his humanistic ideals. He used these terms often when discussing political issues, suggesting that harmony is attainable only through a multiplicity of voices or instruments, each group playing differently yet coming together in an integrated, complex musical composition. Said committed his final years to the West-Eastern Divan, a youth orchestra he founded in 1999 with his friend Israeli-Argentinian composer and pianist Daniel Barenboim. The project brings together young Palestinian, Israeli, and Arab classical musicians to study, rehearse, and perform together.[58] The hope is that the common goal of practicing a composition together and performing in concert will for a moment enable the musicians to transcend the enmity they have developed while growing up in their respective communities. Although Said did not expect the Divan to change political disparities or the deeply rooted prejudices in both societies, it remains an oasis of communal contact, a symbol of coexistence, a collaborative effort to experience worldly aesthetics, and a break in the thick walls erected to separate two societies with "overlapping territories, intertwined histories," and a common destiny.[59]

Like the Divan, convening seemingly conflicting political and social dimensions emphasizes the indelibility of belonging.[60] Despite his commitment to the Palestinian struggle for justice and self-determination, Said paved bridges between intellectuals, artists, and ordinary Jews inside and outside of Israel. Dichotomies of good and bad, black and white, us and them were absent from Said's lexicon. His ability to bring together opposites and embrace the irreconcilable nuances of experience was a mark of Said's personal, academic, and political expressions. Yet he did not shy away from leveling damning critiques at sloppy minimizing theses such as Samuel Huntington's "Clash of Civilizations," Francis Fukuyama's End of History, and Bernard Lewis's "The Roots of Muslim Rage" and What Went Wrong?[61] His warning about the "seductive degradation of knowledge, of any knowledge, anywhere, at any time" is still resonant today.[62]

Said's unfinished work is in persuading intellectuals to heed the call to universal humanism by tearing open the canon to allow texts from multiple traditions, cultures, and locales to commune alongside the Western classics.[63] In making the case for this expansion, Said preached a reconciliatory cosmopolitanism that bridges cultural fissures and sutures "civilizational" cleavages. This spirit of coexistence was evident in his efforts to synergize Palestinian and Jewish identities through mutual recognition of suffering and dehumanization. He often said that "Palestinians were the victims of the victims," suggesting that Jews were best acquainted with and potentially most empathetic to the suffering of Palestinians.[64] Despite the numbing monoliths of nationalism, Said's Palestine symbolized confluence and consilience. Thus, humanism was the embodiment of counterpoint— the harmony of the discordant.

Said's last writings, including On Late Style, increasingly embraced the stylistics of criticism, both implicit and explicit. In these works, his dialogic inventiveness is theoretically unhoused (beyond the descriptors of modernity and poststructuralism). His discussion of Adorno, Mann, Cavafy, Beethoven, Mozart, Bach, Wagner, and Glenn Gould explains the anachronisms and anomalies of creative aesthetic expression during the twilight of life. Said argues that the conditions of lateness often precipitate stylistic virtuosity, rendering the author an amateur intellectual who interrupts prevailing conventions.[65] He reanimates Vico, Auerbach, Rembrandt, Kierkegaard, Ibn Khaldun, Gramsci, Foucault, Garibaldi, and Verdi to emancipate virtuosity and innovation from their pragmatic confinement—revealing their unconventionality and innovativeness and perhaps embodying the exiled exigencies of Said's own late style.[66] His final works, published in two posthumous volumes, gravitate between the contradictory goals of resuscitating a modernist humanism and celebrating the intransigence of amateurism—perhaps engendering Said's unrestrained virtuosity.[67]

FROM REPRESENTATION TO EMANCIPATION

The purpose of the intellectual's societal obligation and responsibility is an axiomatic commitment. This view is central to identifying the metatheoretical paradigms that inform the Saidian method. In much of his writings, Said contended with, exposed, and articulated representation as the notion with the most precarious connection to empowerment. In his view, representation could at once advocate for and disenfranchise emancipatory projects. From the core thematic of literary authorship that he explored in *Beginnings* and the notion of "counterpoint" in his treatises on music, to collective memory in Palestinian life, Said put forth the unequivocal principle that enfranchising emancipation must be coupled with dignifying representation if it is to be fully actualized. For Said, the act of representation is reductive and violent, dismembering and often disempowering the subject of representation.[68] The façade of representation, which appears tranquil, smooth, resolved, and often spectacular—suggesting control and definition—contrasts with the process that produced it. This process infantilizes the subject to the diminutive form and augments the representational image by decontextualizing, dehistoricizing, objectifying, and castrating it. Not only is representation incapable of capturing the cumulative nature of the represented, Said insists "no process of converting experience into expression could be free of contamination."[69]

A key goal of representation is to ready an expression for the sole purpose of consumption, where it is domesticated and rendered safe for assimilation into the self. Said described such domestication during his upbringing in colonial schools reproduced imperial society's representation of Arab history and cultural enclaves as inferior to those of the West. The activity of posing for a family photograph became more about performing identity than about capturing reality (the family's genuine attempt to embody and espouse a European livelihood).

Decrying the earliest examples of representation in his personal life, Said shared in *Out of Place* his father's "unforgiving optical grid," which attempted to project the image of a perfect family in all photographs and videos.[70] He described some of these family photo sessions as "agonizingly long and maddeningly finicky."[71] In this personal history as well as his critique of Orientalism and mediated/visual depictions of Arabness, Islam, and Palestinians, Said lamented the extent to which representational forms such as photography ignore the immediate and fragment lived experience and the memory of it. For Said, photography was more about omission than inclusion, highlighting very little at the expense of much.

Although Said acknowledged the essentialization inherent in photographic imagery, he also recognized that, despite this amputated nature, it provided the only explicit documentation of memory, particularly in the case of the Palestinian experience. The images of his family, as Said attests in *After the Last Sky*, embody family photography as a historical testament, reconstructing Palestine in exile and telling of a Palestinian condition that might otherwise go forgotten.[72] For instance, Said's revisiting of Nazareth as described and narrated via familial memories and refracted through an intertwined history is a meditation on a now-bifurcated, yet confusingly familiar, half-Arab, half-Jewish town.[73]

Photography is a double-edged sword, with the representative image simultaneously conveying both hegemonic and counterhegemonic messages. The photograph is a site where "representation swallows the native up" and provides an opportunity for her rebirth. *After the Last Sky* is Said's exercise of "critical nostalgia," in which representation and narration converge to allow recognition of the excluded.[74] Here Said illustrates the infinite fracture of exiled memory. However, Said's critique of representation, especially in the context of patriarchal imperial conquest and cultural digestion, did not alter his understanding of representation as essential to social existence. The tragedy of Palestine is the victorious rendering of the invisible present, whereby resistance is born out of the mere appearance of the Palestinian.[75]

Representation is at once unavoidable and necessary, as are all units of embodiment and expression, with language being the precursor. Said exposed the disenfranchisement of the other that occurs in representation by authoritative power centers. This default system prohibits any intervention by those being represented and contrasts radically with the alternative system of representation that Said advocated: open-ended, collaborative, communal, interactive, egalitarian, refractory, noncoercive, nonhierarchical, and participatory. His idealized conception of representation combined the cultural critique advocated by Stuart Hall with the dissident self-representational qualities of subjects' participatory action suggested by Fanon and Paulo Freire.[76]

Said leveled his critique at the media and institutions of cultural production by identifying their unparalleled reach, monopolistic domination, and ability to "create" and craft "reality." These institutions enshrine and uphold a hegemonic media structure, format, and style that systematically commodify, decontextualize, and simplify all forms of discourse. As a result, they sharply curtail the possibilities of interjecting or reversing the flow, to the disadvantage of citizenship, cosmopolitanism, and dignified representation for their subjects. Said is somewhat Chomskyan in his discussion of the disparaging ways in which U.S. news media represent and disenfranchise Muslims, Arabs, and their heritage. He decries the fact that the cult of expertise, the cadres of self-professed authorities, and a small group of opportunist native informants are able to uphold a systematized structure that objectifies entire regions, nations, communities, creeds, and ethnicities beyond mediated remedy.[77] Through the mythology of press freedom and openness, the media further

Orientalize the other—notably "colored" peoples or various resistance narratives—by arguing that these have an innate propensity for self-victimization that allows them to exploit the innocent and well-meaning Western media to further their agendas of plight. Beyond the deconstruction of these media discourses and representations, Said saw an urgent need to investigate and expose the "media conglomerates" and institutions that facilitate "pacification, the depoliticization of ordinary life, as well as the encouragement and refinement of consumer appetites."[78]

Said broke with Adorno, Horkheimer, Althusser, Jameson, and Chomsky by asserting the subvertability of these cultural industries and systems of power domination. Although the military-industrial complex infuses the institutions of mediated production with ideology and purpose, he agreed with Raymond Williams that these metalevel epistemologies are not ontologically fixed and are therefore subject to reconfiguration and dismantling.[79] In a Gramscian sense, Said believed in the potential of humanistic critical analysis and participatory resistance to intervene and transform. He embodied this belief as a vocal critic of the monolithic, myopic, and dehumanizing representation of all forms of Palestinian nationalist expression. By demystifying such authoritarian discourses, Said's writings on Palestine ruptured the seemingly harmonious, routinized, and reliable repertory on Palestinianness, unsettling the dominant paradigm, illuminating the contrapuntal nature of self-representation, and permitting dissent.[80]

This subversive humanist role for alternative media can challenge authority: "We today are abetted by the enormously encouraging democratic field of cyberspace, open to all users in ways undreamt of by earlier generations either of tyrants or of orthodoxies."[81] He appreciated this in the integral relationship between the global anti-Iraq war protests and alternative information, with the latter serving as an avenue for public exposure.

By deconstructing systems of discursive power, à la Foucault, and then in his work on the West-Eastern Divan and in Palestinian representation work such as *After the Last Sky,* Said took it upon himself to alter the language of self-embodiment. The subalterity of those inherently disenfranchised from centers of power leaves them meager opportunities for narration. In an act of defiance, Said encouraged narrative discourse on Palestinian identity and became arguably the most influential voice on Palestine through his writings and his ability to inspire and encourage others. His numerous reviews of works by Arab authors and by corrective revisionist thinkers—including Ahdaf Soueif's *In the Eye of the Sun,* Ghada Karmi's *In Search of Fatima,* Mourid Barghouti's *I Saw Ramallah,* and Joe Sacco's *Palestine*—countered the mainstream discourse on Palestine and beyond by calling attention to narratives from the standpoint of the victims.[82]

Hence, by questioning representation, *Orientalism* and *Culture and Imperialism* served as texts of liberation and emancipation, both of the colonized and the colonial mind-sets. Like Frantz Fanon, who identified with foreigners when he was in Martinique and with the colony when in France, Said's vociferous critique of both the colonial and the postcolonial marked a departure from the intellectual politics of allegiance.[83] Instead he spent much of his time disentangling and subverting orthodoxies and dogmas, changing the canonical landscape of various academic disciplines along the way and "de-Orienting" Middle Eastern studies.[84]

The language of justice, human rights, and dissent is often hijacked and co-opted by the establishment. Once the language has been coerced and given new meaning, the intellectual is often left powerless, without the lexical arsenal to speak "truth to power." To refute this practice and regain control of the language, Said sounded the alarm about the ability of power to manufacture collective memory loss through its systematic processes of obfuscation. For him, the continuation and ossification of Orientalist worldviews—from colonial magisterial notes to abuses at Abu Ghraib and Guantanamo—were the greatest threats to memory. In a Gramscian sense, the intellectuals of today's imperial project continue to manufacture consent and identity through abstractions and simplification. In response to an interviewer's question about U.S. President George W. Bush's dichotomization of the world, Said asserted, "The fact that anyone can talk in such huge abstractions—'America' or 'Islam'—makes me want to puncture their pomposity."[85] To restore this memory, he advocated a nuanced critique of the ideological landscape, a ceaseless interrogation of its institutionalizing amnesia, and a disruption of the mechanisms of collective dispossession.

Although his earlier writings were as political as *Orientalism* and were also the subject of debate and contestation, they did not reach beyond literary criticism circles. However, by the time his trilogy had been published—*Orientalism, The Question of Palestine,* and *Covering Islam*—Edward Said had assumed the role of public intellectual and had begun making ripples beyond his discipline, drawing comrades and antagonists alike. His sobering deconstruction of Orientalist discourse, the soundness of his argumentation, the meticulously exhaustive rigor of his analysis, and the pervasive longevity of his opinions have occasionally prompted myopic and counterintuitive efforts to render him irrelevant or to discredit the premise of his treatment in *Orientalism.* As the book etched its place among the iconic canonical texts of critical intellectual writing in the twentieth century, attacks and efforts to demonize Said became more persistent and irrational, seeking to minimize and essentialize him and his ideas.

Said had an acute ability to interpret, assess and explain the perpetual chorus of reproduced, repackaged, and redistributed discourses whose disparagingly Orientalist intonations misrepresented him by decontextualizing his person, his project, and his work. Despite such efforts, more than thirty years since its publication, his landmark work *Orientalism* remains more relevant than ever.[86] The frequent ad

hominem attacks on Said, which continue today and grossly distort his work, justify an effort to situate and historicize him and his oeuvre in the humanistic manner he both employed and emulated. This commitment has become even more important in recent years as some overzealous critics have moved beyond the realm
of discourse and attempted to curtail free thought in academia. Suppression has
come in the form of self-fulfilling tirades of derisive expressions propagated by
pseudo-academic commissars whose efforts have served to suffocate nuance and
democratic principles.[87]

Nonetheless, Said's criticism will outlive its most vocal detractors. This volume
does not aim to counter these concerted attacks. Rather Said's methodical resistance
to and abhorrence of essentialization are themselves the best counterpoint to the
discourses that seek to undermine and misrepresent his work. The universality of
the social justice issues to which he was so committed and the sensitivity with which
he spoke on politics stand as the greatest indictments of paternalistic thinking.

THE BOOK

All representation affects the ability to achieve emancipation, and every emancipatory project must engage and problematize representation. Said's exploration of
the intellectual reflected a degree of self-examination. For him, intellectualism carried the dual responsibility of championing corrective representation and com-
mitting to emancipation. In this regard, Said animated the nomadic qualities of the
exiled intellectual, for whom secular criticism evokes the amateurism of humanistic engagement—a necessary precursor to exposing the disparaging language of representation and pursuing dignified emancipation.

This volume is an attempt to underline the chiasmata in Said's work and to see
beyond the simplistic compartmentalization of his contribution so that we may
improve our understanding of his project. The purpose is not to insinuate discipleship, evoke uncritical sympathy, or sacrifice nuance in search of accessibility.[88]
Rather we hope the essays here will demystify particular aspects of Said's work and
thereby widen the audience for his message. Given that Said was himself an uncompromising critic of orthodoxy, dogmatism, and deification, we have no intention of essentializing or objectifying him; rather we hope that this volume will problematize more than commemorate his contribution.

This collection of essays offers a broad discussion of Said's intellectual legacy,
viewing it through the prism of the thinkers, critics, writers, and activists who know
his work intimately. It expands the analysis of Said beyond disciplinary boundaries,
drawing on his own expansive intellectual terrain and influences and seeking to
chart the impact of his criticism. The book attempts to define the line of thinking
now described as "Saidian." Just as his work traverses borders, the authors in this
volume cross disciplinary boundaries. They are anthropologists, cultural critics,

media scholars, feminist theorists, international lawyers, literary critics, and activists. The breadth of the contributions is a testament to Said's creative capacities and his universal relevance.

The book has three thematic sections, each exploring a trajectory of Said's oeuvre and its intersections with various currents in his quest to engage and critique representation and emancipation. The first focuses on Said's engagement with aesthetics and the colony through the prism of representation, from literary and poetic expression to musical composition and performance. The second group of essays examines Said's poignant observations and meditations on Palestine, Israel, Zionism, and the politics of dispossession. The final essays explore his extensive musings on and embodiment of intellectualism, charting the challenges, conditions, and commitments of the Saidian intellectual at the margins.

During the five years of this book's development, it has taken us on a journey to many cities for interviews, conferences, and meetings. In an attempt to retrace Said's footsteps, and to better explore and express the Saidian utterance, we traveled to Jerusalem, New York, London, Paris, Boston, Istanbul, Alexandria, Chicago, and Berlin. The journey commenced in Cairo because no place seemed more suitable to embark from than the city he loved so dearly but felt like a stranger in. However, more than half a century after his departure from Cairo, Said's intellectual footprints are now discernible in downtown literary gatherings. Even Shalaby's seemingly autobiographical novel *Wekalet 'Attiya* explains his affinity for Said as it mirrors exile in the voice and experiences of its shanty-dwelling protagonist.[89] Shalaby's anonymous narrator, in his struggle to situate his agency on the margins of multiple locales, identities, and literacies, is a Saidian nomad par excellence—from his dislocation and improvisation to his amateurism and criticism. Ironically, it is in the uncompromising and unresolved underbelly of Cairo—Said's first site of estrangement in a lifetime of exile—that his intellectual legacy now finds an embracing "home."

NOTES

1. Khairy Shalaby was born in 1938 to a poor family of Azharites in the governorate of Kafr al-Shaykh in the Egyptian Nile delta. Having spent much of his early life in Egypt's most impoverished and disenfranchised communities, he set many of his seventy books—including novels, plays, short stories, historic tales, and critical studies—in the country's socioeconomic underbelly. Inspired by Yehia Hakki and Naguib Mahfouz, Shalaby is considered by many to be the author of the marginalized. He is at present editor of *al-She'r (Poetry)* and the Library of Popular Studies book series, and he contributes regularly to the literary magazine *Weghat Nazar.* He was awarded the Egyptian National Prize for Literature in 1980–81.

2. Cairo's graveyards from the Mamluk period are now home to hundreds of thousands of people, mostly rural migrants. These sites are commonly known by Egyptians as *arafa,* "the cemetery," and by English speakers as "the city of the dead."

3. Edward Said, *Out of Place* (New York: Vintage, 1999), 193.

4. Edward Said, "Homage to a Belly-dancer: On Tahia Carioca," in *Reflections on Exile and Other Essays* (Cambridge, MA: Harvard University Press, 2000), 346–55.

5. Michael Wood, introduction to *On Late Style: Music and Literature against the Grain,* by Edward W. Said (New York: Pantheon Books, 2006), xv, xvi.

6. For a discussion of Said's relationship with his mother, the person to whom he owed his "earliest interest in music," see the dedication and acknowledgments of *Musical Elaborations* (New York: Columbia University Press, 1991), xi; and Michael Wood's introduction to Said, *On Late Style,* xv–xvi.

7. In Edward Said, *After the Last Sky: Palestinian Lives,* photographs by Jean Mohr (New York: Columbia University Press, 1998), 17, Said laments the absence of any contemporary luminaries: "We have no Einsteins, no Chagall, no Freud or Rubenstein to protect us with a legacy of glorious achievements." During her opening speech of the conference "Counterpoints: Edward Said's Legacy" in Ottawa, Canada, in November 2008, Nahla Abdo of Carleton University declared, "I am proud to say, 'we have Edward Said.'"

8. Said, *Out of Place,* 234.

9. Tony Judt, "The Rootless Cosmopolitan," *Nation,* 19 July 2004, 5.

10. In astronomy, the apogee is the point in the orbit of an object around the earth that is at the greatest distance from the center of the earth. The term also describes the farthest or highest point in a civilization's developmental history.

11. Quoted by Said in *Reflections on Exile,* 185.

12. Said discusses apogee as a mark of peak creative virtuosity, a farthest point from convention, in "Heroism and Humanism," *Al-Ahram Weekly,* 6–12 January 2000, no. 463, http://weekly.ahram.org.eg/2000/463/op10.htm (accessed 22 October 2009).

13. For Said, the limits of theory lay in its inability to accommodate "the essential untidiness, the essential unmasterable presence that constitutes a large part of historical and social situations"; in Edward W. Said, "Traveling Theory," in *The World, the Text, and the Critic* (Cambridge, MA: Harvard University Press, 1983), 241. His use of the term *untidy* suggests an intentionally reflexive and critically rigorous yet seemingly discordant theoretical framework based in humanist humility. A characteristic of all knowledge systems, untidiness became a self-proclaimed method for Said. See Victor Li, "Edward Said's Untidiness," *Postcolonial Text* 1, no. 1 (2004).

14. In "Reflections on Exile," Said speaks of the exile's eccentricity and orphanhood as a source of intransigence: "Clutching difference like a weapon to be used with stiffened will, the exile jealously insists on his or her right to refuse to belong"; in Said, *Reflections on Exile,* 182.

15. See Gilles Deleuze and Félix Guattari, *A Thousand Plateaus,* trans. Brian Massumi (New York: Continuum, 1987).

16. For Said's view of his nomadism, see *Reflections on Exile,* 186. Abdirahman A. Hussein describes this state as "strategic nomadism" and "nomadic eclecticism" in *Edward Said: Criticism and Society* (New York: Verso, 2004), 48. See also Edward Said, *Culture and Imperialism* (New York: Vintage, 1998), 331–32.

17. Nomadism was a source of critical interrogation that spanned much of Said's oeuvre, from his critique of colonial discourses in *Orientalism* to his keynote address on the power politics of scholarly discipleship at the American Anthropological Association conference in 1988; originally published in *Critical Inquiry* 15 (Winter 1988), reprinted in *Reflections on Exile,* 293–316. The nomadism of Palestinian dispossession becomes methodological when it unsettles the political impasses produced by dubious peace initiatives, as Said described in *The Politics of Dispossession: The Struggle for Palestinian Self-Determination, 1969–1994* (New York: Vintage, 1995).

18. Jennifer Wicke and Michael Sprinker, "Criticism and the Art of Politics," in *Power, Politics and Culture: Interviews with Edward W. Said,* ed. Gauri Viswanathan (New York: Vintage, 2002), 162.

19. Said, *World, Text, and Critic,* 23.

20. Edward Said, *Representations of the Intellectual: The 1993 Reith Lectures* (New York: Vintage, 1996), 53.

21. Terry Eagleton also describes Said's intellectualism as "Judaic style"; see his "The Last Jewish Intellectual," *New Statesman*, 29 March 2004, 48–49.

22. Ari Shavit, "My Right of Return: An Interview with Edward Said," *Ha'aretz*, 18 August 2000, reprinted in Viswanathan, *Power, Politics and Culture*, 458.

23. Said, *Reflections on Exile*, 185.

24. Shavit, "My Right of Return," 458. For a more extensive treatment of this quote, see Marc Ellis's essay in chapter 21 of this volume, in which he argues that the establishment of the state of Israel suggests a "return," a symbolic yet paradoxical end to the idea of Jewish exile.

25. See Adel Iskandar's interview with Noam Chomsky in chapter 22 of this volume.

26. Said, *Reflections on Exile*, 184.

27. Terry Eagleton describes Said's preoccupation in "The Last Jewish Intellectual," 8. Quote from Said, *Representations of the Intellectual*, 32. See also Joan Smith, "Cultures Aren't Watertight: Interview with Edward W. Said," *Guardian*, 10 December 2001.

28. Said, *Reflections on Exile*, 176.

29. Theodor Adorno, *Minima Moralia: Reflections on a Damaged Life* (New York: Verso, 2006), 39.

30. Said, *After the Last Sky*, 150.

31. *Edward Said: The Last Interview*, Extended Version, DVD, directed by Mike Dibb (London: ICA Projects, 2004).

32. Ibid.

33. Said, *Reflections on Exile*, 174.

34. Ibid, 170.

35. Said expressed an abstract view of nationalism's liberatory function. In *Nationalism, Colonialism, and Literature* (Minneapolis, MN: University of Minnesota Press, 1990, 73–76, 82), he attested to the dominant role nationalism plays in resistance and decolonization movements but cautioned against its fatally limited nature, its superficial appeal to nativism, and its sloppy usage of the term itself.

36. Said, *Reflections on Exile*, 176. See also Bruce Robbins, "Secularism, Elitism, Progress, and Other Transgressions: On Edward Said's 'Voyage in,'" *Social Text* 40 (Fall 1994): 26. For a critical treatment of the secular in Said's work, see Gil Anidjar, "Secularism," *Critical Inquiry* 33 (Autumn 2006): 52–53.

37. "I Find Myself Instinctively on the Other Side of Power," interview with Edward Said, *Guardian*, 10 December 2001.

38. Said, *World, Text, and Critic*, 29. For an extensive treatment of the term *secular* in Said's work, see Anidjar's "Secularism," 52–77.

39. From Hopkins's 1877 poem "Pied Beauty." Quoted in *Edward Said: The Last Interview*.

40. For Said, human agency was at the core of the humanistic exercise. In "Heroism and Humanism," he defines humanism as "disclosure, it is agency, it is immersing oneself in the element of history, it is recovering rationality from the turbulent actualities of human life, and then submitting them painstakingly to the rational processes of judgement and criticism" (*Al-Ahram Weekly*, 6–12 January 2000). See also his preface to the 2003 edition of *Orientalism* (London: Penguin), xvii, xxii. On the distinction between beginnings and origins, see Said's *Beginnings: Intention and Method* (New York: Columbia University Press, 1985), xvii, 32, 316.

41. Quoted in Yan Hairong, "Position without Identity: An Interview with Gayatri Chakravorty Spivak," *Position* 15, no. 2: 439. While supporting self-determination of the Palestinian people irrespective of outcome, Said expressed a personal distance from the idea of a Palestinian state. He acknowledged that exile had become too deeply entrenched in him to warrant any consideration of his return, yet he disavowed any notion of nationalist purity or essentialization (Said, "Literary Theory at the Crossroads of Public Life," interviewed by Imre Salusinszky, in *Power, Politics, and Culture*, 71).

42. Aamir R. Mufti, "Auerbach in Istanbul: Edward Said, Secular Criticism, and the Question of Mi-

nority Culture," in *Edward Said and the Work of the Critic: Speaking Truth to Power,* ed. Paul A. Bové (Durham, NC: Duke University Press, 2000), 244.

43. Said, *Beginnings,* 19.

44. Said, "Opponents, Audiences, Constituencies, and Community," in *Reflections on Exile,* 118.

45. Edward Said, *Humanism and Democratic Criticism* (New York: Columbia University Press, 2004), 28.

46. Stathis Gourgouris, "*Orientalism* and the Open Horizon of Secular Criticism," *Social Text* 24, no. 2 (Summer 2006): 18–19.

47. While credited with initiating postcolonial theory, Said distanced himself from the term and discipline, applied his criticism of it as a systematic theory and expressed what Terry Eagleton described as "increasing impatience" with postcolonialism (Eagleton, "In the Gaudy Supermarket," review of *A Critique of Post-Colonial Reason: Toward a History of the Vanishing Present,* by Gayatri Chakravorty Spivak, *London Review of Books* 13, no. 10, May 1999). See also Bill Ashcroft, Gareth Griffiths, and Helen Tiffin, *The Empire Writes Back: Theory and Practice in Post-colonial Literatures* (New York: Routledge, 2002), 198.

48. Said, *Representations of the Intellectual,* 77.

49. See Said's "Barenboim and the Wagner Taboo," in *Al-Ahram Weekly Online,* 16–22 August 2001, no. 547, reprinted in his *Music at the Limits* (New York: Columbia University Press, 2008). On 7 July 2001, in a Jerusalem concert of the Berlin Staatskapelle orchestra, Barenboim broke the taboo against performing Wagner in Israel by leading his musicians in an encore performance of the overture to *Tristan und Isolde.*

50. For extensive treatments on Conrad and Austen, see Edward Said, *Joseph Conrad and the Fiction of Autobiography* (New York: Columbia University Press, 2007), and Said's chapter "Jane Austen and Empire" in *Culture and Imperialism,* 80–96.

51. Said, *Orientalism* (1978; repr. New York: Penguin Books, 2003), 9.

52. Ibid., 9–10.

53. Said, *Humanism and Democratic Criticism,* 70.

54. Said, *Representations of the Intellectual,* 82.

55. Ibid., 83.

56. Chinua Achebe, "An Image of Africa," *Massachusetts Review* 18, no. 4 (Winter 1977): 782–94.

57. Said, *Culture and Imperialism,* 76.

58. The West-Eastern Divan is the subject of a 2005 Arte film titled *Knowledge Is the Beginning.* The film shows Said as the interlocutor in various seminars for the Arab and Palestinian musicians. He also spends much of the practice and rehearsal time in quiet observation and contemplation. In one conversation with Barenboim, Said says, "When I saw them [the Divan participants], they all came from different backgrounds . . . Christian, Muslims, higher class . . . When they are playing, their identities are irrelevant." Said noted music's ability to fracture and overcome political impasses, albeit briefly. During sessions in Weimar, where Said led the nightly discussions, he spoke to the Divan participants about their experiential politics until Barenboim looked at him, then at cellist Yo-Yo Ma, and declared, "Shall we play?" Here Said expresses music's unique ability to interrupt the status quo, making it "a bit subversive, even when it seems harmless." For a more extensive treatment of the Divan, see Hakem Rustom's interview with Daniel Barenboim in chapter 13 of this volume.

59. Said, *Culture and Imperialism,* 61.

60. Said, *Representations of the Intellectual,* 32; and Smith, "Cultures Aren't Watertight."

61. For a critique of Huntington, see *Edward Said: The Myth of the "Clash of Civilizations,"* DVD, directed by Sut Jhully (Northampton, MA: Media Education Foundation, 1998); Said's "Adrift in Similarity," *Al-Ahram Weekly,* 11–17 October 2001, no. 555; and Said, "The Clash of Definitions," in *Reflections on Exile,* 569–90.

62. Said, *Orientalism*, 328.

63. Said, *Humanism and Democratic Criticism*, 23, 26, 52–55.

64. Said, "A State, Yes, But Not Just for Palestinians," interviewed by Eric Black, in Viswanathan, *Power, Politics and Culture*, 436. See also Edward Said and Christopher Hitchens, *Blaming the Victims: Spurious Scholarship and the Palestinian Question* (New York: Verso, 2001).

65. Said, *On Late Style*, 133.

66. See Lecia Rosenthal's essay in chapter 27 of this volume, where she reluctantly ventures to situate Said's late style.

67. See Said's posthumously published volumes *Humanism and Democratic Criticism* and *On Late Style*. In chapter 27 of this volume, Lecia Rosenthal grapples with the tension between Said's elaboration of late style's "newness" and his resuscitation of a foregone humanism. Others have remarked that Said's founding of the West-Eastern Divan with Daniel Barenboim appeared to be an expression of his own late style. Indeed if one sees the Divan as an ontologically contrapuntal endeavor and an embodiment of persistent exile, secularity, criticism, counterpoint, and humanism, one can consider it a performance of Said's lateness.

68. Said, *Orientalism*, 272–74. Here Said borrows Roland Barthes' view of language as a deformation to explain the fragmented, disjointed nature of representations.

69. Said, *Humanism and Democratic Criticism*, 49.

70. Said, *Out of Place*, 76.

71. Ibid, 148.

72. See Said and Mohr, *After the Last Sky*, xi.

73. Ibid, ix, 78, 88.

74. See W. J. T. Mitchell, "The Panic of the Visual: A Conversation with Edward Said," in Bové, *Edward Said and the Work of the Critic*, 31–50.

75. Michael Wood, in "Theories of Invisibility: Orientalism and the Question of Palestine," his presentation at the Columbia University November 2008 conference "Orientalism from the Standpoint of its Victims—An Edward Said Conference," proposed that Said was himself an invisible man, repeatedly noting the lack of representation through his assertion, "We [the Palestinians] are there." Wood argues that empire's obfuscation of the native, as in Australia and Palestine, produces a displacement without dislocation or the possibility of relocation. "In what world is it possible to go to war against an invisible people?" He suggests that Palestinians who were not dispossessed or deterritorialized in 1948, 1967, and later are instead subjected to the invisibility of psychic diaspora. As internal "migrants," their presence is terminable, their livelihood revocable, their Israeli citizenship retractable, and their memory erasable. Their existence/invisibility is meant to silence their collective identity and extinguish their nationalist aspirations.

76. In addition to examining identity, representation, and the colony, Said and Stuart Hall often converged in their critique of the Foucauldian approach for failing to recognize the liberational claims of poststructuralism. See Jeff Lewis, *Cultural Studies: The Basics* (Thousand Oaks, CA: Sage, 2008) 174–76, 429. Said shared his interest in the confluence of dissident self-representational and hybrid ideas with Brazilian educator Paulo Freire. Both embraced the importance of counterpoint. Fanon's emphasis on emancipatory action sets another trajectory for collective representation.

77. See Edward Said, *Covering Islam: How the Media and the Experts Determine How We See the Rest of the World* (New York: Vintage, 1997), 36–68, for Said's critique of the cult of expertise and the manner in which mediated representation manufactures and cultivates monolithic identities of the "other." On this topic, Said is theoretically aligned with the writings of Stuart Hall and the Birmingham School of critical cultural studies; he also sheds some light on Chomsky's propaganda model.

78. Gary Hentzi and Anne McClintock, "Overlapping Territories: The World, the Text and the Critic," *Critical Text*, reprinted in Viswanathan, *Power, Politics and Culture*, 63.

79. Said affirms Williams's claim that one can "unlearn" the "inherent dominative mode"; Raymond Williams, *Culture and Society: 1780–1950* (London: Chatto & Windus, 1958), 376.

80. Although Said's contribution to the literature on Palestine is both colossal and indispensable, two notable volumes are *The Question of Palestine* (New York: Vintage, 1992) and *Peace and Its Discontents: Essays on Palestine in the Middle East Peace Process* (New York: Vintage, 1996).

81. Said, preface to *Orientalism*, xxix.

82. Joe Sacco and Edward Said, *Palestine* (Maple Leaf, WA: Fantagraphics Books, 2002), v. Said's introduction to this vivid comic book points to the dissidence of the genre and describes the "terrifying accuracy" and "gentleness" of Sacco's artistic representation, both experiential and fictive, of the underdogs who inhabit the fringes. See also Said and Hitchens, *Blaming the Victims*.

83. See Mathieu Courville, "Genealogies of Postcolonialism: A Slight Return from Said and Foucault Back to Fanon and Sartre," *Studies in Religion* 36, no. 2: 215–40.

84. Hussein, *Edward Said: Criticism and Society*, 34.

85. Smith, "Cultures Aren't Watertight."

86. This became the topic of a plenary at the 2008 Middle Eastern Studies Association convention, which charted *Orientalism*'s lasting influence on the thirtieth anniversary of its publication.

87. Attempts to restrict the circulation of Said's writings within the academy, campaigns to undermine conferences and events in his name, and efforts to discredit his supporters abound—from congressional hearings on Title VI funding where both his person and scholarship were admonished to efforts to undermine a mural commemorating Said at San Francisco State University. Nonetheless, Said's impact within the academy is significant and far-reaching, evidenced by the tens of conferences and memorial lectures worldwide dedicated to his intellectual legacy—including events in Istanbul, Cairo, London, New York, Ottawa, Toronto, Berlin, and Paris. For a discussion of the attacks on Said, see Mathieu Courville, " 'Ivory Towers' or Tower of Babel? A Critical Reading of Martin Kramer," *Critique: Critical Middle Eastern Studies* 15, no. 2 (Summer 2006): 187–99; Stathis Gourgouris, "*Orientalism* and the Open Horizon of Secular Criticism," *Social Text* 24, no. 2 (Summer 2006): 11–20; and Matthew Abraham, "Introduction: Edward Said and After: Toward a New Humanism," special issue, *Cultural Critique* 67 (Fall 2007): 3, 4.

88. One would be hard pressed to find an intellectual in the past century whose memory alone is a source of such heated controversy. Said's memorialization has drawn the enthusiasm of some and the ire of others, even more so than that of his late contemporaries Foucault and Derrida.

89. Khairy Shalaby's 1992 novel *Wekalet 'Attiya*, which won the 2003 Naguib Mahfouz Medal for Literature, was translated into English by Farouk Abdel Wahab and published as *The Lodging House* (Cairo: American University in Cairo Press, 2007).

1

Affiliating with Edward Said

Joseph Massad

Perhaps one of the more important principles that Edward Said abided by in his life and career was the centrality of his role as secular critic. He saw criticism as constitutive of the life of the intellectual, who must "speak truth to power." Indeed, it was his commitment to persistent criticism as a basis for thinking that made him so controversial, whether in the United States, Europe, or the Arab world. Said insisted on affiliative forms of intellectual belonging and community in the expansive sense of the term, forsaking filiative forms as too limiting. The intellectuals and political figures with whom he affiliated and the ideas to which he sought to belong guided his intellectual project of reading and interpreting not only the modern experience of colonizing and colonized subjects but also the way in which both informed his own intellectual constitution and production.

Said believed that the life of an intellectual should be that of a migrant and an exile. He used the term *exile* in a metaphorical sense, referring not to leaving one's physical home but rather to leaving the conventions and accepted truths of one's community, insistently criticizing these truths, and not shrinking from addressing the failures of one's audience, no matter how powerful. In his view, intellectuals must be outsiders "so far as privileges, powers and honors, are concerned."[1] While respectful of religion as a personal relationship to the metaphysical, Said was a committed secularist in his intellectual life. He insisted on being politically godless in an age dominated by the worship of political deities—the "West," Soviet Communism, U.S. imperialism, nationalisms of all varieties, to name the most prominent. His political atheism, however, was not equivalent to neutrality; rather it was an insistent critical stance toward all political religions. He mocked the rites and rituals staged by worshippers of such gods and insisted that these were proof of moral bankruptcy.

Said used the ideas and philosophies associated with these gods but refused to accede to their terms of worship and conversion. This stance was to become his hallmark. Commitment to secular criticism for him was consistent with his conviction that these gods always fail to deliver on their promises and that intellectual life must be lived according to the understanding that "situations are contingent, not . . . inevitable . . . the result of a series of historical choices made by men and women, . . . facts of society made by human beings, and not . . . natural or God-given, therefore unchangeable, permanent, irreversible."[2]

In this sense, Said resisted being enclosed by any type of society, including—and especially—nationality: "Does the fact of nationality commit the individual intellectual . . . to the public mood for reasons of solidarity, primordial loyalty, or national patriotism? Or can a better case be made for the intellectual as a dissenter from the corporate ensemble?"[3] He expected such dissent from Palestinian as well as American intellectuals. "The history of thought, to say nothing of political movements, is extravagantly illustrative of how the dictum 'solidarity before criticism,' means the end of criticism. I take criticism so seriously as to believe that, even in the very midst of battle in which one is unmistakably on one side against another, there should be criticism, because there must be critical consciousness if there are to be issues, problems, values, even lives to be fought for."[4]

Said took this dictum to heart in addressing the politics of Palestinian liberation, posing autocritique as central to its success. In this vein, he launched his attack against the Oslo capitulation. His commitment to the rights of the Palestinian people mobilized his hostility to what he rightly predicted would be the Bantustan solution signed in Oslo and celebrated on the White House lawn. The subsequent metamorphosis of the Palestine Liberation Organization (PLO) into the Palestinian Authority (PA), from a liberation movement into a police authority subcontracted to the Israeli occupation, confirmed his predictions. Moreover, Oslo marked another transformation—with a number of well-known Palestinian intellectuals switching allegiance from national liberation to what came to be known as political pragmatism. They suspended their critical faculties in the name of pragmatism and national unity and were paid handsomely by the PA's new funders. Some quit academic jobs to become full-time advisors to Arafat and his ministers in the PA.[5] This was the fate that Said had feared would befall intellectuals whose vocation was not based on secular criticism.

Said insisted that the intellectual be an amateur, not a professional. He objected to the professional intellectual who views her or his work "as something you do for a living, between the hours of nine and five, with one eye on the clock, and another cocked at what is considered to be proper, professional behavior—not rocking the boat, not straying outside the accepted paradigms or limits, making yourself marketable and above all presentable, hence uncontroversial and unpolitical and 'objective.' "[6] The intellectual amateur, for Said, was "someone who considers that to be a thinking and concerned member of a society one is entitled to raise moral issues at the heart of even the most technical and professionalized activity as it involves one's country, its power, its mode of interacting with its citizens as well as with other societies."[7] The intellectual as amateur, he insisted, should be able to go beyond the professional routine of doing what she or he is supposed to do by asking "why one does it, who benefits from it, how can it reconnect with a personal project and original thoughts."[8]

TRAVELING ORIENTALISM

For Said, these ideas about intellectual life were not merely musings but a way of life. Perhaps the best exemplar of his desire to unsettle rather than to accommodate his audience is *Orientalism*. When the book came out thirty years ago, few books unraveled the archeology of Western identity the way *Orientalism* did. Said's book ingeniously exposed the connections, relationships, modulations, and displacements in Orientalism's production of an Orient that was a ruse for the production of the Occident. If, as Frantz Fanon argued, "Europe is literally the creation of the Third World," Said elaborated on that brilliant summation.[9] Thus, for him, Orientalism was never about the Orient and its identity and culture but about the production of the West and *its* identity and culture—in short, "a kind of Western projection"; the West could not exist if the East were not invented as its antithesis, its opposite, its other.[10]

Edward Said's *Orientalism* excavated a Western epistemological mode of production that projected an Oriental other from its own interiority, externalizing and banishing this other outside the European self as it sought to define itself. The book also tracked the travels of the discipline of Orientalism from Europe to America, where it was "degraded"—a fate that Said predicted would be the fate of much traveling theory. In a much-celebrated essay on this idea, Said wrote that degradation does not have a "moral implication, but rather . . . conveys the lowering of color, the greater degree of distance, the loss of immediate force."[11] If Orientalism (the discipline) in Europe exemplified a type of erudite and sophisticated imperial knowledge, in America, it was degraded to charlatanism.

Said's role as anthropologist of Europe—its cultures, arts, and literatures—catapulted him to the forefront of knowledge production in the Western academy. His book also enraged his detractors, who were appalled by his presumed insolence in subjecting white Europeans to an Oriental gaze. In undertaking his study of Europe, Said, true to his method and contrary to traditional European scholarship on non-Europeans, did not objectify the European but held himself accountable to the very people and cultures he studied and wrote about. This approach is the exact opposite of what Orientalists (and most Western anthropologists) do when they study non-Europeans. As Said wrote, "The Orientalist can imitate the Orient without the opposite being true. What he says about the Orient is therefore to be understood as description obtained in a one-way exchange: as *they* spoke and behaved, *he* observed and wrote down. His power was to have existed amongst them as a native speaker, as it were, and also as a secret writer. And what he wrote was intended as useful knowledge, not for them, but for Europe and its various disseminative institutions."[12] Said's refusal to objectify what he sought to know was precisely why so many Americans and Europeans engaged with and responded to his ideas.

In his partial reversal of European ontological authority, wherein Said, the Oriental, acted as a subject studying Europe and Europeans, Said was careful not to fall into the trap of "Occidentalism," which critics like Sadiq Jalal al-'Azm incorrectly attributed to him.[13] Indeed, even were Said to have objectified the Occident, Occidentalism could not have been the result, given the global racial arrangement of hegemony, control, and power. Orientalism is the discourse of the powerful; the weak lack the power to formulate dominating objectifying discourses, whether of the Occidentalist or any other variety.

The critics most discomfited by *Orientalism* were those who maintained that Said never spoke of the "real Orient."[14] In enacting his critique, Said indeed refused to play the role of native informant, which many critics wanted him to assume. They saw this refusal as arrogance, the willfulness of a subject daring to focus his piercing, albeit nonobjectifying, gaze on Europeans and their systems of thought. *Orientalism* therefore aroused hostility not only because of its method or political critique but also because of the ontological anxiety it induced in Euro-American critics, as much today as when it first appeared in 1978. Moreover, Said well understood that the "Orient" was a category invented by Orientalism, and he saw any attempt to describe a "real" Orient as destined to reinscribe itself within Orientalist discourse. His solution was simple: critical intellectuals must throw the category of "Orient" into the dustbin of history, rather than try to "represent" it "truthfully."

Shattering the European monopoly on dictating subject-object positions, *Orientalism* traveled across disciplines, geographies, and histories. I address each briefly in the paragraphs below.

In traveling through academe, *Orientalism*'s method and epistemological critique were taken up by a number of disciplines, ranging from feminism and gender studies to anthropology, comparative literature, and cultural and postcolonial studies (the latter owes its existence to Said's contributions).[15] In Said's method, the gaze of the other turned around to investigate not only how the other was produced but also how the European self (itself based on many local elisions) was engineered as the universal self. The vigor of Said's method and its ontological boldness were appropriated readily and radicalized, allowing for the study not of blackness but of whiteness, not of femininity but of masculinity, not of homosexuality but of heterosexuality. If Frantz Fanon radicalized George Lukács, as Said observed in "Traveling Theory Reconsidered," Said's own traveling *Orientalism* has been generative of similar radicalization.[16]

In Middle East studies, *Orientalism*'s legacy has been its political critique, not its method. Thus, scores of books on the Middle East have paid homage to Said's work even as they have proceeded with business as usual, Orientalist epistemology and all. For the most part, *Orientalism* remains poorly understood, if not misunderstood altogether, within Middle East studies. Fred Halliday, for example, one of the better-known European Middle East scholars, believes that Said's book simply "identified" the "contestable" claim that there exists "a widespread and pervasive *single* error at the core of a range of literature."[17] In fact, the concept of error is foreign to Said's approach; for him, *Orientalism* was neither a positive nor a positivist project. This fact has apparently eluded many in the field.

Orientalism has also traveled outside America to Europe, Asia, Africa, and Latin America. It has traveled in translation and as a method. Upon its publication in the Arab world in 1981, it became an event, just as it had in America and Europe. Indeed, *Orientalism* and Said's subsequent translated books became part of ongoing Arab intellectual debates not only about Western representations but also about Arab literary production itself.[18] In contrast, some of Said's Western and neoliberal Arab critics suggested that because the book had attracted nativists of all shapes and colors, it was "Occidentalist" and "Khumeiniyist."[19] Said's hostility to nativist appropriations notwithstanding, such critics refused to acknowledge the novelty of *Orientalism* in its new cultural context. Since the nineteenth century, most Arab travelers to Europe had been writing about Europeans in Arabic for an Arab audience. These writers included the nineteenth-century educator Rifa'ah al-Tahtawi and the literary genius Ahmad Faris al-Shidyaq. Both accepted Europe as the new locus of civilization and believed that its identity and that of the Arab East were of a different order. Their books were judged by normative Arab values of the period. Said's *Orientalism* exploded the notion of Orient and Occident; addressed the subjects of its study, Europeans, in one of their own languages; and evaluated them by their own normative evaluative criteria. The book's major achievements in the Arab world were to uncover the production of the European self to an Arab audience that had largely been exposed to European adulatory views of Europeans and to reveal Europeans' production, not merely their representation, of the Oriental.

Orientalism also traveled across time. Thirty years and myriad editions later, it remains in demand. In light of such peregrinations, it is instructive to subject the book to Said's own remarks about "traveling theory." Has *Orientalism*, which is admittedly both theory and criticism, in traveling across time, left its conditions of production and the normative values of its immediate environment to another time, with its own power relations and normative values? It seems to me that this would indeed be the case were it not for a crucial difference—namely, that the conditions and normative values that governed the writing and publication of *Orientalism* in 1978 have changed very little, except in certain corridors of the academy. *Orientalism* was written a decade after the June 1967 war pushed Orientalist discourse to the forefront in America and Europe. If, on the morrow of that war, the *Daily Telegraph* could declare Israel's conquest of the remainder of Palestine and parts of Syria and Egypt as the "triumph of the civilized," the ongoing battles in which America is engaged today can still be seen as part of the "civilized world's" continuous crusades against the uncivilized.[20] Although the academic value of *Orientalism* and recognition of Said have appreciated considerably since 1978, so has the Orientalism to which Said applied his analytical gaze.

We are today in a battle for domination by a superpower that insists on seeing the Orient Orientalistically while itself reflecting all that it finds offensive about this fantastical Orient. If the Oriental bin Laden's logic was that the sacrifice of innocent civilians was justifiable in the service of defeating tyranny, George W. Bush and his cohorts used the same logic in sacrificing many more innocent civilians in Afghanistan and Iraq. If bin Laden is condemned for his religious obscurantism and his belief that God is on his side against the infidels, Bush and his cabal of officials and pundits professed that God was on their side against the evil of the uncivilized. If the Oriental Saddam was feared because of his potential use of (nowhere-to-be-found) weapons of mass destruction against the civilized, Bush was willing to use such weapons against civilians to rid the civilized of the Oriental despot. In this sense, as Arundhati Roy has argued, Bush and bin Laden are each other's doppelgängers.[21] Thus, if Orientalism holds the Arab and Muslim worlds to be static, unchanging, frozen in time, it remains blind to the fact that its own categories and epistemology stand frozen in a time warp.

Although circumstances have changed measurably in the Western academy in the past third century, few circumstances have changed outside it. *Orientalism* has traveled the past thirty years and will continue to travel precisely because the conditions of its production remain unchanged (except in their local details and permutations). The persistence of Orientalism as epistemology has made the book's main goal of demystifying and decoding a Euro-American system of thought as valuable as ever in resisting this increasingly administered and terrorized world.

Said once asked, "What happens to a theory when it moves from one place to another . . . what happens to it when, in different circumstances, and for new reasons, it is used again and, in still more different circumstances, again? What can this tell us about theory itself—its limits, its possibilities, its inherent problems—and what can it suggest to us about the relationship between theory and criticism, on the one hand, and society and culture on the other?"[22] Readers' continuing and growing engagement with *Orientalism* is in itself an answer to Said's important query.

PALESTINE FROM THE STANDPOINT OF EDWARD SAID

If Walter Benjamin thought that "there is no document of civilization which is not at the same time a document of barbarism" and Theodor Adorno insisted that barbarism was internal rather than external to European culture, Said asserted that European culture was defined fundamentally by (though not necessarily reducible to) the colonial venture it unleashed outward.[23] Because of this view, a number of neoconservative members of American academe portray Said as dangerous. The neocons may be right in one sense, for Said's thought is indeed dangerous to those seeking to administer culture, given that much of his work continuously cultivates communities of resistance to self-appointed cultural arbiters. This is precisely what compels Said's enemies to seek to silence his voice.

But if *Orientalism* unsettled people in power, whether in academic life or, increasingly, in political life (recent congressional hearings included discussions of the corrupting influence of Said's *Orientalism* on university students), Said's work and advocacy for the Palestinian cause earned him the enmity of far greater numbers, including fanatics who threatened his life and burned his office. Said's defense of Palestinian rights was never bound by worship at the altar of nationalism, but the opposite: his refusal to accept that Zionism, as a form of nationalism and colonialism, should be a god for intellectuals. He was a good student of Jewish history and spoke regularly, and in the same breath, about historical Jewish suffering and contemporary Palestinian suffering. The fact of nationality never limited his sympathy for oppressed Jews, any more than his secularism and refusal to worship the god of nationalism limited his defense of Palestinians' struggle against their Zionist oppressors.

Edward Said was born in Jerusalem, but this biographical fact merely made Palestine a point of origin for him. Indeed, Said disliked the idea of origins. For him, Palestine *became* a point of departure, or more precisely a "beginning," rather than an origin, a notion he associated with the theological and which therefore had little purchase in his decidedly secular life. For Edward Said, "Beginning is basically an activity which ultimately implies return and repetition rather than simple linear accomplishment, that beginning and beginning-again are historical while origins are divine, that a beginning not only creates but is its own method because it has intention. In short, beginning is making or producing difference ... which is the result of combining the already-familiar with the fertile novelty of human work in language. ... Thus beginnings confirm, rather than discourage, a radical severity and verify evidence of at least some innovation—of having begun."[24] Palestine was a beginning for Said because it involved his active intention: "Between the word *beginning* and the word *origin* lies a constantly changing system of meanings ... I use *beginning* as having the more active meaning, and *origin* the more passive one:

Thus 'X is the origin of Y,' while 'the beginning A *leads to* B.'" Said believed that "ideas about origins, because of their passivity, are put to uses . . . [that] ought to be avoided."[25]

It is because of such uses that Said did not originate *in* Palestine but rather began with it. This distinction is crucial because, as he wrote, "Beginning has influences upon what follows from it: in the paradoxical manner, then, according to which beginnings as events are not necessarily confined to the beginning, we realize that a major shift in perspective and knowledge has taken place. The state of mind that is concerned with origins is . . . theological. By contrast, and this is the shift, beginnings are eminently secular, or gentile, continuing activities. . . . Whereas an origin *centrally* dominates what derives from it, the beginning (especially the modern beginning), encourages non-linear development, a logic giving rise to the sort of multileveled coherence of dispersion we find . . . in the text of modern writers."[26] How then did Said begin? How did Palestine begin for him? How did he begin in and decidedly with Palestine?

Although Said came late to publishing his ideas about musical counterpoint as the basis of reading texts and analyzing historical events (in *Culture and Imperialism),* he had internalized this method much earlier in his scholarship, most eminently in his work on Palestine. For Said, to look at things contrapuntally was to "be able to think through and interpret together experiences that are discrepant, each with its particular agenda and pace of development, its own internal formations, its internal coherence and system of external relationships, all of them coexisting and interacting with others."[27] In *Orientalism,* Said pursued just such an interpretation, insisting that the history of European Jews and the history of anti-Semitism must be read in tandem with the history of the Muslim Orient and the history of Orientalism. In an earlier work, he had asserted, "[The] Palestinian Arabs, who have suffered incalculable miseries for the sake of Western anti-Semitism, really do exist, have existed, and will continue to exist as part of Israel's extravagant cost."[28] In *Orientalism,* he gestured toward the process that linked Palestinians to this history of European anti-Semitism and indeed showed the intimate connection between the history of anti-Semitism and the field of scholarship known as Orientalism.

It is there, at the conjunction of his reading of anti-Semitism and Orientalism, that Said *intended* to begin with Palestine. In *Orientalism,* he began that interrogation by affirming, "What has not been sufficiently stressed in histories of modern anti-Semitism has been the legitimation of such atavistic designations by Orientalism, and . . . the way this academic and intellectual legitimation has persisted right through the modern age in discussions of Islam, the Arabs, or the Near Orient."[29] The way in which Jew and Arab, invented as Semites in European philology as early as the eighteenth century, came to register in the West was best exemplified for Said in the following astute aside by Marcel Proust: "The Rumanians, the Egyptians, the Turks may hate the Jews. But in a French drawing-room the differences between those people are not so apparent, and an Israelite making his entry as though he were emerging from the heart of the desert, his body crouching like a hyaena's, his neck thrust obliquely forward, spreading himself in proud 'salaams,' completely satisfies a certain taste for the Oriental."[30]

Therefore, Said noted that in the wake of the October 1973 War and the oil embargo, Western representations of Arabs showed "clearly 'Semitic' features: sharply hooked noses, the evil mustachioed leer on their faces," and he pointed out that such images were "obvious reminders (to a largely non-Semitic population) that 'Semites' were at the bottom of all 'our' troubles, which in this case is principally a gasoline shortage. The transference of popular anti-Semitic animus from a Jewish to an Arab target was made smoothly, since the figure was essentially the same."[31] Here, Said begins again with the history of anti-Semitism to illustrate his findings about the history of the Arab, and specifically the Palestinian. Said pointed out that in depicting the Arab as a "negative value" and as "a disrupter of Israel's and the West's existence . . . as a surmountable obstacle to Israel's creation in 1948," Orientalist and anti-Semitic representations linked the Arab ontologically to the Jew: "The Arab is conceived of now as a shadow that dogs the Jew. In that shadow—because Arabs and Jews are Oriental Semites—can be placed whatever traditional, latent mistrust a Westerner feels towards the Oriental. For the Jew of pre-Nazi Europe has bifurcated: What we have now is a Jewish hero, constructed out of a reconstructed cult of the adventurer-pioneer-Orientalist . . . , and his creeping, mysteriously fearsome shadow, the Arab Oriental."[32]

These remarks allude to the endemic anti-Semitism that plagues all representation of Arabs today, indeed the displacement of the object of anti-Semitism from the Jew onto the Arab. Much as anti-Semites posited Jews as the purveyors of corruption, as financier bankers who control the world, as violent communist subversives, and as poisoners of Christian wells, many Westerners today view Arabs and Muslims as manipulators of the oil market and therefore of the global financial market, purveyors of hatred and corruption of civilized Christian society, violent terrorists, and possible mass murderers whose weapon of choice is not a Semitic poison but nuclear, chemical, and biological weapons. Thus, activist and documentarian Michael Moore felt justified in telling us in his film *Fahrenheit 9/11* about the portion of the American economy controlled by Saudi money but saw no need to mention the much larger American share of the Saudi economy. In light of Said's work, one cannot understand Orientalism, the Arab, and ultimately the Palestinian without understanding European Jewish history and the history of European anti-Semitism in the context of European colonialism, which made and make all these historical transformations possible and mobilize the discourse that produces them as facts.

To begin with Palestine then is to begin with European Jews, and to begin with

European Jews in modernity is to begin with the history of anti-Semitism. By beginning with these various historical junctures, Said was able to see the emergence of Zionist ideology as a brand of Orientalism and therefore of anti-Semitism that was intrinsic to Europe's colonial project: "By a concatenation of events and circumstances the Semitic myth bifurcated in the Zionist movement; one Semite went the way of Orientalism, the other, the Arab, was forced to go the way of the Oriental."[33] In reading the history of Palestine, of the Palestinians, in conjunction with the history of European Jews, Said could explain how Zionist ideology came to describe Arabs using the same anti-Semitic vocabulary deployed against Jews. This contrapuntal reading allowed him to see that Chaim Weizmann's anti-Arab racism makes sense only in the context of European colonial history: "The common denominator between Weizmann and the European anti-Semite is the Orientalist perspective, seeing Semites . . . as by nature lacking the desirable qualities of Occidentals."[34] Following Said, we can easily see how this common denominator between Zionism and anti-Semitism in the era of colonialism produced the Palestinian *as the Jew,* to the extent that "In his resistance to foreign colonialists the Palestinian was either a stupid savage, or a negligible quantity, morally and even existentially."[35] Said understood Jewish intellectual history as a history of outsiders who effected crucial critiques of European Christian society, and he was saddened by Zionism's continuing attempts to suppress this Jewish tradition by transforming it into a new kind of worship of the state of Israel. The refusal of most Jews to begin again from a position of critique of Zionism, indeed the insistence on beginning again with it, has led to the disappearance of the European Jew as a meaningful ontological category. In this sense, and in line with his understanding of Zionism's displacement of the Jew onto the Palestinian, which was both an ontological and an epistemological reordering, Said told the Israeli newspaper *Ha'aretz* that he considered himself "the last Jewish intellectual."[36]

Said's important gesture allows us to look at the struggles over Palestine in tandem with one another, contrapuntally. If beginning with the modern history of European Jews, one also begins with the history of anti-Semitism, then beginning with the history of Zionism allows one to begin with the transformation of the Palestinian into the Jew. Herein lies the importance of 1948 as another beginning, that of exile and a new form of colonialism. Said made this point in staccato tone: "In 1948, Israel was established; Palestine was destroyed, and the great Palestinian dispossession began."[37] The Palestinian resistance movement, which Said called "Palestinianism" in 1970, also marked a new beginning for the Palestinians. As Said explained, "Palestinianism, then, is an effort at repatriation . . . a transition from being in exile to becoming a Palestinian once again."[38]

But to begin with Palestinianism is also to begin with identity, one that is constantly denied and constantly besieged not only by discourse but also by guns, tanks, and warplanes. As Said explained, "Identity—who we are, where we come from, what we are—is difficult to maintain in exile. Most other people take their identity for granted. Not the Palestinian, who is required to show proof of identity more or less constantly. . . . Such as it is, our existence is linked negatively to encomiums about Israel's democracy."[39]

From Said's standpoint, Palestine and the Palestinians can be apprehended only if one understands the Arab world and Israel as the context and the space within which Palestinians exist. The dislocation of the Palestinians, our dispossession and alienation from our geography, our transformation into wandering and besieged Jews make up the very details of the Palestinian experience. Here is how Said described Palestinian lives: "The stability of geography and the continuity of land—these have completely disappeared from my life and the life of all Palestinians. If we are not stopped at borders, or herded into new camps, or denied reentry and residence, or barred from travel from one place to another, more of our land is taken, our lives are interfered with arbitrarily, our voices are prevented from reaching each other, our identity is confined to frightened little islands in an inhospitable environment of superior military force sanitized by the clinical jargon of pure administration."[40]

In a Western context, Said understood intimately the racial game of civilization that credits the suffering of the civilized and is indifferent to the suffering of "barbarians." He noted, "We have no known Einsteins, no Chagall, no Freud, or Rubinstein to protect us with a legacy of glorious achievements. We have had no Holocaust to protect us with the world's compassion. We are 'other,' and opposite, a flaw in the geometry of resettlement and exodus."[41]

Thus, as the new Jews, our lives must replicate the past life of our oppressors. Said perceived our condition with acuity: "Continuity for them, the dominant population; discontinuity for us, the dispossessed and dispersed."[42] Yet he demanded that the world take notice of our predicament and our tragedy. He described in stark terms the Palestinian condition: "We lead our lives under a sword of Damocles, whose dry rhetorical form is the query 'When are you Palestinians going to accept a solution?'—the implication being that if we don't, we'll disappear."[43] Indeed, many in the Israeli and pro-Israeli camp continue to busy themselves with cataloging the many "missed opportunities" for Palestinians to capitulate, otherwise coded as opportunities for "peace." Said understood well that we could not accept their solutions and that our fight would continue against all attempts to make us disappear. Indeed, Edward Said was central to the struggle to make known the Palestinian narrative.[44] He became a veritable passport for the Palestinian cause, allowing it to cross borders into territories where it was previously denied entry.

Having begun with Palestine, Said began again after the Oslo agreement was signed. His embrace of new beginnings was intimately linked to his aversion to origins. His insistence on the importance of "affiliation" rather than filiation mirrored the distinction he drew between beginnings and origins. Thus, although he was filia-tively connected to Palestine through the accident of birth, he later sought to affili-ate with it—to begin again from a new point. For Said, affiliation offered a conscious choice of belonging, whereas filiation was simply imposed. Although he affiliated with and belonged to the PLO when it represented the Palestinian people's inter-ests, he disaffiliated from it the moment it became an instrument of Zionism. Therein lay his trenchant criticism of Arafat. Said was certainly aware that the PLO of 1968–71 had changed dramatically with the influx of oil money from the Saudis and the Kuwaitis, and from Palestinian businessmen who made their money in the Gulf. However, he continued to read the situation contrapuntally and understood Palestinian limitations in the face of naked power. That the oil money succeeded in preventing the radicalization of the PLO, which was the goal of Arab govern-ments seeking to preserve the modus vivendi with Israel and maintain the stabil-ity of Gulf regimes and imperial oil interests, was ironic. The PLO was the only Third World revolutionary group funded by the most reactionary regimes in the Third World. Yet it carried the only banner that could promise the Palestinian people some redress. When Arafat opted out of that project, Said opted out of the game of prag-matism altogether, offering a renewed vision of the secular democratic state as a decolonized binational state. Comparing the PLO unfavorably with South Africa's African National Congress, as Said often did, was one thing, but witnessing the trans-formation of Arafat from a Mandela-like figure into a Buthelezi was another.[45] In reading the history of Palestine in conjunction with the history of colonialism, especially the settler variety, Said understood that Oslo was Zionism's greatest tri-umph over the Palestinians since the Catastrophe of 1948.

In this sense, Said's notion of secularism—understood as a refusal to believe in infallible gods, not least of which are nationalism and the nation form—is the or-ganizing principle for his notion of beginnings and his rejection of origins as the-ological. Being exiled from dominant ideologies and cultures, including his own, provided Said with the tools to be a critic: one who was inside Palestine and out-side it, inside the West and outside it, and inside the nation and outside it. This role was crucial to his project of being "out of place," physically and intellectually, and of belonging to certain intellectual and political traditions. It defined his sense of be-longing to Palestine and Palestinianness, in both a filiative and an affiliative sense.

Said's pragmatism never compromised his idealism. Understanding the status of Palestine as historical, he never reified it: "The fact of the matter is that today Palestine does not exist, except as a memory or, more importantly, as an idea, a po-litical and human experience, and an act of sustained popular will ... [It is the mil-lions of Palestinians] who make up the question of Palestine, and if there is no coun-try called Palestine it is not because there are no Palestinians. There are."[46] Thus, for Said, to begin with Palestine is to begin with the understanding that "the strug-gle between Palestinians and Zionism [is] a struggle between a presence and an interpretation, the former constantly appearing to be overpowered and eradicated by the latter."[47] Said demonstrated his hermeneutical skills as a critic to disassemble the web of representations that Orientalism and anti-Semitism mobilized through Zionism. His attempt to read Palestine from a Canaanite perspective contra Michael Walzer was deeply informed by his interpretive skills. He mounted this analysis not by reducing a form of perspectivalism to relativism but by repeating the logic of Zionism to retell its story differently. If Zionism insisted on playing a prehistorical archeological game, positing fantastically the ancient Hebrews as the progenitors of modern European Jews, Said smugly posited the tale of the earlier native Canaanites, conquered as they were by the invading foreign Hebrews, in ways reminiscent of the Palestinian experience.[48] Polemics aside, and he *was* a master polemicist, Said insisted that for Palestinians, Zionism constituted but part of the chain of historical invasions of Palestine, from the Crusaders to the Ottomans, Napoleon, and the British. He insisted, therefore, on reading Zionism not only in its European environment but also from the standpoint of its Palestinian victims.

In light of these beginnings, it is crucial to consider also how Said *saw* Palestine. Said's literariness and engagement with the discursive informed his analysis of how Palestine and the Palestinians emerged within European Orientalist thought and its Zionist correlate. But he did not limit his investigations to the discursive, he also drew on the visual, whether in the imaginary dimension of thought and fantasy, visual representation in literature itself, or concrete visual representations and artistic productions of the worlds that Europe constructed, including Palestine. How did visual representations begin to read the Palestinian situation for Said? Can such representations provide a venue to look at Palestine and Zionism from the standpoint of the Palestinians? It is in considering these questions that the centrality of the visual and its interpretation lies for Said when looking at the Palestinian Question. If Michel Foucault, who fascinated Said, began his historical and philosophical inquiries with the visible, the seeable, and then moved to the discursive, the sayable, Said began with the discursive and then moved to the visible. His book *After the Last Sky* is an introduction to the dialectics of seeing and blindness and a look at the critic's role of appreciating and interpreting the visual. It is in a sense an explication of how the visual could begin to read Palestine and how Said himself could begin again with Palestine through the visual. Because seeing is not a simple photochemical response but a hermeneutical exercise, Said delved into the question of how he, a Palestinian, could see Palestinians through the eyes of a Swiss photographer. What is inside and what is outside, what is interior (and anterior) to the representation in a photograph and what remains outside it? In these junctures, Said located his intervention. While fully appreciative of the aesthetic value of photography, Said apologetically justifies the role of the critic as a reader of the social text inscribed by visual representations. For him, Jean Mohr's photographs, around which he constructed *After the Last Sky*, demanded an interpretation. In looking at pictures of shepherds, and of Palestinian women in the field, for example, Said explains how the process of interpretation begins:

> [The photographs] are all, in a troubling sense, without the marks of an identifiable historical period. And for that matter, they could be scenes of people anywhere in the Arab world. Placeless. Yet all the photographs are of working people, peasants with a hard life led on a resistant soil, in a harsh climate, requiring ceaseless effort. We—you—know that these are photographs of Palestinians because I have identified them as such; I know these are Palestinian peasants because Jean has been my witness. But in themselves these photographs are silent; they seem saturated with a kind of inert being that outweighs anything they express; consequently they invite the embroidery of explanatory words.[49]

Said insists that his reading is one of many and that others can and do read them differently. One of the first readings of a photograph is giving it a title, such as the one titled "Shepherds in the field." Mindful of his Western audience and the influence of Orientalism on them, Said explains,

> You could add, "tending their flocks, much as the Bible says they did." Or the two photographs of women evoke phrases like "the timeless East," and "the miserable lot of women in Islam." Or, finally, you could remember something about the importance to "such people" of UNRWA [United Nations Relief and Works Agency], or the PLO—the one an agency for supplementing the impoverished life of anonymous Palestinians with the political gift of refugee status, the other a political organization giving identity and direction to "the Palestinian people." But these accumulated interpretations add up to a frighteningly direct correlative of what the photographs depict as "alienated labor," as Marx called it, work done by people who have little control of either the product of their labor or their own laboring capacity.[50]

In piling up possible interpretation upon possible interpretation in this passage, Said is trying to demonstrate both the centrality of hermeneutics in making possible multiple readings of aesthetic products and their social texts and its inadequacy as an exercise in dominating or in resisting domination. Thus, he concludes the above paragraph by asserting, "After such a recognition [that of alienated labor], whatever bit of exotic romance that might attach to these photographs is promptly blown away. As the process of preserving the scenes, photographic representation is thus the culmination of a sequence of capturings. Palestinian peasants are the creatures of half a dozen other processes, none of which leaves these productive human beings with their labor intact."[51]

Said is aware that certain readers of the visual want only one immediate meaning. Such visual fundamentalists can and often do marshal a theological approach to the visual in the interest of establishing facts or propping up claims. Although Said and Mohr attempt in *After the Last Sky* to begin again viewing Palestinians differently, Orientalism and Zionism had begun almost a century earlier to look at Palestinians through other visual prisms. Said discusses that "most famous of early-twentieth-century European books about Palestine," *The Immoveable East* by the Alsatian Philip Baldensperger.[52] To Said, the notable feature in this inaugural effort was that "it is magisterial in its indifference to the problems of interpretation and observation."[53] He felt the same about the work of Finnish archeologist and anthropologist Hilma Granquist. Reading these writers and "seeing their photographs and drawings, I feel at an even greater remove from the people they describe. . . . What I think of when I read . . . Baldensperger is the almost total absence of Palestinian writing on the same subject. Only such writing would have registered not just the presence of a significant peasant culture, but a coherent account of how that culture has been shaken, uprooted in the transition to a more urban-based economy."[54] Said believed that his own book was beginning to register such a presence, uncomfortable as it was, both discursively and visually.

But if the struggle over Palestine is a struggle over interpretation, of what lies outside Zionist representations, both visual and discursive, and what lies within them, then the visual, given the apparent immediacy of its images and its apparent independence from the discursive, where Said's expertise lay, could only evoke in the literary Said a sense of "panic," as he told W. J. T. Mitchell in a now-famous interview about the visual arts.[55] There, he reflected on his approach to writing *After the Last Sky*. First he described the emotional responses that Jean Mohr's pictures provoked in him: "I spent weeks and weeks making a selection of the photographs from his enormous archive . . . I wasn't really looking for photographs that I thought were exceptionally good, as opposed to ones that were not exceptionally good. I was just looking for photographs that I felt provoked some kind of response in me. I couldn't formulate what the response was. But I chose them."[56] Said then grouped the pictures in four piles, which ultimately set the stage for the four chapters of his book. Ultimately, the photographs provided a visual referent around which Said could weave a Palestinian narrative: "I was really more interested in how they corresponded to or in some way complemented what I was feeling."[57] Said was not saying that the visual and the discursive, or as the interview said, "the seeable and the sayable," are reducible to one another, or merely capable of symmetrical representations in different modes. Far from it. He was insisting on the "correlative" nature of the seeable and the sayable, "not in the sense of interchangeable but in the sense of one doing something that the other can't do . . . and if you remove one, then something is missing in the other."[58] Indeed, Said was most impressed with Foucault precisely because the latter "would begin with the visible—in other words, it was the visible that made possible the sayable."[59] However, he did not think that the visual should be fetishized or made into an idol to be worshipped. Such fetishization was directly opposed to his secular commitments. Said's oft-repeated citation from the twelfth-century monk Hugh of Saint Victor is instructive:

> It is, therefore, a source of great virtue for the practiced mind to learn, bit by bit, first to change about invisible and transitory things, so that afterwards it may be able to leave them behind altogether. The man who finds his homeland sweet is still a tender beginner; he to whom every soil is as his native one is already strong; but he is perfect to whom the entire world is as a foreign land. The tender soul has fixed his love on one spot in the world; the strong man has extended his love to all places; the perfect man has extinguished his.[60]

This quote exemplifies both Said's resistance to nationalist belongings and his insistence on his central notion of "secular criticism," which allowed him to render sayable and seeable much that had been rendered silent and pushed outside the visual frame in the Palestinian experience. Said sought to make the Palestinian narrative sayable and the Palestinians themselves visible to a world that insisted on not seeing or hearing them. His lament about the deafening silence of most American and many European intellectuals on Palestine stemmed from his insistence that the intellectual must begin and begin again when reading a social, a literary, and indeed a visual text. For him, a just resolution of the Palestine Question would usher in a new beginning, discursively and visually, for a global politics of affiliation with the oppressed, not least because Israel is the last settler colony standing in Asia and Africa.

Said's interest in the tension between the filiative and the affiliative attracted him to the brilliant work of Palestinian artist Mona Hatoum. In an essay he wrote for Hatoum's installation exhibit The Entire World as a Foreign Land, an understanding that Said shared, he wrote:

> Her work is the presentation of identity as unable to identify with itself, but nevertheless grappling the notion (perhaps only the ghost) of identity to itself. This is exile figured and plotted in the objects she creates. Her works enact the paradox of dispossession as it takes possession of its place in the world, standing firmly in workaday space for spectators to see and somehow survive what glistens before them. No one has put the Palestinian experience in visual terms so austerely and yet so playfully, so compellingly and at the same moment so allusively.[61]

Hatoum's arrangement of objects in her installation, objects that are familiar and utterly unfamiliar at the same time, is important, affecting how they impress themselves on the viewer:

> In another age her works might have been made of silver or marble, and could have taken the status of sublime ruins or precious fragments placed before us to recall our mortality and the precarious humanity we share with each other. In the age of migrants, curfews, identity cards, refugees, exiles, massacres, camps and fleeing civilians, however, they are the uncooptable mundane instruments of a defiant memory facing itself and its pursuing or oppressing others implacably, marked forever by

changes in everyday materials and objects that permit no return or real repatriation, yet unwilling to let go of the past that they carry along with them like some silent catastrophe that goes on and on without fuss or rhetorical bluster.[62]

This quality of Hatoum's visual art makes it "hard to bear (like the refugee's world, which is full of grotesque structures that bespeak excess as well as paucity), yet very necessary to see an art that travesties the idea of a single homeland."[63] For Said, Hatoum's art spoke loudly, as his own writings do, against the ugly horrors of the Oslo capitulation, which American, Israeli, and Palestinian plastic surgeons spent (and continue to spend) countless hours in the operating room beautifying: "Better disparity and dislocation than reconciliation under duress of subject and object; better a lucid exile than sloppy, sentimental homecomings; better the logic of dissociation than an assembly of compliant dunces."[64] These words of Said insistently echo Hatoum's visual assertions.

In such conjunctions between the textual and the visual, we see how Said began with Palestine. In insisting on new beginnings in reading literary and visual texts about Palestine and the Palestinians, Said offered a new language and a new vision, not only to non-Palestinians but also and particularly to Palestinians—a way to speak about and see Palestine and the Palestinians from different historical angles and in different geographic contexts. Resisting his initial panic at the visual, Said engaged with it and uncovered layers of the Palestinian experience that his literary engagement did not permit him to see. In his literary works, Said's attention to the Arab and Western contexts for the Palestinian struggle was his hallmark. He insisted on reading the European Jewish struggle against anti-Semitism contrapuntally with the Zionist struggle to colonize and dominate the Palestinians, just as he insisted on reading the Palestinian struggle against Zionist colonialism alongside trenchant criticism of Arab regime politics and the politics of the Palestinian leadership. This analysis informed his study of visual representations of, and by, Palestinians, which simultaneously revealed and concealed everyday lived experience as well as the overall political context of the Palestinian condition. In photographs, the camera dominates and captures Palestine and its native population, on the one hand showing Palestinians resisting its power, looking back at the photographer and challenging his or her attempt to capture them, and on the other, looking away from the camera and refusing the very terms of such representations. Indeed, Said's analysis of the visual is another Palestinian attempt to resist Orientalist and Zionist capturings. In his literary studies of Europe and its culture, he turned the "camera," his gaze, back on the Western Orientalists seeking to represent and photograph the non-European. His method of contrapuntal reading thus allowed him to contemplate secular solutions to the Question of Palestine that few others could offer. When we view Palestine from the standpoint of Edward Said, we see that his indispensable legacy constitutes a new beginning in the struggle to see and speak about

Palestine, to belong to the Palestinian idea, to be a critic of discursive and visual representations of the Palestinian experience.

TRAVELING THEORISTS

Said's stance on Palestine influenced many scholars in the emerging field of post-colonial studies, which grew out of his critique of Orientalism. Yet the reaction of these scholars to his work has not been uniform. Whereas most share his analysis of colonialism and its settler variety, some have espoused Zionist positions, criticizing the right-wing policies of various Israeli governments or political figures while insisting that Zionism is legitimate in itself. I have discussed elsewhere the short-comings of such an approach in the telling case of Kwame Anthony Appiah. In his book *In My Father's House,* Appiah was offended only by Meir Kahane, suggesting that Kahane's thought was contaminating an otherwise pristine Zionism and the "moral stability of Israeli nationalism."[65]

Homi Bhabha, who is widely seen as one of the major scholars in the field along-side Said and Gayatri Chakravorty Spivak, recently made an important contribution to this line of argument. Unlike the latter two, however, he appears to be committed to depoliticizing deeply political questions.

In a recent "tribute" to Edward Said, Bhabha represented him as a passionate Oriental whose rational faculties retreated before emotion:

> There is much to agree with [in Said's arguments], but much to question also. The high Saidian style speaks with a moral passion that sometimes sacrifices analytic precision to polemical outrage, and his singular commitment to the Palestinian cause could create a severe hierarchy of historical choices. Said's desire to snatch some shred of dignity for his diasporic and misrepresented peoples led him, at times, to pass over distinctions, to resist shades of meaning and interpretations that might have widened the circle of empathetic dialogue.[66]

To illustrate this charge, Bhabha reports that Said, though unequivocally condemnatory of Palestinian suicide bombings as a form of resistance, nonetheless offers an explanation for it, saying that it is

> a direct, and in my opinion, a consciously programmed result of years of abuse, powerlessness and despair . . . the response of a desperate and horribly oppressed people, [which] has been stripped of its context and the terrible suffering from which it arises . . . the location of Palestinian terror—of course it is terror—is never allowed a moment's chance to appear . . . so remorseless has been the focus on it as a phenomenon apart, a pure, gratuitous evil which Israel, supposedly acting on behalf of pure good, has been virtuously battling.[67]

The problem with this analysis, according to Bhabha, is that it ignores Hamas's "perilous strategies of political control within the Palestinian camp" and, most importantly, ignores the fact that this approach "internally destabilizes the emergence of any representative Palestinian leadership that could have the power to negotiate a just and lasting peace on behalf of a united Palestinian people."[68] Bhabha, who as a "postcolonial" critic is presumably also anticolonial, never relates the Zionist enterprise or Israeli occupation to colonialism, which leads him to call not for an end to Israel's colonization and occupation but for a negotiated "just and lasting peace" (terms borrowed from U.S. State Department pronouncements that also never mention colonialism or occupation). And despite Bhabha's attempts to avoid references to "colonialism" in his text, it lurks behind every criticism that he levels against Said: "Said's rage sometimes drives him toward a dark two-dimensionality," presumably that of colonialism and anticolonialism.[69] Yet Bhabha seems blind to his own "dark two-dimensionality"—namely, his view that Hamas and Sharon are equally objectionable, on the one hand, and his implicit support for a U.S.-sponsored capitulation dubbed "peace," on the other.

The question of Said's "rage" is hardly a Bhabhaesque invention. Standard Zionist attacks on Said have always criticized his "rageful" and "angry" tone, in contrast to the cool, rational tone taken by Zionists (and, in this case, by Bhabha).[70] Thus Bhabha, positioning himself as the more careful and nuanced observer who, unlike Said, can perceive "shades of meaning," suggests that he is not encumbered by the emotional passions dogging Orientals of the Said variety. Moreover, it would seem that Said, like all Orientals (Bhabha excepted), had mortgaged his reason for the benefit of his passion, as he is at pains to grasp philosophical abstractions: Said, according to Bhabha, was "quite chary of my taste (as he saw it) for conceptual complexities and theoretical abstractions!"[71]

Rejecting the irrational rebarbative solution of Said, Bhabha tells us that his presumably dispassionate "vision" of a solution for the Palestinian condition "would be based on a shared awareness that the territorial security of a peoples [sic] is more relevant today than a nationalistic demand for territorial *integrity*."[72] If this notion sounds suspiciously like the Israeli government formula that makes "security" paramount and self-determination secondary, that is because it is. Realizing that this Israeli recipe may not be sufficient to convince us in itself, Bhabha proceeds with his "own speculations": "The time may soon be past for staging the Palestinian-Israeli conflict on a global scale, as the rallying cry of the Zionist-Jewish 'project' or the pan-Arab 'cause,' because these movements focus too much on the divisive 'origins' of the conflict rather than concern themselves with the local lives and regional experiences of communities who live in the shadow lines of everyday conflict."[73]

Again, if this sounds like Zionist argumentation, or like a white American reproach to African Americans—urging the oppressed to forget the past, avoid becoming "stuck" in it, and focus on the present situation instead—that is because it is. The fact that Zionist colonialism has, since its inception, driven Palestinians off their lands using European Jewish racial privilege to justify its colonial venture, and that it continues to do so, seems immaterial to Bhabha. That he calls for a binational state does not mean that he endorses Said's solution, for Bhabha's binational state will not undergo decolonization. For him, the problem remains one of "conflict," not of colonialism. The "conflict" is between competing nationalisms, not between colonialism and national liberation. His refusal to distinguish between settler-colonizing nationalism and anticolonial nationalism is clear in the following assertion: "Despite their enormous political differences, both political bodies [the Israeli government and the PA] participate in forms of 'traditional nationalism' that are purist and provincial."[74] Such assessments could explain why Bhabha is so popular in some leftist Israeli academic circles.[75] Perhaps Said's concept of what happens to theory when it travels should be applied to *theorists* when *they* travel, becoming "tamed" and "domesticated."

Whatever praise Said receives in Bhabha's dubious tribute is, at best, of a phatic order. Significantly, Bhabha did not share his views of Said's ideas on Palestine and Zionism during Said's lifetime but chose the occasion of his death to voice them. Bhabha, whose entire oeuvre, as many of his critics have argued, is about coding passing as resistance, today represents the right wing of postcolonial studies. He fails to appreciate that many of the colonized refuse his recipe of "mimicry," no matter how "ambivalent," as a liberationist strategy.

INTELLECTUALS AS PERFORMERS

Said's intellectual life was not only about particular struggles against injustice and oppression but also about the struggle to know. He was most concerned about the degradation of knowledge as technicians in the guise of intellectuals disseminated ideas, whether in the televised and print media or in government parlance. He opposed the cult of the expert in society: experts need to be certified by powerful institutions and to speak their language, at which point they cease to be intellectuals. Their role then becomes one of closing debate, not opening it; of serving power, not challenging it; of humoring authority, not speaking truth to it. For Said, "the intellectual ought neither to be so uncontroversial and safe a figure as to be just a friendly technician nor should the intellectual try to be a full-time Cassandra, who was not only righteously unpleasant but also unheard. . . . But the alternatives are not total quiescence or total rebelliousness."[76]

Said's intellectual life was guided by his radical opposition to ignorance and by his unwavering commitment to fighting injustice. Everything he wrote revolved around these two axes. As a tireless fighter for justice for the Palestinian people, he refused to compromise with racist half measures that kept the Palestinians oppressed while freeing Israel from moral and actual responsibility. In his defense of Islam and Muslims against the onslaught of American racist pronouncements, his principled analysis was not shaken by the events of September 11. He continued to defend Islam as "religion" *and* "culture" against the monstrous misrepresentations of the Western media and Western governments, insisting on humanizing Muslims and Arabs in the face of absolute dehumanization. He did so while condemning the killing of civilians, whether by suicide bombers or by the U.S. military. His hostility to individuals (Arabs, Europeans, and Americans) who hired themselves out to the highest bidders was consistent with his commitment to informed knowledge and with his opposition to a world dominated by jejune technicians disseminating ignorance as knowledge for the right price.

Said spoke against intellectuals who gave up their gods readily when a crisis in their belief system occurred and exchanged them for other gods, whom they worshipped in the same way. He discerned this phenomenon in those who supported communism and then transferred allegiance to U.S. imperialism, in those who championed Trotskyism or fundamentalism and then switched to liberalism or neoconservatism, and in Arab intellectuals who championed Arab and Palestinian anticolonial nationalism and then switched to support U.S. imperialism and its Zionist subsidiary. For him, such intellectuals had developed the "despicable habits of collecting rewards and privileges from one team, only . . . to switch sides, then collect rewards from a new patron."[77]

To him, such individuals were the antitheses of intellectuals. He asked,

Why as an intellectual did you believe in a god anyway? And besides, who gave you the right to imagine that your early belief and later disenchantment were so important? In and of itself, religious belief is to me both understandable and deeply personal: It is rather when a total dogmatic system in which one side is innocently good, the other irreducibly evil, is substituted for the process, the give-and-take of vital interchange, that the secular intellectual feels the unwelcome and inappropriate encroachment of one realm on another. Politics becomes religious enthusiasm . . . with results in ethnic cleansing, mass slaughter and unending conflicts that are horrible to contemplate.[78]

Said understood that the new god for most technicians is the West. "For the secular intellectuals," he insisted, "*those* gods always fail."[79]

Said's interest went beyond defining the role of intellectuals: "In the outpouring of studies about intellectuals there has been far too much defining of the intellectual, and not enough stock taken of the image, the signature, the actual intervention and *performance,* all of which taken together constitute the very lifeblood of every real intellectual."[80] Said's peregrinations into the world of music are instructive in this regard. He was fascinated by the question of performance in general and by musical performance in specific.[81] For him, a musical performance was "rather like an athletic event in its demand for the admiringly rapt attention of its spectators."[82] He pointed to the similarities between essayists and performers as commentators on a work of art, a novel, a musical composition, yet although he wrote with much depth about essayists and composers, he wrote with equal vigor about novelists and performers (especially pianists). His literary fascination with the novelist over the critic and his musical fascination with the performer over the composer come through in his interest in Glenn Gould, Arturo Toscanini, Maurizio Pollini, and Alfred Brendel, among others. I do not mean to suggest that Said was not interested in composers, about whom he wrote quite a bit, but merely that his fascination with performers was of a different order.

In discussing performance as "an extreme occasion," Said stated, "We should begin by noting how the extreme specialization of all aesthetic activity in the contemporary West has overtaken and been inscribed within musical performance so effectively as to screen entirely the composer from the performer."[83] Unlike Beethoven, Mozart, Chopin, and Liszt, who performed their own compositions, modern performers perform the work of others and are rarely composers themselves. (Pierre Boulez and Leonard Bernstein are exceptions, but they are not known principally for performing their own works.[84]) For Said, this marked a major change: "Performance cut off from composing therefore constitutes a special form of ownership and work."[85] Thus, one could see Said himself not only as a composer of his own work but also as a performer of the work of others, of which he took possession. If Gould appropriated Bach and Pollini appropriated Chopin, then Said, in performing the works of Vico, Gramsci, Lukács, Adorno, Césaire, Auerbach, Fanon, Foucault, and many more, took ownership of their work and *affiliated* with it, accenting certain ideas over others and rearranging the score to produce different music.[86] Indeed, Said addresses this idea in "Traveling Theory Reconsidered," where he discusses the transformation that the work of Lukács underwent in the hands of Adorno and Fanon: "To speak here only of borrowing and adaptation is not adequate. There is in particular an intellectual, and perhaps moral, community of a remarkable kind, affiliation in the deepest and most interesting sense of the word."[87]

READING SAID MUSICALLY

Said was fascinated by the connection between memory and music, by how "remembrances of things played" are enacted. Indeed, he criticized some piano performances for veering off their structured programs: after reaching a climax in the finale, some pianists would take away one's remembrance of the performance with an encore that destroyed the structure of the program the listener had just enjoyed.[88] Clearly Said, unlike Adorno, did not think that radio, television, and recordings of musical performances meant a regression in listening *tout court*, nor did he fully agree with Benjamin that mechanical reproducibility leveled the original and the copy. He remained fascinated by the evanescence of sound in concert performances, which are unrepeatable by definition.[89] The question of temporality was ever present in his understanding of performance as an extreme occasion. He praised Umm Kulthum's musical forms for being "based upon an inhabiting of time, not trying to dominate it. It's a special relationship with temporality."[90] The quintessential example of such temporality was Glenn Gould, whose reluctance to perform public concerts after 1964 was the emblematic mark of his fame.[91] Said's fascination with Gould had as much to do with Gould's genius per se as it did with how the musician's genius enveloped his personal life, making him the eccentric performer he was.

Said, as is well known, had high aspirations in his youth of becoming a concert pianist. As late as 1993, he gave two concerts with his friend Diana Takieddine (one at the Miller Theater in New York, the other at Georgetown University in Washington, D.C.) to packed audiences. The two played a range of piano pieces, including ones by Mozart, Schubert, and Chopin. Said loved Chopin and strongly disagreed with those who saw him as a "salon" composer with "effeminate" style.[92] A few years ago I mentioned to Said that I enjoyed John Field's nocturnes more than Chopin's and that I liked less Chopin's Nocturne no. 2 than Field's no. 1 (both in E-flat major), which Chopin quoted extensively; Edward was furious and yelled at me about my utter ignorance of Chopin's beauty!

Music for Said was inspiring. When he played Schubert's *Fantasie in F Minor* (op. 103) for a film about him shot in 2002 and produced by Salem Brahimi *(Selves and Others: A Portrait of Edward Said)*, his face quivered with every note that his hands transposed on the keyboard. Significantly, Schubert wrote his *Fantasie* (a piano duet) in the last year of his short life. One of the most moving parts of *Fantasie* is a beautiful and sad musical phrase, which Schubert, as in Proust's "little phrase," refuses to let go of. In Proust's *À la recherche du temps perdu*, a sonata for violin and piano composed by the fictional composer Vinteuil, in which a lovely "petite phrase" recurs again and again, haunts the imagination of Swann (Proust's most cultured and refined character) and leads him into the register of memory, where true love is encoded for him. In *Fantasie,* the music veers into more majestic terrain, traveling a spectrum of emotions and moods, but it always comes back and succumbs to the somber "little phrase" that structures it. The effect is as if Schubert did not want to end the piece and wanted to cling to the beauty and sadness of that "little phrase," which kept pulling him back, until the very end. Perhaps Schubert's attachment reminded Said of his own attachment to Palestine, which, no matter how far from it he ventured into academic, literary, and musical terrains, always pulled him back. Indeed, Said continually made connections and references to Palestine, even in his more esoteric essays about literature, theory, or music. *Fantasie* might also have served as a premonition for Said that the performance would be his swan song.

Said had sensed his mortality drawing near for some time. This sense found expression in his commentary on Mozart's Da Ponte operas, which he concludes with a note about Mozart's affinity with and consciousness of his own mortality: "In [*Così fan tutte*], death is rendered less intimidating and formidable than it is for most people. This is not the usual, conventionally Christian sentiment, however, but a naturalist one; death as something familiar and even dear, a door to other experiences." Written in 1997, Said's text betrays his sense of impending death. "Yet [death's] prospect also induces a sense of fatalism and lateness—that is, the feeling that one is late in life and the end is near."[93]

One could perhaps read Said himself musically. Although we might view his ideas as chordal compositions when read as an oeuvre, he was careful to present them in arpeggiated form as well, making certain that every element and every note was *elaborated* in a Gramscian sense.[94] Thus, when each chord was played, it could be appreciated for its synchronously performed constituent components, as a totality.

As he wrote in his memoir, Edward Said felt "out of place" much of his life, but he created an intellectual place, even an intellectual world, where he could belong and where he called upon others to join him. The place that Said created had a new language, a new syntax, and a new vocabulary, to which those who, like him, felt out of place in a terrifyingly unjust world could belong. Affiliating with Edward Said is then an affiliation with the place he created, the principles that guided his life, and the causes for which he fought.

NOTES

This chapter modifies and expands on two earlier articles: "The Intellectual Life of Edward Said," *Journal of Palestine Studies*, no. 131 (Spring 2004): 7–22; and "Beginning with Edward Said," in *Belonging, The Catalog for the 7th International Biennial of Sharjah*, curated by Jack Persekian and edited by Kamal Boullata (Sharjah, United Arab Emirates, 2005).

1. Edward W. Said, *Representations of the Intellectual: The 1993 Reith Lectures* (New York: Vintage, 1996), 53.

2. Ibid., 60–61.

3. Ibid., 32.

4. Edward W. Said, "Secular Criticism," in *The World, the Text, and the Critic* (Cambridge, MA: Harvard University Press, 1983), 28.

5. On the transformation of Palestinian intellectuals, see my "Political Realists or Comprador Intelligentsia: Palestinian Intellectuals and the National Struggle," *Critique*, Fall 1997.

6. Said, *Representations of the Intellectual*, 74.

7. Ibid., 82.

8. Ibid., 83.

9. Frantz Fanon, *The Wretched of the Earth* (New York: Grove Press, 1968), 102.

10. Edward W. Said, *Orientalism* (New York: Vintage, 1978), 95.

11. Edward Said, "Traveling Theory," in *The World, the Text, and the Critic*, 236.

12. Said, *Orientalism*, 160.

13. See Sadiq Jalal al-'Azm, "Orientalism and Orientalism in Reverse," *Khamsin* 8 (1980): 5–26.

14. Fred Halliday, for example, complained that Said focused on "discourses *about* the region, not the societies and politics themselves"; see Fred Halliday, *Islam and the Myth of Confrontation* (London: I. B. Tauris, 1996), 201. See my review of Halliday's book in the *Journal of Palestine Studies*, no. 102 (Winter 1997): 112–14.

15. On Said's influence on the field of anthropology, see Nicholas B. Dirks, "Edward Said and Anthropology," *Journal of Palestine Studies*, no. 131 (Spring 2004): 38–54. On Said's impact on comparative literature, see Timothy A. Brennan, "Edward Said and Comparative Literature," 23–37, in the same issue.

16. Edward W. Said, "Traveling Theory Reconsidered," in *Reflections on Exile and Other Essays* (Cambridge, MA: Harvard University Press, 2001).

17. Halliday, *Islam and the Myth of Confrontation*, 210.

18. Sabry Hafez, "Edward Said's Intellectual Legacy," *Journal of Palestine Studies*, no. 131 (Spring 2004): 76–90.

19. Hazim Saghiyyah, the guru of the Arab neoliberals, wrote a deeply unlearned book about Said's *Orientalism* in which he dubbed it part of the rising Khumeiniyist cultures (note the plural). See his *Thaqafat al-Khumayniyyah: Mawqif min al-Istishraq am Harb 'ala Tayf?* (The Cultures of Khumeinyism: An Attitude towards Orientalism or a War against a Specter?) (Beirut: Dar al-Jadid, 1995).

20. The *Daily Telegraph* article is cited in David Hirst, *The Gun and the Olive Branch: The Roots of Violence in the Middle East* (New York: Nation Books, 2003), 344.

21. Arundhati Roy, "The Algebra of Infinite Justice," *Guardian*, 29 September 2001.

22. Said, "Traveling Theory," 230.

23. See Walter Benjamin, "Theses on the Philosophy of History," in *Illuminations, Essays and Reflections*, ed. Hannah Arendt (New York: Schocken Books, 1968), 256; Max Horkheimer and Theodor Adorno, *Dialectic of Enlightenment* (New York: Continuum, 1972); and Edward W. Said, *Culture and Imperialism* (New York: Knopf, 1993).

24. Edward W. Said, *Beginnings: Intention and Method* (1975; repr. New York: Columbia University Press, 1985), xvii.

25. Ibid., 6.

26. Ibid., 272–73.

27. Said, *Culture and Imperialism*, 36.

28. Edward W. Said, *The Politics of Dispossession: The Struggle for Palestinian Self-Determination, 1969–1994* (New York: Pantheon, 1994), 10.

29. Said, *Orientalism*, 262.

30. Said, *Orientalism*, Proust quoted on 293.

31. Ibid., 286.

32. Ibid.

33. Ibid., 307.

34. Ibid., 306.

35. On the transformation of the Palestinian into the Jew, see my "The Persistence of the Palestinian Question," *Cultural Critique*, no. 59 (Winter 2005): 1–23. Quote from Said, *Orientalism*, 306.

36. Ari Shavit, "My Right of Return: An Interview with Edward Said," *Ha'aretz*, 18 August 2000.

37. Edward W. Said, *After the Last Sky: Palestinian Lives*, photographs by Jean Mohr (New York: Pantheon, 1986), 18–19.

38. Edward W. Said, "The Palestinian Experience, 1968–1969," in *The Politics of Dispossession*, 4.

39. Said, *After the Last Sky*, 16.

40. Ibid., 19–20.

41. Ibid., 17.

42. Ibid.

43. Ibid., 46.

44. See his "Permission to Narrate," in Said, *The Politics of Dispossession*, 247–68.

45. On the effects of Oslo on the Palestinian national movement, see my "Repentant Terrorists, or Settler-Colonialism Revisited: The PLO-Israeli Agreement in Perspective," *Found Object*, no. 3 (Spring 1994): 81–90; and my "Return of Permanent Exile," *Critique* 14 (Spring 1999): 5–23.

46. Edward W. Said, *The Question of Palestine* (New York: Vintage, 1979), 5.

47. Ibid., 8.

48. Edward W. Said, "Michael Walzer's Exodus and Revolution: A Canaanite Reading," *Grand Street* 5 (Winter 1986): 86–106; and Michael Walzer, *Exodus and Revolution* (New York: Basic Books, 1984).

49. Said, *After the Last Sky*, 92.

50. Ibid., 92–93.

51. Ibid., 93.

52. Ibid., 94.

53. Ibid.

54. Ibid.

55. W. J. T. Mitchell, "The Panic of the Visual: A Conversation with Edward W. Said," in *Edward Said and the Work of the Critic: Speaking Truth to Power*, ed. Paul A. Bové (Durham, NC: Duke University Press, 2000), 31.

56. Ibid., 35.

57. Ibid., 36.

58. Ibid., 43.

59. Ibid.

60. Edward W. Said, "Reflections on Exile," in *Reflections on Exile*, 185.

61. Edward W. Said, "The Art of Displacement: Mona Hatoum's Logic of Irreconcilables," in *Mona Hatoum: The Entire World as a Foreign Land* (London: Tate Gallery Publishing, 2000), 17.

62. Ibid.

63. Ibid.

64. Ibid.

65. Kwame Anthony Appiah, *In My Father's House: Africa in the Philosophy of Culture* (Oxford: Oxford University Press, 1992), 43. See my "The 'Post-Colonial' Colony, Time, Space and Bodies in Palestine/Israel," in *The Pre-Occupation of Post-Colonial Studies*, ed. Fawzia Afzal-Khan and Kalpana Seshadri-Crooks (Durham, NC: Duke University Press, 2000).

66. Homi K. Bhabha, "Untimely Ends," *Artforum*, February 2004, 19.

67. Ibid.

68. Ibid., 20.

69. Ibid.

70. On Zionist descriptions of Said's rage, see Ella Shohat, "Antinomies of Exile: Said at the Frontiers of National Narration," in *Edward Said, A Critical Reader*, ed. Michael Sprinker (Oxford: Blackwell, 1992), 125–28.

71. Bhabha, "Untimely Ends," 20.

72. Ibid., emphasis in original.

73. Ibid.

74. Ibid.

75. See Ella Shohat, "The 'Postcolonial' in Translation: Reading Said in Hebrew," *Journal of Palestine Studies*, no. 131 (Spring 2004): 55–75.

76. Said, *Representations of the Intellectual*, 69.

77. Ibid., 112.

78. Ibid., 114.

79. Ibid., 121. For a study of Said's overall views of religion, see William D. Hart, *Edward Said and the Religious Effects of Culture* (Cambridge: Cambridge University Press, 2000).

80. Said, *Representations of the Intellectual*, 13.

81. See Rashid Khalidi's interview with Daniel Barenboim, "A Musical and Personal Collaboration," *Journal of Palestine Studies*, no. 131 (Spring 2004): 91–97.

82. Edward W. Said, *Musical Elaborations* (New York: Columbia University Press, 1991), 2.

83. Ibid.

84. Ibid., 2–3.

85. Ibid., 5.

86. For Said's explication of the terms *filiation* and *affiliation,* see his "Secular Criticism," 16–25.

87. Said, "Traveling Theory Reconsidered," 452.

88. Edward W. Said, "Remembrances of Things Played: Presence and Memory in the Pianist's Art," in *Reflections on Exile,* 222–23.

89. See Theodor Adorno, "On the Fetish Character in Music and the Regression of Listening," in *The Essential Frankfurt School Reader,* ed. Andrew Arato and Eike Gebhardt (New York: Continuum, 1993), 270–99; and Walter Benjamin, "The Work of Art in the Age of Mechanical Reproduction," in *Illuminations,* 217–51. For Said's brief discussion of mechanical reproducibility, see "The World, the Text, and the Critic," in *The World, the Text, and the Critic,* 32–33.

90. *Power, Politics, and Culture: Interviews with Edward W. Said,* ed. Gauri Viswanathan (New York: Pantheon Books, 2001), 100.

91. Said, *The World, the Text, and the Critic,* 32. See Said's discussion of Gould in *Musical Elaborations,* 22–34.

92. Said, *Musical Elaborations,* 60.

93. Edward W. Said, "*Così fan tutte* at the Limits," *Grand Street* 62 (Fall 1997): 106.

94. For Said's explication of Gramscian elaboration, see his "Reflections on American 'Left' Literary Criticism," in *The World, The Text, and The Critic,* 170–71.

PART ONE

On Colony and Aesthetics

For histories are there to prove
That none of another breed
Has had a like inheritance,
Or sucked such milk as he,
—WILLIAM BUTLER YEATS,
"THE GHOST OF ROGER CASEMENT"

See how in the blacksmith's shop
The flame burns wild, the iron glows red;
The locks open their jaws,
And every chain begins to break
—FAIZ AHMAD FAIZ, "SPEAK"

2

Edward Said Remembered on September 11, 2004

A Conversation with Gayatri Chakravorty Spivak

Interviewed by Ben Conisbee Baer

GAYATRI CHAKRAVORTY SPIVAK (GCS): There is something strangely appropriate that we sit in New York on this day remembering Edward Said. He was an eminent New Yorker, deeply involved in the life of New York. By geopolitical circumstance, he could not be located in a "real" place called Palestine. He was technically an Arab American, but it is difficult to think of him as American. But it seems completely appropriate to think of him as a New Yorker.

This is to make a distinction between city-states—being of New York—and nation-states—being American. Now that nation-states are being disempowered and disenfranchised under globalization, the stand-off between cities and nations is being reinvented. Even as, in the new information society, certain megacities are becoming more important on their own, in an earlier dispensation, urban identities and national identitarianisms were in conflict in other ways. That conflict played out in Edward Said's existence. September 11 touched him in two ways. As a New Yorker, he was touched by a successful terrorist strike for the first time.

How did it touch him as an Arab?

He wanted, some day, to be able to claim a Palestinian national identity. In that context, he had started talking about the use of state terror long ago. People envious of his courage called him the Professor of Terror in print, and that label pained his gentle, vulnerable spirit.

For example, in the 1980s, in "The Essential Terrorist," in *Blaming the Victims*, he argued that, as a word and concept, *terrorism* had acquired an extraordinary status in American public discourse. In a certain sense, that was the only period when he was occupied with definitions of terrorism. His thinking in those days takes on a peculiar appropriateness now. Many of his early speculations have acquired a different kind of relevance and importance, with a different nuance from when he first wrote them.

BEN CONISBEE BAER (BCB): *In what ways does Said's early work on Orientalism and the "othering" of the Middle East have a different resonance now?*

GCS: When *Orientalism* became important for postcolonial studies, it led to a greater historical interest in literary studies. The first wave of the study of Orientalism focused on British imperialism in India. Strangely, it did not have as great an impact on French work. Of course, Said has an enormous following in France. Yet French literary criticism did not take a new turn as a result of *Orientalism,* even though the most important orientalizing figures in *Orientalism* are also the French.

Orientalism influenced the study of early modern Britain, the work of Stephen Greenblatt, the rise of the New Historicism. Harold Aram Veeser's forthcoming book on Said will make the connections clear.[1] Let me now simply say that the connections between British Empire studies and *Orientalism* were somewhat counterproductive. India's negotiated independence had been in existence for over fifty years. The questions of U.S. foreign policy in Israel and Israel's policy toward Palestine were peripheral to the literary-critical sphere of *Orientalism.*

The influence of *Orientalism* went into the metropolitan postcolonial approach, where the study of representation—how the writer constructs the other—became connected with ethnic studies (and the metropolitan migrant figure we learned to call diasporic). The initiators of this subdisciplinary tendency could learn from the basic presuppositions of *Orientalism.* Today the connection with West Asia is coming clearer. This is the post-9/11 change. *Orientalism* equals racial profiling equals the demonization of Islam. Despite the fact that Said was both a political writer and a literary critic, earlier the connection between these two roles was not seen as clearly. Many of the South Asian or South Asianist or early modernist postcolonialists did not spend a great deal of time opposing U.S. foreign policy on the West Bank.

Today *Orientalism* has new significance because the war on terror relies on constructing terrorists. CNN and the newspapers show us narrative instantiations. The invasion of Iraq depended on constructing a modern state as a terrorist state, a rogue state, in order to advance U.S. geopolicy.

BCB: *How do you see the relationship between the two types of otherness? As you point out,* Orientalism *is mainly about othering negatively, constructing a hostile other to bolster the self. The other that comes from the Lévinas-Derrida post-phenomenological tradition makes representation possible as a more positive event.[2] How does that aspect enter the political arena?*

GCS: Let me now speak of Edward Said as an academic intellectual. He was an altogether serious teacher. He was associated with Columbia University throughout his teaching life. He did not take his academic responsibility lightly. And as a teacher and an academic, he did not feel that the postphenomenological tradition was the best way to devise the relationship between politics and literature.

In the philosophical tradition that you describe, the self emerges in relation to an outside. In Lévinas's work—though the idea does not come through in the English translation so much—the area of the other is a relief map. That is why Lévinas uses so many different words for various kinds of others. *Exteriority* is the subtitle of his first influential book. After the Second World War, Lévinas concluded that to be able to think the ethical, after such a catastrophe, in a reaction to terror, one must think of the human subject as emerging only through a complicated set of relationships—I use the more ordinary-language word *relationships* because we are talking about Edward Said rather than about Lévinas—relationships, then, with exteriority, what lies outside.

I like to think that when Edward Said examined how one constructs a manageable other, which allows the imperialist self to establish itself, he was actually discussing how the particular historical phenomenon fits in the big taxonomy, which is a form of philosophical description. That is the connection I suggest. I do not believe Said himself would have made this type of connection. The reader needs to decide if the connection is worth making.

Lévinas was a supporter of the state of Israel. While he was writing *Totality and Infinity*, he also wrote essays—collected in *Difficult Freedom*—in which he was embarrassingly vocal against "Asiatic hordes." I have pointed out elsewhere that in these papers, Lévinas denies the Muslim the right to the Abrahamic; he forecloses the Muslim out of the Abrahamic. From this point of view, Lévinas is an example of Orientalist representation and exclusion. The connections are complicated.

Derrida has suggested that Lévinas's uncritical support of the politics of the state of Israel may stem from his failure to distinguish between the narrow sense and the general sense of the notion of "the third," which is implicit in the concept of the face-to-face.[3] There is, to paraphrase Derrida, a silence in Lévinas on this philosophical obligation or task. Again, a complicated question. Edward Said's historical example of othering and Lévinas's idea that the self can emerge only in relationship with an outside are not in binary opposition. You can situate Said taxonomically within the Lévinasian taxonomy, just as you can use Lévinas's ideas as an illustration of Said's argument.

BCB: *From the mid-1980s on, when the subdiscipline now called postcolonial studies was emerging, you and Edward Said and Homi Bhabha were often lumped together as the triumvirate that invented it. I know that none of you*

*were really attempting to institutionalize postcolonial studies. But in what sense
was this a shared project for you, especially with Said?*

GCS: My solidarity with Edward Said related to the politics of West Asia. Because
of the division between the postphenomenological ways of thinking and what
was at the end of the day a more enlightened British way of thinking, our
theoretical undertakings were not as closely related as some of our readers
thought. However, I believe that the reader is generally more correct. If, therefore, the readers perceive a connection, a historical connection, a theoretical
connection, then perhaps they are more right than we have been. After all,
our writings are in the public domain. So I like to think that perhaps there
are connections between Bhabha's work, Said's work, and mine that we as
individuals did not see as clearly.

Said's "Abecedarium culturae," which came out in *TriQuarterly* in 1971,
was the first thing of his that I read. I did not know him then. (I have written
about this in *Critical Inquiry*.) I met him in 1974. I felt that this extremely
intelligent reader was being less than fair to the people he was reading, people
who then were still called structuralists: Foucault and Derrida and people like
that. And I actually made notes in the margin—my editor had sent the piece
to me—to show where decisions to translate seemed tendentious. That's where
we began. However, right from the start, we were completely as one in the
politics of Palestine. The readers may be right. But we perceived our connections as political rather than as literary-critical.

"Abecedarium culturae" became part of Said's first book, *Beginnings*. Between *Beginnings* and *Orientalism*, between 1975 and 1978, an immense
change took place, and it was a political change. The critical methodology
that informs *Beginnings* remained in place. *Orientalism* is different because
its critical method is informed by the realization that the problems are more
substantive than formal, although this notion has not dislodged the theoretical assumptions. These assumptions were thickened by the substantive project of recognizing a political use for them. In those years, the sociology of
knowledge was an important issue: the realization that knowledge is socially
produced rather than learned by straightforward investigation. Said was a
child of his times.

BCB: *You seem to be pointing to a difference in levels, two complementary things
going on at the same time—the political and the literary-critical—in both your
and his work, and you, at least, see the solidarity as being more on the political
level. What relationship do you see between your two spaces of activism?*

GCS: This is a difficult question, but we did think about it. In Said's *After the Last
Sky*, he comes across as deeply concerned about the Palestinian subaltern. He
is not interested solely in high-level politics. I don't distinguish myself from
him in this interest in the subaltern. Our ways of going about it were different.

His ways were perhaps more effective. The attempt to change and form public opinion with well-researched commentary on political moves by involving the highest level of political intervention and talented young musicians in superbly trained international collaboration can, I want to hope and believe, be more effective. My attempt, more idiosyncratic yet based on firmly held convictions, has many fewer chances of being effective. My idea is that unless one changes the desires and capacities to judge in the largest sector of the electorate in the global south, no change in policy will ever be sustained by anything that can be called a democracy of, for, and by the people. But this attempt is a foolhardy one. Its chances of success are remote, although I think that maintaining its continuity is important. One never closes the schools. Vanguardism must be persistently supplemented by this sort of textural involvement that supports the structures.

Although Said has been more effective in moving large numbers of people. Under the Bush administration in the United States and its relationship to West Asia, historically, these chances now seem to be fewer, or diminished. But this situation is just a historical happenstance. I hope that the administration will change, even against all the straws in the wind. I hope that the nature of these murderous politics will change. They can change. In my project, however, the hope for change is either low or not there. You cannot measure the importance of this work by the prospect of predictable change. This view is a difference between Said and me.

BCB: *Did you ever discuss these issues with him in such terms?*

GCS: No, no, because these efforts of mine are completely hands-on and therefore very limited. I've been doing this for about twenty-two years. In the first few years, I had so little hope that I thought this work was not worth talking about. It is a hopeless enterprise, although full of all kinds of joys. It *is* very real; it certainly takes a lot of time. I look for recruits, but the standards for recruitment are at least as high as admission into Columbia, although of a different kind.

So, in spite of all these very real features, and the children moving haphazardly toward high school, I had no idea in the first few years whether such an impractical idea would ever catch on. So I didn't talk about it at all, although I could feel, as could others, that changes were happening in my attitude toward my work as a whole, the world as a whole, and toward other kinds of politics and activism.

Every time that I came back from a teacher-training session, I was appalled by how ignorant people are about that other need. On one occasion, this feeling bore too strong a mark. I let the secret out in public and so was invited to address Amnesty International. But by then the idea of initiating a conversation with my friend when I had so long remained silent was not possible. This was 2002, the year before he died. Something had held me back earlier as well:

I did not feel free to discuss this at all. When he asked me, "What is it that you do when you go to India?" I gave him a slightly frivolous answer, so in 2002, I believed that chapter, that possibility, was closed. I regret it, because he certainly listened carefully if he felt that something was worth listening to. It would have been interesting to check it out with him. And of course there is a relationship between my long critical intimacy with all the developments in recent French theories or interpretation and the way this work emerged. Not in the way of applying theory, but in a sort of recognition after the fact. Sometimes the theoretical presuppositions were themselves modified. I don't know if I could have persuaded him. He was difficult to persuade, but perhaps I could have said something about the usefulness of this approach.

Mind you, if you look at *Culture and Imperialism,* in its nooks and crannies you see that Said was not completely impervious to the seductions of deconstruction. Talking about the work of the Subaltern Studies group of historians of South Asia and commenting on the work of Ranajit Guha, he notices that such intellectuals are more interested in deconstructing than in destroying, and he says that the key is knowing how to read, as the deconstructionists say. You do get such bits here and there, which show that he did not completely put them aside as immoral nihilists.

BCB: *As you suggest, in* Culture and Imperialism, *Edward Said began tentatively to use the terminology of certain "poststructuralist" thinkers, such as Deleuze and Guattari's "nomadology" from* A Thousand Plateaus.[4] *What are your wider thoughts on his attempt to put such concepts to work in his writings?*

GCS: I think he belonged to a completely different mind-set, Ben. When I read Kant's newspaper essay "What Is Enlightenment?" and come across the description of the enlightened subject as the scholar who writes for all time and all people, I think of Edward Said. That was his mode, as he himself made clear in *Representations of the Intellectual.* When Kant talks about the relationship of the enlightened scholar to his place of work—Kant was himself a professor—we are sometimes surprised to see that the freedom of the enlightened scholar relates more to his published work than to his everyday relationship to the university. This point relates to Said's comfortable relationship with Columbia and the courageous truth telling of his writings.

BCB: *Do you think Said's work has made an opening for feminist scholars of postcolonialism?*

GCS: I think you can use Said's work for feminism, but I don't think it directly carries feminist content.

To come back in closing to the anniversary of 9/11, we miss Edward Said as a general presence. Ernesto Laclau phoned from London, having just read of further horrors of the U.S. occupation of Iraq. "Gayatri, your colleague," he began, and we both knew of whom he was speaking, "whom I did not know very well," he continued, "although I was going to have a conversation with him this year, is sorely missed in a situation like this one. He gave us ideas about how to think and how to fight against what's happening." That voice is not heard any more. As a general presence, a person who reacted in ways that taught us things, he was important to us.

I met former Columbia provost Jonathan Cole by chance on the street. He told me he had just finished writing a book. I asked him what the book was about. He said, "It's about the way in which the university has lost its franchise as a place of education in contemporary society." I said, "Strange that one would have to justify the university as a place of education; it's like justifying the nonburning of libraries. I miss Edward." Cole was a close friend of Edward's. He said, "I knew, of course, that I would miss him, but I did not realize that I would miss him quite so much." This need for his presence in the current post-9/11 destruction of free society in the United States is teaching us afresh how important he was.

NOTES

These explanatory notes were made by interviewer Ben Conisbee Baer.

1. Harold Aram Veeser, *Edward Said: Life, Politics, and Thought* (New York: Routledge, forthcoming in 2010).

2. "Postphenomenological" philosophy, as we call it here, emerged in the writing of thinkers who had a critical intimacy with the work of Edmund Husserl and Martin Heidegger in particular. Jacques Derrida and Emmanuel Lévinas drew implications from the philosophies of Husserl and Heidegger that they both enabled and suppressed in their work. For example, Husserlian phenomenology sought to track the elusive presence of the object as it is intended by consciousness, or as it appears to the "I." Lévinas brings out the ethical dimension of the phenomenological analyses of the encounter with the "otherness" of what appears to the "I." In effect, he claims that this alterity is the very thing that allows me to be me, binding me to it in a relationship of responsibility even as it is finally unknowable. This is not the "other" in the more Saidian sense of being "othered": turned into an object of knowledge that supports an imperialistic or orientalizing project. Derrida elaborates on Husserl, Heidegger, and Lévinas in multiple arenas too broad to summarize here. A useful overall account of these relations appears in Simon Critchley, *The Ethics of Deconstruction* (West Lafayette, IN: Purdue University Press, 1999).

3. Jacques Derrida, *Adieu to Emmanuel Lévinas* (Stanford, CA: Stanford University Press, 1999).

4. Gilles Deleuze and Félix Guattari, *A Thousand Plateaus,* trans. Brian Massumi (London: Athlone, 1992). The authors define *nomadology* as a way of knowing and doing; they differentiate it from the "State," which they view as a monolithic and law-bound entity. The nomadological approach is extrastate, mobile, strategic, pluralizing, and boundary crossing, akin, perhaps, to Antonio Gramsci's "maneuvering war" but more generalized. It may describe movements as heterogeneous, such as nongovernmental organizations and criminal gangs, or be used more literally to describe the nomads and exiles unassimilated to the institutional structures of nation-states. Despite Said's cautious usage, the speculative inflation and sometimes uncritical celebration of anything "nomadic" has proceeded apace in the intervening years.

3

Beginnings Again

Michael Wood

I

There is a temptation, given the directions and importance of Edward Said's later work, and missing as we now do the sanity and the passion of his thinking about the Middle East, to treat his literary work as subordinate to his political essays and to see his early work as a mere prelude to what was to come. Or even to see his literary work as bluntly political and to forget the early writing altogether. We have *Orientalism*, first published in 1978, and we have Said's further pathbreaking studies in postcolonial theory and practice, along with his indefatigable commentaries on the changing and threatened fate of the Palestinians. The rest is silence, a season before the beginning.

I don't believe that we need to resist this temptation entirely, at least in its milder form, even though it rests on a false chronology and an untenable division: Said had been writing about Arabs and Israelis since 1970, and he continued to write about music and literature until he died.[1] A look at Said's literary studies allows us to see the long continuities, to find a certain sense of politics therein, and to see the theory of imperialism in unlikely places. Without the later work we should perhaps not be so interested to read, in Said's book on Joseph Conrad, a version of his Harvard dissertation, published in 1965, of "an imperialism of ideas, which easily converts itself into the imperialism of nations," or to learn, in a 1967 essay on R. P. Blackmur and Georges Poulet, that "criticism is notorious for its imperialism, carried out in the name of understanding."[2] The first time Said used the famous quotation from Marx that became one of the epigraphs to *Orientalism*—"They cannot represent themselves, they must be represented"—was in the 1976 essay "On Repetition," and the context was European social class rather than the West's invention of the East.[3]

In another 1967 essay we note the significance to Said of the work of Merleau-Ponty, which he never disavowed but repeatedly reworked. "Merleau-Ponty's central philosophic position," Said says, "is that we are in the world before we can think about it." A little later, he comments on the philosopher's statement "The world is not what I think, but what I live through."[4] *World* and *worldliness* were enduring terms for Said, almost magically freighted concepts that he invoked again and again when he wanted to indicate the poverty or shortcomings of a theory or a view. Literary criticism, he suggests in *The World, the Text, and the Critic,* especially Anglo-American literary criticism, is too keen to turn away from the world, to forget the "materiality" of literature, "the text's situation in the world." "Worldliness does not come and go." It is not a synonym for our slackest idea of history, "the impossibly vague notion that all things take place in time." Things do take place in time, but we haven't said enough if we don't say more: "Literature is produced in time and in society by human beings, who are themselves agents of, as well as somewhat independent actors within, their actual history."[5]

In the early work we can see the first formulations of later thoughts, and we can watch those thoughts begin their career of alteration and repetition. Said's later argument, for example, was not that "an imperialism of ideas easily converts itself into the imperialism of nations" but that the imperialism of nations makes profound and effective (and often unobserved) use of the imperialism of ideas. Similarly, although Said continued to believe that "we are in the world before we can think about it," he refused the antitheoretical implications of this claim. It is because thought comes late to us that we so desperately need it, that it becomes an unrefusable obligation of the conscious life.

The concepts of rescue and completion, which Said explored in his early work and never abandoned, are also important in this context. He first encountered both notions in Conrad, and they are essential not only to his view of Conrad's career but also to his sense of his own. In an 1899 letter, which Said cites both in his Conrad book and in *Beginnings* (1975), the novelist described his work as an unmoving monster. "Its eyes are baleful; it is as still as death itself—and it will devour me . . . I am alone with it in a chasm with perpendicular sides of black basalt. Never were sides so perpendicular and smooth and high . . . There's no rope long enough for that rescue."[6] Though no rope is long enough, Conrad manages to put the monster to rest by finishing his novel. And then, of course, the monster wakes when the novelist starts another. But the writer who can't be rescued may himself be a rescuer, as Conrad suggests in an essay on Henry James: "The creative art of a writer of fiction may be compared to rescue work carried out in darkness against cross gusts of wind swaying the action of a great multitude. It is rescue work, this snatching of vanishing phases of turbulence, disguised in fair words, out of native obscurity into a light where the struggling forms may be seen, seized upon, endowed with the only possible permanence in this world of relative values—the permanence of memory."[7]

The writer turns turbulence into words, drags it into light, and makes it memorable—a view that Said shared not only of Conrad's work but of writing generally, or of all writing that is not merely functional. The fact that the writer could and does fail is an essential part of this adventure. "He had failed," Said says of Conrad's prose at those moments when it goes slack or vacant, "to rescue meaning from his undisciplined experience."[8] But Conrad didn't always fail, whatever the novelist himself thought. "The achievement of Conrad's life," Said says, "was that he had actively borne a full burden of felt order and disorder." This is the achievement of his *life*, we note; but he had made writing his life, and his fictional characters, in Said's view, constantly try to rescue their pasts through narrative, "to interpret what, at the time of occurrence, would not permit reflection." They live in "an atmosphere that exudes the feeling of something wrong, which has to be examined or recollected or relived or worked out."[9]

We can easily see how these activities—rescuing meaning, bearing a burden of feeling, belatedly interpreting, reliving, or working out an old error—bring with them the idea of incompletion, and indeed Said made a large claim for the importance of this concept, "that inherent yet necessary incompleteness of all human endeavour which is the basis of humanism."[10] Again, he found a fabulous quotation from Conrad to signal the point. "And besides, the last word is not said,—probably shall never be said. Are not our lives too short for that full utterance which through all our stammerings is of course our only and abiding intention?"[11] Humanism is a failing dream of a full utterance. But it fails, ultimately, by the highest standards. Along the way it has many modest successes—and all the more successes because it knows its own incompleteness.

II

But now we must register some resistance to the temptation to assimilate Said's earlier and later work, and for three excellent reasons: because the earlier work is important in its own right; because it belongs to a particular historical moment, which it both reflects and illuminates; and because it alters our view of the later work. Each of these reasons is, of course, closely implicated in the others, but I separate them here for clarity of discussion.

In a 1976 essay, published a year after *Beginnings*, J. Hillis Miller classified Said's work, along with that of a few others, as "uncanny criticism."[12] This criticism might also be thought of as radical—another of Said's most cherished words—because it refused the tired conventions and "given assumptions" of the time, above all Said's notion that criticism is "the confrontation of an inquiring critic with a resisting text—that is, between a flexible subject and a completed object."[13] For Said, as we have just seen, neither text nor person could be completed, and we shouldn't pretend they can. But Miller, whom Said cites in his preface to the 1985 edition of *Beginnings*, says that for the uncanny critics, "the moment when logic fails in their works is the moment of their deepest penetration into the actual nature of literary language, or language as such."[14] This statement certainly applies in important ways to Paul de Man, Geoffrey Hartman, and Miller himself; but in *Beginnings* Said refuses this particular implication, thereby showing us precisely what is new and demanding about his critical thinking. He is seeking "something rather unlike literary history, or *explication de texte,* or cultural generality." He aims to isolate a problem—in this case, the question of what it means to begin—explore related examples and evidence, find an appropriate discursive language, and finally allow his quest to "learn from itself, to adjust to and change itself in progress."[15] But this process involves no failure of logic. On the contrary, Said repeatedly celebrated rationality when many of his peers were eagerly embracing an intuitive skepticism. French structuralism, for Said, whatever its flaws and limitations, was "an exemplary rational and contemporary recognition in explicit critical terms of the need to make a beginning."[16] Indeed, we might say, it was an exemplary rational recognition of the contemporary uses of reason. Whatever the discontinuities and difficulties of practicing a new history, Michel Foucault and others believed "that rational knowledge is possible, regardless of how very complex—and even unattractive—the conditions of its production and acquisition."[17] Said suggested, "Structuralism has demonstrated the value of determinedly rational examination, has displaced the prior mystique of mere appreciation passing itself off as scholarship."[18]

Yet Said's stance was close enough to the skepticism of his contemporaries for his idea of rational knowledge to seem difficult, even puzzling. It was full of contradictions. On several occasions in the late 1960s when I heard Said lecture on repetition, say, I was convinced that the subject was originality. And vice versa. For him, to begin was always to begin again, and so in one sense not to begin at all: "Paradoxically, an interest in beginnings is often the corollary result of not believing that any beginning can be located."[19]

Repetition includes the idea of anticipation as well as the idea of return. Repetition and originality are opposed, but not always, because originality implies a first loss as well as a first start, and each concept may turn into the other.[20] Said's key terms do not simply have opposites, or imply their opposites. They *are* their opposites; they become themselves by wrestling with their doubles, as if they were not words at all but tormented characters in Conrad. We have to pay attention, Said says in a brilliant, seemingly casual definition of reading, "to what the words drag along with them, whether that is the memory of the writing or some other, hidden, and perhaps subversive opposite."[21]

Like William Empson, Said evokes Freud's seminal essay "The Antithetical Meaning of Primal Words." Indeed, Freud, along with Kierkegaard and Nietzsche, was an essential figure in Said's intellectual formation, a genuine *maître à penser:* the pages on Freud in *Beginnings* are among the most deeply felt and intensely worked. Said also had another master closer to hand: his Princeton teacher R. P. Blackmur, who typically thought several things at once and was adept at catching the movements of his own mind in language. In the early essay I cite above, Said comments, "Blackmur himself survives the momentary sense of his terms."[22] These antecedents are important, but more important still, I believe, is the sheer intimacy with which Said lived his sense of contradiction. He was an exemplar of a habit of thought even more than a product of formal education; he combined lived experience—that of a Palestinian whose education, begun in Egypt, continued in the United States— with a particular set of formative influences that were comparative, cosmopolitan, and dialectical. I have mentioned Empson, and Said did too, but only in passing. Said's writing also bears a certain resemblance, in the sense of opposites fiercely entangled in each other, to the work of Derrida. But finally the practice of contradiction in Said doesn't resemble Empson's ambiguity, or his definitions of so-called complex words, and Said did not call for a Derridean deconstruction of binary oppositions. He thought in the way he needed to think, which called for him to insist on logic rather than confront its failure. Logic sustains our contradictions and helps us be clear about them. It would be pleasant, perhaps, if such contradictions could be dissolved or resolved. Or perhaps it wouldn't. Perhaps contradiction is like incompletion, a feature of being alive and awake. Contradiction is what we live with and through, and logic allows us to see how we are living.

What I call the practice of contradiction is evident everywhere in Said's early work (and less and less in the later work) and is best illustrated by a look at the central argument of *Beginnings*. One appealing and characteristic aspect of this argument is the notion that to begin means, among other things, to discover or invent the beginning you didn't know you had. This element of discovery certainly applies to all the literary figures Said cares about, but he also names Freud, Nietzsche, Kierkegaard, and Lévi-Strauss as thinkers who "define the characteristically human in terms of what we might call the possibility of an alternative, or a second time."[23] In other words, we don't have a first chance until we find the second. This dizzying thought helps us understand why Said mentions Borges as often as he does. But of course the dizzying thought, on reflection, is also the soundest rational sense. How could we count to one if we couldn't at least count to two?

"A beginning is already a project under way," Said wrote, and "a beginning is often that which is left behind."[24] These quotes paint two slightly different pictures of what we might call the lateness of beginnings. Should we say, to adapt Merleau-Ponty's phrase, that we have always begun before we can think about it? Said would accept this proposition, I assume, but only as a preparation for an important next step: we haven't really begun until we have begun to think about beginning. We need to discover or invent an intention for our projects; without it, any endeavor will be orphaned, "like a foundling, awaiting an author or a speaker to father it, to authorize its being."[25] Here Said comes particularly close to the skeptics he opposes.

Consider these opposing claims: beginnings do exist in reality, although we cannot always identify them; no beginnings occur in reality, because the very idea of a beginning is a fiction. Said thought the first claim to be both dogmatic and metaphysical, a version of "radical inauthenticity."[26] Reality is under no obligation to supply beginnings just because we are in the habit of believing in them. The second claim, Said suggested, has to be respected, and at one point he says, "A beginning might well be a necessary fiction."[27] The second claim overlooks (and the first claim assuages too easily) our practical and moral need for beginnings. We can't do without them, whether they are fictional or not. Said now makes his crucial distinction in the book between beginnings and origins. Beginnings are active, he says, and origins are passive. A beginning is a human intention; an origin is a theological postulate.[28] A beginning is something we may have to invent; an origin is something we cannot know but must accept. At this point, Said's argument takes on its most paradoxical but also profoundly humanist form. Some beginnings, he suggests, are practical points of departure and are thus both invented and real, first conceived and then acted upon. "A beginning is a formal appetite imposing a severe discipline on the mind." These beginnings are accompanied by, caught up in, a more purely mental activity, both a longing and an anxiety, where the very thought of beginning is always just beyond our reach, because wherever we look, we find only the already begun. This second class of beginning represents the unknown, but "the unknown remains with us to haunt us from its horizon even after we have consciously begun." This is Said's way of mediating between, or collapsing, the two claims about beginnings. Yes, beginnings exist, but they are human inventions and choices, like, we might say, opening a railway or getting married. And no, these choices are not completely new beginnings, because they were in many senses already under way before we took them on. A beginning, then, is both a practicality and a sort of phantom, and when we put these two manifestations together, we see that we have *necessary* fictions rather than necessary *fictions*. Or rather, we go beyond fiction. Fiction and reality meet up in the notion that what is indispensable may also be wrong. But then we feel its wrongness, and we know it won't always be wrong, only unprovable. In this notion skepticism becomes vigilance rather than mere indulgence in doubt or what Said calls "manic hopelessness." Action makes the fiction real, and the fiction reminds us that reality could have been different. Said concludes the second chapter of *Beginnings* with this statement: "In this space certain fiction and certain reality come together as identity. Yet we can never be certain what part of identity is true, what part fictional. This will be true as long as part of the beginning eludes us, so long as we have language to help us and hinder us in finding it, and so long as language provides us with a word whose meaning must be *made* certain if it is not to be wholly obscure."[29]

III

"Theory is a cold and lying tombstone of departed truth," Conrad wrote. Said doesn't openly dissociate himself from this statement, although his comment on it ("as if to say that truth itself consisted entirely of the movement immediately connected to the person performing the action") suggests a different direction of thought.[30] For Conrad, theory is whatever gets between us and a fabulous realm beyond interpretation, where words are no longer needed and where our imaginations and our egos express themselves without mediation. "What is that realm?" Said asks in *The World, the Text, and the Critic.* "It is a world of such uncomplicated coincidence between intention, word, and deed that the ghost of a fact, as *Lord Jim* has it, can be put to rest."[31] This quote is a splendid example of Said's antithetical thinking because Conrad's novel says precisely the opposite. The narrator remarks that it is "impossible to lay the ghost of a fact," alluding to the fact of another man's disgrace.[32] Yet, of course, Said is right, having leapt ahead of the merely literal. This impossibility is the sort that would vanish in Conrad's imagined, alternative realm, the place where intentions, words, and deeds are one. One of the strengths of Said's criticism is his ability to be extremely sympathetic to such a vision while remaining perfectly clear about the degree of desperation this fantasy implies.

A refusal of theory then looks like a refusal of reality, as Said began to argue in the later 1960s. Theory, properly understood, would rescue the study of literature from triviality, or its worldlessness. Once again dismissing "appreciation" as an appropriate mode of serious criticism, along with "methodologies" and "techniques," Said insisted that theory "is more generous and capable of finer strictness than either alternative."[33] But what is theory, apart from a representation of everything that complicates dreams of immediacy? Perhaps we should ask what it *was*, in the late 1960s and early 1970s, when Said was writing on this subject, because "each historical moment produces its own characteristic forms of the critical act, its own arena in which critic and text challenge one another."[34] Theory, in Said's view, would connect text and world, without underrepresenting either. It would pay close attention to words, but not only to words, and above all it would see that literature is a place of worldly confrontation, not scholarly peace—always remembering that the association of scholarship and peace is itself something of a fantasy. "Oriental texts," for example, would no longer "inhabit a realm without development or power, one that exactly corresponds to the position of a colony for European texts and culture," and we would give up "the fallacy of imagining the life of texts as being pleasantly ideal and without force or conflict."[35] This notion is very attractive, but theory still sounds like a panacea, and we cannot easily see what is theoretical about it. I shall not attempt a full-scale accounting of the many meanings of the word *theory* in the American academy thirty or forty years ago, but we can benefit from glancing at its principal zones or regions. In the first instance, "theory" meant French thought in literature, anthropology, philosophy, psychoanalysis. Later it came to include the work of Walter Benjamin and the Frankfurt School; and later still it embraced Russian Formalism.

Second, "theory" meant an interest in disciplines and movements that were not themselves literary: not just the areas I've mentioned but also social theories and practices like Marxism and feminism. In this sense, theory represented a breakout from a closed and complacent academic world, although Said was always keen to remind us that this attention to other modes of thought and action was characteristic of modernism at its best and most inquisitive. Eliot raided anthropology and the study of religion for his poems, and Empson thought constantly about new developments in science and mathematics. Lionel Trilling, Said remarks, "the critic whose work in the United States had most assuredly placed English studies centrally on the literary agenda, spoke of a modern literature that included Diderot, Mann, Freud, Gide and Kafka."[36] Thus "theory" in the American 1960s and 1970s represented a renewed and newly inflected internationalism but not an entirely fresh start—a perfect Saidian beginning, in other words. "Criticism in America today," Said wrote in 1976, "is more cosmopolitan than it has been since the first two decades of this century."[37] Third, "theory" meant self-awareness about the discipline and the profession of literary study, a willingness to ask all the difficult questions that had been swept under the carpet or locked away and lost. What is literature? Why do we need literature? What is it for? Whom is it for? How is it different from history? From philosophy? Theory was a sophisticated way of making the old, crude 1960s demand for "relevance," or at least a way of answering those who made such a demand. Of course, plenty of heated argument had taken place in the supposedly quiet times before "theory" arrived, especially about the respective merits of historical and formal approaches to literary texts. But this period also saw a curious and protracted consensus about the terms of the argument and a distinct inclination to get on with the daily job without addressing the large issues. Such an approach has its virtues, of course, but these virtues are not everlasting, and if one clings to them too long, they look like avoidance.

An anecdote may help evoke this period. During the oral examination of a Ph.D. candidate, the question arose of animal imagery in the novels of D. H. Lawrence— a subject not at the cutting edge of literary studies in the 1970s but one that might still have yielded interesting results—the candidate first listed the occasions on which rabbits figure in Lawrence's fiction. We then moved on to horses. My colleagues seemed completely satisfied by this analysis-free series of appreciative mentions. Then, as if there were no other kind of literary question in the world, one of my colleagues kindly said to the candidate, "And are there any other animals you would like to talk about?" At that moment I understood the appeal of "theory." Until then I had thought some theorists were interesting and some not; I thought the same about traditional scholars. I also thought that "theory" was not a single thing that we had automatically to be for or against. But this example certainly highlights the appeal of "theory," whatever it is, as long as it encourages questions and an active, even troubled engagement with literary study. Theory's questions might be abstruse, and at times even inane. But they at least require us to think about them, whereas those fictional animals could be pulled out of a book without a second's analytical consideration.

In some parts of *Beginnings*, we may now feel that Said was following a fashion that didn't suit him. The talk about texts and textuality seems a little fussy, as if Said thought he had to acknowledge an almost infinite indirectness before he could return to the direct connections that interested him. But his arguments about "adjacency" and "molestation" are powerful, and they carry out in detail the deep practice of contradiction I have described. The quality that Said admires in his chosen modernists—Joyce, Yeats, and Mann, as well as Conrad and the thinkers I have mentioned—the element that he sees as the great adventure of their period, is their determination to refer "to other works, but also to reality and to the reader, by adjacency, not sequentially or dynastically." Later in the book, he says, "Instead of a source, we have the intentional beginning, instead of a story a construction." Said eloquently insists that the modernists sought something "beyond the reach of genealogy," a world of "words, children, ideas" all "freed from the domination of a single original cause, like the father or the image."[38] Sometimes Said writes of the replacement of fathers by brothers, but this figure is perhaps still a touch too genealogical. The modernists, often with great difficulty, sought to replace inheritance by creative choice, and we today might want to begin again by selecting entirely new fathers for ourselves, rather than refusing fatherhood altogether. We need only refuse genealogy as doom, as unavoidable nature.

The European novel as a genre, in Said's view, performs the prehistory of this adventure. It mimes genetic life, as if a literary form could offer a kind of biology, and it owes its astonishing successes to the deep attraction of this idea. But the novel as a form also knows that it is faking, pulling off an immense cultural trick, whereby worlds of artifice will be taken as merely natural. Said calls this knowledge "molestation." "Molestation . . . is a consciousness of one's duplicity, one's confinement to a fictive, scriptive realm, whether one is a character or a novelist."[39] He cites three "special conditions" for the rise of narrative fiction in Europe: a doubt about the authority of the voice that is speaking (a fear of being fictional, we might say, or of writing only fiction); a sense that whatever truths may be available to us can be approached only indirectly; and "an extraordinary fear of the void that antedates private authority."[40] I don't think this triple claim makes historical sense. It is too broad, exceptions are too easily found, and the argument has a whiff of anachronism, as if Nietzsche and Freud had crept into the eighteenth century and moved all the furniture. But the whole picture of authority and molestation—an authority that secretly craves molestation, a molestation that often shores up the authority it seeks to bother—offered a remarkable fable of modernism to Said. From the eighteenth century until the early twentieth, a great adventure had taken place: a long new beginning that was rational and hopeful despite its clashes with despair and unreason.

IV

The words "after theory" are in the air now, and even Said came to believe that theory had taken a wrong turn, that at least in the American academy, it had gone sadly quietist and conservative. There is something both touching and amusing about Said's remark, in his 1985 preface to *Beginnings*, that he "can only plead guilty" to failing to predict that "theory" too, just like the old approaches, could be used to "purge" literary texts of their worldliness and set them apart in hermetic isolation.[41] Was this quietism already implicit in French structuralism and its successors? Many have thought so, and Said himself repeatedly pointed to structuralism's difficulty in dealing with "change and force." But he persisted in believing not only in the "vitality of modernism" but in the "radical spirit" of what came to be called theory. "At its best," he said, "radical criticism is exactly like all radical activity: full of its own changing, and haunted by its opposite."[42]

Said would say now, I think, that the world "after theory" is not full enough of its own changing, and indeed is perhaps not changing enough. And we could utter the words "after theory" in a tone of embarrassment rather than triumph. What if we haven't "begun," in Said's sense, with theory or half of what it offers us? What if we have simply made "theory" mean too many things and have been in too great a rush to believe we have mastered the difficult thought of our time? What if we have thought we were radical because we stirred up the academy but all the while have been letting the world go by? Whenever we return to these questions, we shall find in Said's work a model and an encouragement, a working example of what radical criticism can be.

It is in this sense that Said's early work can illuminate the later, preventing us from letting it settle into orthodoxy. We need to remember how restless and inquiring Said's cast of mind was and how devoted he was to the unreconciled in life and literature and music. Such a career can have no teleology, no steady progress toward a final achievement, no completion. And it can't produce coherent notions of earliness and lateness. The continuities we find in Said's work reflect not a smooth persistence but a series of tense entanglements between what is literally early and literally late. His very idea of late style—his book on this subject appeared in 2006—involved not serenity and wisdom but continuing creative disturbance. "Each of us," he wrote, thinking of figures like Rembrandt, Matisse, Bach, and Wagner, "can readily supply evidence of how it is that late works crown a lifetime of aesthetic endeavor. . . . But what of artistic lateness not as harmony and resolution, but as in-transigence, difficulty and unresolved contradiction?"[43] And what of critical late-ness not as ripeness and singleness of thought but as commitment to a practice full of change and haunted by what could never be finished?

NOTES

1. Among Said's writings on Arabs and Israelis, see, for example, "The Arab Portrayed," in *The Arab-Israeli Confrontation of June 1967: An Arab Perspective,* ed. Ibrahim Abu Lughod (Evanston, IL: North-western University Press, 1970), 1–9; "The Palestinian Experience," *Columbia Forum* (Winter 1970); "A Palestinian Voice," *Middle East Newsletter,* October–November 1970; "The Crisis in the Middle East: An Exchange," *Columbia Forum* 13, no. 1 (Spring 1970): 45 (reply to Sholomo Avineri's response to Said's "The Palestinian Experience" [1970]).

2. Edward W. Said, *Joseph Conrad and the Fiction of Autobiography* (Cambridge, MA: Harvard University Press, 1966), 140. The 1967 essay is reprinted as "Sense and Sensibility: On R. P. Blackmur, Georges Poulet, and E. D. Hirsch," in Said, *Reflections on Exile and Other Essays* (Cambridge, MA: Harvard University Press, 2000), 15–23.

3. "On Repetition" is reprinted in Edward W. Said, *The World, the Text, and the Critic* (Cambridge, MA: Harvard University Press, 1983), 123.

4. Said, *Reflections on Exile,* 5.

5. Said, *The World, the Text, and the Critic,* 148, 151, 35, 152.

6. Said, *Joseph Conrad and the Fiction of Autobiography,* 55. See also *Beginnings: Intention and Method* (New York: Basic Books, 1975), 129.

7. Said, *Joseph Conrad and the Fiction of Autobiography,* 10.

8. Ibid., 4.

9. Ibid., 82, 88, 94.

10. Said, *Reflections on Exile,* 14.

11. Said, *The World, the Text, and the Critic,* 44.

12. J. Hillis Miller, "Beginning with a Text," *Diacritics* 6 (Fall 1976): 2.

13. Said, *Beginnings,* 193–94.

14. Ibid., xvii.

15. Ibid., 3–4.

16. Ibid., 281.

17. Ibid., 283.

18. Ibid., 335.

19. Ibid., 5.

20. "The actuality of the narrative process is repetition, it is true, but it is not the repetition of back-ward but of *forward* recollection"(ibid., 87–88). "Narratives . . . create another sense altogether by re-peating, by making repetition itself the very form of novelty" (ibid., 87). "Originality in one primal sense, then, has to be loss, or else it would be repetition" (*The World, the Text, and the Critic,* 133).

21. Said, *Beginnings,* 75.

22. Said, *Reflections on Exile,* 22.

23. Said, *Beginnings,* 262.

24. Ibid., 13, 29.

25. Ibid., 48.

26. Ibid., 78.

27. Ibid., 50.

28. Ibid., 6, 372.

29. Ibid., 76, 78, 39, 78.

30. Said, *Joseph Conrad and the Fiction of Autobiography,* 27.

31. Said, *The World, the Text, and the Critic,* 95.

32. Joseph Conrad, *Lord Jim* (London: Penguin, 1972), 150.

33. Said, *The World, the Text, and the Critic,* 128.

34. Said, *Beginnings,* 195.

35. Said, *The World, the Text, and the Critic,* 47.

36. Ibid., 142.

37. Ibid., 141.

38. Said, *Beginnings,* 10, 66, 171.

39. Ibid., 84.

40. Ibid., 92.

41. Ibid., xviii.

42. Ibid., 335, 376, 75.

43. Edward W. Said, *On Late Style: Music and Literature against the Grain* (New York: Pantheon, 2006), 7.

4

Side by Side

The Other Is Not Mute

Laura Nader

In *Culture and Imperialism* (1993) Edward Said describes the Western cultural imagination that inspired Europeans to extend their rule across the globe and that fed their belief in their right and obligation to dominate other peoples. Said also followed and identified an "oppositional strain" in a number of writings that sought to expose this system of domination and point out its imperialist assumptions and insidious effects. Such effects stemmed from the justification of Western ambitions and took the form of slow cultural decolonization in many areas of the world. Even in the 1950s when I sought to fulfill my graduate requirements at Harvard University, traces of these effects remained. I was told that only two foreign languages—French and German—were considered civilizational in the university's canon; Arabic did not qualify. In Algeria at that time Arabic was forbidden as a formal language of instruction and administration. In *Culture and Imperialism* Said argued for mutual respect and coexistence and highlighted the anthropological truism that human beings have been intertwined and connected since the start, always digesting each other's discoveries. In this chapter, I explore this "oppositional strain" further. My goal is to delineate a line of thinking, sometimes summarized as *coexistence*, that has long and deep roots in the East. This notion defines a manner of engagement that runs side-by-side or eye-to-eye and refuses hierarchy, recognizing human beings as equal but malleable and therefore capable of difference.

The author would like to thank Saddeka Arebi, Ayfer Bartu, Monica Eppinger, Brad Erickson, Chris Hebdon, Jesse Sanford, Rik Pinxton, and many other students and colleagues who have discussed the issues raised in this essay.

CAN CULTURES COMMUNICATE?

When Edward Said came onto the public scene, he surprised many British and American publics. Thanks to his voice, the Other—in this case the Arab Palestinian—was not mute. He had a special voice that incorporated high English and American culture as well as his own high Arab culture of literature and politics, poetry and novels. Said had a deep knowledge of both cultures that allowed him to initiate a dialogue with Western scholars, but the balance between him and British and American intellectuals was skewed in his favor (or one might say "not in his favor" for the same reason). His Other had a constricted understanding of contemporary Arab culture.

I first met Edward Said at an American Enterprise Institute (AEI) roundtable in September 1976. We were on a panel with Samuel Huntington and Mustafa Safwan titled "Can Cultures Communicate?" (American Enterprise Institute 1976), a two-day conference in Washington, D.C., on Arab and American cultures. In his opening statement Said said, "Arab culture is not widely known in this country. The problems of translation are many, but that is only part of it. If you were to ask a generally literate American about what is now taking place culturally in the Arab world—in poetry, in fiction, in the arts generally—he would be very hard put to name a single figure of any importance. That is to say, of any importance to the Arabs"(American Enterprise Institute 1976: 2). He continued, "America as a cultural entity to the Arab world is rather different from the reverse. . . . The general Arab image of America and the West has been one of wonder and of some admiration, which in the past few decades has, for the most part, soured" (4). He spoke of a long history of cultural attitudes, which could be described as Western stereotypes now filtered into American culture:

> This "schism" between words and actions or reality in Arab culture has been made by people who do not know the language. These generalizations about the way Arabs think and the way Arabs speak, and the difference between them, are made on the basis of a few free-floating generalizations about Arab society and Arab mentality. In any other situation, one would openly call this racist. You cannot characterize a culture according to some norm that you impose on the relationships between words and actions and say, "It is perfectly clear that Arabs really never mean what they say." . . . Words and actions differ in all societies. . . . But to make an arbitrary judgment and say it is greater in Arab societies and less great in Sweden and in the United States is perhaps a rather dangerous form of generalization, which leads to nothing productive. (American Enterprise Institute 1976: 8–9)

Indeed, Said was correct: no culture has a monopoly on the gap between word and deed, nor are there adequate measures of such phenomena, although there probably should be. The tendency to see one's own culture as the most logical, the most beautiful, the most whatever is a phenomenon that anthropologists refer to as ethnocentrism. This type of cultural bias seems to be the grounds for Said's later elaborate and damning refutation of Huntington's book *The Clash of Civilizations*. His contention with the term *civilization* is particularly noteworthy.

In another section of the 1976 dialogue, Said pointed out that the relationship between the West and the Arab world is strange in that it is perceived not as a relationship between two contemporary cultures but as one between a contemporary culture and a classical culture. Whatever knowledge Americans have of Arab culture is skewed toward classical culture and focused on people like Ibn Khaldoun, Averroes, and medieval philosophers, writers, and poets: "So Americans know nothing about the modern Egyptian novel, for example, or about modern Syrian poetry. A most peculiar sort of time lag exists in the world today. . . . Everything to be found in Arab society appears degenerate somehow, a degraded version of the great classical past" (American Enterprise Institute 1976: 12).

In his public lecture, Said commented, "Preceding the Gulf War on Iraq, books on ancient Iraq and Babylonia were being made available by publishers, not books on the modern and contemporary history. I would say that even Arab intellectuals like Ibn Khaldoun and Averroes are widely unknown as well as the Arabo-Islamic contributions to the West overshadowed as they were by Orientalists writing on the backwardness and stagnation of Islam" (American Enterprise Institute 1976: 8).

Said also criticized a lack of Arab purpose in understanding the United States in any systematic way. In his view a deep knowledge of both cultures was necessary for informed dialogue and mutual respect. This view was both the moral ground on which Said stood and an expression of his own cultural traditions, and of course, it was a major irritant for his critics, who might ask: Is there any value to the argument that the West's search for knowledge about Arab society, literature, religion is cast through the same prism of the colonial gaze? So although engagement with the Other takes place, little understanding follows.

In a 1992 article, Ella Shohat, herself an Arab Jew living between two cultures, explained what is so threatening about Edward Said's style of presentation and representation:

> Spokespersons such as Said, Ibrahim Abu-Lughod, James Zogby, and Rashid Khalidi defy the stereotypical Arab look of thick mustaches, hooked noses, or halting English and heavy Arab accent. They can also speak within the American media's discursive norms. Said, whose area of academic specialization is not Middle Eastern studies but English and Comparative Literature, presents an entirely "mainstream" image. Since Arabs have consistently been represented as antithetical to all things Western, the idea of a spokesperson on Palestinian-Arab rights intimately aware of Western culture is extremely disturbing, particularly for the Israelo-centric politics of representations. The point is a sensitive one for Israel's self-image and for official Israeli propaganda, which, along the lines of the culture of Empire, portrays "Arabs" as ignorant of Western civilization. Historical encounters between Arabs and the West, for example dur-

ing the "Golden Age" in Iberia and during the two hundred years of colonial rule, are minimized. Such representation has been especially crucial for a nation-state that is geographically situated in the Middle East but whose imagery constantly revolves around the "West." (Shohat 1992: 128)

Especially in his later years and particularly in his visits to Egypt, Edward Said urged his fellow Arabs to study and understand the culture of the West (Said 1993: 294) and advocated the establishment of departments of American studies in Arab universities. Said, however, was not the first to point out the necessity of understanding the culture of those with whom dialogue is essential.

STUDYING EUROPE

In the early nineteenth century, Muhammad Ali recognized a need to understand Europe and particularly the French after the Napoleonic invasion of Egypt in 1798. In 1826 an Egyptian delegation, with Rifa'ah Al-Tahtawi as its imam, was sent to France. Al-Tahtawi spent five years in Paris (1826–31) and in 1834 published the first ethnographic study of "a strange land with strange customs." The book, written for the Egyptian populace, was an attempt to begin a dialogue about a compromise between East and West and to consider the possibilities of forging a harmonious relation between equal, if different, parts. For Al-Tahtawi the West was a place for exchange, for mutual reflection, for interactivity. Although his French teachers of translation wanted to convert him to their notion of what it is to be civilized, the dialogue he conducted with himself in his book reveals that he was not a total convert and had not become an apostle of European modernity and development. He made comparisons explicit, by pointing out or turning upside down the arrogance of positional superiority he found around him. He made clear that he knew the Arabs were the teachers of the Europeans, yet he was forthright in his admiration for French notions of freedom, justice, and equity. By the time one completes a reading of An Imam in Paris (2004), as it is called in its first English translation, one senses the possibility of exchange between two different yet similar cultures—similar because of our common humanity. The opportunities engage the mind, offering possibilities of coexistence.

Al-Tahtawi's view reminds one of Said's, except that Said wrote after more than a hundred years of imperialism and colonialism whereas Al-Tahtawi was entangled with the modernizing project. Nevertheless, both found themselves between two civilizational modes (or as Said would say, "living in two cultures or two languages"). Both were empowered by firsthand knowledge of Europe and the Arab world. Both recognized the need to distinguish between and connect logical thought and emotion. But Said had experienced colonialism firsthand, so modernization was not his priority as it was for Al-Tahtawi. For Said, the notion of modernity had little utility because he refused to internalize the Western idea of the developmental inferiority of Arab society. But for Al-Tahtawi, this project of modernization was apparently the justification for his stay in France. Furthermore, while Said viewed his own identity as contrapuntal rather than fixed, Al-Tahtawi saw himself as transitory and instrumental in his communication with the Other.

In "The Resonance of the Arab-Islamic Heritage in the Work of Edward Said" (1992), Ferial Ghazoul wrote perceptively about Said's method of revising distortions in Western discourse to arrive at a fresh way of looking at the power dimension. For example, he discussed the Irish poet Yeats and the Palestinian poet Mahmoud Darwish in the same article and looked at Foucault in tandem with Ibn Khaldoun, comparing them in order to undermine the parochialism of Western thought, to unmask prejudice disguised as intellectual product.

Said often challenged the "Western canon." In a lecture at Cambridge in 2002, he said that humanism cannot be truly humanist if it does not account for humanistic production outside the Western canon (Said 2004). He could not have done any of this critique if he had been enclosed in the Middle Eastern studies paradigm. And neither could Al-Tahtawi have gained the insight that comes from comparison had he not, as a student of translation, understood both French and Arabic. As he observed, "When it comes to word plays, expressions, and the multiple usage of them, ornate rhetorical figures based on pronunciation, French is devoid of all this. What in Arabic is seen as embellishment, the French sometimes perceive as weakness." In sum, he said, "All of the elegance of an Arabic text disappears once it has been translated" (2004: 182). His recognition that each language has its specific conventions of usage that do not always translate came from his comparison of the two languages. Yet, though language differences are a path to understanding, as they were for both Al-Tahtawi and Said, cultural patterning occurs on a foundation of similarity. In general, such an orientation is more common among Arab and other Middle Eastern intellectuals.

If one reads Amin Maalouf's *The Crusades through Arab Eyes* (1984) as a counterpoint to the Orientalism described by Said, one finds no evidence that Muslims believed that the Crusader Franj were inherently inferior. The Arab historian Usama Ibn Munqidh believed the Franj could become equals through the civilizing influence of his society precisely because their barbaric actions were not seen as signs of inherent or perpetual inferiority. As Ibn Munqidh wrote, "Their barbarian mores were gradually being refined by contact with the Orient" (Maalouf 1984: 129). Al-Jabarti's *Chronicle of the French Occupation of Egypt* (1975) presents scenes of episodic chaos and human depravity, but the wronged party, his Egyptians, are nowhere valorized. In fact the description of an orgy of looting is anything but a sympathetic depiction of Coptic, Muslim, or Jewish Egyptians.

Al-Jabarti's view of the Napoleonic invasion is a tonic to the one-sided gaze of Egyptian coffeehouses by Edward William Lane's *The Manners and Customs of the*

Modern Egyptians (1923), written in 1836. In Lane's book, the coffeehouse is a fixed scene entirely separate from the eyes of the observer. He does not see his own reflection in the mirror (Naddaf 1986). However, Al-Jabarti's work, like the magnetic stimulus of Said's *Orientalism,* contributes to a conversation on Orientalism and Occidentalism. Whereas Al-Jabarti holds the French in high regard by virtue of their discipline, organization, and unity, qualities whose lack he laments in his countrymen, he also holds them in contempt. Yet, despite the antipathies, one sees no suggestion either in Maalouf's sources or in Al-Jabarti's writing that the Arabs considered themselves inherently superior to the Europeans, as is found in the intended or unintended racist ideology of some Orientalist writings. Rather the Arab historians display the reciprocal gaze of the Arab/Muslim East, which evokes the old formulation of the People of the Book to recognize that Muslims, Christians, and Jews share the same God and the same religious foundations.

FOUNDATIONS OF SIMILARITY

If racism entails a worldview that groups people hierarchically in ways that predicate the inherent and heritable superiority and entitlement of the dominant group, Arab observers seem free of such superiority. This latter tradition, of which Edward Said was a part, lends itself more easily to open dialogue based on assumptions of similarity. Such suppositions may explain why Arabs and Arab Americans on talk shows often preface their remarks with "We are human beings too." Arab/Muslim professed commitments to equality and the absence of hierarchy signal inclusion rather than exclusion, a reflexive comparison. To understand new things, we have to describe them in words we already know and understand. Thus, the exact moment of comparison is also the moment of analysis, and a variety of theoretical lenses allow nuanced images that are both complex and specific, reflecting an ambiguity and multiplicity of perspectives.

In another nineteenth-century Arab observation, this time on European music, Ahmad Faris recognized the cultural within the realm of habit, which is something learned and is therefore not inevitable: "If music were a redundancy of Logic it would be practiced uniformly even as logic is one of its canons. Yet, people differ widely within: the melodies favored by the Arabs do not move others; nay, the Arabs themselves differ from one another, the Egyptians being unmoved by Syrian melodies—and European melodies leave them all unmoved" (Cachia 1973: 43). Throughout the commentaries Faris applies his own sensibilities and categories to highlight the arbitrary nature of musical cultural practices.

According to Hayden White, "In Said's worldview, things exist side-by-side with one another, not in hierarchies of relative reality or ordered series of dynastically related groups" (cited in Said 1992: 109). In this spirit Said exclaimed, "I make a systematic defense of the non-European civilizations. They were communal societies.... They were democratic societies.... They were cooperative societies, fraternal societies. I make a systematic defense of the societies destroyed by imperialism" (Said 1992: 38).

THE DOUBLE GAZE

Commentaries on the West acknowledge the problems of privileging Western writings and also acknowledge the fact that peoples of different civilizations were not the silent or frozen partners that most Westerners still make them out to be. Introducing a different or additional kind of representation disrupts the polar "Us and Them" systems and blurs the boundaries and distinctions. Such a double gaze may provide accounts of the uniqueness of different cultures while illuminating the overlapping and interconnected nature of world history. For this reason, the problem of Orientalism should not be posed as a problem of representation; rather, it is a particular system of representation, not an inevitable result when peoples encounter each other. Unlike Orientalist infrastructures, there are no organized institutions, no hegemonically organized scholarship which could be labeled as "Occidentalism." Alternatively, people on the other side of these encounters have not been mute, nor have they shied away from making singular observations about the Western world. Interactions between peoples have taken place since the beginning of world history. In this sense, one can speak of "Occidentalisms," non-Western perceptions of the Western world, whatever "West" might have meant. So a project of Occidentalism is my way of enhancing Said's initial work, although Said himself argued that the dominant global presence of the West disallows equivalence and prevents a dignified Occidentalism. Occidentalism is not a remedy for Orientalism, nor is it a mirror image of Orientalism. It simply acknowledges that populations throughout time have acted upon their constructions of others and have done so in highly variable ways, even within the same culture and despite asymmetries in power.

Comparative analysis is particularly important in anthropological attempts to understand encounters between different peoples. Juan Cole (1992) argues that most negative images of the Middle East among nineteenth-century Europeans derived from a contrastive approach. Europe was rational, orderly, and virile; the East was irrational, stagnant, and effeminate. Said notes such contrasts in examining the tendency of Orientalist literature to dichotomize the human continuum into we/they contrasts. Comparison and contrast are inevitably coupled, but they are not the same. To admit difference without likeness might well be seen as faulty and ideological. As Cole suggests, even when European observers' comparisons were actually "reflexed contrasts," Muslim festivals and attendance at shrines recalled Roman Catholic practices for Protestant British colonial officers; British prime minister Anthony Eden read Egyptian president Gamal Abdel Nasser as Mussolini (Cole 1992:

9). Reading comparative commentaries on the West in Occidentalist literature can make one think of the ways in which other cultures are like one's own while giving Others their place within a common human heritage. As the boundaries between Us and Them blur, one can more easily see that We and They are part of the same history (Wolf 1982). Claude Lévi-Strauss indicated as much in 1974, describing "that crucial moment in modern thought when thanks to the great voyages of discovery, a human community which had believed itself to be complete and in its final form suddenly learned . . . that it was not alone, that it was part of a greater whole, and that in order to achieve self-knowledge, it must first of all contemplate its recognizable image in this mirror" (326). Unfortunately, the Orientalist system of representation does not provide that mirror and indeed should not be identified with representation per se. However, we might see a project on Occidentalism as a project in discovery. How should we react to elite commentary on the West (from Arab historians of the Crusades to contemporary Moroccan elites) stating that "the West, they have no culture, no civilization but they do have technology" (as a visiting Moroccan dignitary said to me)?

In a piece on Edward Said's public intellectualism, Tim Brennan (1992) writes of Said's defense of scholars who synthesize vast amounts of materials to reach plausible generalizations:

> Such scholars strive toward ever-widening horizons of intellectual work in order to generalize, to encourage the "virtues of the roving intelligence, the need for comparative studies, the totality that is not totalizing," the inquiry that is "free" in the necessarily ambiguous sense of that term . . . Originality is not the most important demand made of an intellectual. . . . Said played down the qualities of uniqueness or revelation, on which most professional fame is based, in pursuit of something more basic: finding one's priorities. . . .
>
> . . . Said sees contradictions everywhere, and urges us to internalize them by projecting, in good philological fashion, into the full experiences of others. (83, 84)

And Brennan sees this statement as a rallying cry for future work.

This spirit, which perhaps for chauvinistic reasons I call anthropological, enables Said to make provocative observations. In his comments on Western studies of the Middle East and the use of monolithic concepts like "Islam" or "the Arabs," he noted, "People who profess to know the Middle East . . . take an immediate political event . . . and for an ultimate understanding of it, they take a couple of passages from the Koran or from some twelfth-century jurist, and say, 'If you really want to understand what is going on, you have to go back to these lines.' . . . The equivalent of such folly is to say, 'If you really want to understand what is taking place in the Congress on the energy bill, you have to read the New Testament very carefully, and then everything will be clear to you'" (American Enterprise Institute 1976: 16–17). Such a critique is likely to come from someone who understands both cultures and uses a comparative frame to uncover the eye that sees.

SIDE BY SIDE

In 1994 I wrote an essay about comparative consciousness. In it, I pointed out that although anthropology has seen a variety of comparative traditions, I support an inclusive anthropology that is not solely about non-Western, colonial, or isolated island societies. I suggested that the subject for anthropology is human existence in all its diversity, including all cultural forms found on the globe: in the suites, in the streets, in the villages, on the steppes, in the cities, in the institutions, and in the mind. Similarly, this inclusive tradition embraces many kinds of intellectuals, not just European and American ones. Anthropology, I reminded my colleagues, not only includes the whole earth today but covers the entire period of human existence. In this sense, I suggest that Edward Said had an anthropological turn of mind, even though he was sometimes critical of anthropological works, as I have also been.

The particularistic approach in which the native is mute can be distinguished from the universalistic one that allows for the Other's Other and thereby enables us to see ourselves better. Denial, a social disease related to ethnocentrism, makes us unaware of the special lenses through which we look at life. We need "to know as much about the eye that sees as the object seen" (Kluckhohn 1949: 16). If in looking at Egyptian women's lives Western feminists get caught up in clitorectomy (Morsy 1991), we miss the opportunity to examine the phenomenon of breast implants in the United States, for example. If the Daniel Pipes of the world look only at militant Islam, they miss the insights that come with looking at militant Islam together with militant Christianity and Judaism. If we debunk comparison, we throw out possibilities for examining those dimensions of the human experience that are shared, such as the militancy of all world religions or the repression of women in all patriarchal societies, ours included. Without comparison, we not only practice moral imperialism, but we literally lose consciousness and become victim to the bounds of thinkable thought (Chomsky 1985). The need for increased consciousness of comparative methodologies is compelling precisely because of current political controversies that may be fueled by facile generalizations about how Muslims treat their women, for example.

The term *comparative consciousness* implies that people are sometimes not conscious of comparison, although the act of thinking comparatively is probably universal. In travel or journalistic observations, comparison is sometimes implicit and sometimes explicit, depending on the context. But comparison is always part of the observational substratum and always bears a dialectical relationship to the political and cultural world. Said's point was not that Orientalist scholars purposely "misrepresent" the Middle East but that the Western political-intellectual culture that surrounds scholarship on the Orient links such representations logically to imperialism.

Comparisons that squeeze the unique into the narrow definitions of scientific variables gloss over both hegemonic and counterhegemonic influences, thereby neglecting historical processes and papering over implicit comparisons attached to the observer as instrument. Over the past several decades, all of us have become more sophisticated about the manner in which knowledge is created. The observers of the West I have mentioned are all members of elite classes, and their firsthand encounters serve up different impressions than they would have formed from a distance or even would form today.

A look at changing perceptions of women illustrates the stimulus of firsthand encounters. That women have been at the core of cultural encounters between West and East is by now obvious. The condition and status of women are especially central to Eastern and Western patriarchal societies. Women's concepts of themselves, and their means of evaluating other societies, are often expressed in the most superficial manner, as in commentary such as "they are overcovered or they are undercovered" in their clothing habits. Given the symbolic centrality of women within or between societies, discourse about them is bound to be politicized and subject to contests about nationality, cultural authenticity, development, reform, state construction, and more. However, images of women have not solely been the creation of men.

By the end of the nineteenth century, a variety of Western women had visited or lived in the Middle East, as wives of the increasing numbers of Western officials, doctors, engineers, and businessmen who traveled there to represent Western interests. Like their male counterparts, most women who left records of their impressions of the Middle East used their own culture as a yardstick by which to judge their host countries. However, one common theme, which will ring strangely to contemporary feminists, was that Muslim women had significantly greater independence and more rights than Western women; moreover, these writers saw the Muslim Middle East as more humane than the Christian West. The reader of these accounts gets the sense that these Western women, trapped in their own forms of subjugation, thought that Oriental lives might be preferable to their own. Using the perspective of both gender and class, Billie Melman's *Women's Orients* (1992) analyzes British women's travelogues on the Middle East between 1821 and 1914. Among these visitors were the eighteenth-century aristocrat Mary Wortley Montagu, who recorded the fulfilling opportunities available to Turkish women, and travelers who re-created the harem in the image of the feminine, autonomous middle-class European household. Melman embeds her argument in plural Orientalism. Today, the situation has turned around so dramatically that no one doubts which view of the Oriental woman prevails today: that of the independent Oriental woman or that of the repressed one. Social and historical interpretations are not immune from control via the dynamics of power, and the nineteenth-century women in Melman's book used their depictions of the Other to comment indirectly on the image and status of women in Britain, Western Europe, and the United States. Muslim women also used such strategies to promote change.

Two Turkish sisters spent six years in Europe in the early part of the twentieth century. One of these sisters, Zeynep Hanoum, corresponded with a British friend, Grace Ellison. A collection of the letters she wrote to Ellison between 1906 and 1912 (Ellison 1913) provides a fascinating early critique of Western feminist theory, offering a unique example of the interplay of "Eastern" and "Western" images. Hanoum's letters make critical comments on education, the political situation in turn-of-the-century Turkey, the idea of progress, and the condition of women both in Turkey and in Europe. Hanoum's stay in Europe prompted reflections about her life and life in the countries she visited. Her main concern was the condition of women, specifically freedom of women, a notion that underwent a tremendous transformation during her stay in Europe and her exchanges with Grace Ellison, a leading feminist of the time.

In her introduction to the collection, Ellison writes,

> I too, own my inability to come any nearer a solution of this problem (women's suffering in Turkey). I, who through the veil have studied the aimless, unhealthy existence of these pampered women, am nevertheless convinced that the civilization of Western Europe for Turkish women is a case of exchanging the frying-pan for the fire. . . .
>
> Be warned by us, you Turkish women I said to them, painting the consequences of our freedom in its blackest colors, and do not pull up your anchor till you can safely steer your ship. My own countrymen have become too callous to the bitter struggles of women; civilization was never meant to be run on these lines, therefore hold fast to the protection of your harems till you can stand alone . . .
>
> The time has not yet come for the Turkish woman to vindicate her right to freedom; it cannot come by mere change of law, and it is cruelty on the part of Europeans to encourage them to adopt Western habits which are part of a general system derived from a totally different process of evolution. (1913: xvi, xvii, xviii)

Europe, Hanoum's dream, means freedom for her, and the first step in claiming this freedom is the symbolic removal of the veil. Gradually, however, her new life loses its glamour. Her letters chronicle a series of disappointments, specifically European failures to live up to the idea of progress and to improve the condition of women, which she sees as signs of the ignorance of Europeans. She is struck by the questions Europeans ask her: "In costume we are on a level with Paris, seeing we buy our clothes there; and as regards culture, we are perhaps more advanced than is the West . . . How little we are known by the European critics" (Ellison 1913: 39). Her bewilderment and anger are also apparent in her response to the question "How many wives has your father?" She responds, "As many as your husband, Madam" (49). She wishes that "nine out of every ten of the books written on Turkey could be burned! . . . What nonsense has been written about the women!" (49). She also finds European women lacking in grace and unwilling to take advantage of the unbounded opportunities they have. This observation leads her to reflect on the price that Turkish women pay if they adopt the Western model of "freedom" and "emancipation": "No longer can they do what they feel for fear of compromising a 'social position.' Is not the gaiety of their lives worse than the monotony of ours? Often times they have to sacrifice a noble friendship to the higher demands of social exclusiveness. How strange and insincere it all seems to a Turkish woman" (118).

After her visit to the English Parliament, Hanoum writes, "But, my dear, why have you never told me that the Ladies' Gallery is a harem? A harem with its latticed windows! The harem of the Government! No wonder the women cried through the windows of that harem that they wanted to be free. . . . How inconsistent are you English! You send your women out unprotected all over the world, and here in the workshop where your laws are made, you cover them with a symbol of protection" (Ellison 1913: 194).

She reflects further on the Ladies' Club: "The silence of the room was restful, there was an atmosphere of peace, but it is not the peace which follows strife, it is the peace of apathy. Is this, then, what the Turkish women dream of becoming one day? Is this their idea of independence and liberty? . . . A club, as I said before, is after all, another kind of harem" (Ellison 1913: 186–88). And when she is about to leave Europe after six years, she makes clear her disappointment and skepticism. Zeynep Hanoum caught on to the key problem of "modernization." What does the West have to offer? What should be the compromise between European and Turkish ways? What are the consequences of making a compromise? She asks, "Do you remember with what delight I came to France, the country of *Liberté, Egalité,* and *Fraternité?* But now I have seen those three magic words in practice, and the whole course of my ideas has changed! . . . How dangerous it is to urge those Orientals forward, only to reduce them in a few years to the same state of stupidity as the poor degenerate peoples of the West" (Ellison 1913: 237–39).

A well-honed comparative consciousness leads one to question basic assumptions and opens a world of discovery. Hanoum recognized Western women's apparent freedom, a trap of heavy burdens, and after weighing individualism against solidarity, she expressed her preference for the latter. She painted herself into the picture, observing the way in which she was treated as a "living spectacle" (Ellison 1913: 50), and faulted herself for sometimes making judgments too quickly. She also found similarities: "The Englishmen remind me of the Turks. They have the same grave demeanor, the same appearance of indifference to our sex, the same look of stubborn determination, and like the Turk, every Englishman is a Sultan in his own house" (288). At the same time she saw Europeans as shallow, impolite, and most unforgivably, inhospitable. She described France, where she stayed the longest (in Paris), as an "exaggerated democracy" and wrote that French cemeteries reminded her of home. Her letters remind us how people define themselves through interaction with each other; their encounters with others set the stage for reflexive comparison, often changing their perspectives as the context changes with the specifics of history. Such encounters lead not to general conclusions but to new questions and new analyses, which may not be new at all, except to one's self, prompting an exercise in self-discipline.

A FINAL NOTE: THE CLASH OF IGNORANCE

If one thinks of truth as a strict correspondence between representation and the real world, one must take Orientalisms and Occidentalisms with a grain of salt. If one is interested in the observer's view of the relationship between two entities, one learns that no truth exists outside of history. Specific writings produce their own discourses for truth making. The examples I present here are part of the human archive of memories that have much to do with what is happening in the world today and what may happen tomorrow. Listening to contemporary news reports on Iraq, for example, makes one recall Said's observation that in any other situation, such reporting would openly be called racist. Cross-cultural dialogue should aim not to determine the accuracy of individual assessments but to make sense of the conditions in the East and West that influence these impressions and determine their impact, whether it be imperialism, political and cultural colonialism, religious fervor, or in Iraq, the American/British invasion and occupation of 2003.

Any interaction between different groups of people has a power dimension that plays out in overlapping and interconnected histories. Unfortunately, area studies have severed regions from one another in the scholarly mind, so they are almost never studied in relation to one another. This narrow, geographic focus perpetuates dichotomies and stereotypes and fosters radical separation and opposition. Similarly, the terms *third world* and *fourth world* imply a global order, a neat division of the world into clear and simple zones, each with a fixed place in a hierarchy. Yet cultures and societies are not abstract, oppositional, static, and sealed units that function in isolation, or fit along an evolutionary spectrum from the barbaric to the civilized. No first world exists independently from the third world; a third world exists in every first world and vice versa. In addition, all countries are developing.

Commentaries on the West provide a critique, sometimes startling, that could enlighten us about other human possibilities and help avoid what Edward Said called "the clash of ignorance" in a 2001 article. After all, the contemporary human condition is the result of thousands of years of cumulative encounters. Europeans borrowed the jacket and trousers from the Mongols! A system of side-by-side representations seems to me more productive of dialogue about war and peace, or about state and stateless terrorism, or about women's conditions than do detached, objective analyses or the European system of Orientalism described so passionately by Edward Said.

WORKS CITED

Al-Jabarti, A. 1975. *Napoleon in Egypt: Al-Jabarti's Chronicle of the French Occupation, 1798.* Trans. Shmuel Moreh. Princeton, NJ: Markus Wiener.

Al-Tahtawi, R. 2004. *Al-Tahtawi—An Imam in Paris.* Intro. and trans. Daniel L. Newman. London: Saqi Press.

American Enterprise Institute. 1976. "Can Cultures Communicate?" Roundtable moderated by E. Stewart, with Samuel P. Huntington, Laura Nader, Nustafa Safwan, and Edward Said, 23 September 1976, Washington, D.C.

Brennan, T. 1992. "Places of Mind, Occupied Lands: Edward Said and Philology." In *Edward Said: A Critical Reader.* Ed. M. Sprinker. Cambridge: Blackwell Publishers, 75–95.

Cachia, P. 1973. "A 19th Century Arab's Observations on European Music." *Ethnomusicology* 17 (1): 41–51.

Chomsky, N. 1985. "The Bounds of Thinkable Thought." *Progressive,* October.

Cole, J. 1992. *Comparing Muslim Societies: Knowledge and the State in a World Civilization.* Ann Arbor: University of Michigan Press.

Ellison, G. 1913. *Zeynep Hanoum: A Turkish Woman's European Impressions.* London: Seeley, Service and Co.

Ghazoul, F. 1992. "The Resonance of the Arab-Islamic Heritage in the Work of Edward Said." In *Edward Said: A Critical Reader.* Ed. M. Sprinker. Cambridge: Blackwell Publishers, 15–29.

Kluckhohn, C. 1949. *Mirror for Man: The Relation of Anthropology to Modern Life.* New York: McGraw-Hill.

Lane, E. W. 1923. *The Manners and Customs of the Modern Egyptians.* New York: E. P. Dutton.

Lévi-Strauss, C. 1974. *Tristes Tropiques.* Trans. John and Doreen Weightman. New York: Atheneum Press.

Maalouf, A. 1984. *The Crusades through Arab Eyes.* Trans. J. Rothchild. New York: Schocken.

Melman, B. 1992. *Women's Orients: England and the Middle East, 1718–1918—Sexuality, Religion and Work.* Ann Arbor: University of Michigan Press.

Morsy, S. 1991. "Safeguarding Women's Bodies: The White Man's Burden Medicalized." *Medical Anthropology Quarterly* 5 (1): 19–23.

Naddaf, S. 1986. "Mirrored Images: Rifa'ah al-Tahtawi and the West." *Alif,* no. 6 (Spring).

Nader, L. 1992. "Comparative Consciousness." In *Asserting Cultural Anthropology.* Ed. R. Borofsky. New York: McGraw-Hill.

Said, E. W. 1978. *Orientalism.* New York: Pantheon.

———. 1992. *Edward Said: A Critical Reader.* Ed. M. Sprinker. Cambridge: Blackwell Publishers.

———. 1993. *Culture and Imperialism.* New York: Alfred A. Knopf.

———. 2001. "The Clash of Ignorance." *Nation,* October, 11–13.

———. 2004. "The Changing Bases of Humanistic Study and Practice." In *Humanism and Democratic Criticism.* New York: Columbia University Press, 43–55.

Shohat, E. 1992. "Antimonies of Exile: Said at the Frontiers of National Narrations." In *Edward Said: A Critical Reader.* Ed. M. Sprinker. Cambridge: Blackwell Publishers, 121–43.

Wolf, E. 1982. *Europe and the People without History.* Berkeley: University of California Press.

5

Edward Said and Anthropology

Nicholas B. Dirks

Despite, or perhaps because of, Edward Said's enormous impact on the discipline of anthropology, he was not always welcomed as a friendly critic. For some anthropologists, he was the embodiment of the unpopular notion that the discipline would forever be tainted by its colonial origins. Said was hardly the first to call attention to the colonial origins—and continuing entailments—of anthropology, but something about the challenge he held out made many anthropologists uncomfortable, defensive, and reactive. When Edward Said was invited to the annual meetings of the American Anthropological Association (AAA) as an anthropological interlocutor in November 1987, his critical reflections about the implications of U.S. imperialism for the discipline, in which he noted the persistence of colonial forms of knowledge and the need for explicit political engagement, were not uniformly well received. According to one observer, "Respondents angrily and vigorously pointed out the vast radical literatures and personal political histories that contradicted Said's vision."[1] This was not the hero's welcome that one might have expected given the critical importance of *Orientalism* for the anthropological project.

When Edward Said published his pathbreaking *Orientalism* in 1978, he articulated the most compelling polemical critique of scholarship in colonial ideas and legacies that had so far been made. After this work, it seemed impossible to study the colonial world without making explicit or implicit reference to his critique that both our sources and our basic categories and assumptions (as anthropologists, historians of the colonial world, area-studies experts, etc.) have been shaped by colonial rule. Said made the case that the Orient qua Orient was constituted by the collaboration of power and knowledge in the context of Western colonial rule. When Said used the term *Orientalism,* he meant it in a number of interdependent senses.

86

In one sense, it referred to the colonial establishment's tendency to view the Orient as Europe's other, a land of exotic beings and exploitable riches that existed primarily to service the economy and the imagination of the West. He also used the term to describe a much more sophisticated body of scholarship—embodied in practices such as philology, archaeology, history, and anthropology—that glorified the classical civilizations of the East (while glorifying even more the scholarly endeavors of the West that made possible their recuperation and study) but suggested that all history since the classical age was a story of decline, degradation, and decadence. Orientalism, whether in the guise of colonial cultures of belief or more specialized subcultures of scholarship, shared fundamental premises about the East that denigrated the present, denied history, and repressed any sensibility of contemporary political, social, or cultural autonomy and potential in the colonized world. The result of this thinking, Said suggested, was the relentless Orientalization of the Orient, the constant reiteration of tropes conferring inferiority and subordination.

The importance of this critique was hardly lost on anthropologists, who were already well aware of the colonial context of much early anthropological knowledge, not to mention the extent to which much anthropological work continued to privilege ideas of exoticism, otherness, and the primitive. Yet, at the 1987 AAA meeting, attendees were clearly ambivalent about the implications and scope of the *Orientalism* critique. On that occasion, the panelists certainly addressed questions of colonialism and imperialism, but their responses suggested a residual resistance to the kind of totalizing epistemological critique made by Said, even as some respondents were concerned about Said's lack of reference to Marxist critiques of imperialism within the discipline. If Said's position was seen as too heavily weighted toward epistemological and political concerns rather than economic or material ones, he at least addressed the ways in which the political crises of anthropological practice and knowledge had moved into literary and philosophical domains. As a professor of English and comparative literature, Said had been distressed to see historical and political issues treated as questions of reading and writing. In fact, the 1980s saw the political engagements of the Vietnam era give way to a focus on literary theory and narrative method. And Said was correct, if rhetorically mischievous, in observing that "few of the scholars who have contributed to such collections as *Writing Culture* or *Anthropology as Cultural Critique*—to mention two highly visible recent books—have explicitly called for an end to anthropology as, for example, a number of literary scholars have indeed recommended for the concept of literature."[2] In pointing out that the crisis of representation had come to dominate recent anthropological writing—both of the books he named had been published in 1986—Said was especially well positioned to complain about the literary turn: "Few of the anthropologists who are read outside anthropology make a secret of the fact that they wish that anthropology, and anthropological texts, might be more literary or literary theoretical in style and awareness, or that anthropologists should spend more time thinking of textuality and less of matrilineal descent, or that issues relating to cultural poetics take a more central role in their research than, say, issues of tribal organization, agricultural economics, and primitive classification."[3] Said seemed horrified to realize that the message that many anthropologists took away from *Orientalism* was that they should pay greater attention to the poetics of colonialism than to the politics of anthropology.

However, the panelists at the AAA meetings were less concerned about the critique of literary theory than about the relationship of colonialism to anthropology, both in affecting the constitution of the discipline and in suggesting a relationship between colonialism and capitalism. In making the charge that "the recent work of Marxist, anti-imperialist, and meta-anthropological scholars . . . nevertheless reveals a genuine malaise about the sociopolitical status of anthropology as a whole,"[4] Said asked why, for instance, the author of one "remarkable book" that provided a model for a new kind of critical "historical anthropology" made an impassioned case for the importance of anthropology as a discipline. At a time of evident "paradigm exhaustion," how could the ultimate refrain come down to concern about the survival of anthropology?[5] Said also argued that the original and important work of anthropologists such as Marshall Sahlins and Eric Wolf lacked both critical self-reflection (and, by implication, significant critical engagements with the colonial sources for much of their historical work) and awareness of the contemporaneous politics of representation ("Who speaks? For what and to whom?").[6] Anthropologists might retreat into textuality, or they might practice varieties of Marxist political economy, but in both cases, they seemed to evade the historical and political reasons that made the postcolonial field increasingly inhospitable to older forms of ethnographic fieldwork. And in their protestation of the importance of their guild, they seemed to betray anxieties that Said intuited had to do with the foundational politics of anthropology. Whether Said meant to overstate the case or not, the responses of his fellow panelists made clear that he had hit upon something sensitive and that anthropology, for all its contemporary merits in the panoply of American social sciences, still had difficulty engaging the genealogical burden of its colonial origins. In this chapter, I reflect on Said's impact on and his legacy to anthropology, but I do so in the larger context of recalling the depth and persistence of the disciplinary anxiety that emerged around *Orientalism*.

Said did not in fact pay a great deal of attention to the history of anthropology in *Orientalism*. The historical polemic he mounted there was directed primarily against the structural and largely discursive collaborations between the academic traditions of textual, philological, and civilizational study, on the one hand, and the formal political and institutional mechanisms of colonial rule, on the other. He mentioned anthropology either as part of area studies or as one of the social scientific disciplines, along with history and political science, critical to postwar academic delineations of the areas of the world that had earlier been left to textual scholars or colonial administrators. True, he criticized the reductive culturalism of the anthropology of thinkers as different as Claude Lévi-Strauss and A. L. Kroeber—in its uses by influential Orientalist scholars such as Gustav von Grunebaum.[7] However, Clifford Geertz was one of the few scholars to emerge from Said's polemic with honorable mention. Said praised Geertz's scholarship for moving beyond the field of Orientalism "defined either canonically, imperially, or geographically. . . . The anthropology of Clifford Geertz . . . is discrete and concrete enough to be animated by the specific societies and problems he studies and not by the rituals, preconceptions, and doctrines of Orientalism."[8] When, in his subsequent essay, "Orientalism Reconsidered," he sharply criticized Geertz's "standard disciplinary rationalizations and self-congratulatory clichés about hermeneutic circles," he was not recanting his earlier comments so much as giving vent to his more troubling sense that anthropologists were repeating the political delusions of philosophical and literary theories and preoccupations that stressed meaning and interpretation over the clamorous demands of politics and history.[9] And he took care to use this concern as a backdrop for his praise of Johannes Fabian's *Time and the Other*.[10] In light of his criticism of hermeneutic circles, Said suggested, "Fabian's serious effort to redirect anthropologists' attention back to the discrepancies in time, power and development between the ethnographer and his/her constituted object [is] all the more remarkable."[11] Nevertheless, anthropology played a negligible role in Said's writings until his participation in the AAA meetings in 1987.

Despite this, Said did not have to comment directly or extensively on anthropology to connect the central concerns of his book to the historical and theoretical entailments of anthropology in colonial history or in Orientalism as a field, and a tradition, of scholarship. Besides, Said's critique of area studies had struck close to home, because anthropology had played a significant role in the development and elaboration of many of the central activities of area studies, both as a general field of study and as a discrete institutional activity within university area institutes or centers. Indeed, postwar anthropology expanded largely because of political and academic recognition of its critical role in the study of the postcolonial world. Said, of course, was hardly the first critic either to suggest the need for political and historical interrogation of the discipline or to link it to Orientalism, but, as we have seen, he struck a nerve. Anthropological reviewers often accepted the importance of Said's criticisms, only to counter with the charge that he essentialized Orientalism as much as it had essentialized the Orient and that he left no role for the true Orient to emerge in any account or to speak back. Various reviews and commentaries counterattacked Said for the very sins he had attributed to the imperial West and to the traditions of Orientalist scholarship.[12] To these critics, Said was both a Nietzschean postmodernist and a political polemicist, subject in either case to excess, contradiction, and ruthless disregard for the facts. But that these charges have been made throughout the thirty years since the book's publication reveals something more fundamental: *Orientalism* was not just an important intervention; it played a key role in the reconceptualization of anthropology in the second half of the twentieth century.

If Said's central arguments had been anticipated by others, perhaps most notably by Anwar Abdel-Malik, one of the most important anthropological anticipations of his work was by Talal Asad in *Anthropology and the Colonial Encounter*.[13] Asad, who assembled the essays in the volume from a conference he convened at the University of Hull in 1972, noted that the subject of colonialism, particularly its relations with anthropology, had been largely ignored in British social anthropology. Reacting to those who insisted that the discipline had grown out of the "ideas and ideals of the Enlightenment," Asad wrote, "Anthropology is also rooted in an unequal power encounter between the West and Third World which goes back to the emergence of bourgeois Europe; an encounter in which colonialism is merely one historical moment. It is this encounter that gives the West access to cultural and historical information about the societies it has progressively dominated, and thus not only generates a certain kind of universal understanding, but also re-enforces the inequalities in capacity between the European and the non-European worlds."[14] Here was the germ of a sweeping critique, made more insistent by his subsequent observation that although anthropologists legitimately lay claim to the "sympathetic recording of indigenous forms of life that would otherwise be lost to posterity . . . they have also contributed, sometimes indirectly, towards maintaining the structure of power represented by the colonial system."[15] And in his own introduction to the volume, Asad took this argument further, proposing a complementary relationship between Orientalist scholarship and anthropological writing: "For the orientalist's construct, by focusing on a particular image of the Islamic tradition, and the anthropologist's, by focusing on a particular image of the Africanist tradition, both helped to justify colonial domination at particular moments in the power encounter between the West and the Third World . . . by refusing to discuss the way in which bourgeois Europe had imposed its power and its own conception of the just political order on African and Islamic peoples, both disciplines were basically reassuring to the colonial ruling classes."[16]

Despite the care with which Asad made his argument, his central point was frequently interpreted as the charge that anthropologists had been the handmaidens of colonial rule, and interventions by anthropologists as various as Del Hymes and Robert Scholte were taken the same way. When the charge was taken seriously, anthropologists—British social anthropologists in particular—defended themselves by providing personal and institutional histories that shed a very different light on the history of the discipline. Significantly, Asad did not in fact suggest direct and intentional collaboration, nor was he primarily interested in assigning blame. He predicated his critique of colonialism on a larger analysis of "the dialectic of world power." Anthropologists could not have done much more than reinforce existing arrangements and understandings whether they had wished to do so or not. He wrote instead, "I believe it is a mistake to view social anthropology in the colonial era as primarily an aid to colonial administration, or as the simple reflection of colonial ideology. I say this not because I subscribe to the anthropological establishment's comfortable view of itself, but because bourgeois consciousness, of which social anthropology is merely one fragment, has always contained within itself profound contradictions and ambiguities—and therefore the potentialities for transcending itself."[17] In any case, his primary concern was the effects of colonialism on anthropological knowledge: "That such contributions were not in the final reckoning crucial for the vast empire which received knowledge and provided patronage does not mean that it was not critical for the small discipline which offered knowledge and received that patronage." Characteristically, this more subtle point received little direct attention until much later.[18] Besides, Asad did not move to a more constructivist epistemological critique because, in this volume at least, he did not grant the kind of power to knowledge that Edward Said—following Foucault as well as Nietzsche—insisted upon.

Asad's argument that anthropologists had reified colonial images of colonized societies was nevertheless severe and well ahead of its time. Another writer who departed early from the common view was the anthropological historian Bernard Cohn, who had begun writing searing essays in the late 1950s about the political entailments of what he called a colonial sociology of knowledge. In his early historical essays, Cohn demonstrated in multiple ways how revenue and tenurial arrangements, legal codes and institutions, and other expressions of what we now call "colonial governmentality" were fundamental to Britain's conquest and rule of India.[19] And he demonstrated that many of the associated colonial understandings and policies had come to be taken as fundamental truths about India, not only in its period of colonization but throughout its civilizational past. In anticipation of some of Said's arguments about the character of colonial knowledge as a discursive formation, Cohn wrote in 1968, "The orientalists and the missionaries were polar opposites in their assessment of Indian culture and society but were in accord as to what the central principles and institutions of the society were. They agreed that it was a society in which religious ideas and practices underlay all social structure; they agreed in the primacy of the Brahman as the maintainer of the sacred tradition, through his control of the knowledge of the sacred texts. . . . There was little attempt on the part of either to fit the facts of political organization, land tenure, the actual functioning of the legal system or the commercial structure into their picture of the society derived from the texts."[20] Cohn demonstrated the productive nature of these (mis)understandings. In discussing caste, for example, he proposed that the colonial decennial census of India, in the hands of administrator-scholars such as H. H. Risley, not only canonized the idea of India as a land of caste—"India was seen as a collection of castes; the particular picture was different in any given time and place, but India was a sum of its parts and the parts were castes"—but also made caste a much more important institution for the development of local social movements and political mobilization.[21] Cohn went on to write important essays on a wide variety of issues relating to colonial forms of knowledge, from the generative significance of early colonial grammars to the symbolic economies imposed in spectacular state functions meant to represent British authority and its hegemony over Indian elites. His abiding sense of the need to historicize anthropology was in large part the fruit of his recognition that anthropology in India had been significantly shaped by the colonial encounter.

If Cohn's influence on historians of colonialism has been deep, especially on those writing about the British colonial history in India, other anthropologists have become much better known for their advocacy of history. For example, Cohn's colleague in Chicago, Marshall Sahlins, embraced history in a series of books that arose from his work in Hawaii and Polynesia. In doing so, however, Sahlins not only kept structuralism as a guiding framework and emphasized culture as a key idea, but he also minimized the role of colonialism except as a distorting effect of capitalism on the proper understanding of "natives" and "others."[22] For Sahlins, history was primarily about the reproduction of structure, and change was the conjunctural result of cultural encounters that transform basic structure through a logic driven by the culture of capitalism. In the founding myth of his own historical anthropology, Sahlins narrated the story of how Captain Cook unwittingly sailed into the mythological topos of the Hawaiian god Lono, only to find himself the all-too-material victim of ritual sacrifice—an event that prompted imperial retribution and ultimately the colonization of the island. Many anthropologists saw Sahlins's seminal analysis of this historical moment as a signal revision of anthropology's traditional aversion to temporality and history, but the subsequent critique by Gananath Obeyesekere, however provisional its historical conclusions, made clear that all was not well in the land of historical anthropology.[23] Although the debate was at one level a rehearsal of the larger debate about culture versus practical reason, and at another, a vitriolic exchange about "native" versus "anthropological" knowledge, it was perhaps more fundamentally about the relationship between colonial power and colonial knowledge, the very terms that became inescapable after the publication of Orientalism.

Obeyesekere argued that Sahlins read historical sources literally and that despite his great knowledge of the archival materials, he did not read colonial texts "contrapuntally," in relation to the systematic interests—in both the material and the ideological senses—of colonial power.[24] Moreover, Obeyesekere charged Sahlins with buying into a general Western myth of the European man as "god" in the eyes of "natives." The more general implication of this critique, of course, is that contemporary anthropological understandings of culture—however critical and revised—reproduce older colonial notions that have circulated as stereotypes about the cultures of colonized peoples. Obeyesekere used his own work in and personal knowledge of Sri Lanka to predicate his suspicion, occasioning the most aggressive of Sahlins's polemical retorts, but the more important point is his questioning of Sahlins's relative absence of suspicion about the accounts of explorers, traders, missionaries, and colonial administrators.[25] Indeed, as Said had insisted, the historical archive was itself a sediment of the history of colonial institutions, ideas, and investments. And if this archive was in part the result of the legitimizing project of colonialism, postcolonial anthropological projects could not use it unproblematically to certify their cultural analyses. Sahlins, who quipped in a recent essay that anthropology would be better off left un-Said, is singularly resistant to the notion that anthropology has been significantly affected by its colonial past, reacting against the demand that the epistemological terrain of anthropology be interrogated solely in relation to colonial forms of knowledge.

Sahlins's reaction to the influence of Said anticipated the reactions of other anthropologists who share neither Sahlins's structuralism nor his commitment to the constitutive idea of culture. We cannot ignore the fact that Said wrote *Orientalism* at least in part as a literary scholar informed by the theoretical insights of Foucault and even Derrida, though he made clear his deep debt to Gramsci and saw himself in a serious genealogical relationship with Vico (as does Sahlins). *Orientalism* is in some ways profoundly Foucauldian, and we must remember that Foucault was still a very new and undigested force in anthropology when *Orientalism* was published in 1978. The anthropologist Paul Rabinow had by then begun writing on Foucault, but the implications of Foucault's critical histories of the disciplines, his complex sense of discourse, and his insistence on the inextricably productive relationship of knowledge and power had yet to make their mark in the published record of disciplinary thought. In an essay published the same year as *Orientalism,* Said wrote a brilliant commentary on the reading strategies of Derrida and Foucault, showing their similarities and differences, evaluating their approaches to the study of texts, and explaining why Foucault was ultimately much more useful for his project than Derrida was.[26] Said was nevertheless concerned about Foucault's lack of a theory of historical change and his failure to build a Gramscian understanding of hegemony into his model of discourse. At the same time, Foucault's work had opened up new ways to conceptualize the systematic character of writing that embodied different trajectories, histories, and intentions yet participated significantly in and was determined by the colonial project. As Said wrote in *Orientalism,* "I have found it useful here to employ Michel Foucault's notion of a discourse, as described by him in *The Archaeology of Knowledge* and in *Discipline and Punish,* to identify Orientalism. My contention is that without examining Orientalism as a discourse one cannot possibly understand the enormously systematic discipline by which European culture was able to manage—and even produce—the Orient politically, sociologically, militarily, ideologically, scientifically, and imaginatively during the post-Enlightenment period."[27] However, Said could not dispense with his commitment to the significance and consequence of individual action, whether in politics or in writing. Although he deployed Foucault's notion of discourse, he also asserted his belief in the "determining imprint of individual writers upon the otherwise anonymous collective body of texts constituting a discursive formation like Orientalism."[28] In the end, his historicist understanding of texts was perhaps most significant; the point for Said was that "the unity of the large ensemble of texts I analyze is due in part to the fact that they frequently refer to each other: Orientalism is after all a system for citing works and authors."[29] In short, discourse for Said was neither theoretical fancy nor simple shorthand for taking a few examples as the whole; it was a historical phenomenon of staggering actuality.

Said has been taken to task by many critics, anthropologists, and others for the internal inconsistencies of his text. On the one hand, he was clearly a secular humanist; on the other, he was indebted to Foucauldian poststructuralism and hailed, as was Foucault, by the siren of Nietzschean critique. He was an eloquent critic of the essentializing tendencies of Orientalist discourse but himself essentialized not just that discourse but both the Orient and the Occident. He was sympathetic to the aspirations and intentions of some Orientalists, but he ultimately consigned them to the tyranny of their historical moment. He suggested that Orientalist discourse had worked to "orientalize the Orient," but he nowhere suggested how that occurred. He invited oppositional strategies of representation for the brute realities of Oriental life, yet seemed to ignore the task of finding more adequate ways to give accounts of, and for, the Orient. And he critiqued representation while saying that representation alone could not aspire to the conditions of truth; if all representation is doomed, why bother?

This last charge, and another above it, grew out of Said's extraordinary reflections on the life and work of Louis Massignon, whom he admired greatly. In *Orientalism,* Said praised Massignon for having "reconstructed and defended Islam against Europe on the one hand and against its own orthodoxy on the other. This intervention—for it was that—into the Orient as animator and champion symbolized his own acceptance of the Orient's difference, as well as his efforts to change it into what he wanted."[30] Said is curiously forgiving of Massignon's almost heroic "will to knowledge over the Orient." And he defends him against the charge by some Muslim scholars that he "misrepresented Islam as an 'average' or 'common' Muslim might adhere to the faith," in short as one who engaged the "object" of scholarship as a vital and living tradition in which the political stakes were well removed from the usual perspectives of the colonizing agent or gaze. Most curious of all, Said's defense of Massignon occasions his own rumination on the ultimate impossibility of representation: "The real issue is whether indeed there can be a true representation of anything, or whether any and all representations, because they *are* representations, are embedded first in the language and then in the culture, institutions, and political ambience of the representer . . . We must be prepared to accept the fact that a representation is *eo ipso* implicated, intertwined, embedded, interwoven with a great many other things besides the 'truth,' which is itself a representation." These reflections lead Said to comment more generally about the theoretical frame of his general argument. "My whole point about this system is not that it is a misrepresentation of some Oriental essence—in which I do not for a moment believe—but that it operates as representations do, for a purpose, according to a tendency, in a specific historical, intellectual, and even economic setting. In other words, representations have purposes, they are effective much of the time, they accomplish one or many tasks." He explains that the relationship between individual will or intention and institutional structure or effect is complex and fraught and that the ideal of pure knowledge is as impossible as destruction of the will to knowledge by the contingencies of political power and appropriation. For Said, however, this acknowledgment robs individuals neither of their responsibility nor their significance, and he insists that he means neither to "dehumanize Massignon . . . nor [to] reduce him to being subject to vulgar determinism."[31]

Of Said's early reviewers, James Clifford was the most perceptive and sympathetic, in part because he recognized the power of Said's reading of Massignon. In his careful essay on *Orientalism,* Clifford traced Said's ambivalences—about representation and truth, structure and agency, society and the individual, poststructuralism and humanism, among others—and expressed appreciation of the moments of textual strain for what they revealed.[32] He recognized that Said's humanism was as deep as his historicist insistence on the discursive character and political implication of French and British Orientalist scholarship. And although he averred that Said's "methodological catholicity" blurred his analysis, he dismissed neither the power of Said's arguments nor their importance for anthropology. At the same time, Clifford was uncomfortable with what seemed to be left of the anthropological idea of culture. In the face of Said's attack on oppositional distinctions, Clifford asserted, "There is no need to discard theoretically all conceptions of 'cultural' difference, especially once this is seen as not simply received from tradition, language, or environment but also as made in new political-cultural conditions of global relationship . . . However the culture concept is finally transcended, it should, I think, be replaced by some set of relations that preserves the concept's differential and relativist functions and that avoids the positing of cosmopolitan essences and human common denominators."[33] Clifford's own ambivalence about the culture concept, or at least his critical sense of its emergence and manifold misuses in the professional genres of anthropological writing, has been forcefully argued in other influential essays. But here we see his residual commitment to the concept itself, both in its articulation of difference and in its demand for a relativist worldview. Significantly, Clifford departed from Said in both his concern about the totalizing implications of the Orientalism critique and his identification of the problematic universalism of Said's humanism.

Clifford's review makes clear that Said in some ways went well beyond the earlier critiques of Asad, Cohn, and other anthropological critics of the role of colonialism in their discipline. This departure was in part because Said came from outside the discipline and in part because in raising the crisis of representation to a new level, he attributed productive capacity to knowledge itself. For the same reasons, however, many who considered themselves Said's fellow travelers in their political critiques of American foreign policy reacted against Said's privileging of epistemology, sometimes with marked antipathy. Micaela di Leonardo has argued, for example, that Said's problem is his anti-Marxism and his consequent failure to appreciate the larger issues of capitalism, relations of production, and class. Di Leonardo accuses Said of "willful blindness" about the "veritable global flood of Marxist work on imperialism," and she objects in particular to his failure to appreciate the power of Eric Wolf's work. But di Leonardo has no brief for the culture concept, especially as refashioned in the work of someone like Clifford. She notes that in Clifford's "lyrical yet hagridden definition" of the ethnographic encounter, he "misses both informants' and ethnographers' institutional connections, up to the level of differing citizenships and differential power (by class, race, gender) as citizens."[34] So, in the end, Said is too poststructuralist for di Leonardo, too humanist for Clifford, and, for many anthropologists, too concerned about the epistemological legacies that colonialism left to anthropology.

Yet Said's influence has been as enduring as it has been troubling. A perusal of anthropological journals reveals that right up until his death, Said was generating critiques, responses, and reflections on the capacity of the anthropological enterprise to survive *Orientalism*. In August 1990 *Anthropology Today* published a critical essay on Said by Michael Richardson, "Enough Said," in which Richardson asserted that Said's idealism and hypertextualism distracted him from appreciating the manifest importance of responsible engagement with the reality of the Orient. Tellingly, however, Richardson expressed approval of the following quote by Simon Leys: "Orientalism could obviously have been written by no one but a Palestinian scholar with a huge chip on his shoulder and a very dim understanding of the European academic tradition."[35] The following year, Nicholas Thomas took Richardson to task in the same journal, both for misreading Said's critique and for ignoring anthropology's reliance on ideas of exoticism, otherness, and intransitive distance between the subject and object of knowledge. Characteristically, Thomas took for granted the need to take seriously Said's call for a different kind of critical anthropology "that is concerned with the formation of anthropological knowledge in the context of colonial histories and contemporary imperialism."[36] Thomas was less interested in applying Said's critique literally to anthropology than in thinking with it. For example, he questioned the way in which much humanist and self-critical anthropology, which continued to use the culture concept to animate social description, subordinated the "lives, cultures, and societies [of the people described]

to the purposes of metropolitan rhetoric: the interests of healthy skepticism or relativistic cultural criticism at home thus make the other admissible primarily as a
corrective to some aspect of 'our' thought."[37] And in an essay published just a few
months later in *Cultural Anthropology*, Thomas produced one of the most trenchant and forceful critiques of this reliance on notions of cultural difference, exoticism, alterity, and ideas of otherness. Writing against ethnography, Thomas sharply
demonstrated the unacceptable politics of the pervasive rhetoric about the distinctive mission of anthropology and pointed out that many historical anthropologists and others were indeed taking up Said's challenge and beginning to make
cognate empirical demonstrations of the need for a radically new theoretical ar-
mature for the discipline.[38]

Despite the explosion of critical work on colonialism, colonial knowledge, and
the politics of anthropology during the 1980s and 1990s, the debate about Said continued as well. During those years, Said was taken to task by others outside anthropology for his apparent anti-Marxism, even as some people within anthropology (most vocally, Lewis) accused Said, along with many others, of conspiring to
give anthropology a bad name.[39] Increasingly, scholars have associated Said's name
with the general field of postcolonial studies, and ironically many have assumed
that Said was merely calling for the establishment of a form of identity politics in
which only the "self" could represent the "self."[40] However, although Said welcomed
(even as he helped to inspire) the huge theoretical shifts in the American academy
that altered usage of the terms *self* and *other* that had predicated so much of the anthropological enterprise, he was no champion of the identity politics that often went
along with this change. Indeed, Said was aghast when people used identity politics
in his name to reduce historical, political, theoretical, and epistemological questions to simple assertions of ontology. His resistance may have seemed paradoxical to some critics, but his humanism was precisely what made him suspicious of
the rising chorus of identity claims in the academy. And his enduring critical sensibility was what allowed him to learn from writers such as Conrad and caused him
to react to "native" successors to Conrad such as Naipaul. Indeed, Said often invoked Adorno's great line, noting that one had to be steeped in a tradition to hate
it properly, and he always preferred to "hate" the classics rather than find alternatives that failed to bring him aesthetic pleasure along with opportunities for critical
engagement.

Much to Said's chagrin, *Orientalism* was such a monumental work that it overshadowed much of his later academic writing, in particular *Culture and Imperialism*,
which he published in 1993.[41] This sprawling book was at once a sequel to *Orientalism* and a different project altogether. Said bristled when he read others who
claimed to go "beyond" *Orientalism*, implying that he had not. In *Culture and Imperialism*, Said discussed various expressions of resistance to imperialism, and he
demonstrated the force of Fanon's famous phrase "Europe is literally the product

of the third world." On the one hand, he dealt with myriad colonized and post-colonial writers who had "written back," complicating, resisting, transforming, and hybridizing the force of Orientalism's discursive hegemony. Of course, at the same time he delineated the forces faced by any resistance effort. He again offered his critical assessment of America's position in the world, particularly its involvement in the then-recent Gulf War, and noted the rise of a newly uncontested—because of the fall of the Soviet Union—"new world order." Viewing this domination as clearly imperial in its extent and ambition, he was as cogent and insightful as ever about the way in which the United States established its imperial forms and legitimated them with often-unprecedented military, political, and economic aspirations. On the other hand, he developed an extraordinary argument that called attention to the centrality of empire in the formation of "Europe." Using readings of Austen, Thackeray, Dickens, among others, Said demonstrated that empire enabled the rise of the British novel as much as it enabled the rise of the British state and its economy. With his characteristic turn of phrase, he wrote, "Without empire, I would go so far as saying, there is no European novel as we know it."[42] But this phrase was not just a polemical flourish: he showed that the conventional story of Britain/Europe's autonomous cultural development in the eighteenth and nineteenth centuries not only was inextricably connected to imperial wealth and possession but also was able to maintain its general invisibility because of the extent to which empire was taken for granted in the writings and cultural expressions of that time and place.

If in *Orientalism* Said argued that the Orient was literally produced as a cultural as well as a political object or essence, in *Culture and Imperialism* he suggested that the Occident—or the metropole—had managed to produce itself only through the instrumentalities of imperial history. The implication was that the Occident had to make the Orient "other" and render it so different that its contribution to modernity and European culture would somehow be unthinkable. In these terms, the two books present two sides of the same coin; they are both sustained efforts to unthink the curious effect of imperialism—to make imperialism simultaneously natural and benign, acceptable and invisible. Many in the academy saw this argument as the final assault on the literary canon—even dead white women like Jane Austen were imperialists—and regularly accused Said of reading empire everywhere (a charge he happily acknowledged, though as a consequence of world history rather than personal prejudice). Yet those who actually read the book were forced to realize that Said was deeply invested in the great works of art that make up the canon. Even as he advocated expanding comparative literature to be global rather than merely European, he continued to be a passionate and sensitive reader of the traditional texts; perhaps in some circles, this appreciation made his interventions all the more dangerous and difficult to accept.

Outside of literary studies, Said's proposals in *Culture and Imperialism* seem somewhat less revolutionary, because a number of scholars in history and anthropology at the time had begun to demonstrate different ways in which the colonial world constituted a "laboratory of modernity." These scholars argued that the colonial encounter was made up of a set of histories that not only produced many of the commodities that have become critical to the modern world but also engendered fundamental ideas of citizenship, political rights, culture, race, sexuality, health, urban planning, and state discipline.[43] Curiously, anthropologists seemed to find it easier to write empire back into the metropole than did most scholars of literature or history, who still see Europe's cultural and political achievements as *sui generis* and continue to treat the idea of Europe as sacrosanct. Nevertheless, some of Said's early proposals continue to provoke anxiety within the discipline of anthropology, which I am sure would please him. Yet we can see the impact of Said's work throughout the contemporary anthropological world, particularly in the U.S. academy, where anthropology is increasingly international. Anthropologists—only a small sample of whom appear in this essay—have contributed important insights into the cultural, political, social, and economic effects and legacies of colonial history. Indeed, colonialism is accepted as a major subject of anthropological inquiry, even as recognition of colonial forms of knowledge continues to bedevil even the most postcolonial debates about cultural difference, moral relativism, identity, or for that matter, the significance of globalization. Of course, not all of this intellectual ferment can be credited to the influence of Edward Said and *Orientalism*. But Said clearly made an important and productive—if often also troubling—difference in the field, and for that influence alone, anthropology, in my hybrid view at least, is forever in his debt.[44]

NOTES

An earlier version of this chapter appeared under the same title in the *Journal of Palestine Studies* 33, no. 3 (Spring 2004): 38–54.

1. Micaela di Leonardo, *Exotics at Home: Anthropologies, Others, American Modernity* (Chicago: University of Chicago Press, 2000), 47.

2. Edward Said, "Representing the Colonized: Anthropology's Interlocutors," *Critical Inquiry* 15 (Winter 1989): 208.

3. Ibid.

4. Ibid.

5. Ibid., 209.

6. Ibid., 212.

7. Edward Said, *Orientalism* (New York: Random House, 1997), 296–98.

8. Ibid., 326.

9. Edward Said, "Orientalism Reconsidered," *Race and Class* 27, no. 2 (1985): .5

10. Johannes Fabian, *Time and the Other: How Anthropology Constitutes Its Object* (New York: Columbia University Press, 1983).

11. Said, "Orientalism Reconsidered," 6.

12. See, as one of many such examples, Michael Richardson, "Enough Said: Reflections on Orientalism," *Anthropology Today* 6, no. 4 (August 1990): 16–19.

13. Talal Asad, ed., *Anthropology and the Colonial Encounter* (London: Ithaca Press, 1973).

14. Talal Asad, introduction to ibid., 16.

15. Ibid., 17.

16. Talal Asad, "Two European Images of Non-European Rule," in Asad, *Anthropology and the Colonial Encounter*, 18.

17. Introduction to Asad, *Anthropology and the Colonial Encounter*, 17.

18. As an excellent, if very recent, example, see Peter Pels and Oscar Salemink, eds., *Colonial Subjects: Essays on the Practical History of Anthropology* (Ann Arbor: University of Michigan Press, 1999).

19. Bernard S. Cohn, *An Anthropologist among the Historians and Other Essays* (Delhi: Oxford University Press, 1987).

20. Bernard S. Cohn, "Notes on the History of Indian Society and Culture," in ibid., 146.

21. Ibid., 147. Cohn, "The Census, Social Structure and Objectification in South Asia," in Cohn, *An Anthropologist among the Historians*, 224–54.

22. Marshall Sahlins, *Islands of History* (Chicago: University of Chicago Press, 1985).

23. Gananath Obeyesekere, *The Apotheosis of Captain Cook: European Mythmaking in the Pacific* (Princeton, NJ: Princeton University Press, 1992).

24. The term *contrapuntal*, of course, is Said's.

25. For Marshall Sahlins's response to Obeyesekere's charge, see his *How "Natives" Think: About Captain Cook for Example* (Chicago: University of Chicago Press, 1995).

26. Edward Said, "The Problem of Textuality: Two Exemplary Positions," *Critical Inquiry* 4, no. 4 (Summer 1978): 673–714.

27. Said, *Orientalism*, 3.

28. Ibid., 23.

29. Ibid.

30. Ibid., 272.

31. Ibid., 272, 272, 273, 274.

32. James Clifford, "On Orientalism," in *The Predicament of Culture: Twentieth-Century Ethnography, Literature, and Art*, 255–76 (Cambridge, MA: Harvard University Press, 1988; review first published in *History and Theory* in 1980).

33. Ibid., 274–75.

34. Di Leonardo, *Exotics at Home*.

35. Richardson, "Enough Said," 18.

36. Nicholas Thomas, "Anthropology and Orientalism," *Anthropology Today* 7, no. 2 (April 1991): 7.

37. Ibid.

38. Nicholas Thomas, "Against Ethnography," *Cultural Anthropology* 6, no. 3 (August 1991): 306–22.

39. On Said's supposed anti-Marxism, see, for example, Sumit Sarkar, "Orientalism Revisited: Saidian Frameworks in the Writing of Modern Indian History," *Oxford Literary Review* 16 (1994): 205–24; and Aijaz Ahmad, *In Theory: Classes, Nations, Literatures* (London: Verso, 1992).

40. In 1999, to give a rather more complex example of how writers have approached this issue, Vassos Argyrou published "Sameness and the Ethnological Will to Meaning" in *Current Anthropology* 40: S29–S41, in which he took Said's critique as a starting point. However, he then argued that the ethnological effort to find "sameness" invariably invokes difference instead, reproducing an inherent commitment to typological and analytic differentiation that in some ways becomes an apparent contradiction only when subjects are viewed as "natives" (who must distrust both sameness and difference as aspirations when engaged in ethnological work at home). In effect, Argyrou argued that representation is less an epistemological than an ontological crisis, brought into focus when one of the "others" confronts a variety of still-pervasive but unspoken assumptions about the relationship between identity and

anthropological knowledge. I suspect that Said would have granted the force of the argument but questioned its premises.

41. Edward W. Said, *Culture and Imperialism* (New York: Knopf, 1993).

42. Ibid., 69.

43. Bernard Cohn observed some years ago that "the process of state building in Great Britain, seen as a cultural project, was closely linked with its emergence as an imperial power"; Cohn, *Colonialism and Its Forms of Knowledge* (Princeton, NJ: Princeton University Press, 1995), 3. Cohn noted that many of the projects of state building in both countries—the documentation, legitimation, and classification— "often reflected theories, experiences, and practices worked out originally in India and then applied in Great Britain" (ibid., 4). Many others have done foundational work on the metropolitan effects of colonial history. See, for example, Ann Stoler, *Race and the Education of Desire* (Durham, NC: Duke University Press, 1995); Paul Rabinow, *French Modern: Norms and Forms of the Social Environment* (Cambridge, MA: MIT Press, 1989); John Comoroff and Jean Comoroff, *Of Revelation and Revolution* (Chicago: University of Chicago Press, 1991). Also see the discussions in Nicholas B. Dirks, ed., *Colonialism and Culture* (Ann Arbor: University of Michigan Press, 1992); Gyan Prakash, ed., *After Colonialism: Imperial Histories and Postcolonial Displacements* (Princeton, NJ: Princeton University Press, 1995); and Ann Stoler and Frederick Cooper, *Tensions of Empire* (Berkeley: University of California Press, 1997).

44. I close this essay on a personal note, however, because my relationship to anthropology was originally mediated by Bernard Cohn, who died two months to the day after Said, in the autumn of 2003. I was trained by Cohn as a historian of South Asia at the University of Chicago in the 1970s. Though Cohn had been hired a decade earlier to head the South Asia history program, he was an anthropologist by early training and primary professional experience. He introduced me to the idea that social and cultural history could learn from anthropology, both as a way of reimagining the historical archive and as a theoretical repertoire from which to draw. An early champion of interdisciplinarity, he often quipped that he didn't care what your discipline was as long as you were ashamed of it. Cohn, as I've noted, was sharply critical of his own discipline of anthropology for continuing to inscribe colonial assumptions and categories of thought in approaching broad questions about relations between the "West" and the "East." Largely because of Cohn's influence, I first read *Orientalism* with a sense of recognition, primed to reimagine the larger story of the disciplines—and of Orientalist scholarship and the area-studies establishment—through Said's much more sweeping argument. Said was always far more engaged in public political debate than Cohn was, even as his style of academic intervention was both more impassioned and more theoretically attuned. But Cohn was the one who made clear to me that the story Said was telling about Orientalism and colonialism was a far more general story, with major implications throughout and across the disciplines of history and anthropology, as well as across contexts and cultures.

6

The Critic and the Public

Edward Said and World Literature

Timothy Brennan

Edward Said's authority was always ultimately literary. It is important to appreciate this fact and not underestimate it. His status in such varied fields as history, geography, music criticism, political commentary, exposé journalism, and the Palestinian movement defers to the place of honor he precociously established within comparative literature between 1966 and 1975, and he consistently relied on literature and the tropes of literary criticism to express his political and social imagination during his *anni mirabili* (1975–92).

Yet for him literature remained largely "autonomous," capable of being evaluated as either good or bad depending on its degree of timelessness or antinomian energies.[1] Prose masterpieces (a word from which he would not have flinched) were a place of refuge from the world, not merely an index of their immersion in its antagonistic material interests. They were verbal inventions whose social value was nonutilitarian and internally sufficient, although not only so. These views are paradoxical at two extremes because they escape both a customary notion of literary engagement and its opposite—the semanticization of politics that permeated most literary and linguistic theories in the decades of his rise to prominence.

Said not only evoked and proposed but also embodied the privileged social role of criticism in an age of science, but he did so without, on the one hand, descending into the antimodern aesthetic rejectionism of the conventional "literary man"— exemplified by precursors like F. R. Leavis—or, on the other, accepting the neatly inverted homology of that stance in French poststructuralist theory. The latter offered instead a hypermodern, oracular commentary on the systems of discourse (which uncomfortably shared, in his opinion, many of science's quasi-theological finalities). In a generous and accretive idiom, filled with conversational asides and wide-ranging archival detours, he methodically crafted a literary discourse that displaced texts from their textuality, recasting them in the sensual mold of the intellectual act. Not enough attention has been paid to how Said made literary criticism authoritative, but this accomplishment lies at the heart of his contribution to comparative literature.

THE SAIDIAN PERSONA

Said dwelled on the term *authority* in his first important critical undertaking, *Beginnings* (1975), in which he examined its etymology by relating it to *authorship:* the intentional act of intellectual will. Highlighted in the book's subtitle, *Intention and Method,* the concept was crucial to his reinvention of the field of comparative literature, not least because it so clearly diverged from prevalent emphases on linguistic anonymity—the production of subjects through inherited and imposed linguistic determinations. To this end, he sought not only to author a body of written texts but to offer a life-model of intellectual conduct, and his redefinition of comparative literature was the instigating factor for the larger enterprise. Said's discovery (calling it an invention would be inaccurate) lay not so much in a new principle of reading or a novel thematization of texts as in a *method.* Although he presented this method in a nonprescriptive manner, it reached out to intellectuals who wished to attain (in his words) "mass density and referential power."[2]

The palpable curiosity of humanists, their command of speech, and unpredictable range of reference, he proposed, were potent acts of authorial self-fashioning that gave them advantages over the arid specialists of the military, the market, and the media. The person of the critic burst forth with the excitement of knowing, and in that sense Said's writing has always been biographical, consisting almost entirely of savoring with the reader the representative lives of remarkable individuals—Raymond Schwab, Glenn Gould, Tahia Carioca, Jonathan Swift, Giambattista Vico. But his writing is also, and not only in his memoirs, autobiographical. It relies on the creation of a persona, which in his case was a peculiar combination of invention and circumstance.

Let us not forget that Said, for instance, worked throughout his career at Columbia University in a department of English *and* comparative literature—an unusual hybrid given that the academy usually segregates English from comparative literature as well as from "foreign language" departments. But by conjoining these fields at Columbia, he made it more difficult to maintain the impregnability of the Anglo-Saxon canon. Columbia, moreover, was among the first American universities to recognize comparative literature as a discipline, naming George Woodbury as the nation's first professor of comparative literature in 1892—a fact Said self-consciously cited more than once while deriding the bogus "universal values" of Woodbury's "gentleman scholars," who supposedly worked "above the sphere of politics."[3] But more importantly, Said fell curiously between generations.[4] He came of age only after the first wave of post–World War II émigrés from Europe had established themselves in American academia and before the rather different Nietzschean and Heideggerian impulses of continental theory took hold in American academic literary circles, which until that point had been preoccupied with a "new critical" mode of formalist close reading.

Despite its importance, the Saidian persona, both as inheritance and self-creation, has frequently been misinterpreted. Almost without exception, Said the man is cast in terms of his Palestinian identity and exile, with no allowance for the fact that he was an American as well, and one whose multilingual background was, after all, ambiguous. He spent the entire first half of his career in willing and untroubled assimilation; his childhood and early schooling in Lebanon, Palestine, and Egypt gave way to a gentlemanly privilege in Ivy League venues that was no less instrumental in constructing his identity (just as it was decisive in giving him tools to speak). Commentators on Said's work in the United States consequently misunderstand his sense of "home," which is far less literal than positional, less filiative than political. Exile for him was ideational as well as physical, which is why he spoke approvingly at one point about the "executive value of exile" that some writers have been "able to turn into effective use."[5] The personal accidents of life affect understanding, of course, but Said was particularly eager to insist that they do not constitute positions. Nor was the opposite the case. Ideological *positionings* are not immune from the same type of repugnant inflexibilities that can attach to the bonds formed by conditions of birth. In this vein, rejecting the "systems" of Northrop Frye and Foucault, Said once observed that even affiliative (which is to say, ideological or positional) structures are dangerous when they "more or less directly reproduce the skeleton of family authority supposedly left behind when the family was left behind. The curricular structures holding European literature departments make that perfectly obvious."[6]

The entire matrix of meanings we associate with " 'home,' belonging, community," he further argued, is intimately bound up with the "assurance, confidence, the majority sense" necessary for the "power of the State."[7] This is a characteristic Saidian move. Home refers not only to a site of origin but to the comfort of belonging among those of the same social outlooks and opinions in a sublime national-cultural conformity. His aim in this construct, among other things, was to reject the filiative authority accorded him as an exilic Palestinian while conceding his privileged status in the United States, which he criticized precisely as an insider, albeit from a special perspective. He also explored the compelling need in an era of sectarian resurgence and nationalist manias "to produce new and different ways of conceiving human relationships."[8] His point, however, was not that we need a form of transnationalism, as we call it today—he continued to believe in the necessity of national movements—but that we need to flee sectoral categories altogether:[9] "[The intellectual is a] wanderer, going from place to place for his material, but remaining a man essentially *between* homes. . . . Such notions as 'exteriority' and 'in-betweenness' . . . do not refer to a sort of fellow-traveling critical eclecticism. Rather, they describe a transformation that has taken place in the working reality of the self-conscious writer."[10] This shifting of the locational (being) to the positional (believing or knowing) takes place throughout Said's work.

Said by disposition and biographical positioning chafed against the readerliness—the effete literary appreciation of the aristocratic amateur—to which he was, paradoxically, drawn. His critical acuity derived from the same "mixture of styles" that occurred when clerical Latin gave way to the vernaculars in traditional European philology, instinctively merging the traditional intellectual's confident ease with a demotic and popular instinct. Between 1969 and 1975, in a two-pronged move, he developed an arsenal of arguments against the older humanist formalism of the leading critics of his youth (including his own dissertation advisor, Richard Blackmur), and later against those he largely considered their avatars: the tamed insurrectionaries of a textualist "theory." To understand his accomplishment, we need to grasp his success in articulating this conflictual position—a polemic posing as a negotiation—which was quite unlike that of his contemporaries and was frequently misunderstood by them.

As we have seen, Said's redrawing of comparative literature suggested a more ambitious set of propositions than a theory of literature per se. Even in the one book that appears to address the field directly, *Culture and Imperialism* (1993), he moves from an exegesis of André Gide and George Antonius to preoccupation with imperial geography and place as territory, undermining the idealist emphasis on the concepts of "hybridity" and "migrancy" that were fashionable at the time of the book's publication. His now-overused term *contrapuntal criticism,* for example, was an alternative to hybridity, conjuring images less of mixture and mutual complicity than of independently directed harmonizations and contacts.[11] At any rate, we would be wrong to see his contribution as merely expanding the English literary canon into French, Arabic, North African, and Indian spaces, or bringing the postcolonial studies of his supposed creation into contact finally (and belatedly) with the Euro-bastion of academic romance criticism.[12] He chipped away at the edifice of traditional comparative literature in a more indirect and atmospheric fashion—by presenting a unified portrait of critical activity by way of intertwined concepts such as the "gentile" intellect, "sequential" versus "philosophical" reasoning, the "primitive mind," "secularity," and the "transitive intelligence." These concepts forcefully, although not neatly, coalesced in his work, and because his authority was vast enough to make these gestures a discourse more or less consciously taken on by other critics after him, they made later movements of comparative literary redefinition thinkable.

As an intergenerational oddity, Said apprenticed in comparative literature at a

time when two divergent influences were revitalizing the field: a translated and updated continental philology and, a couple of decades later, deconstruction.[13] Among
the many ways to assess Said's academic achievement, one way is certainly to say
that he outmaneuvered the latter by reinterpreting the former in a more global and
theoretically adept idiom.

A RESPONSE TO WAR

In its contemporary form, comparative literature is a post–World War II creation,
even if its origins are evident much earlier. Already implicit in John Dryden's comparative study of genres such as satire, drama, and philosophical and epic poems
(1631–1700) or in Nicolas Boileau-Despréaux (1636–1711), the term enters the critical lexicon in Charles Augustin Sainte-Beuve (1840), although its contemporary
sense already appeared completely formed in Goethe's notion of *Weltliteratur*
(1827).[14] Still, as René Wellek and Austin Warren point out in *Theory of Literature*
(1949), the field had undergone a series of fissures, particularly following World
War II. These fissures resulted from the field's competing impulses: on the one hand,
to compare the literatures of different languages; on the other, to identify "literature in its totality, with 'world-literature,' with 'general' or 'universal' literature."[15]

In the nineteenth century, these apparently volatile motives were conjoined under a grand taxonomic ordering of essential shared components. The physical features of the literary species were identified in a descriptive compulsion: that is, the
concise characterization of genre *as such*, of style *as such*, and the modes of criticism (critical editions, literary history, *explication de texte*, aesthetics, linguistics,
bibliography, etymology and comparative grammar)—an impulse on display in
Wellek and Warren's book itself, in Northrup Frye's *Anatomy of Criticism* (1956),
Auerbach's *Introduction to Romance Philology* (1943), and, in a revisionary allusion
to both, Said's "Secular Criticism" (1983), which opens with a listing of the four
modes of commonly practiced literary study.

Requiring an arduous and daunting display of erudition and linguistic specialization, and usually considered the province only of a gifted elite or the foreign born,
comparative literature in practice tended to be misunderstood and misregarded.
Such study became the fate of "utility players," of students forced to take on tasks
normally performed by several professors, teaching a little grammar here and a little theory there and displaying a versatility often taken for dilettantism.[16] Particularly because undergraduates are usually unable to keep up with the field's withering demands on knowledge, the central rationale of the discipline—linguistic
multiplicity—was mocked by the widespread teaching of classics in translation. The
comprehensive categorization of genres, or the intricate comparison of literary language across millennia, dissolved into introductory courses on literary appreciation. Above all, faced by the single-minded mission of national literature depart-

ments, comparative literature (despite its inherent generalism) tended in the 1970s
and 1980s to be seen as a residual space and became the home of the austere and
monothematic concerns of a finely wrought "theory." In this mode and despite a
crisis of identity wrought by the non-West's emergence into the European literary
imagination, its massive sweep could find a common disciplinary language.[17]

These centrifugal pressures were the outcome of comparative literature's divergent authority based on various continental sources, both literary and political. One
popular view holds that the field is essentially the creation of the postwar immigration to the United States of venerable and erudite European critical masters.[18]
However, this view slights the antagonisms among the émigrés and underplays
(while at times mentioning) the immigration's Cold War setting—the impetus to
institute comparative literature as a kind of eclectic area studies for war-torn Western Europe. As for the antagonisms, although the émigrés shared some common
ground, little linked the updated humanist philology and historicism of Erich Auerbach and Leo Spitzer, the new critical positivism of Wellek, Theodor Adorno's ironiz-
ing variant of left-Hegelian critical theory, or the Nietzschean antihistoricism of Paul
de Man, especially given the latter's return to the conventional topics of English and
German Romanticism. In Cold War area studies, comparative literature played a
homologous but exactly inverted role. Its purpose was to produce an aesthetically
sophisticated, nonconfrontational modality that would reduce the sociological evidence of a whole people—as in philology—to a set of aesthetic attributes.

If this range of disciplinary imperatives sounds somewhat bewildering and self-
contradictory, some of its substance is captured by the clash of two towering figures
who have had a profound effect on comparative theory in the postwar period. On
the one side is Mikhail Bakhtin, a Christian revolutionary populist schooled in the
ecstatic energies of the early Soviet Union. Rejecting the Russian formalists, he countered their preference for the play of poetic language with a blunt and unmistakable *prosaics*—his coinage for the historical study of prose rather than poetic forms.
He theorized literary language as it had been creatively disrupted by the popular
speech of lower classes and forgotten linguistic communities. On the other side
stands Roman Jakobson, the emissary of Russian formalism to the West and the
exalted representative of structuralism during the advent of "theory" in the American academy.

Said was one of the few American critics in the decades after the 1960s who was
conversant, at the level of sensibility, with both these traditions, although he stubbornly refused to engage with Bakhtin (whose outlook, although very different, re-
sembled his own in its discomfort with the rigid formalisms and aestheticism reigning in his own era).[19] Only Said's work shows an understanding of these schools'
incompatible stakes or an effort to judge their offerings in a vision of the whole. As
a result, he was able to suggest what comparative literature in its boldest moments
might actually compare. In *Orientalism* (1978), for instance, he had written about

the institutions of intellectual image making, about the standards and rules by which civilizational values are created, and about the apparatus of knowledge that intellectuals create as well as the effects they have through mediation. It was only a small step to speak later, as a literary scholar, about "a connection in terms of arms trade and counterinsurgency theories . . . between the contras, the Saudi Arabians and the Israelis," and to observe in the same passage the need for a "theoretical and intellectual perspective" that would allow critics to explore such connections "through what I would call a kind of globalism in the study of texts."[20]

But Said did not diagnose comparative literature as such. He was not particularly interested in its institutional history, and he never said openly that comparative literature is always a response to war. Of course, the conventional view has been to point out that the modern version of the field emerged from the crises of World War II, mostly because of German scholars' effort to keep the spirit of Europe alive at the moment of its near extinction. But this view overlooks the fact that Goethe's *Weltliteratur* was conceived in the wake of the Napoleonic invasions and flourished again at the turn of the century, on the eve of World War I. In 1830, Goethe wrote, "There has for some time been talk of a universal world literature and rightly so, for the nations, flung together by dreadful warfare, then thrown apart again, have all realized that they had absorbed many foreign elements, and become conscious of new intellectual needs."[21]

In reply to a coming century of revolutionary upheaval and territorial re-mappings on the European continent, rhythmically shadowing the conquest and re-conquest of colonial possessions, comparative literature developed a distinctively cosmopolitan rhetoric. Goethe, taking his cue, according to Fritz Strich, from the "world of trade and commerce," envisioned literature as a "common world-council," emphasizing its "unifying, human or contemporaneous character" as against the purities of strict national literatures.[22] This cosmopolitan thrust resurfaced at the end of the nineteenth century in the lead-up to World War I, when alongside the brewing disgruntlements following the Berlin conference, the Prussian military buildup, and the Russian confrontations with Britain over Afghanistan, the field received its first official institutional recognition, through the creation of chairs or lectureships in comparative literature in 1891 at Harvard, 1896 at Zurich, 1897 at Lyon, 1899 at Columbia, and 1910 at the Sorbonne.[23] Despite contemporary accounts of Auerbach's and Spitzer's "making of comparative literature," the conditions of their emergence were far from unique.

SAID AND THE NEW REFORM

Said, too, composed *Orientalism* in the immediate aftermath of the Vietnam War and shortly before the wave of colonial explosions that were to cap that momentous finale (only a year after *Orientalism*'s publication) in Nicaragua, El Salvador,

Grenada, the Philippines, and Iran. At times a Goethean mood, prompted by an urgent sense that a storm was brewing, took hold of his writings on comparative literature. Whether critical adversaries or public nemeses, the enemy had to be studied "as was the case with the postwar Auerbach and some of his peers." With a deft sense of the long term, they managed "to overcome bellicosity and what we now call 'the clash of civilizations' with a welcoming, hospitable attitude of humanistic knowledge designed to realign warring cultures in a relationship of mutuality and reciprocity."[24]

However, Said did not really invent the revival of Goethe's concept of *Weltliteratur*. Strich (1942), and later Auerbach (1958), took on this task.[25] But Said acted as their attorney at an early date, announcing to American literary circles that Goethe's initial gesture must now take a more vigorously non-Western turn. But Said encouraged and sustained its original expansion into realms that exceeded literary language (Auerbach was quite clear about this goal). His Auerbachian declaration of purpose came not only in the form of his translation (with Maire Said) of Auerbach's "Philology and *Weltliteratur*" in 1969 but also in a protracted elaboration of methodological tasks that was nothing less than a program, as I suggest below.[26]

There is substantial evidence that Said was the first to articulate the concerns of the new movement in comparative literature that took shape in the early 1990s as postcolonial studies ushered in an atmosphere of canonical revision. When his ideas eventually found echoes, they often appeared to have come unmoored from his two-pronged approach. Thus a degree of ambiguity attended discussions of his influence: Had he called a trend—predicting before others the inevitable direction of literary studies? Or had his lessons, repeated over two decades (1969–92), so filled the landscape that he had single-handedly molded a sensibility, rendering it impossible for the next generation of comp lit reformers to speak without reproducing ideas he had already written into the record?

The *locus classicus* of this new reform (inspired by ideas that have led recently to a renewed interest in "world literature") seems to be Charles Bernheimer's influential anthology, *Comparative Literature in the Age of Multiculturalism* (1992), a succinct and valuable assessment officially composed for the American Comparative Literature Association.[27] The anthology traverses the postwar history and future options of the field by collating arguments scattered in Said's writing throughout the 1970s and then programmatically laid out by him as early as 1982. All the critiques and sources, both in Said originally and then in the anthology, have a twofold thrust: a disciplinary emphasis on breaking out of "national and linguistic identities," wondering whether literature "may . . . adequately describe our object of study," and the desire that "comparative study should [not] abandon the close analysis of . . . formal features."[28] But the most obvious borrowing lay in an incipient disenchantment with "theory," which the anthology places in the context of "the

Reagan-Bush years." Following Said's earlier lead, Bernheimer expresses his fatigue at theory's "suspicious vigilance" in making formulaic "comparisons that always collapsed into difference" while turning its declared interest in extrinsic meanings of literature into subtly "intrinsic" ones.[29] This comment is an unmistakable (although perhaps unwitting) echo of Said's complaints during the previous decade about the retreats of theory, which he elaborated in *Beginnings* and *The World, the Text, and the Critic*. It was, he argued in 1983, no accident that this turn coincided with "the age of Reaganism," which had produced in the academy "a priestly caste of acolytes and dogmatic metaphysicians."[30]

Comparative literature required a rationale to lift it from its status as the humanities' disciplinary "remainder." *Orientalism* might seem to have provided this rationale in its new non-Western emphasis, but actually the non-Western gesture had been an aspect of comparative literature from the start.[31] Even Goethe, according to Strich, did not consider world literature to be synonymous with European literature. Moreover, "in the decade after 1810," as Said pointed out, "[Goethe] became fascinated with Islam generally and with Persian poetry in particular."[32]

To be sure, Auerbach's modernization of philology did not clearly retain this aspect of the Goethean emphasis, and Said was perturbed enough at one point to pronounce Auerbach "no longer tenable" on the grounds that Auerbach's precious Europe was better seen in terms of what E. P. Thompson had called "Natopolis"—a collection of countries that had long dominated peripheral regions where "new cultures, new societies and emerging visions of social, political and aesthetic order now lay claim to the humanist's attention."[33] He complained that during Auerbach's wartime exile in Turkey, "there was no discernible connection between [him] and Istanbul at all; his entire attitude while there seems to have been one of nostalgia for the West."[34] But this statement was less a concession than a pedagogical tease. More than any modern critic, Auerbach exhibited the mastery of the history of rhetoric necessary to win adherents to a program of comparative literary expansion. Said, in one of his last pieces of writing, described Auerbach's style in words he would have loved for others to use about his own: an "unruffled, at times even lofty and supremely calm, tone conveying a combination of quiet erudition allied with an overridingly patient and loving confidence in his mission as scholar and philologist." With obvious emulation, Said described Auerbach's life work as comprised of a "handful of deeply conceived and complex themes with which he wove his ample fabric" and pointed out that Auerbach condemned the "failure of German literature to confront modern reality," as Said had American literature from his earliest days as a young professor.[35]

His links to Auerbach, then, went much deeper than adopting the latter's atmospheric humanism. Both saw the expansion of literary study into new canonical territories as one of the first, but least essential, imperatives of disciplinary transformation. The more important task was to grasp that "literature" was now extraliterary—that is, though devised at a time when leisured reading performed the true, anthropological function of value formation, the field now achieved its ends via more disparate forms of knowledge.[36] Auerbach was invaluable for constructing a method that acted as a wedge against the "division of intellectual labor" that Said took to be a pernicious "cult of professional expertise" designed to force intellectuals to sell themselves "to the central authority of a society."[37] *Beginnings* was the first of Said's books to lay out a case for the conclusions he had drawn from his apprenticeship in modern philology. It was a case for what might be called intellectual generalism.

LEFT PHILOLOGY

One must remember this strain of generalism—filtered through Auerbach but not (despite a widespread view) identical to his—when assessing retrospectively the meaning of *Orientalism*. The book is less about conflicting cultural values, or the comparative severity of Western and Eastern tyrannies (modern or ancient), than about the institutional creation and re-creation of discourse as an intellectual force of will. Said investigates Orientalism without freezing either East or West in the molds so prevalent in the U.S. press. But perhaps the more salient point is that for Said, the ideological bludgeon of "Orientalism" is not so much a civilizational taint or genetic prejudice from which, say, the white race suffers as a matter (as he later wrote in *Culture and Imperialism*) of "positional superiority." European knowledge production vis-à-vis the Orient took the form it did *because it could*. Europe (and later the United States) controlled the land, the trade, the government registers, and the means of disseminating information. In brief, the process painstakingly described in *Orientalism* is one in which no one could counter the dominant European view, and this lamentable hegemony gradually gave way to the belief, backed up by otherwise sensitive scholarship, that no one need question it. Said takes pains to describe the self-generating system of images and values that professional intellectuals in a specific social setting devised and propagated. For a variety of complicated reasons, those settings were incomparable, which is why one cannot posit, with pretentious balance, an Occidentalism to offset Orientalism.

Said sought to document intellectuals' role in the formation and legitimation of state policy. Yet he did not see this involvement purely as a matter of bad faith. Rather, *Orientalism* charts the inescapable fact of dominance in the act of amassing information on an "area" whose coherence is predicated on an internal, or domestically defined, set of attitudes. Within this frame, the outlooks of many journalists, commentators, and academics, argues Said, are deeply similar to one another in that they all pursue policies of expansion, forcible inclusion, and appropriation, albeit in different ways. The Orientalist system of knowledge conceals its assumptions by easing its audience into a mass of intricate details and documentary "proof" that serve the original concept. The finesse of scholarship is not a unique or elite realm for Said; his whole effort is to make it naked. The formidability and grandeur of scholarship, he suggests, bears an inverse relationship to the more basic questions that prejudice makes elusive: Why is one only an "Oriental" only in the West, never in the Orient itself? Why have the subjects never been given (as Said was to write in a later essay) "permission to narrate"?

Said never rests on the point that European literary critics or contemporary area studies experts got the Orient wrong: he states only that their Orient took no account of the Orientals' ordering of themselves. He does not argue, for example, that there is no such thing as a "real" Orient or that it has a life only in "discourse." Rather, he does not pretend to describe that brute reality to which he repeatedly refers and to which he gives priority of place. His point, by contrast, is that Western intellectuals are relatively indifferent to that reality and have proceeded confidently to build and elaborate on ideas and images based on those that have preceded them, never looking beyond this constellation of value. The book, in short, is about how intellectuals create a reality.

Given this stance, one would expect Said to welcome a brand of Marxism, however defined, not least because so much of his formative thinking was deeply invested in Marxism (although this has not been widely acknowledged). As early as 1966, in his very first published piece, he expressed admiration for the work of Lucien Goldmann, whose argument "stands in the center of a highly challenging and flowing pattern, a 'dialectic,' whose every detail sustains and is sustained by every other detail."[38] Many of his most insistent motifs—among them, his repudiation of the phenomenologists' "lonely ego," the "rigorous intellectual effort" that forms the inner coherence of an author's work, and the value of "historical consciousness"—are all emergent here. At this moment, in the presence of the dialectical tradition, which he then deliberately connected to *les sciences humaines* of Dilthey, Vico, and Auerbach, he established his own continuity of thinking with Marxism.[39] He was excited about Goldmann's theory of the way "in which individual parts can be said to make up a whole greater than a mere sum of its parts"—a view, he argued, that led away from a monadic consciousness to a relational "group consciousness," which is not simply Hegelian but philological.[40]

The point is probably lost on those who already "know" Said to be the founder of postcolonial theory's politics of discursivity, but we need to recall what he wrote about dialectics on the eve of *Orientalism*'s appearance almost a decade later in 1978:

> I have a great deal of sympathy for what [Marxist groups within the Modern Language Association] are trying to do, but I think it is a fundamental misjudgment of reality to base one's political work on an unsituated effort to show that Marxism is principally a reading technique. . . . What I am saying is that . . . to turn a literary or intellectual project immediately into a political one is to try to do something quite undialectical. But to accept the form of action prescribed in advance by one's profes-

sional status—which in the system of things is institutionalized marginality—is to restrict oneself politically and in advance.[41]

In this passage, he clearly rejects not Marxism's extremes but its timidity in the American context. In that spirit, he returned to Goldmann almost a decade later, in "Traveling Theory," in an effort to translate the meaning of Goldmann's dialectics.[42] He analyzed the "tamings" of reading over time as texts passed from one to another social circumstance—particularly, how the concepts of reification and totality passed from Lukács to Goldmann to Williams and Foucault, undergoing a transgression in the process. Dialectics—a term he ridiculed and whose associations with a ponderous philosophical politics from which he sought to distance himself—reasserts itself in his thinking in the mid-1970s, just as he was finishing *Orientalism*, in a review of Béla Királyfalvi's study of Lukács's *Aesthetik*, where he considered the Hungarian's logic to be "Hegelian in its dynamism, but more radical . . . in its thrust into totality."[43] Although Said's reliance upon these strains of thought cannot be doubted, he resisted embracing them—strategically perhaps, but thereby leaving his thoughts to the interstitial comments of a long-term dialogue: "Marxism has . . . always struck me as more limiting than enabling in the current intellectual, cultural, political conjuncture" (he was writing in 1992).[44] The unexpected point is that Said always saw tight linkages between these influences, one drawn from the left of European theory and the other from the philological substratum of comparative literature, even though the latter in others' hands would have had a merely liberal flavor.

It is remarkable, for example, that no one has observed that Said's discovery of the invaluable work of Vico—which he apparently came to through Auerbach—almost certainly derived from Lukács's "Reification" essay in *History and Class Consciousness*, which may explain why his reading of Vico struck contemporary critics (like Hayden White) as "baffling." Even without the clear documentation we have of Said's fascination with Lukács (I myself took seminars on Lukács with Said in 1981), we can see that the "Reification" essay forcefully articulates the primary themes of Said's attacks on the "system" thinking of theory that permeates *Orientalism*. The following passage from Lukács's essay precisely captures the point Said made repeatedly, in very similar words, in *Orientalism* and *The World, The Text, and the Critic*: "The ideal of knowledge represented by the purely distilled formal conception of the object of knowledge, the mathematical organization and the ideal of necessary natural laws all transform knowledge more and more into the systematic and conscious contemplation of those purely formal connections, those 'laws' which function in—objective—reality *without the intervention of the subject*."[45]

This focus is not a merely passing one in Lukács's text, of course; it is the principal idea of the essay, and Lukács repeatedly grounds this view in the work of Vico, whom the essay presents (much as Said does) as an alternative to the "antinomies" of thought in the Western idealist tradition. This tradition, for both men, fails to concretize the image of the thinker in his or her social context and is therefore unable to see why thought that violates the political interests of the theorist is, for that reason, literally unthinkable (hence, the "antinomy"). One cannot help hearing echoes of the following passage, which is far from unusual in Lukács's text, in Said's work: "[Hegelian thought] signals a change in the relation between . . . freedom and necessity. The idea that we have made reality loses its more or less fictitious character: we have—in the prophetic words of Vico . . .—made our own history and if we are able to regard the whole of reality as history (i.e., as *our* history, for there is no other), we shall have raised ourselves in fact to the position from which reality can be understood as our 'action.'"[46]

Indeed, I even suggest that the core ideas of Said's critical work on the political implications of scholarship as an act of intellectual will and consciously chosen influences and emulations are based directly on his reading of Lukács's critique of Vico. He shares with Lukács and Vico the idea that history is made, that it actually took place, and that it can be remembered and accurately (or inaccurately) represented. Said was not a philosophical thinker, and he never worked through the texts of Hegel or Hegelians. When he dismissed dialectics (as he did from time to time in print), he did so with a pedestrian understanding of its methods and with a received, commonsensical understanding of its doctrinal role in unsupple political movements of various sorts. With much more conviction and energy, he associates poststructuralism with "system-thinking," a collection of theories against which he fought a sustained battle in a number of books and essays.[47] Just before his death he again acknowledged, more clearly than before, that the work of Auerbach, one of the most obvious intellectual sources, "arose from the themes and methods of German intellectual history and philology; it would be conceivable in no other tradition than in that of German romanticism and Hegel."[48]

BIOGRAPHY AND METHOD

Said's arguments have carried rhetorical weight not only because they are more accessible than deconstruction to a variety of disciplines in the humanities and social sciences but also because they are backed by a carefully prepared method. When well-known critics confidently announced as late as 1988 that "Paul de Man is taken as emblematic of what comparative literature tries or wishes to be," they expressed a consensus that Said disparagingly refused to accept.[49] As he wrote in "Roads Taken and Not Taken in Contemporary Criticism," "The critical method—Auerbach's, Spitzer's, Blackmur's, Barthes', or Poulet's—is effective because every aspect of language is significant. . . . A vast range of possibilities immediately opens out. Are these linguistic significations intentional, are they all equal, is one signification more determined historically or sociologically than another, how do they influence each other?"[50]

Although "theory" thought of itself as the only force treating the linguistic artifact with complexity and depth, Said argued in 1975 that despite its impressive philosophical resources, theory does "not seem to be interested as much as I would like in the sheer semantic thickness of a literary text," which is evident only by involving oneself in history, anthropology, political theory, and the conditioning forces of one's time and place.[51] Poststructuralism was, he felt, simplistic when compared to more situated, materialist analyses attentive to literary form.

This strategy of indirection, although not without a confrontational or polemical edge, recast the slogans of theory in an alien tradition, allowing the reader to see theory's vaunted "ruptures" as the insights of earlier, generally better-equipped scholars. To take only one example, Said's inaugural term *beginnings* was far from innocent; it set itself up as a foil to deconstruction's "critique of origins" and structuralism's death of the author, although without engaging either in open combat. Said essentially critiqued Eurocentrism from within humanism in the name of a departure from the "airless and technically lucid finality characterizing [the] structural *critifact*[s] of theory."[52]

Said sympathized with Auerbach in that the latter's original insights have often wrongly been taken to be the former's contributions. For example, although scholars commonly associate the idea of "worldliness" with Said, the proposition comes from *irdischen*, Auerbach's term in *Dante, Poet of the Secular World*. ("Secularity"— another supposed Saidian coinage—is simply a rendering of the same word.) Auerbach also provided Said with the original terms of complaint against academic specialization.[53] But if the left Hegelian tradition and Auerbach begat Said, Giambattista Vico begat Auerbach, and despite the fact that Said obviously considered the German's work closely, the Italian's commanded the greatest space in his thinking. Few have appreciated the depths of this connection or the role it played in Said's method: his greatest, though osmotic, influence on comparative literature.

In the movement from Goethe to George Woodbury, comparative literature was taken over by the evolutionary manias of nineteenth-century Europe and its obsession with "science" as taxonomic system. Villemain first used the term *literature comparée* (1829) as an analogy to Cuvier's *anatomie comparée* (1800).[54] The comparative approach to scholarship, according to one recent scholar, "developed by the towering Romantic theorists, especially Herder and the Schlegels, becomes a comparative *method* . . . when 'Romantic conceptions fell into discredit, and ideals from the natural sciences became victorious, even in the writing of literary history.'"[55] Attentive readers of *Orientalism* will remember that Cuvier is the great villain of the book, the advocate of a "system" adopted by the bad philology of Ernst Renan, which Said contrasted with the expansive and humane philology of Raymond Schwab.

Above all, Vico's work allowed Said to pursue his strategy of indirection. Residing conveniently outside the contemporary critic's range of reference, Vico carried with him no offensive connotations, yet his entire career was an attempt to obliterate the unsavory attractions of Descartes (whom he despised). Descartes was the perfect twin embodiment of French philosophical idealism and scientific arrogance. Almost as if he were acting as Said's proxy, Vico propounded a "new" science—history—which was antipathetic to a notion of originality as "rupture." Confronting claims to novelty, Vico observed, according to Said, that "only by reproducing can we know what was produced and what the meaning is of verbal production for a human being: this is the quintessential Vichian maxim."[56] He perfectly anticipated Said's method in basing his etymological approach on complementarity: the lateral rather than the linear and sequential, the concept of beginning as a repetition of worthy precursors, the conception of language as "the rewriting of history," and the unfolding of a thesis not in prophetic explosions but in "a gradually developing exemplary discourse."[57]

Vico gave Said a decidedly secular authority as well. His vision was a "frighteningly godless one," a "human vision" of "an excruciatingly gentile mind"—in other words, a mind "which has been denied the fully integrated revelation accorded the Hebrews [creating instead] a neutral, amoral, and beautiful *mundus* of the mind that is—as he is always ready to remind us—only an imagistic economy for the real thing."[58] To evade the stigma of embracing the Hegelian tradition that had empowered many of his twentieth-century objects of emulation (for example, Antonio Gramsci, Adorno, Raymond Williams, Joseph Needham), Said shrewdly returned to a prior historical moment and to an icon who had himself infused Romanticism with its colloquial and historical energies. But the return was filled with the shadow-plays of an ongoing contemporary debate, which was not lost on discerning readers. When Said spoke, for instance, of Vico's "primitive men" who had discovered the "utilitarian inner function of language"—driving home Vico's points that "in the very act of understanding the world man was in reality understanding himself" and that "the language that a man speaks . . . makes the man and not man the language"—he intended to render the "discursive regime" of Foucault less phatic and ominous and to place him in continuity with a richer and more crowded past.[59] In this way, Said deliberately transformed Foucault's point into a colloquial truth of profound and unimpressive normality.

Said did not, however, want to make a new god of philology; he wished only to eschew "both intellectual positivism, the conceit of the philologists, and universal systematizing, the conceit of the philosophers."[60] Yet it is also true that the resources available for humanists in Reagan's America were not altogether equal. As a model, philology offered advantages not unlike theory's "eternal truths": Philology treated "contingent, historical truths at their basic level: it conceives of man dialectically, not statically."[61] As a slowly developing force, Said's prolific and richly layered demonstration of methodological alternatives slowly became a discursive pole of attraction. In the past decade, as postcolonial studies have evolved into the study of world literature, his arguments appear finally to have carried the day, thanks to the ways in which his scholarship has substantially, if not visibly, transformed comparative literature.

NOTES

A version of this essay originally appeared as "Edward Said and Comparative Literature," *Journal of Palestine Studies* 33, no. 3 (Spring 2004): 23–37. I have revised the piece and added a new section for this volume.

1. Jennifer Wicke and Michael Sprinker, "Interview with Edward Said," in *Edward Said: A Critical Reader*, ed. Michael Sprinker (Cambridge, MA: Blackwell, 1992), 250: "It seems to me that works like *Moby-Dick* or *Mansfield Park* or *Gulliver's Travels* are autonomous literary texts . . . I haven't at all given that idea up. For me these works first of all represent a kind of private experience of pleasure in reading and reflection."

2. Edward W. Said, *Orientalism* (London: Penguin, 2003), 20.

3. Ibid., 235. See also Edward Said, *Culture and Imperialism* (New York: Knopf, 1993), 45–46: "The first American department of comparative literature was established in 1891 at Columbia University, as was the first journal of comparative literature."

4. I am indebted to Gauri Viswanathan for this suggestion.

5. Edward W. Said, "Secular Criticism," in *The World, the Text, and the Critic*, 248–67, 8.

6. Ibid., 23.

7. Ibid., 10–11.

8. Ibid., 17.

9. For his mixed views on nationalism, see Wicke and Sprinker, "Interview with Edward Said," 231–32.

10. Edward Said, *Beginnings: Intention and Method* (Baltimore: Johns Hopkins University Press, 1975), 368–70.

11. Ironically, some people have taken *Culture and Imperialism* to be Said's definitive statement on literature, for it does not measure up to other books in his oeuvre. Apart from rehearsing his early-career arguments less forcefully than other works, the book never explores the extensive literature available on imperialism as a cultural and economic complex, and it even states (quite inaccurately) that no one before him had examined the relationship of culture to imperialism. Whereas elsewhere he adopts a language of nonclosure as a form of resistance to "system," here this language appears to avoid the difficult task of working through conflicts. In a concessionary gesture very much at odds with his bracing tone in *The World, the Text, and the Critic*, he repeatedly indulges in the pious "two superpowers" language of the Cold War (an unconvincing stance, needless to say, during the first U.S. invasion of Iraq and after the official fall of communism). Not coincidentally, his assessments of "theory" take on a very different, almost uncritical resonance, as if he feels compelled to pay homage to the hegemony of the times, which was particularly evident in the decade of the 1990s (see 57 especially).

12. "Supposed" creation because he distanced himself from the field of postcolonial studies, never using the term to describe his work. I consider Said's antagonistic relationship to this field he supposedly "invented" in "The Illusion of a Future: *Orientalism* as Traveling Theory," *Critical Inquiry* 26, no. 3 (2000): 558–83.

13. Until the beginning of the twentieth century, philology was practically indistinguishable from the field of study that we today call classics (the study of the literatures of ancient Greece and Rome). In the nineteenth century, such study was a ponderous and formidable scholarly enterprise comprising linguistics, comparative grammar, and the European vernaculars. For a full account of its history and

defining features, see Erich Auerbach's *Introduction to Romance Languages & Literature*, trans. Guy Daniels (New York: Capricorn Books, 1961 [1943]). For a contrasting view written with an eye to Said, see Paul de Man's "Return to Philology," in *Resistance to Theory* (Minneapolis: University of Minnesota Press, 1986), 21–26.

14. François Jost, *Introduction to Comparative Literature* (Indianapolis: Pegasus, 1974), 9.

15. René Wellek and Austin Warren, *Theory of Literature* (New York: Harcourt Brace, 1949), 40–41.

16. Charles Bernheimer, ed., *Comparative Literature in the Age of Multiculturalism* (Baltimore: Johns Hopkins University Press, 1995).

17. Wlad Godzich wrote of "the sudden uncertainty surrounding the very object of our study" in "Emergent Literature and the Field of Comparative Literature," in *The Comparative Perspective on Literature: Approaches to Theory and Practice*, ed. Clayton Koelb and Susan Noakes (Ithaca, NY: Cornell University Press, 1988), 20.

18. See, for example, Natalie Melas, *All the Difference in the World: Post-coloniality and the Ends of Comparison* (Stanford, CA: Stanford University Press, 2007), 65–68; David Damrosch, "Auerbach in Exile," *Comparative Literature* 47 (Spring 1995): 97–117; and F. Anthony Appiah, "Geist Stories," 53–54, and Emily Apter, "Comparative Exile: Competing Margins in the History of Comparative Literature," 86–88, both in Bernheimer, *Comparative Literature in the Age of Multiculturalism*.

19. Said's mentor, Raymond Williams, describes qualities in Bakhtin that were often applied to Said as well. See *The Politics of Modernism: Against the New Conformists* (London: Verso, 1990). As I argue in "Places of Mind, Occupied Lands: Edward Said and Philology," in *Edward Said: A Critical Reader*, 74–95, Said's "moral order of space" from *Culture and Imperialism* resembles Bakhtin's idea of the "chronotope," and Bakhtin's well-known (although frequently mangled) idea of the "dialogic" nature of language is reflected in Said's idea of the "overlapping territories" of intellectual life.

20. Wicke and Sprinker, "Interview with Edward Said," 242.

21. Fritz Strich, *Goethe and World Literature* (London: Routledge and Kegan Paul, 1949), 32.

22. Ibid., 9, 11.

23. Jost, *Introduction to Comparative Literature*, 13.

24. Edward W. Said, "Introduction to the Fiftieth Anniversary Edition" of *Mimesis: The Representation of Reality in Western Literature*, by Erich Auerbach, trans. Willard R. Trask (Princeton, NJ: Princeton University Press, 2003), xiv.

25. For an early mention of Said's reliance on Auerbach, see Paul A. Bové, *Intellectuals in Power: A Genealogy of Critical Humanism* (New York: Columbia University Press, 1986), 1–38. For the first detailed examination of the Auerbach connection as well as Said's relationship to philology, see Brennan, "Places of Mind, Occupied Lands," 74–95. Recent reconsiderations of this theme include Emily Apter, "Global Translation: The 'Invention' of Comparative Literature, Istanbul, 1933," *Critical Inquiry* 29 (Winter 2003): 253–81, which delves into the Turkish context of Auerbach's writing during the war.

26. Erich Auerbach, "Philology and *Weltliteratur*," translated with an introduction by Maire Said and Edward Said, *Centennial Review* 13, no. 1 (Winter 1969): 1–17.

27. Examples of the trend toward "world literature" in postcolonial studies include Alamgir Hashmi, *The Commonwealth, Comparative Literature and the World* (Islamabad: Gulmohar, 1988); Roberto Schwarz, *Misplaced Ideas: Essays in Brazilian Literature* (London: Verso, 1992); Franco Moretti, *Modern Epic* (London: Verso, 1996); Timothy Brennan, *At Home in the World: Cosmopolitanism Now* (Cambridge, MA: Harvard University Press, 1997); Pascal Cassanova, *La République Mondiale des Lettres* (London: Verso, 1999); Emily Apter, *Continental Drift* (Chicago: University of Chicago Press, 1999); Neil Lazarus, *Nationalism and Cultural Practice in the Postcolonial World* (Cambridge: Cambridge University Press, 1999); and David Damrosch, *What Is World Literature?* (Princeton, NJ: Princeton University Press, 2003).

28. Bernheimer, "The Bernheimer Report, 1993," in Bernheimer, *Comparative Literature in the Age of Multiculturalism*, 42–43. Some of the anthology's essays, unlike the report itself, depart dramatically

from Said's method of working. Anthony Appiah's "Geist Stories," which opens the volume, is instructive in this respect. He begins with an anecdote about being invited as a young professor to attend a public lecture by René Wellek on his Ivy League campus. Unexpectedly detained, he is unable to make the lecture, entering the hall to hear (or, as he says, "thinks" he hears) Wellek's concluding sentence about the "life of spirit" in history. While conceding that he didn't actually attend the lecture, Appiah is undeterred. Alluding to Wellek's "mittel Europaïsch" pronunciation, Appiah dismisses Wellek along with the intellectual enterprise he shared with several earlier generations, extending from German Romanticism through the liberation movements of nineteenth-century Europe that were inspired by the French events of 1789. He renders all this as nothing: poof! the topic of a jest. He dispatches a lifetime's work as tainted Hegelian meandering and blustery Euro-arrogance (the word *spirit* or *Geist* is sufficient to convey all of this to him in a flash). This gesture could not be farther from Said's careful preparation in the profession, which took early account of this star-crossed tendency in American intellectual life and attempted to curb and redirect it.

29. Bernheimer, introduction to *Comparative Literature in the Age of Multiculturalism*, 5, 6.

30. Said, "Secular Criticism," 3–5.

31. R. K. Dhawan, *Comparative Literature* (New Delhi: Bahri Publications, 1987).

32. Said, "Introduction to the Fiftieth Anniversary Edition," xv.

33. Said, "Secular Criticism," 21.

34. Wicke and Sprinker, "Interview with Edward Said," 230.

35. Said, "Introduction to the Fiftieth Anniversary Edition," x, xix, xxxi, xx. There is an "absence in America of such universal novelistic figures as Solzhenitzyn, or the Egyptian Naguib Mahfouz, or Gabriel García Márquez—writers for whom mimesis with a profoundly moral social engagement is still potent." Said, "Contemporary Fiction and Criticism," *Tri-Quarterly* 33 (Spring 1975): 255.

36. Edward Said, "Roads Taken and Not Taken in Contemporary Criticism," in *The World, the Text, and the Critic*, 151; and Edward Said, "Interview," *Diacritics* 6, no. 3 (Fall 1976): 41.

37. Said, "Secular Criticism," 2. See also Said, "Interview," *Diacritics*, 38: "To some extent we are technicians doing a very specialized job; to a certain degree also we are keepers of, kept by, and tutors to the middle and upper classes, although a great deal of what we are interested in as students of literature is necessarily subversive of middle class values."

38. Edward Said, "A Sociology of Mind," *Partisan Review* 33, no. 3 (Summer 1966): 444.

39. Ibid., 448, 447, 445, 444.

40. Ibid., 444.

41. Said, "Interview," *Diacritics*, 39.

42. Edward Said, "Traveling Theory," in *The World, the Text, and the Critic*, 238.

43. Edward Said, "Between Chance and Determinism," *Times Literary Supplement*, 6 February 1976, 67.

44. Wicke and Sprinker, "Interview with Edward Said," 260. Said then specifically addresses the expressions of Marxism within the Palestinian movement: "Take the Popular Front, which declares itself a Marxist movement . . . They could be described in other ways, but those of a classical Marxist party they are not. Its analyses are not Marxist. They are essentially insurrectionary and Blanquist, dispiriting to the organization of the PFLP [Popular Front for the Liberation of Palestine] and also 'the masses,' whom they seem to address. They have no popular base, never did" (ibid.).

45. Georg Lukács, "Reification and the Consciousness of the Proletariat," in *History and Class Consciousness* (Cambridge, MA: MIT Press, 1971), 128 (emphasis by Lukács).

46. Ibid., 145.

47. I discuss Said's view of poststructuralism in more detail in "The Illusion of a Future: *Orientalism* as Traveling Theory," *Critical Inquiry* 26 (Spring 2000): 558–83.

48. Said, "Introduction to the Fiftieth Anniversary Edition," xii.

49. Godzich, "Emergent Literature," 13. I use the word *disparagingly* in light of his characteristic comment in the Wicke and Sprinker interview: "I've been very conscious, for example, of not wanting to impose myself on students in the way in which people like de Man and other members of the (now defunct) Yale School have done, to become part of a school, to formalize what it is that I do in teachable ways or anything like that" (248).

50. Said, "Roads Taken and Not Taken," 147–48.

51. Said, "Interview," *Diacritics,* 32.

52. Said, "Roads Taken and Not Taken," 152.

53. See Said, "Introduction to the Fiftieth Anniversary Edition," xvi.

54. Wellek and Warren, *Theory of Literature,* 38.

55. Melas, *All the Difference in the World,* 83.

56. Said, *Beginnings,* 357.

57. Ibid., 337.

58. Edward Said, "Vico: Humanist and Autodidact," *Centennial Review* 11, no. 3 (1967): 341, 351.

59. Ibid., 348.

60. Ibid., 352.

61. Said and Said, introduction to Auerbach, "Philology and *Weltliteratur,*" 2.

7

Affiliating Edward Said Closer to Home

Reading Postcolonial Women's Texts

Denise deCaires Narain

There is no Archimedean point beyond the question from which to answer it;
there is no vantage outside the actuality of relationships among cultures, among
unequal imperial and non-imperial powers, among us and others; no one has
the epistemological privilege of somehow judging, evaluating, and interpret-
ing the world free from the encumbering interests and engagements of the on-
going relationships themselves. We are, so to speak, of the connections, not
outside and beyond them.

—EDWARD SAID, *CULTURE AND IMPERIALISM*

Someone is going up the stairs, barefoot, so it is not a footfall I hear, but the
clatter of a bucket and broom. It is someone whose name I once knew but who
now remains nameless. One of the many who taught me my first words, my
first songs, which flowers tasted sweet, which plants were not for tasting, the
right grain for birds, the language of the seasons. Someone nameless taught
me the first verse of the Lankan national anthem which is still all I know of
it. I sing along and remember her. Nameless but not forgotten. The closest
connections are often anonymous. The identity of love.

—MINOLI SALGADO, "HEART"

In the first epigraph, Said's emphasis on the connectedness of cultural worlds is part
of an exhortation to "fellow Americans" to recognize the role of America as "*the*
dominant outside force" in most, if not all, parts of the formerly colonized world
and to acknowledge the responsibilities that attach to such power. "In short, we face
as a nation the deep, profoundly perturbed and perturbing question of our relationship to others—other cultures, states, histories, experiences, traditions, peoples,
and destinies. We are, so to speak, *of* the connections, not outside and beyond them.
And it behooves us as intellectuals and humanists and secular critics to understand

the United States in the world of nations and power from *within* the actuality, as participants in it, not detached observers."[1]

Here he presents the United States both as *home* and, in the extent of its power and control, as *the world*. Beyond this specific reference to America and Americans, Said generally posits the ideal critic/intellectual as one who occupies a somewhat paradoxical position of "situated worldliness": a position that refuses the dubious security of nativism and embraces homelessness and the condition of exile as an enabling space while acknowledging that texts and other cultural artifacts do not transcend the political, historical, and cultural circumstances of their production and consumption. The critic/intellectual is, in Said's construction, *necessarily* mobile and at home in the world. By offering the second epigraph, I draw attention to connections of a more personal and emotional kind, those of "the heart, the hearth and home." In "Heart," Minoli Salgado recalls her closeness in childhood to a servant in the family home to acknowledge more intimate instances of connection across difference.

In this chapter, I explore the implications of these two rather different avenues for connection between distinct cultural worlds and suggest possible resonances between them. Said argued repeatedly that "nativism is *not* the only alternative. There is the possibility of a more generous and pluralistic vision of the world." But although he recognized that "moving beyond nativism did not mean abandoning nationality," his engagement with "native" or "local" cultures was fairly limited, even in *Culture and Imperialism,* which explicitly addressed this omission.[2] Said's almost exclusive engagement with Western canonical literature also means that women's writing and questions of gender receive fairly scant attention. Despite these elisions, his work remains suggestive in reading for that "more generous and pluralistic vision of the world."

Said's insistent reminders of the connections between cultures and his affirmation of the critic's tasks of recognizing, working through, and extending those connections is particularly useful to postcolonial feminism. That Said prefers to invoke the role of the "critic" and "intellectual" rather than that of the theorist is also pertinent: feminist postcolonial scholarship, like feminist scholarship more generally, has tended in recent times to adopt a rather sternly purist position about its function as "Theory." The grandstanding that results has not been conducive to fostering the solidarities between women across differences that many feminists argue for. Said's work offers suggestive ways forward, and I suggest that his emphasis on contrapuntal readings and on the shared historical contexts of our worlds, which he evocatively refers to as "overlapping territories, intertwined histories," can be deployed in a reading of contemporary postcolonial women's texts in ways that both invigorate feminist inquiry *and* help align Said's work more closely with women's writing than is usually the case.

Mildred Mortimer, in "Said and Djebar: A Contrapuntal Reading," acknowledges the limited extent of Said's attention to the work of women writers, noting that when he does affirm Assia Djebar's *L'Amour, La Fantasia,* he does so in a footnote. Nonetheless, she argues, "Rather than fault Said for myopic vision . . . I propose to read his work as an invitation to postcolonial writers to extend and develop his analyses of Orientalism and imperialism."[3] I find the generosity of such an approach persuasive. In what follows, I discuss a selection of postcolonial women's texts in order to explore the relevance of Said's contrapuntal method of reading to these texts and to suggest trajectories for extending the application of his insights. Said's work, beginning with *Orientalism,* focused on the dominant role of the West in constituting Western culture as normative while inscribing "other" cultures as inferior. Although *Culture and Imperialism* attempted to shift the emphasis away from an exclusive focus on Western canonical texts toward a broader range of non-Western forms of culture, this maneuver was only partially convincing. If embracing *filiative* ties, anchored in fixed ideas of one's genealogical and geographic place in the world, are "to accept the consequences of imperialism too readily," as Said wrote, then *affiliation* extends the possibilities for attachments and suggests that such attachments are a matter of reflection and choice. Many readers critiqued *Culture and Imperialism* for not extending its affiliations to more Third World or non-Western texts. In a tribute to Edward Said, David Lloyd draws attention, among other things, to some of the tensions and ambiguities in Said's ideas of "filiation" and "affiliation" and suggests that, "indeed, it is not entirely clear that Said himself ever entirely escaped the filiative force-field of his own affiliation to the body of Western culture to which, over and again, he returned with such complicated affection."[4]

Rather than focusing on the inscription of imperialism within canonical Western culture, this chapter seeks to reorient, if not evade, the "force field" of Western culture by turning to textual examples that center on relationships between women of unequal social status within particular postcolonial locations. Specifically, I look at how the selected texts represent the figure of the servant and explore the intimacies, possibilities, and ambiguities of such representations. Said's work is not an obvious choice for such a focus, given the elisions I've noted. Further, as L. H. M. Ling argues, "Said remained intriguingly unreflective . . . about home. In focusing almost exclusively on 'the exilic condition,' home became an assumption, an unquestioned origin, a reified way of being. Said did not theorise on how home may relate differently to different subjectivities like daughters and servants in contrast to sons and patriarchs. His contrapuntal method registered seemingly disparate events or conditions or cognitions of being but he did not see an underlying commonality binding them, perhaps producing them."[5]

There have, of course, been other feminist critiques of Said's oeuvre. Reina Lewis, in *Gendering Orientalism,* states the case quite categorically: "For Said, in *Orientalism* at least, Orientalism is a homogenous discourse enunciated by a colonial subject that is unified, intentional and irredeemably male."[6] Valerie Kennedy, in her critical introduction to Said's work, sees sharp irony in Said's inability to make connections between the "othering" processes at work in Orientalism and the very similar processes that feminist scholars have charted in analyzing the distortions generated by patriarchal regimes of knowledge. Like Lewis, Kennedy suggests that the lack of attention paid to Western women in Said's interrogation of Orientalist discourse seriously compromises the work: "Western women have no place in his analysis of the 'white middle-class Westerner.' As a representative of imperial and postcolonial political and economic power, the latter is identified unambiguously as 'he.' Arab women are even more dramatically excluded from the Orientalist stereotype he quotes here and from the text as a whole."[7]

Neither the afterword Said wrote for the 1994 edition of Orientalism nor the preface for the 2003 edition engages directly with any feminist challenges to the male-centeredness of his project in Orientalism, which suggests that Said remained convinced that, as he said in an interview with Raymond Williams, "in the relationships between ruler and the ruled in the imperial or racial sense, race takes precedence over both class and gender. . . . I have always felt that the problem of emphasis and relative importance took precedence over the need to establish one's feminist credentials."[8]

The rather dismissive reference to "feminist credentials," with its suggestion of faddishness, is disappointing, but given the obvious and inevitable predominance of male writers in the canon of literature that Said addresses, it is not surprising that women do not feature more centrally in his work. As Jane Miller and others have argued, the exclusion of women in Orientalism was a structural problem, requiring a structural solution.[9] The parallels between "feminist" and "nativist" critiques of Said's work (to use shorthand) converge around the elision of "the native," "the woman," and "the woman native" in both Orientalism and Culture and Imperialism (though in the latter, Said does address the question of native agency).

Kennedy offers a tentative defense of Said's elision of the "non-Western woman": "To be fair to Said, this is not easy, either in practical or conceptual terms. Evidence about non-Western women is less easily accessible than that relating to either Western men or women. Theorizing about non-Western women has also proved tricky for Western feminists, who have been accused by Gayatri Spivak and Chandra Talpade Mohanty, among others, of reducing them to the stereotype of victim."[10]

I agree with Kennedy that representing "the other woman" has posed problems for feminism, but I argue that this issue has proved to be more than just "tricky." It has fractured feminist work in quite emphatic ways and has had an inhibiting, if not paralyzing, effect on the kinds of texts discussed and issues raised in feminist discourses. In Going Global: The Transnational Reception of Third World Women Writers, to take a fairly recent example, Marnia Lazreg argues,

> Given the politics of reception of Other women's work and speech, it is crucial to ask whether "Western" audiences, feminist or otherwise, should insist on the knowability of these women. The many conferences, seminars and courses devoted to these

Other women have not yielded a deeper understanding of them. Generalizations and stereotypes still flourish, and for some societies (such as the Middle East) these stereotypes seem to hold greater sway than they did *before* the advent of academic feminism. . . . The triumphant discourse is but a discourse with global ambitions. *What we need is the expression of reality by those who live it and on their terms.*[11]

In this argument, Lazreg indicts Western feminist scholarship as itself an Orientalizing discourse. In doing so she extends the remit of Said's *Orientalism* and builds on the seminal essays of Chandra Mohanty, Gayatri Spivak, and others. Spivak's "Can the Subaltern Speak?" identifies in painstaking detail the difficulty, if not impossibility, of attempting to speak for "the" subaltern woman. The essay was a crucial intervention and remains one of the most frequently cited essays in postcolonial feminist discourses. But the pessimistic conclusion of that essay, that "the subaltern cannot speak," despite all the contingent considerations Spivak has since presented to qualify that conclusion, has, I believe, contributed to a kind of paralysis in feminist scholarship, making scholars reluctant to read and write about "Third World" women's texts or to address the possibility of dialogue with (or about) "the Other woman." Lazreg's argument that we need the "expression of reality by those who live it" is suggestive but clearly begs more questions than it answers.

A growing number of feminist critics are now challenging this pessimistic determinism. For example, Vron Ware in "What Other Way to Speak?" makes a strong argument for finding other ways to *hear* as well as to speak *to* (rather than *about*) the other woman.[12] Another recent example is Sarah Ahmed's *Strange Encounters: Embodied Others in Post-Coloniality,* which argues persuasively against silence as an acceptable response to the difficulties of engaging with the other woman, "[Silence], as a response to the feminist and postcolonial critiques of universalism, assumes that the best way to avoid speaking for others is to avoid speaking at all . . . [it] also functions as a kind of solipsism that confirms the privilege that it seeks to refuse (I can only speak about myself, or I can only speak about the impossibility of my speaking) . . . Cultural relativism assumes distance and difference in order precisely not to take *responsibility* for that distance and difference."[13]

Ahmed suggests that one of the ways we might "take responsibility" for the differences that separate women is to attend to the structures through which women are *already* connected. "We need a politics that works with what is already assimilated, for example, which accepts that the encounters implicit in the gendering of the international division of labour already mediate how it is possible for women to encounter other women in different nation spaces at all."[14]

Attending to the ethical implications of existing relationships between women involves issues of labor—and the question Who works for whom? It also involves paying attention to more intimate—and perhaps ambiguous—encounters than are usually implied in Said's work. The figure of the servant provides a resonant and suggestive focus here.

The servant functions in many postcolonial texts as a crucial intermediary. Positioned between "the people" and the ruling elite (whether "colonial" or "postcolonial"), the servant provides "domesticated" access to the "ordinary people," the subjects invariably assumed to be the proper focus of postcolonial studies (at least in its earliest manifestation).[15] Bruce Robbins—in his study of servants in nineteenth-century British fiction, *The Servant's Hand*—argues, "Organized around the massive fact that one speaker is powerful and the other powerless, dialogues between master and servant can be reduced to a handful of standard types."[16]

Despite the relatively marginal function of servants in the texts, however, these figures are powerfully resonant. Rather than focusing on the fidelity of the representation of servants to the supposed "reality" of servants' lives, as demanded by realist prose, Robbins argues for readings that are attuned to the play of language so that the text becomes "a medium or arena of political skirmishing, alive with the turbulent significance of moves and countermoves." In pursuing such an approach, Robbins draws parallels between the "othering" of the domestic working class in the novel and of Arabs in Orientalist discourse and cites (approvingly) the following lines from Said's *Orientalism*: "The things to look at are style, figures of speech, setting, narrative devices, historical and social circumstances, *not* the correctness of the representation nor its fidelity to some great original."[17] Rather than reading the limited representations of the servant available in English fiction as "the sign of a monotonous exclusion," Robbins suggests that their function in narrative "can be investigated as the site of unknown and perhaps surprising confrontations." He acknowledges the need to make a distinction between the treatment of Arabs in Orientalist discourse and treatment of the serving class in novelistic discourse, and he cites Said's reference to "the almost total absence in contemporary Western culture of the Orient as a *genuinely felt and experienced* force."[18] The implication is that the ubiquity of servants in certain nineteenth-century households and the intimate nature of their work within those households indeed makes them a "genuinely felt and experienced force." In a further intertextual link, in *Culture and Imperialism*, Said consolidates the parallels between the marginality of the Orient and of the servant: "As a reference, as a point of definition, as an easily assumed place of travel, wealth and service, the empire functions for much of the European nineteenth century as a codified, if only marginally visible, presence in fiction, very much like the servants in grand households and in novels, whose work is taken for granted but scarcely ever more than named, rarely studied (though Bruce Robbins has recently written on them), or given density."[19] Neither Said nor Robbins develops a more substantial connection between each other's studies of the marginal but powerfully constitutive presence of empire and servants, respectively, but clearly this discussion of the difficulties of representation intersects directly with some of the debates within postcolonial feminist discourse. How might these concerns with representation relate to the many texts by postcolonial women writers that explicitly seek to invest the servant woman with a powerful "vocal agency" and physicality with which to challenge dominant culture? In these texts, servants often embody a distinctly "native" resistance to the operations of colonial power and act as symbols of the text's alignment with "home" and "home/land." How might Robbins's argument apply in a postcolonial context in which this desire to represent "the people" is often an *explicit* aim and focus? How might we explore Said's ideas of filiation and affiliation through texts that seek to represent solidarity with the other woman? Can the postcolonial woman writer *hear* the subaltern, if she cannot make her *speak?*[20]

Jean Rhys's novel *Wide Sargasso Sea* provides a familiar and instructive starting point.[21] The novel attempts to rescue the demonized white Creole figure, Bertha Mason, from Brontë's *Jane Eyre* and to write a more credible life for her. In doing so, Rhys foregrounds the colonial history that Brontë's text elides and, to use Said's term, writes *contrapuntally*. So, where Brontë implies that Bertha's wild, animalistic behavior can be explained by biology and geography, Rhys suggests that *History* is the determining force. Although Antoinette is a white Creole and from a plantation-owning family, her place in this history is not one of unequivocal power and privilege, given the political and economic decline of the plantocracy at the time in which the novel is set. The marriage that eventually leads to her breakdown and fiery end at Thornfield is the result of a trade-off with the man (the never-named Rochester figure) who offers her respectability as well as the opportunity to "whiten up" (as an Englishman, his "whiteness" is altogether more powerful and respected than hers). The postemancipation context of the novel is a crucial determinant of what happens in the narrative, and this history precludes any relationship between Antoinette and her childhood friend, Tia, the daughter of one of the servants, beyond the immediate parameters of childhood and the family home at Coulibri. When the house is set on fire and Antoinette and her family are forced out, Tia refuses to give the recognition that Antoinette's backward glance signifies and instead throws a sharp stone, which draws blood and decisively ruptures any illusion that Antoinette may have entertained of belonging with Tia. The violent history of slavery and its aftermath also set the limits on the relationship between Antoinette and her "nurse," Christophine.

A good deal of the critical debate surrounding *Wide Sargasso Sea* has centered on Rhys's representation of the relationships between Antoinette and Tia and between Antoinette and Christophine. Kamau Brathwaite argues that Rhys, as a white Creole, is too far removed from the social realities of the black West Indian population to be able to represent their realities convincingly.[22] Gayatri Spivak comes to a similar conclusion in "Can the Subaltern Speak?" though the process by which she arrives at this conclusion is more convoluted than Brathwaite's. Benita Parry refuses "Spivak's deliberated deafness to the native voice" and points to a useful distinction between her own reading and Spivak's, "While allowing that Christophine is both speaking subject and interpreter to whom Rhys designates some crucial functions, Spivak sees her as marking the limits of the text's discourse, and not, as is here argued, disrupting it."[23]

Although both Spivak and Parry offer insightful readings, I argue that *Wide Sargasso Sea* cannot be made to render so definitive a position on the subaltern woman as either critic would wish. Both readings elide the *intimacy* of the relationship between Christophine and Antoinette in pursuit of an ideologically driven argument that reinstalls a binary categorizing of subjects that the text—both intentionally and inadvertently—questions. In other words, the literary text does not force us to choose but allows these positions to resonate. Jonathon Culler's succinct reminder of the distinctiveness of literary discourse is helpful here: "If literature helps to make us self-conscious agents, it does so by promoting thick description over simplifying principle, so that potential conflicts of value and principle may emerge."[24]

This argument does not forget that the novel revolves around a binary opposition between the "white" and "black" worlds represented by Antoinette and Christophine. Although the women clearly have affection for each other, their encounters are always mapped in terms of the services Christophine provides for Antoinette. Rhys's novel, then, constructs Antoinette and Christophine in neatly distinct ways: Antoinette, although a passionate lover when she feels loved, is more often presented as fragile, vulnerable, and anxious about who she is and where she belongs. The "voice" distinguishing her narration is that of the internal monologue, and when her utterances are public, they are often fragmented and tentative. Christophine, by contrast, is a solidly grounded presence in the text. She is the only reliably welcoming figure for Antoinette, whom she attempts to jolt out of her passivity with words such as, "A man don't treat you good, pick up your skirt and walk out. Do it and he come after you." Christophine's pithy language is described by the husband as "horrible," but he recognizes her as a "fighter" as she astutely exposes the political implications of his attempts to maneuver his wife into madness.[25]

The text also gives Christophine an alternative source of knowledge and power in the form of Obeah and distinguishes her from both Antoinette and the husband by the forcefulness with which she asserts herself and by her awareness of that power. She bargains hard to rescue Antoinette and even asks for a sum of money so that she can take Antoinette away to Martinique (and "other places").[26] This "female elopement" with its promise of a happy ending is denied, and Christophine is forced to make her exit—but not until the husband reasserts his patriarchal power by invoking the Law. Christophine's assertion of worldly wisdom or "worldliness" is curtailed by the husband's power to *world* his words.

Wide Sargasso Sea ultimately presents the servant as having more power than her charge, a reversal that may appear to willfully ignore history. This power derives partly from Christophine's role of surrogate mother, but to my mind the role reversal has a stronger explanation that rests on an understanding of colonial and imperial history; this history shapes the novel and positions Christophine as the *rightful*, and indeed *righteous*, claimant to the homeland. Antoinette, by contrast, proclaims her affiliation with the *landscape*, but both her need to lay claim to it and the aestheticized nature of the claim belie the anxiety that attends it. In other words, Rhys confirms that Christophine belongs *without question* to the West Indies but endows Antoinette's sense of belonging with none of that ethical certainty. Instead, Antoinette's fate is firmly tethered to the textual world of *Jane Eyre*, not just in the obvious intertextual link but also the text's construction of her through modernist literary conventions of character construction: she is psychologically complex and has an "interiority" that allows the reader to inhabit her consciousness. By contrast, Rhys constructs Christophine in a manner that privileges presence and vocal agency so that she is seen (and heard) from the outside. Both women indicate a clear understanding of the demonizing impact of colonial relations, but Christophine declares this understanding ("No chain gang, no tread machine, no dark jail either. This is free country and I am free woman"), while Antoinette interjects short parries and halting asides.[27] Where the construction of Antoinette is "thickened" by familiar literary signifiers, Christophine is apprehended largely as a political subject.

We could easily conclude (in line with Brathwaite) that this textual economy is the result of a failure on Rhys's part to imagine outside of the racially hierarchized world of her time. A letter Rhys wrote to Diana Athill might seem to corroborate this view: "The most seriously wrong thing with Part II is that I've made the obeah woman, the nurse, too articulate. I thought of cutting it a bit, I will if you like, but after all no one will notice. Besides there's no reason why one particular Negro woman shouldn't be articulate enough, especially if she's spent most of her life in a white household."[28]

In this comment, Rhys appears to be confounded by the power of her own construction, but she also implies that the servant's ability to speak articulately and to analyze can be explained only by her exposure to the white people she serves and from whom she imbibes knowledge. "The eavesdropping servant," as Robbins reminds us, is a familiar dimension of the servant in literary fiction. But Rhys also argues that "no one will notice," indicating her awareness that the conventions for the reception of literary texts preclude serious attention to the servant.

A section of Rhys's unfinished autobiography, *Smile Please*, touches on some of these ambiguities and tensions. In the third chapter, "Meta," Rhys describes her own childhood nurse: "And now it is time to talk about Meta, my nurse and the terror of my life. She had been there ever since I could remember: a short, stocky woman, very black and always, I thought, in a bad temper. I never saw Meta smile. *She always seemed to be brooding over some terrible, unforgettable wrong.*"[29]

Rhys implies that this "terrible unforgettable wrong" is linked to her in a way she never makes explicit but that she dramatizes in the image of Meta violently shaking her by the shoulders (because her parents have forbidden Meta to slap her), while the child yells breathlessly, "Black Devil, Black Devil, Black Devil!"[30] Meta also tells the young Rhys stories of zombies, soucriants, and werewolves (loups-garous) that leave the child terrified (into adulthood): "I can't remember who took her place, or if anyone did. But in any case it was too late, the damage had been done. Meta had shown me a world of fear and distrust and I am still in that world."[31]

This extraordinary exchange between nurse and child conveys powerfully the collision of cultural worlds that underpins the encounter. Rhys's upbringing, like that of many white Creoles at that time, included strict prohibitions against involvement in Creole practices—whether speaking Creole, dancing in the carnival, or singing calypsos.[32] This taboo may well have rendered "that world" all the more desirable—and other sections of Smile Please suggest as much. But despite recognizing the impact of black cultural practices both on her own imagination and as a force of political importance, Rhys appears unable to construct a literary form in which to fully inscribe "that world." The second chapter of Smile Please, titled "Books," concludes with another scene involving Meta:

> My nurse, who was called Meta, didn't like me much anyway, and complete with a book it was too much. One day she found me crouched on the staircase reading a bowdlerised version of the Arabian Nights in very small print.
> She said, "If you read so much, you know what will happen to you? Your eyes will drop out and they will look at you from the page."
> "If my eyes drop out I wouldn't see," I argued.
> She said, "They drop out except the little black points you see with."
> I half believed her and imagined my pupils like heads of black pins and all the rest gone. But I went on reading.[33]

This charged exchange reiterates Rhys's perception of the boundedness of the cultural worlds of the child and the nurse, conveying powerfully the terms in which those boundaries are mapped: the world of the spoken word collides with that of the scripted word. Although these autobiographical fragments indicate an awareness of the cultural power of both worlds, Rhys appears unable in her *fiction* to transcend the boundaries between these worlds. The reader, however, adopting Said's contrapuntal method, *can* allow these worlds to resonate against each other to transgress the limitations of Rhys's text.

It is not entirely whimsical to note that the text the child reads is Arabian Nights— and not, say, Middlemarch, or indeed, Jane Eyre. Arabian Nights, a text so significant in Said's mapping of Orientalism, offers both the oral dissemination of stories and a profoundly gendered power struggle. It appears in a wide range of postcolonial women's texts of varied provenance and is a recurring strand in Ahdaf Soueif's collection of short stories, Aisha.[34] Space does not permit me to elaborate on this redeployment of Arabian Nights except to note the ways that these writers seek to evade any re-Orientalizing impulses, even as they reorient the tales from feminist perspectives. *Aisha*, a collection of eight loosely connected stories, alternates (with the exception of two of the stories), between the worlds of Aisha, a middle-class academic, and Dada Zeina, her nurse. As in *Wide Sargasso Sea*, the relationship between nurse and child in *Aisha* is one of trust and affection, although the characters' respective worlds are starkly opposed. Aisha, whose parents are both academics, lives in a book-centered world. The living room walls are covered with books: "All are to be treated with great respect and never torn or folded or scribbled in or put face downwards or looked at while eating in case you drop food on them."[35]

Later in the same story, the *Arabian Nights* figures as an emblem of Orientalist literary discourse: "My mother has a problem with me. I am finishing my books too quickly. We get home from school and long before bed-time I have finished the books from the library and am demanding more. In desperation she lets me browse among her books. I pick out a heavy red and gold volume of the *Arabian Nights*. 'It's all right,' she assures my father, 'it's only the Lane edition.' And I enter yet another new world. A world of Oriental souks and magic and Djinnis."[36]

The mother considers the Lane edition of *Arabian Nights* "safe"; Said incidentally refers to it as an "uninspired translation."[37] The parents are presented as "modern" and liberal, explaining the rationale for their decisions patiently and kindly. Interestingly, this liberalism does not allow Aisha to form relationships across cultures (she is not allowed to conduct a friendship with the Indian boy she meets on the boat from Egypt to England), nor does it allow her to acquaint herself with "traditional" Egyptian culture or to listen to the stories Dada Zeina relates:

> Her nurse looked at her meaningfully and the child thrilled. Here she was: an accomplice, a grown-up. Her baby sister and brother were asleep inside, but she was eight years old and sitting up on the balcony listening to her nanny's story. And it would be like this every Wednesday night when her parents went out. So long, of course, as she was careful and kept her secret. "She's a good girl," Dada Zeina always said to the other nurses in the club, "she never carries tales to her mother." And although in some deep corner inside she was uneasy, feeling the bribe in her words, she still felt proud, and anxious to keep those privileged story-telling hours. Besides, she didn't want to carry tales. She had asked her mother once how women did the joy-cry and her father had said it was something that only vulgar people did.[38]

The child's enthrallment to Zeina's stories is heightened because she and her nurse are taking part in a forbidden exchange and are accomplices in challenging the authority of the parents and the cultural order they represent. In other moments in the stories, Dada Zeina is the one sworn to secrecy, as Aisha sneaks out in "high and secret heels."[39] "The Wedding of Zeina" and "Her Man" focus on Zeina's world and her location in that world, which is "exposed." "The Wedding of Zeina" describes Zeina's violent induction into married life at the age of fifteen, including the way her aunts hold her down so that her body hair can be removed in preparation for the prewedding virginity test. Conducted by the groom-to-be, her nineteen-year-old cousin who is a butcher, the "test" is successful, and the young man waves around the bloodied bandaged finger with which he has penetrated the girl, to the shouts of joy of the women and the firing of the uncles' guns.

Although narrated in the third person, much of the story is in the form of Zeina's spoken account to the child, with occasional reminders of Aisha's illicit presence: "Aisha was quiet. 'We ought to go to bed before your parents come back,' said her nanny. 'Oh no,' eyes enormous, 'they're at the ballet. They won't be back before twelve at least. Please, *please* go on. What happened next?' "[40] When Zeina describes the aunts pulling off her knickers, Aisha's response again reminds the reader of the force and *difference* of the parents' cultural mores and the way this heightens the child's (and the reader's) sense that the nurse's stories are "sensational" and "vulgar": "The little girl sat very still. She had the strangest, warmest, gentlest, tingling feeling between her legs and her heart was pounding in both fear and pleasure. This was forbidden. Her parents never ever said 'knickers,' always 'culottes' and her nurse, in deference to them, said 'kollott,' but now, now she was using the other, the 'vulgar' word."[41] "Her Man," which follows immediately from "The Wedding of Zeina," is also narrated in the third person, and Zeina is again the focus of the narrative, although this story is uninterrupted by the presence of Aisha. The story opens with Zeina ruefully contemplating her bad luck because her husband has just taken a younger second wife, Tahiyya, despite the fact that she (Zeina) is "young and full of youth and pretty, with eyelashes black as night even without kohl and a face fair and full of light and smooth as silk. What thighs. What legs."[42]

In the husband's absence, the women of the household counsel Zeina to contain her anger or risk losing her husband and remind her that "the shade of a man is better than that of a wall."[43] In the end, Zeina uses what might easily be described as "feminine wiles" to regain control of her marriage: when a storm sends the frightened younger wife to Zeina's room for comfort one night, Zeina's comforting caresses slide into full-scale seduction as she sees Tahiyya as she imagines her *husband* sees her in the act of love: "Tahiyya's eyes were closed, her mouth half open and her forehead gleamed with sweat. So this was what she was like with him. This was what he now found waiting in bed for him every night. It must make him feel really proud. Make him feel like the master of men. Zeina stopped stroking and pinched the inside of Tahiyya's thigh hard. The girl only moaned and shifted slightly opening her legs. Then Zeina had her idea."[44] Zeina continues to make love to the younger woman and, at the height of her pleasure, bites her hard enough to leave a bruise, which is then displayed, on her husband's return, as evidence of Tahiyya's infidelity. In "The Wedding of Zeina," the aunts use a similar wile: they bite the young Zeina's upper thigh to force her to open her legs for the virginity test. In both examples, women are presented as complicit in maintaining the very "traditions" that symbolize their oppression within patriarchal culture.

One could argue that these two stories present images of "the Third World woman" that fit precisely the exoticized, homogenized stereotype against which postcolonial feminists have argued so powerfully: "This average third world woman leads an essentially truncated life based on her feminine gender (read: ignorant, poor, uneducated, tradition-bound, domestic, family-oriented, victimized etc.). This, I suggest, is in contrast to the (implicit) self-representation of Western women as educated, as modern, as having control over their bodies and sexualities, and the freedom to make their own decisions."[45]

Indeed, Soueif said as much herself in an interview:

"The Wedding of Zeina" and "Her Man" were the first things I ever wrote, and at that time I wasn't really aware of "the politics of reception." . . . These are the two stories that I feel most distant from now, but they got me a lot of attention in England and were very popular. I think that in itself tells us something about this whole question. . . . It tells us, I suppose, that there is a certain amount of, I hesitate to use the term "exoticization," because again that wasn't something that I was doing consciously. *If it's there at all, it's because genuinely for me these stories describe an exotic world.* So, in the sense of what I was doing, I was doing something genuine and real. I was turning into fiction stories or fragments of stories that I had heard.[46]

In this comment, Soueif explicitly addresses the kinds of tensions that were implicit in Rhys's attempt to "translate" the cultural power she recognized in Meta's cultural world into that of Meta's fictive counterpart, Christophine, in *Wide Sargasso Sea. Aisha* was first published in 1983 when feminism was in expansive mode, receptive to representations of the "Other" woman but not yet anxiously questioning how that "Other woman" might be encountered, recognized—or heard. The emphasis on finding a voice in the heyday of 1980s literary feminism often rested on an assumption of transparency of "voice." Clearly such "innocent representation" has been called into question by a variety of theorists and critics, and these interventions, as I argued at the start of this chapter, have made a definitive impact on feminist inquiry. Nonetheless, Soueif's equivocation above and the anxious tone of her commentary on some of the stories in *Aisha* indicate the continuing difficulty of staging encounters between women and expose the knotty intimacies that must be negotiated if we take seriously Said's suggestion that "we are, so to speak, of the connections, not outside and beyond them." But it perhaps also exposes the limited range of "connections" implied in Said's arguments and foregrounds the risks Soueif takes in writing cultural differences when these are experienced "up close and personal" in the home—and then disseminated widely "abroad."

In a review of *Aisha,* Said wrote, "There is a remarkably productive, somewhat depressing tension between the anecdotal surface of modern, Westernised Egyptian life and the troubling, often violent but always persisting traditional forms beneath. . . . Instead of politics we are given strange dislocations that are caused by that unresolved tension between what is traditionally Muslim and Egyptian and what is Western and modern."[47]

In reading the distinction between the "modern" and the "traditional" in the Egyptian cultures in *Aisha* as one between "surface" and what lies "beneath," Said elides Soueif's deliberate juxtapositions and connections in the collection. Compounding this oversight, he implies that Soueif presents these encounters between "traditionally Muslim" and "Western and modern" worlds as *apolitical* ("instead of politics"). The obvious (and troubling) implication is that feminism isn't politics and that sexual politics had no impact on the ideology of imperialism, colonialism, or nationalism. In his review of *Aisha,* Said appears unable to see the unresolved tensions in the stories as a productive space in which "the modern" and "tradition" connect and from which a broader political platform might be imagined.

I prefer to read the tension between the "worlds" in *Aisha* less censoriously than either Saïd or Soueif suggests. In the last story in the collection, significantly titled "The Nativity," Soueif takes the encounter between the worlds of tradition and modernity—as signified by Zeina and Aisha, respectively—to a dramatic conclusion. In this story, Aisha is unhappily married and childless and is being pressured by her family and by Zeina to try to correct the latter circumstance and, in the process, perhaps save the marriage. The wider implication of this situation is that despite differences of class and culture, the two women share experiences of gendered oppression. Zeina persuades Aisha to visit the shrine of Sidi Abul Suoud, dismissing the suggestion that stories of saints and masters belong to childhood: "They're our familiars, my darling, our masters. And we have to please them or they clamp on our heads and never let us rest. You know all this. I've told you a thousand stories since you were tiny. And you used to listen and ask for more."[48] When they visit the shrine, Aisha is exposed to a world she has so far encountered only via the *Arabian Nights.* Watching women supplicants dancing in various states of rapture, she whispers to herself, "It's a Bacchanalia," and in another scene she takes herself to task for attempting to draw parallels between the dance and a poem she's memorized: "Aisha, you know so much more about Art than Life." This interpretation is then extended more sternly in the "voice-over" that (indicated by the use of italics) frames this story and intervenes with an authoritative commentary at crucial moments: "Yes. How strange that you should have read about it; that as a child you should have brooded over pictures in big, fat books. While I waited. All those years I waited. And then you dismissed it all. You decided it was a world that had happened long ago, long ago in far-off places. *By what right did you decide? With what knowledge?* And now? Will you see that it is here? That all the time it was here? On your doorstep, waiting for you?"[49] The identity of this superomniscient narrator is never explicitly revealed, but he performs as the voice of one of the masters "riding" Aisha. Said finds this device unconvincing, "as if the author had decided that she couldn't leave Aisha to descriptive realism but at the last minute had to point out the presence of a significant narrative process."[50] Although the use of this "voice-over" is slightly awkward, its function as a "significant narrative process" is more suggestive than Said implies, for it maps precisely the limits of realism for the writer who seeks to negotiate between worlds long held separate by definitive conventions for representation.

The dénouement of "The Nativity" takes Aisha's encounter with "traditional" Egyptian culture further: a butcher, Farag, helps Aisha and Zeina make their way through the crowd and offers to introduce Aisha to the nativity of Sidi Ali. Aisha agrees to meet him, ignoring Zeina's warnings: "He's not like men you know. He's not like those foreigners or the boys at school or the Gezira Club. You don't know anything about this type. I *come* from a family of butchers and I know how their minds work."[51] Farag rapes Aisha, and the story ends dramatically with Aisha, now pregnant, on a hospital bed struggling for her life.[52] The penalty for transgressing sociocultural boundaries is presented in stark terms. And, although this approach may resonate with Said's comment that "Soueif is perhaps uncritically attached to the idea of making each story build to a final, usually clever 'point,'"[53] I prefer to emphasize the way in which this narrative impasse indicates the difficulties and risks of representation that Soueif had to negotiate in staging this cultural encounter— however unsatisfactory its execution and dénouement.

In a review of Said's memoir, *Out of Place*, Soueif draws parallels between the circumstances of Said's life and hers: "Said is there just ahead of me. And other things too: the life lived simultaneously in English and Arabic, the imagining of oneself into the comics or novels we read, *the response to the different and authentic energy in the conversation and company of maids and drivers.*"[54]

Both Said and Soueif have, in various places, acknowledged the privileged circumstances of their respective backgrounds. Both writers have also worked, with commitment and persistence, to establish political affiliations beyond this privilege: Said, in his extensive writing on Palestine; and Soueif, in her biting journalism on the recent "wars on terror." Bearing such dedicated work in mind, I believe that a more accommodating critical response is demanded than Soueif herself offers in a retrospective comment on the two stories in *Aisha*: "But, reading them now, I can see that they do present Egypt or the East in terms that perhaps the West is comfortable with: as a world that is very traditional, very close to magic, ritualistic, a little brutal, and very sensual—our world as perceived by aficionados of the *Arabian Nights*. And that is possibly why they struck a chord immediately. Because, that was the Eastern world that the West was comfortable with and wanted to read about."[55]

Soueif's self-critique is clearly well intended; as she says earlier in this interview: "I wasn't really aware of 'the politics of reception.'" But her disavowal of these two stories is also marked by ambivalence: she hesitates over applying the word *exoticization* to these stories because, "*If it's there at all, it's because genuinely for me these stories describe an exotic world.*" Again, I think we can read these tensions more generously and recognize the desire for connections across class boundaries (however flawed). Perhaps in doing so we may also refuse to be hijacked by the monotonous and predictable argument about delivering "what the West wants to hear." Perhaps, too, we may become more attuned to other kinds of "worldliness," allowing the worldly wisdom of figures such as Christophine and Zeina to impact the more familiar and stylish worldliness of the cosmopolitan exile in postcolonial discourse?

Said's memoir, *Out of Place*, resonates intriguingly with Soueif's concerns in *Aisha*.[56] Said's preface begins, "*Out of Place* is a record of an essentially lost or forgotten world" and then describes the processes and journeys he undertook in writing the book.[57] He describes a visit to his former neighbors during a trip to Cairo in 1998, during which he was told that somebody was waiting in the kitchen to see him. Said quickly recognized the "small, wiry man" dressed in the style of an "Upper Egyptian peasant" as Ahmad Hamed, "our *suffragi* (butler) for almost three decades, an ironic, fanatically honest and loyal man whom we had all considered a member of the family."[58] Ahmad did not immediately recognize Said: "No, Edward was tall, and he wore glasses. This isn't Edward." Eventually Edward convinced Ahmad of his identity:

> Suddenly we fell into each other's arms, sobbing with the tears of happy reunion and a mourned, irrecoverable time. He talked about how he had carried me on his shoulders, how we had chatted in the kitchen, how the family celebrated Christmas and New Year's, and so on. *I was astounded that Ahmad so minutely remembered* not only the seven of us—parents and five children—but also each of my aunts, uncles, and cousins, and my grandmother, in addition to a few family friends. And then, *as the past poured out of him,* an old man retired to the distant town of Edfu near Aswan, I knew again how fragile, precious, and fleeting were the history and circumstances not only gone forever, but basically unrecalled and unrecorded except as occasional reminiscence or intermittent conversation. This chance encounter made me feel even more strongly that this book . . . had some validity as an unofficial personal record of those tumultuous years in the Middle East.[59]

Said does not provide much information about Ahmad Hamed other than describing his role as the family's *suffragi* and telling us that Ahmad is now retired and is dressed in the style of a peasant (in dark robe and turban). But the emotional intensity of the meeting is remarkable. This intensity stands out from the cool detachment of the prose in the body of the memoir: no other encounter is described with such immediacy and drama (though clearly the text documents many highly charged situations and relationships). Throughout the memoir, Said refers to various drivers, servants, and cooks, but although these references are always warm and affectionate, they are seldom detailed and never sustained. Given the relatively fleeting and undocumented presence of servants in the memoir, the encounter between Said and Hamed, so dramatically evoked in the preface, resonates even more intriguingly. Said's suggestion, for instance, that Hamed was "considered a member of the family" seems uncharacteristically naïve, given the importance he ascribes to "family" (the "proper" family) in shaping his life. The trope of "the family" is deployed habitually in several postcolonial texts in describing the accommodation or appropriation of servants, so Said's reference to the family is unsurprising in this context. The disappointment is that the encounter between Said and Hamed is not staged more centrally, and its implications assessed more thoroughly, which could have rendered a more textured and more complete picture of the loss of home and homeland in Palestine that Said otherwise documents so thoughtfully. And why, given Hamed's intimate connection with the Said family and involvement in the daily running of the household, was Said so astounded that Hamed remembered him and his entire extended family in such detail? Said's statement that "the past poured out of him" is also interesting, suggesting an elemental, natural quality to Hamed's delivery of stories about the past and a sense that he operates *as* the past for Said. If Hamed is figured as embodying the past, it is through a *spoken*, and therefore elusive, account of the past. Said's words suggest the ephemeral nature of the oral: "fragile, precious, and fleeting . . . not only gone forever, but basically unrecalled and unrecorded except as occasional reminiscence or intermittent conversation."[60] The impetus for the memoir, then, is consolidated around an idea of recalling, recording, and documenting an idea of the past that Hamed symbolizes so intensely.

In her 2002 memoir, *In Search of Fatima*, Ghada Karmi implies an even more intense association of the past with the family servant, Fatima.[61] Karmi explicitly consolidates her memories of home and homeland in the figure of Fatima: "It was a curious thing, when I look back, that not long after we reached Damascus no one spoke about Fatima or Muhammad or the house or even Jerusalem. It was as if only I preserved their memory. . . . My allegiance to Fatima, to our house and to my childhood became a private affair, my secret to cherish and protect."[62] Karmi does not "find" Fatima in this memoir ("Our house was dead, like Fatima, like poor Rex [the family's dog], like us."[63] But the inscription of Fatima as a central figure in the narrative, structuring the painful quest to return home—and to the homeland—recognizes the importance of the personal in shaping the political and in connecting the meanings of "home" and "homeland." Said recognized precisely this connectedness in the blurb he provided for Karmi's memoir, noting that it "has a wonderfully subtle way of showing how in thousands of different ways the political and the personal intermesh." Karmi's memoir, then, provides a productive intertext with Said's. Although her text does not provide a detailed and sustained account of Fatima's life, it does signal an awareness of the intimate imbrication of Fatima's life in her own and a desire to recognize and inscribe that connection.

In "Edward Said and the Politics of Dispossession," Karmi again draws attention to the role of servants. In this testimonial, Karmi argues that "the general parameters of Arab existence were inescapably colonialist. . . . These influences dominated his upbringing. When the Said family left Jerusalem in 1947, they went to Cairo where he attended an English-style school. *Arabic was forbidden at home, except when speaking to the servants.* As Said himself noted, during his adolescent years this caused a split in his sense of identity, from which he never recovered."[64]

Said's work responds to this "split" in manifestly diverse ways, but I draw attention to one trajectory *not* taken, less to critique than to extend Said's ongoing relevance. Toward the end of the preface to his memoir, Said concludes that "the main reason . . . for this memoir is of course the need to bridge the sheer distance in time and place between my life today and my life then."[65]

The "sheer distance" between "now" and "then," "here" and "there" is crystallized in the emotional encounter between Said and Hamed. That Said could not speak or write about—or chose to leave unspoken—the resonances and implications of this encounter may indicate the difficulties of negotiating "difference" when it is located so close to home. It may also be a consequence of Said's primary focus in the memoir on that bigger loss of *homeland*—and the huge political implications of that loss. Indeed, *Out of Place* shows that recognition of the Palestinian cause was a powerful point of return and reconnection for Said. However, I suggest that the encounter between Said and Hamed, the family *suffragi*, resonates beyond its designated place in the preface, where it is figured as "a prompt," endorsing the author's reason to write. The problems of comparing across the genres of fiction and memoir notwithstanding, one cannot help but read Soueif's complex representation of the servant figure as evidence of a commitment to exploring the kind of personal and intimate connections that Said tends to sidestep in *Out of Place*. It is also tempting to attribute Soueif's willingness *to get close to* the other, to use Sarah Ahmed's phrase, as much to gendered differences between the authors and texts as to generic differences. In Soueif's *Aisha,* the gendered oppression of women provides a connection that cuts across class differences, though it does not erase those differences. Said's memoir appears strangely uncurious and unreflective about the lives of the servants whose presences regularly punctuate the text. The "unresolved tension" between "the modern" and "the traditional" that Said refers to in his review of *Aisha* cannot simply be resolved textually: fiction and memoir are necessarily privileged genres, but they can resonate with the presence(s) of subjects historically excluded from such privileged textual forms. So, although Said's work does not offer us dedicated attention to questions of gender or explorations of the kind of close encounters across class differences that Rhys's and Soueif's texts focus upon, his oeuvre, in all its contradictory richness, remains suggestive for postcolonial feminisms. Said's insistence on the connectedness of cultures and on the need to affiliate beyond the immediate circumstances of one's nativity may not have engendered affiliations in his work that are as close to "home" as we may want. But his insights continue to

provide resonant clues for reading across difference and extending affiliative possibilities in our own critical practices as postcolonial feminists. In that process, perhaps, we can also affiliate Said closer to home.

NOTES

Epigraphs: Edward Said, *Culture and Imperialism* (London: Vintage, 1994 [1993]), 65, my emphasis;
Minoli Salgado, "Heart," *Wasafiri*, no. 42 (Summer 2004): 42, my emphasis.

1. Said, *Culture and Imperialism*, 64, 65.

2. Ibid., 277. Of course, Said's writing on Palestine focuses heavily on the specific realities of Palestinians, but his writing about *writing* seldom incorporated this material.

3. Mildred Mortimer, "Said and Djebar: A Contrapuntal Reading," *Research in African Literatures*
36, no. 3 (2005): 55.

4. David Lloyd, "La Rigeur Dans Le Desepoir," in "Edward Said: Tributes," ed. Amitava Kumar and
Michael Ryan, special issue, *Politics and Culture*, no. 1 (2004), http://aspen.conncoll.edu/politicsand
culture/page.cfm?key=301 (accessed 13 July 2009).

5. L. H. M. Ling, "Said's Exile: Strategic Insights for Postcolonial Feminists," *Millennium Journal of
International Studies*, no. 36 (2007): 136.

6. Reina Lewis, *Gendering Orientalism: Race, Femininity and Representation* (London: Routledge,
1996), 17.

7. Valerie Kennedy, *Edward Said: A Critical Introduction* (Cambridge: Polity Press, 2000), 43–44.

8. Raymond Williams, "Appendix: Media, Margins and Modernity (Raymond Williams and Edward
Said)," in *The Politics of Modernism: Against the New Conformists*, ed. Raymond Williams (London: Verso,
1994 [1989]), 265–73.

9. See Jane Miller, *Seductions: Studies in Reading and Culture* (London: Virago, 1990); and Sara Mills,
Discourses of Difference: An Analysis of Women's Travel Writing and Colonialism (London: Routledge,
1991).

10. Kennedy, *Edward Said*, 44.

11. Marnia Lazreg, "The Triumphant Discourse of Global Feminism: Should Other Women Be
Known?" in *Going Global: The Transnational Reception of Third World Women Writers*, ed. A. Amireh
and L. Suhair Majaj (New York: Garland, 2000), 37–38, my emphasis.

12. Vron Ware, "What Other Way to Speak?" (paper presented at Women and Others: Re-thinking
Gender, Race, and Empire, a symposium at the University of Alabama, Tuscaloosa, 2005).

13. Sarah Ahmed, *Strange Encounters: Embodied Others in Postcoloniality* (London: Routledge, 2000),
166–67, emphasis in original.

14. Ibid., 177.

15. If, as the quotation marks indicate, an idea of "the people" is a constructed one, this fact may
help explain the drift away from class as a major focus within postcolonial studies.

16. Bruce Robbins, *The Servant's Hand: English Fiction from Below* (Durham, NC: Duke University
Press, 1993), 59.

17. Ibid., 8, 9.

18. Ibid., 8, 9, 19, my emphasis.

19. Said, *Culture and Imperialism*, 75.

20. I am aware that in Spivak's argument, the servant would not, strictly speaking, be deemed subaltern but would more properly be described as a "domesticated other." See "Three Women's Texts and
a Critique of Feminism," in *Race, Writing and Difference*, ed. Henry Louis Gates, Jr. (Chicago: University of Chicago Press, 1985), 243–61.

21. Jean Rhys, *Wide Sargasso Sea* (London: Penguin, 1983 [1966]).

22. E. K. Brathwaite, "A Post-cautionary Tale of the Helen of our Wars," *Wasafiri* 11, no. 22 (Spring 1995): 69–78.

23. Benita Parry, "Problems in Current Theories of Colonial Discourse," in *Postcolonial Studies: A Materialist Critique* (London, Routledge, 2004), 23, 22.

24. Jonathon Culler, "The Literary in Theory," in *What's Left of Theory: New Work on the Politics of Literary Theory,* ed. J. Butler, J. Guillory, and K. Thomas (London: Routledge, 2000), 281.

25. Rhys, *Wide Sargasso Sea*, 91, 71, 133.

26. Ibid., 131.

27. Ibid.

28. F. Wyndham and D. Melly, eds., *Jean Rhys Letters: 1931–1966* (London: Andre Deutsch, 1984), 297.

29. Jean Rhys, *Smile Please: An Unfinished Autobiography* (London: Penguin, 1984 [1979]), 29, my emphasis.

30. Ibid., 31–32.

31. Ibid., 32.

32. See, for example, the account by Phyllis Shand Allfrey, a Dominican writer and friend of Rhys's, of the prohibition on speaking patois. Indeed, Allfrey's father was a member of the League for the Suppression of Patois. Lizabeth Paravisini-Gebert, *Phyllis Shand Allfrey: A Caribbean Life* (New Brunswick, NJ: Rutgers University Press, 1996), 26.

33. Rhys, *Smile Please,* 28.

34. Ahdaf Soueif, *Aisha* (London: Bloomsbury, 1995 [1983]).

35. Soueif, "Knowing," in *Aisha,* 63.

36. Ibid., 79.

37. Edward W. Said, *Orientalism* (London: Penguin, 1987), 164.

38. Soueif, "Knowing," 87.

39. Soueif, "The Nativity," in *Aisha,* 141.

40. Soueif, "The Wedding of Zeina," in *Aisha,* 89.

41. Ibid., 88.

42. Soueif, "Her Man," in *Aisha,* 95.

43. Ibid., 98.

44. Ibid., 107.

45. Chandra Mohanty, "Under Western Eyes: Feminist Scholarship and Colonial Discourses," *Feminist Review* 30, no. 1 (1988): 61–88, 65; (1991): 56.

46. Joseph Massad, "The Politics of Desire in the Writings of Ahdaf Soueif," *Journal of Palestinian Literature* 28, no. 4 (Summer 1999): 74–90, 86, my emphasis.

47. Edward W. Said, "Edward Said Writes about a New Literature of the Arab World," *London Review of Books,* 7–20 July 1983, 8.

48. Soueif, "The Nativity," in *Aisha,* 142.

49. Ibid., 147, 156, 147, my emphasis.

50. Said, "Edward Said Writes," 8.

51. Soueif, "The Nativity," 167.

52. The story renders the rape in less blunt, more ambiguous terms than this summary suggests.

53. Said, "Edward Said Writes," 8.

54. Ahdaf Soueif, "Becoming Edward Said," *Mezza Terra* (London: Bloomsbury, 2004), 255, my emphasis.

55. Ahdaf Soueif in Joseph Massad, "The Politics of Desire in the Writings of Ahdaf Soueif," *Journal of Palestinian Literature* 28, no. 4 (Summer 1999): 86.

56. Edward Said, *Out of Place: A Memoir* (London: Granta, 1999).

57. Ibid., xi.

58. Ibid., xii.

59. Ibid., xiii, my emphasis.

60. Ibid., xv.

61. Ghada Karmi, *In Search of Fatima: A Palestinian Story* (London: Verso, 2002).

62. Ibid., 139.

63. Ibid., 450.

64. Ghada Karmi, "Edward Said and the Politics of Dispossession," *Al-Ahram Weekly,* 9–15 October 2003, http://weekly.ahram.org.eg/2003/659/op13.htm.

65. Said, *Out of Place,* xiv.

8

Translating Heroism

Locating Edward Said on Ahdaf Soueif's The Map of Love

Katherine Callen King

Edward Said asserts in *Orientalism* that he, unlike Michel Foucault, believes in the "determining imprint of individual writers upon the otherwise anonymous collective body of texts constituting a discursive formation like Orientalism."[1] This imprint justifies paying a lot of attention to individual authors, not only of scholarly but also of literary work, so that one can detail "the dialectic between text or writer and the complex collective formation to which [the] work is a contribution."[2] When he turns to the modern American version of Orientalism, he laments the fact that its "social-science" approach utterly neglects the literature of the cultures it is interpreting. Such neglect is unfortunate, he says: "Since an Arab poet or novelist . . . writes of [their] experiences, of [their] values, of [their] humanity (however strange that may be), [their work] effectively disrupts the various patterns (images, clichés, abstractions) by which the Orient is represented. A literary text speaks more or less directly of a living reality . . . its force is in the power and vitality of words that, to mix in Flaubert's metaphor . . . tip the idols out of the Orientalists' arms and make them drop those great paralytic children—which are their ideas of the Orient— that attempt to pass for the Orient."[3]

In his 1994 afterword Said discusses several creative writers, such as Salman Rushdie, C. L. R. James, Aimé Césaire, Derek Walcott, and the Irish collective Field Day, whose work has reappropriated the historical experience of colonialism and transformed that which had been based on the geographical separation of peoples into "a new aesthetic of sharing and often transcendent re-formulation."[4] He thus implies that poetry, fiction, and drama do the same work as criticism and theory, but perhaps with more "power and vitality."

Edward Said met Egyptian novelist and scholar Ahdaf Soueif in 1981 and quickly became both her personal friend and her intellectual mentor. As Soueif said recently in a lecture at Georgetown University, "I listened to him speak and was consciously learning from him . . . his positions were some of the major things I was interested in, and so I was greatly influenced by him."[5] This influence is clear in her novel *The Map of Love,* her "homage to Edward," which vividly subverts several specific Orientalist paradigms that Said exposed.[6] Impressed as much by his character—"his inclusivity, all encompassing humanity, and enthusiasm"—as by his intellectual and political positions, Soueif not only infuses her narrative with Said's critical theory but also creates two heroic protagonists to embody the man himself.[7] I am interested in exploring both the resulting heroization of Said and the activist implications of translating this controversial public intellectual into accessible fiction.

Soueif's novel weaves a love story into the political struggle between imperialist Britain and occupied Egypt at the turn of the twentieth century. Both the love and the struggle are echoed by parallel contemporary events near the turn of the twenty-first century. The novel's political themes include racism, sexism, diaspora, and oppression, both internal (by fundamentalist religion and the police) and external (by the Ottoman, French, and English forces, and, currently, the World Bank). The love story adds, on a more optimistic note, the theme of border crossing through cross-cultural relationships and translation (of Arabic into English, of Islamic culture to the "West"). The love story seduces; the political one is a call to action.

The story contains many "heroes," who in this novel are those who are open to other cultures and speak out against injustice. One of them is Amal al-Ghamrawi, the narrator, who re-creates an episode in her family's history at the turn of the twentieth century and thereby develops the strength to fight injustices in modern-day Cairo. Amal re-creates history by translating, organizing, and setting in context ninety-year-old letters and diaries brought to her in Cairo by a long-lost American cousin, Isabel Parkman, who becomes a vehicle for much of the modern-day cross-cultural translation. Both women find counterparts in the story that Amal half translates, half imagines about their forebears: a "heroic" English woman, Anna Winterbourne (Isabel's great-grandmother), who comes to Egypt in 1900; and a "heroic" Egyptian woman, Layla al-Baroudi (Amal's grandmother), an activist for women's rights. The two women develop an intimate friendship, and when Anna marries Layla's lawyer brother, Sharif al-Baroudi, they live as sisters until Sharif's assassination some eleven years later.

Culturally open yet with a fierce desire for national independence and social justice, Sharif al-Baroudi is the character who comes closest to being a genuine hero in *anyone's* book. He is a darkly handsome romance figure transposed into a politically deromanticized Egypt, a Byronic hero who wields his knowledge of the law like a scimitar and puts himself in the front line of danger through his principled and unremitting eloquence. Like Layla and Anna, Sharif has a modern counterpart, Amal's brother, 'Omar, a charismatic Arab American pianist, renowned New

York conductor, and political activist. Although somewhat less developed than Sharif, 'Omar shares his grand-uncle's fearless dedication to social justice and national independence, in this case for Palestine, his mother's homeland. As we will see, both fictional heroes share much with the renowned scholar, music critic, and tireless Palestinian activist to whom this volume of essays is dedicated.

Soueif introduces her reader to key Saidean ideas that undergird the novel's political poetics through Sharif al-Baroudi. Near the beginning of his relationship with Anna, Sharif asks, "Which is better? To take action and perhaps make a fatal mistake—or to take no action and die slowly anyway?" Anna's answer reveals that she is his true intellectual partner: "I believe you have to know yourself first—above all."[8] How is this answer relevant to the question? Consider Antonio Gramsci's Delphic dictum: "The starting-point of critical elaboration is the consciousness of what one really is and is 'knowing thyself' as a product of the historical process to date, which has deposited in you an infinity of traces without leaving an inventory. . . . Therefore it is imperative at the outset to compile such an inventory."[9]

Said quotes this passage in his introduction to *Orientalism* to explain that in "many ways my study of Orientalism has been an attempt to inventory the traces upon me, the Oriental subject, of the culture whose domination has been so powerful a factor in the life of all Orientals."[10] So too throughout *The Map of Love*, Soueif shows Egyptians debating who they are, drawing both on history and on current events, and she shows Amal continually researching a little-studied period between two well-known revolutions and similarly moving back and forth between past and present.[11] To increase her capacity to imagine the past and thus to make Anna's story truly visible to Isabel, Amal spends hours delving into newspaper archives for print stories and microfilmed photos that will uncover political realities normally hidden from a tourist's view. Soueif thereby makes the point that understanding these political realities is a conscious process that takes hard work, whether one is Egyptian or a foreigner, showing through the "powerful and vital" medium of fiction what Said demonstrates through literary criticism: there is no "essence," either "Oriental" or "Western," that can be automatically known.[12] Because Amal is the one making discoveries, we might say that the novel is "compiling an inventory" for Egyptian readers, but it is also, very importantly at this moment in time, "compiling an inventory" for readers in England and America.[13] As Amal learns more about her history, as tourists Anna and Isabel get to know Egyptians better, so too do "Occidental subjects" get to know both Egyptians and themselves better.

Near the end of the novel Soueif has Sharif al-Baroudi write an article that, given its fictional date of 1911, could well be interpreted as a blueprint for Said's *Orientalism*. Sharif writes that the East holds two attractions for the West: an Economic desire for resources and a yearning—be it Religious, Historical, and/or Romantic— for the land of the Scriptures, the Ancients, exotic Fable.[14] He delineates four typical reactions to the *reality* of Egypt that are very similar to Said's analysis of travel literature and the pronouncements of politicians, and then, like Said, he shows how religious, historical, and romantic feeling actually serve the economic interest.[15] Also like Said, Sharif talks about the invisibility of real modern Egyptians to the European eye and about Europeans' insistence that intellectual Egyptians get their ideas from elsewhere and are not representative of the mass of their people.[16] We can compare this analysis to Said's in *Orientalism:* "Thus any deviation from what were considered the norms of Oriental behavior was believed to be unnatural; Cromer's last annual report from Egypt consequently proclaimed Egyptian nationalism to be an 'entirely novel idea' and 'a plant of exotic rather than of indigenous growth.'"[17]

Finally, again like Said, Sharif concludes his article with a plea to end the felt division between "East" and "West" that imperialism has promoted: "If there are elements of Western Culture in us, they have been absorbed through visiting your countries, learning in your institutions and opening ourselves to your culture. There we have been free to choose those elements that most suited *our own* history, *our* traditions and aspirations—that is the legitimate commerce of humanity. Our only hope now—and it is a small one—lies in a unity of conscience between the people of the world for whom this phrase itself would carry any meaning."[18]

Said's work similarly affirms that "cultures and civilizations are so interrelated and interdependent as to beggar any unitary or simply-delineated description of their individuality," and he praises the "idea of rethinking and re-formulating historical experiences which had once been based on the geographical separation of peoples and cultures."[19] Said concludes the original 1978 version of *Orientalism* with the following vision: "Without 'the Orient' there would be scholars, critics, intellectuals, human beings, for whom the racial, ethnic, and national distinctions were less important than the common enterprise of promoting human community."[20]

Soueif's Sharif qualifies his vision of hope with the phrase "it is a small one."[21] In his chapter "Orientalism Now" and in his afterword, Said demonstrates both that such a hope for unity exists and that it remains nearly as small at the end of the twentieth century as it was at its beginning.[22] Noting that "systems of thought like Orientalism, discourses of power, ideological fictions—mind-forg'd manacles— are all too easily made, applied, and guarded," he cautions that the "answer to Orientalism is not Occidentalism. No former 'Oriental' will be comforted by the thought that having been an Oriental himself he is likely—too likely—to study new 'Orientals'—or 'Occidentals'—of his own making."[23]

Some have not heard and others have not heeded Said's warning, and the world is currently experiencing some horrific effects of a clash between Orientalism and an equally virulent Occidentalism. Soueif, perhaps alerted by the dismaying Islamist response to *Orientalism,*[24] seeks to prevent her readers from replacing the manacles of Orientalism with those of Occidentalism by bringing to life a cadre of historical English and French progressives. Anna's letters mention, sometimes merely in passing, at least sixteen men and women who are sympathetic to the Egyptian

people, describing them at dinner parties, in Parliament, and in the press vocifer-
ously opposing the hypocrisy, cruelty, and shortsightedness of the Empire's overseas policies. In addition to re-creating this "living reality," Soueif twice has her characters draw an explicit moral from the existence of this group of European "heroes."
First, when Anna weeps over the unjust executions, imprisonments, and whippings
of the men of Denshwai and says she is ashamed of being British, Sharif responds,
"No. . . . This is not to do with being British. [Prosecutor] Al-Hilbawi is Egyptian,
and so is [Judge] Ahmad Fathi Zaghloul. And your Mr. Barrington and Mr. Blunt
are British."[25] Later Anna plans to translate Theodore Rothstein's book into Arabic
because "even if it contains nothing that is new to the Egyptians, it should serve to
remind them that not all Englishmen are their enemies."[26]

Although *The Map of Love* may at this point seem to be simply an extended political tract, it is very much more than that. Soueif makes her (and Said's) political
message emanate naturally from the living, breathing reality of compellingly complex characters. Sharif and Anna in particular are not only complex but they engage in a wonderfully romantic love affair and then a marriage that, by intermingling deep sensuality with equally deep intellectuality, demonstrates that heeding
Said's call to eliminate the "East/West" dichotomy can be sexy on all levels. Just as
romance served the colonial purpose of economic exploitation, so Soueif makes
romance serve her postcolonial one of liberation. As Hala Halim has observed,
"Given the current trend of translating nineteenth-century Orientalist texts into
Arabic, *The Map of Love* will provide an admirable example of how one Egyptian
writer has re-written this material to produce her own counter-narrative."[27]

Most readers probably do not need Soueif to point out that Sharif-al Baroudi's
literary lineage is the Brontë sisters' "Mr. Rochester and Heathcliff, and all the characters we find in [early twentieth-century romance] novels—tall, dark, handsome,
enigmatic, a stranger, proud, aloof, yet [with] depths of sensitivity and empathy and
passion and tenderness, and so on."[28] Soueif has translated this generic romance
figure into "a real genuine Egyptian" and she uses Amal, translator of English novels, to draw her readers' attention to this fact: "In Layla's account of [Sharif] I see
my own brother, and in Anna's I find the dark, enigmatic hero of Romance."[29] English and American readers will recognize this hero and therefore will feel that they
are allowed to read this Arab hero at least partly through their "Western" perspective. In turn, Arab readers who have read recent translations of romance novels may
be pleased to find an Egyptian who is really Egyptian in a role that, according to
Soueif, often is filled by a "completely fake" Easterner.[30]

Through Sharif, Soueif gilds her modern activist with Romance, and through
'Omar, Soueif manages to gild Said himself. In addition to having Amal "see" her
brother in Layla's account of Sharif and having Isabel "see" 'Omar in Sharif's portrait,[31] Soueif deploys several parallel details to force her reader to connect her two
fictional figures. For example, Sharif ends his first "arranged" marriage after six

months because of intellectual incompatibility—one of Soueif's feminist touches—but he is able to secure his bride's family's honorable consent only because of the political danger his family faces after the 1882 uprising in which Sharif's father and uncle participated.[32] Similarly, 'Omar's first short marriage ends with the 1967 Israeli-Arab war, when, as 'Omar explains to his mother, both he and his wife "discovered I was an Arab."[33]

Soueif slyly has Amal consider speaking to 'Omar about editing and republishing Sharif's article under his own name.[34] In this way, we return to Said via 'Omar. Soueif gives 'Omar a Jerusalem birthplace to match Said's.[35] Her character, like Said, identifies as Egyptian, American, and Palestinian.[36] 'Omar, a concert pianist, is the charismatic conductor of the New York Philharmonic, which led one internet wag to term 'Omar a combination of Said and Zubin Mehta. True, but those who read *The Nation* also know Said as a concert pianist and music critic in his own right.[37] 'Omar's literary output will also have a familiar ring to fans—or foes—of Edward Said: Soueif says that 'Omar has written three books on the Palestinian question: *The Politics of Culture, A State of Terror,* and *Borders and Refuge.*[38] Soueif portrays him as an activist in the Palestinian cause, not only through his writing but also through free concerts in Ghazzah, Jericho, and Qana.[39]

Sharif and 'Omar share with Said an activism against Occupation, and they also share his refusal either to make concessions to public opinion or to adhere blindly to a party or nationalist group. Said was an advisor to Yasir Arafat in the 1970s and 1980s but refused to join the Palestine Liberation Organization. He joined the Palestine National Council (PNC), of which Arafat was chair, in 1977, but he resigned in 1991, citing lack of democratic process. In 1993 he denounced Arafat's signing of the Oslo accords, calling instead for a single secular state to which Palestinians who had been expelled in 1948 could return. Said thus became persona non grata not only to Zionists but also to Arafat's supporters and to Hamas's Islamists.[40] As Said's alter ego, 'Omar has a similar experience: "And then, with the world celebrating another diplomatic triumph, another reluctant handshake on the White House lawn, he broke with the PNC. He was the spectre at the party, telling anyone who would listen that Oslo would not work, could not work."[41]

A few pages later, fictional year 1997, 'Omar is in Ramallah at the Conference of National Unity sponsored by the Palestinian Authority. Amal comments that her brother "hates seeing the Resistance turn into the Authority," and continues, "My brother speaks his mind, and he speaks it where it will be heard—and dangerous."[42] When 'Omar returns from the conference, he condemns Arafat for having eleven security forces and for using "torture and bonebreaking just as much as the Israelis."[43] He asserts that Hamas is now the only political party with credibility, but he cannot support it: "One cannot approve of fundamentalists—of whatever persuasion."[44] Such sentiments will be familiar to anyone who has kept up with Said's political writing.

By creating both ancient and modern "Saids," Soueif roots contemporary events in the Egyptian tradition of resistance to oppression. According to Said, such intellectual roots are important because "a standard imperialist misrepresentation has it that exclusively Western ideas of freedom led the fight against colonial rule, which mischievously overlooks the reserves in Indian and Arab culture that *always* resisted imperialism, and [it] claims the fight against imperialism as one of imperialism's major triumphs."[45] Soueif puts the lie to such misrepresentation by returning again and again to the 1882 nationalist revolution against British domination led by Egypt's Colonel Ahmed 'Urabi and Mahmoud Sami Pasha al-Baroudi (a historical figure who appears as Sharif's uncle in the novel).[46] This revolution demanded, according to one of Soueif's modern Egyptians, "the ending of foreign influence, the payment of the Egyptian debt . . . an elected parliament, a national industry, equality before the law, reform of education, and allowing a free press to reflect all shades of opinion."[47] It was put down by the British, who then sent in Lord Cromer to head a colonial government that lasted over seventy years. Soueif also mentions the 1919 revolution, in which she makes Layla an active participant, and the student movements of the 1970s as part of the indigenous tradition of struggle for freedom and democracy.[48]

Imperialist ideologies often claim to bring backward countries into the modern era, but Soueif points out that for Egypt, at least, imperialism did just the opposite.[49] Egyptian men like Sharif—and women like his sister Layla—attempt to set up cultural institutions, reform the legal code, and emancipate women, but they are thwarted by Cromer at every step.[50] As Soueif pointed out in a talk on *The Map of Love*, "Colleges of engineering and agriculture, and so on, were all instituted by Mohammed Ali, back in the thirties and the forties of the nineteenth century. The great drive toward modernisation was being carried out bit by bit during the nineteenth century, and it was really with the British occupation that it came to a stop."[51] Sharif, one of whose projects is an art institute, expresses anger that the British budget will fund some technical education "to produce clerks and workers," but "it does not permit an extra piastre for any project to do with culture or education."[52] She depicts him as frustrated at the "time . . . being lost. The generations that should have been educated, the industries that should have been introduced, the laws that should have been reformed."[53]

The effects of Occupation continue to retard legal reform today. Soueif prefigures the modern situation in a scene in which the wealthy Prince Yusuf says that he is reluctant to use his private fortune to fund the art school because of Islamist opposition, to whom such a donation would signify "collusion with the British to import evil European arts into the country, to train our young men into them."[54] Soueif elaborates on the Occupation's strengthening of Islamists later in one of Anna's letters: "People who would have tolerated the establishment of secular education, or the gradual disappearance of the veil, now fight these developments because they feel a need to hold on to their traditional values in the face of the Occupation. While the people who continue to support these changes have constantly to fight the suspicion that they are somehow in league with the British."[55] Soueif's fictional modern-day Egyptian progressives are still hampered by this legacy of British Occupation, still fighting a double battle against fundamentalism and an undemocratic regime that "tries to outbid the Islamists in the religious stakes."[56]

By including such scenes, Soueif adds to the inventory of "traces" left by European domination. First, they let her Egyptian readership know themselves not only as resisters to Occupation but also as early embracers of secularism and the arts. Embracing secularism and the arts, what Said might call "worldliness," becomes in fact a mode of resisting imperialism and is at least as authentic as Islamism and nationalism. Second, they let Soueif's European and American readership understand that supporting the invasion, either verbal or physical, of another people's cultural or physical space does not promote modernization.[57]

Although the harms of turn-of-the-twentieth-century colonialism and of its turn-of-the-twenty-first-century legacy are depressingly constant, Soueif's reader can perhaps take hope from the equally unrelenting struggles to alleviate them. The harms may be the true "enduring Oriental reality," but in the novel the struggles also represent an enduring *human* essence.[58] As we know from progressive history books, journals, and newscasts, and as Said himself has made clear, there always have been and there always will be people who risk their well-being and even their lives for the sake of social justice. Soueif's heroic protagonists exemplify such people.

Amal asks her brother, who, like Said, has received death threats, to be careful.[59] 'Omar's romantic forebear Sharif is also asked to be careful by his wife: "It is not only the British who dislike you. The Khedive does not like you, you have turned down government posts, resigned from the Council. . . . The Turks know that you want Egypt independent from them, and now you are also involved in Shukri's campaign against the settlements in Palestine. The Islamists hate you for your position on education. We *know* there are more radical nationalists who think your way is too cautious, too slow."[60]

Four years later a friend warns Sharif that he has "stood too much alone. Particularly in the last few years."[61] After Amal reads Layla's account of Sharif's assassination, by whom—Zionist or Islamist, British or Egyptian, "Westerner" or "Easterner"—we never learn, she begins to worry even more about 'Omar, who is on his concert tour in the Palestinian territories. For he is, she muses, "a solitary figure. . . . Beloved by many, hated by many, but essentially solitary. . . . alone in that no-man's land between East and West."[62] Sharif's and 'Omar's isolation links them to the hero of English romance and also to epic heroes in both Asian and European traditions.[63] But for those intimate with Said's writing and thinking, it links them as well to the intellectual, as described in *Representations of the Intellectual,* the Reith lectures Said gave for the BBC in 1993.[64] There he describes the true—that is, public (as opposed to the corporate or private)—intellectual as an outsider who questions "patriotic nationalism, corporate thinking, and a sense of class, racial or gender privilege"; a person who dissents "against the status quo"; an "eloquent, fantastically courageous and angry individual for whom no worldly power is too big and imposing to be criticized"; "someone whose whole being is staked on a critical sense, a sense of being unwilling to accept easy formulas" and who is therefore "neither a pacifier nor a consensus builder"; and, most controversially and famously, one who puts solidarity second to "criticism."[65] We can explain this last qualification by Said's firm belief "that the intellectual belongs on the same side with the weak and unrepresented," that "even among the oppressed, there are also victors and losers," and that feelings of solidarity might "narcotize the critical sense" and perhaps loosen one's hold on "standards of truth about human misery and oppression."[66] Said's aversion to solidarity is so strong that he can conceive the intellectual's position as a sort of exile: "While it is an *actual* condition, exile is also for my purposes a *metaphorical* condition. Even intellectuals who are lifelong members of a society can, in a manner of speaking, be divided into insiders and outsiders: those on the one hand . . . who can be called yea-sayers; and on the other hand the nay-sayers, the individuals at odds with their society and therefore outsiders and exiles so far as privileges, power, and honors are concerned."[67]

Soueif's two male protagonists are created from this same mold. Sharif and 'Omar are allied to family, friends, and other independent thinkers but refuse to align with the privileged classes to which they have access; they are committed to a nationalist cause and the oppressed but decline to toe any party line that might dull their critical sense and allow a double standard to creep in. To use Said's words, they "stand between loneliness and alignment" as perfect representations of the courageous intellectual.[68]

By listing the many groups who are suspect in the assassination of Sharif and by portraying the death threats against 'Omar, Soueif takes to their logical extreme Said's use of words like *courage, risk, exposure,* and *difficulty,* which in *Representations of the Intellectual* he links to the intellectual's risking status, wealth, and community but not death. Among the literary heroes that Said chose to illustrate the intellectual's vocation, only one dies, and this death is not attributed to the character's "deeply confrontational intellect" except in a metaphorical way.[69] Although Said cites Malcolm X as an example of the intellectual's oppositional consciousness, he does not evoke the assassination and in fact criticizes as "quite impossible absolutism" Julien Benda's belief that the real intellectual will "risk being burned at the stake, ostracized, or crucified."[70] Despite the death threats that Said and no doubt many of the intellectuals he discusses had received, his analysis does not so much heroize past and present intellectuals (and certainly not himself) as explain why the public should value the contributions of the unpopular intellectual.[71] Most intellectuals in England and the United States are, after all, not killed for their annoying speech. To Said, the biggest threat to the intellectual is not death but co-optation by power.[72]

Said the expository writer aims primarily at his readers' intellect; Soueif the novelist aims also at intellect, but her path flows through the heart. She appears to want the reader to value the intellectual as a *person* and to fear losing him or her. Soueif shows Amal, the reader, translator, and imaginer of the past, mourning the death of Sharif "with fresh grief" and then turning her worried thoughts to her absent brother, incommunicado for some days while giving concerts in the West Bank and Jordan.[73] Amal tries to take comfort in the fact that she has often worried needlessly about 'Omar in the past, but the novel ends on an unsettling note, as a baby's wail evokes in her a "sudden fear . . . so strong that it jolts her off the sofa and to her feet" with the cry "'Omar! . . . My Brother . . . !"[74] Given the identification Soueif has encouraged the knowledgeable reader to make between Sharif, 'Omar, and Said, we must interpret this unsettling ending both as an expression of fear for Said, who was alive when the novel was published, and as a validation of his true heroism, a recognition that, like a true hero, he was risking his life for principle.

To move from the sublime to Hollywood, I cannot resist asking what relationship might exist between Romance hero(es) 'Omar/Sharif and Omar Sharif, glamorous, romantic, sexy Egyptian/Hollywood movie star. Soueif, no doubt aware that Michel Shalhoub, who reinvented himself as Omar Sharif, was Said's detested older schoolmate at prep school, may have chosen these names primarily for their lofty associations in Arabic culture, but she may also have introduced the movie star's glamorous persona as part of her seduction.[75] While readers are picturing Omar Sharif's romantic persona, especially in the role of Prince Ali in *Lawrence of Arabia*, Soueif makes sure they see a consistently principled political activist smoldering beneath those dark brows. Near the end of the film, Ali abandons force to enter a newly created legislature. He says he has learned from the message Lawrence preached when he first came to Arabia; Lawrence meanwhile has gone over the edge into a seemingly permanent violence. Some viewers of the film might have interpreted these reverse trajectories as Ali's learning civilized ways from the best part of the English Lawrence, while Lawrence learned barbarity from his Arabian experience. They are, however, unlikely to retain this interpretation once they discover the long tradition of Egyptians with indigenous political agendas depicted in *The Map of Love*.

The romance of *Lawrence of Arabia*, however, may live on in a more positive way. Those of Soueif's readers who are aware of Edward Said's writings and biography but have not experienced his own glamorous persona will perhaps visualize Omar Sharif in the role of the novel's activist intellectual. Though the association would not likely please Said, this merging of personas might strengthen the allure of political activism for Soueif's readers—activism not with a scimitar or gun but with pen and voice, not on the battlefield but in the court of public opinion. It might help readers respond to the romance and the challenge Said found in the activist intellectual life: "It is a spirit in opposition, rather than in accommodation, that grips me because the romance, the interest, the challenge of intellectual life is to be found in dissent against the status quo at a time when the struggle on behalf of under-represented groups seems so unfairly weighted against them."[76] Soueif cleverly reappropriates the romantic name chosen by an ambitious movie star, transforming it into a vehicle for the truly *sharif* ("noble") public intellectual. Will the real 'Omar Sharif please stand up?

The activist implications of translating this controversial real-life figure into accessible fiction should be coming into focus by now. For Soueif, who is a professional translator as well as a novelist and political commentator, translation per se has activist implications. One cannot, she thinks, "view the act of selecting, translating and publishing a work as simply a literary act. . . . It has to be viewed as both an act of culture and of political significance." She views translation as an "intersection between cultures" and believes that the translator is "translating not words, nor information" but "an entire culture."[77] "In *The Map of Love*," she says, "there is a constant attempt to render Arabic into English, not just to translate phrases but to render something of the dynamic of Arabic, how it works, into English. So, there is the question of how to open a window into another culture, and is it doable?"[78] Three characters in the novel are themselves translators, and for two of them, Anna and Layla, the motivation is not only to open windows into another culture but also to galvanize opposition to imperialist policies that are oppressing and distorting the culture. Anna's starting point is "confidence in public opinion; that if only people can be made to see, to understand—then wrongs can be undone, and history set on a different course."[79] Her goal is to enable the powerless to speak their own truth to the powerful: "The fact that it falls to Englishmen to speak for Egypt is in itself perceived as a weakness; for how can the Egyptians govern themselves, people ask, when they cannot even speak for themselves? They cannot speak because there is no platform for them to speak from and because of the difficulties with language. By that I mean not just the ability to translate Arabic speech into English but to speak as the English themselves would speak, for only then will the justice of what they say—divested of its disguising cloak of foreign idiom—be truly apparent to those who hear it."[80] Translation, then, can help change "the hearts and minds" of a dominant people in two ways: first, by making audible the voices of a subordinate people, it can engender respect for them as thinkers, and second, it can allow their experiences to be judged by a universal standard of justice.[81]

The word "justice" in Soueif's passage reminds me of one of Said's descriptions of the intellectual in *Representations of the Intellectual*. The intellectual, "an individual endowed with a faculty for representing, embodying, articulating a message, a view, an attitude, philosophy or opinion to, as well as for, a public," represents "all those people and issues that are routinely forgotten or swept under the rug. The intellectual does so on the basis of universal principles: that all human beings are entitled to expect decent standards of behavior concerning freedom and justice from worldly powers or nations, and that deliberate or inadvertent violations of these standards need to be testified and fought against courageously."[82] I am reminded too of the penultimate sentence in Soueif's recent obituary for her longtime friend: "He believed that ordinary people, all over the world, still cared about truth and justice."[83] Soueif's passage in *The Map of Love*, then, follows Said in representing the "power" to whom the intellectual speaks "truth" as the public—not the leaders of a nation but the people who elect those leaders.[84]

The public is also, obviously, the audience for novels, which can do on an imaginative level what intellectual analysis and criticism can do on an intellectual level. Soueif combines the two kinds of work by making two of her major protagonists the kind of courageous intellectuals that Said celebrates in *Representations of the Intellectual*. For me, Soueif's choice of protagonist and mode of representation have the same activist importance that she assigns to translation, and, in fact, I see them as essentially the same process. Just as a translator's choice of what and how to translate from one language to another matters politically, it is significant that Soueif translates a character that many perceive as "embarrassing, contrary, even unpleasant" (I refer both to the intellectual in general and to Edward Said in particular) into the idiom of Gothic romance, a familiar genre in which the reader presupposes that such a character will turn out to be worthy of love in the end.[85]

In doing so, Soueif contributes modern, more positive counterparts to the fictional intellectuals Said evokes in the first essay/lecture of *Representations of the Intellectual*. There Said describes literature as "modern life seen as a novel or drama and not as a business or as the raw material for a sociological monograph"; this form is the best way to illustrate "how it is that intellectuals are representative . . . of a quite peculiar, even abrasive style of life and social performance that is uniquely theirs."[86] For Said these fictional intellectuals—Turgenev's Bazarov *(Fathers and Sons)*, Joyce's Stephen Dedalus *(Portrait of the Artist as a Young Man)*, and Flaubert's Moreau and Deslauriers *(Sentimental Education)*—can represent an enduring reality.[87] In counterpoint, Soueif brings a historic figure into fictional existence, pouring the original into a simplified generic mold, in order, paradoxically, to allow his complex ideas to reach the ears of even the most reluctant audience.

Early in her novel, Soueif establishes the metaphor of seeing through another person's eyes, a mundane trope that both translates Said's concept of Orientalist texts citing each other and performs what these texts failed to do vis á vis the objects of their scrutiny.[88] Anna explicitly tries to see things through her father-in-law's progressive eyes, and she is therefore able to take seriously things like the anti-Occupation newspaper *al-Liwa*, which Lord Cromer pronounces of no significance and dismisses as a product of French interference.[89] This metaphor appears again when Anna tells Sharif that if she had joined a Cook's tour she "would have seen things through [her] companions' eyes."[90] To use Soueif's own trope, I believe that she, the translator, gives us the eyes to see Edward Said, whose relentless and effective critique of U.S. foreign policy and racist thinking earned him many enemies, not as a monstrous enigma—part "West," part "East," like a mythic centaur who belongs to no real species—but as a recognizable generic hero fighting the enemies of *human* civilization.[91]

Soueif has translated the intellectual, who is often disprized, if not despised, in American and English culture, into a public hero worthy of awe, and she has also given literary—that is, immortal—flesh to a particular intellectual who, despite being demonized by many, after his death inspired countless personal encomia from his "3000 close friends."[92] Said's name and ideas will live on in his awesome body of published work; his persona and ideas will endure and reach millions more in the "living reality" of Soueif's fiction.

NOTES

1. Edward Said, *Orientalism* (New York: Random House, 1978); reprinted with a new afterword (New York: Vintage Books, 1994), 23.

2. Ibid., 24.

3. Ibid., 291.

4. Ibid., 351.

5. Lecture and discussion about *The Map of Love* at the Marino Family International Writers' Workshop, Georgetown University, Washington, D.C., 10 September 2005, as reported to me via e-mail by Adel Iskandar.

6. Ibid.

7. Quotations from ibid. My argument is predicated on the idea that any reader familiar with the career and writings of Edward Said will recognize him behind one of the characters—'Omar al-Ghamrawi—but in addition to demonstrating a strong relationship with a second protagonist, I hope to show that 'Omar is far more than "loosely based on" Said, as Joseph Massad says in an excellent pre-publication review essay and interview, "The Politics of Desire in the Writings of Ahdaf Soueif," *Journal of Palestine Studies* 28/4, no. 112 (1999): 82.

8. Ahdaf Soueif, *The Map of Love* (New York: Anchor Books, 1999), 215.

9. Said, *Orientalism*, 25. Partially quoted from Antonio Gramsci, *The Prison Notebooks: Selections*, trans. and ed. Q. Hoare and G. Nowell Smith (New York: International Publishers, 1971), 324. The last phrase is translated by Said himself from *Quaderni del Carcere*, vol. 2, ed. Valentino Gerratana (Turin: Einaudi Editore 1975), 1363.

10. Said, *Orientalism*, 25.

11. See Joseph Massad on this period between the 1882 'Urabi revolt and the 1919 revolution, which also includes the beginning of the Zionist project. As he says, Soueif "transforms history into a guide for the present" (Massad, "The Politics of Desire," 82).

12. Said criticizes Orientalism for suggesting "both an enduring Oriental reality and an opposing but no less enduring Western essence" (*Orientalism*, 333) and suggests that a major reason for this false position is that "Orientalism failed to identify with human experience, failed also to see it as human experience" (328).

13. Soueif and her mother have translated the novel into Arabic. Even the English version of her work has been well received by the Arab world, where "readers have said that even though the writing is in English, that this is an authentic Arab voice" (quoted in Massad, "The Politics of Desire," 89).

14. Soueif, *The Map of Love*, 481.

15. Ibid., 481–83. Sharif's first response, "stay and try to ignore, focuses on historical or religious

claims (such as those of Palestine). Compare Said's analysis of Chateaubriand (Said, *Orientalism*, 170–75). The second response, "try to change it," focuses on challenging the "Colonial Enterprise" and justifications like the "White Man's Burden," which fits with Said's analyses of colonialism and cultural imperialism. Compare Said's analysis of and quotations from Lord Balfour, Lord Cromer, and Rudyard Kipling (Said, *Orientalism*, 33, 226–54). The third response, to "leave," receives no elaboration, nor does the fourth, "try to understand," except as the reason Sharif is writing the article.

16. "Europe simply does not see the people of the countries it wishes to annex" (Soueif, *The Map of Love*, 483). The idea that intellectual Egyptians are somehow different from the general Egyptian population receives elaboration elsewhere in the text. One of Anna's letters describes Lord Cromer's response to the Egyptian newspaper, *al-Liwa*, as nonrepresentative of Egyptian thought: "Lord Cromer merely said it was a publication of no significance, paid for by the French, and read only by the 'talking classes'" (ibid., 67). Harry Boyle, Oriental Secretary at the British Agency, later claims that the *effendis* (the educated class) are not real Egyptians (ibid., 98).

17. Said, *Orientalism*, 39.

18. Soueif, *The Map of Love*, 484, emphasis added.

19. Said, *Orientalism*, 347, 351.

20. Ibid., 328.

21. Soueif, *The Map of Love*, 484.

22. "I shall conclude briefly by saying that although the animosities and inequities still exist from which my interest in Orientalism as a cultural and political phenomenon began, there is now at least a general acceptance that these represent not an eternal order but a historical experience whose end, or at least partial abatement, may be at hand" (Said, *Orientalism*, 352).

23. Ibid., 328.

24. *Islamist* is the word currently used to designate fundamentalist Islam, which, like fundamentalist Christianity, calls for religion-based governance of the community's cultural and political life. In discussing the reception of *Orientalism*, Said says he most regrets that some readers perceived it as anti-Western (ibid., 330). He thoroughly discusses and rebuts the "caricatured permutations" that make up this alleged anti-Westernism (ibid., 330–45).

25. Soueif, *The Map of Love*, 429.

26. Ibid., 465.

27. Hala Halim, "Translating Egypt," review of *The Map of Love* by Ahdaf Soueif, *Al-Ahram Weekly* 442 (12–18 August 1999), http://weekly.ahram.org.eg/1999/442/bk1_442.htm (accessed 28 May 2009).

28. Ahdaf Soueif, "Talking about *The Map of Love*," transcript of a book talk at Brunel University, London, on 28 February 2000, *EnterText* 1.3 (2000): 102, http://people.brunel.ac.uk/~acsrrrm/entertext/1_3_pdfs/soueif_1.pdf (accessed 28 May 2009).

29. Ibid.; Soueif, *The Map of Love*, 254–55. Amal often refers in novelistic terms to the story she is translating, and at one point she compares her feeling for Anna to her feeling for Dorothea Brooke (Soueif, *The Map of Love*, 26). Compare Isabel's response to a portrait of Sharif that depicts his eyes as "proud and aloof and yet, if you look carefully, sad also" (178).

30. Soueif, "Talking about *The Map of Love*," 102.

31. Soueif, *The Map of Love*, 178.

32. Ibid., 151, 269.

33. Ibid., 334.

34. Ibid., 488.

35. Ibid., 21.

36. Ibid., 21, 50; compare Said's descriptions of himself in his autobiography, *Out of Place: A Memoir* (New York: Vintage Books, 1999), xii, 289–93. Like 'Omar and Sharif, Said's first marriage was "short-lived and unhappy" (256). Said is reticent about his first marriage, mentioning it a few times only in

passing (282, 284), but in her Georgetown University talk, Soueif commented that 'Omar's experience was reminiscent of Said's (lecture and discussion on *The Map of Love* at the Marino Family International Writers' Workshop, reported to me in e-mail from Adel Iskandar). I do not know whether she was referring to Said's marriage or his profound reaction to the "shock" of the 1967 war (Said, *Out of Place*, 293).

37. See *Out of Place* (281, 291) for Said's account of his piano studies and his final rejection of a professional career in music. In addition to articles in *The Nation*, Said has published two books that combine his literary and musical interests: *Musical Elaborations* (New York: Columbia University Press, 1993) and *Parallels and Paradoxes: Explorations in Music and Society* with Daniel Barenboim, ed. Ara Guzelimian (New York: Pantheon Books, 2002).

38. Said's books on the Palestinian situation include *The Question of Palestine* (1979), *After the Last Sky: Palestinian Lives* (1986), *The Politics of Dispossession* (1995), *Peace and Its Discontents* (1996), *Covering Islam* (1997), and *The End of the Peace Process* (2000).

39. Soueif, *The Map of Love*, 391.

40. See Said, *The Politics of Dispossession: The Struggle for Palestinian Self-Determination, 1969–1994* (New York: Vintage Books, 1995), xxiv–xxvi. Highlights of this description of his relationship to the Palestinian national movement: "I was a partisan, yes, but a joiner and a member, no" (xxiv). "I was savagely attacked by both Fatah and the Popular Front for talking about the need for a recognition of Israel and accepting a two-state solution" (xxv). "In 1984, both Shafiq and I were roundly denounced by the Fatah dissidents . . . and threatened with death for our 'treasonous' rallying to Arafat" (xxvi).

41. Soueif, *The Map of Love*, 330.

42. Ibid., 344.

43. Ibid., 356.

44. Ibid., 357.

45. Edward Said, *Culture and Imperialism* (New York: Vintage Books, 1994), 23.

46. For examples of this, see ibid., 136, 158, 204, 223–24, 227, 268–69, 275–76, 335, 349, 365–66, 383.

47. Soueif, *The Map of Love*, 227.

48. Ibid., 173–74, 221, 224. At one point the 1919 green flag of national unity shelters 'Omar's infant son Sharif from the sun (ibid., 480–81). Hala Halim may be right that this episode is an example of "too many coincidences spoil[ing] the novelistic broth" (Halim, "Translating Egypt," 4–5), but it does hammer home the point that the struggle for freedom in Egypt is traditional, handed down from parent to child, rather than imported.

49. Compare Said (*Orientalism,* 347) on Paul Johnson's 1993 essay "Colonialism's Back—And Not a Moment Too Soon."

50. See Terri Beth Miller's "Behind the Veil" for a good analysis of Soueif's method of wresting "a woman-centered story of Egypt from the grasp of patriarchal narrative" ("Behind the Veil: Deconstructing 'Woman' in Ahdaf Soueif's *The Map of Love,*" *Interculture* 2 (January 2005): 9, www.fsu.edu/~proghum/interculture/vol2.html (accessed 30 May 2009).

51. Soueif, "Talking about *The Map of Love,*" 106.

52. Soueif, *The Map of Love,* 262.

53. Ibid., 263.

54. Ibid., 264.

55. Ibid., 384.

56. Ibid., 229.

57. During a discussion after readings from *The Map of Love* at Brunel University in London, Soueif was asked why she had not commented more on "how Islam oppresses women." Soueif offered a two-part answer. First, she said, Islam need not oppress women; second, Euro-American feminist agitation against Islam and clitoridectomy has actually set back Egyptian feminism and the movement against

clitoridectomy, "whereas if it had just been left alone, it was going to go. We were working on it." ("Talking about *The Map of Love*," 108–9.)

58. Compare Said, *Orientalism*, 328, 333.

59. Said talks about death threats and how his office was set on fire in Edward Said, "Between Worlds," *Reflections on Exile and Other Essays* (Cambridge, MA: Harvard University Press, 2000), 564; originally published in the *London Review of Books*, 7 May 1998).

60. Soueif, *The Map of Love*, 416. Sharif resigns from the Egyptian Legislative Council in 1905 (395), and in 1907 he refuses to join any of the four political parties that have sprung into being after the resignation of Lord Cromer (433–34).

61. Ibid., 496.

62. Ibid., 515. Compare Said's account of his experiences in "Between Worlds," 564–68, and his description of the "individual intellectual vocation" in "On Lost Causes," in *Reflections*, 552–53.

63. Think of Gilgamesh on his fearsome journey through the wilderness and his absolute refusal to accept a "normal" way of life (see *The Epic of Gilgamesh*, trans. and ed. M. G. Kovacs [Stanford, CA: Stanford University Press, 1989], 85n1). Even more aptly, think of Achilles in Book One of *The Iliad*, dashing the scepter to the ground and excoriating not only the rapacious great king Agamemnon but also the compromising lesser kings who fail to join him in mutiny against the violation of an important social principle. The epic hero knows what he needs to do and is willing to die rather than capitulate to something he does not believe in.

64. Edward Said, *Representations of the Intellectual: The 1993 Reith Lectures* (New York: Pantheon, 1994).

65. Ibid., xiii, xvii, 8, 23, 32.

66. Ibid., 22, 41, 41, xii. On the effects of solidarity on the critical sense, Said also wrote, "Although there is inestimable value to what an intellectual does to ensure the community's survival during periods of extreme national emergency, loyalty to the group's fight for survival cannot draw in the intellectual so far as to narcotize the critical sense, or reduce its imperatives, which are always to go beyond survival to questions of political liberation, to critiques of the leadership, to presenting alternatives that are too often marginalized or pushed aside as irrelevant to the main battle at hand. Even among the oppressed, there are also victors and losers" (41).

67. Ibid., 52–53. See Neil Lazarus's critique of Said's "metaphorical construal of intellectualism as exile" as "modernist nostalgia" in "Representations of the Intellectual in *Representations of the Intellectual*," *Research in African Literatures* 36, no. 3 (2005): 118–19. Lazarus feels, perhaps correctly, that Said dismisses too decisively "the possibility of solidaristic critical practice" (119).

68. Said, *Representations of the Intellectual*, 22.

69. Ibid., 15. Turgenev's Bazarov dies of an infectious illness due to his own carelessness and the incompetence of a village doctor (Ivan Turgenev, *Fathers and Sons*, trans. Harry Stevens, *The Vintage Turgenev*, vol.1 [New York: Vintage Books, 1950], 337–38). Said says that Bazarov's "peremptoriness and defiance as an intellectual lift him out of the story, unsuited to it and somehow not fit for domestication" (Said, *Representations of the Intellectual*, 16).

70. On Malcolm X, see Said, *Representations of the Intellectual*, xvii. On Julien Benda, see ibid., 6–7.

71. Said's discussion is also, of course, a spine-stiffening castigation of intellectuals prone to using their talents in professional service to authority (be it national or ideological) rather than in amateur service to "the weak and unrepresented" (ibid., 22). For Said's contrast between the professional (motivated by profit, i.e., status or wealth) and amateur ("fueled by care and affection"), see ibid., 65–83, esp. 73–74, 82–83.

72. Ibid., 18, 35, 41, 121.

73. Soueif, *The Map of Love*, 510.

74. Ibid., 516.

75. *Sharif* means "noble" in Arabic, and can be used as a proper name just as English speakers might use Earl, Duke, or King. We could thus translate '*Omar Sharif* as "noble '*Omar*." The Jerusalem site known to English speakers as Temple Mount is known as al-Haram al-Sharif ("noble sacred space") to Arabic speakers, and within al-Haram al-Sharif is the Mosque of 'Omar, which is also known as the Dome of the Rock. This mosque and the sanctuary that encloses it, which form one of the most holy sites in Islam, illustrate the powerful connotations of the names chosen both by Soueif and by Shalhoub.

76. Said, *Representations of the Intellectual*, xvii.

77. Quoted by Tariq Hassan-Gordon, reporting on a talk by Soueif at the American University in Cairo, 17 October 2001: "Novelist Highlights the Dangers in Translating Arabic," *Middle East Times* 43 (26 October 2001), www.metimes.com//2001/10/26/novelist_highlights_the_dangers_in_translating_arabic/7837/ (accessed 30 May 2009).

78. Massad, "The Politics of Desire," 85.

79. Soueif gives these words to her turn-of-the-century protagonist Anna Winterbourne. Gayatri Spivak says something similar in her essay "The Politics of Translation," in *The Translation Studies Reader*, ed. Lawrence Venuti (New York, NY: Routledge, 2000), 399–400.

80. Soueif, *The Map of Love*, 481.

81. Quotations from ibid., 399.

82. Said, *Representations of the Intellectual*, 11–12.

83. Ahdaf Soueif, "Edward Said: My Friend," *Guardian*, 26 September 2003, www.ahdafsoueif.com/Articles/Edward_Said_My_Friend.pdf (accessed 30 May 2009).

84. Some have criticized Said's oft-repeated credo that the duty of an intellectual is to speak truth to power, saying that power already knows the truth; others have defended the statement, saying that it means to speak in the face of power. See Lazarus, "Representations of the Intellectual," 119–20, for an interesting discussion of these points of view. Soueif seems, correctly I feel, to blend the latter interpretation with the democratic ideal of placing power in the hands of the people.

85. Quotation from Said, *Representations of the Intellectual*, 12.

86. Ibid., 14.

87. Although these literary protagonists lack the activist component that Said insists on elsewhere, they do thoroughly affirm a *sine qua non* for the intellectual life: a commitment to "intellectual freedom" and to engaging in intellectual activity for its own sake rather than in order "to fortify ego or celebrate status" (ibid., 17, 20).

88. See Said, *Orientalism*, 23.

89. Soueif, *The Map of Love*, 66–67.

90. Ibid., 212.

91. Soueif is by no means alone in viewing Said as a larger-than-life hero. Stathis Gourgouris, who also knew the man personally, has described him as "a warrior. His life restores meaning to this otherwise bankrupt word. He was indefatigable and invincible. He fought against his own illness with the same determination he fought on the side of justice and humanity for his entire life. Even until his final week, he lived according to a rhythm that would exhaust people much younger than him and totally healthy. He traveled incessantly. And even though obviously in the last years his body had lost its gigantic capacities, still he never gave you the sense of a person who needed the hours of rest that every traveler needs.... Limits got on his nerves, except the limits of humanity which he saw violated everywhere." See Gourgouris, "Edward Said—Remembrance for Memory," Athens, 30 September 2003, www.edwardsaid.org/articles/20030930001.Stathis.Gourgouris.html (accessed 5 November 2003).

92. Soueif, "Edward Said: My Friend."

9

Edward Said and the
Poetry of Decolonization

Jahan Ramazani

"The earth is closing on us, pushing us through the last passage," begins a poem written in Arabic by Mahmoud Darwish; it famously ends with the questions, "Where should we go after the last frontiers? Where should the birds fly after the last sky?"[1] In Darwish's poem, which distills Palestinian uprooting, dispossession, and exile in elemental images of earth, space, stars, and sky, the Palestinian predicament becomes a nightmarish flight from entombment in the earth and a desperate search for a place to call one's own. Edward Said quoted this poem in an homage to Darwish and later used the evocative phrase "after the last sky" as a book title. In his tribute to Darwish, published in 1993, Said describes the sometime member of the Palestine Liberation Organization Executive Committee as "Palestine's unofficial national poet." Yet in a passage that is tantamount to a self-description, Said vigorously distinguishes Darwish's "mordant wit, fierce political independence, and exceptionally refined cultural sensibility . . . from the frequent coarseness of Palestinian and Arab politics." Said continues: "In Darwish, the personal and the public are always in an uneasy relationship, the force and passion of the former ill-suited to the tests of political correctness and policy required by the latter." Although Said rejected the formalist separation of literature from the world, his view of the aesthetic—as suggested by his Adornian praise for the "strained and deliberately unresolved quality" of Darwish's later poetry—sternly avoids the propagandistic. Said was fascinated not so much by Darwish the political spokesperson as by Darwish the vexed and introspective poet, who achieved representative status in the quest for Palestinian self-determination precisely by refusing to subordinate his idiosyncrasies to the collective. Comparing Darwish to the Irish poet W. B. Yeats, the Saint Lucian poet Derek Walcott, and the countercultural American Jewish poet

Allen Ginsberg, Said claims in his essay that these Anglophone poets "possess that irresistibly rare combination of incantatory public style with deep and often hermetic personal sentiments" and that Darwish achieves "a harassing amalgam of poetry and collective memory, each pressing on the other."[2] Later, in a posthumously published book, Said similarly admires the "late style" in the work of the Greek Alexandrian poet Constantin Cavafy, which renders contending moods and views "without resolving the contradiction between them," instead holding "them in tension, as equal forces straining in opposite directions."[3]

As a lifelong advocate of Palestinian and worldwide decolonization and as a critic devoted to the painstaking analysis of literary works, Said reflects on Darwish's and Cavafy's poetry in terms that raise large questions: What is the role of poetry in decolonization—a massive historical process associated less often with verse than with political movements and violent acts of resistance, with boycotts, strikes, rallies, and marches? How can poetry, without subordinating personal independence and unresolved ambivalences to collective aspirations, aid and advance decolonization? Moreover, how can the transnational affinities and reach of poetry, linking Darwish's work with that of Yeats, Walcott, and Ginsberg, be reconciled with the culturally specific imperatives of decolonization? These and related issues remain inadequately explored in poetry criticism and in postcolonial studies, even though the struggle to decolonize large swaths of the globe has been a defining feature of the twentieth and twenty-first centuries and even though poetry stands to yield as much insight into cultural decolonization as do other literary genres. Said's work is helpful in engaging these questions, when we bring his ideas about "decolonizing cultural resistance" into dialogue with poetry criticism. Although Said admired Darwish, Cavafy, and other non-Anglophone writers, he seldom wrote about Arab or Palestinian poets other than Darwish; the literature to which he devoted most of his critical career—a preference shaped by his British colonial education in Egypt—was literature written in English. Because the British Empire was, as Said observed, by far the largest and most populous among its European competitors, the Anglophone poetry it spawned is a rich and rewarding field for consideration.

As a literary critic, Said might seem an unlikely source for reflections on Anglophone poetry and decolonization, given his career-long preference for the novel and his fame as the theorist of Orientalism. Near the beginning of his landmark book *Orientalism* (1978), he states forthrightly that he is bracketing the "brute reality" of the "lives, histories, and customs" of the East to focus on "the enormously systematic discipline by which European culture was able to manage—and even produce—the Orient."[4] That book's Foucauldian vision of Orientalist discourse is so tightly sealed that it admits little adversarial friction or contestation. Fifteen years later, Said published *Culture and Imperialism* (1993), the work on which I focus here, in which he revisited and even corrected the monolithic conceptualization of his earlier book. "What I left out of *Orientalism*," Said conceded, "was that response to

Western dominance which culminated in the great movement of decolonization all across the Third World."[5] Although *Culture and Imperialism* remains largely concerned with Orientalism, Said also wanted to make space for the other side of the story, especially in his long third chapter, "Resistance and Opposition," in which he gave pride of place to a poet, in the reprinted essay "Yeats and Decolonization" (1988). As one might expect of the world's most eloquent proponent of the Palestinian struggle, Said knew that, contrary to Gertrude Stein's aphorism "there is no there there," there *is* a there there, beyond the Orientalist construct: wherever the tentacles of empire reach, resistance mobilizes itself.[6]

Decolonization, in its most obvious sense, is a word for a formal, legal, and political process, but Said's primary argument in *Culture and Imperialism* is, as his title suggests, "that culture played a very important, indeed indispensable role," both in extending and securing empire and in eroding and undermining it.[7] At times Said represents the relation between cultural and political decolonization as a two-step process: "After the period of 'primary resistance,' literally fighting against outside intrusion, there comes the period of secondary, that is, ideological resistance." As "secondary" resistance, cultural and ideological works extend and legitimize a fundamentally political and military process. The "cultural effort to decolonize . . . goes on long after the political establishment of independent nation-states" and "persist[s] well after successful nationalism has come to a stop." At other times Said represents these two forms of resistance as simultaneous and interwoven: "in the overseas *imperium* the massive political, economic, and military resistance was carried forward and informed by an actively provocative and challenging culture of resistance."[8] According to this second model, literary and other cultural works have a primary role to play in propelling decolonization. The dissonances between such statements indicate the difficulty of theorizing the causality and chronology of cultural and political decolonization in different parts of the world, at different times. The lines of influence usually remain murky between a particular work and a resistance movement, no matter how proudly worried Yeats may have been when he asked in his late poem "Man and the Echo" if an early play of his had sent out "Certain men the English shot" and had thus fomented a violent Irish uprising against British rule.[9]

Whether prior to, simultaneous with, or subsequent to political decolonization, what exactly is cultural decolonization? Said ascribes distinct but interrelated tasks to "decolonizing cultural resistance." One of the first, he says, is "to reclaim, rename, and reinhabit the land." Other aspects of decolonizing cultural resistance, such as the assertion of communal identity, are "quite literally grounded on this poetically projected base."[10] Said does not explain what he means by "poetically," but it is striking that decolonization is for him at root a poetic enterprise: it involves re-creating the land by renaming it and thus imaginatively and linguistically repossessing it. By resonantly invoking, reciting, and remythologizing place names, Yeats, Derek

Walcott, Lorna Goodison, Kamau Brathwaite, A. K. Ramanujan, Wole Soyinka, and other Anglophone poets can thus be seen as participating in a central task of cultural decolonization—not, as we might expect, angrily taunting or satirizing the colonizer but renaming and remapping topography. "If there is anything that radically distinguishes the imagination of anti-imperialism," Said says, sounding much like Frantz Fanon, "it is the primacy of the geographical element. Imperialism after all is an act of geographical violence," which begins experientially, for the colonized, with "loss of the locality to the outsider."[11] But whereas Fanon gives violence an almost mystical role in forming communal identity, Said's emphasis is on reimagining geography, the *poiesis* of giving places their names.[12]

A second key task of cultural decolonization, according to Said's analysis, is to re-create and reclaim a communal history, and in this respect Said again builds on Fanon's *Wretched of the Earth*. Much as the empire has expropriated the land, displacing native names, myths, and attachments, so too has it marginalized and disfigured indigenous narratives of the past, subordinating them to "the Western powers' monumental histories."[13] Decolonization involves reimagining and reintegrating a mythical and historical past for the indigenous community, repopulating that past with a different cast of heroes, heroines, and perhaps even villains. Among Anglophone poets, Yeats revives mythical Irish histories, Ramanujan traces the fantastically heterogeneous elements of the past that circulate through him and other South Asians, and Goodison thinks back through her family history to her enslaved great-grandmother:

a guinea woman
wide eyes turning
the corners of her face
could see behind her [14]

To enable the emergence of freshly reconstituted communities and national identities, decolonization thus requires nothing less than the imaginative remaking of both space—the once expropriated topography—and time—the collective historical experience of that place.

This account of cultural decolonization may well seem to overlap substantially with nativist and nationalist views, and indeed Said is loath to underestimate the importance of such formations in resisting colonialism and breaking the grip of empire. Yet at the heart of his description of cultural decolonization, he also emphasizes, perhaps surprisingly, a transnational humanism—the pervasive and "noticeable pull away from separatist nationalism toward a more integrative view of human community and human liberation."[15] Echoing elsewhere Fanon's critique of nationalist "separatism and mock autonomy" as the internalization of colonialist oppression, Said cites Césaire's *Cahier* to suggest that postcolonial independence is no more than a starting point on the way to the "real work": "nothing less than the

reintegration of all those people and cultures, once confined and reduced to peripheral status, with the rest of the human race."[16] Decolonization is in Said's view
crippled, narrow, and insufficient, unless it "refuses the short-term blandishments
of separatist and triumphalist slogans in favor of the larger, more generous human
realities of community *among* cultures, peoples, and societies."[17] Decolonization requires the actual and the poetic repossession of a land and a history, but to succeed,
this struggle must be recognized as part of a larger, transnational, human struggle,
which crosses boundaries among colonized populations and even between colonizer and colonized. Said witheringly condemns "remaining trapped in the emotional self-indulgence of celebrating one's own identity."[18] Despite the many postcolonial critiques, by Chinua Achebe and others, of humanist "universalism" for
cloaking Eurocentrism and despite localist anxieties that it effaces cultural specificity, Said asserts that transnational secular humanism is crucial to "a more generous
and pluralistic vision of the world."[19] He exhorts us to "acknowledge the massively
knotted and complex histories of special but nevertheless overlapping and interconnected experiences."[20]

Said viewed this knotting along two theoretical vectors. First is the horizontal
vector of connections and affiliations among decolonizing groups: fundamental to
cultural and political resistance are reciprocal recognitions and affiliations across
cultural and national lines.[21] Such transnational and intercultural recognitions are
"poetic" insofar as they involve the figurative construction of likeness, of similitude.
Indeed, the work of many postcolonial poets—even those not discussed by Said—
bears out his analysis. Walcott horizontally identifies the ambivalent Caribbean cultural struggle against empire with that of the Irish—in his words, "colonials with
the same kind of problems that existed in the Caribbean. They were the niggers of
Britain" (ten years before the more famous remark by Roddy Doyle's character in
The Commitments, "The Irish are the niggers of Europe").[22] Similarly, Goodison
builds poems around the transnational affinities between South African and Ja-
maican feminisms; Agha Shahid Ali sees the mirror image of South American atrocities and disappearances in those of his native Kashmir; and the Yorkshire poet Tony
Harrison identifies the blackness of his working-class boots with the blackness of
Césaire's negritude.[23]

Second, Said accentuates the vertical entanglements between colonizer and colonized, which are so extensive that their cultures, histories, and realities are ultimately inseparable. Thus, postcolonial poets such as Ali, Brathwaite, Wole Soyinka,
Goodison, and Christopher Okigbo redeploy the core strategies of Euromodernist
poetry—the translocalism, mythical syncretism, heteroglossia, and apocalypticism
of Yeats, Eliot, and Pound—in service to their own decolonizing struggles against
local cultural hegemonies (British Victorian norms enforced in the schools by local elites).[24] Mocking "tribalism" and other identitarian views that require, for example, "Arabs to read Arab books, use Arab methods, and the like," Said approv-

ingly cites the view of one of his intellectual heroes, C. L. R. James, that "Beethoven belongs as much to West Indians as he does to Germans, since his music is now part of the human heritage."[25]

As we might expect from the terms of his praise for Darwish, when Said discusses particular instances of the literature of decolonization, he shies away from patriotic huzza, and he avoids placing some writers on the side of heroic and revolutionary resistance while viewing others as its antithesis. His most extended discussion of a "poet of decolonization" is hesitant and conflicted. Said's Yeats sometimes leans in the "nativist" and "nationalist" direction, his early work standing "at a threshold it cannot cross," even his later work stopping "short of imagining full political liberation."[26] At other times Said hails Yeats for his cross-national affinities with other poets of decolonization—Tagore, Senghor, Césaire, Darwish, Neruda— and suggests that the poet exemplifies, especially in his later work, a movement "beyond national consciousness" toward a fuller, transnational conception of "*liberation.*"[27] Yeats's ambivalently decolonizing work, according to this reading, cannot be limited either to nativism or to its supposed antithesis.[28]

Said is sometimes caricatured as a shrilly one-dimensional and partisan writer, but as a theorist of decolonizing cultural resistance, the reverse is true. The complexity of his thinking becomes especially evident when we compare it with other critical statements on the poetry of decolonization, unmentioned by Said. According to the authors of a major work on the subject, *Toward the Decolonization of African Literature,* the task of cultural decolonization is to throw off all European influences and paradigms, "to end all foreign domination of African culture, to systematically destroy all encrustations of colonial and slave mentality."[29] Chinweizu and his coauthor condemn poets such as Soyinka, J. P. Clark, and the early Okigbo for having "assiduously aped" European models, importing foreign imagery, diction, forms, and attitudes.[30] At the same time, they praise poets such as Okot p'Bitek, Kofi Awoonor, and the later Okigbo for using authentic African imagery, genres, and models, and thus helping to build a distinctive African national consciousness, based in "the separate and autonomous status of African literature," purged of foreign contaminants.[31] For Said, by contrast, cross-cultural affiliations and identifications are central to the poetry of decolonization. When he writes of Césaire, for example, he claims that the core of the poet's work is not the *ressentiment* of an overzealous nativism but "affectionate contention" with Western precursors.[32] Citing Fanon's warning that nativist resistance risks replicating the old colonial order in reverse, Said states, "The dangers of chauvinism and xenophobia ('Africa for the Africans') are very real. It is best when Caliban sees his own history as an aspect of the history of *all* subjugated men and women, and comprehends the complex truth of his own social and historical situation."[33] In another important book on the subject, *History of the Voice,* Kamau Brathwaite also attacks assimilated writers for retarding cultural decolonization, while hailing nativist writers for advancing it.

Among the poets he believes have been unfaithful to West Indian forms and experience are Claude McKay, one of whose sonnets "could have been written by a European"; George Campbell, whose ode lacks "any unique element in terms of the Caribbean environment"; and even Louise Bennett, whose Creole poetry uses a "Scots tune" for rhythm.[34] Although Brathwaite argues that a poetry of decolonization must be rooted in native rhythms and the local environment, he offers, ironically, cogent evidence for an alternative view when he cites the decisive influence of T. S. Eliot's recorded voice in awakening West Indian poets like himself to their own Caribbean speech rhythms.[35] By this measure, colonial importation and literary decolonization—instead of being steps in a linear movement toward liberation—are entangled and even inextricable. Said, who in *Culture and Imperialism* openly adapts Eliot's model in "Tradition and the Individual Talent" of the pastness and yet presence of the past, writes that: "to ignore or otherwise discount the overlapping experience of Westerners and Orientals, the interdependence of cultural terrains in which colonizer and colonized co-existed and battled each other through projections as well as rival geographies, narratives, and histories, is to miss what is essential about the world in the past century."[36]

Said's cross-national, cross-cultural, cross-hemispheric vision of decolonization thus helps illuminate the complex ambivalences and hybrid texture of postcolonial poetry. Walcott, for example, can rage at England's Renaissance writers as "Ancestral murderers and poets" and attack them for their complicity in an empire guilty of "the abuse / Of ignorance by Bible and by sword," yet recognize "That Albion too was once / A colony like ours."[37] Similarly, in "The Stranglehold of English Lit.," the Malawian poet Felix Mnthali launches an angry critique of a canonical British novelist, anticipating Said's more nuanced reading of her in *Culture and Imperialism:*

> Your elegance of deceit,
> Jane Austen,
> lulled the sons and daughters
> of the dispossessed
> into a calf-love
> with irony and satire
> around imaginary people.[38]

Slavery "made Jane Austen's people / wealthy beyond compare!" but, from Mnthali's perspective, Austen's sly fiction has blinded modern Africans to the ravages of empire. In attacking Austen, however, Mnthali's poem draws on a more recent European paradigm—the agonistic, modernist apostrophe to a dead canonical writer, such as Pound's to the "detested," "pig-headed" Whitman in "A Pact."[39] Like Walcott's lyric, Mnthali's Janus-faced poem instances the often resistive relation of postcolonial poets to writers who are seen as cultural agents of British imperial expansion and these poets' more affiliative, if still revisionary, relationship with modernist poets—Pound, Eliot, Yeats—whose ambivalent response to the earlier British canon enables their own.

Further, Said's transnationalist view can help us understand and embrace a wide range of poets of decolonization, whether they are nativists or cosmopolitans; whether they are writers in Standard English or writers in creoles, pidgins, and local vernaculars; and whether they are decolonizers of genre, meter, and form or decolonizers of historical and political content. "The extraordinary formal precision and virtuosity of these poems," said Said of *The Country without a Post Office*, "as well as their often searing imagery, derive from Agha Shahid Ali's responses to Kashmir's agony. But this is poetry whose appeal is universal, its voice unerringly eloquent."[40] Like many other poets of decolonization, Ali wrote both in Western forms, such as the canzone and free verse, and in non-Western forms, such as the ghazal, one of which he dedicated to Said, using Darwish's phrase "after the last sky" in an epigraph and within the poem. This ghazal, "By Exiles," ends each couplet with the *radif*, or refrain, "by exiles" and intricately interconnects Said's fate as a Palestinian exile with Ali's as a Kashmiri exile—"two destinies at last reconciled by exiles." In the echoic repetitions of this form, the exilic destinies of a poet and a critic from two embattled, non-self-governing homelands are made to rhyme. The image of a shawl draped on Said's piano—"By the Hudson lies Kashmir, brought from Palestine"—punningly enacts a double geographic displacement (Kashmir is surreally translocated to New York via Palestine) and serves as the intimate basis for this ghazal's linkage of Kashmiri and Palestinian exile.[41] The personal and the public interlock, as Said indicates of Darwish, and in other poems, Ali achieves what Said calls, also in reference to Darwish, "a harassing amalgam of poetry and collective memory." Ali suffers both the military ravages of Kashmir and the more private agonies of a lover's or a mother's death. Western and non-Western forms and public and private griefs converge when Ali closes "Lenox Hill" with the defiant claim that his private mourning for the loss of his mother exceeds even Kashmir's collective, national grief—a distinction that nevertheless further intertwines the two kinds of bereavement:

> For compared to my grief for you, what are those of Kashmir,
> and what (I close the ledger) are the griefs of the universe
> when I remember you—beyond all accounting—O my mother?[42]

"Lenox Hill" hypnotically circulates its rhyme words in accordance with the dictates of the Italian form of the canzone, yet this sonic and verbal repetition also recalls Ali's use of the *radif* in his many poems that follow the conventions of the Persian and Urdu versions of the ghazal. An elegy, the poem invokes the Western tradition of poetic mourning, yet Ali also habitually associated the elegiac with Urdu poetry and culture—even as he also found it in Eliot's *Waste Land*. "Partly because of empire," Said writes, "all cultures are involved in one another; none is single and pure, all are hybrid, heterogeneous, extraordinarily differentiated, and unmonolithic."[43] Said's nuanced attention to the "hybrid" and "heterogeneous" texture of literary works, instead of distracting him from the geopolitical analysis for which he is best known—not poems but politics, not culture but coercion—made him all the more alert to the brutal simplifications of imperial policy. Take, for example, this prescient statement on American self-deception in *Culture and Imperialism,* written more than a decade before the U.S.-led invasion of Iraq. The U.S. government's supposedly well-intentioned schemes to "make the world safe for democracy . . . especially in the Middle East," never succeed, Said states, "because they trap the planners in more illusions of omnipotence and misleading self-satisfaction (as in Vietnam), and because by their very nature they falsify the evidence."[44] In the posthumously published *Humanism and Democratic Criticism,* Said cites Cavafy's famous poem about how an empire needs "barbarians" to construct its identity and legitimacy, even if it must deform reality to do so: "the regretful last line of Cavafy's splendid poem 'Waiting for the Barbarians' suggests, in its lapidary irony, how useful a hostile Other is in such circumstances—'they were, those people, a kind of solution.'"[45] Regrettably, some recent policy makers—far from recognizing that "all cultures are involved in one another," "hybrid, heterogeneous," "unmonolithic"—have split the world into civilization and barbarism, terrorists and democratizers, here and over there. We are reminded of what is torn and shredded by such ideological machinery when we explore, with Said's guidance, the subtly interwoven and ineluctably cross-cultural fabric of the poetry of decolonization.

NOTES

A version of this essay is published in my book *A Transnational Poetics* (Chicago: University of Chicago Press, 2009), part 2 of chapter 7. I wish to thank Namita Goswami, who organized a symposium on Said at DePaul University at which I first presented a version of this paper.

    1. Quoted in Edward W. Said, "On Mahmoud Darwish," *Grand Street* 12, no. 48 (1993): 115.
    2. Ibid., quotes from 112–15.
    3. Edward W. Said, *On Late Style: Music and Literature against the Grain* (New York: Pantheon Books, 2006), 148.
    4. Edward W. Said, *Orientalism* (1978; New York: Vintage-Random House, 1979), 5, 3.
    5. Edward W. Said, *Culture and Imperialism* (New York: Knopf, 1993), xii.
    6. Gertrude Stein, *Everybody's Autobiography* (1937; New York: Cooper Square Publishers, 1971), 289.
    7. Said, *Culture and Imperialism,* 221.
    8. Ibid., 209, 213, 222.
    9. W. B. Yeats, "Man and the Echo," in *The Poems,* rev. ed., ed. Richard J. Finneran, vol. 1 of *The Collected Works of W. B. Yeats,* ed. Finneran and George Mills Harper (New York: Macmillan, 1989), 345.
    10. Said, *Culture and Imperialism,* 226.
    11. Ibid., 225.

12. Frantz Fanon, "Concerning Violence," in *The Wretched of the Earth*, trans. Constance Farrington (New York: Grove Press, 1963), 35–106.

13. Said, *Culture and Imperialism*, 215. In Fanon's words, colonialism "turns to the past of the oppressed people, and distorts, disfigures, and destroys it" (*Wretched of the Earth*, 210).

14. Lorna Goodison, "Guinea Woman," in *Selected Poems* (Ann Arbor: University of Michigan Press, 1992), 64. See A. K. Ramanujan's "Elements of Composition" and "Small-Scale Reflections on a Great House" in *The Collected Poems of A. K. Ramanujan* (Delhi: Oxford University Press, 1995), 96–99, 121–23.

15. Said, *Culture and Imperialism*, 216.

16. Edward W. Said, "The Politics of Knowledge," in *Reflections on Exile and Other Essays* (Cambridge, MA: Harvard University Press, 2000), 378–79.

17. Said, *Culture and Imperialism*, 217 (emphasis in original).

18. Ibid., 229.

19. Ibid., 230.

20. Ibid., 32.

21. Ibid., 196.

22. Derek Walcott, "An Interview with Derek Walcott," conducted in 1977 by Edward Hirsch, *Contemporary Literature* 20, no. 3 (1979): 288; Roddy Doyle, *The Barrytown Trilogy: The Commitments/The Snapper/The Van* (New York: Penguin, 1995), 13. See also Walcott, "Leaving School" (1965), in *Critical Perspectives on Derek Walcott*, ed. Robert D. Hamner (Washington, DC: Three Continents Press, 1993), 32.

23. See, for example, Lorna Goodison, "Bedspread," in *Selected Poems*, 67–68; Agha Shahid Ali, "I See Chile in My Rearview Mirror," in *A Nostalgist's Map of America* (New York: Norton, 1991), 96–99; Tony Harrison, "On Not Being Milton," in *Selected Poems*, 2nd ed. (London: Penguin, 1987), 112.

24. See my "Modernist Bricolage, Postcolonial Hybridity," in *Modernism and Colonialism: British and Irish Literature, 1889–1939*, ed. Richard Begam and Michael Valdez Moses (Durham, NC: Duke University Press, 2007), 287–313; and in *Modernism/Modernity* 13, no. 3 (2006): 445–63.

25. Said, *Culture and Imperialism*, xxv.

26. Ibid., 234, 238.

27. Ibid., 230.

28. See my Yeats chapter in *The Hybrid Muse: Postcolonial Poetry in English* (Chicago: University of Chicago Press, 2001).

29. Onwuchekwa Jemie Chinweizu and Ihechukwu Madubuike, *Toward the Decolonization of African Literature* (1980; Washington, DC: Howard University Press, 1983), 1.

30. Ibid., 163, 170.

31. Ibid., 195, 10.

32. Said, *Culture and Imperialism*, 212.

33. Ibid., 214.

34. Edward Kamau Brathwaite, *History of the Voice: The Development of Nation Language in Anglophone Caribbean Poetry* (London: New Beacon Books, 1984), 21, 23, 35.

35. Ibid., 30–31.

36. Said, *Culture and Imperialism*, xx.

37. Derek Walcott, "Ruins of a Great House," in *Collected Poems, 1948–1984* (New York: Farrar, Straus, and Giroux, 1986), 20.

38. Felix Mnthali, "The Stranglehold of English Lit.," from *Echoes from Ibadan* (Ibadan, privately printed, 1961), reprinted in *The Penguin Book of Modern African Poetry*, 4th ed., ed. Gerald Moore and Ulli Beier (London: Penguin Books, 1998), 172–73.

39. Ezra Pound, "A Pact," in *Personae* (New York: New Directions, 1949), 91.

40. Edward W. Said, as quoted on the back cover of Agha Shahid Ali, *The Country without a Post Office* (1997; New York: Norton, 1998).

41. Agha Shahid Ali, "By Exiles," in *Call Me Ishmael Tonight: A Book of Ghazals* (New York: Norton, 2003), 28–29. On Ali's "tangled literary and cultural loyalties" in this and other ghazals, including Ali's echo of "exiled by exiles" from Said's essay on exile, see David Caplan, *Questions of Possibility: Contemporary Poetry and Poetic Form* (New York: Oxford University Press, 2005), 53–59. On Ali's hybridizing use of refrain and return, as well as a reading of this ghazal, see Malcolm Woodland, "Memory's Homeland: Agha Shahid Ali and the Hybrid Ghazal," *English Studies in Canada* 31, nos. 2–3 (2005): 249–72.

42. Agha Shahid Ali, *The Rooms Are Never Finished* (New York: Norton, 2002), 17–19.

43. Said, *Culture and Imperialism*, xxv.

44. Ibid., xviii–xix.

45. Edward W. Said, *Humanism and Democratic Criticism* (New York: Columbia University Press, 2004), 36. See also his more extended discussion of Cavafy in *Late Style*, 142–48.

10

Edward Said in
Contemporary Arabic Culture

Sabry Hafez

In his *Representations of the Intellectual,* Edward Said suggests that "as an intellectual I present my concerns before an audience or constituency. But this is not just a matter of how I articulate them, but also of what I myself, as someone who is trying to advance the cause of freedom and justice, also represent. I say or write these things because after much reflection they are what I believe; and I also want to persuade others of this view."[1] This statement makes an important point about the identification between the "self," its concerns, the discourse emanating from its intellectual activities, and the role it aspires to play in the world. Said emphasizes this vital ingredient: "There is therefore this quite complicated mix between the private and the public worlds, my own history, values, writings and positions as they derive from my experience, on the one hand, and on the other hand, how these enter into the social world where people debate and make decisions about war and freedom and justice."[2] Therefore, if we are to understand Said's intellectual legacy, his appeal for the Arabic culture, his cultural project, and its impact on the Arabic culture, we must be keenly aware of this "quite complicated mix." The unique mix that went into the making of this remarkable individual appealed, for many reasons and on many levels, to Arab intellectuals and enabled them to take pride in interacting with his cultural project. It is also the reason for Said's wider appeal to intellectuals in the previously colonized countries in Asia, Africa, and Latin America.

As an Arab-Western intellectual, Edward Said was heir to, or a product of, the complex and often painful process of the Arabs' interaction, or rather fascination, with the West. For many Arab intellectuals, Said is an Arab embodiment of the main object of desire of the whole Arabic culture, the West. Hence they can safely embrace him without inviting accusations of betraying their identity or alienating themselves from their culture. If the individual is a product of his/her culture, it is not fair to claim that Said is a product of the Arabic culture, which has been burdened for decades with defeat, tyranny, and schizophrenia while struggling to liberate itself from their shackles. He is the product of the best strand of the rational, liberal humanitarian Western culture, and particularly that of its most powerful languages, the hegemonic English language and to a lesser extent, the French and German ones.[3] This description applies not only because he did not write a single text in Arabic, despite his admirable effort to regain his Arabic language and his joy in speaking it as he sought to recapture his national identity.[4] It is so also because, as we shall see, his cultural formation took place through an English-language education, from Victoria College in Cairo to the Ivy League universities of the United States. Naturally, his intellectual project is a product of this highly rational strand of the Western culture. When Ferial Ghazoul, one of Said's students, planned a special issue of her journal, *Alif: Journal for Comparative Poetics*,[5] to explore the interesting strand of intellectual influences and connections that illuminate Said's project, she found no single Arab intellectual connection. It was easy to trace Said's interaction with ideas from Giambattista Vico, Friedrich Nietzsche, Karl Marx, Antonio Gramsci, Michel Foucault, Raymond Williams, Theodor Adorno, Georg Lukács, Frantz Fanon, Erich Auerbach, Maurice Merleau-Ponty, and other Western intellectuals, but finding an Arab intellectual of their caliber whose ideas or discourse played a role in his project was difficult. This point in no way denies the role played by Arabic culture in the Western renaissance or the impact of Andalusia's flourishing Arabic culture on European literature and thought. In fact, Said endeavored to remind the West of its indebtedness to earlier Arabic culture and to disseminate some of its modern achievements. Indeed, in his work one finds many references to Al-Hallaj, Ibn Hazm, Ibn Khaldun, Jamal al-Din al-Afghani, George Antonius, Jurji Zaydan, and a number of his Arab contemporaries. Yet one is hard put to identify a significant intellectual connection with any of them, apart from the impact of his fellow Palestinian, Ibrahim Abu-Lughod, which was more political and personal. Although we find little significant Arab contribution to Said's intellectual project, Said, as this chapter elaborates, made significant contributions both to Arab causes, such as Palestine, freedom, and justice and to the Arab intellectual scene.

Certainly, Said became, particularly after revisiting his Palestinian identity following the 1967 war, an eloquent voice of dissent in his Western culture, and this activism enhanced Arab intellectuals' identification with him and his appeal in the Arabic culture. But toleration, if not celebration, of difference and dissent is an integral part of liberal rational Western practice while being relatively alien to Arabic public life. From the time of the old sultans to that of contemporary despots and subaltern dictators, the Arabic public arena has been marked by conforming and co-opting practices, with most intellectuals perpetually struggling to gain the blessings of those in power and show one's subservience to them.[6] Even more, Arabic culture, particularly in its recent history, has seen a tidal wave of intellectuals using their connections with the state to crush and discredit their intellectual opponents. This lamentable situation enhanced the allure of Said in Arabic culture, making him stand out as a dissenting intellectual who "speaks truth to power" rather than subjugating truth to the service of those in power. In this respect, Said is perhaps the best product so far of the Arab interaction with the West.

ARAB-WESTERN INTERACTION

Interactions between the Arab world and the West have a long history, but the modern phase of the relationship, from which Said emerges, goes back to the turn of the nineteenth century and the famous French expedition to Egypt in 1798.[7] This brief encounter with the West had a seismic cultural impact on the Arabs, shaking them out of their insular and regressive existence and catapulting them into the modern world.[8] Some countries, as well as individuals, responded with ambitious programs of modernization, while others recoiled from the shock by returning to the traditional past. The initial success of those who selected the path of modernity in the first half of the nineteenth century led to wide acceptance of this trajectory by countries and individuals alike. The Arab world at the time was keen to catch up with the West, particularly Europe, and modeled its modern project on it. Although the last decades of the nineteenth century witnessed the colonialization of many Arab countries, this aggression did not dampen the will to progress or the open acceptance of many Western values, institutions, and ideas.[9]

Traditionalists equated modernization with Westernization, perceiving it from the outset as a process of undermining Islam and its Arabic culture, and they launched an assiduous attack against it. Yet the first few decades of the twentieth century saw an enthusiastic embrace of Western models in most aspects of Arab social and cultural life. Arabs embraced Western, mainly European, educational and legal systems, Western dress, and European codes of conduct, and they developed the necessary infrastructure for cultural transition. The results were a marked change in the intellectual climate and the genesis of modern Arabic narrative genres, such as the novel, the short story, and drama.[10] They also went to the West in large numbers, particularly the Levantines, and Edward's father, Wadi' Said (1895–1971), was one of these émigrés. He left Palestine for the United States in 1911 and lived there until 1920.[11] During his time in the United States, two Arabic journals edited by Levantine emigrants were published, indicating how sizable the Arab community was in America.[12] Like Wadi' Said, many Arabs from Lebanon, Syria, and Palestine went to the Americas and embraced the social and cultural life there. But the most telling aspect of Said's father's experience in the United States is his total adoption of the West. He changed his name to William, became an American citizen, enrolled in the U.S. army, and participated in World War I in France in 1918.

Although Wadi' Said returned to Palestine in 1920 at the insistence of his mother, and married in the traditional Arab way in 1932, his adoption of the Western model governed the rest of his life. His decision to identify with Western ways was clearly reflected in the naming of his children and in their education.[13] He was an Arab Christian of a Protestant denomination, and his sense of being a minority, even within the small Christian Arab community, led him to take certain pride in his American citizenship, which all his children enjoyed but his wife did not. At this time, the United States was the paragon of freedom and modernity and the champion of oppressed nations and minorities, a far cry from the America of the present time.

By the time he left the United States, one of the most influential, innovative literary movements in modern Arabic culture had started in New York. In 1920 a group of Levantine intellectuals established al-Rabitah al-Qalamiyyah (the Pen Association) headed by Jibran Khalil Jibran (1883–1931).[14] The establishment of this group as the first Mahjar movement was the Levantine equivalent of the Egyptian al-Diwan Group.[15] It is not a mere coincidence, that while Jibran and his colleagues— some of whom had been publishing cultural periodicals such as *al-Sa'ih* (1912–24?) and *al-Funun* (1913–18) for years before—al-Diwan Group emerged in Cairo in the same year. Both groups were the culmination of a long process of development from neoclassical verve to romantic sensibility, which started at the beginning of the century with Jibran's *'Ara'is al-Muruj* (Prides of the Meadows, 1906) and *Al-Arwah al-Mutamarridah* (*Rebellious Spirits*, 1908), and the highly sentimental works of Mustafa Lutfi al-Manfaluti (1872–1924).[16] The Pen Association and al-Diwan Group both grew out of genuine cultural needs, although they developed their work and ideas in isolation of each other, yet both strongly embraced Western romantic notions and adapted them to Arabic cultural conditions. When 'Abbas Mahmud al-'Aqqad (1889–1964), the leading figure of al-Diwan Group, discovered the work of the Pen Association, he strongly identified with it and perceived it as a vindication of his group's ideas, which were meeting strong resistance in Egypt. He republished some of the work of members of the Pen Association in Egypt and collected the critical articles of Mikha'il Nu'aimah in the latter's first book, *Al-Ghurbal* (The Sieve, 1923).

In his introduction to Nu'aimah's book, al-'Aqqad states clearly that the Pen Association developed parallel ideas to those of his group, but with more flare, sophistication, and maturity. This comment is an implicit confession that firsthand contact with the West was highly appreciated at the time and viewed with great admiration. Al-Diwan Group was equally driven by cultural and patriotic agendas, which limited its impact to Egypt, whereas the Pen Association had a literary focus and had firsthand contact with many of the major works of European romanticism. This emphasis broadened its appeal and made it highly influential in many Arab countries, from Iraq to Tunisia. However, the two movements consolidated the hold of Western romantic ideas, innovative literary enterprise, and rational thought on the vibrant field of modern Arabic literature. By the beginning of the following decade, their combined endeavor triumphed with the formation of the Apollo Group in 1932, the first pan-Arab romantic movement.[17] Thus the actions and attitudes of Edward Said's father were representative of a wide range of activities and endeavors taking place at the time in the Arab world. The adoption of Western models was all encompassing, affecting the way of life as much as cultural modes of expression and thought. This effect was particularly pronounced among the Christian minorities of the Arab world, who felt a stronger affinity with the West than did their Muslim counterparts.[18] This statement is in no way an indictment of the Christian minorities; it simply notes a fact. Undoubtedly, their sociocultural background enabled them to play a significant role, particularly in Greater Syria, in the struggle against European occupation and the formation of Arab nationalism. They also played a momentous role in changing and modernizing the Arabic language and mobilized the Arabic grammatical laws of derivations to absorb new words and concepts into the system without upsetting it. In a sense, they made classical Arabic conducive to the demands and rubrics of modernity.

A WESTERN FORMATION

Edward Said was born in Jerusalem in 1935, but despite his American citizenship, he was not brought up in America, whose Arab community was brimming with romantic liberalism. He spent his childhood and the early years of his cultural and educational formation in colonial Egypt of the 1930s and 1940s, with intermittent visits to and vacations in Palestine.[19] At the time Egypt, and particularly Cairo, was a turbulent place full of contradictions and teeming with social and political movements that spanned the political spectrum, from the Muslim Brothers to the Communists. But Edward was neither aware of nor touched by any of this upheaval, for he was raised in the protective cocoon of the liberal, cosmopolitan Egypt of foreigners and minorities. He enjoyed the comforts of a well-to-do middle-class family and the benefits of solid private education. As a young boy in the mid-1940s, he was shocked when Mr. Pilley, the British secretary of the Gezira Club, called him an Arab. "Arabs aren't allowed here, and you're an Arab."[20] Yet there was what Said later called "a fatalistic compact between my father and myself about our necessarily inferior status. He knew about it, I discovered it publicly for the first time face to face with Pilley, yet neither of us saw it as worth a struggle of any kind, and that realisation shames me still."[21]

The events of the following years saw the Palestinian Nakba, the loss of his home, and the uprooting of many of his relatives, but the young boy was protected from its tragedy by his father's wealth and his American citizenship. He went first to an English school in 1941, then to Cairo School for American Children in 1946, and then to the Victoria College in 1949, the school for children of the colonial elite.[22]

In 1951 he went to the United States, and after a year in Mount Hermon, he enrolled at Princeton. He then went to Harvard for his postgraduate studies, which culminated in his doctoral thesis on Joseph Conrad in 1963.[23] This education and cultural formation established his strong foundation in Western literary culture and methodology, and ironically enhanced his appeal to Arab culture and intellectuals two decades later. But it also took him away from the "inferior status" of the "Arab." His father warned him, upon his arrival in America, "in the United States one should stay away from the Arabs. They will never do anything for you and they will pull you down . . . They'll always be a hindrance. They neither keep what is good about Arab culture, nor show any solidarity with each other."[24] Edward seems to have heeded his father's advice: he neglected his Arabic language and culture, specialized in English and comparative literature, and pursued a scholarly career in American academia.

Yet the nagging sense of being "out of place" continued to haunt him, and the accumulation of "hurt" and "injustice" finally caught up with him and drove him back to his culture.[25] One can now read Said's career retrospectively and see how his acute sense of being an "exile" and "out of place" motivated his existential choice of Conrad—who, like himself, experienced both geographic and linguistic displacement—as the topic of his doctoral dissertation. Said shared with the writer the perspective of a decentered self, capable of seeing the culture of the "other" from within and from outside at the same time. Conrad also raised issues of identity, uprooted and broken histories, subjectivity, and the dynamic tension between cultures, powers, and people.

Said's sense of exile and "hurt" also drove him, at an early stage of his career, to break new ground. The 1950s and 1960s in American academia were dominated by the all-"American" approach of New Criticism, which most young scholars accepted without questioning. In a move highly unusual for a young scholar writing his dissertation, Said rejected the methodology of the New Criticism, finding its treatment of the text as a "verbal icon" autonomous from its context and divorced from the author's history, identity, and experience to be an inadequate tool for unlocking the hidden meanings of Conrad's work. Instead of adopting New Criticism's textual analysis and linguistic investigation of the text, Said opted for the more sophisticated approach of uncovering and articulating the essence of the consciousness at work in the text. He selected the phenomenological approach of the Geneva School, which eschewed formalist or objective methods in favor of a phenomenological study of the work that sought to constitute an author's worldview from his literary language.[26] Adherents to this approach see in the literary work the essence and structure of human consciousness as shaped by the author's history, identity, vision, and experience, and they read in it the sedimentation of all these elements in a transsubjective mode of understanding that does not divorce the text from its author or its history. Said found the sensitive hermeneutic strategy of this approach, which probes the work for signals that disclose the structure of consciousness, more conducive to the underlying sense of displacement and exile in Conrad's texts. For the Geneva School, the author's projection of imaginative worlds is the key to his existential identity, so the critic's task is to identify recurring patterns of space-time experience in the author's work. Said found this idea attractive in articulating the underlying structure of consciousness that attracted him to Conrad.

NEW BEGINNINGS

Using such a new approach in the American academy, with its unique blend of existential and phenomenological criticism, Said established his academic credentials from an early age. His cumulative work in the nine years between the publication of his doctorate and the appearance of his accomplished book *Beginnings* in 1975 established him as an erudite scholar with unique methodology, profound insight, and sensitive critical judgment.[27] These were the years of the rise of literary theory in America, and instead of following in the footsteps of the Russian formalists, French structuralists, or deconstructionalists (whose theories he had nonetheless deeply absorbed), as many of his contemporaries did, Said developed a unique theoretical genealogy.[28] He neither rooted his project in the semiotic structuralist genealogy that led eventually to deconstruction, as the Yale critics did, nor in Marxist literary theory, as Fredric Jameson and others did. He was already ahead of his American colleagues in his early rejection of New Criticism and his selection of the Geneva School approach for his doctorate. But with the publication of his *Beginnings: Intention and Method*, he established his reputation as an original scholar who developed his own path.

In his intransitive *Beginnings* he rooted his work in the overlooked work of Giambattista Vico, whose *The New Science* (1725) questions the universality of knowledge and the certitude of accepted convictions and establishes the historicity of these concepts. He then combined this concept of knowledge with the archaeology of Michel Foucault after subjecting it to a rigorous Nietzschean questioning of its origin and purpose. From this analysis he posited his unique theory of "the novel as beginning intention." By the time he wrote *Orientalism*, he had modified this theoretical approach by adding a geographical dimension through the work of another Italian intellectual, Antonio Gramsci, who gave the national identity and geographical locations their important role in our perception of culture and thought. The use of Gramsci's work and the dialogue with his ideas coincided with Said's discovery of the work of the Frankfurt School and particularly that of Theodor Adorno and Walter Benjamin. In his later work, Said became much closer to Adorno, his ideas and critical method, than to any other thinker. Not only did Said share Adorno's passion for music and admire his great writing on it, but he also admired the breadth, variety, and individuality of his thinking and his ability to blend the creative, critical, and philosophical elements in a lucid and impossibly simple style. The same can be said about Said. More importantly, if Adorno has offered us through his "negative dialectics" the theory of the untheorizable in philosophy and music, Said has achieved a similar theorization in the literary field. Like Adorno, Said came to emphasize the importance of individual honesty and passion, reject orthodoxy, and defend the virtue of *nicht mitmachen*, not playing along or compromising in the name of expediency. Those who knew Said would recognize the Adorno-like uncompromising stance in the activities of his later years, particularly in his politics.

ORIENTALISM'S NEW PATH

The disastrous defeat of 1967 and the encounter with Ibrahim Abu-Lughod played a decisive role in Edward Said's intellectual reorientation toward his Arab identity and culture.[29] Abu-Lughod recruited Said to the AAUG (Association of Arab American University Graduates) and asked him to write his first text on an Arab topic.[30] Said wrote an article for a special issue edited by Abu-Lughod of *Arab World,* the Arab League's monthly published in New York. Some scholars speculated that this piece was the seed from which *Orientalism* germinated, because the article raises the question of representation, or rather misrepresentation, of a whole culture. In his homage to Abu-Lughod, Said settled this issue: "I used the occasion to look at the image of the Arabs in the media, popular literature and cultural representations going back to the middle ages. This was the origin of my book *Orientalism,* which I dedicated to Janet and Ibrahim."[31] But from that time on, Said's interest in and engagement with the Arab world in general, and the Palestinian question in particular, never ceased.

However, we should not reduce Said's reengagement with the Arab world to this moment, for the process was a lengthy one, as he indicates in his memoir, *Out of Place.* It simmered under the surface of his many interests for a long time until the demands of a questioning Arab like Abu-Lughod and then the cataclysmic events of the wars provided a conduit for its development. Said was a highly driven individual who was keen to excel and to consolidate his academic achievement through major theoretical work before taking off in a new direction.[32] Not until 1978 was the book that made his international reputation, *Orientalism,* published. He wrote the book without interruption in less than a year, and it is doubtful that *Orientalism* would have been written if not for the 1967 and 1973 wars and Said's greater involvement in Palestinian politics. Another important influence was the year between these wars that Said spent in Beirut finishing *Beginnings* and perfecting his Arabic.[33] But no doubt the coverage of these two wars in the Western media and the synergy between the words and actions of the Occidental establishment motivated his grand project by directing his attention to the wide gulf between the reality of the Orient and its representation in Western discourse. This confluence of events led him to provide us with the most compelling narrative available of European humanism's complicity in the colonial project of subjugating and misrepresenting the Orient. *Orientalism* married the theoretical acuteness and acumen of *Beginnings* with the inventory of hurt and injustice suffered by the Orient. This combination gave the book's powerful theoretical postulations a strong moral underpinning that not only made it relevant to a large number of wronged cultures but also appealed to the humanistic drive at the heart of liberal Western culture.[34]

Although Said had gained recognition in the field of English literature and modern languages before the publication of *Orientalism*, he had made little or no impact outside these circles and was entirely unknown in the Arab world. The breadth of this groundbreaking book's coverage and the originality of its thesis quickly made it an international success. It soon became the cornerstone of a larger project of deconstructing colonial discourses and practices to analyze their impact on culture and politics, values and perception, literature and identity. With his two subsequent books, *The Question of Palestine* (1979) and *Covering Islam* (1981), Said fleshed out his theory of Orientalism with case studies vindicating its methodology and opening the floodgates to the many postcolonial case studies that followed and continue to flow today. The wide debate triggered by this project has continued to grow and has given rise to the flourishing disciplines of postcolonial criticism, cultural criticism, and new historicism.

Orientalism introduced Said to the Arab world. Unfortunately, it was badly translated into Arabic; as Radwa 'Ashur, a professor of English literature and an accomplished novelist and critic, writes in her able study of Said's work, "The Arabic translation of *Orientalism* is confused, ambiguous and suffers from many problems, the most obvious of which is the transformation of a lucid and enjoyable book into a difficult text laden with incomprehensible terminology."[35] Aside from obfuscating his brilliant argument, the translation had a negative impact on his legacy and on the perception of his work in Arabic culture and among its intellectuals. The book was the first of Said's to be translated into Arabic and the thick verbosity, pretentious terminology, and confused vocabulary of the translation associated Said with a type of sterile and problematic language that was the hallmark of the coterie of Adonis, a clique that clung to Said for some time and complicated perceptions of him in Arab intellectual circles for years, until he successfully shook it off.[36]

Thanks to the opacity of the translation, many ardent opponents of modernity and Westernization in the Arab world—the Islamicists and traditionalists who by virtue of their ideology are the natural enemies of Said's cultural and ideological stance—exuberantly embraced the book. They perceived it as a new rendering of their traditional attack on the Orientalists, one that articulated in the language of their adversaries their grievance and sense of injustice and hurt vis-à-vis the West. That they saw a text so radically at odds with their approach in this way was ironic, for their attack had been historically motivated by religious convictions and their belief that Orientalists aimed to undermine Islam and distort its image.[37] Thus, instead of seeing Said's seminal work as exposing (and undermining) the basis and motivation of the Orientalist discourse, they considered it the latest in a series of diatribes against the misrepresentation of Islam in European discourse.[38] In the process, they completely overlooked Said's most persuasive argument—about the dialectics of knowledge and power, the complicity of discourse in the dynamics of hegemony and imperialism, and the fabrication of an inferior Orient as justification for its subjugation and conquest. Overlooked, too, was the book's insight into how Europeans viewed the Orient as an absolute "Other," inferior and exotic. More importantly, Said's implicit call for the Orient to represent itself and purge its culture of the traces and sedimentation of the Orientalist legacy was lost.[39]

   Though the message of Said's *Orientalism* was distorted in Arabic intellectual circles—and indeed among the wider public through the traditionalists' widely disseminated misrepresentation of his main thesis as a kind of identity politics—the book did spark a wider debate on the issues it addressed. A meaningful discussion ensued among Arab scholars who had read the book in its original English or French translation, and their number grew with time.[40] In addition, some of the Western writings on the book were translated into Arabic in the 1990s in a way that redressed the balance. Thanks to these efforts, which eventually corrected the earlier misunderstanding of *Orientalism,* and as a result of the dissemination of Said's later writings and growing engagement with Arab politics, his impact on the Arab intellectual scene is now compared to that of the early pioneers of engagement with Western discourse in Arabic culture—towering figures like Rifa'ah Rafi' al-Tahtawi (1801–73), Ahmad Faris al-Shidyaq (1804–87), and Khayr al-Din al-Tunisi (1810–90), whose contributions radically changed the terms of cultural interaction with Western discourse. Indeed, Said's trajectory from a deep concern with Western culture to an equally profound interest in Arabic issues gave many intellectuals great hope and impetus.

SAID'S TRAVELING THEORIES

Whatever the damage caused in Arab intellectual circles by the misrepresentation of *Orientalism,* it was soon overcome by Said's erudition, range, élan, and prolific productivity. The publication in 1983 of *The World, the Text, and the Critic,* which contains some of his most astute theoretical essays, coincided with the launch in Cairo of *Fusul,* the first journal in Arabic dedicated to literary criticism and literary theory.[41] *Fusul* soon became a pan-Arab cultural forum for theory and critical debates, and within a few years it had energized the Arabic critical scene and invigorated its voracious quest for theoretical investigation. It changed the nature of Arabic critical discourse and conducted a far-reaching dialogue with many strands of modern critical theory, particularly structuralism, Russian formalism, Marxism, deconstruction, reception theory, and psychoanalytic interpretation of literature.

In the early years of *Fusul* the names of Roland Barthes, Michel Foucault, Jacques Derrida, Jacques Lacan, Wolfgang Iser, Walter Benjamin, Terry Eagleton, and Fredric Jameson were encountered far more frequently than Said's. *Fusul* also translated works by many of these literary theorists in its pages, but nothing by Said.[42] This regrettable situation was soon corrected with the relaunch in Ramallah, in the early 1990s, of the Palestinian quarterly *Al-Karmal*, which translated a number of Said's important critical essays.[43] Even in *Fusul*, with the maturation of contemporary Arabic critical discourse, Said and his ideas gained more currency, as did those of Mikhail Bakhtin, Antonio Gramsci, Pierre Bourdieu, and Gilles Deleuze. This shift occurred as the ephemeral appeal of structuralism—with its susceptibility to imitative reproduction of its tenets—wore off. Arabic criticism had to go through this less demanding phase of theorization, borrowing, and adaptation—and what Said called the "remorseless indignation of orthodoxy and the expression of tired advocacy"[44]—before grappling with the critical theories of the newer group of critics, with their more subtle and complex critical insights.

The publication of Said's famous articles "Traveling Theory" and "Traveling Theory Reconsidered" dealt a sharp blow to the prevailing tone of Arab critics, who had long contented themselves with simply replicating Western theory or, at best, applying its tenets to Arabic texts.[45] The encounter with Said's "traveling theory" encouraged many to shake off their dependency on, even enslavement to, these theories. More specifically, Said in these two articles argues against turning literary theory into a cultural dogma, which, appropriated by schools or institutions, can quickly acquire the status of authority, erecting walls around itself and becoming the closed domain of specialists and acolytes. He argues instead for a more attractive alternative, a theory of permanent dissonance, deconsecration, decentralization, and demystification, a Gramscian counterhegemony that rejects enslavement to dominant systems. According to Said, any study of the way in which theories travel reveals the inevitability of change and transformation at every junction of the journey and in every aspect of the theory—techniques of dissemination, communication, and interpretation. And with his belief in noncoercive human community, he thinks this is as it should be. Theory, as he states in the second essay, "is to travel, always to move beyond its confinements, to emigrate, to remain in a sense in exile ... [in] a geographical dispersion of which the theoretical motor is capable ... [in a] movement [that] suggests the possibility of different locales, sites, situations for theory without facile universalism or over-general totalizing."[46]

Just as Said called upon the Orient to represent itself and speak out in *Orientalism*, here he argues for the critic's liberation from the dogma of theory. He observes that in "the Arab world there is this tendentious reliance on and even blind replication of unitary theories without a clear effort to change these theories to something relevant to the Arab culture."[47] Many Arab critics, such as Ceza Qasim (Egypt), Muhammad Barrada (Morocco), Ferial Ghazoul (Iraq), Yumna al-'Id (Lebanon), Subhi Hadidi (Syria), and Fakhri Salih (Jordan), to mention but a few, embraced his call and spoke out on the need to liberate Arabic critical discourse from the grip of Western theory and the drudgery of imitation. It is no longer viable to import Western literary theory or apply it blindly to Arabic literary phenomena or texts. Nonetheless, it is easier to reject the tyranny of universalism, as Said has shown us, than to make a lasting contribution to its modification and change. Thus, though many Arab critics have understood Said's lesson that "no one today is purely one thing," the task of bringing creativity, originality, and sophistication to literary theory while taking into account cultural plurality is still in its infancy in Arabic critical discourse.[48]

Many Arab critics also understood Said's aversion to linear subsuming histories and a unitary sense of identity, as well as his preference for a contrapuntal approach sensitive enough to deal with the complexity of historical experience. "All cultures," he wrote, "are involved in one another; none is single and pure, all are hybrid, heterogeneous, extraordinarily differentiated, and unmonolithic. This, I believe is as true of the contemporary United States as it is of the modern Arab world."[49] Admittedly, practicing contrapuntal criticism without the advantage of Said's multicultural erudition and talent for "musical elaborations" is difficult. Nonetheless, precisely because of Said's approach, Arab critics are now more confident in using critical notions without being bound by them. The growing sophistication of Arabic critical discourse is in part due to Said's contribution, and this greater sophistication in turn generates wider appreciation of his work.

CULTURAL CRITICISM

It is natural, therefore, that Said's next major work, *Culture and Imperialism* (1993), which saw the culmination of his critical project of deconstructing the Western narrative, received considerable attention in Arab intellectual circles long before it was translated into Arabic. The book was extensively reviewed in the Arabic press and quoted in academic papers, and it inspired several academic studies. In a paper delivered at a conference in Cairo in January 2004, Radwa 'Ashur enumerates several academic projects inspired by Said's approach that young researchers have undertaken in Egyptian universities. A recent example of the book's impact was a January 2004 conference organized by the Egyptian Society of Literary Criticism that took as its main theme *al-Naqd al-Thaqafi*, "cultural criticism."[50] Arab intellectuals are increasingly using the term *al-Naqd al-Tahqafi* to refer to the critical approach associated with the work of Said. They are showing a marked preference for Said's cultural criticism over the "postcolonial" strand of his work, *Naqd ma Ba'd al-*

Isti'mar, that is preferred in the West. The most obvious reason for this preference is the deep-rooted Arab sense of cultural confidence that derives from an often exaggerated pride in its classical legacy. This attitude is buttressed by the tendency to understate colonialism's impact on Arabic culture. Unlike many colonized countries that adopted "the language of the colonizer" in their writing, Arabic culture has a sustained literary history and a pride in its language and cultural integrity that was not eroded by colonialism. With the notable exception of Algerian works, the bulk of the Arab world's cultural output, even during the period of colonialism, was written in Arabic and was marked by the quest for national identity and resistance to colonialism.

The work of those Arab intellectuals who did write in French or English, even those that achieved prominence in the West, tended to be dismissed by the Arab intellectual mainstream as marginal contributions to the languages in which they were written rather than seen as Arab cultural products. In addition, the early fascination with Western genres, which led a writer like Naguib Mahfouz, for example, to aspire in the 1940s to emulate Sir Walter Scott's historical novels, and in the 1950s, to mirror the European realistic novel, has dwindled and receded. By the 1970s and 1980s, Mahfouz was conducting a creative intertextual dialogue in his novels with archetypal Arabic narrative form. For example, he drew on the folk epic in his 1977 *Malhamat al-Harafish (Harafish)* and his 1982 novel *Layali Alf Layla (Arabian Nights and Days),* and he mimicked the dictionaries of the notables in his fascinating 1987 novel *Hadith al-Sabah wa'l-Masa' (Talk of Morning and Evening).*[51] This shift to a creative dialogue with Arabic narrative forms and genres enriched Arabic literature, and Said played an important role in promoting the mature examples of Arabic narrative, using his enormous symbolic capital and influential position in the cultural field to lend credence to many works of Arabic literature. Among the many writers he introduced to the wider literary audience are Naguib Mahfouz, Ahdaf Souief, Gamal al-Ghitani (Egypt), Mahmoud Darwish, Mourid al-Barghouthi (Palestine), Al-Tayyib Salih (Sudan), Halim Barakat (Syria), and Ilyas Khoury (Lebanon).

By a pleasant concurrence, Arabic literature's renewed interest in older Arabic narrative forms and genres coincided with the introduction of Said's critical contribution. As a result, the Arab intelligentsia embraced his cultural criticism, seeing it as a more comprehensive approach to culture and criticism than existing approaches, given that it brought together history, geography, the notion of knowledge and power, and critical insight. Thus "cultural criticism," in contrast to the postcolonial strand of Said's thought, does not confine itself to issues of representation, instead reaching for a more comprehensive reading of the text. The Western response to Said's project, in contrast, generally rests on readings of the colonized work written in the main languages of the colonizers, English and French.

Arab critical discourse is increasingly embracing Said's contribution not only for its perceptive critical insights but also for its effort to liberate Arab criticism from the drudgery of subsisting on the crumbs of Western theory. In particular, Arab critics have come to believe that the absence of an all-encompassing theory of Arab culture led to the adoption of imported theories, making Arab scholars' methodology derivative and ultimately trapping them in a methodological nexus against which they rebelled. When Said's theory became known in the Arab world, scholars saw it as a genuine Arab contribution that assumed a world of creativity and equality and thereby offered a way out of the methodological dependency on the West. Though well aware that Said's contribution was deeply rooted in Western thought and methodology—and indeed was created in a Western language—they looked to the subversive power of its rebellion against the reigning orthodoxy and methods in literary criticism. Because of Said's towering accomplishment, the trajectory of his intellectual output, and his increasing involvement in Arab cultural and political affairs, he was a role model for many Arab intellectuals during the last decade of his life. Such a figure was vital for the Arab culture at this time, when it suffered a low ebb culturally and politically and was often the target of Western abuse. Said, much to his dismay, was often treated as a paragon of wisdom, with people taking his every word as an inspired and insightful revelation. The role of the intellectual who speaks truth to power is Said's most appealing and lasting contribution to the Arabic cultural scene.

SPEAKING TRUTH TO POWER

Traditionally, ever since Abu-Zarr al-Ghifari refused to be co-opted by the Ummayad caliphs in the eighth century, Arabic culture has revered the oppositional intellectual who articulates the unsaid and speaks truth to power. But since the death of the critic, dramatist, and short story writer Yusuf Idris (1927–91) and the co-option and silencing of most Arab intellectuals, the Arabic cultural scene has lacked the voice of a strong and effective oppositional intellectual with the stature, recognized achievements, and moral authority to speak truth to the corrupt subaltern powers that dominate culture and politics in today's Arab world. In filling this role, Said may have made his most appealing and lasting contribution to the Arabic cultural scene.

Said summarized the situation in the Arab world during recent decades as follows: "In the Arab world, the brave, if airy and sometimes destructive, pan-Arab nationalism of the Nasser period which abated during the 1970s has been replaced with a set of local and regional creeds, most of them administered harshly by unpopular, uninspired minority regimes. They are now threatened by a whole array of Islamic movements. There have remained, however, a secular cultural opposition in each Arab country; the most gifted writers, artists, political commentators, intellectuals are generally a part of it, although they constitute a minority many of whom have been hounded into silence or exile."[52]

Said was well aware that this sorry state of affairs was the product of the unholy alliance between the corrupt political regimes in the oil-rich states and in the United States. He was equally aware of the impact of this alliance on secular intellectuals and of the lasting damage inflicted on their secular project and on the wider political and cultural world. The secular cultural opposition suffered most from the deterioration of the political scene and from cultural expediency that often approached dependency. This lamentable situation, in which intellectuals were co-opted to an extraordinary degree, undermined the legitimacy of the intelligentsia in the eyes of its constituency. Most Arab "intellectuals" were stuck in the habit of mind that Said called "avoidance"—"that characteristic turning away from a difficult and principled position which you know to be the right one, but which you decide not to take. You do not want to be too political; you are afraid of seeming controversial; you need the approval of a boss or an authority figure; you want to keep a reputation of being balanced, objective, moderate."[53] These considerations take an even cruder form in the Arab world, where the risk is not simply that an outspoken critic will seem controversial but that he or she will be persecuted, harassed, imprisoned, or barred from working or publishing.

In this context a rapid series of tragic developments took place in the region that had dizzying effects on readers and intellectuals alike. As the political situation rapidly deteriorated in the Arab world, with Arab regimes losing their legitimacy in the eyes of their people, the gulf between people's feelings about national, social, and political issues and the actions and discourse of their governments was as wide as it had been in modern time. The secular intellectuals found themselves pressed between the hammer of the illegitimate regimes (which co-opted or silenced them) and the anvil of the rising Islamic fundamentalism (which marginalized their role and deprived them of their natural constituency). Both readers and secular intellectuals sought a figurehead, or rather a fearless vocal intellectual, as a rallying point. They needed an intellectual who could speak for the people whom Frantz Fanon, a vital source of Said's thought, called "the wretched of the earth"—the oppressed and the marginalized—but they also yearned for an ethical approach to politics based on real justice, one that would make life human and possible in the face of a pernicious moral vacuum. Who else but a towering figure like Said could put down the barons of American media with devastating elegance and panache and defend Arabic culture:

> The Nahda brought freedom from the religious texts, and surreptitiously introduced new secularism into what Arabs said and wrote. Thus contemporary complaints by New York Times idiot-savant Thomas Friedman and tired old Orientalists like Bernard

Lewis who keep repeating the formula that Islam (and the Arabs) need a Reformation have no basis at all, since their knowledge of the language is so superficial and their use of it non-existent as they show no acquaintance whatever with actual Arabic usage where the traces of reformation in thought and practice are everywhere to be found.[54]

In his last decade Said played such a role, not only by his distinguished intellectual project, which probed the central relationships between history, narrative, and politics, but also by his active involvement in the Palestinian question. The intellectual, for Said,

> is an individual with a specific public role in society that cannot be reduced simply to being a faceless professional, a component member of a class just going about her/his business. The central fact for me is, I think, that the intellectual is an individual endowed with a faculty for representing, embodying, articulating a message, a view, an attitude, philosophy or opinion to, as well as for a public . . . whose place it is publicly to raise embarrassing questions, to confront orthodoxy and dogma, rather than to produce them, to be someone who cannot easily be co-opted by governments or corporations, and whose raison d'être is to represent all those people and issues that are routinely forgotten or swept under the rug.[55]

This quote could as easily describe Said himself and his role in the Arab intellectual scene at the time. His blistering attack on institutions' cynical reliance on Orwellian "newspeak" to disguise the truth and stifle morality and justice was among his prized achievements. A deafening silence and intellectual vacuum lay beneath the din of official media and the stifling jargon of conformity, making the Arab public hungry for a vocal and authoritative voice. And at just this time Said became an active presence on the cultural scene, writing regular columns and articles in Arabic for *Al-Hayah* and in English for *Al-Ahram Weekly*.[56] Although most of these articles were political journalism, rather than scholarship, their level of discourse put them on a par with his literary essays, which continued to appear in Arabic translation. Said's literary and cultural project certainly undermined the bastion of regressive traditional power and helped to detonate a wider cultural debate. He was an Arab intellectual who was independent from the establishment both economically and politically, and he was a person of achievement and international fame who was willing to mobilize on behalf of an ongoing struggle and his embattled community.

Said was without doubt a vociferous public critic of these powers. But to play the role that the Arab public demanded of him, he was keen to demonstrate the importance of reconciling "one's identity and the actualities of one's own culture, society, and history to the reality of other identities, cultures, peoples. This can never be done simply by asserting one's preference for what is already one's own: tubthumping about the glories of 'our' culture or the triumphs of 'our' history is not worthy of the intellectual's energy, especially not today when so many societies are comprised of different races and backgrounds as to resist any reductive formulas."[57] In other words, he felt strongly about the need to reeducate the public to bring it along with him. We may not be able to measure the success of his effort, but his message is continuing to find voice in the writing of many Arab intellectuals, particularly critics. In his recent books, the Egyptian critic Jabir 'Asfur draws on Said's work to develop a new language and critical idiom.[58] In addition, two major Arabic periodicals have recently dedicated issues to his work.[59]

Although Said's project is passionately persuasive, it defies closure and certainty. Its purely secular orientation increases its appeal both to intellectuals and to the wider public in the Arab world. His intellectual orientation further enlarges his constituency, lending legitimacy and authenticity to his work and making it relevant to contemporary Arabic culture. Indeed, his intellectual trajectory in some ways parallels that of Arab culture in the modern period, first showing unquestioning acceptance of the Western model and submitting to the process of reeducation in its schools. But upon suffering cumulative "hurt" and "injustice" at the hands of the West, both Said and Arabic culture began to rethink the unconditionality of this acceptance. The parallel ends there, of course, for in the Arab world, this questioning led some to reject the West totally and more generally gave way to regression and despondency. To this situation Said brought fresh air with his secular criticism, penetrating insight, and courage.

In the years to come, Said's impact on the Arabic culture, as elsewhere, is sure to grow and flourish. The changes he has already engendered cannot, or may I say should not, be easily reversed. I base this prediction both on the growing interest in his work in the Arab world since his departure and on Said's notion that "all criticism is postulated and performed on the assumption that it is to have a future."[60] The future of his work seems secure as we see growing interest in his accomplishments in the Arab world, not only in his political work and moral stance but also in his most difficult theoretical texts. Michael Wood, in his introduction to Said's posthumously published *On Late Style*, argues that Said's premature departure took place in his middle period rather than his late period. Yet he poses an interesting question:

> Is this to say that Said himself didn't have a late style? He certainly had the politics and morality he associated with late style, a devotion to the truth of unreconciled relations, and in this sense his own work joins the company of the essays, poems, novels, and operas he writes about. But lateness is not all, any more than ripeness is, and Said found the same politics and morality, the same passions, in other places and persons; indeed they are his own earlier politics and morality and passion. Lateness 'elucidates and dramatizes,' as he says in another context, makes it hard for us to go on with our delusions.[61]

But one can confidently say that Said's work, not only his literary and musical criticism, where he made a lasting contribution, but also his writing on politics, morality, and the intellectual, will make it hard for Arabic culture and Arab intellectuals to go on with their delusions.

NOTES

A shorter version of this chapter appeared as "Edward Said's Intellectual Legacy in the Arab World," *Journal of Palestine Studies* 131/33, no. 3 (Spring 2004): 76–90.

1. Edward Said, *Representations of the Intellectual: The 1993 Reith Lectures* (London: Vintage Books, 1994), 9.

2. Ibid.

3. My emphasis in this chapter is on one strand, because Said himself devoted a large part of his intellectual project to fight the other negative strands in Western culture.

4. For a detailed account of Said's profound relationship with the Arabic language, see his eloquent essay "Living in Arabic," published posthumously in *Al-Ahram Weekly*, Cairo, 12–18 February 2004.

5. See "Edward Said and Critical Decolonization," ed. Ferial J. Ghazoul, special issue, *Alif: Journal of Comparative Poetics*, American University in Cairo, no. 25 (2005).

6. Of course, such practices are not reserved for the Arab world; the West is also full of bigotry and narrow-mindedness.

7. Interactions between the Arab world and the West started in the seventh century and reached their peak in the ninth and tenth centuries. This period saw the expansion of Arabic culture in the Islamic world, great cultural development, and growing awareness of the importance and acquisition of knowledge, regardless of its origin. It started with the translation of Greek, Syriac, Aramaic, and Hellenic works into Arabic, first during the Umayyad period and then during the Abbasid Caliphate. In 830, Bayt al-Hikma (House of Wisdom) was established to translate mostly Western works. This phase saw great acculturation, translation of the Greek canon, and assimilation of many of its tenets into an ever-expanding Arabic culture. The culture was in control of this project, for the source of the knowledge it was acquiring was absent and played no rule in the culture or in the process of interaction. The mirror image of this phase took place after the Crusades, between the twelfth and fifteenth centuries, when Europeans adopted and translated, particularly into Latin, Arabic knowledge and works in large numbers. The interaction in these two phases was marked by peaceful interchanges, with the self dealing with the knowledge of an absent other and setting its own pace and agenda. But this situation changed in the third phase of the Arabs' interaction with the West, which started with the nineteenth century and continues to this day. This period, to which Said devoted considerable study in *Orientalism*, is marked by tension, conflict, colonialism, and power politics.

8. Although I devoted a book-length study (*The Genesis of Arabic Narrative Discourse: A Study in the Sociology of Modern Arabic Literature* [London: Saqi Books, 1993]) to the complexity of the process of change and modernity, showing how its seeds germinated long before the turn of the nineteenth century, here I note the French expedition as a significant milestone along this long road.

9. Apart from Algeria, which was colonized in 1830, most of the Arab countries fell under the yoke of colonialism in the last two decades of the nineteenth century.

10. For a detailed study of the process of cultural transition see my *Genesis of Arabic Narrative Discourse*.

11. For a detailed account of Said's father's time in the United States, read chapter 1 of Edward W. Said, *Out of Place: A Memoir* (London: Granta Books, 1999).

12. These journals were *al-Sa'ih*, edited by 'Abd al-Masih Hadad (1881–1950), and *al-Funun*, edited by his fellow Palestinian Nasib 'Aridah (1887–1946).

13. In addition to Edward, whose Western name was a burden, as he tells us in the opening pages of *Out of Place*, were Gerald, Rose-Mary, Jane, Joyce, and Grace Said.

14. Other members of the group were Mikha'il Nu'aimah (1889–1978), Nasib 'Aridah (1887–1946), Rashid Ayyub (1881–1941), 'Abd al-Masih Hadad (1881–1950), and Amin al-Rihani (1867–1940).

15. The main members of this group are 'Abbas Mahmud al-'Aqqad, Ibrahim 'Abd al-Qadir al-Mazin (1890–1949) and 'Abd al-Rahman Shukri (1886–1958), who was the most poetically gifted of the three. Shukri also was the one who introduced his group to the major works of English romanticism after his return from two years in England.

16. Many scholars view the poet Mutran Khalil Mutran (1872–1949) as a forebear of romanticism through his poetry and his journal, *Al-Majallah al-Misriyyah* (1900).

17. This group formed in Cairo but had members from most Arab countries. It disseminated many Western romantic ideas and called for freeing poetry from traditional and archaic molds.

18. Muslims couched their rejection of Western ideas mostly in Islamic terminology and hence remained alien to Christians in the Arab world.

19. Three years after his birth, another Mahjar group of Levantine intellectuals, *al-'Usbah al-Andalusiyyah* (the Andalusian League), formed in 1932 in São Paulo. The famous members of the group were Iilya Abu-Madi (1890–1957), Rashid Salim al-Khuri (1887–1984), Ilyas Farahat (1893–1977), Fawzi al-Ma'luf (1899–194?), and Michel Ma'ruf.

20. Said, *Out of Place*, 44.

21. Ibid., 45.

22. For more of Said's reflections on his life in Egypt, see "What Cairo Means to Me," an interview conducted in 1994 by Mona Anis in Cairo; and "Edward Said: Optimism of the Will," by Mona Anis, also from 1994. Both were reprinted in an *Al-Ahram Weekly Online* special memorial issue on Said, no. 657 (24 September–1 October 2003).

23. His doctoral thesis was later published as his first book, *Joseph Conrad and the Fiction of Autobiography* (1966; repr. New York: Columbia University Press, 2007).

24. Said, *Out of Place*, p. 229.

25. For several instances in which he felt "hurt" and "injustice," see ibid., 248.

26. The major critics in the Geneva School are Marcel Raymond, Georges Poulet, and Jean-Pierre Richard. Their work draws on the phenomenological philosophy of Edmund Husserl, the existential phenomenology of Martin Heidegger, and the perceptive phenomenology of Merleau-Ponty. They developed the early phenomenological criticism of Roman Ingarden into a complex approach that probes texts for key signs and recurring metaphors to elaborate the structure of consciousness.

27. Many of Said's early papers appeared years later in his *Reflections on Exile and Other Literary and Cultural Essays* (London: Granta Books, 2001). Edward Said, *Beginnings: Intentions and Method* (London: Granta Books, 1975).

28. European literary theory was introduced to the American academy by Roman Jakobson (1896–1982), who was a member of the Russian Formalist School and the Prague Linguistic Circle before emigrating to America and working in its academy in the 1940s. But his brand of formalism and semiotic analysis had little influence in intellectual circles until the early 1960s, when French structuralism was on the rise and Yale critics, particularly Paul De Man and Michael Riffatere, made structuralism and particularly deconstruction fashionable in America for some time.

29. See Said's account of this encounter and the impact of his friendship with Abu-Lughod on his life and thought in his homage to Abu-Lughod: "My Guru: The Death of a Palestinian Intellectual," *London Review of Books*, vol. 23, no. 24 (13 December 2001), 19–20.

30. Salman Abu-Sittah relates the story from Abu-Lughod's point of view. Abu-Lughod told him of

his first encounter with Edward Said in the 1950s at Princeton University. He introduced himself to Said as a Palestinian, and Edward jumped off his chair saying, "Me too." At the height of the anti-Arab media hype in America in 1968 and upon the establishment of the AAUG, Abu-Lughod remembered his first brief encounter with Said and asked him to write about the misrepresentation and distortion of the Arab character in English literature. When he received the article, which was Said's first academic text on an Arabic topic, he was very impressed with its depth and erudition. See *Al-Kutub-Wijhat Nazar*, no. 61 (February 2004): 80.

31. Said, "My Guru," 19.

32. The major works that established his academic reputation during this period were *Beginnings* and most of the studies that appeared later in his *The World, the Text, and the Critic* (Cambridge, MA: Harvard University Press, 1983).

33. In his interview with Subhi Hadidi, Edward Said describes his return to his Palestinian identity, his sabbatical in Beirut, his study of the Arabic language in 1972, and the 1973 war as the major inspirations for his book. See Subhi Hadidi, ed., *Ta'qibat 'ala al-Istishraq* (Postscripts on Orientalism, 1996).

34. This is not the place for a detailed study of this influential book and its impact on the international academic scene, but it has been covered in other chapters of this volume.

35. The book was translated into Arabic by Kamal Abu-Deeb as *Al-Istishraq: al-Ma'rifah, al-Sultah, al-Insha'* and published in Beirut by Dar al-Ilm Lil-Malayin in 1981. Many years later, in 2002, it was translated by Muhammad Inani and published in Cairo by Al-Hay'ah al-'Ammah lil-Kitab. For the quote, see Radwa 'Ashour, "Hikayat Edward," *Al-Kutub Wijhat Nazar*, no. 85, Cairo (November 2003): 14.

36. Adonis is a Syrian Alawite poet and critic who played, with several others, a significant role in modernizing Arabic poetry. But in order to perpetuate his poetic achievement, he devoted his critical effort to justify his poetic approach and encouraged younger poets to follow in his footsteps. He launched a journal, *Mawaqif,* to create a supporting cultural trend. In the 1980s, with the rise of oil-rich countries and their ascending role in Arab media, he published a laudatory book on Muhammad Ibn Abd al-Wahab, the regressive Saudi theologue, positing him as one of the pillars of Arab modernity. Adonis was promptly appointed cultural advisor to *Al-Hayah,* an Arabic daily owned by the regressive and oil-rich Saudis. He wrote a weekly column for the publication and helped recruit many writers, including Said, to contribute to its cultural pages. Adonis introduced one of his disciples to Said who translated *Orientalism* and *Culture and Imperialism*. With Said's wider involvement in Arab culture and his awareness of the political and cultural ramifications of his association with Adonis's coterie, he decided to distance himself from this clique and to find a better translator for his subsequent work.

37. For examples of such traditionalist attacks on Orientalists, see Husain al-Harrawi, *al-Mustashriqun wa-l-Islam* (Orientalists and Islam, 1936), Bint al-Shati', *Turathuna al-Thaqafi bayn Aydi al-Mustashriqin* (Our Cultural Legacy in the Hands of Orientalists, 1957), Najib al-'Aqiqi, *al-Mustashriqun* (The Orientalists, 1965), and Malik Ibn Nabiyy, *Intaj al-Mustashriqin wa-Araruh fo rhe Fikr al-Islami al-Hadith* (The Work of the Orientalists and Its Impact on Modern Islamic Thought, 1969).

38. See for example 'Abd al-Rahman Badawi, *Mawsu'at al-Mustashriqin* (Encyclopedia of the Orientalists, 1984), Salim Yafut, *Hafriyyat al-Istishraq* (Archaeology of Orientalism, 1989), and Salim Humaish, *al-Istishraq fi Ufuq Insidadih* (Orientalism in Its Closed Horizon, 1991).

39. The main exception is Sadik Jalal al-'Azm, "Orientalism and Orientalism in Reverse," *Khamsin,* no. 8, London (1981).

40. See, for example, Salim Yafut, *Hafriyyat al-Istishraq* (Archaeology of Orientalism, 1989), Salim Humaish, *al-Istishraq fi Ufuq Insidadih* (Orientalism in Its Closed Horizon, 1991), Falih 'Abd al-Jabbar, *Al-Istishraq wa-l-Islam* (Orientalism and Islam, 1991).

41. *Fusul: Majallat al-Naqd al-Adabi* (Fusul: A Journal of Literary Criticism) is a quarterly that appeared in Cairo in 1982 and soon became a pan-Arab cultural forum for theory and critical debates.

42. Later on, and soon after his death, *Fusul* corrected this and devoted an issue to the work of Ed-

ward Said, following in the footsteps of other serious cultural periodicals, such as *Alif: A Journal of Comparative Poetics*, Cairo, no. 25 (2005); and *Weghat Nazar*, Cairo, no. 85 (November 2003).

43. See, for example, *Al-Karmal,* nos. 48, 49, 68, and 72–73, which all contain translated essays by Said. Syrian critic Subhi Hadidi was instrumental in properly introducing many of Said's serious texts and ideas to the Arab reader.

44. Said, *Reflections on Exile,* 452.

45. Said, *The World, the Text, and the Critic,* 226–47. Said, "Traveling Theory Reconsidered," 436–52.

46. Said, "Traveling Theory Reconsidered," 452.

47. Hadidi, *Ta'qibat 'ala al-Istishraq,* 142.

48. Edward Said, *Culture and Imperialism* (London, Chatto & Windus, 1993), 407.

49. Ibid, xxix.

50. Radwa 'Ashur, paper presented at the History and the Text conference organized by the Faculty of Letters and Humanities of Kairoun University, Tunisia, 2003.

51. See Naguib Mahfouz, *Malhamat al-Harafish* (Harafish, 1977); *Layali Alf Layla* (Arabian Nights and Days, 1982); and *Hadith al-Sabah wa-'l-Masa'* (Talk of the Morning and Evening, 1987). The Arabic versions, which I consulted for this chapter, are published by Maktabat Misr in Cairo; English versions are published by the American University in Cairo Press.

52. Said, *Representations of the Intellectual,* 86.

53. Ibid., 74.

54. Edward Said, "Living in Arabic," *Al-Ahram Weekly,* http://weekly.ahram.org.eg/2004/677/cu15 .htm (accessed 6 June 2009).

55. Said, *Representations of the Intellectual,* 9.

56. Toward the last years of his life, Said was clearly aware of the equivocal position of publishing in *Al-Hayah* and the mixed messages in writing for a Saudi-owned paper. Adonis was the one who persuaded Edward Said to write for *Al-Hayah* in the first place. But Said increasingly felt uncomfortable and expressed this discomfort to me during a long walk in Warwick one morning. He justified the action by his need to communicate with the wider Arab audience that this newspaper reached. His political stance was unequivocal, but publishing his views in this newspaper led to misunderstanding and ambiguity. It is difficult to assess the full impact of these articles on the Arab reader without further study.

57. Said, *Representations of the Intellectual,* 69.

58. See Jabir 'Asfur, *Nazariyyat Mu'asirah* (Contemporary Theories, 1998), in which he deals directly with Said's many works, and *Afaq al-'Asr* (Horizons of Our Time, 1997). Both works are published by Cairo's Egyptian Book Organization.

59. See "Edward Said: His Impact on the World and on US," special issue, *Al-Adab* (December 2003); and *Al-Karmal,* no. 78 (Winter 2004).

60. Stathis Gourgouris, "The Late Style of Edward Said," *Alif: Journal of Comparative Poetics,* Cairo, no. 25 (2005): 168.

61. Michael Wood, introduction to *On Late Style: Music and Literature against the Grain,* by Edward Said (London: Bloomsbury, 2006), xvii. The Said quote is from Said's *Musical Elaborations* (New York: Columbia University Press, 1993), 21.

11

"Long, Languorous, Repetitious Line"

Edward Said's Critique of Arab Popular Culture

Anastasia Valassopoulos

We have never understood (or if we have, we have turned away from its les-
sons) the value of what it is that we are as a people and culture, and have stead-
fastly put our faith (a heritage from colonialism) in the white master or in
middle-men.

—EDWARD SAID, "CULTURAL POLITICS"

In "Cultural Politics," which he wrote for the Egyptian newspaper *Al-Ahram Weekly* in 2000, Edward Said articulated an emotive yet practical direction for Arab cultural production: that it cease to foreground restrictive positions on sociopolitical *realities* and return, promptly, to aesthetics and form. While emphasizing this return as crucial for the survival of Arab culture in the global cultural market, Said himself, in the article, returned to a more conservative formulation of *good* cultural production. This tension has consistently been present in Said's commentary on popular culture. As I argue here, Said seemed unwilling to reconcile his desire for the proliferation and distribution of cultural products from the Arab world with his strong opinions of those products. I have found this tension to be highly productive: on the one hand, it rigorously questions any celebratory view of popular culture outside of its sociopolitical context; on the other hand, it asks consumers and producers of this culture to refrain from sterile and uncreative sociopolitical commentary, which Said called "spin."[1]

In "Cultural Politics," Said put forward a convincing example of the type of cultural product that represents Arab cultural life at its best. However, as we will see, he does not use the term *popular culture* when he discusses elements that others commonly call "popular" or "media" culture. Distancing himself to avoid allegations of elitism (although such allegations have been forthcoming from a variety of critics working in literary theory and popular culture), Said reframes his discus-

191

sions as analyses of politics and culture rather than aesthetics per se.[2] He writes, "I simply wanted to state a highly schematic version of my own aesthetic philosophy at the beginning in order, in a sense, to make clear that what I shall be saying in what follows is not intended as and cannot be an extended discussion of aesthetics, but of politics and culture."[3]

Positioning himself as a supporter of the Arab cultural scene, Said names writers and artists who have been prolific in the English-speaking world (such as Ahdaf Soueif and Mona Hatoum) yet bemoans the absence of indigenous Arab artists from the global cultural scene. He concedes that the Arab world has produced a number of distinguished artists, though he does not make a distinction between so-called high culture and popular culture. Although Arab writing in particular, according to Said, has been dealt a bad hand by international academics and intellectuals (he mentions Coetzee's review of Mahfouz in particular in "Cultural Politics"), a pressing need exists to make more primary material (films, novels, poetry) available to a wider audience: "What we need is an immediately available infusion of contemporary Arabic cultural production in the English-speaking world (now at the centre of the world cultural debate), and that simply is not there."[4]

Interestingly, Said does not distinguish between forms of cultural production, seeking only to emphasize the need for sizeable coverage. Pointing out the unbridled potential of powerful cultural media to influence popular thought, Said provides a reading of Youssri Nasrallah's 1999 film *Al Madina*. His enthusiasm and respect for the film's achievements provide clues to his theoretical perspective on popular culture in general.

In praising Nasrallah's film's appeal to the English-speaking world, Said notes,

> *Al-Madina* makes no concessions to what might be considered exoticism. This is *not a film delivering local colour,* nor is it about a particularly Arab/Egyptian predicament, *nor is it explicable in socio-economic or ethnographic terms* of the sort that would take such things as globalisation and the Third World into account. All of these elements are there of course—it is the story of a young Egyptian lower-middle-class man who wants to be an actor—and its language, images, and manner are obviously Egyptian. Yet its appeal and the level of its aesthetic existence assume a much larger and more universal audience as well as a far greater ambition and reach. Most important, *the appeal of the film is filmic,* so to speak, and not dependent on cultural explanations that are required to understand or in some way excuse and explain it by some special code.[5]

This comment is crucial not for what it teaches us about the film in question but for the insight it provides into Said's overall approach to popular culture: its remit and its function. We might say, productively, that Said emphasizes and promotes an appreciation of Arab culture in which the *Arabness* of that culture (read a particular formulation of politics and/or socioeconomics) is not its defining principle. I have argued elsewhere that form and technique are too often ignored in favor of easily digestible nuggets of information about the *reality* of the Middle East.[6] Though Said may never have satisfied those who wanted him to take up popular culture as an academic subject for scrutiny and to provide it with a critical paradigm, we can perhaps look to some of his journalism in *Al-Ahram* and in more recent writing and interviews to ascertain the degree to which he has nevertheless attempted to influence a method of critique of popular culture (whether the popular culture of the Arab world or that of the West). As we will see in the examples to follow, Said was chiefly interested in forms and techniques within art forms that speak to larger organizing principles across disciplines and across geopolitical divides. His comments on *Al Madina* make clear that he appreciates the fact that it operates on a sophisticated level as *film*. What he appreciates is something quite complex—cultural artifacts that are not "dependent on cultural explanations" but that somehow elide the necessity for oversimplified contextualization to address a pedantic and unimaginative audience. Instead, he seems to argue for conceiving connections through "filmic" proficiency (intertextual allusions, filmic technique, and so on). Though he seems to make the elitist assumption that the tools for enabling filmic recognition are readily available to all, Said nevertheless makes a crucial point: "This is not to say, however, that *Al-Madina* dodges political questions or issues that are difficult and complex: on the contrary, it doesn't but rather they are *integrated into the film as part of its aesthetic*, rather than ideological and/or socio-cultural, structure."[7]

Said here calls for an appreciation of the forms that culture takes: not simply as a means to an end (constructing political sound bites) but as an end in itself. However, making his distinction, though admirable, is not an easy or clear assignment. We are being asked to have faith in Said, the cultural intellectual, in his opinion of what the film achieves and how it achieves it. However, closer inspection reveals that it is almost impossible for Said to advance an objective view of the film and for readers or viewers to reach a consensus of the "filmic" qualities of the film outside of the narrow confines of cultural theory. Where Said provides an illuminating reading of the film's attempt to chart new territory, one can also imagine an entirely *other* ideologically or socioculturally driven reading of the film. Said's *method*, however, is important: his drive to seek broader alignments within the film illuminates the potential of the film to address global aesthetic concerns rather than fulfill a documentary role. Looking back at earlier instances of Said's cultural critique, one can trace his approach and understand the discrepancies that arise when aesthetics (presented as objective) are actually formed at the personal/emotive level even while they claim to function at the public level. In this chapter, I take a close look at several of Said's pieces—"Homage to a Belly-Dancer: On Tahia Carioca" and his 1999 obituary for Tahia Carioca, "Farewell to Tahia"; his opening remarks to a Marcel Khalifé concert in 2002; and his foreword to Joe Sacco's graphic novel *Palestine*—to explore why certain accusations of "elitism" have found their way into critiques of Said and why this charge may not take into account the complexities of studying popular culture while simultaneously consuming it—an issue that Said was well aware of. Indeed, his articulation of his negotiation of this consumption may well be his most important contribution to the field of popular culture critique.

In "Farewell to Tahia," Said's obituary for the popular Egyptian belly dancer and actress Tahia Carioca, he writes, "Every culture has its *closed off areas,* and in spite of her overpowering and well-distributed image, Tahia Carioca inhabited, indeed *was,* one of them."[8] Exalting in the memory of Carioca, Said compares her to another popular figure, this time the singer Umm Kulthum.[9] In a deft move that highlights his difficulty with commemorating one figure, Said, though ostensibly seeking to contextualize Carioca, ends up using his critique of Umm Kulthum, whom he generally dislikes, to make wider comments about certain strands in Arab music and culture:

> The only other entertainer on her level [Carioca's] was Umm Kulthum, the great Qur'anic reciter and romantic singer whose records and videos (she died in 1975) continue to have a world-wide audience today, possibly even greater than she had when she was alive. . . . I found her 40-minute plus songs insufferable and never developed the taste for her . . . but *for those who like and believe in such cultural typing* she also stood for something quintessentially Arab and Muslim—the long, languorous, repetitious line, the slow tempi, the strangely dragging rhythms, the ponderous monophony, the eerily lachrymose or devotional lyrics, etc.—which I could sometimes find pleasure in but never quite come to terms with. Her *secret power* has eluded me, but among Arabs I seem to be quite alone in the feeling.[10]

Here, Said dexterously removes himself from the populace—from all other Arabs. Though he is by no means alone in his disapproval of Umm Kulthum and what he claims she represents, his formulation of cultural typing suggests that he alone is immune to it. "Those" whom Said disagrees with are millions of Arabs across the world, and yet their tastes and experiences are rhetorically sidelined. In this passage, Said appears to write *his* history of Arab culture (his appreciation for Tahia Carioca) rather than open up the possibilities (for his readers) of *living* its variety— a variety that he craves and argues for in "Cultural Politics":

> For the past half century or so there has been considerable artistic ferment in the Arab world. Not only has there been one unquestionably great novelist (Mahfouz) but a whole range of other writing, drama, dance, cinema, sculpture, painting and music that attests to an enormous artistic production. This has included classical work, as well as popular art. To mention names almost at random like Taha Hussein, Um Kulthum, Adonis, Youssef Chahine, Tayib Salih, Nizar Qabbani, Abdel-Rahman Munif, Mahmoud Darwish, Mohamed Abdel-Wahab, Tahia Carioca, Katib Yacine, Tawfiq El-Hakim, Saadi Youssef, Elias Khoury is only to begin to scratch the surface of a whole massive formation that has *graced* the Arab world and *engaged* literally millions upon millions of ordinary citizens.[11]

Although Said praises cultural figures from the Arab world in this passage, in "Farewell to Tahia" he offers a verdict on his favorite dancer by placing her in opposition to his least favorite musician (given that he could have invoked any number of other dancers and musicians, his choice of Umm Kulthum seems even more stark). The two performers share little common ground, formally, which makes this comparison particularly interesting. Rather than attempting to explore a wider range of experiences and invoking codes of appreciation similar to those he expressed for Nasrallah's *Al Madina,* Said here reveals, through his own attempt at cultural appreciation, how complicated it is to address all forms of popular culture as if they have equal aesthetic value. Said is perhaps revealing the risks of commenting on popular culture without a methodically conceived critical context. While building on the image of Tahia Carioca, Said provides nuanced observations that are overwhelmingly positive, yet he forgoes the opportunity to broaden the scope of his inquiry and place a potential rival in aesthetic context: Why was Umm Kulthum's music so popular? Why were people so enamored of her? What values did she ascribe to? Instead, Said takes this opportunity to make clear his allegiance for one thing and not another. Perhaps his point is that the appreciation and idolatry of popular cultural icons is openly dependent on a rivalry between its protagonists (thus, without the rivalry, there is very little); Said participates in this discourse by offering support to Tahia—support that seems wholly derived from Said's very personal experience of her:

> Through the cinema and later television Tahia was known to every Arab partly because of her stunning virtuosity as a great dancer—no one ever approached her unrivaled mastery of the genre—and her colorful, thoroughly Egyptian playfulness, i.e. the word-play, gestures, ironic flirtatiousness synonymous with the country's sparkling and engaging reputation as the Arab world's capital when it comes to such matters as pleasure, the arts of desire and an unparalleled capacity for banter and sociability. . . . What she did was obviously performed inside an Arab and Islamic setting but was also *quite at odds, even in a sort of tension with it.* . . . You couldn't take Tahia out of a Cairo night-club, stage, or wedding feast . . . she is entirely local, untranslatable, commercially unviable except in those places, for the short time (20 to 25 minutes at most) her performance would normally last.[12]

Said finds it impossible, or unnecessary, to explain fully how Carioca works "at odds" with the predominant Arab and Islamic setting. Presumably her popularity constitutes a closed-off area insofar as others, the "foreigners, visiting scholars [and] intelligence agents" cannot understand her or the conditions of her existence.[13] The appreciation of Carioca however, seems to come exclusively from a personal, unashamedly eroticized experience of viewing one of her performances. In "Homage to a Belly-Dancer" Said speaks favorably of Umm Kulthum, calling her a "great singer."[14] However, he claims that one could not really *"enjoy* looking at the portly and severe Um Kalthoum," whereas one could very much enjoy looking at belly dancers like Tahia Carioca.[15] Said describes his memory of going to see her as a young boy: "Her diaphanous veils were laid over the modified bikini that was basic to the outfit without ever becoming its main attraction. The beauty of her dance was its connectedness: the feeling she communicated of a spectacularly lithe and well-shaped body undulating through a complex but decorative series of encumbrances made up of gauzes, veils, necklaces, strings of gold and silver chains."[16]

This description makes us privy to a very personal and sensual perspective that likely drives the contemplation and appreciation of Tahia Carioca. A more efficient *contextual* explanation for the popularity of the two women *is* possible, and I have attempted one elsewhere, though I am well aware that it does not fully explain the rise to fame of both these women.[17] Perhaps Said is attempting to alert us to the possibility of continually contextualizing and theorizing popular culture, but this approach could never adequately capture the allure of one public figure over another. In his illuminating introduction to a Marcel Khalifé performance, Said describes why he admires Khalifé's work: "[He is] the only major musician in the Arab world singing in Arabic, to compose his songs using contemporary Arab poetry, and he doesn't resort to what most singers do today in Arabic—that is to say, *sentimental or unimportant, nugatory, trivial lyrics.*"[18]

Said alludes to a trend within Arabic popular music that he cannot appreciate. This quality of "soporific sentimentalism" seems to distract from the social and political potential of music. In contrast, Said pays tribute to Khalifé's performances on the oud and to the positive association of his music with the poetry of Mahmoud Darwish. Said's description of himself as a man who "know[s] a lot about music" makes it difficult to argue against him.[19] Yet Walter Armbrust clearly questions this type of positioning in his discussion of the varying interpretations of "vulgarity" in *Mass Culture and Modernism in Egypt*. Discussing the well-known singer Ahmad Adawiya, he notes that "simultaneous conflicting commentary" about the singer is not unusual. Whereas one listener called him a "popular singer," another called him a "vulgar singer."[20] Equally, where Said attempts to develop an ambitious entreaty, as in the case of *Al Madina* or in his introduction to Khalifé, the extradiegetic connections that he proposes can turn hollow when scrutinized for objectivity. In fact, Said is not immune to the potency of the image and the shifting ground beneath cultural figures in the popular imaginary. In "Homage to a Belly-Dancer" Said describes returning to Egypt after a fifteen-year absence, excited and thrilled to be attending a play starring Tahia Carioca:

> The play was an overwhelmingly long and vulgar farce about a group of Egyptian villagers who has a delegation of Soviet agricultural experts foisted on them . . . It began at about 9:30, but I could only endure two-and-a-half hours (i.e. half) of its idiotic badinage.
>
> No small part in my disillusionment was what had become of Tahia. She had the

role of the loudest, toughest village woman . . . gone was the tawny seductress, the grace-
ful dancer who was all elegance and perfectly executed gesture. She had turned into a
220-pound swaggering bully; she stood with her hands on her hips unreeling insults.[21]

This passage reveals the extent to which certain personable qualities appeal to the
viewer.[22] However, Said *is* attentive to the difficulties of separating a critical response
from an "emotional" or "affective" response. In replying to an interview question
about how one can respond to the pervasive nature of popular culture, Said noted,

> It seems to me that a much more interesting approach would be to look at the soci-
> ology of the form itself, to look at the construction of the media conglomerates, the
> industry, and the formal tools used, which make up, as you know, an extremely so-
> phisticated apparatus reduced to rather simple ends: pacification, the depoliticization
> of ordinary life, as well as the encouragement and refinement of consumer ap-
> petites . . . I wonder whether that isn't best dealt with allusively, and whether the effort
> of looking at this kind of stuff shouldn't really come from a quite serious study of the
> history and sociology of literature in the wider political and social context. . . . Co-
> operation between the media and the state is quite unique to our time. I think it's go-
> ing to define politics in the future.[23]

Perhaps Said deemed this idea of a grouping, at the heart of the idea of the reception and enjoyment of popular culture, to be underpoliticized. In the preoccupation with popular culture, we might become lost and lose track of the social and
the political (he admired Khalifé's work for keeping these elements in focus). Rather
than becoming involved in cultural production that asks the individual to think outside himself, popular culture may seem democratic (for all) yet promote selfish individuality, inducing a "soporific sentimentalism."[24]

Said, however, may also be playing a discursive game and defying us to construct
a reliable position from which to discuss popular forms. With canonical or literary
forms, one can argue, as Said does, that these works are immune from the demands
and tastes of consumers. As popular culture participates in a consumerist cycle, Said
may never have entertained the idea of undertaking a serious critique of popular
culture. Not able to deny the vast influence and pervasive presence of popular forms,
however, he focused on a popular form of his choosing in order to reveal the dangers in attempting objective critiques of popular forms:

> The main problem I have and don't have any answer to, is that it's strange that, for ex-
> ample the music of my own Arab and Islamic tradition means relatively little to me . . .
> I've never been interested in or compelled by it as something to study, although I know
> it well and have always listened to it. The same is roughly true of popular music. Pop-
> ular culture means absolutely nothing to me except as it surrounds me. I obviously
> don't accept all the hideously limited and silly remarks made about it by Adorno, but
> I must say it doesn't speak to me in quite the same way that it would to you or to my
> children. I'm very conservative that way.[25]

Armbrust, writing in 1996, perceived this negation as a betrayal of the potential in the serious study of modernist and popular discourses emerging in the Middle East. "In Egypt the texts that have received the least academic scrutiny are not the primordial utterances of the noncolonized, but those produced and disseminated in the new media: cinema, television, radio, cassette tapes, lowbrow magazines. Much of this material is implicated in nationalist and modernist discourses, but both the arbiters of metropolitan Third World canons and their critics consider it unworthy of comment" (in a footnote, Armbrust identifies Said as one such critic).[26]

Armbrust here gestures toward critics such as Said for being uninterested in popular culture because they do not deem it worthy of examination. Though this stance is a considered criticism that points to the self-imposed limits of postcolonial critics like Said, we could argue that these critics' priorities were to interrogate representation and to dissect the institutionalized structure that massified and popularized culture in the first place. Said was not alone in giving precedence to these priorities. For example, Israeli and Palestinian studies have not, until recently, been very open to the academic investigation and critique of popular culture. Rebecca Stein and Ted Swedenburg, in their important edited collection *Palestine, Israel and the Politics of Popular Culture*, significantly highlight the growing importance of scholarly studies of popular culture, particularly in a geographical area most often distinguished by political, socioeconomic, and, more recently, religious discourses and debates in the public sphere. Their most significant point is that "an attention to popular culture configures both politics and history differently, providing a significant alternative to some of the political narratives and paradigms that have dominated academic, activist and popular discourse on Palestine and Israel."[27] I would want to extend this argument to much of the Arab world and to begin to imagine the study of popular culture in the Arab world as an extension of Said's work rather than an opposing endeavor. We can concede that the area of Israeli-Palestinian studies has, perhaps rightfully so, been dominated by political narratives. Said's fear that popular culture could provide only a staid and crude understanding of sociopolitical complexity, though not unfounded, is perhaps now a little dated. It is no coincidence that much current academic work into popular forms of cultural production from and about the Arab world rehearses and extends the paradigms that Said put forward thirty years ago in *Orientalism*. Indeed, I suggest that Said heralded the possibility of developing nuanced scholarship on popular culture. If Said himself was restrained in the area of popular culture critique, preferring instead to focus on its pitfalls, perhaps the time was not yet right for a critical focus on certain trends in cultural production. We know from his 1991 work *Musical Elaborations* that he was very interested in the "transgressive elements in music," particularly in classical music, jazz, and rock. On classical music, Said wrote,

In short, the transgressive element in music is its nomadic ability to attach itself to, and become part of, social formations, to vary its articulations and rhetoric depending on the occasion as well as the audience, plus the power and the gender situations in which it takes place. In this respect Western classical music in particular can usefully be regarded as one of the products of intellectual labour that Gramsci analyzed as constituting what he called the "elaboration" of Western civil society. Seen in this slightly alienating way, music shares a common history of intellectual labour with the society of which it forms so interesting and engaging an organic part.[28]

This passage highlights Said's interest in the composition of music that can, in part, be free from "socially tyrannical pressures."[29] Nevertheless, a review of Stein and Swedenburg's pioneering collection shows that contemporary studies of popular culture and popular music may be able to figure out which seemingly socially tyrannical pressures, even while implicated in capitalist structures, may actually constitute the raw materials for making transgressive cultural products. Intuitively, Stein and Swedenburg argue that until recently, no one could imagine a scholarship of Israeli-Palestinian popular culture: "For scholars concerned primarily with questions of nationalism and national conflict in Palestine and Israel, the global circuits of the popular cultural commodity have further removed it from the scholarly agenda. Popular culture, in all these approaches, is deemed epiphenomenal to questions of politics and power."[30]

Arguing for the need to leave behind this unproductive mode of engagement, in order to think critically about "culture-power relations," Stein and Swedenburg suggest moving away from "classic Marxist analysis, in which mass production and commodification are thought to render the cultural form 'inauthentic.'"[31] We could argue that Said, in his unwillingness to enter into complex debates on the nature of popular culture, preferring to deal with its "sociology," was suspicious of its claims to authenticity, a claim that could not be accommodated by his methodological discursive perspective. Although in "Cultural Politics" he expresses his desire that Arab culture gain exposure globally, he resists further categorization of forms. One notable exception to this stance, though, is Said's introduction to Joe Sacco's graphic novel *Palestine*. Linking his love of comics to his memories as a child, Said writes,

> My incongruously Arab protestant family and education in the colonial post World War Two Middle East were very bookish and academically very demanding. An unremitting sobriety governed all things. These were certainly not the days either of television or of numerous easily available entertainments. Radio was our link to the outside world, and because Hollywood films were considered both inevitable and somehow morally risky, we were kept to a regimen of one per week. . . . Comics played havoc with the logic of a+b+c+d and they certainly encouraged one *not* to think in terms of what the teacher expected or *what a subject like history demanded*.[32]

Said most admires Sacco's powerful drawings and narratives because "there is no obvious spin, no easily discernible line of doctrine."[33] In both Sacco and Carioca, Said appreciates their ability to appear to move outside of normative politics (whatever these happen to be at the time they create their work). Said's reading of Sacco's and Carioca's art is, if nothing else, a testament to his ability and openness to engage as widely as possible with a variety of cultural forms when he *has something to say* about their politics. In "Counternarratives, Recoveries, Refusals," Mustapha Marrouchi painstakingly traces Said's multiple engagements with culture and politics and indexes the long critical history of Said's work. His thoughts about Said's methods of interpretation are useful here, not so that we may recycle Said's interpretive tools at will but so that we may better remember Said's willingness to critique unfashionable or contested subjects in music, history, and other cultural forms:

> Said's *ijtihad* and *tafss'ir* (explanation), almost his leading characteristics, are configurations the modern reader finds hard to sketch but that, in the future, would constitute the indispensable grids to which we and our culture become legible. Not that there is anything nightmarish about this world of Said's, in the crude sense in which other critics have drawn it. Said breathes into his world the vitality of poetic prose, cultural politics mixed with deep philosophical reflections on masterpieces such as *Kim, Heart of Darkness,* and *Aida.* He understands their dichotomies and is particularly effective on what he terms the "sheer link" between a work of art, for instance Jane Austen's *Mansfield Park,* and its context, where the passing reference to the distant slave plantation on Antigua becomes the trope for the representation of Mansfield Park itself in all its intimacy and grace. He draws attention not so much to *how* to read as to *what* is read and *where* it is written about and represented.[34]

Said's interest in a broader cultural context and in situating the experience of culture constitutes an "indispensable grid" for conceiving how aesthetics, if elucidated, can open rather than shut down cultural debate. Marrouchi contends that Said's strategy as an intellectual—his methods—endure across cultural critique: "Far more than Foucault or even Williams, and more persistently than any Third World intellectual, Said has been that other fine instance of the *strategic* intellectual, theorist as mediator and interventionist, political activist, and commentator, bringing the more arcane *l-mi'rifa* (knowledge) to bear on questions of televisual imagery and culture."[35]

Clearly Said's preface to Joe Sacco's work shows an engagement with popular culture on the level of art and politics. Rather than measure the impact of Sacco's work in terms of political correctness, he discusses how the historical impact of this popular genre, its appeal and broad remit, allows it to achieve a political message that has eluded the most overtly political of forms: it gives an immediate and ruthless voice to the questions and predicament of Palestine. In this way, Said reveals that to politicize the popular is to recognize its potential.

Said was nothing if not balanced in his treatment of his consumption of culture, whether he focused on well-known artists or on figures in Arab popular culture. In *On Late Style,* Said alludes to this idea:

> I think it is right to therefore see Adorno's extremely intense lifelong fixation on third-period Beethoven as the carefully maintained choice of critical model, a construction made for the benefit of his own actuality as a philosopher and cultural critic in an enforced exile from the society that made him possible in the first place. To be late meant therefore to be late for (and refuse) many of the rewards offered up by being comfortable inside society, not the least of which was to be read and understood easily by a large group of people.[36]

To be popular then, Said seems to say, one need not always accommodate the present—all of what is popular *now*—in one's work. Instead, the creator of cultural products needs to choose his or her battles and provide "critical model[s]" for the rest. In understanding this position, we can begin to situate Said's refusal to deal at large with the overwhelming content of Arab popular culture within a larger framework, recognizing that he often found himself dealing with unpopular material and paid the price for doing so. Writing of artistic late style, with specific reference to the poetry of Cavafy, he notes, "The prerogative of late style [is that] it has the power to render disenchantment and pleasure without resolving the contradiction between them. What holds them in tension, as equal forces straining in opposite directions, is the artist's mature subjectivity, stripped of hubris and pomposity, unashamed either of its fallibility or of the modest assurance it has gained as a result of age and exile."[37]

In his mind, then, the achievement for the artist and critic is to hold firm to the objects and ideas that he or she does choose to ponder over and critique—without denying that other subjects are being left out. In this way, the focus need not fall on what is left out of criticism but rather on what is to be learned from the criticism that is performed. The choice that the poet or artist makes is equal to that of the critic—and this choice cannot and need not always sit comfortably within a defined and assured political position, though it may be accountable to this position.

Writing on the lasting impact of *Orientalism,* Marrouchi has said, "The indeterminacy in the authority of Western knowledge brought about by *Orientalism* has provoked us to rethink the modern West from the perspective of the Other, to go beyond Orientalism itself in examining the implications of its demonstration that the East/West opposition is an externalization of an internal division in the modern West. Even if Said's work performs this task inadequately, the proliferation of writing back with a vengeance would be unimaginable without it."[38]

NOTES

Epigraph: Edward Said, "Cultural Politics," *Al-Ahram Weekly Online*, 4–10 May 2000, http://weekly.ahram .org.eg/2000/480/cu2.htm (accessed 12 June 2009).

1. Edward Said, introduction to *Palestine*, by Joe Sacco (London: Jonathan Cape, 2003), iii.

2. Among the writers who have accused Said of elitism are Aijaz Ahmed, *In Theory: Classes, Nations, Literatures* (London: Verso, 1992); Walter Armbrust, *Mass Culture and Modernism in Egypt* (Cambridge: Cambridge University Press, 1996); and Hsu-Ming Teo, "Orientalism and Mass Market Romance Novels in the Twentieth Century," in *Edward Said: The Legacy of a Public Intellectual*, ed. Ned Curthoys and Debjani Ganguly (Carlton, Victoria: Melbourne University Publishing, 2007).

3. Said, "Cultural Politics."

4. Ibid.

5. Ibid. (emphasis mine).

6. Anastasia Valassopoulos, *Contemporary Arab Women Writers: Cultural Production in Context* (London: Routledge, 2007), 126.

7. Said, "Cultural Politics" (emphasis mine).

8. Edward Said, "Farewell to Tahia," *Al-Ahram Weekly Online*, October 7–13, 1999, http://weekly .ahram.org.eg/1999/450/cu4.htm (accessed 12 June 2009).

9. Though I have elsewhere discussed Umm Kulthum's background and popularity, in this chapter, I discuss Said's views on her only to make a point about method. See Anastasia Valassopoulos, " 'Secrets' and 'Closed Off Areas': The Concept of *Tarab* or 'Enchantment' in Arab Popular Culture," *Popular Music and Society* 30, no. 3 (2007): 329–41.

10. Said, "Farewell to Tahia" (emphasis mine).

11. Said, "Cultural Politics" (emphasis mine).

12. Said, "Farewell to Tahia."

13. Ibid.

14. Edward Said, "Homage to a Belly-Dancer: On Tahia Carioca," in *Reflections on Exile and Other Essays* (Cambridge, MA: Harvard University Press, 2002), 346.

15. Ibid., 347.

16. Ibid., 348.

17. Valassopoulos, " 'Secrets' and 'Closed Off Areas.' "

18. Edward Said, "Introduction by Edward Said," *Rock-Paper-Scissors*, 29 April 2002 (emphasis mine), www.rockpaperscissors.biz/index.cfm/fuseaction/current.alt_press_release/project_id/242/alt_ release/261.cfm (accessed 12 June 2009). Marcel Khalifé is a well-known Lebanese oud player whom Said very much admired. Khalifé is known for composing music to accompany the poetry of the late Mahmoud Darwish.

19. Ibid.

20. Armbrust, *Mass Culture and Modernism in Egypt*, 180.

21. Said, "Homage to a Belly-Dancer," 351.

22. Predictably perhaps, Carioca was redeemed in Said's eyes years later when he met her and learned of her unlikely involvement in political and social activism. She proved to be a savvy and knowledgeable woman who had played a central role in the cultural life of Egypt. Said makes no mention of his earlier disappointment in the obituary.

23. *Power, Politics, and Culture: Interviews with Edward W. Said*, ed. Gauri Viswanathan (London: Bloomsbury, 2005), 63–64.

24. Said, "Introduction by Edward Said."

25. *Power, Politics, and Culture*, 144–45.

26. Armbrust, *Mass Culture and Modernism in Egypt*, 4.

27. Rebecca L. Stein and Ted Swedenburg, eds., *Palestine, Israel and the Politics of Popular Culture* (Durham, NC: Duke University Press, 2005), 11.

28. Edward Said, *Musical Elaborations* (New York: Columbia University Press, 1993), 70.

29. Ibid., 71.

30. Stein and Swedenburg (eds.), *Palestine, Israel and the Politics of Popular Culture*, 1.

31. Ibid., 15, 1.

32. Sacco, *Palestine*, i–ii (emphasis mine).

33. Ibid., iii.

34. Mustapha Marrouchi, "Counternarratives, Recoveries, Refusals," in *Edward Said and the Work of the Critic*, ed. Paul Bové (Durham, NC: Duke University Press, 2000), 213.

35. Ibid., 227.

36. Edward Said, *On Late Style: Music and Literature against the Grain* (New York: Pantheon Books, 2006), 21–22.

37. Ibid., 148.

38. Marrouchi, "Counternarratives, Recoveries, Refusals," 195.

12

Edward Said and Polyphony

Rokus de Groot

These basically conventional ornaments manage somehow to communicate a speechless, contentless eloquence.
—EDWARD W. SAID, *MUSICAL ELABORATIONS*

A gifted pianist, Edward Said gave music a privileged place in his life. In 1999, together with Daniel Barenboim, Said brought together young Arab and Israeli musicians to play as *one* orchestra. The West-Eastern Divan Workshop, named in honor of Goethe's famous poem, was devised to dissolve, if only temporarily, political polarity through musical cooperation.[1]

Said was one of the few post–World War II intellectuals to accent his work with ideas on music forms. Until the mid-twentieth century, music-oriented intellectuals were commonplace, as evidenced in the writings of Arthur Schopenhauer, Friedrich Nietzsche, Henri Bergson, Ernst Bloch, Susanne Langer, and Theodor Adorno. Music gave Said ample occasion to reflect on matters such as the relationship between the private and the public, between the dominant and the alternative, and between aesthetics and ethics. In this chapter, I concentrate on a key concept in Said's reflections on music, *polyphony*—as a musical practice, a personal guide for intertwining his musical and cultural backgrounds, and a metaphor for humanist emancipation.

MUSIC'S LOSS OF AUTHORITY

Although music played such a creative role in Said's thought, he often confronted what he saw as a growing gap between classical music and the larger cultural environment, which he attributed to "the decreasing frequency of music as a subject in the curriculum of liberal education, the decline of amateur performance . . . , and the difficulty of access to the world of contemporary music."[2] Said had repeatedly deplored this cultural situation in the West, in which music is the least-known art among the generally educated public and intellectuals alike. He saw classical music as largely marginalized. Dismayed and puzzled by this situation, Said believed that music was losing its authority.[3]

In discussing the receding importance of music in intellectual discourse, Said spoke of "a kind of apartheid," unique to our time and very different from the status of music in the nineteenth century.[4] He identified two modern-day audiences for classical Western music and its successors: corporate and wealthy people who tend to be rather conservative and do not want new music; and a small and declining number of people who are knowledgeable about music and are interested in new developments. He related this situation to Theodor Adorno's account of the negative teleology of twentieth-century Western classical music: "So autonomous has music become with Schönberg . . . that it has withdrawn completely from the social dialectic that produced it in the first place."[5] Instead of being representative of society, like the music of the triumphant nineteenth-century bourgeoisie, classical music had come to represent the *inability* to function within the society: "The true new music is the music that cannot be performed and cannot be heard."[6] In his writings on music, Said strongly resists the decline of interest in classical music and makes the case for recovering music's proper role in intellectual debate.

MUTENESS AND MUSIC AS PRIVATE/PUBLIC

As Said grew older, he became increasingly interested in the problem of aesthetics: "I think there is a definite branch of human activity, . . . the aesthetic, which has its own privileges, which has its own domain, which I am interested in preserving."[7] On many occasions, he followed up this statement by pointing out that the aesthetic is not immune to sociocultural affiliations, albeit with paradoxical phrasings: "The aesthetic work, for all its irreducible individuality, is nevertheless a part—or, paradoxically, not a part—of the era in which it was produced and appeared."[8]

He emphasized and even defended the privacy and pleasure of listening to and playing music for oneself.[9] In this context he noted Proust's statement that the principle of art is personal, individual, and original. Books are "l'oeuvre de la solitude et les *enfants de silence*" ("the work of solitude and the children of silence"); in a later publication, he completed this quotation, adding "produced at the expense of everyday intercourse."[10]

Furthermore, to Said, music's "muteness" had a connection to a negative side of silence. He saw muteness and silence as ambiguous qualities, because he connected them to the Gramscian phenomenon of the subaltern—"those whose struggle against the dominant mode has hitherto either been confined to silence or misrepresented in the confident accents of the directive class."[11] Later in the same essay, he speaks of the silence of colonized people, and "colonial silence."[12] Elsewhere, he wrote that for an intellectual to be silent is the worst condition, largely because he related this state to being silenced either by coercion or in withdrawal.[13] We may hear in Said's work the connection between (classical, and especially instrumental) music's muteness and the possibility for this medium to drift off to the position of the subaltern, with the concomitant loss of authority.

The privateness of music and its artistic autonomy are furthered, Said observed, by the notion that music is not denotative and does not share a common discursivity with language.[14] He even spoke of the "muteness" and "allusive silence" of music: "In its instrumental form music is a silent art; it does not speak the denotative language of words, and its mysteriousness is deepened by the fact that it appears to be *saying something.*"[15] Many times Said expressed puzzlement about this side of (Western classical) music: "Beyond the ultra-individuality of the experience, how does one give it a kind of resonance beyond itself? How does one give it a kind of extension?"[16]

At the same time, Said adamantly demystified the nineteenth-century concept of so-called absolute music, the idea that music is a purely autonomous art. To him, music was not at all separate from political and social processes, despite this having been taken for granted for at least a century.[17] Rather, he held that Western classical music "shares a common history of intellectual labor with the society of which it forms so interesting and engaging an organic part," constituting, in Gramsci's words, the "elaboration" of Western civil society.[18] Said's principally secular stance prevented him from idealizing or idolizing music as "absolute," as the most direct expression of the "divine" or "World Soul." To him, music was essentially manmade: "That's my idea about secularity: that you don't rely on some outside miracle, outside force like the divinity, but that man makes his own history."[19]

In his reflection upon Proust's À la recherche du temps perdu, Said links the private and public aspects of music: "Music is of fundamental interest therefore because it represents the rarity, uniqueness, and absolute individuality of art [in terms of work, artist, performance, auditor/reader/spectator], as well as its intermittent, fragmentary, highly conditional, and circumstantial existence."[20] Indeed, in line with his insistence on aesthetics as a realm of human activity in its own right, he is not suggesting that the practice and understanding of music could or should be reduced to the sociopolitical sphere. In his humanistic perspective, music, and more generally the aesthetic, should be able to function as a voice of *resistance*, "as an indictment of the political . . . , a stark contrast, forcefully made, to inhumanity, to injustice."[21] Expressing his interest in that which can neither be resolved nor reconciled, Said concludes, "For me, as somebody who cares so deeply about music, a very important part of the practice of music is that music, in some profound way, is perhaps the final resistance to the acculturation and commodification of everything."[22]

Music, then, has the potential to serve as a powerful "contrapuntal" voice in the texture of human expressions. We see this notion in Said's humanistic advocacy of alternatives: "But for intellectuals, artists, and free citizens, there must always be room for dissent, for alternative views, for ways and possibilities to challenge the tyranny of the majority and, at the same time and most importantly, to advance human enlightenment and liberty."[23] Said highlighted this *contrapuntal* voice with great poignancy in his analysis of late style.[24]

Evidently, he did not believe that all music functions in this way. A lot of music has become, in a Gramscian sense, "traditional," denoting the attitude of intellectuals who serve the institutional order and work for enterprises and corporations to help these bodies organize their interests to gain power and consolidate their control.[25] Music in the hands of a "hired agent" cannot function as a contrapuntal voice; instead, it stresses the monophony of corporate power.

AMATEURISM AND TRANSGRESSION

Edward Said wrote about music as a passionately committed *amateur* intellectual. He gave the term *amateur* a clearly positive intonation: "[Amateurism is] literally, an activity that is fueled by care and affection rather than by profit and selfish, narrow specialization," or more elaborately, "the desire to be moved not by profit or reward but by love for and unquenchable interest in the larger picture, in making connections across lines and barriers, in refusing to be tied down to a specialty, in caring for ideas and values in spite of the restriction of a profession."[26] Amateurism was a matter of well-considered choice for Said; ultimately the public role of the intellectual should be one of an "outsider, 'amateur,' and disturber of the status quo."[27]

A remarkable resonance exists between Said's amateurism and his notion of *transgression,* with both suggesting the idea of making connections across lines and barriers. Furthermore, Said viewed music as a transgressive medium par excellence: "In short, the transgressive element in music is its nomadic ability to attach itself to, and become part of, social formations, to vary its articulations and rhetoric depending on the occasion as well as the audience, plus the power and the gender situations in which it takes place."[28] Thus, to deal with music in an amateur manner seems apt given Said's contention that transgression is a key characteristic of the medium. The paradox is that music, so suited to amateur intellectual treatment, is probably the most specialized among the arts.

Said brought this conception of music to practice, acting not only as a political critic but also as an amateur, when he established the West-Eastern Divan Workshop, which uses music as a medium to transgress the political and military abyss between Palestinians and Israelis. This act may be viewed in the transgressive spirit of Goethe, about whom Said remarked, "Art, for Goethe especially, was all about a voyage to the 'other,' and not concentrating on oneself." Said believed that such a spirit was much needed in our time, because "there is more of a concentration today on the affirmation of identity, on the need for roots, on the value of one's culture and one's sense of belonging."[29]

LACK OF COUNTERPOINT

To gain a fuller understanding of Said's reflections on music, one must begin with his account of a childhood experience. The first concert he ever attended was a recital by the grand diva of Arabic music, the still-legendary singer Umm Kulthum. Said described his impressions in an interview in 2000:

> It was a dreadful experience for me. I think I was eight or nine. . . . It did not begin until 10 o'clock at night. I was half asleep. I was a kid. And there was this great crowded theatre. There did not seem any order to it. The musicians would wander on stage, sit down and play a little bit, wander off, and then come back, and finally *she* would appear. And they would sing together with her orchestra. And her songs would go on for forty to forty-five minutes. And to me there was not the kind of form or shape [I was used to in relation to Western classical music], it seemed to be all more or less the same. And the tone was mournful, melancholic. I did not understand the words. Above all what I missed, I realize now, was counterpoint. It is very monophonic music. I think it is designed to send people, not exactly into a stupor, but it would induce a kind of melancholic haze, which people like. And I found it very disturbing. Mentally it made you inactive. [My assessment of this music practice] is entirely subjective. So I very early on rejected it and began to focus exclusively on Western music, for which I hungered more and more.[30]

Said's response bears a striking resemblance to the way Western listeners, well versed in Western classical music, used to judge music from the Middle East. In fact, Said's judgment was surprisingly stereotypical and prejudicial toward Oriental music generally and the Arabic variety specifically.

A Palestinian by birth, Said was raised by parents who were ardent lovers of Western music, so this kind of music accented much of his youth. Conversely, although his maternal uncle played the *ud* at family gatherings in Lebanon, Said had little exposure to Arab music. His parents did not possess Arabic records; they collected only Western classical music records (mainly Beethoven, Mozart, Rossini, some Bach, Wagner, and Richard Strauss).

Five decades later, in *Musical Elaborations,* Said returned to Umm Kulthum's art, with new thoughts on the recital he had witnessed as a boy:

> The first musical performance I ever attended as a very small boy (in the mid-1940s) was a puzzling, interminably long, and yet haunting concert by Umm Kulthoum, already the premier exponent of classical Arabic song. I had no way of knowing that her peculiar rigor as a performer derived from an aesthetic whose hallmark was exfoliating variation, in which repetition, a sort of meditative fixation on one or two small patterns, and an almost total absence of developmental (in the Beethovenian sense) tension were the key elements. The point of the performance, I later realized, was not to get to the end of a carefully constructed logical structure—working through it— but to luxuriate in all sorts of byways, to linger over details and changes in text, to di-

gress and then digress from the digression. And because, in my preponderantly Western education (both musical and academic) I seemed to be dedicated to an ethic of
productivity and of overcoming obstacles, the kind of art practiced by Umm Kulthoum
receded in importance for me.[31]

This passage is key in Edward Said's work. He shows that, raised especially by his
mother with Western classical music, he had internalized its values and standards.
For many years, he had believed that his mid-1940s experiences with Umm
Kulthum's music had "either been superseded by substantial changes in my taste or
forgotten and left behind in a past with which I no longer have an active connection."[32] Significantly, he emphasized in Umm Kulthum's art the lack of the element
he so valued in Western classical music: counterpoint. And he became acutely aware
of the significance of counterpoint through this baffling early engagement with Arab
music.

POLYPHONY

In music, polyphony is the simultaneity of two or more melodic lines (designated
as "voices" or "parts") that, heard simultaneously, differ in their melodic and rhythmic shapes, and sometimes in timbre as well.[33] Usually this concept goes together
with that of equality between voices; no part dominates another.[34] The more interesting practices of polyphony ensue from voices with articulate identities; as we shall
see below, these identities are transformed as the voices engage in polyphonic play.
One amazing aspect of polyphony is the fact that the large amount of simultaneous
melodic-rhythmic activity often sounds well ordered. How do voices maintain their
difference without being independent of each other?

Indeed, classical Western polyphony is not simply an indifferent simultaneous
display of several melodies. It certainly does not imply complete independence of
the participating voices. Polyphony has two dimensions: the contrapuntal one and
the harmonic one.[35]

The contrapuntal dimension relates to the melodic and rhythmic difference between simultaneous voices. The simultaneity of voices results in a variety of melodic
relationships (counter, oblique, and parallel motions, with a preference for the
former two), as well as in rhythmic disparity.[36] In classical Western polyphony, the
participant voices are attuned to each other. Part of this mutual attuning belongs
to the harmonic dimension. The concept of harmony applies to the pitch relationships between the simultaneous voices, according to norms for euphony and variety in the particular music tradition. Harmonic is not the same as harmonious. In
fact, a great deal of dissonance between voices may occur. Another aspect of mutual attuning is the rhythmic complementarity and disparity between voices.

Harmonic norms, and by consequence harmonic acceptability, differ considerably from one musical practice to the other, historically and synchronically. In Renaissance polyphony, for example, the attuning of the voices to the overall harmonic structures and processes is articulated in terms of consonance and dissonance, in which consonance is the principle reference. In contrast, the musicologist Charles Seeger developed the concept of *dissonant* polyphony to promote "a purifying discipline."[37] In his turn, Pierre Boulez considerably extended the notions of voice and harmony. Voices may consist in themselves of complex "structures" (this is the term Boulez uses), which consist of agglomerates of pitches, durations, or timbres, or of groups of voices.[38] For Boulez, the concept of harmony was not limited to classical tonal or preclassical modal pitch relationships. He introduced the notion of "multiplied harmony," which is expressed as a system of degrees of density.[39]

Counterpoint is a defining characteristic of polyphony. Pierre Boulez used the term *responsibility* to characterize the ways in which the voices in polyphony relate to each other, shape each other (as in melodic and rhythmic complementarity), and contribute to overall textures and processes (particularly in the harmonic dimension).[40] He used the word in its literal sense of "ability to respond." Responsibility in counterpoint is thus actualized in two dimensions of ordering: the relation between one voice and each of the others (contrapuntal), and the relation between the individual voice and the collective of voices (harmonic). Together the voices articulate the harmonic framework, and they may transgress it individually as well. Boulez emphasized that this aspect of responsibility is what allows polyphony to distinguish itself from monody, heterophony, and homophony.[41]

Because of this "ability to respond," the voices may be perceived as transforming each other continuously. Through their harmonic interference, they elicit sonorous aspects in each other that one could not hear if the voices were sung or played separately. The listener may even become aware of *new* voices that are not performed as such. Apart from occurring when fundamentals, and their overtones, interfere with one another, this perception of new voices may also happen when voices cross each other in pitch position *(Stimmtausch)*, thereby causing them to temporarily lose their original identity (that is, how they sound separately). In the latter instance, fresh melodic formations may be perceived, arising out of fragments of these crossing voices.[42]

Predicting what will happen between voices upon sonic interference is difficult, depending on the performance space, the position of the listener, and other factors. One example of such interference is *resonance*. When a fundamental pitch and its overtones in one voice happen to be harmonically in agreement with pitches in other voices, these pitches may sound more emphatic and stable than others. Or a dissonant relationship between voices can bring out rich and even chaotic spectrums of overtones, prompting unforeseen dynamic sonic processes.

Counterpoint and polyphony are not restricted to Western musical traditions, though they are (or rather have been) characteristic of them; polyphony is also practiced in Central Africa and Polynesia. When we take polyphony in the general sense—as the simultaneous unfolding of two or more voices, each with its own identity yet each also with a "responsibility" for the other(s), as well as for the ensemble of voices—we can extend the concept, transgressing the limits of the common form of *melodic* polyphony in the West before 1900. The extended concept includes rhythmical or even timbric voices. This form of polyphony can embrace Arabic and Indian music traditions too if one considers the relationships between vocal or instrumental solo parts, on the one hand, and percussion ones, on the other.[43] If the West has developed a high art of polyphony, it does not hold exclusive claim to it. In the spirit of Said's concept of transgression, we can view this polyphonic art as a legacy to humanity at large, available for elaboration in any musical tradition and open to further metaphorical interpretation.[44]

SAID AND ARABIC AESTHETICS: ELABORATION VERSUS DEVELOPMENT

Said's account of his experience at Umm Kulthum's recital, however, is not the whole story. Later in his life, this experience kept returning to his mind, together with his revived interest in Arab culture. At the end of the passage above, Said concluded, "But of course it [the art of Umm Kulthum] only went beneath the surface of my conscious awareness until, in recent years, I returned to an interest in Arabic culture, where I rediscovered her, and was able to associate what she did musically with some features of Western classical music."[45]

Though Said felt that Umm Kulthum's art lacked counterpoint, his experience of this very music eventually seemed to function for him as a counterpoint especially to the Austro-German classical music traditions.[46] Perhaps the experience of Umm Kulthum's music planted the seed for Said's later articulations of "alternatives" to dominant Western schemes, both in music and music philosophy. Eventually the contact with Arabic music also enabled Said to detect alternatives *within* Western music.

We can unpack these arguments by concentrating on Said's observations in *Musical Elaborations* (1992), a volume that includes his 1989 Wellek Library Lectures in Critical Theory at the University of California, Irvine. His music criticism mainly focuses on works from Western classical music between Bach and Schönberg, but his perspective is certainly not exclusively Western. In this book, the reader meets discussions of musical details that betray a perspective much more attuned to Arab aesthetics than to a Western classical one. For example, Said makes an amazing remark about ornamental turns in classical and romantic music by composers such as Schumann, Brahms, Wagner, and Richard Strauss: "These basically conventional ornaments manage somehow to communicate a speechless, contentless eloquence I find very difficult to explain."[47]

A large part of the compositions Said discusses in *Musical Elaborations* are variations: Bach's *Goldberg Variations*, Mozart's *Duport Variations*, Beethoven's *Diabelli Variations*, the Theme with Variations for Piano opus 18 by Brahms, Elgar's *Enigma Variations*, the *Metamorphosen* by Richard Strauss, Rzewski's Piano Variations on "The People United Will Never Be Defeated." Said's interest in these works is revealing in that they display characteristics more typical of the tradition of Umm Kulthum than of Western classical aesthetics. As far as the latter are concerned, the sonata form, as it appears in the first movements of symphonies, is a much more prestigious and central musical format than the variational one. The sonata form emphasizes—in Said's terms—"developmental tension" and "carefully constructed logical structure," rather than "exfoliating variation. . . . luxuriating in all sorts of byways, lingering over details . . . digressing."[48] This second set of qualifications presented by Said as characteristic of Arab music describes the Western *variation* compositions quite well.

To an extent, this attention to variational compositions is a symptom of Said's resistance against the core of Austro-German classical music: the (first-movement) sonata form. This form is an overall process to which every part contributes: the exposition with the first and second themes, creating tension through differences in key and melodic-rhythmic content; then the development section, which heightens key and thematic tensions; and finally the recapitulation, in which first and second themes return, but now in the same key.

Edward Said tends to portray the sonata form as one of unequal power relationships, placing it against the background of Western cultural ideologies and largely passing over transgressions within actual sonata practice. As a result, the relevant texts sometimes acquire a touch of Occidentalism:

> So much of the discipline of music is severe and rigorous, so much of it dominative and specialized . . . that it is no wonder that sonata form, which can be read and is frequently described as a disciplinary essentialization of coercive development, achieved so great an authority in classical nineteenth century compositional and performance techniques. The model for the sonata form, is, I think, pedagogic and dramatic: what we have in it is a demonstration of authoritative control in which a thematic statement and its subsequent development are worked through rigorously by the composer. . . . Thus themes undergo development, there is a calculated alternation of dominant and tonic keys, and a clangorous affirmation of the composer's authority over his material is achieved.[49]

This characterization makes the sonata what Umm Kulthum's music and non-Western classical music in general are precisely *not*. For Said, *variation forms* in Western music are an alternative and even a countertradition. Earlier in this essay, I pointed to the significance of the fact that, in spite of the apparent dismissal of his early experience with Arab music, Said gives this countertradition special attention.

In Western music, Said considered the aesthetics and music of Olivier Messiaen to be a crucial symbol of the alternative.[50] Messiaen's work does not rely on the central values of the main Western musical tradition because it does not base itself on "development, control, inventiveness, and rhythm in the service of forward logical control. Instead his work emphasizes repetition and stasis." This music is an "anti- or non-narrative alternative to the mainstream tradition"—that is, it is not a case of "mastering time according to a linear model" but instead offers music as "statement and infinitely possible variations."[51] In discussing Messiaen's work, Said observes, "From the different, private perspective of a contrary artist, however, music is an- other way of telling . . . , digressive, reiterative, slower in its effects because built up through the whole series of affirmations and associations that come with not focusing on getting through time but of being *in* time, experiencing it together, rather than in competition, with other musics, experiences, temporalities."[52] This wording is strikingly similar to his description of his early experience with Umm Kulthum's art. Moreover, the evident partiality of this characterization, and even identification with it, is unexpected. His orientation is clearly expressed in the title of the book we ex- plore here: it speaks not of musical *developments* but of *elaborations*.

Said detects attempts toward this countertradition within the heart of Western classical music, pointing to Beethoven's fascination during his third creative period with fugal and variational forms, which he saw as "his way of getting away from the coerciveness of sonata form, opening music out exfoliatively, elaboratively, con- templatively."[53] In countertradition, he suggested, disciplined organization of mu- sical time is dissipated and delayed.[54]

It is striking that Said connected the concept of countertradition not only with variational forms in the usual sense but also with the contrapuntal mode. Indeed, one may view textures of polyphony—especially homogeneous ones, which, as in canons and fugues, use only one melodic shape—as forms of variation; variation occurs in an overlapping instead of a consecutive way. He paraphrases polyphony as "contrapuntal" to the model of the authoritative sonata form: "You think of and treat one musical line in conjunction with several others that derive from and re- late to it, and you do so through imitation, repetition, or ornamentation—as an an- tidote to the more overtly administrative and executive authority contained in, say, a Mozart or Beethoven classical sonata form."[55]

Interestingly, we can find a connection between this description of polyphony and another favorite concept of Said's, elaboration. Textures of homogeneous po- lyphony show explicit processes of elaboration because the parts are each other's overlapping variants. But also in a more general way, polyphonic voices modify each other in endless and unexpected ways due to (psycho-)acoustic and syntactical in- terferences between the perceived simultaneous voices. In the latter instance, elab- oration is implicit. Polyphony often constitutes such a complex texture that it eludes cognitive grip, and one can listen to it many times without being able to cognitively exhaust the sonorous processes. The voices have, so to speak, a mutually elaborative effect. If one had to choose the musical texture most likely to defy a single authori- tative listening, polyphony would be a convincing candidate.[56]

CRITIQUING WESTERN MUSIC PHILOSOPHY

Said contrasted the dominant and the alternative not only in music but also in music philosophy and cultural criticism. In his introduction to *Musical Elaborations*, he clearly describes his perspective as "the consciousness of a non-Westerner, for whom the remorseless totalizing to be found both in Adorno and in Thomas Mann's *Doktor Faustus* is an instigation for thinking about *alternative* patterns."[57] One senses a relationship here between Said's assessment of these authors and his concept of the "totalizing" classical-romantic sonata form. In fact, Said hints at such a relationship at the end of the introduction to his book: "I believe, *not all* music can be experienced as working toward domination and sovereignty, just as not all music follows the awesomely invigorating patterns of sonata form."[58]

Many passages in *Musical Elaborations* actively resist the concept and practice of totalization. For example, after a lengthy critical discussion of Adorno's work and of *Doktor Faustus,* Said observes, "All retrospective historical analyses, whether of music or of any other human activity, that judge, theorize, and totalize simultaneously, that say in effect that one thing like music = all things, or all musics = one big summarizing result . . . , seem to me to be intellectually and historically flawed."[59] Said even labels the theories of Thomas Mann, Foucault, and Adorno Eurocentric or imperial. In his eyes, "They resemble each other in projecting no escape from, and no real alternative to those . . . patterns [as observed in European history of thought]."[60] No social system, no historical vision, no theoretical totalization, no matter how powerful, can exhaust all the alternatives or practices that exist within its domain. Transgression is always a possibility.[61]

Even so, Said does not relegate aesthetic traditions to mutually exclusive spheres. He firmly rejects a focus upon "purely" European, Jewish, black, or Muslim traditions—not only because the notion of purity has no reality for him but also because he does not accept any principle of separate essentialization that purifies types and turns them to universals. He demonstrates time and again the hybrid nature of cultures.[62]

Though Said is certainly partial to the *alternative,* he also expresses great esteem for Adorno's criticism and the Austro-German music tradition. Far from rejecting these traditions, he simply does not believe in according them a privileged, dominating position.[63]

ALTERNATIVE CONCEPT OF TIME

In Said's writing, the musical countertradition seems to involve a concept of time, different from the one induced by dominant practices in Western classical music as connected with the sonata form.[64] Said relates this alternative tradition to the experience of a certain slowness, a feeling of leisure, an invitation to reflect, contemplate, and become aware of endless possibilities for rich sonorous relationships. In contrast, he related "dominant" time to the sense of duty and the ethic of productivity.

We have met this alternative concept already in Said's comments on Messiaen, whose countertraditional music he describes as being *in* time rather than trying to get through time. As "another way of telling," from "the private perspective of a contrary artist," "digressive, reiterative, slower in its effects," it does not compete with other music, experiences, and temporalities but enables us to experience them all together.[65]

Elaboration—the characteristic feature of the alternative—"can be transformative and reflective, . . . it can occur slowly."[66] In a similar fashion, he describes Bruckner's Ninth Symphony as "leisurely, majestic unfolding" and Richard Strauss's *Metamorphosen* as "a lateral movement outward, expanding slowly and contemplatively, . . . the work's majestically and inward self-contemplation."[67]

Remarkably similar expressions appear in Said's description of his first live experience of a great "foreign" symphony orchestra, a 1951 concert by Furtwängler and the Berlin Philharmonic in Cairo: "And the thing that I remember, in particular, was his [Furtwängler's] feeling for time. It was a new concept of time, because, for me, time had always been connected to duty and chores and things I was supposed to do. Here, all of a sudden, time was transformed into all the possibilities of organized musical sound and a beautiful plasticity, which I'd never before experienced in quite that way and with such a large number of people all at once."[68]

Again, the temporal concept of leisure and slowness—related to the experience of a countertradition within Western art music as well as an alternative way of composing and listening to that music—echoes Said's observations about Umm Kulthum's recital. In the latter, he further noted the contrast between the sense of time he was educated in (which made him dedicated to an ethic of productivity and overcoming obstacles) and the great Arabic singer's nondirectional but rather "luxuriating," "digressing" approach to time. This sense of time is also underlined in Said's description of Umm Kulthum's performance as "interminably long."

Finally, we can find a link between the alternative concept of time and polyphony. To appreciate the interferences between simultaneous voices, and the resulting multiple mutually elaborative effects in acoustics and syntax, one must take ample time to listen to the intricacies of counterpoint.[69]

COUNTERPOINT BETWEEN MUSICAL TRADITIONS

To Said, counterpoint has played a role not only within the confines of single musical works or traditions but also between traditions. We have seen that the art of

Umm Kulthum, although apparently locked away by its witness for decades, played an important role for Said as an *alternative,* as a contrapuntal voice to Western classical music. In Said's personal history, Western and Arabic music became intertwined traditions, allowing him to detect new ways of listening to both Arabic and Western classical music. Said's depiction of Middle Eastern music, such as Umm Kulthum's, as nondevelopmental, used to bear the Orientalist mark of rejection. However, to Said, this characteristic later provided a starting point for protesting the dominant tendencies in Western classical music and offered the envisaging of musical and cultural alternatives.

In fact, Said confirmed that his alternative ways of listening to Western classical music were inspired by his early contact with Arabic music. He wrote that his experience of Brahms's Variations opus 18 was "threaded through" with the singing of Umm Kulthum and other non-Western music traditions—along with Western ones.[70] "What I find interesting here is how many of my own earlier musical experiences persist and keep returning, despite my conscious feelings that they have either been superseded by substantial changes in my taste or forgotten and left behind in a past with which I no longer have an active connection."[71]

Looking back on his life in 2000, he did not consider the coexistence of the Arab and English-American parts of his life to have created a schizophrenic condition. In fact, in his later years, he used the musical notions of polyphony and counterpoint to characterize the relationships between these life "voices."[72]

Said ends *Musical Elaborations* with an "amateur" reflection on *Metamorphosen* by Richard Strauss, a composition that seduced him to present a utopian perspective. The descriptive terms that Said used for the seminal experience of Umm Kulthum's singing recur, but now in a positive key. He is struck by the central role in *Metamorphosen* of reiteration and variation: "The reiterative variational techniques are sustained by a conscious affirmation of how musical time can become the subject of a musical treatment more concerned with its own internal complexities than with dramatic control."[73]

Said writes that he experiences Strauss's composition as elegiac. Does he hear a reminder of his childhood in *Metamorphosen?* Is his personal history resonating with his vision of a humanistic utopia? Maybe the memory of the pre-1948 Arab world plays a part in his imagination of this music, a world in which Said could travel freely between Cairo, Lebanon, and Palestine. This world was a "continuous country," basically one culture, with Arabic as *lingua franca;* a world that he experienced as one of unity in diversity, in which he experienced the customs and behaviors of the grocers and handymen in different cities as variations but not opposites; and a world that, in his young eyes, was not set in the key of "dramatic control."[74] "In the perspective afforded by such a work as *Metamorphosen,* music thus becomes an art not primarily or exclusively about authorial power and social authority, but a mode for thinking through or thinking with the integral variety of human cultural practices, generously, noncoercively, and, yes, in a utopian cast, if by utopian we mean worldly, possible, attainable, knowable."[75]

MUSICAL POLYPHONY AS HUMANISTIC EMANCIPATION

Said went further still and suggested polyphony as a *humanistic model*. "It seems to me that the basic humanistic mission today, whether in music, literature, or any of the arts or the humanities, has to do with the preservation of difference, without, at the same time, sinking into the desire to dominate."[76] His humanism is one of alternatives, always with room for dissent and ultimately geared to furthering human (rational) enlightenment and liberty.

A "difference," for Said, is an identity or a tradition, but not in the usual sense. He takes these notions as contrary to the common practice in which difference is employed to affirm identity, often with a tendency toward domination or subjection. Said did not favor conceiving differences (identities or traditions) as pure, or worse, as things that should be made "pure." An identity "is itself made up of different elements. But it has a coherent sound and personality or profile to it."[77] A humanist community is one that overcomes divisions without destroying the differences.[78]

Said's work offers ample potential for viewing polyphony as a promising, even alluring representation of a humanist community, to serve as an emancipatory model. I will now assess from a social perspective the various aspects of polyphony in music that have been discussed above.

Respect for Difference without Domination within a Shared Harmonic System

We have seen that musical polyphony requires simultaneous voices with a clear definition. None of these voices dominates another. Variety of simultaneous melodic motions is characteristic. However, this variety does not amount to the mere coexistence of the heterogeneous. On the contrary, in music the relationship between polyphonic voices is one of mutual melodic, rhythmic, harmonic, and timbric "responsibility"—in other words, a relationship of mutual attuning. Contrapuntal and harmonic responsibility, in particular, expresses itself in constantly changing complementarities and disparities. Polyphony is the unfolding of intertwining histories between voices within a shared harmonic—though not necessarily harmonious—framework.

To conceive polyphony metaphorically as a social model entails the welcoming of difference—without which polyphony is impossible—as well as the eagerness to involve oneself in the endless richness of ever-changing mutual responses between voices. Though one voice may seem temporarily more prominent—but not dominant—than others, this role changes between the participants and is not lasting. Musical polyphony can indeed serve as a humanistic model in this sense: it involves no tyranny of majority or minority and dissident voices are always in play, as are alternative ways to listen to the voices' musical interrelationships.

In applying a metaphorical interpretation of polyphony, we can view the shared harmonic framework (by virtue of which the contrapuntal voices can interact) from Said's intercultural perspective, which included a commitment to radical secular humanism and to "amateurism" in the true sense of the word. Thus, the "harmonic. dimension" may be understood as mutual respect, the joyful readiness to interact in complementarity and disparity, and, basically, love. Just as in polyphony *harmonic* does not mean *harmonious,* so love, in Said's view, would not necessarily imply the reconciliation of contradictions but an enhanced sensitivity of them.

Of course, relating the notion of humanist emancipation metaphorically to the harmonic dimension, which in polyphonic music used to be exacting, needs more thought. Questions of an ethical nature arise: Who should devise this "harmonic dimension" (which, as in music, will be continuously redefined by the participants)? How can participants reach a temporary consensus about it? How can the community recognize the exacting nature of harmony (again, not harmoniousness, since dissonance is an important part of it) without allowing it to become oppressive? Indeed, how can participants jointly create a framework of harmonic reference that both stays open to change and keeps serving mutual attuning?

The "Alternative" Time Concept

Said developed the idea of alternative time in relation to countertraditions to classical music, both non-Western and Western. He also found the concept favorable to the appreciation of musical polyphony, which requires time to reflect, contemplate, and become joyfully aware of the plethora of possibilities of sonorous relationships. This notion of time involves a sense of leisure, commensurate with a certain slowness in the unfolding of sound textures and processes.

This idea is clearly translatable to a humanistic community, which offers an alternative to a time concept of duty and productivity. In a nonhumanistic world, a "monophonic" ethic of pressure to produce creates a chronic sense of a lack of time. This sense of lack is comparable to the experience of being a prisoner—creating a feeling of isolation (as an individual or as a group) depriving people of the possibility to reflect and to mature. In fact, to inspire a constant sense of time shortage is an efficient, totalizing means for economic corporate power to exert dramatic control and to make people, seemingly voluntarily, into slaves. This economizing of time is a modern variant of systematic social suppression. In contrast, Said's alternative time concept is emancipatory. Variation, elaboration, luxuriation, and digression appeal to the faculties of individual discovery, reflection, and enjoyment. Thus, the listener can open up to the inexhaustible richness of possibilities, in playful contrapuntal response to others' individual expressions, and, most importantly, in a spirit of intellectual and sensuous maturation.

Dissidence

In counterpoint, especially in the case of J. S. Bach, individual voices frequently provide moments of dissidence, when the logic of their melodic motion comes into conflict with the prevailing harmonic structure suggested by (some of) the other voices. The roles of either emphasizing or countering overall harmonic structures shift constantly between voices.

As a metaphor for sociocultural and political situations, this musical ensemble of behaviors fits into Said's humanistic ideal. He believed that humanist community offers "room for dissent, for alternative views, for ways and possibilities to challenge the tyranny of the majority and . . . to advance human . . . liberty."[79]

Polyphonic textures are dissident from the listener's point of audition. While allowing constant shifts of attention from one voice to another, the textures continuously defy complete cognitive grip. One may well learn to appreciate this feature as conducive to freedom, as it undoes the drive to control, while listening may yet orient itself to the harmonic dimension of polyphony. This musical dissidence holds rich possibilities for metaphoric application to the idea of humanistic emancipation.

Transgression

Polyphony thrives when articulated with well-defined melodic, rhythmic, or timbric identities. At the same time, the richness of sonorous and syntactical interference between simultaneous voices, including special procedures like *Stimmtausch*, create multiple mutually elaborative effects, which often blur the definition of the original voice identities. This process grants the listener ample opportunity to develop "nomadic abilities" of attention. Polyphony stimulates perceptive transgression, which actualizes itself in the listener's mobilizing of perspectives on the sound texture. This aspect of polyphonic listening, too, can be seen as a model of Said's view of transgression as an emancipatory component of radical humanism.

CONCLUSION

We can see in Said's work a two-sided view of emancipation in the realm of music. First, he sees promise for music to undergo re-emancipation as a significant voice in the intellectual debate and in society at large. He does so by underlining music's eminent privateness, calling attention to polyphony as a highly evolved discipline in the field of aesthetics, and viewing music as possibly the final resistance to the general commodification at work in society. Second, he sees potential for music to assume a public role and to serve as a model for the humanistic emancipation of society, in the metaphorical sense. In this metaphorical realm, polyphony offers a mutually attuned multivoicedness and an alternative nontotalizing time concept. Moreover, counterpoint yields benefits as a musical practice, especially if offered in general education from an early age. In this way, I read Said's work on music as a contrapuntal expression to Adorno's negative teleology.

To Edward Said, music was not merely an abstract, formal model for humanist emancipation. He involved himself in the art as an amateur—motivated by love, joy, and passion. This stance resonates with his description of polyphony as joyful. If music is to serve as a model for humanistic emancipation, it is in the spirit of Said that love and joy should sound through it. Actually, this embrace of joy would transform music into a privileged model. I further suggest that, for music to serve as a model for humanistic emancipation, music education is essential.[80] Children should become familiar with the art from a very early age—with exposure to both its private and its public aspects and with opportunities to experience both its emotional and its intellectual potential.

Teachers would need to look beyond the likes and dislikes of pupils, which are often molded by powerful music industries and confined by exacting peer group leaders. One challenge is to develop the ability to transgress fixed ideas about the connection between musical practices, on the one hand, and sociocultural, national, generational, and gender affiliations, on the other, while recognizing their existence.[81] Other challenges are to develop in children a sensitivity to music as a contrapuntal voice in the fabric of voices in society, a possible route of resistance— and a field of formidable intellectual articulation. This wider education could end the gradual and perpetual shrinking away from incorporating specialist knowledge of music into education.

This re-emancipation of music would require a major change in present-day practices. Music has been accorded rather menial roles, serving as a mood regulator, a filler of feared emptiness, an identity marker, a means of constructing role models, a servant to the self-advertisement of popular stars, and a hired agent for corporate interests. Gramsci would term most of these tasks "traditional," in that they serve the prevailing hegemony; they favor the "monophony" of economic primacy and do not further a spirit of "counterpoint."

Music educators will need to refrain from stifling music by verbal or visual domination and to find ways to teach music lovingly and joyfully as a discipline in its own right. Music may play a role as counterpoint in society if people learn to find eloquence in its muteness.[82]

Edward Said and polyphony have an intricate history. His predilection for counterpoint in Western classical music made him dismiss the Arab musical art of Umm Kulthum in his youth. But his once-concealed Arabic background returned and eventually enabled him to formulate a powerful criticism of Western classical music and music aesthetics (especially in relation to Adorno), open up unexpected ways of "alternative" listening to that music, detect both Western and non-Western musical countertraditions, and rediscover his Arab heritage. A fundamental personal musical experience—first emphasizing the discrepancy between Arab and Western classical musical traditions and later developing an intermusical counterpoint between them—allowed him to transgress—both personally and as a universalist scholar—the divide that kept them apart. To him, two worlds that had been separated for so long responded to each other in a larger humanistic texture. Finally, Said's work opens the door to the idea that polyphony may serve metaphorically as an emancipatory model for a secular humanist global community. Polyphony became a way of thinking for him, giving him an "ability to respond" to and deal creatively with the contradictions between his complex cultural backgrounds. It enabled him to articulate his own, unmistakably "different" voice.[83]

NOTES

A much shorter version of this text appeared as "Perspectives of Polyphony in Edward Said's Writings," in *Edward Said and Critical Decolonization*, ed. F. J. Ghazoul (Cairo: American University in Cairo Press, 2007), 219–40.

1. The West-Eastern Divan Workshop took place in 1999 at Weimar, which was then the cultural capital of Europe. Along with Arab (from various national backgrounds) and Israeli musicians, a smaller group of German musicians participated. The organizers included cello player Yo-Yo Ma. The event celebrated the 250th birthday of Goethe and was named after this poet's *Der west-östliche Divan*, written after he had acquainted himself with translations of Persian literature and published in 1819.

2. E. W. Said, "The Virtuoso as Intellectual," in *On Late Style: Music and Literature against the Grain* (London: Bloomsbury, 2006), 115–16.

3. E. W. Said and D. Barenboim, *Parallels and Paradoxes: Explorations in Music and Society*, ed. A. Guzelimian (New York: Pantheon Books, 2002), 137.

4. Ibid., 130.

5. E. W. Said, *Reflections on Exile and Other Essays* (Cambridge, MA: Harvard University Press, 2002), 515. This passage relates Thomas Mann's *Doktor Faustus* to Adorno's *Philosophie der Neuen Musik*.

6. Said and Barenboim, *Parallels and Paradoxes*, 131; see also 130. Edward Said mostly deals with classical Western music and its successors, and seldom with jazz, pop, or rock music. He finds premonitions of the shift in classical music in the last works of Beethoven: "The whole question of affirmation and communication has become very problematic. . . . And I think that symbolizes the moment when music really moves out of the world of everyday exertion, of effort, of human solidarity and struggle, into a new realm, which symbolizes the obscurity of music to contemporary audiences today. In other words, music becomes a highly specialized art" (ibid., 142).

7. Edward Said, interview by Michaël Zeeman, in Felix Meritis, Amsterdam; copyright Dutch broadcasting company VPRO, 2000. Broadcast by Dutch television September 28, 2003, to commemorate the passing of Said.

8. Said, "Glimpses of Late Style," in *On Late Style*, 134.

9. Said holds that despite its reification, the art of music does preserve the connection between pleasure and privacy. On this point, he disagrees with Adorno, "for whom in the totally administered society no person is exempt from ideological coercion." *Musical Elaborations* (London: Vintage, 1992), xvi.

10. Ibid., 93; he discusses Proust's *Contre Saint-Beuve* (Paris: Gallimard, 1971), 303. For his embel-

lishment on Proust, see E. W. Said, "From Silence to Sound and Back Again: Music, Literature, and History," in *Reflections on Exile*, 519.

   11. Said, "From Silence to Sound," 523.
   12. Ibid., 524.
   13. E. W. Said, *Representations of the Intellectual: The 1993 Reith Lectures* (New York: Vintage, 1994), 69.
   14. Said, *Musical Elaborations*, 40.
   15. Said, "From Silence to Sound," 517. On many occasions, Said expressed his wonder about this element of muteness: "Anyone who has written or thought about music has of course confronted the problem of meaning and interpretation, but must always return to a serious appraisal of how music manages in spite of everything to preserve its reticence, mystery, or allusive silence, which in turn symbolizes its autonomy as an art." (*Musical Elaborations*, 16; see also 75).
   16. Said and Barenboim, *Parallels and Paradoxes*, 156.
   17. Said, *Musical Elaborations*, xii. In various writings, Said analyzed parallelisms between music's allegedly autonomous status and its social, political, and cultural embedding and effect. See, for example, "Adrian Leverkühn's pact with the devil is therefore a peculiarly apt fable for a musician whose technical interests replicate the parallelism possible between the least denotative and most formal of the arts, music, and life conceived in a Nietzschean mode amorally, beyond good and evil" (ibid., 46). And later: "Music's fundamental muteness allows Mann, as it allows Leverkühn and Adorno . . . to see in the imitative, contrapuntal, and intoxicating knowledge of music an allegory for the catastrophic collapse of a great civilizational achievement" (ibid., 47–48). Said adds his assessment of the effect of Adorno's and Mann's views on music: "The terms of discussion have largely been shut down by an overlapping theory of history and music that relies on the occult, transgressive aspects of music to interpret history and, conversely, the deterministic and 'objective' character of history to interpret music" (ibid., 49).
   18. Ibid., 70; see also 15.
   19. Said and Barenboim, *Parallels and Paradoxes*, 73.
   20. Said, *Musical Elaborations*, 75.
   21. Said and Barenboim, *Parallels and Paradoxes*, 168. Said suggests that this aspect of resistance is what people respond to in Beethoven's music.
   22. Ibid., 168.
   23. Said and Barenboim, *Parallels and Paradoxes*, 181. Said has consistently taken this stance. Consider the following examples. "The intellectual . . . [represents] an individual vocation, an energy, a stubborn force engaging as a committed and recognizable voice in language and in society with a whole slew of issues, all of them having to do in the end with a combination of enlightenment and emancipation or freedom" (*Representations of the Intellectual*, 73). "One of the main intellectual activities of our century has been the questioning, not to say undermining, of authority" (ibid., 91). This leads to the pressing question, "How does the intellectual address authority: as a professional supplicant or as its unrewarded, amateurish conscience?" (ibid., 83).
   The tension in musical practices between the private and the public is a particular instance of a more general characteristic of the intellectual. Said observed the positioning of the intellectual from a personal perspective: "There is therefore this quite complicated mix between the private and the public worlds, my own history, values, writings and positions as they derive from my experiences, on the one hand, and, on the other hand, how these enter into the social world where people debate and make decisions about war and freedom and justice" (ibid., 12).
   24. Said, *On Late Style*.
   25. Said, *Representations of the Intellectual*, 4.
   26. Ibid., 82, 76. See also Said, *Musical Elaborations*, xvii.
   27. Said, *Representations of the Intellectual*, x.

28. Said, *Musical Elaborations,* 70. He later comments that music transgresses "into adjoining domains—the family, school, class and sexual relations, nationalism, and even large public issues" (ibid., 56).

Said also reflected on transgression as a concept of secular humanism: "Secular transgression chiefly involves moving from one domain to another, the testing and challenging of limits, the mixing and intermingling of heterogeneities, cutting across expectations, providing unforeseen pleasures, discoveries, experiences" (ibid., 55).

29. Said and Barenboim, *Parallels and Paradoxes,* 11. Transgression as a guiding concept also challenges the maintenance of cultural canons, which in Said's opinion tends to set limits and priorities too rigidly and too hierarchically (*Musical Elaborations,* 60).

30. Said, interview by Zeeman.

31. Said, *Musical Elaborations,* 98.

32. Ibid., 98.

33. In musical parlance about polyphony and counterpoint, "voice" is not restricted to vocal parts; it includes instrumental ones as well, and in the twentieth century, groups of parts (related to other such groups). "Voice" here refers to a sequence of sounds that meet criteria of coherence specific to a particular music tradition.

34. In other words, the voices differ from the perspective of simultaneity. Viewed paradigmatically, the melodic lines may be identical (though often transposed in pitch) or (highly) similar. This type of counterpoint may be termed *homogeneous* or *monothematic* (or, to use a more encompassing term, *homogeneous polyphony*); it typically occurs in canons (in the sense of musical procedures in which the presentation of the same melody in various parts overlaps) and in fugues. When a high degree of difference exists between voices, again paradigmatically, this occurrence may be called *heterogeneous* or *polythematic polyphony.* See H. W. Zimmermann, "Über homogene, heterogene und polystilistische Polyphonie," *Musik und Kirche* 41, no. 5 (1971): 218–28.

Johann Sebastian Bach's musical legacy constitutes a very high art of polyphony, in both its homogeneous and heterogeneous forms. Awe-inspiring examples of the latter appear among his *Choralvorspiele* for organ; listen, for example, to "Herr Gott, nun schleuß den Himmel auf" and "Hilf, Gott, daß mir's gelinge," the latter with a combination of homogeneous and heterogeneous polyphony. But homogeneous polyphony may offer considerable differentiation among parts, too. Thus, in Contrapunctus I of Bach's *Kunst der Fuge,* most presentations of the melodic subject deviate from the expected standard form. The work also contains interesting combinations of homogeneous and heterogenic polyphony. The third variation of Bach's *Goldberg Variations*—a composition, as performed by Glenn Gould, on which Said commented extensively—presents two treble melodic parts in canon (that is, they share the same melody, albeit shifted in time) and one highly capricious bass part that does not resemble the other ones at all. Glenn Gould's 1982 recording makes me acutely aware of the heterogeneous polyphony in the piece. He imparts the bass part with the quality of a muttering bass clarinet and plays it somewhat more loudly than the canonic voices. This "alternative," even "dissident" way of performing is undoubtedly what attracted Said to Gould. Later in the chapter, I write at length about Said's interest in the ornamental versus the large-scale structural.

35. The term *contrapuntal* derives from Latin *punctus contra punctum,* "note against note," which betrays the role of script as a technological device for developing counterpoint in the history of Western music. As I point out later, however, contrapuntal music practices are by no means limited to traditions that use written notation. Counterpoint does also occur in the texture of homophony, a musical texture of melodic differentiation and rhythmic sameness between simultaneous voices.

36. Oblique motion entails the fixation or repetition of a given pitch in one voice, while the melody in another voice rises or falls.

37. C. Seeger, "On Dissonant Counterpoint," *Modern Music* 7, no. 4 (1930): 25–26. Seeger presented

a didactic design that reversed the rules for classical Western counterpoint: the requirement of conso-nance on certain syntactical positions, like the ends of phrases, was turned into the requirement of dis-sonance. This approach applied not only to melody but also to rhythm, which also could be made "dis-sonant." Among the composers who were inspired by this notion and developed it in their own ways were Ruth Crawford-Seeger and Carl Ruggles. Also, Dutch composer Matthijs Vermeulen (1888–1967) developed a type of dissonant polyphony by changing the norms for harmonic relationships. He shifted the normative reference within the overtone series from proximity to the fundamental pitch to distance from it.

38. In fact, in Renaissance polyphony, a voice is a complex phenomenon as well: a totality of fun-damental tones and overtones (harmonics) that often gives rise to unpredictable interferences between voices.

39. P. Boulez, *Boulez on Music Today*, trans. S. Bradshaw and R. R. Bennett (1963; repr. London: Faber and Faber, 1971), 117–18. Again, this approach is a generalization of the concepts of consonance and dissonance, because consonant chords are acoustically less dense than dissonant ones, both in fun-damentals and in overtones.

40. "We must now study the concept of polyphony, which is distinguished [from monody, ho-mophony, and heterophony] . . . by the responsibility which it implies from one structure to another" (*Boulez on Music Today*, 118).

41. *Monophony*: the performance of a single melodic line, by one voice or by several voices; *hetero-phony*: simultaneous variation of the same melodic line in two or more voices; *homophony*: the perfor-mance by two or more voices of different melodic lines, simultaneously identical in rhythmic structure.

42. This impression of new voices occurs between the upper voices in the third variation of Bach's *Goldberg Variations*.

43. In North Indian classical music, apart from rhythmical polyphony, melodic-timbric polyphony may occur. For example, in performances for more than one *shenai* (a double-reed instrument), usu-ally one player responds to the solo lines of another through shifting drones, as an accompaniment. More-over, a polyphonic play may arise between melodic (vocal or instrumental) solo parts, and quasi-melodic patterns played on the two percussion instruments that together compose the *tabla*, especially the *bayan* part of the couple.

44. Composers have frequently used the concepts of polyphony and counterpoint in a metaphori-cal sense. Thus, Matthijs Vermeulen viewed his "polymelody" or "authentic horizontalism" in an eman-cipatory, utopic way as a totality of equal social relationships. See T. Braas, *De symfonieën en de kamer-muziek van Matthijs Vermeulen: Poëtica en compositie* (Amsterdam: Donemus, 1997), ch. 2, para 4. It is in a metaphorical sense that we will further explore the significance of polyphony in Said's work.

45. Said, *Musical Elaborations*, 98.

46. *Austro-German* is Said's term, in ibid.

47. Ibid., 86; see also 85. Said gives examples from Brahms's Theme with Variations op. 18, Schu-mann's *Frauenliebe und Leben*, Wagner's *Tristan und Isolde*, and Strauss's *Capriccio*.

48. Said, *Musical Elaborations*, 98.

49. Ibid., 100. This chapter focuses on Said's concept of (first-movement) sonata form. In classical-romantic practice, we typically find many transgressions of the strict sonata form; to invent such trans-gressions was likely a challenge for composers. At the same time, one should keep in mind that the sonata form was theoretically formulated in a time *after* the Vienna classical masters practiced their art; thus, the notion of transgression is relative indeed. See C. Rosen, *The Classical Style: Haydn, Mozart, Beethoven* (London: Faber and Faber, 1971; rev. ed. 1976).

50. Said, *Musical Elaborations*, 99. Said quotes Boulez, who suggests that Messiaen offers a para-digm "to think things through together, heterophonically, variationally" (ibid., 97, referring to P. Boulez, *Orientations: Collected Writings*, ed. M. Cooper [London: Faber and Faber, 1986], 406–7).

51. Said, *Musical Elaborations*, 99, 101.

52. Ibid., 100.

53. Ibid., 101.

54. Ibid., 102.

55. Ibid., 102.

56. In line with the extended concept of polyphony I unfold earlier in the present text, this statement also applies to West African and other polyrhythmic music practices. When Said uses the concept of counterpoint metaphorically, he often does so in a context of dissidence and resistance; see, for example, Said, *On Late Style*, 21, about Adorno's work as a contrapuntal voice.

57. Said, *Musical Elaborations*, xv.

58. Ibid., xvii. Said criticizes not only the sonata form but also Wagner's system of *leitmotiven* in this way, offering the following comment about this system: "as Thomas Mann's Doctor Faustus was so powerfully to grasp, [it] could be seen as directly symbolic of totalitarianism" (ibid., 46; see also 45).

59. Ibid., 49–50.

60. Ibid., 51.

61. Ibid., 55.

62. Ibid., 53.

63. One of Adorno's concepts that Said takes issue with is the Hegelian temporal perspective of a totalizing historical teleology. He suggests that a spatial or geographical alternative would be more true to the diversity and distribution of human activity (ibid., xiv).

64. However, in the Western new music of the twentieth century, alternative time concepts superseded the dominant nineteenth-century one.

65. Said, *Musical Elaborations*, 100.

66. Ibid., 102.

67. Ibid., 102, 103.

68. Said and Barenboim, *Parallels and Paradoxes*, 17.

69. That these alternatives became dominant in Western classical music itself, especially after Claude Debussy (1862–1918), is striking. In most twentieth-century textbooks on the history of Western music, this topic receives ample attention. See, for example, R. P. Morgan, *Twentieth-Century Music* (New York: Norton), 40–50. Music scholars have considered this phenomenon both the effect of and the condition for Western interest in non-Western musical traditions. Even before Debussy, "alternatives" were present in Western music, particularly in relation to the concepts of the archaic (Arcadia), the world of the folk (Pastorale), nature (in the romantic sense, in contrast to the urban world), and the exotic. See C. Dahlhaus, *Die Musik des 19. Jahrhunderts*. Neues Handbuch der Musikwissenschaft, Band 6 (Wiesbaden: Laaber, 1980); translated by J. Bradford Robinson as *Nineteenth-Century Music* (Berkeley: University of California Press, 1989). To this list we can add a fifth concept: the world of magic (usually connected with chromaticism as an autonomous system, as in the work of Wagner and Rimsky-Korsakov). See also my "Jonathan Harvey's Quest of Spirit through Music," *Organised Sound* 5, no. 2 (2000): 103–9; and "The Concept of Extended Modality in Recent Works by Ton de Leeuw," in *Oideion: The Performing Arts World-wide* 2, ed. W. van Zanten and M. van Roon (Leiden: Research School CNWS, 1995), 93–112; and "Oriental Identities in Western Music," in *Redefining Musical Identities: Reorientations at the Waning of Modernism*, ed. R. de Groot and A. van der Schoot (Zwolle: ArTEZ, 2007), 87–99.

70. Said, *Musical Elaborations*, 97.

71. Ibid., 97–98.

72. Said, interview by Zeeman. The term *schizophrenia* is suggested by the interviewer.

73. Said, *Musical Elaborations*, 103.

74. Said spoke at length about this period of his life in the Zeeman interview. See also Said, *Musical Elaborations*, 103.

75. Said, *Musical Elaborations,* 105.

76. Said and Barenboim, *Parallels and Paradoxes,* 154.

77. Ibid.; see also 155.

78. Said, interview by Zeeman.

79. Said and Barenboim, *Parallels and Paradoxes,* 181.

80. Dr. Eleni Lapidaki of Aristotle University, Thessaloniki, Greece, made me aware of the importance of music education during her participation as a guest researcher in the Department of Musicology, University of Amsterdam, spring 2004.

81. In *Parallels and Paradoxes,* Barenboim makes an interesting point in a discussion with Said about
the transgression of musical identities. As the men talk about the different sonorous qualities of symphony orchestras, Barenboim observes, "What is wonderful about this German sound—as it is of the
French sound or the Italian sound—is that it can be understood, felt, and expressed by anyone."

82. During a presentation I gave on the idea of musical polyphony as a homologous model for, or
a parallel to, a (utopia of) radical humanist society, Karin Bijsterveld suggested that the notion may be
considered—and criticized—as a "homophonic" or even "monophonic" approach instead of a "contrapuntal" or "polyphonic" one. Sonic Interventions, a conference of the Amsterdam School for Cultural
Analysis, March 30, 2005, University of Amsterdam.

However, we cannot expect that music will be totally emulated in sociopolitical practices. Let us
treat music—and models based on it—as a "contrapuntal" voice, in exacting and challenging relationships to society.

83. Edward Said's fascination with counterpoint and polyphony is apparent in his writings. For
example, he admires Glenn Gould's polyphonic—or "integrated," to use his word—performance qualities, as a pianist, as an intellectual, as a writer, and as a film and television personality. This polyphonic
orientation is evident in Gould's work as a pianist: in his characteristic practice of playing, conducting,
and humming/singing at the same time (Said, *Musical Elaborations,* 21–34). In his writings, Said often
rejects cultural and political practices that seek to exclude voices and are deaf to "counterpoint." See especially his *Culture and Imperialism* (New York: Knopf, 1993).

PART TWO

Palestine, Israel, and Zionism

Without consideration, without pity, without shame they have built great and high walls around me.

—CONSTANTINE P. CAVAFY, *WALLS* (1896)

13

The Arab/Jewish Counterpoint

An Interview with Daniel Barenboim

Interviewed by Hakem Rustom

And though the whole world sink to ruin,
I will emulate you, Hafiz, you alone!
Let us, who are twin spirits, share pleasure and sorrow!
To love like you, and drink like you,
Shall be my pride and my life-long occupation.

—GOETHE, WEST-EASTERN DIVAN

Music has an intimate life with politics. It is unthinkable that a political project would be influential and resonant without the legitimacy and power of music and the arts. For Edward Said and Daniel Barenboim, to make music was to defy silence and physical laws.[1] From their first meeting in London, the two forged a friendship that would nurture a most extraordinary humanist project. The West-Eastern Divan Workshop aimed to show that through music, diversity and difference could co-exist despite the rigid omnipresence of nation-states and monolithic nationalisms. With the Divan, they sought to transcend physical and emotional barriers and bring together Israelis and Arabs to perform together, in the belief that the arts generally, and music in particular, provide an alternative model for human understanding.[2]

It was in Weimar that the idea of the West-Eastern Divan was inspired. Weimar is the city of the acclaimed German poet Johann Wolfgang von Goethe, whose interest in world literature informed his extended poem *West-Eastern Divan,* in which he imagines himself in a conversation with the Persian poet Hafiz. This poem became inspirational to the Divan because it represents a poetic dialogue between cultures and languages, particularly between Western Europe and the region called "the Orient" at Goethe's time. Said and Barenboim explained that the name of the orchestra "stems from the fact that Goethe was one of the first Germans to be truly interested in other countries—he started learning Arabic when he was over 60."[3] In

2002, the Divan found its home in Andalusia, Spain, a region that beginning in the eighteenth century witnessed a renaissance galvanized by the coexistence of Jews, Christians, and Muslims during much of the 700-year Arabo-Muslim rule.

Whereas Weimar stands only a few kilometers away from a Nazi concentration camp where thousands of Jews were brutally killed, Andalusia witnessed the Catholic wars that cleansed the Iberian Peninsula of its Muslim and Jewish populations. The Divan aspires to acknowledge and transcend these cataclysmic times, revive examples of coexistence, and remind us of their fragility. This is with the hope that Israelis and Palestinians would learn from Jerusalem's own complex and polyphonic history—unconfined to one nation or religion. As Said stated, "If it weren't for the rich emblematic status of Palestine and Israel none of this would have been possible since it is because the complex issue itself, whose core from my point of view is the struggle for Palestinian human rights in a land sanctified by the three great monotheistic religions, is so fertile with possibilities, ones that reach into culture, history, politics and personal relations that we have been able to do what we do."[4]

In August 2003 and upon the invitation of the Autonomous Regional Government of Andalusia, the Barenboim-Said Foundation was established in Seville, only weeks before Edward Said's death on 25 September in New York. The foundation emphasizes the importance of music education for dialogue and reconciliation. Besides managing the Divan, the foundation supports musical initiatives in the Palestinian Occupied Territories, in cooperation with the Edward Said National Conservatory of Music (so named after Said's death), and it inaugurated the Edward Said Music Kindergarten in Ramallah to foster the musical talents of Palestinian children at an early age.

Said and Barenboim had different backgrounds and conflicting narratives of history. Said often articulated this difference by saying that they had "parallel narratives" that were similar yet could not meet or be reconciled.[5] They acknowledged the injustices committed against each other's people: Said narrated the destruction of European Jewry while discussing Jewish history's impact on Palestine; Barenboim narrated the destruction of Palestine and Palestinian society through the creation of Israel. The two men did, however, disagree on many fundamental issues, such as the redemptive aspect of Zionism, the foundation of the Jewish state after the Holocaust, and the Oslo Accords. Said was an adamant critic of Zionism and its fixation on creating an exclusive state for the Jews, a project that was conceived long before the Holocaust.[6] Barenboim, in contrast, regards Zionism as an emancipatory necessity for the Jews after centuries of European anti-Semitism and the Nazi regime's mass destruction of Europe's Jewry.[7]

The men also had conflicting views on possible solutions in Israel and Palestine: Said saw the Oslo agreement as an end to the two-state solution and began advocating one binational state for Arabs and Jews with the same borders as pre-1948 Palestine. Barenboim favors a state in which Jews are a majority, yet he parts from the Israeli establishment by advocating a federation between a Jewish-Israeli state and an Arab-Palestinian one.[8] Perhaps Barenboim's acceptance of an honorary Palestinian passport best reflects his view of coexistence. In "Dual Citizenship," he states, "The citizens of Israel have just as much cause to be alert to the needs and rights of the Palestinian people (both within and outside Israel) as they do to their own. After all, in the sense that we share one land and one destiny, we should all have dual citizenship."[9] Through this stance, Barenboim critiques the binational state yet affirms a Palestinian identity that must manifest itself in an independent political entity. Whereas Said desired a single state for two nations, Barenboim wishes for two states in a single nation in which the Arab and Jewish futures are inseparable.

Whether the friends envisioned one or two states, they were both uncompromising critics of both the Israeli and the Palestinian establishments. Said and Barenboim were condemned by Palestinians and Israelis, respectively, for their political stands. In his *London Review of Books* article "Lost between War and Peace," Said discusses his visit to the Occupied Territories in 1996 and the banning of his books by the Palestinian Authority for his criticisms of Yasser Arafat after the Palestinian leader signed the Oslo Accords. In turn, Barenboim, during an address to the Knesset after receiving the Wolf Prize in 2004, criticized Israel's occupation and divided the monies of the prize between music education projects in Israel and the Palestinian Occupied Territories.[10] Later, Barenboim was denounced by Limor Livnat, the Israeli education minister at the time, as a "real anti-Semite" for refusing to give an interview to an Israeli Army Radio reporter because she wore a military uniform to an event attended by Palestinians.[11]

The Barenboim-Said relationship was complex and cannot be reduced to the usual dichotomies and labels. Their common affinity for European classical music was the force that brought them together. They both saw music in a broader perspective, as Barenboim said: "We can learn a lot about ourselves [from music] . . . about the human being, about politics, about society, about anything that you choose to do."[12] From this understanding, and despite the orchestra members' preexisting animosities, the Divan enabled Syrians, Egyptians, and Palestinians to meet with Israelis and, with one heart and one mind, to play the same score harmoniously. Said and Barenboim intended for the Divan to perform in every country represented in the orchestra. After many complications, the orchestra eventually performed in Ramallah in 2005, breaking yet another taboo for Israelis and Arabs alike. In Ramallah, Barenboim summed up the purpose of the visit: "I am not a politician, have no political ambitions, but I have strong feelings about what is happening in the region. I came here to reach a hand, to learn."[13]

Paul Smaczny's documentary film *Knowledge Is the Beginning* shows that despite the glowing success of the Divan, the interactions between Arab and Israeli musicians were not free of emotional and intellectual hardships. For example, Mohammed, an Egyptian musician, discovered that his father and that of an Israeli participant fought on opposite sides of the same war. After Barenboim performed at the Friends

School in Ramallah, a girl came up to him and said, "You are the first thing I see that comes from Israel that is not a soldier or a tank."[14] Said once asked, "Who knows how far we will go, and whose minds we might change?"[15] Perhaps those encounters would have answered Said's question; they also explain why toward the end of his life he considered the Divan to be one of his most significant accomplishments.[16]

Realizing that Palestinian and Israeli, Jewish and Arab histories are intertwined, Said and Barenboim saw their futures also as inseparable. They acknowledged this inseparability in dedicating the Divan to carving out an alternative means of dialogue and coexistence. This alternative way met with many bureaucratic, cultural, and political hurdles. But with Said and Barenboim's friendship as a metaphor and radiant example, the will to overcome has triumphed and remains unhindered. Said once exclaimed, "The beauty of the friendship with Daniel is that there is no such thing as the end of the road." Just as Barenboim saw in Said a resilient and valiant counterpart, the late Palestinian intellectual acknowledged the maestro as "a man for whom obstacles are there to be toyed with along the way," and to whom "no difficulty cannot be surmounted."[17]

The contradictions and multivocality in their friendship embodied the idea of counterpoint; the two men were each other's interlocutors, moving in opposition and in unison, carving a space that evoked the complexities and contradictions but also the harmonies of reality. After all, music, like their vision for the future of Israel/Palestine, is contrapuntal.[18] Their joint vision was recognized by the award of the 2002 Principe de Asturias Concord Prize for working "selflessly and praiseworthily to promote coexistence and peace."[19]

Today, more than ten years after the first Weimar orchestra workshops in 1999, and despite the ever-harrowing political situation in the Middle East, the Divan has not only persevered but also flourished, performing in concert halls worldwide to resounding acclaim.

On a cold afternoon a year after Said's passing, on October 14, 2004, I sat with Daniel Barenboim in his office at the Berlin Staatsoper, where he spoke about his friendship and work with Edward Said and the future possibilities for Israelis and Palestinians.

· · ·

HAKEM RUSTOM (HR): *Mr. Barenboim, I wish to start with your statement in "Remembering Edward Said" in which you wrote: "The Palestinians have lost a formidable defender, the Israelis a no less formidable adversary, and I a soul mate." What did you mean? Can you elaborate on this statement?*

DANIEL BARENBOIM (DB): He was a soul mate on many levels—some personal, others intellectual, and some in partnership in the work we did together. On the personal level, we were very close friends. We spoke nearly every day on the phone, we enjoyed similar things in life, starting of course with music, but we also enjoyed many other pleasures like gastronomy and cigars. I think we had a similar sense of humor, which was very handy, especially when life was not as we planned it to be, like during his horrible illness. His ability to laugh and joke about so many things, including his health, was very handy for me too. Having a very similar sense of humor, we had a lot of fun together. We had the pleasure of sharing many important and less important matters, which was a source of great joy to me.

On the intellectual level, I don't think I've ever had, nor will I ever find, somebody who could be as intellectually stimulating as he was for me, starting from his ability to relate to and make connections between so many disciplines. This could be seen in his books *Culture and Imperialism* and *Orientalism,* where he relates literature to politics. He was a pioneer to be able to see these connections, to look at literature with a political eye and at politics with a cultural eye. As a result of the intellectual stimulus and the personal friendship, we were able to work together extremely well and to found the West-Eastern Divan that people refer to as an orchestra. It is not an orchestra; it is much more than that. It is more like a workshop that gives young musicians from different countries of the Middle East a forum to come and study music and then play in concerts. The idea of the West-Eastern Divan comes from Goethe's work of the same title, since he was one of the first Europeans to enjoy and learn from ideas coming from other civilizations.

MEETING EDWARD SAID

HR: *I want to bring you back to memory, to June 1993 when you first met Edward Said in a hotel lobby in London. Do you remember this encounter?*[20]

DB: I remember it because it was so unexpected. I was checking in at the Hyde Park Hotel on Mayfair. I was sitting in the hotel lobby, and a gentleman came to me and introduced himself, saying, "My name is Edward Said." Of course, I knew who he was . . .

HR: *You knew him?*

DB: Yes, of course I knew who he was, although I had not met him before. He said very nice things about my music making and told me about the many concerts at which he had been present, especially those in New York. And then he mentioned that he had read my writings about the Middle East and the Israeli-Palestinian conflict, and he said they were very original, I think he said "courageous," for an Israeli to express in public.

We started talking in the lobby. I think it was one o'clock or one-thirty; he was running to an appointment, and I was about to go to a rehearsal, so we arranged to meet that afternoon. We agreed to meet at five o'clock and have tea and chat and from that day on we became inseparable.

HR: *What did you know about him before this encounter?*

DB: I knew that he was a professor of comparative literature at Columbia University. I knew that he wrote about music but not in detail; I hadn't read any of that work. I knew about *Orientalism*, and I had read his name in various publications on the conflict. But I knew him mostly as a university professor.

HR: *After coming to know him on a personal level, would you say he was the person you pictured him to be?*

DB: I can't tell you because I hadn't formed a picture of him as a person before I met him.

HR: *How would you describe Edward Said to someone who never met him? In other words, who was Edward Said in your eyes?*

DB: Edward Said was a person of immense intellectual clarity; he was able to really follow the development of his own thoughts in total clarity. He was also very courageous about the intellectual power he possessed, because he was not afraid to say whatever he thought, no matter where he was. In that sense he had a great image. He was someone highly intelligent and deeply sophisticated, and everybody was able to see that immediately. To measure his work, I would say that Edward was not a tactician, he was a strategist. In other words, he would not say, "On this occasion I'd better not say that," but rather "I am not afraid of not achieving my goal by saying the wrong thing." He had his firm positions and acted according to his knowledge. In that sense, he was fearless.

He was an extremely well-dressed gentleman. There was something of a dandy about him, which somehow did not go hand in hand with his image as a professor, a Palestinian, or an intellectual. He was not an absentminded professor; he was not dirty with cigarette smoke, like so many intellectuals of that time. He was always respectably well dressed. And for somebody who was so preoccupied with essentials, he spent a tremendous amount of thought and time on outward appearances too. People who concern themselves so much with essential things often don't care about how they look, but he did care very much. I am not trying to be complimentary, but I am trying to paint a picture of Edward Said, the author of *Culture and Imperialism* and *Orientalism;* Edward Said, the professor; Edward Said, the fighter for the Palestinian cause.

HR: *What do you mean? Can you expand on this?*

DB: Given that he was a fighter for the Palestinian cause, you wouldn't expect him, or anyone focused on a cause, to be a properly dressed gentleman who spent a tremendous amount of time and money on his handmade shoes. When I went to Vienna one time, he said to me, "Please, will you do me a favor? There is one shop there where they make my shoes . . ." I asked him: "Edward, why don't you buy your shoes at home?" He said: "No, no, I have to have my made-to-measure shoes." And they were tremendously expensive! I know because I had to pay for them once, and I didn't have enough cash, and the shoemaker did not accept credit cards. Then I had to wait one week to be paid by the Vienna Philharmonic! You wouldn't really associate this kind of behavior with a Palestinian intellectual fighter or a professor at a university. That was the mixture that was Edward!

HR: *Did he seem paradoxical to you?*

DB: I don't know, I don't know!

EDWARD SAID AND ISRAEL/PALESTINE

HR: *In your opinion, what did Said mean to Palestinians?*

DB: First, he restored a sense of dignity to the Palestinians. He did this by lifting up not only their morale but their aspirations. No society in the world is made up solely of good or bad people. I am sure that there are bad Palestinians and bad Israelis, as there were good Germans during the Nazi regime, etcetera. Whatever I say does not, of course, apply to all Palestinians but to all thinking Palestinians. Edward Said gave them a sense of dignity by giving them an intellectual base to their sometimes primitive thinking. He was able to fight for the Palestinian cause in the center of the Western world using Western intellectual weapons; this was a unique characteristic. He was also able to distinguish the Palestinian destiny from that of the rest of the Arab world when and where it was necessary. He was able to show the connection between Palestinians and the Arab world, but he was also able to articulate the singularity of Palestinian history, of Palestinian destiny, of Palestinian art, of Palestinian literature; the Palestinians were not just "the Arabs."

HR: *He was very keen on articulating the suppressed Palestinian narrative . . .*

DB: Yes, they are not just "the Arabs." He was a very sophisticated thinker, and I think his intellectual approach was a very important tool. He also had great educational importance in that he told the Palestinians what he thought. He had the courage to tell Palestinians that they had to understand the psychological aftereffects of the Jewish tragedy of the twentieth century, that it could not just be ignored. He showed that the Palestinians had to have this knowledge to be able to come to terms with Israelis. Similarly, Israelis have to come to terms with the existence of a Palestinian people and a Palestinian destiny. In other words, Edward achieved this moral authority in the world primarily due to two factors: his knowledge and, just as importantly, his ability and courage to say whatever he thought to any audience. He didn't mince words with the Israelis, but he also didn't mince words with the Palestinians or the rest of the Arab world. And this is why he was criticized in Palestine; this is why for a long time, his books were forbidden. I don't know what the position is now. Do you know if they are still banned?

HR: *No, I don't think so. In the aftermath of the second Intifada, he is no longer seen as a threat to the Palestinian Authority. His books were banned right after Oslo, when he called for Arafat's resignation. But after Said passed away, there were many posters of him in Palestinian cities, and he was honored by many Palestinian institutions, including Arafat himself!*

DB: Yes, when he died, everybody tried to act as if they were his greatest friends and admirers.

HR: *Even those who had never read him!*

DB: No, much worse: even those who read him and criticized him! But he was no longer there physically. They could pick up something that he said or wrote out of context because now they didn't fear being corrected by him. It is as simple as that!

HR: *And what did Said mean to Israelis?*

DB: For the Israelis, of course, he was their greatest adversary because in some areas, he was an advocate of the Palestinians. He was their adversary with great intellectual understanding and knowledge. He was not just a populist or primitive protester; he was well founded. In this century of hate, in which the Palestinians are the victims of the victims, I think he was one of the first important people in the Arab world to recognize the Holocaust and the way it changed not just the history of the Jewish people but the necessities of the Jewish state. He showed an understanding and sensitivity that very few Arabs have. This fact put his criticism of the Israeli government's handling of the Palestinian issue on a completely different platform, one of understanding and empathy. He was able to demonstrate that the present Israeli government was shortsighted for not seeing the needs of another minority. Coming from that angle gives someone a forceful moral authority. Instead of saying that the creation of the state was a mistake, that 1948 was a catastrophe and Israel should now get out, his way was that of knowledge and sensitivity, which was much more difficult for Israelis to deal with.

HR: *Is that why you recently stated that many Israeli leaders would want to forget the existence of Edward Said?*

DB: Yes, for this reason he was an intellectual threat in many ways. The conflict is so complex—more complex than most people think because it has so many angles: there are historical and religious angles as well as political ones. He was able to deal with all of them, even the social aspects, the social justice or injustice. He made it very uncomfortable for Israelis.

HR: *What were your perceptions of the Palestinians before you knew and worked closely with Edward Said?*

DB: I don't think that I have changed my perceptions so much. In fact, a lot of what I have said is in the second edition of the first book I wrote, *My Life in Music,* which came out before I met Edward, but of course the friendship with

Edward gave me a much more detailed understanding of the situation on many levels, including the political level. Edward was from the start ferociously opposed to the Oslo Accords. You know, I have to admit, like many people in the world, I didn't foresee the dangers at that moment.

HR: *Most people didn't agree with him at the time.*

DB: And I still don't agree with Edward a hundred percent. I think that although the problem with Oslo lies, of course, partly in the way it was constructed, it lies just as much, if not more, in the way it was implemented. I think the implementation or lack of implementation of Oslo was worse than its construction. I think something much more positive could have come out of Oslo than what did. On that we disagreed. But he was proven right!

HR: *Before you knew Edward, what was your relationship to the conflict in Israel/Palestine?*

DB: I was not as active obviously, just as Edward was not as active on the constructive part as he was on the critical part. But he was not active in the same way that he later became active with the Divan, where he saw the opportunity to create something positive despite the conflict and a way to change things.

My first *awakening*, if you want, was . . . I have to go back a little bit; I grew up in Israel. When I moved to Israel in 1952, I was ten, and I stayed there until I finished school, for eight years. At that time our generation was not aware of many aspects of the conflict; the Israeli narrative was the only one present then. I think this was dramatically changed by the 1967 War and by the work of the New Historians. In retrospect, we can see clearly defined steps in the development of the relationship between Israelis and Palestinians: one between 1948 and 1967, the second between 1967 and 1995 or 1996.

HR: *Until Oslo?*

DB: Until after Oslo, and then the battle of the Second Intifada. I am not trying to distribute guilt or criticism. So in the 1950s we were the children who lived in ignorance of the existence of another narrative. I think the individuality of the Palestinians within the Arab world is much stronger now than it was in 1952 or 1960 because of the many different relationships with Israel—because Palestine was partitioned, because it came under Israeli control in 1967, and because of all that happened afterward.

But my first *awakening* was in 1969, when the Israeli prime minister, Golda Meir, said that a lot of people speak about Palestinians, but there is no such thing as Palestinians, and that we are the Palestinians—we the Jews, Israel. She said we were living on land called Palestine before, and we were the Palestinians.

HR: *Isn't this statement from Golda Meir what triggered Edward Said politically? He once commented that upon hearing Meir's comments, he wanted to embark*

on *"the slightly preposterous challenge of disproving her"* and to articulate a nar-
rative that was not heard very much and was even suppressed.[21]

DB: Yes, I think you are probably right. I think Edward became actively involved
after the 1967 War, but not as much as he was after 1969. At that time, I became very interested in so many aspects of the conflict. One of them, but
not one of the most important, was my roots in music. I come from an art
where development and expression are always tied to time; there are eight
bars for this phrase, sixteen bars for that phrase, and it takes a lot of time
to establish the presence of the rhythmical, melodic, or harmonic figure. In
other words, as musicians, we deal with time. We express musical content
through melody, harmony, and rhythm, but only in the time that is necessary
for them.

When you deal with philosophy, you deal with content. Whether you are
dealing with Kant, Kierkegaard, Aristotle, or Sartre, it makes no difference;
you are dealing with ideas, and you can take the time you need to elaborate
your ideas and represent them. But you are not necessarily in contact with
the time element that influences the implementation or development of ideas.
And therefore I would say that the element of time is not uppermost, whereas
it is ever present in my work. I can understand why, from the 1970s on, people
in the Arab world maintained that a great injustice was done in 1948.

HR: *Do you agree with that view?*

DB: Partly, partly, I will come to that. But all the Arab leaders that I've read from
that time believed that they had suffered in 1948, in 1956, and in 1967 but
that they have a different tempo from that of the Israelis. In other words, the
Israelis are ahead now, but in the long run, time is on the side of the Arabs. I
was young and became more and more interested in the element of time. Of
course, I increasingly realize that it was not just a question of time—whether
time was on Israel's side or the Arabs' side—but that time was influencing the
development—and now I say even the existence—of Israel because of the
demographics.

So from the 1970s on, I became more and more interested in the conflict
and more aware of the fact that we were moving from a situation of no choice
toward a situation of conscious choice—a choice for the future of the Jewish
people after the Second World War and in our relationship with the Palestinians. The choices that were made then were in fact not only unacceptable
but particularly unacceptable, because people who suffered the cruelty, the
unimaginable cruelty, of the Holocaust had to have another degree of sensitivity to the pain and to the destiny of the Palestinian people.

HR: *What role did time play in the political situation?*

DB: The Arabs felt that time was on their side, and the Israelis felt that time was
on their side. I started to ask how this was possible. Why? What drove each

side to think that? Then I realized that Arabs thought that in the end, Israel would remain a small enclave in the large Arab part of the world. And Israel would be defeated if nothing else by the demographics. Israel felt that time was on its side because it was creating a highly developed society with high technology, medicine, culture, and so many other things that were not a regular part of this part of the world.

HR: *Let us go back to the period after your first meeting with Said. In the years between that meeting and starting the Divan in 1999, when you spent time with Said, what did you discuss? What did you talk about? What role did politics and the Israel/Palestine conflict play in your discussions?*

DB: Well, we talked a lot about the conflict, about the fact that both peoples hated it. But their destinies were inextricably linked, and the refusal to see this fact kept each side from seeing the suffering of the other. A part of the conflict is symmetrical, but other parts of the conflict are asymmetrical, and it is clear that one side is the conqueror and the other is the conquered. And the conqueror has a moral and historical responsibility. The conqueror has quite a lot more to lose.

HR: *Than the conquered?*

DB: Yes, more than the conquered, because the conquered has lost much in the act of being conquered. He therefore has much less to lose and much more to gain. We talked about all of these things. And we talked a lot about music. A lot about music!

EDWARD SAID AND MUSIC

HR: *Edward Said once said, "Daniel and I have in common a fixation on the ear rather than the eye."*[22] *Do you agree?*

DB: Absolutely.

HR: *What did he mean by that?*

DB: That both of us are more sensitive to the expression that is coming to the ear, through music, than that coming to the eye, through paintings, for instance. Edward knew a lot about painting; he knew more about painting than I do, but he was not primarily a visual person.

HR: *Were your favorite composers, if you have any, his as well? So did you differ musically?*

DB: Hardly! We shared, I think, most things. We had no serious disagreements.

HR: *And as a pianist, how would you describe him?*

DB: Edward was a very talented musician; he was a very talented pianist. Edward did not practice in the years I knew him, so he was not able to play as well as he could have otherwise. I think if Edward had spent the 1950s, 1960s, and 1970s working on the piano and playing, he would have been more than a fine professional pianist. More than very fine, because he had a very good facility also.

HR: *I'd like your opinion on a quote by Edward Said. While speaking about the limitation of partition as a solution of multiple nationalities, he said, "It's like someone telling you, 'Okay, the way to learn a musical piece is to divide it into tinier and tinier units, and then suddenly you can put it altogether.' It does not work that way."*[23]

DB: I hope he will forgive me, but I disagree completely with this musical strategy. When you see a musical piece for the first time, you have to break it down into smaller units to understand it. You have to deconstruct it, to compose it backward, so musically, I don't really see it.

As for the situation you mentioned, I don't see a one-state solution from the Palestinian side now either. I think the answer has to be a two-state solution. Whether the two-state solution will stay for sixty years or more is something else. It is very possible that if they are in a federation then there will be no need for the two states anymore. People are going to accept that. But to use a musical metaphor, you cannot go from the first subject to the second subject without a transition, so the two-state solution would exist with the idea of federation. Time will tell whether such a state would be only a transitional entity or whether it would survive.

HR: *At Said's first memorial, you described him as "a musician's soul in the deepest sense of the word."*[24] *What did you mean by that?*

DB: A musician has to integrate all the different aspects of music into a piece. You cannot deal only with the rhythm, or melody, or harmony, or structure, because the minute you say "only," a piece ceases to be music. Music is the integration of all the aspects that make it. This is the extraordinary thing about music, and it is the paradox of music. Music ultimately expresses itself only through sound. If I were able to explain to you a Beethoven symphony in words, the symphony would not be necessary anymore. But the fact that I cannot articulate a Beethoven symphony in words means that it can be expressed only through sound. Yet the sound alone is not meaningful, and this brings you full circle again. This is the problematic aspect of music.

THE WEST-EASTERN DIVAN

HR: *How was the idea of the Divan conceived?*

DB: Neither by Edward nor by me. In 1998, maybe 1997, the European Union announced that Weimar would be named the cultural capital of Europe for 1999. The man who was running the program to showcase the city's culture, Bernd Kaufmann, came to see me and asked me to help him. I was extremely busy with my other commitments at the time, as I was then artistic director of the Berlin Staatsoper. As artistic director, I was in charge of not only the music but the whole artistic policy of the house. I was also artistic director of the Chicago Symphony, and I was very active in Bayreuth. I was conducting at least two operas a year, and I was playing the piano, so I didn't really have room for anything else. It was too much, and there was no way for me to do it.

But he was very stubborn and very charming. He caught me off guard because he came to visit me in Bayreuth during the rehearsal period, when my evenings were free. We had a very leisurely dinner starting at eight o'clock and ending at two or three o'clock in the morning, so we had a lot of time. He was a fascinating fellow, very charming, very stubborn in the best sense of the word. He asked me, "Why is Weimar so important to you?" "Well," I said, "because Weimar represented the best and the worst in German history: the best because it is the city of Goethe, Schiller, and Wagner; and the worst because it is only five kilometers away from the Buchenwald concentration camp." And then, believe it or not (you know the feeling when you speak before you actually know what you are going to say?), I heard myself saying, "We can use that to bring together Israelis and Arabs!" Because in the end, the state of Israel was created as a result of the Holocaust, and the Palestinian problem was created, not solely but partly, as a result of the creation of the state of Israel. So, if you want, this would now come full circle and it may be the best way of repairing some of the injustices of the Nazis. The Germany of today could provide help for both peoples and the rest of the Arab world through this Weimar culture.

I said this without any practical idea to back it up, but he immediately caught on: "Okay, let's do that." And before I knew it, he had set the whole mission in motion through the Goethe Institute, the cultural office of the German foreign ministry. In August, we received more than two hundred applications from young musicians in the Arab world alone. We had to decide on the Arab side because we did not know the musical standards in Arab countries. I knew those in Israel: the Israel Philharmonic and the youth orchestras. But what did I know about Cairo? About Damascus? Nothing! And I didn't want simply to pay lip service to the idea—having nine Israelis and one Arab just to say we have Arabs! The project had to be based on equality.

And so we started the project, and I told him that I had to conduct auditions.

HR: *So the initial concern was the standard for the participants?*

DB: Yes, but there was no point in making decisions either numerically or qualitatively. There was no point in putting three Israelis and only one Arab in the orchestra, and there was no point in taking some Arabs who were not good enough, because they would feel uncomfortable and the Israelis would be uncomfortable. The Divan was not for political profit; it was not a political seminar nor a political workshop. The lesson of the Divan was equality: we, you and I, play in the orchestra; you are an Arab, and I am an Israeli. We are more or less on the same level; before a piece of music, we are equals. Then we can coexist. If one of us is much better than the other, we cannot coexist. The idea is actually very simple.

HR: *Do you feel your work with the Divan now is more challenging than it was with Edward Said?*

DB: Of course!

HR: *In what way?*

DB: He was the figure that represented the other side. The hope was that the Arab people would have the great Edward Said, the Palestinian intellectual. But also we wanted the Israelis to see someone of that level from the other side; this aspect was very important. It is difficult to do that alone.

HR: *And do you now plan to take the Divan to the West Bank or even to Arab capitals like Cairo?*

DB: Yes, we definitely want to go to Ramallah.[25]

HR: *Will this happen for sure? Is it possible?*

DB: Now I can tell you that we are planning to go to Ramallah; we'll see if anybody will impede that plan. Edward and I shared the belief—totally, completely, and absolutely—that the full dimension of Divan would come to the fore the day the Divan could perform in all the countries that are represented in it. For the Divan to show the world its fullest message, it has to play in Beirut, Damascus, Amman, Ramallah, Tel Aviv, Jerusalem, and Cairo. Until it does that, it will be something in exile.

HR: *In exile?*

DB: Yes, of course. It is in exile, and it is in exile because it cannot go home.

HR: *On exile, you once said that you often felt at home while with Edward Said. What is home in that sense?*

DB: We felt the same. He was at home lecturing at Columbia University, but he was not at home. I am at home making music here in Berlin or in Chicago, but I am not at home. This sense is what we had in common—not nostalgia but a sense of being able to be at home in what we do yet have a longing for somewhere else that was our home.

HR: *You mean a state of exile in the metaphorical sense, as he called it.*

DB: Yes.

HR: *Where do you feel most at home?*

DB: I really feel at home musically, wherever I play, I really do. Let me repeat the cliché that I feel at home wherever I can make music. It is true. I feel at home in Jerusalem—not in the Jerusalem of today but in a vision of Jerusalem that is the center for culture and—if you want—for religion too. The latter does not apply to me because I am not a religious person; I feel at home in the vision of a Jerusalem that realizes its historical, religious, moral, and cultural possibilities.

HR: *What would you say about Jerusalem's becoming, as some want it to be, a multinational city?*

DB: My answer depends on how you define a "multinational" city. That it has to belong to Israel, yes. That it has to belong to Palestine, yes. But I am not a politician! You know, part of the problem of the conflict for me is that there are certain rights that neither side is willing or able to forgo. You have to have enough understanding about the other side's position on why it doesn't want to forgo. Both must solve this before implementation. I could say that West Jerusalem can be Israeli, and East Jerusalem can be Palestinian maybe, I don't know. My job is not really to propose solutions. But I know that for Jerusalem to develop its full potential, it has to be able to provide the whole world with the elements the world sees in it. How you solve it politically is not really my field.

THE FUTURE OF ISRAEL/PALESTINE

HR: *When you talk about the orchestra, you seem to be saying that it is an analogy or even a microcosm of the one-state solution. Is that so?*

DB: No, not necessarily a one-state solution. Why? Equality of rights does not mean a one-state solution. It could be a two-state solution.

HR: *Edward Said was an advocate of the one-state solution.*

DB: Edward was in and out with that. When I met Edward, he was an advocate of the one-state solution. Then he advocated the two-state solution when he realized that the one-state solution was not going to work after Oslo. In the last two or three years of his life, he went back to the one-state solution, for the same reason that he changed his idea from one-state solution to two-state solution.

His process was actually very interesting; he changed from the one–state solution to the two–state solution because he felt that the only way to give the Arabs equal rights and an equal fate was to give them what the Israelis have— namely a state. But the situation on the ground was worsening, and he saw that the emergence of a real, autonomous, independent, Palestinian state was becoming less and less likely, so he went back to the one-state solution.

HR: *Did you agree with Said in that area?*

DB: We disagreed on that . . .

HR: *Which solution do you favor now?*

DB: Now I think that it is too late for a two-state solution and that the one-state solution will not work. Now I feel that the solution has to begin with a two-state solution, but the two states have to be federated in some way. First, the conditions have to be created for the Palestinian state. You cannot have a Palestinian state in pockets created by the Israeli government. And therefore you need the two-state solution to underscore the understanding that there have to be viable geographical conditions for a Palestinian state. However, after what we have been through all these years, especially during the past five or six years, I think that even if the Israeli government, in the present or in the future, created the conditions for a Palestinian state alongside an Israeli state on the pre-1967 borders with some modifications, it would first need to find a solution for the Jerusalem question and the refugee problem. I don't think the two-state solution can work now with the current amount of hatred and vengeance.

I don't know if this view is justified. I am just trying to look at the facts, and that would be the only solution for me: creation of a Palestinian state with the necessary geographic and other conditions for it to be part of a federation with Israel from the beginning; this solution would force Israel and the Palestinian state to cooperate in every possible area from the very first day. Otherwise, it will not work. What the demography would then do or not do is something else. Something along the lines of Benelux.

LAST MEETING

HR: *Would you take us to your last meeting with Edward Said?*

DB: It was in August 2003, just a month before he passed away. He was in very bad health, but he was determined to come to Spain, and he came and he was wonderful. He talked with the youngsters a number of times and talked on very important subjects: the conflict, the war, also music and the world of culture. And he came to rehearsals and he came to the concerts. He was wonderful!

HR: *That was the last time.*

DB: Yes. And then I spoke to him on the phone. I was in Chicago, and I spoke to him every day. I had arranged to go to New York to see him the following Sunday, which was my first free day. But on Tuesday I heard that he went to the hospital, so I flew immediately to see him. He passed away that Thursday morning.

HR: *Did you attend the funeral in New York?*

DB: Yes.

HR: *After this long friendship, what did you feel then? What was going on in your mind?*

DB: Well, I was obviously very, very sad. I had a sense of loss. However, I also felt that what he brought into this world and what he represented had to stay and that his friends and admirers have a duty to continue his work.

HR: *If you could communicate something to Edward Said now, what would it be?*
DB: Keep working! Keep working up there! Keep working and send us the waves! *Khalas!*
HR: Khalas! *Thank you very much, Mr. Barenboim.*
DB: I wish you had not come. I wish he was still here! There would have been no need for you to come! But I am very glad that you came. And if the situation were not what it is, then the Divan would not have been necessary. Good musicians from Cairo would come to Tel Aviv and from Tel Aviv would go to Damascus. There would be no need for this West-Eastern Divan.
HR: *So something good is coming out of undesired situations?*
DB: Of course.

NOTES

Epigraph: Goethe, "Unbegrenzt" (Uncircumscribed), from the *West-Östlichen Divan* (West-Eastern Divan), in *Goethe: Selected Verse*, ed. David Luke (New York: Penguin Books, 1986), 237.

1. See the discussion in Daniel Barenboim and Edward W. Said, *Parallels and Paradoxes: Explorations in Music and Society*, ed. Ara Guzelimian (London: Bloomsbury, 2003), 30.

2. In the speech he delivered upon receiving the Principe de Asturias prize in Oviedo, Spain, October 2002, Said commented, "Strange though it may seem, it is culture generally, and music in particular that provide an alternative model for the conflict of identities"; http://fundacionprincipedeasturias .org/en/multimedia/20 (accessed 11 August 2009). See also Said's comments in Paul Smaczny, *Knowledge Is the Beginning* (Warner Classics, 2005), DVD.

3. "Information Dossier," 2004, Barenboim-Said Fundación, Seville, Spain, p. 3.

4. Edward Said, "Memory, Inequality and Power: Palestine and the Universality of Human Rights" (lecture, University of California, Berkeley, 19 February 2003); the text is courtesy of Mariam C. Said. A version of the lecture was later published under the same title in *Alif: Journal of Comparative Politics* 24 (2004): 15–33.

5. Mariam C. Said told us that Said often used the phrase "parallel narratives" to explain the difference between him and Barenboim (personal communication, New York, November 2008).

6. See, for example, Said's "Zionism from the Standpoint of its Victims," *Social Text*, no. 1 (Winter 1979): 7–58; reprinted in Said's *The Question of Palestine* (New York: Vintage, 1992). "My Right of Return: An Interview with Edward Said," *Ha'aretz*, 18 August 2000; reprinted in *Power, Politics and Culture: Interviews with Edward W. Said*, ed. Gauri Viswanathan (New York: Vintage, 2002), 457–58. And "Freud, Zionism, and Vienna," *Al-Ahram Weekly*, 15–21 March 2001, no. 525, http://weekly.ahram .org.eg/2001/525/op2.htm (accessed 11 August 2009).

7. See Barenboim's online journals "Daniel Barenboim on Dual Citizenship" and "60 Years: Daniel Barenboim on Israel," www.danielbarenboim.com/journal.htm (accessed 11 August 2009).

8. Ibid.

9. Barenboim, "Daniel Barenboim on Dual Citizenship."

10. In the Knesset speech on 9 May 2004, Barenboim said, "Does the condition of occupation and domination over another people fit the Declaration of Independence? Is there any sense in the independence of one at the expense of the fundamental rights of the other? . . . Can the Jewish people whose history is a record of continued suffering and relentless persecution, allow themselves to be indifferent to the rights and suffering of a neighboring people?" The full statement appears in Barenboim's online journal: www.danielbarenboim.com/journal_wolfprizespeech.htm (accessed 11 August 2009).

11. "Livnat Denounced Barenboim as 'Real Anti-Semite,'" *Jerusalem Post*, 4 September 2005.

12. Daniel Barenboim, "In the Beginning Was Sound," BBC Radio, 2006 Reith Lectures, Lecture 1, 7 April 2006.

13. Smaczny, *Knowledge Is the Beginning*.

14. Ibid.

15. See Said's speech upon receiving the Principe de Asturias prize, http://fundacionprincipedeasturias .org/en/multimedia/20 (accessed 11 August 2009).

16. Rod Usher, "Hearts and Minds," *Time*, 25 August 2002.

17. Said's quotes are from a conversation he and Barenboim had with David Sells on *BBC Newsnight*, August 2003.

18. At the fourth Reith Lecture that Barenboim gave in Ramallah, "Meeting in Music," he explained this contrapuntal essence as the site where "different notes and voices meet, link to each other, either in joint expression or in counterpoint, which means exactly that—counterpoint, or another point." See Rokus de Groot's essay, chapter 12 of this volume.

19. "Minutes of the Jury" for the 2002 Concord Prize, http://fundacionprincipedeasturias.org/ en/awards/2002/daniel-barenboim-1/jury (accessed 11 August 2009). For a recording of Said's prize-acceptance speech, see http://fundacionprincipedeasturias.org/en/multimedia/20; for Barenboim's speech, see http://fundacionprincipedeasturias.org/en/awards/2002/daniel-barenboim-1/speech (both accessed 11 August 2009).

20. For Said's recollections of his meetings with Barenboim, see Edward W. Said, "Daniel Barenboim (Bonding across Cultural Boundaries)," in *Music at the Limits*, 259–64 (New York: Columbia University Press, 2008).

21. Edward Said, "The Arab Portrayed," *The Arab-Israeli Confrontation of June 1967: An Arab Perspective*, ed. Ibrahim Abu-Lughod (Evanston, Ill.: Northwestern University Press, 1970).

22. Barenboim and Said, *Parallels and Paradoxes*, 5.

23. Ibid., 14.

24. Daniel Barenboim, "The Maestro," trans. from Spanish by Kimberly Borchard, September 2004, www.danielbarenboim.com/journal_maestro.htm (accessed 11 August 2009). See also "The Maestro," *Al-Ahram Weekly*, 4–10 November 2004, no. 715.

25. The Divan performed for the first time in Ramallah on 21 August 2005. The Ramallah Concert was featured in Paul Smaczny's film *Knowledge Is the Beginning*.

14

Speaking Truth to Power

On Edward Said and the Palestinian Freedom Struggle

Ardi Imseis

In his 1993 Reith lectures, "Representations of the Intellectual," Edward Said provided what I consider one of his most important intellectual contributions.[1] In the lecture "Speaking Truth to Power," Said pondered "how the intellectual confronts the question of power and authority" to make the point that the task of the intellectual qua intellectual cannot properly be fulfilled under the corrupting influence of self-interest beholden to such elements.[2] Although intellectuals necessarily possess beliefs, loyalties, and affiliations that are shaped by the societies of which they are a part, and in that way are no different from most other individuals, Said held that intellectuals differ from others in the felt need to constantly question power and to challenge its use to further the narrow interests of the few who wield it, usually at the expense of various minorities or voiceless outsiders. Power and authority, in this sense, include the political/nationalist establishment, mainstream media, religious order, and corporate interest, among other things, and it is the imperative of the intellectual to maintain an arms-length from these influences in order to fulfill what is essentially a contrarian role in society.

When the intellectual succumbs to the pull of such forces, however, hypocrisy becomes the order of the day, and the resulting conflict of interest casts a long shadow over much of his or her work. Said denounced such hypocrisy as a plague on the intellectual, deriding the propensity of those whose cultural chauvinism, for instance, leads them to "pontificate about abuses in someone else's society and to excuse exactly the same practices in one's own."[3] Citing Alexis de Tocqueville as "a classic example of this"—we are told that the nineteenth-century French intellectual was not as given to criticizing his own government's persecution of Algerian Muslims in the 1830s and 1840s as he was to criticizing America's abuse of native

Americans and African slaves—Said argued that the "inevitable conclusion" for the intellectual is "that if you wish to uphold basic human justice you must do so for everyone, not just selectively for the people that your side, your culture, your nation designates as okay."[4] For Said, true intellectuals could never be "fawning" servants of power and interest but rather should be persons with "an alternative and more principled stand that enables them in effect to speak the truth to power," the personal consequences be damned.[5]

The exhortation to speak truth to power was essentially Said's motto in public life, and as one of the twentieth century's most profound public intellectuals, he was its standard bearer par excellence. One of his great contributions was to affirm, not merely through his writings but by personal example, that we all have more than a passing role to play in holding power and authority to account. Nowhere was this belief more evident than in the enormous energy he invested in the cause of justice and freedom in Palestine. Over four decades, Said stood out as one of the most eloquent and forceful voices for the Palestinian people and its quest for liberation. Because of what he described as the "complete hegemonic coalescence between the liberal Western view of things and the Zionist-Israeli view," Said always maintained (and denounced the fact) that Palestine's case was uniquely one in which "fear of speaking out about one of the greatest injustices in modern history has hobbled, blinkered, [and] muzzled many who know the truth and are in a position to serve it."[6] Said chose the alternative course, emphasizing that "despite the abuse and vilification that any outspoken supporter of Palestinian rights and self-determination earns for him or herself, the truth deserves to be spoken."[7]

Looking back on his work on Palestine, one can discern three (among many, I hasten to add) distinctive roles that Said played in advancing the discourse on the subject. First, he had an enormous impact as a *narrator* of the contemporary Palestinian experience. Perhaps the most marked feature of his contribution was his stubborn insistence that the Palestinian people be addressed on their own terms and that they be acknowledged by the world at large as a people possessing agency and the capacity, like all other peoples, to represent themselves. Second, Said was an exemplary *critic* of power, not only of Zionist and Western power but also of Arab and Palestinian power. One of the testaments to the character of the man was his absolute refusal to allow his own identity and affiliations to confine his thoughts or cloud his judgment when he saw a need to criticize leaders, particularly those within his own communities, whether Arab or American. Third, Said played an important role as a *visionary*, for he was able to foresee, long before most, various solutions for bringing about a just and lasting peace between Palestinians and Israelis. Viewed with hindsight, these solutions now seem axiomatic to many scholars, activists, and policy makers familiar with the conflict. The common theme in these three roles was that Said took very seriously his position as an intellectual and the concomitant duty imposed on him to speak the truth to power.

SAID AS NARRATOR

The importance of a people asserting their collective voice in representing themselves in the public domain, whether in cultural, social, economic, or political fora, and particularly in the case of a colonized, oppressed, or subjugated people, was a subject that preoccupied the great South African antiapartheid activist Steve Biko. In treating the subject of Black Consciousness in 1971, he explained to fellow antiapartheid activists that his philosophy had very much "to do with correcting false images" of black Africans "in terms of our culture, education, religion [and] economics," and that "there is always an interplay between the history of a people, i.e. the past, and their faith in themselves and hopes for their future."[8] In noting that the privileged "whites can only see us from the outside and as such can never extract and analyse the ethos in the black community," Biko counseled that black South Africans "must therefore work out schemes not only to correct this, but further *to be our own authorities rather than wait to be interpreted by others.*"[9] Of course, in the South Africa of his day, Biko's ideas posed a considerable threat to the apartheid system and the worldview it stood for. With such thoughts banned from expression of any kind by the ruling authorities, they were uttered by Biko at great peril, as was tragically confirmed by his brutal murder at the age of thirty while in South African police detention after conviction under the now-infamous Terrorism Act. That Biko persisted in preaching Black Consciousness in the face of substantial threats to his personal well-being, however, speaks volumes of the courage sometimes required in daring to represent the oppressed and those whom the powers that be would just as soon wish away or dismiss as nonpersons, subhuman, simply not like "us."[10]

That Biko's example was well understood by Said was evident in the manner in which he represented the Palestinian people and its enduring struggle for freedom. In the context of that struggle, the issue of representation has been central and generally shaped by two distinct but related paradigms, both characterized by an attempt to impose a master narrative on Palestinians: one focused on effacing the reality of Palestine and its people; another on portraying Palestinians in such negative terms as to cast doubt on their very humanity and thereby render them unworthy of consideration. Said took serious issue with both of these paradigms and regarded them as major contributing factors that helped rationalize the actual effacement of much of Palestine in 1948 and the continuous subjugation of the Palestinian people thereafter. To him, they were to be treated as challenges that had to be met with an effective counternarrative if Palestine and its people were to continue to exist in the historical record at all, let alone reconstitute themselves as a nation in their native land.

The first of these is what one may call an "imperial paradigm." This paradigm was shaped by the Palestinian encounter with European imperialism in the first half of the twentieth century and by the international order it spawned in the quarter century after World War II. A marked feature of this encounter was that the international system "divided peoples into different levels of 'civilization' according to which international legal rights were awarded to those regarded as most advanced."[11] A stark example of this was article 22 of the Covenant of the League of Nations, concluded at the Paris Peace Conference on 28 April 1919, which provided that the "well-being and development" of the peoples of the former colonies of the defeated Axis powers formed "a sacred trust of civilization."[12] Under article 22, because such peoples "were not yet able to stand by themselves under the strenuous conditions of the modern world," the League established the mandate system in order that their "tutelage" could "be entrusted to advanced nations."[13] As for the colonies and territories formerly administered by the Ottoman Empire, including Palestine, article 22 provided that they had "reached a stage of development where their existence as independent nations can be provisionally recognized subject to the rendering of administrative advice and assistance by a Mandatory [power] until such time as they are able to stand alone."[14] While it is true that article 22 bears tremendous import for having provisionally recognized the political independence of Palestine at a time when Zionist settlers constituted a very small minority of the population of the country,[15] the unmistakable paternalism and contempt expressed by the Great Powers through it toward the Palestinians as people "not yet able to stand by themselves," not capable of confronting "the strenuous conditions of the modern world," and therefore requiring the "tutelage" of "advanced nations" were matters that helped propagate a narrative of effacement that deeply troubled Said. The following passage from *The Question of Palestine* is demonstrative:

> All the transformative projects for Palestine, including Zionism, have rationalized the denial of present reality in Palestine with some argument about a "higher" (or better, more worthy, more modern, more fitting; the comparatives are almost infinite) interest, cause or mission. These "higher" things entitle their proponents not only to claim that the natives of Palestine, such as they are, are not worth considering and therefore nonexistent; they also feel entitled to claim that the natives of Palestine, and Palestine itself, have been superseded definitively, transformed completely and beyond recall, and this even while those same natives have been demonstrating exactly the opposite. Here again the Arab Palestinian has been pitted against an undeniably superior antagonist whose consciousness of himself and of the Palestinian is exactly, *positionally,* superior.[16]

Through such reflections, Said not only denounced the callous worldview of imperial Europe toward the Oriental Other but also helped deconstruct the dominant narrative of the international system and the state-centered legal and political order upon which it had been based. Despite centuries of lived history, this system continued to regard non-Europeans as subservient natives unworthy of standing in the "modern world."

Another obvious example of this denigration is the Balfour Declaration of 2 November 1917, by which the Zionist movement secured a commitment from the British government to help establish a "Jewish national home" in Palestine: "His Majesty's Government view with favour the establishment in Palestine of a national home for the Jewish people, and will use their best endeavours to facilitate the achievement of this object, it being clearly understood that nothing shall be done which may prejudice the civil and religious rights of *existing non-Jewish communities* in Palestine, or the rights and political status enjoyed by Jews in any other country."[17] Of course, at the time the declaration was issued, Great Britain had no sovereignty or control over Palestine, the country still being under the administrative control of the Ottoman Empire. But the violation of the *nemo dat* principle aside, this historical fact mattered little to the colonial culture that shaped, influenced, and imposed a narrative in which Palestine and Palestinians were simply rubbed out.[18] Palestine's indigenous Arabs then accounted for roughly 92 percent of the country's population, "facts about which there could be no debate," as Said often put it.[19] Nevertheless, Lord Balfour chose to obfuscate reality by referring to them as the "existing non-Jewish" community, as though they, not the Zionist settlers for whom the declaration was issued, constituted the minority. One is here reminded of Said's observation that language is "a highly organized and encoded system which employs many devices" to express "not 'truth' but representations," which are ultimately informed by the "culture, institutions, and political ambience of the representer."[20] That such was the case with Balfour's choice of language was a matter he himself felt little compunction admitting. In a memorandum to Lord Curzon dated 11 August 1919, Balfour stated, "In Palestine we do not propose even to go through the form of consulting the wishes of the present inhabitants of the country. . . . The four great powers are committed to Zionism and Zionism, be it right or wrong, good or bad, is rooted in age-long tradition, in present needs, in future hopes, of far profounder import than the desire and prejudices of the 700,000 Arabs who now inhabit that ancient land."[21]

For Said, more than the declaration itself, it was the *idea* behind Balfour's decision to issue it that was cause for great concern. Said viewed the declaration "as part of a history, of a style and set of characteristics centrally constituting the question of Palestine as it can be discussed even today," and he lamented the fact that this "style" took "for granted the higher right of a colonial power to dispose of a territory as it saw fit."[22] In doing so, Said encouraged the re-presence, if you will, of the Palestinians into history, as living, breathing subjects whose very existence as a nation was being plotted against for the sake of "age long tradition" not in the least bit related to them. He rejected the "brute, politically manipulated disproportions between natives and non-natives" made acceptable by the "rationale" of men like Balfour—namely that Zionism "as a superior idea to that of sheer number and presence [i.e. of indigenous Palestinians] *ought to rule* in Palestine."[23]

Other examples of the imperial paradigm continued to emerge long after the demise of British power and the onset of the age of human and peoples' rights in the post–World War II era. Indeed, it was in the "postcolonial world" that "elements of the old order through which the West assume[d] a centrality against the periphery of the ex-colonies" were replicated in the international institutions that evolved.[24] The U.N. General Assembly's recommended partition of Palestine in 1947, whereby the one-third Jewish-settler minority was granted approximately 57 percent of the territory of Palestine, leaving only 43 percent for the indigenous Palestinian two-thirds majority, was such an example.[25] Another was U.N. Security Council Resolution 242 of 22 November 1967, which affirmed the principles of "a just and lasting peace in the Middle East," including the achievement of "a just settlement of the refugee problem," meaning, of course, the *Palestinian* refugee problem.[26] But Said's deconstruction of the resolution, with its master narrative of Palestinian nonexistence (how could "anonymous refugees" have any *real* national rights? he wondered), helped us identify what was essentially a repackaging of the old imperial system in the garb of the "enlightened" new world order.[27] If, as Said noted, "by the end of the seventies there was not a progressive political cause that did not identify with the Palestinian movement," it could only have been due to the emergence of the Palestine Liberation Organization (PLO) in 1964 and the subsequent introduction of a Palestinian counternarrative during the decolonization period. From that point forward, Palestinians were to "be [their] own authorities," as Biko put it, and Said would play a direct role in shaping the narrative of their national liberation movement as a member of its "parliament in exile," the Palestine National Council (PNC), from 1977 to 1991.

A second phenomenon that has shaped how the Palestinians and their freedom struggle have been represented is what one may call the "Zionist paradigm." In *The Question of Palestine,* Said explained:

> What we must again see is the issue involving representation, an issue always lurking near the question of Palestine. I said earlier that Zionism always undertakes to speak for Palestine and the Palestinians; this has always meant a blocking operation, by which the Palestinian cannot be heard from (or represent himself) directly on the world stage. Just as the expert Orientalist believed that only he could speak (paternally as it were) for the natives and primitive societies that he had studied—his *presence* denoting their *absence*—so too the Zionists spoke to the world on behalf of the Palestinians.[28]

This point was central to Said's understanding of the Palestine problem, and he always sought to affirm, in one form or another, that from their earliest encounters with political Zionism, the Palestinians were the object of a conscious effort to strip them of the right to narrate their own politics, their own history, even their own existence. For if such an existence were acknowledged in any manner, it would be impossible for Zionism to reconcile its own master narrative of a scattered, pioneering, victimized people answering the call to "redeem" a desolate "land no one wanted."[29] As Said noted, "In order to mitigate the presence of large numbers of natives on a desired land, the Zionists convinced themselves that these natives did not exist, then made it possible for them to exist only in the most rarefied forms."[30]

One of the earliest examples of such representations was the Zionist slogan that Palestine was a "land without a people for a people without a land," a myth propagated by Israel Zangwill, a contemporary of Theodor Herzl, Zionism's "founding father."[31] Nur Masalha, one of today's leading Palestinian historians, has noted that the land-without-a-people myth "not only justified Zionist settlement but also helped to suppress conscience-pricking among Israeli Jews for the dispossession of the Palestinians before, during and after 1948: if the 'land had been empty,' then no Zionist wrongdoing had taken place."[32] As Masalha notes, "For the Zionist settler who is coming to 'redeem the land' the indigenous people earmarked for dispossession are usually invisible."[33] In *Culture and Resistance,* Said concurred ("We are an invisible people") and added anecdotally that for many Israelis, "it is a very difficult thought to accept, that you are there not because you're a great, heroic figure escaping the Holocaust, but you are there largely at the expense of another person who you've displaced or killed or driven away."[34]

Another example is former Israeli prime minister Golda Meir's 1969 exclamation that "it was not as though there was a Palestinian people in Palestine considering itself as a Palestinian people and we came and threw them out and took their country away from them: they did not exist."[35] In *The Politics of Dispossession,* Said noted that after Meir had "set the general tone" with this statement, he viewed his "most specific task . . . to make the case for Palestinian presence, to say that there *was* a Palestinian people and that, like all others, it had a history, a society, and, most important, a right to self-determination."[36] "In other words," as he put it, "to try to change the public consciousness in which Palestine had no presence at all."[37] Of course, the "public consciousness" that most concerned Said in this respect was that of the West, particularly in the United States, where popular ignorance of the Palestinians and their plight had become widespread in the decades following Meir's fabrication. As a Palestinian American, Said was particularly troubled by this, as demonstrated in the following passage from *Orientalism:* "The life of an Arab Palestinian in the West, particularly in America, is disheartening. There exists here an almost unanimous consensus that politically he does not exist, and when it is allowed that he does, it is either as a nuisance or as an Oriental. The web of racism, cultural stereotypes, political imperialism, dehumanizing ideology holding the Arab or the Muslim is very strong indeed, and it is this web which every Palestinian has come to feel as his uniquely punishing destiny."[38] It is noteworthy that Said's "own experiences" in dealing with this destiny in part led to his writing *Orientalism,* by all accounts his most influential work.[39] In doing so, he helped illustrate the effect to which deconstructionist methodologies could be put in countering narratives imposed on peoples for whom power purports to speak.

Where the Zionist master narrative has been unable to rely on effacement to deal with the Palestinians, it has turned to dehumanization. Said lamented the record of unspeakable denigrations of the Palestinians as "two-legged vermin," "drugged roaches in a bottle," and "grasshoppers" who must be "crushed," as well as the more frequent references to the Palestinians as a "demographic threat" and "ticking bomb" commonly found in mainstream Israeli media today.[40] One of the more politically damaging representations in this narrative has been the image of the Palestinian as "terrorist," a representation that has persisted for decades and has gained increased currency from events in Israel and the occupied Palestinian territory (OPT) since the outbreak of the Second Intifada in September 2000, as well as from the so-called global war on terror that erupted following the 11 September 2001 attack on the United States. In *Blaming the Victims*, Said exposed the rationale for incorporating the charge of "terror" or "terrorism" into the master narrative: "The main thing is to isolate your enemy from time, from causality, from prior action, and thereby to portray him or her as ontologically and gratuitously interested in wreaking havoc for its own sake."[41] Using this formula, the Palestinian "terrorist," acting only out of a primordial desire to kill, is much easier to condemn, denounce, and eschew as anathema to order, liberty, and freedom—essentially to "our" way of life. In *The Politics of Dispossession,* Said continued, "The very indiscriminateness of terrorism, actual and described, its tautological and circular character, is antinarrative. Sequence, the logic of cause and effect as between oppressors and victims, opposing pressures—all these vanish inside an enveloping cloud called 'terrorism.'"[42]

Said's counternarrative offers a method to roundly condemn taking advantage of the vague and nebulous character of the term *terror* to "justify everything 'we' do and to delegitimize as well as dehumanize everything 'they' do."[43] It forces all concerned to ask the harder if not obvious question "why" before judging the other for resorting to violence. At the same time, it does not accept or justify violence for its own sake or for political ends, and it absolutely rejects the use of all forms of violence *by anyone* against civilians or noncombatants anywhere.

Beyond countering the representations rooted in imperialist and Zionist discourse, though, Said regarded the Palestinian people and its struggle for freedom as symbolic of a more universal, human struggle against oppression, injustice, and exploitation. This view added a valuable element to the counternarrative that he helped cultivate and that continues to be a prominent feature of the discourse of the disenfranchised the world over. For Said, the global appeal of the Palestinian cause was a direct result of the link between European colonialism and the rise of Zionism in the late nineteenth century, both of which "appealed to a European audience for whom the classification of overseas territories and natives into various uneven classes was canonical and 'natural.'"[44] "That is why," Said wrote, "every sin-

gle state or movement in the formerly colonized territories of Africa and Asia today identifies with, fully supports, and understands the Palestinian struggle."[45] But
shared historical experience was not the only reason for Said's conception of Palestine as a concept far greater than itself. Ironically, for him, Palestine's status as a festering colonial problem in the age of the so-called postcolony, neglected and protracted, rendered its allegorical value all the more poignant. Said saw Palestine as
more than a freedom struggle capable of capturing the popular imagination; he also
saw it as a door to a brighter future for us all:

> No one who has given his energies to being a partisan has ever doubted that "Pales-
> tine" has loosed a great number of other issues as well. The word has become a sym-
> bol for struggle against social injustice.... There is an awareness in the nonwhite world
> that the tendency of modern politics to rule over masses of people as transferable,
> silent, and politically neutral populations has a specific illustration in what has hap-
> pened to the Palestinians—and what in different ways is happening to the citizens of
> newly independent, formerly colonial territories ruled over by antidemocratic army
> regimes. The idea of resistance gets content and muscle from Palestine; more usefully,
> resistance gets detail and a positively new approach to the microphysics of oppres-
> sion from Palestine. If we think of Palestine as having the function of both a place to
> be returned to and of an entirely new place, a vision partially of a restored past and
> of a novel future, perhaps even a historical disaster transformed into hope for a dif-
> ferent future, we will understand the word's meaning better.[46]

I think that this aspect of Palestine had the greatest resonance for Said, perhaps
because he was the quintessential exile, a citizen of the world, a product of far more
than Palestine itself. In the end, this internationalist, universalist, secular, humanist outlook on Palestine and its potential was one of the most important elements
of Said's counternarrative on the place, its people, and its cause.

SAID AS CRITIC

A natural outgrowth of Said's exhortation to speak truth to power was the role he
assumed in public life as power's consummate critic. If speaking truth to power was
the reason for illuminating subaltern narratives and presence, holding power's
agents, their intentions and methods up to public scrutiny was necessary to carve
out the space for accounting for such narratives in their own right. In the context
of the Palestinian freedom struggle, Said devoted considerable energy to a critical
reading and understanding of Zionism. For him, Zionism was more than an abstract ideal that called for the creation of a "body corporate" of the Jews in Palestine, to use Theodor Herzl's term; it was the product of a certain historical context
and a set of values and forces that had *consequences,* not only for its Jewish adherents but also for the non-Jewish natives of the place Zionism coveted, colonized,
and eventually transformed.[47] In *The Question of Palestine,* Said devoted a full chap-

ter to deconstructing Zionism from "the standpoint of its victims," and he begins
the chapter with the following important observation:

> It is frequently argued that such an idea as Zionism, for all its political tribulations
> and the struggles on its behalf, is at bottom an unchanging idea that expresses the
> yearning for Jewish political and religious self-determination—for Jewish national
> selfhood—to be exercised on the promised land. Because Zionism seems to have cul-
> minated in the creation of the state of Israel, it is also argued that the historical real-
> ization of the idea confirms its unchanging essence and, no less important, the means
> used for its realization. Very little is said about what Zionism entailed for non-Jews
> who happened to have encountered it; for that matter, nothing is said about where
> (outside Jewish history) it took place, and from what in the historical context of nine-
> teenth-century Europe Zionism drew its force. To the Palestinian, for whom Zionism
> was somebody else's idea imported into Palestine and for which in a very concrete
> way he or she was made to pay and suffer, these forgotten things about Zionism are
> the very things that are centrally important.[48]

Thus, for Said, Zionism was more than an emancipatory idea for persecuted European Jewry, a fact he readily acknowledged. Rather, it was Zionism's simultaneous
affiliation with, organic connection to, European imperialism and colonialism that
mattered the most, an appreciation of which was required if a full and fair understanding of the idea was at all possible.[49] Of course, Said was not the first to identify this aspect of Zionism; Walid Khalidi and Ibrahim Abu-Lughod, among others,
had done so years earlier.[50] However, he deconstructed and articulated it in a more
critical fashion than anyone before him.

His formula was set out in *The Question of Palestine*, where he counseled the importance of examining "effective political ideas like Zionism" from both a genealogical standpoint ("in order that their provenance, their kinship and descent, their
affiliation both with other ideas and with political institutions may be demonstrated") and from a practical standpoint (as a system of "accumulation of power,
land, ideological legitimacy" on the one hand, and "displacement of people, other
ideas, prior legitimacy," on the other).[51] It was this contextual, multilayered, epistemological approach to understanding Zionism as an *idea* that was the hallmark
of his role as one of its most public critics. For him, no idea, movement, culture, or
civilization could be understood in simple terms, and he was greatly troubled by
the tendency of many self-styled intellectuals to essentialize and simplify Zionism's
relationship with its Palestinian Other (Zionism was essentially "good," whereas
Palestinians were essentially "bad").[52]

One particularly demonstrative example of this is to be found in an interview given
by prominent Israeli "New Historian" Benny Morris to Ari Shavit of the Israeli daily
Ha'aretz on 9 January 2004.[53] Morris, of course, gained notoriety with the 1987 publication of *The Birth of the Palestinian Refugee Problem, 1947–1949*, in which he defini-

tively demonstrated, among other things, that the Palestinians had been expelled and/or forced to flee during the 1948 war by Zionist forces.[54] Corroborating much of the Palestinian historical narrative, Morris's revelations earned him the unwanted opprobrium and eventual boycott of much of the Israeli academic establishment. Following the 2004 printing of the revised edition of his seminal work, Morris told *Ha'aretz* that further research into Israel Defense Force archives had revealed that "there were far more Israeli acts of massacre" during the 1948 war "than I had previously thought. . . . To my surprise, there were also many cases of rape," a "large proportion" of which "ended with [the] murder" of the Palestinian victims.[55] Notwithstanding these harrowing findings, the following exchange between Morris and Shavit reveals the extent to which power and the ideas that fuel it, in this case Zionism from the standpoint of Morris, essentializes its victims and can be regarded by its adherents as important enough to justify even the darkest of deeds:

> *Shavit:* Benny Morris, for decades you have been researching the dark side of Zionism. You are an expert on the atrocities of 1948. In the end, do you in effect justify all this? Are you an advocate of the transfer of 1948?
>
> *Morris:* There is no justification for acts of rape. There is no justification for acts of massacre. Those are war crimes. But in certain conditions, expulsion is not a war crime. I don't think that the expulsions of 1948 were war crimes. You can't make an omelet without breaking eggs. You have to dirty your hands.
>
> *Shavit:* We are talking about the killing of thousands of people, the destruction of an entire society.
>
> *Morris:* A society that aims to kill you forces you to destroy it. When the choice is between destroying or being destroyed, it's better to destroy.
>
> *Shavit:* There is something chilling about the quiet way in which you say that.
>
> *Morris:* If you expected me to burst into tears, I'm sorry to disappoint you. I will not do that.
>
> *Shavit:* So when the commanders of Operation Dani [an Israeli military operation in which thousands of Palestinians were ethnically cleansed from their homes by Zionist forces in 1948] are standing there and observing the long and terrible column of the 50,000 people expelled from Lod *[sic]* walking eastward, you stand there with them? You justify them?
>
> *Morris:* I definitely understand them. I understand their motives. I don't think they felt any pangs of conscience, and in their place I wouldn't have felt pangs of conscience. *Without that act, they would not have won the war and the state would not have come into being.*
>
> *Shavit:* You do not condemn them morally?
>
> *Morris:* No.
>
> *Shavit:* They perpetrated ethnic cleansing.
>
> *Morris:* There are circumstances in history that justify ethnic cleansing. I know that

this term is completely negative in the discourse of the twenty-first century, but when the choice is between ethnic cleansing and genocide—the annihilation of your people—I prefer ethnic cleansing.

Shavit: And that was the situation in 1948?

Morris: That was the situation. That is what Zionism faced. *A Jewish state would not have come into being without the uprooting of 700,000 Palestinians. Therefore it was necessary to uproot them. There was no choice but to expel that population.* It was necessary to cleanse the hinterland and cleanse the border areas and cleanse the main roads. It was necessary to cleanse the villages from which our convoys and our settlements were fired on.

Shavit: The term "to cleanse" is terrible.

Morris: I know it doesn't sound nice but that's the term they used at the time. I adopted it from all the 1948 documents in which I am immersed.

Shavit: What you are saying is hard to listen to and hard to digest. You sound hard-hearted.

Morris: I feel sympathy for the Palestinian people, which truly underwent a hard tragedy. I feel sympathy for the refugees themselves. But if the desire to establish a Jewish state here is legitimate, there was no other choice.[56]

Difficult though it may be, let us leave aside Morris's supposed sympathy for the Palestinian people. For our limited purposes, only the following of his claims is relevant: that in 1948 the ethnic cleansing of the vast majority of Palestine's indigenous Christian and Muslim Arab inhabitants by Zionist forces was completely justified, indeed *required,* so that Zionism could fulfill its goal of establishing a Jewish state in that land. In *The Question of Palestine,* a full twenty-five years before Morris made his startling proclamations, Said helped us understand power's propensity to justify the unjustifiable by examining what Zionism meant for its Palestinian victims. Referring first to a passage in *Heart of Darkness* (where Conrad writes, "The conquest of the earth, which mostly means the taking it away from those who have a different complexion or slightly flatter noses than ourselves, is not a pretty thing when you look into it too much . . . What redeems it is the idea only; an idea at the back of it; not a sentimental pretence but an idea—something you can set up, and bow down before, and offer a sacrifice to"),[57] Said makes the following observation:

> The power to conquer territory is only in part a matter of physical force: there is the strong moral and intellectual component making the conquest itself secondary to an idea, which dignifies (and indeed hastens) pure force with arguments drawn from science, morality, ethics and a general philosophy. Everything in Western culture potentially capable of dignifying the acquisition of new domains—as a new science, for example, acquires new intellectual territory for itself—*could* be put at the service of colonial adventures. And *was* put, the "idea" always informing the conquest, making it entirely palatable.[58]

And so it was through an analysis of the idea of Zionism and its provenance that Said offered an alternative understanding of why, how, and on what grounds its adherents used it to justify their treatment of the Palestinians, rendering all of its practical effects for them, no matter how unspeakable and tragic, perfectly acceptable and palatable to the conscience. Between Conrad and Morris, the power of an idea, in this case the idea of Zionism, is laid bare; it is, alas, a trump card to be played over all other considerations. What Said's reading enabled was the deconstruction of Zionism first as an idea and second as a system aimed at the actual effacement of Palestine and the subsequent creation of Israel in its place. But his analysis can apply to virtually every act the state of Israel has undertaken with respect to the Palestinian people to this day. Take, for example, the expropriation of Palestinian land, or the construction of the wall in the West Bank, or the erection of Jewish-only settlements and bypass roads in the OPT, or the imprisonment without charge or trial of Palestinian detainees, or the extrajudicial killing of stone-throwing Palestinian youth. All these actions are manifestations of modern Zionism's interaction with its Palestinian Other; taken separately, viewed in a vacuum, one can justify each of them to varying degrees, as is done regularly by Israeli government officials or supporters of Israel, as necessary to keep Israel and the Jewish people "secure." But what Said offered, with his critical reading not only of Zionism's acts but more importantly of Zionism as an idea, was a framework for viewing such acts through the prism of its victims, a way to see continuity in the treatment of these victims—not because Israel requires security, nor because Palestinians are terrorists, but finally because if Zionism as an idea is in the end worth anything, such acts are necessarily justified, even required.[59]

But of course, Said's role as critic did not stop at Zionism or Israel. Anyone familiar with his writings on Palestine knows he was equally intent on calling American power to account, in particular for the role that successive U.S. administrations had played in the conflict.[60] To be sure, Said never let his criticism of American foreign policy in the Middle East cloud his understanding and appreciation of the complexity of American history, culture, and society. But he was tenacious and fearless in taking a stand against what he saw as unabashed American duplicity in its support for Israeli policies against the Palestinian people, not to mention U.S. support for numerous autocratic regimes in the Arab world. As someone who intimately understood the global appeal and power of American "ideals" (I concede that the construct is distinctly anti-Saidian), Said decried the U.S. tendency to pursue policies of democracy at home and dictatorship abroad in the Middle East. Following the method and approach of Noam Chomsky, Said always took great pains to illustrate to his American audience his view that U.S. foreign policy was not only bad for the Palestinians and, ultimately, for Israel, but also inherently anti-American and supremely counterproductive for American interests in the region. In *Culture and Resistance*, he put it thus:

I think that most Arabs and Muslims feel that the United States hasn't really been paying much attention to their desires, but has been pursuing its policies for its own sake,
without much in the way of explanation or attempts to somehow justify them. And
above all, pursuing these policies not according to many of the principles that the
United States proclaims are its own: democracy, self-determination, freedom of
speech, freedom of assembly, and its commitment to international law. It is very hard,
for example, to justify the thirty-four-year-old occupation of the West Bank and
Gaza—140 Israeli settlements and roughly 400,000 settlers brought with the support
and financing of the United States—and say this is part of U.S. adherence to international law and U.N. resolutions. So all of this is a record that keeps building up in an
area in which—and here we come now to the really sad part—the rulers have been
supported by the United States against the wishes of the people. And there is a general sense in which the United States is flouting its own principles in order to maintain such governments and regimes in power and really have very little to do with the
large number of people who are dominated by these regimes.[61]

Of course, through his writings Said frequently noted that the American approach to the region bore no small resemblance to the imperial policies pursued
by Britain and France in the first half of the twentieth century. The conflict between
British legal obligations to the Palestinians under the Covenant of the League of
Nations and British promises to the Zionists in the Balfour Declaration is one such
example. Another is the manner in which Britain and France surreptitiously dismembered the ailing Ottoman Empire into spheres of influence through the infa-
mous Sykes-Picot Agreement of May 1916, the obvious (not to mention anomalous)
contours of which remain with us to this day. The main difference between American power and that of its British and French progenitors was in the level of its sophistication, itself a product of its contemporaneous emergence with the age of human rights and information—both considerable impediments to the more raw
exercise of power characteristic of centuries past, and thereby requiring a developed expertise in the Machiavellian use of image, language, and ideas. Said's criticism of America's exercise of power in dealing with the Palestinian problem was
important because of his ability to identify and deconstruct its "neo-imperial" penchant for deploying a sort of Orwellian doublespeak to mask the real intent and
effect of American policy in the region. In *The Politics of Dispossession*, Said observed that "one of the most ominous developments in the Middle East since the
era of avowedly secret agreements by the powers on the disposition of spheres of
influence has been the rise of a public policy consisting of the traditional *Realpoli-
tik* but incorporating the terminology of a liberal mutual interest, respect, and assistance platform against extremism and disorder; even as the far less evident underside of that platform is a thoroughly ruthless instrument for quashing or containing
the slightest social restiveness or protest."[62]
Using this framework, Said offered a critical view of how the considerable moral

force of such important ideas as "freedom," "liberty," "democracy," and most important for our purposes, "peace" had been turned on its head to explain in as altruistic terms as possible a policy that is in effect the antithesis of those ideas. The net effect of this vernacular of "liberal mutual interest," as Said termed it, has been to silence dissent, for if one is against the policies of America and its friends in the region, one necessarily finds oneself pitted *against* liberty, freedom, democracy, and peace.

This deconstruction of American foreign policy in respect to the Palestine problem was most evident in Said's writings in the years following the 1993 signing of the Declaration of Principles on Interim Self-Governing Arrangements (DOP) between Israel and the PLO and the onset of the now-defunct Oslo "peace" process. Contrary to what mainstream political pundits in London, New York, Paris, and Washington portrayed as the dawn of a new era, Said argued was in fact a drastic turn for the worse—a "Palestinian Versailles," fashioned and supported by "incompetent" Palestinian leaders and "dishonest" Israeli and American negotiators.[63] Under Oslo, Israel and the PLO undertook to conclude a number of interim agreements over a five-year period (1993–99) that would lead to a final settlement of their conflict based on the "land-for-peace" formula outlined in U.N. Security Council Resolutions 242 (1967) and 338 (1973). Whereas the basis of the Oslo process was the PLO's recognition of "the right of the State of Israel to exist in peace and security," the government of Israel offered little more than recognition of "the PLO as the representative of the Palestinian people," stopping short of express recognition of the right of the Palestinian people to self-determination in a state of their own or of the then twenty-six-year-old military occupation of the OPT, with its attendant destruction of Palestinian lives and property.[64] Instead, the Oslo process centered on the creation of a quasi-autonomous Palestinian Authority (PA), established to administer selected local and civil affairs for the majority of the Palestinian population in the OPT (taxation, education, health, etc.), which was itself divided into three separate jurisdictions, Areas "A", "B" and "C."[65] At no point during the Oslo years did the PA's limited authority extend beyond the various noncontiguous portions of Areas A and B (amounting to just over 21 percent of the total area of the OPT, or just 5 percent of the total area of historical Palestine).[66] At the time of this writing, it is questionable whether these areas continue to exist in practical terms, having been run over by Israel's military offensive in March 2002 and effectively kept under siege ever since.[67] In contrast, and notwithstanding a commitment in Oslo that "neither side shall initiate or take any step that will change the status of the West Bank and the Gaza Strip pending the outcome of permanent status negotiations," since 1993, Israel has more than doubled the number of its settlers in the OPT through continued construction of illegal Jewish settlements, bypass roads, and, most recently, the wall in the West Bank (declared illegal by the International Court of Justice in July 2004).[68] With these actions, Israel has consolidated its control over the area, with no discernible reduction in support from the United States.[69] In fact, U.S. support intensified during the Second Intifada, which has caused unprecedented levels of Palestinian suffering, including through the Israeli imposition of a regime of siege, curfew, and closure on the besieged Bantustan-like enclaves in which the Palestinians have effectively been corraled since 1993 and culminating in the Israeli assault on the Gaza Strip in December 2008–January 2009. The result: over 6,000 Palestinians and 1,000 Israelis killed; over 31,500 Palestinians and 6,800 Israelis injured;[70] and a Palestinian economic recession described by the World Bank as "among the worst in modern history," with unemployment increasing from 10 percent in September 2000 to an average of 41 percent during 2002, and the number of Palestinians living below the poverty line of $2 per day during the same period rising from 20 percent to over 50 percent of the population. In the Gaza Strip alone during the same period, "unemployment exceeded 46 percent of the workforce and the poverty level rose to 68 percent."[71] Israel's September 2005 withdrawal of its approximately 8,000 settlers from the Gaza Strip has not resulted in any major improvement of the socioeconomic or human security of Gaza's population, nor incidentally has it ended Israeli occupation.[72]

It is in this general context that Said questioned the meaning of the term *peace* as bandied about by the United States and its "junior partner," particularly during the Oslo years.[73] In *Peace and Its Discontents*, he lamented that "American 'peace' in the Middle East" has meant "the subordination of all regional and local issues to the United States" and its interests, which he saw as effectively identical to those of Israel in the conflict between Zionism and the Palestinians.[74] In *From Oslo to Iraq and the Road Map*, Said bemoaned that for years "the United States has underwritten Israel's intransigence and brutality" in the form of "$92 billion and unending political support, all for the world to see"; "ironically," he wrote, this support was far stronger "during, rather than either before or after, the Oslo process."[75] His analysis of the positions the United States took during the Oslo process called into serious question Washington's self-styled designation as the "honest broker" between Israel and the Palestinians, the duplicity of which was symbolized, in Said's view, by the presence in the Clinton and Bush II administrations of a "small cabal of individuals, all of them unelected and therefore unresponsive to public pressure," many with well-known public ties to the Zionist lobby in the United States or otherwise known as staunch public supporters of Israel.[76] Although these people—men such as Martin Indyk and Dennis Ross, among others—did not for Said "symbolize a conspiracy," they personified for him "an aggressively unbroken continuity in U.S. Middle East Policy" that had to be called to account if justice was to be achieved for all involved.[77] In the context of the Oslo process, this continuity manifested itself in, for instance, the automatic support Israel received from the United States for Prime Minister Ehud Barak's so-called "generous offers" at the Camp David Summit of July 2000, as well as in the parameters President Clinton put forth at Taba in

January 2001.[78] In commenting on Clinton's proposals (calling them a "warmed-over Israeli intention to perpetuate control over Palestinian lives and land for the foreseeable future"), Said criticized their "underlying premise" that "Israel needs protection from Palestinians, not the other way around."[79] This premise, Said emphasized, was something that has informed and continues to inform official American approaches to the conflict up to the present, the "vision" of President George W. Bush as outlined in the so-called Middle East road map being no exception. That document, vague as it is, is still heavily imbued with the notion that it is democratic Israel, not the dispossessed, colonized, militarily occupied Palestinians, that is under constant military attack and therefore in need of peace and security. As Said noted in respect to the road map, "the real onus is placed on the Palestinians . . . who must keep coming up with the goods in rapid succession" (e.g., PA "reform," end to "Palestinian violence," "incitement," etc.), "while the military occupation remains more or less in place," with Israel in full control.[80] According to this "vision," the problem is not Israeli dispossession, colonization, or occupation of Palestinians or their land, but rather Palestinian "corruption," "violence," and "terror," which must be put to an end before the Israelis can return to negotiations with the Palestinians—in essence, before "peace" can be achieved. In this sense, one might view the road map as an obvious throwback to the American "rejectionist" approach to "peace" in the Middle East (to borrow a notion from Chomsky) prevalent in the 1970s and 1980s. This approach rejected negotiations with the PLO, rejected Palestinian statehood, and rejected even the slightest pressuring of Israel to end its occupation or construction of settlements in the OPT, let alone an acknowledgment of its responsibility for the creation of the Palestinian refugee problem.[81] In the end, Said's criticism of official American approaches to "peace" confirmed the need for Israelis and Palestinians to move beyond the doublespeak—that "liberal mutual interest" must line up against "extremism and disorder"—to make an honest and principled commitment simply to do justice to others based on universal standards of law and morality.

Importantly, this call of Said's did not stop with his criticism of Zionism and the United States. It was just as evident in his scathing treatment of leaders and governments in the Arab world. As a fiercely secular liberal who had for many reasons been disaffected by the general malaise of the contemporary Arab Middle East, particularly in the years after the fall of Palestine and the decolonization period, he spent considerable energy commenting upon and criticizing its leaders and governing ethos in the Arabic-language press. As with other of his writings, his foremost concern as an independent free-thinking intellectual was to provide a catalyst for forward-looking change in the Arab world, which he considered vital to the struggle for justice and freedom in Palestine.

One of the issues that most troubled Said in this respect was the manner in which Arab regimes and official Arab institutions expressed their opposition to Zionism and Israel. From 1948 onward, this opposition took the form of a total rejection and boycott of the "Zionist entity," a pretender-state and imperial usurper of Arab patrimony and rights, the struggle against which was the paramount duty of every Arab citizen—man, woman, and child. Said strongly criticized this policy as a hopeless, bankrupt approach to dealing with what Israel and Zionism had wrought on the Palestinian and Arab peoples. He believed that this approach had contributed to the gradual militarization, despotism, and tyranny of the Arab state system in the post-1948 period. In *The Question of Palestine,* Said derided this image of Israel perpetuated in the Arab world:

> Israel has tended to appear as an entirely negative entity, something constructed for us for no other reason than either to keep Arabs out or to subjugate them. The internal solidarity and cohesion of Israel, of Israelis as a people and as a society, have for the most part eluded the understanding of Arabs generally. Thus to the walls constructed by Zionism have been added walls constructed by a dogmatic, almost theological brand of Arabism. Israel has seemed essentially to be a rhetorical tool provided by the West to harass the Arabs. What this perception entailed in the Arab states has been a policy of repression and a kind of thought control. For years it was forbidden ever to refer to Israel in print; this sort of censorship led quite naturally to the consolidation of police states, the absence of freedom of expression, and a whole set of human rights abuses, all supposedly justified in the name of "fighting Zionist aggression," which meant that any form of oppression at home was acceptable because it served the "sacred cause" of "national security."[82]

As an alternative to this "policy of repression" and "thought control," Said counseled an open and frank engagement with Israel ("what earthly use is there in pretending that it doesn't exist?" he wondered), and with its principal sponsor, the United States.[83] The intention was not only to escape the shroud of ignorance in which the Arab states had enveloped their societies as regards these two formidable powers in their midst, but just as importantly, to remove the pretense of the daunting enemy at the gates, thereby opening up internal Arab governing structures and policies to public scrutiny and accountability for the manner in which they had for far too long held their own citizens in utter contempt. In this respect, Said often wrote of the need for Arabs to seriously study Israel and the United States, to undo having "literally made [the Arab world] more passive, more unable to respond to what America and Israel unilaterally decide to do" in the region.[84] Likewise, he decried the punishment by various Arab states of the few people in the Arab world—journalists, academics, literary figures, and the like—who dared to follow the call to engage Israel as a reality or who simply recognized the obvious futility in continuing to ignore it; he called the so-called "crime" of "normalization" a "stupid concept" that had been "overused either to divert attention from Arab indifference to the Palestinians or to attack other Arabs or to promote ignorance."[85] Tellingly, the matter of confronting Israel's existence was, for Said, symptomatic of a larger problem: "At issue is the right to free thought and expression and, underlying that, the right to be free of ludicrously enacted restrictions against individual freedom."[86] It was therefore little wonder that in *From Oslo to Iraq* he expressed his deep consternation with how "such rubrics as homosexuality, atheism, extremism, terrorism, and fundamentalism have been overused much of the time without sufficient care or nuance, just so that critics of the ruling groups could be silenced or imprisoned."[87] He then issued the following sober warning, no less important for its call for ordinary citizens in the Arab world to speak truth to power than for the glimpse it offered into the seriousness with which he took universal values and justice:

> As the Arab world spins into further incoherence and shame, it is up to every one of us to speak up against these terrible abuses of power. No one is safe unless every citizen protests what in effect is a reversion to medieval practices of autocracy. If we accuse Israel of what it has done to the Palestinians, we must be willing to apply exactly the same standards of behavior to our own countries. This norm is as true for the American as for the Arab and the Israeli intellectual, who must criticize human rights abuses from a universal point of view, not simply when they occur within the domain of an officially designated enemy. Our own cause is strengthened when we take positions that can be applied to all situations, without conditions such as saying "I disagree with his views, but" as a way of lessening the difficulty and the onus of speaking out. The truth is that, as Arabs, all we have left now is the power of speaking out, and unless we exercise that right, the slide into terminal degeneration cannot ever be stopped. The hour is very late.[88]

Of course, the urgency of this call to speak out was most present in Said's disparagement and condemnation of PLO decision making leading up to and following the conclusion of the DOP. For Said, the Oslo Accords were a "Palestinian capitulation" to Israeli power, a disaster of epic proportions, second only to the Nakba of 1948.[89] After decades of Palestinian dispossession, exile, colonization, and persecution, he could not bear the idea that the best that could be achieved was Israel's halfhearted recognition of the PLO and the establishment of a quasi-autonomous local authority over Palestinian towns and villages in the OPT. This "solution" effectively relieved Israel of the burden of such oversight (which, as the occupying power, it is legally obligated to ensure while leaving the occupation intact). In his analysis, the only thing the Palestinians received at Oslo was "a series of municipal responsibilities in Bantustans controlled from the outside by Israel," whereas Israel had secured "official Palestinian consent to Israeli occupation."[90] As for the core Palestinian rights—political self-determination, an end to the occupation, sovereignty in East Jerusalem, the return of the refugees—these were, and continue to be, unaddressed, left to some future round of negotiations—when, where, and between whom no one really knows.

Although many people early on doubted that these would be the bitter fruits of

Oslo, history proved Said correct. For this great "surrender" of Palestinian rights, Said never forgave Yasir Arafat, his small coterie of Oslo "negotiators," or the rest of the PLO functionaries who returned from exile in Tunis to assist in the endeavor.[91] In his scathing criticism of the pro-Oslo PLO leadership, one is reminded of Frantz Fanon's reflections on the "pitfalls of national consciousness" in his classic work, *The Wretched of the Earth*: "The battle against colonialism does not run straight away along the lines of nationalism. . . . It so happens that the unpreparedness of the educated classes, the lack of practical links between them and the mass of the people, their laziness, and let it be said, their cowardice at the decisive moment of the struggle will give rise to tragic mishaps."[92]

For Said, the "tragic mishap" for the Palestinians was Oslo, and he was unrelenting in calling to account those Palestinian leaders who were responsible for it. In *Peace and its Discontents*, he noted,

> After laboriously constructing the unity of Palestinians everywhere, bringing together the Diaspora and the 800,000 Palestinian citizens of Israel, as well as the residents of the occupied territories, the PLO by a stroke of the pen [i.e., at Oslo] split the three components apart, accepting the Israeli designation of Palestinians as only the encaged residents of the territories. No other liberation movement in the twentieth century got so little—roughly 5 percent of its territory. And no other leaders of a liberation movement accepted what in effect is permanent subordination of their people. . . . Arafat and his Palestinian Authority have become a sort of Vichy government for the Palestinians. Those of us who fought for Palestine before Oslo fought for a cause that we believed would spur the emergence of a just order. Never has this ideal been further from realization today.[93]

As life for the Palestinians of the OPT seriously deteriorated during the Oslo years, Said lamented that the PA had "become a byword for brutality, autocracy and unimaginable corruption," not to mention a collaborative tool of Israel in the consolidation of its hold over the OPT and, ultimately, over Palestinian lives.[94] Increasingly, Said focused his criticism on Arafat's leadership, openly questioning the competence, intentions, and integrity of the man who had previously enjoyed the intellectual's support and loyalty ("I felt that Arafat was genuinely a representative of Palestinian nationalism, far transcending his actual role as a human being," he said).[95] Like Fanon's warning against so-called anticolonial nationalists who "mobilize the people with slogans of independence, and for the rest leave it to future events," Said decried Arafat's continual "abuse," in the absence of a detailed plan, of "old slogans like 'a Palestinian state' and 'Jerusalem our capital'" when Oslo had in fact brought the Palestinians farther from, not nearer to, those goals.[96] So harsh was Said's criticism of Oslo and the PLO that in August 1996, the PA minister of information (and subsequent coauthor of the highly touted Geneva Initiative), Yasir Abed Rabbo, banned Said's books in the OPT on the orders of Arafat.[97] The following passage in *From Oslo to*

Iraq, written during the Second Intifada, is indicative of the view Said had come to hold of Arafat and of the quality of Palestinian leadership around him after Oslo:

> Arafat is finished: why don't we admit that he can neither lead, nor plan, nor do anything that makes any difference except to him and his Oslo cronies who have benefited materially from their people's misery? He is the main obstacle to our people's future. All the polls show that his presence blocks whatever forward movement might be possible . . . A leader must lead the resistance, reflect the realities on the ground, respond to his people's needs, plan, think, and expose himself to the same dangers and difficulties that everyone experiences. The struggle for liberation from Israeli occupation is where every Palestinian worth anything now stands: Oslo cannot be restored or repackaged as Arafat and Company might desire. It's over for them, and the sooner they pack and get out, the better for everyone.[98]

Unlike its predecessor of 1987–92, the Second Intifada was accurately regarded by Said as "an intifada against Oslo and against the people who constructed it," including Arafat and his back-room negotiators. Said was unremitting in his belief that

> these people should now have the decency to stand before their people, admit their mistakes, and ask (if they can get it) for popular support if they have a plan. If there isn't one (as I suspect), they should then have the elementary courtesy at least to say so. Only by doing this can there be anything more than tragedy at the end of the road . . . They must now explain publicly what they thought they were doing [through Oslo] and why they did it. Then they must let us express our views on their actions and their future. And for once they must listen and try to put the general interest before their own, despite the millions of dollars they have either squandered or squirreled away in Paris apartments and valuable real estate and lucrative business deals with Israel. Enough is enough.[99]

Of course, the spirit in which Said presented these and other criticisms of Arafat's rule was very different from that of the disingenuous demands currently en vogue in Western diplomatic circles—demands for "PA reform" or "Hamas recognition of Israel" as a prerequisite for a resumption of the "peace" process with scarcely a word about the centrally important issue of Israel's decades-old military occupation of Palestinian land, which "remains more or less in place."[100] Rather, he sought a complete and total winding up of the PA, along with Oslo, and perhaps more importantly, the collective defeatist mind-set of Palestinian leadership that he believed had led to the problem in the first place. In a ringing tone similar to that of Biko's call for South Africans to embrace Black Consciousness in their struggle against apartheid, Said derided "the sense of capitulation toward Israel and the United States . . . now so prevalent among our political elites," which "derives in the end from an absence of self-confidence," "a spirit of passivity," a mentality of "servility," and, alas, "a total absence of self-knowledge."[101] In calling for a new leadership and daring to hope for a brighter future despite the compounded difficulties created by

Oslo, he reminded his people that it was not enough to demand that Arafat and his PA hangers-on "resign as incompetent but that any future leaders must have a sense of self-dignity as well as a real knowledge of Israel and the United States. What we must have in other words are decolonized minds, not men and women who can neither liberate themselves nor their own people."[102] The most important indication that Palestinians in the OPT may have taken this message to heart was the landslide victory of Hamas in the Palestinian Legislative Council (the legislative branch of the PA) in January 2006. Said, of course, was no Islamist. But few can question that the election results were a complete vindication of his critique of the Palestinian leadership under the ousted nationalist Fatah party, whose personalities were responsible for Oslo and its dreadful aftermath.

SAID AS VISIONARY

Said did not, of course, embark on the criticism of power merely for criticism's sake. The point behind it all was to find a better way of thinking and approach, to constructively move on, and in a manner that would guarantee peace and justice for Palestinians and Israelis alike. In addition to embracing his roles as narrator and critic, Said possessed a unique ability not only to identify, broadly speaking, what needed to be done to achieve peace and justice but perhaps more importantly to articulate it—and to do so long before such ideas became the accepted norm in political, diplomatic, and media circles.

At the base of Said's vision was his unyielding belief in the "unassailable" morality and justness of the Palestinian cause.[103] The problem for the Palestinians, he believed, was that they had for far too long been abandoned by the international community and, in more recent years, severely ill served by their leaders. Throughout his writings, particularly in the last decade of his life, Said made little secret of the influence that the South African liberation struggle had on his worldview, in particular, what he came to believe was "the only alternative" to continued conflict in Palestine/Israel.[104] At the heart of this alternative was the proposition that in order "to counteract Zionist exclusivism," the Palestinians would have to seize the moral high ground just as Nelson Mandela's African National Congress (ANC) had, to "assert our common humanity as Jews and Arabs."[105] Although the Israelis had power without end to deploy against the Palestinians, and although the dispossessed, colonized, and occupied Palestinian people had a legal and moral (though not absolute) right to resist by force if necessary, continued violence was not a realistic or useful option for either party. On this point, Said was unequivocal: "Neither the Palestinians nor the Israelis have a military option against each other. Both peoples must learn to live in peace, and in mutual acknowledgement of each other's history and actuality."[106] And as much as he denounced Israeli violence against his people, Said was equally as adamant about condemning Palestinian violence against Israeli civilians. He often made it a point to indicate that although he considered suicide bombings to be a direct "result of years of abuse, powerlessness, and despair," these acts were "reprehensible" and could never "be part of a program for national revival since what they promote is negation for its own sake."[107] Said was keenly aware that even "a just cause can easily be subverted by evil or inadequate or corrupt means."[108]

It was in recognition of the futility of violence, the failures of Oslo, and the fact that in such a world the task of bringing peace to this particular region could not reasonably be entrusted to any Israeli or American leader, nor to the likes of the old-guard PLO leadership, that Said called for "a different avenue of approach."[109] This required the sort of mass, grassroots, international, and nonviolent mobilization of Palestinians that had, in Said's view, never really been tried before.

> Successful liberation movements were successful precisely because they employed creative ideas, original ideas, imaginative ideas, whereas less successful movements (like ours, alas) had a pronounced tendency to use formulas and an uninspired repetition of past slogans and past patterns of behavior. Take as a primary instance the idea of armed struggle. For decades we have relied in our minds on ideas about guns and killing, ideas that from the 1930s until today have brought us plentiful martyrs but have had little real effect either on Zionism or on our own ideas about what to do next. In our case, the fighting is done by a small brave number of people pitted against hopeless odds: stones against helicopter gunships, Merkava tanks, missiles. Yet a quick look at other movements—say, the Indian nationalist movement, the South African liberation movement, the American civil rights movement—tells us first of all that only a mass movement employing tactics and strategy that maximizes the popular element ever makes any difference on the occupier and/or oppressor. . . . Only a mass movement that has been politicized and imbued with a vision of participating directly in a future of its own making, only such a movement has a historical chance of liberating itself from oppression or military occupation.[110]

Thus, with the South African parallel in mind, Said counseled the Palestinian people to energetically seek out global partnerships with other peoples from whom a nonviolent liberation struggle in Palestine could draw strength, most importantly "the partnership of like-minded Israelis and diaspora Jews who understand that you cannot have occupation and dispossession as well as peace with the Palestinian people."[111] Peace and reconciliation were clearly dependent on the success of such a Jewish-Palestinian partnership, and believing the "moral dimension" to be "our only field of struggle," Said recognized that the initiative would have to come from the militarily and politically weaker Palestinian side, whose case "gains its moral stature by its humane dimensions, its sincere willingness for coexistence, its firm belief in respecting the rights of others."[112] To this end, Said emphasized that Palestinians "must show Israel and its supporters that only a full acknowledgement by them of what was done to us can bring peace and reconciliation," but "also that we must always be very clear in our understanding of Jewish suffering and in making it apparent that what binds us together is a common history of persecution."[113] This common history represented a bridging narrative of sorts, whereby "Jewish tragedy," epitomized by the Nazi holocaust of the Jews, "led directly to the Palestinian catastrophe" in 1948—neither "equal to the other" but each equally worthy of reverence and understanding by the other.[114] In the end, Said asserted that the "only way of rising beyond the endless back-and-forth violence and dehumanization is to admit the universality and integrity of the other's experience and to begin to plan a common life together."[115]

Said first articulated his vision of that common life in 1980, when he first publicly advocated a two-state solution based on U.N. Security Council Resolutions 242 (1967) and 338 (1973) and a division of mandatory Palestine between the Jews and Arabs.[116] At the time, and although discussion of such ideas had taken place within PLO circles as early as 1974, the notion was dismissed by Israel, which had complete control over all of historical Palestine; and by most Palestinians, who continued to insist on the complete liberation of the country and the establishment of a democratic, secular state for all its inhabitants, Arab and Jew. Although Said believed that the Palestinian people were justified in rejecting the original partition of Palestine in U.N. General Assembly Resolution 181 (II) of 29 November 1947, given their status as indigenous inhabitants and their numerical superiority over the Zionist settler community (the Palestinians then constituted two-thirds of the population and owned 96 percent of the land), his pragmatism and desire for peace compelled him to recognize the need for two independent states to coexist in the land: "I accept it because I consider it to be a reality . . . I don't believe in dispossessing people; you'd have to find a mode of sharing."[117]

For his espousal of the two-state solution, Said was "attacked from all sides," including both the Israeli and Palestinian.[118] Nonetheless, the outbreak of the First Intifada in December 1987 and the subsequent adoption by the PNC of the two-state solution at its nineteenth session in Algiers in November 1988 provided him with added impetus to advance his convictions. From that point on, the "nub of the question," as he put it, was "the end of the occupation, since national self-determination, from either the Israeli or the Palestinian point of view, is incompatible with the domination of one people by another, in which one people enjoys all the rights, the other none."[119] If peace were to become reality, Israelis had to be convinced of the imperative of ending the occupation and making way for the establishment of a Palestinian state in the West Bank and the Gaza Strip:

> Palestinians present themselves as interlocutors with the Israelis for peace. We are not
> an inconsiderable people, and our achievements in education, business, science, and
> engineering testify to intelligence, will and foresight. We say to the Israelis and to their
> U.S. friends, live with us, but not on top of us. Your logic, by which you forecast an
> endless siege, is doomed, the way all colonial adventures have been doomed. We know

that Israelis possess a heritage of suffering, and that the Holocaust looms large over their present thought. But we Palestinians cannot be expected merely to submit to military rule and the denial of our human and political rights, particularly since our attachment to Palestine is as significant, as deep and as lasting as theirs. Therefore we must together formulate the modes of coexistence, of mutuality and sharing, those modes that can take us beyond fear and suffering into the future, and an extraordinarily interesting and impressive future at that.[120]

Eventually, the "two-state" vision espoused by Said was accepted by every major party to the Arab-Israeli conflict, including the Israelis and the Americans: it became the basis for negotiations first at Madrid in 1991 and then at Oslo in 1993. Since that time, the diplomatic community has embraced the notion of the "two-state solution" as the only acceptable basis for the "final and comprehensive settlement of the Israel-Palestinian conflict."[121]

The onset of the Oslo process and its attendant effects on the landscape of Palestinian space in the OPT compelled Said to rethink his views on the two-state solution. While the notion of shared sovereignty in two separate states presupposed a mutual respect for the territorial integrity of the neighboring state, Said pointed to Israel's massive geographic and demographic transformation of the OPT in the years following the conclusion of the DOP as effectively having spoiled any possibility of an independent, contiguous, and viable Palestinian state in the West Bank and the Gaza Strip. A series of developments between 1993 and 2006 led him to this conclusion: a massive influx of Israeli settlers into the OPT, causing their number to more than double, from some 200,000 to well over 400,000; the rapid construction of hundreds of kilometers of additional settler-only bypass roads connecting the settlements with Israel; the presence of some 200 Israeli military bases/posts throughout the OPT; the erection of the wall; the destruction of the Palestinian village-road network; and the imposition of a complex regime of closures, curfews, and a South-African style "permit system" that severely limited Palestinian freedom of movement. As a result, the Palestinian inhabitants of the West Bank were confined in "227 non-contiguous islands," and the Palestinians of the Gaza Strip were left to fester in one of the most densely populated and impoverished places on earth.[122] According to the U.N. special rapporteur on human rights in the OPT, John Dugard, this situation led to the development of "an apartheid regime worse than the one that existed in South Africa."[123]

As Said saw these events unfold, he abandoned the two-state solution in favor of an idea that he considered "the only long-term solution" to the Palestinian-Israeli conflict: one state for Jews and Arabs—a binational state—that would inhabit all of the former Mandate of Palestine.[124] In Power, Politics, and Culture, he explained that any attempt to solve the problem by carving a Palestinian state out of the remains of the OPT is doomed to fail "because the Israelis have now sunk their tentacles on the land of [the] Palestinians":

By their own aggressive zeal, the settler movement and the Israeli government and army have in fact involved themselves so deeply in Palestinian life that in my opinion there is no separation between them, or only the separation of apartheid. But demographically there are two populations living together. In about ten years there will be demographic parity [between Palestinians and Israelis living within Mandate Palestine]. Therefore the only conclusion to be drawn from this is to devise a means where the two peoples can live together in one nation as equals—not as master and slave, which is the current situation.[125]

For Said, the equation was simple: because Israeli colonization of the OPT had been so effective in integrating the West Bank and Gaza Strip into Israel, the establishment of an independent Palestinian state had effectively been rendered a nonoption (at best it would be "a tiny rump; it's not worth it," Said wrote).[126] If one factored in the Palestinians' economic dependence on Israel and the projected demographic parity between Jews and Arabs in Mandate Palestine, one could hardly dismiss the inevitability of the one-state model. Of course, Said was not naive. He well understood the considerable obstacles in the way of establishing such a state, not least of which, in his view, was the strength of respective Israeli and Palestinian nationalisms, the former with its emphasis on the need to protect the "Jewish character" of the state and the latter with its long-felt desire to exercise sovereignty freely in its own land. Nevertheless, Said's "sense of realism" led him to conclude in the last decade of his life that "the only way this problem is going to be settled, as in South Africa, is to face the reality squarely on the basis of coexistence and equality," one person–one vote, and equality for all.[127] "I know it seems like a long shot," he said, "but I think within the working out of the history and the unfolding of time, it becomes a more and more attractive idea."[128]

Unlike his vision and advocacy of the two-state solution, Said's one-state vision of peace did not see widespread acceptance among the international community during his lifetime. Nevertheless, he was correct that it would become "more and more attractive" over time. During the past decade, the idea has taken root among a significant number of thoughtful people on both sides of the conflict, and it has even gained favorable attention among some of the Palestinian political elite.[129] Although the future of the one-state solution remains unclear, an objective consideration of each of the variables that compelled Said to adopt it reveals the potential power and attractiveness of the idea, not to mention the extent of Said's foresight in identifying it and articulating it for us as resolutely as he did.

CONCLUSION

The late Palestinian jurist Henry Cattan wrote, "Just as a disease cannot be treated without knowledge of its cause, so also the Palestine Question cannot be resolved unless there exists a full and proper knowledge of its dimensions."[130] More than any other individual of his generation, Edward Said contributed to the advancement of knowledge about every dimension of the Palestine problem, leaving an indelible mark on those who genuinely desire that peace and justice be done in the Middle East. At the heart of his approach was his deeply held belief in the duty of the intellectual to be a contrarian force in a world that has too often seen the unscrupulous exercise of power. His call to speak truth to power was not merely directed at ivory-tower elites; it was also a rallying cry, an attempt to awake in one and all a culture of dissent. Said believed that such a culture was critical to the healthy development of humanistic, democratic, universal values upon which the freedom and cooperation of all peoples rest.

To this end, Said's tripartite role as narrator, critic, and visionary in addressing the Palestinian freedom struggle was interwoven with the intellectual imperative to speak truth to power. The quintessential exile, Said always sought to stand apart from the interests of authority, which, in turn, provided him with the intellectual and public space in which to call authority to account. Although none of this activity earned him widespread popularity among the elite, Said was unmoved by such considerations and pressed on to narrate Palestinian presence and criticize Zionist, American, and Palestinian policy makers, all the while daring to envision a better future for them all. His main goal throughout was to seek justice and freedom for the Palestinian people, based on principles of universalism, humanism, law, and morality, and to do so in a manner respectful of the same interests and rights of their main protagonists, the Jewish people of Israel. His was a world in which everyone mattered equally *and had to be treated as such* if a durable and tangible peace was to be forged. Whether or not Said's considerable work in this field will yield the fruits it merits is unknown. What is known, however, is the scope and seriousness of the challenge he put to us all: that women and men of conscience must continue to speak truth to power so that power's victims might have their stories told, their histories acknowledged, and their rights to liberty, justice, and freedom realized.

NOTES

The opinions I express here are exclusively mine and do not represent the opinions or views of the United Nations organization or of the United Nations Relief and Works Agency (UNRWA). I would like to thank Michael Lynk and others for their comments on an earlier draft of this essay.

1. The lectures were subsequently published by Random House under the same title. See E. W. Said, *Representations of the Intellectual: The 1993 Reith Lectures* (New York: Vintage Books, 1994).

2. Ibid., 85.

3. Ibid., 92.

4. Ibid., 93.

5. Ibid., 97.

6. E. W. Said, *The Question of Palestine*, 2nd ed. (New York: Vintage Books, 1992), 37; Said, *Representations of the Intellectual*, 101.

7. Said, *Representations of the Intellectual*, 101.

8. Steve Biko, *I Write What I Like: A Selection of His Writings*, 2nd ed. (London: Bowerdean Publishing, 1996), 52.

9. Ibid., 52–53 (emphasis added).

10. It is telling that Biko chose to name the column in which most of his writings appeared "I Write What I Like," the title eventually given to the book containing his most pivotal work. Although Biko was forced to write the column under a pen name because of the strict South African laws prohibiting free speech, his refusal to allow the authorities to censor his thoughts personifies the type of fortitude that Said demanded of intellectuals as critics of power.

11. J. Strawson, "Reflections on Edward Said and the Legal Narratives of Palestine: Israeli Settlements and Palestinian Self-Determination," *Penn State International Law Review* 20, no. 2 (Winter 2002): 374.

12. Covenant of the League of Nations, article 22, as quoted in H. Cattan, *The Palestine Question* (London: Croom Helm, 1988), 369.

13. Ibid.

14. Ibid.

15. In 1918, there were approximately 700,000 Palestinians, and only 56,000 of them claimed Jewish religious identification. See T. Mallison and S. Mallison, *The Palestine Problem in International Law and World Order* (London: Longman, 1986), 25.

16. Said, *The Question of Palestine*, 15.

17. Balfour Declaration, as quoted in Mallison and Mallison, *The Palestine Problem*, 427 (emphasis added).

18. *Nemo dat quod non habet*: a principle of English common law that "one cannot give what one does not possess."

19. On the population statistics, see Mallison and Mallison, *The Palestine Problem*, 25. Quote from Said, *The Question of Palestine*, 17.

20. E. W. Said, *Orientalism* (New York: Vintage Books, 1979), 21, 272.

21. As quoted in Said, *The Question of Palestine*, 16–17.

22. Ibid., 16.

23. Ibid., 18.

24. Strawson, "Reflections on Said," 363–64.

25. U.N. General Assembly Resolution 181 (II), 29 November 1947; Cattan, *The Palestine Question*, 36.

26. U.N. Security Council Resolution 242, 22 November 1967.

27. E. W. Said, *The Politics of Dispossession: The Struggle for Palestinian Self-Determination, 1969–1994* (New York: Pantheon Books, 1994), 141.

28. Said, *The Question of Palestine*, 39.

29. N. Masalha, *The Politics of Denial: Israel and the Palestinian Refugee Problem* (London: Pluto Press, 2003), 11. The quote is from a speech that former Israeli prime minister Yitzhak Shamir delivered before the Madrid Peace Conference in October 1991. Masalha (8) notes that it draws on the classic Zionist concepts of "land redemption" (*geolat adama* in Hebrew) and "land conquest" (*kibbush adama*).

30. Said, *The Question of Palestine*, 19.

31. Masalha, *The Politics of Denial*, 12. See also N. Masalha, *A Land without a People: Israel, Transfer and the Palestinians, 1949–1996* (London: Faber and Faber, 1997).

32. Masalha, *The Politics of Denial*, 11.

33. Ibid., 12.

34. E. W. Said, *Culture and Resistance: Conversations with Edward W. Said*, interviews by David Barsamian (Cambridge, MA: South End Press, 2003), 20–21.

35. *Sunday Times*, 15 June 1969, as quoted in Cattan, *The Palestine Question*, 219–20.

36. Said, *The Politics of Dispossession*, xvi.

37. Ibid.

38. Said, *Orientalism*, 27.

39. Ibid.

40. Said, *The Politics of Dispossession*, 138; A. Shavit, "Survival of the Fittest" (interview with Benny Morris), *Ha'aretz Magazine*, 9 January 2004, 16–17. See also I. Pappe, "Ingathering," *London Review of Books*, 28 April 2006.

41. E. W. Said and C. Hitchens, eds., *Blaming the Victims: Spurious Scholarship and the Palestinian Question* (London: Verso, 1988), 154.

42. Said, *The Politics of Dispossession*, 257.

43. Ibid.

44. Said, *The Question of Palestine*, 69.

45. Ibid.

46. Ibid., 125.

47. Theodor Herzl, *The Jewish State* (New York: Dover Publications, 1988), 83.

48. Said, *The Question of Palestine*, 56–57.

49. For instance, in *The Question of Palestine*, Said notes, "For whatever it may have done for Jews, Zionism essentially saw Palestine as the European imperialist did, as an empty territory paradoxically 'filled' with ignoble or perhaps even dispensable natives; it allied itself, as Chaim Weizmann quite clearly said after World War I, with imperial powers in carrying out its plans for establishing a new Jewish state in Palestine, and it did not think except in negative terms of 'the natives,' who were passively supposed to accept the plans made for their land; . . . in formulating the concept of a Jewish nation 'reclaiming' its own territory, Zionism not only accepted the generic racial concepts of European culture, it also banked on the fact that Palestine was actually peopled not by an advanced but by a backward people, over which it *ought* to be dominant" (81–82).

50. See Walid Khalidi, ed., *From Haven to Conquest* (Beirut: Institute for Palestine Studies, 1971); Ibrahim Abu-Lughod, ed., *The Transformation of Palestine: Essays on the Origin and Development of the Arab-Israeli Conflict* (Evanston, IL: Northwestern University Press, 1971).

51. Said, *The Question of Palestine*, 57.

52. A perfect example of this aspect of Said's approach to Zionism is his critique of Samuel Huntington's "Clash of Civilizations" thesis, in which, Said wrote, the "personification of enormous entities called 'the West' and 'Islam' is recklessly affirmed as if hugely complicated matters like identity and culture existed in a cartoonlike world where Popeye and Bluto bash each other mercilessly, with one always more virtuous pugilist getting the upper hand over his adversary." Said derided Huntington for having little "time to spare for the internal dynamics and plurality of every civilization, or for the fact that the major contest in most modern cultures concerns the definition or interpretation of each culture, or for the unattractive possibility that a great deal of demagogy and downright ignorance is involved in presuming to speak for a whole religion or civilization. No, the West is the West, and Islam Islam"; E. W. Said, *From Oslo to Iraq and the Road Map* (New York: Pantheon Books, 2004), 119–20.

53. Shavit, "Survival of the Fittest," 44.

54. B. Morris, *The Birth of the Palestinian Refugee Problem, 1947–1949* (Cambridge: Cambridge University Press, 1987).

55. Ibid., Shavit, "Survival of the Fittest," 44.

56. Shavit, "Survival of the Fittest," 44.

57. Said, *The Question of Palestine*, 77.

58. Ibid.

59. This mind-set, Said noted in *From Oslo to Iraq*, allows one to make sense of the Israeli insistence

on continuing to colonize the very territory from which it claimed it intended to withdraw during the Oslo process. If, on the one hand, peace requires handing the OPT over to the Palestinian people, then why the persistence in constructing settlements, building bypass roads, demolishing homes, and confiscating land? What explains, to use Said's words, this "total irreconcilability with what the Jewish state wants—peace and security, even though everything it does assures neither one nor the other" (128)? He suggested that the answer lay in the continuing and unyielding influence of the idea of Zionism on Israel's leaders and institutions, who apparently have been unable to reconcile themselves with the folly of it all.

60. Ibid., 21–23.

61. Said, *Culture and Resistance*, 105–6.

62. Ibid., 207.

63. E. W. Said, *Peace and Its Discontents: Essays on Palestine in the Middle East Peace Process* (New York: Vintage Books, 1996), 7, 16, and 152.

64. G. Watson, *The Oslo Accords: International Law and the Israeli-Palestinian Peace Agreements* (Oxford: Oxford University Press, 2000), 315–16. See generally E. W. Said, "Palestinians Under Siege," in *The New Intifada: Resisting Israel's Apartheid*, ed. R. Carey, 27–44 (London: Verso, 2001); see also I. Brownlie and G. S. Goodwin-Gill, "Opinion: The Protection Afforded by International Humanitarian Law to the Indigenous Population of the West Bank and the Gaza Strip and to Foreign Citizens Therein, with Particular Reference to the Application of the 1949 Geneva Convention Relative to the Protection of Civilian Persons in Time of War," Oxford Public Interest Lawyers, September 2003, www.unhcr.org/refworld/docid/3ae6b36d2.html (accessed 30 July 2009).

65. Under the Israeli-Palestinian Interim Agreement on the West Bank and Gaza Strip (Taba, 28 September 1995) 36 ILM. 551 (1997) [hereafter Interim Agreement], the PA was to exercise internal security and civil authority in Area A and Israel was to exercise external security authority. In Area B, the PA would exercise civil and limited security authority, and Israel would exercise overarching internal security authority. Finally, Area C would be under complete Israeli authority.

66. See PLO Negotiations Affairs Department, Map of Israeli and Palestinian Security Controlled Areas, www.nad-plo.org/images/maps/pdf/palisr.pdf (accessed 11 September 2004).

67. Portions of the Gaza Strip constitute a limited exception to this 2002 Israeli encroachment. In the area, a coterie of PA, Hamas, Islamic Jihad, and other smaller armed Palestinian groups vied for control until Hamas took over in June 2007. In August and September 2005, the state of Israel withdrew its settlers and permanent military installations and forces from the Gaza Strip in a unilateral act it termed "disengagement." Israel has since asserted that its occupation of the Gaza Strip has come to an end, including its corresponding international legal obligations toward the Palestinian civilian population. The Israeli position notwithstanding, under the law governing foreign military occupation, the Gaza Strip remains occupied territory and Israel the occupying power. Under international law, occupation of a territory is determined by the "effective control test," which is spelled out in article 42 of the 1907 Hague Regulations Respecting the Laws and Customs of War on Land (18 October 1907, 36 Stat. 2277, 1 Bevans 631; entered into force 26 January 1910). Article 42 provides that "territory is considered occupied when it is actually placed under the authority of the hostile army." In applying this test, the following guidelines apply: (a) the number and distribution of occupying forces in the territory is immaterial to the question of continued effective control (thus, territory can be controlled through all or a combination of air and sea power and deployment of limited ground forces on the perimeter); (b) the existence of local/indigenous authorities administering portions of the territory does not preclude the continued effective control of an occupying power over the whole of the territory (for example, through administrative control over the population); and (c) so long as an occupying power retains the ability to exercise effective authority over territory from which it has withdrawn, that territory remains occupied. Despite the removal of Israeli settlers and military installations from the Gaza Strip, the state of Israel has re-

tained effective control over the Gaza Strip's borders, airspace, and territorial waters. Moreover, Israel continues to maintain ultimate administrative control over Gaza's population registry, tax system, and fiscal policy. Finally, Israel retains, and has exercised to devastating effect since the disengagement, the "right" to reenter Gaza at will, which is not in accordance with accepted principles governing the use of force under the Charter of the United Nations (59 Stat. 1031, TS 993, 3 Bevans 1153; entered into force 24 October 1945). See "Legal Aspects of Israel's Disengagement Plan under International Humanitarian Law," Policy Brief, Harvard Program on Humanitarian Policy and Conflict Research, September 2004; www.reliefweb.int/library/documents/2005/hpcr-opt-26jul.pdf (accessed 27 July 2009); *Report of the Special Rapporteur of the Commission on Human Rights, John Dugard, on the Situation of Human Rights in the Palestinian Territories Occupied since 1967*, U.N. Doc. E/CN.4/2006/29 (17 January 2006); and *Disengaged Occupiers: The Legal Status of Gaza* (Gisha Legal Center for Freedom of Movement, January 2007).

68. Quote from Interim Agreement, article 31(7).

69. Said, *From Oslo to Iraq*, 128. On the illegality of the wall in the West Bank, see "Legal Consequences of the Construction of a Wall in the Occupied Palestinian Territory," Advisory Opinion (ICJ, 9 July 2004), 43 ILM 1009.

70. The figures for deaths of Palestinians and Israelis come from B'Tselem, Israeli Center for Human Rights in the Occupied Territories, current to 26 December 2008; B'Tselem, Statistics, www.btselem.org/English/Statistics/Casualties.asp (accessed 5 January 2008). The figures for injuries of Palestinians are from the Palestine Red Crescent Society, current to 30 June 2007; Palestine Red Crescent Society, Total Daily Number of Deaths and Injuries, www.palestinercs.org/modules/cjaycontent/index.php?id = 15 (accessed 5 January 2008). The figures for injuries of Israelis come from the Magen David Adom as reported by the Israeli Foreign Ministry, current to 1 May 2006; see Israel Ministry of Foreign Affairs, Victims of Palestinian Violence and Terrorism since September 2000,www.mfa.gov.il/MFA/Terrorism-+Obstacle+to+Peace/Palestinian+terror+since+2000/Victims+of+Palestinian+Violence+and+Terrorism+sinc.htm (accessed 5 January 2008).

71. World Bank, *West Bank and Gaza Update*, August 2004, 3.

72. See note 67.

73. Said, *Peace and Its Discontents*, 89.

74. Ibid., 88.

75. Said, *From Oslo to Iraq*, 128.

76. Ibid., 256. Said, *Peace and Its Discontents*, 7–88.

77. Ibid. See also J. J. Mearsheimer and S. M. Walt, *The Israel Lobby and U.S. Foreign Policy* (New York: Farrar, Straus and Giroux, 2007).

78. On the myth of Barak's "generous offers," see T. Reinhart, *Israel/Palestine: How to End the War of 1948* (New York: Seven Stories Press, 2002), 21–60. On Clinton's proposals, see ibid., 219.

79. Said, *From Oslo to Iraq*, 38.

80. Ibid., 280.

81. Ibid., 282.

82. Said, *The Question of Palestine*, 87–88.

83. Said, *From Oslo to Iraq*, 82.

84. Said, *Peace and Its Discontents*, 89–90. In one of his many exhortations about the need for Arab study of Israel and the United States, Said wrote, "I find it puzzling that given American and Israeli hegemony in the region there is still not a single university department in any Arab country, including the Occupied Palestinian Territories, in which American and Israeli societies are studied and taught" (89).

85. Said, *From Oslo to Iraq*, 82.

86. Ibid., 82–83.

87. Ibid., 83.

88. Ibid., 83–84.

89. Said, *Peace and Its Discontents*, 7. *Nakba* is Arabic for "catastrophe." Palestinians use the term to describe the fall of Palestine in 1948 and the ethnic cleansing of the Palestinian nation from its historical homeland.

90. E. W. Said, *The End of the Peace Process: Oslo and After* (New York: Pantheon Books, 2000), 14.

91. Ibid.

92. F. Fanon, *The Wretched of the Earth*, trans. Constance Farrington (New York: Grove Press, 1963), 148.

93. Said, *Peace and Its Discontents*, 156, 159–60.

94. Said, *From Oslo to Iraq*, 184.

95. *Power, Politics, and Culture: Interviews with Edward W. Said*, ed. G. Viswanathan (New York: Pantheon Books, 2001), 397.

96. Fanon, *The Wretched of the Earth*, 150; Said, *From Oslo to Iraq*, 28.

97. Said, *The End of the Peace Process*, 106–7.

98. Said, *From Oslo to Iraq*, 96–97.

99. Ibid., 31.

100. Ibid., 279–80.

101. Said, *Peace and Its Discontents*, 98.

102. Ibid., 99.

103. Said, *The End of the Peace Process*, 197.

104. Said, *From Oslo to Iraq*, 48–51.

105. Ibid., 50.

106. Said, *The Politics of Dispossession*, 157.

107. Said, *From Oslo to Iraq*, 194; Said, *The End of the Peace Process*, 194.

108. Said, *From Oslo to Iraq*, 187.

109. Ibid.

110. Ibid., 29–30.

111. Ibid., 41.

112. Said, *The End of the Peace Process*, 197.

113. Ibid., 197–98.

114. Ibid., 207.

115. Ibid., 208.

116. T. Judt, foreword to Said, *From Oslo to Iraq*, xv.

117. Cattan, *The Palestine Question*, 39; Said, *Power, Politics, and Culture*, 289.

118. Judt, foreword, *From Oslo to Iraq*, xv.

119. Said, *The Politics of Dispossession*, 143.

120. Ibid.

121. "A Performance-Based Road Map to a Permanent Two-State Solution to the Israeli-Palestinian Conflict," www.reliefweb.int/w/rwb/nsf/vID/4F7C106BC695F26185256D180075EBBF?OpenDocu ment (accessed 21 September 2004).

122. M. Bishara, *Palestine/Israel: Peace or Apartheid* (London: Zed Books, 2002), 136, 139.

123. A. Benn, "U.N. Agent: Apartheid in Territories Worse than in S. Africa," *Ha'aretz*, 24 August 2004.

124. Said, *Culture and Resistance*, 63.

125. Said, *Power, Politics, and Culture*, 434.

126. Ibid.

127. Ibid., 435.

128. Ibid.

129. See, for instance, V. Tilley, *The One State Solution: A Breakthrough for Peace in the Israeli-Palestinian Deadlock* (Ann Arbor: University of Michigan Press, 2005); A. Abu Nimah, *One Country: A Bold Proposal to End the Israeli-Palestinian Impasse* (New York: Metropolitan Books, 2006); L. Abu-Odeh, "The Case for Binationalism," *Boston Review*, December 2001–January 2002, http://bostonreview.net/BR26.6/abu-odeh.html (accessed 27 July 2009); A. Shavit, "Cry the Beloved Two-State Solution," *Ha'aretz*, 15 September 2003. On the reception by the Palestinian political elite, see G. Sussman, "The Challenge to the Two-State Solution," *Middle East Report*, www.merip.org/mer/mer231/sussman.html#_ftn22 (accessed 27 July 2009).

130. Cattan, *The Palestine Question*, viii.

15

Edward Said and the Palestine Question

Avi Shlaim

Edward Said was an extraordinarily versatile and prolific scholar whose work ranged across academic disciplines. Although his principal field was comparative literature, he was also a student of culture and society. His 1978 book, *Orientalism*, exposed the ideological biases behind Western perceptions of "the Orient" and helped create a distinctive subfield that came to be called postcolonial studies. In addition to these literary pursuits, Said was a pianist of concert-playing standard and a leading music critic. Last but not least, he was a politically engaged intellectual and the most eloquent spokesman for the dispossessed Palestinian people.

Edward Said's attachment to the Palestinian cause had deep emotional roots. He was born in Jerusalem in late 1935 to a wealthy Christian Palestinian family and spent his childhood in an area of the city that is today an opulent Jewish district. In December 1947, after the United Nations vote for the partition of Palestine, the family moved to Cairo, where Said's father already had a branch of his business. The immediate family was thus spared the worst ravages of the catastrophe, which turned more than 700,000 Palestinians into refugees. But the cataclysmic quality of this collective experience, of the catastrophe, or *Nakba* in Arabic, seared itself in the boy's mind.

Although Said was only twelve years old at the time and had no more than a semiconscious awareness of the event, he later recalled some memories with special lucidity. One was that many of the members of his extended family, on both sides, "were suddenly made homeless, some penniless, disoriented, and scarred forever." He saw some of them again after the fall of Palestine, "but all were greatly reduced in circumstances, their faces stark with worry, ill-health, despair." Yet they bore their suffering not so much as a political but a natural tragedy. This circumstance etched itself in Said's memory with lasting results, mostly because he saw faces that had once been content and at ease become worn with the cares of exile and homelessness. "Many families and individuals had their lives broken, their spirits drained, their composure destroyed forever in the context of seemingly unending, serial dislocation."[1] For Said, this disruption had the greatest poignancy.

The second thing that Said recalled was the one person in his family who somehow managed to pull herself together in the aftermath of the Nakba. She was his paternal aunt Nabiha, who devoted her life to working with Palestinian refugees in Cairo. In the memoir of his childhood, *Out of Place*, Said gives a vivid account of this formidable relative who never discussed the political aspects of the dispute in his presence. A middle-aged widow with some financial means, Nabiha saw it as her lifelong task to help the refugees—by battling with the indifferent Egyptian bureaucracy, getting their children into schools, cajoling doctors into giving them treatment, finding jobs for the men, providing constant sympathy and support for the women. For Nabiha, being Palestinian imposed a duty to assist the unfortunate refugees, many of whom ended up penniless, jobless, destitute, and disoriented in the neighboring Arab countries. From her, Said learned that whereas everyone was willing to pay lip service to the cause, only a few people were prepared to do something practical about it. She remained an exemplary figure, a person against whom he measured his own efforts and always found them wanting.[2]

Although he was born in Palestine, Edward Said spent most of his life in the United States, progressing steadily through Princeton and Harvard universities to become chair of the English and Comparative Literature Department at Columbia. Until his early thirties, he was too focused on his academic career and on his passion for music to take much interest in the politics of his homeland. It was the trauma of the Arab defeat in June 1967 that, by his own account, shook him out of his earlier complacency and reconnected him to his people. Despite the shattering consequences of the defeat, which set in motion a new wave of refugees, Said felt invigorated by the Palestinian national movement, whose influence began to spread throughout the Arab world in the aftermath of the June War: "We were the first Arabs who at the grass-root level—and not because a colonel or a king commanded us—started a movement to repossess a land and a history that had been wrested from us."[3]

Said's direct involvement in the tangled history of the Palestinian national movement is not easy to summarize. He first met Yasir Arafat when the chairman of the Palestine Liberation Organization (PLO) came to the United Nations in 1974. He translated Arafat's speech from Arabic into English, and he became acquainted with the various officials of the PLO at the time, notably Shafiq al-Hout and the famous poet Mahmoud Darwish. During the 1980s, Said became publicly identified with Arafat, especially in Europe and the United States, where he began to be called upon regularly by the mainstream media. Said faced a difficult choice. He could defend the PLO and Arafat as the main instruments of the Palestinian struggle against the overwhelmingly hostile media, which treated the struggle as nothing more than terrorism and anti-Semitism. Or he could join in the general racist chorus in the United States of attacks on the Palestinians, Islam, the Arabs, and Arab nationalism in general. Said chose the former, and as a result, he was fiercely attacked by right-wing American Jews, one of whom gave him the soubriquet "the Professor of Terror."[4]

Gradually, Said started to play a more active role as a spokesman for the Palestinians. In 1974, he became a member of the Palestinian National Council (PNC), the nearest thing to a representative assembly of the Palestinians in exile. Elected as an independent intellectual, he steered clear of the endemic factional struggles and used his authority to try to influence the overall direction of the movement. He rejected the policy of the armed struggle and argued for recognition of the state of Israel.[5] In 1979, Said expounded his moderate philosophy in print in *The Question of Palestine,* in which he sought to counter the massive accumulation of lies, distortions, and willful ignorance that surrounded the Palestinian struggle at the time. Yet Said was savagely attacked by both the mainstream Fatah and the more radical Popular Front for the Liberation of Palestine for urging the recognition of Israel.[6]

Said was well ahead of his colleagues in conceding that the Jews had some historic claim to Palestine. However, he did not see this claim as exclusive to Israel, and it most certainly did not entail the right to dispossess the Palestinians. Nevertheless, Said's position differed significantly from that of the hard-liners, who insisted on an exclusive Palestinian right to the whole of historic Palestine. Said's anticolonial critique of Israel took into account the persecution of the Jews in Europe and the strong impact of the Zionist idea on the European conscience. He understood that the Holocaust meant that Israel could not be judged by exactly the same standards as other nations. But he could not see why the Palestinians should be deprived of their natural rights because of crimes against the Jews that they had not perpetrated.[7] Thus, Said's compassion for Jewish suffering was accompanied by the demand that Israel recognize its own culpability for the plight of the Palestinians. In a public debate with Salman Rushdie in the late 1980s, in a phrase that was to become famous, Said described the Palestinians as "the victims of victims."[8]

In *The Question of Palestine,* Said returned to this fundamental injustice. The Palestinians, he noted, had not only been associated with opposition to Zionism but were viewed variously as the "heart" of the Middle East problem, terrorists, and intransigents. But ultimately they had had extraordinarily bad luck: in making their strong case for resisting colonial invasion of their homeland, they had to go up against "the most morally complex of all opponents, Jews, with a long history of victimization and terror behind them."[9] The absolute wrong of settler colonialism, he pointed out, was greatly diluted by its use to straighten out the destiny of the Jews at the expense of the Palestinians. Yet despite its trenchant critique of Israeli nationalism, *The Question of Palestine* should be read as an essay in reconciliation.

Although Said's calls for accommodation and peaceful coexistence earned him the displeasure of Arab radicals and gained him few adherents on the Israeli side, he never abandoned the struggle. On the contrary, he articulated his inclusive vision at every conceivable opportunity. In 1983, he was unable to attend the PNC meeting in Algiers, but he sent a long memorandum to the attendees, arguing that they should accept the reality of Israel if they were to be able to resist and limit its dominance over the Palestinian homeland and if they were to be able to put forward a clear goal of their own.[10] The world must see, he wrote, that "the Palestinian idea is an idea of living together, of respect for others, of mutual recognition between Palestinian and Israeli." This sentence encapsulates Edward Said's thinking. It summarizes the most consistent theme in his voluminous writing on the subject, from *The Question of Palestine* to the last article.

One of the most unfortunate aspects of the dispute, in Said's view, was that even the word *peace* acquired a sinister meaning for the Arabs. According to the standard Zionist narrative, Israel fervently desired peace, whereas the Arabs—ferocious, vengeful, and gratuitously bent on violence—did not. The reality was rather more complicated and therefore difficult to convey to the uninformed public: "In fact, what was at issue between Israelis and Palestinians was never peace but the possibility for Palestinians of restitution of property, nationhood, identity—all of them blotted out by the new Jewish state."[11] Moreover, for the Palestinians, peace on Israel's terms meant accepting the military verdict of 1948, the loss of their society and homeland.

Preserving the Palestinian national identity was all-important. Said described his "most specific task" as simply to make the case for a Palestinian presence in a world that tended to deny it. The task was to insist, again and again, that "there was a Palestinian people, and that, like all others, it had a history, a society, and, most important, a right of self-determination."[12] Like his friend Mahmoud Darwish, Said repeatedly reasserted the distinct identity and the presence of his people. The constant refrain in one of Darwish's best-known poems is "Sajjil Ana 'Arabi"—"Take note, I am Arab." Said's writings convey the same insistent message on behalf of the Palestinian people, not as individuals but as a collective entity.

If asserting the Palestinian presence was one key task, mapping out a path to reconciliation between the Palestinians and their opponents was another. Said's ideas about paths to peace, however, were neither fixed nor consistent. His thinking about a settlement evolved constantly as he took into account the changing reality on the ground. One can discern four main phases in Said's thinking and writing on the subject. Initially, he favored a one-state solution, a binational state for Jews and Arabs that would include the whole of historic Palestine. Then, at the PNC meeting in 1988, he advocated a two-state solution, based on the partition of Palestine. In 1993, at the time that the Oslo Accord was signed, he came out decisively against the two-state solution that was implicit in the agreement. Finally, toward the end of his life, he reverted to the one-state solution. His thinking had come full circle.

In *The Question of Palestine,* Said set forth the rationale for a one-state solution with great clarity and conviction. The 1967 war, he observed, placed the question of Palestine in a direct adversarial position vis-à-vis Israeli Zionism. The moderate forces in the Palestinian resistance movement formulated an idea and a vision that broke away sharply with all past ideas in its camp: the notion of a single secular democratic state for Arabs and Jews covering the whole of Palestine. Although this idea was derided in some quarters as a propaganda ploy, Said considered it tremendously important for the following reason:

> It accepted what generations of Arabs and Palestinians had never been able to accept— the presence of a community of Jews in Palestine who had gained their state by conquest—but it went further than mere acceptance of Jews. The Palestinian idea posited what is still, to my mind, the only possible and acceptable destiny for the multicommunal Middle East, the notion of a state based on secular human rights, not on religious minority exclusivity nor ... on an idealized geopolitical unity.... The ghetto state, the national security state, the minority government, were to be transcended by a secular democratic polity, in which communities would be accommodated to one another for the greater good of the whole.[13]

Two major events in the 1980s led Said to reexamine his position and to move from a one-state to a two-state solution. First, following the Israeli invasion of Lebanon in 1982, the PLO was forced to move its headquarters from Beirut to Tunis. The organization's stature was so diminished and it became so enfeebled and reclusive that it was incapable of providing effective political leadership. Then, in December 1987, the First Intifada erupted in Gaza and rapidly spread to the West Bank. It was a spontaneous, full-scale civilian uprising against Israeli rule that took the PLO leaders in Tunis by complete surprise. The Intifada refocused world opinion on the plight of the Palestinians. It gave them the status of a people dispossessed and under brutal military occupation. A group of Palestinian moderates began to argue for a bold initiative to translate the success of the Intifada into a more lasting political achievement. Edward Said was one of them.

In the months leading to the crucial PNC meeting in Algiers in November 1988, Said discussed with his colleagues the wisdom of abandoning the rhetoric of the liberation of Palestine by armed struggle and offering a historic compromise based on the partition of the country. Even after the PLO's expulsion from Lebanon and the loss of its last front against Israel, it continued to pretend that the goal was the liberation of Palestine. To the majority of Jews and Americans, the liberation of Palestine was synonymous with the extermination of the state of Israel. Said saw no point in maintaining a formula that was neither possible nor really true to the goal. He believed that this was the most significant moment in Palestinian life since 1948 and that the issue had to be faced head-on.[14]

The PNC drafted a Palestinian declaration of independence, and Yasir Arafat asked Said to translate it from Arabic into English.[15] On 15 November 1988, a majority vote of the PNC carried the motion: divide historic Palestine into two states, one Israeli and one Palestinian. The PNC formally recognized Israel's right to exist, it accepted all relevant U.N. resolutions going back to November 1947, and it opted unambiguously for a two-state solution to the dispute between the two nations. The vote essentially transformed the Palestinian national movement from a liberation movement to an independence movement. To claim, as Christopher Hitchens has done, that Edward Said was the intellectual and moral architect of this mutual-recognition policy is an exaggeration.[16] But Said certainly contributed to this revolution in Palestinian political thinking. He was bitterly disappointed, however, that this move to moderation elicited no response from Israel and prompted only a short-lived dialogue between the PLO and the United States.

In June 1992, Edward Said visited Israel and Palestine. The trip was his first visit to the area since 1947, and it turned out to be an eye-opener. For the first time, he saw the grim reality of life under Israeli occupation. He was struck by the scope and solidity of the Jewish settlements on the West Bank and by the pervasive presence of Israeli soldiers. These firsthand observations planted doubts in his mind about the viability of an independent Palestinian state alongside Israel. The Israeli presence looked too deeply entrenched to be rolled back. Israeli settlements across the green line gave every appearance of being there to stay, and the two communities seemed too closely intertwined to be separated. As a result of the visit, Said was no longer confident that the two-state solution was a realistic option.[17]

Just as Edward Said was moving away from the two-state solution, the Tunis-based PLO leadership decided to embrace it. Secret negotiations in the Norwegian capital culminated, on 13 September 1993, in the signature of the Declaration of Principles for Palestinian Self-Government, better known as the Oslo Accord. In an article in the *London Review of Books*, Edward Said launched a frontal assault on the Oslo Accord. Some of the criticisms focused on Arafat's autocratic, idiosyncratic, and secretive style of management. Others dissected the substance of the deal. The most basic criticism was that the deal negotiated by Yasir Arafat did not carry the promise, let alone a guarantee, of an independent Palestinian state.

"Let us call the agreement by its real name," thundered Said, "an instrument of Palestinian surrender, a Palestinian Versailles." His description of the signing ceremony mixed contempt and anger in roughly equal measure: "The fashion-show vulgarities of the White House ceremony, the degrading spectacle of Yasir Arafat thanking everyone for the suspension of most of his people's rights, and the fatuous solemnity of Bill Clinton's performance, like a 20th century Roman emperor shepherding two vassal kings through rituals of reconciliation and obeisance: all these only temporarily obscure the truly astonishing proportions of the Palestinian capitulation."[18]

In a series of newspaper articles, Said argued that the Oslo Accord compromised the basic national rights of the Palestinian people as well as the individual rights of the 1948 refugees. He lambasted Arafat for unilaterally canceling the Intifada, failing to coordinate his moves with the Arab states, and introducing appalling disarray within the ranks of the PLO. "The PLO," wrote Said, "has transformed itself from a national liberation movement into a kind of small-town government, with the same handful of people still in command."[19] The clear implication was that Arafat and his corrupt cronies had sacrificed principle to grab power. Furthermore, this agreement was not a deal between two equal parties: on the one hand was Israel, a modern state and a military superpower; on the other hand was the PLO, a leadership in exile with no maps, no technical expertise, no territorial base, and no friends. "All secret deals between a very strong and a very weak partner," wrote Said, "necessarily involve concessions hidden in embarrassment by the latter. . . . The deal before us smacks of the PLO leadership's exhaustion and isolation, and of Israel's shrewdness."[20]

Said's critique of the Oslo Accord may have seemed unduly harsh and pessimistic at the time, but it was fully borne out by subsequent events. Indeed, the critique was almost prophetic. The accuracy of Said's predictions is surprising: he even surprised himself. One explanation for his prescience is that he read the text of the declaration of principles very carefully—and he was a past master in analyzing texts. Reading the text made it patently clear that this accord was not the product of negotiations between equals: Israel had imposed its will on the PLO. The document made no mention of Palestinian self-determination or sovereignty or an end to the expansion of Jewish settlements.[21] Not only were Said's judgments vindicated, but to his chagrin, his worst fears came to pass. The Oslo Accord had inspired high hopes of an independent Palestinian state living in peace and security alongside Israel. Seven years later, however, the agreement was in tatters and the hope had all but evaporated amid the violence and the bloodshed of the Second Intifada.

In the years after the conclusion of the ill-fated Oslo meeting, Edward Said gradually reverted to his initial position—namely, that the only fair and viable solution to the dispute between Arabs and Jews was a secular binational state over the whole of Palestine, from the Jordan River to the Mediterranean Sea. A single state would address the root problems of the conflict, the problems created by the 1948 war, especially the right of return of the Palestinian refugees, whereas the Oslo Accord of 1993 and Oslo II of 1995 offered only partial solutions to the problems created by the 1967 war. Said recognized that emotions on both sides were strongly against a single state, but he considered a binational democratic state to be the only real alternative to the bloody impasse of the Al-Aqsa Intifada.

The outbreak of the Second Intifada in September 2000 signified the final failure of the Oslo Accord to bring about a genuine reconciliation between the two communities. The main flaw in these accords, according to Said, was their total obliviousness to the interests of the Palestinian people, as well as their enhancement of Israel's position by propaganda and relentless political pressure. Said called the Oslo peace process a phony peace because it perpetuated the inequality between the Palestinians and the Israelis. The Israelis were allowed sovereignty, territorial integrity, and self-determination; the Palestinians were not.

In a long series of articles in the Western and Arabic press, subsequently gathered in the book *The End of the Peace Process*, Said returned again and again to two main themes. One theme was the consequences of the Oslo Accord. Here he painted a discouraging picture of the deteriorating situation in the aftermath of Oslo: the increase in Palestinian poverty and unemployment, the restrictions on freedom and the abuses of human rights, and the continuation of the worst aspects of the Israeli occupation, including land appropriation and settlement expansion. A second and related theme was disenchantment with Yasir Arafat and the Palestinian Authority. Said could be blunt in his comments on Israel and the United States, but he reserved his most scathing criticisms for Arafat and his tight band of loyalists, excoriating them for their subservience to Israel, venality, corruption, lack of accountability, and fatal yet characteristic mix of incompetence and authoritarianism. "Yasir Arafat," in Said's bitter conclusion, "neither has the vision nor courage to lead anyone anywhere except into more poverty and despondency."[22]

Disappointment with Oslo and with the Palestinian participants in it led naturally and logically to the fourth and final stage in the evolution of Edward Said's thinking on solutions to the Palestinian-Israeli dispute: advocacy of a binational state. He spent the last few years of his life trying to develop an entirely new strategy of peace, a new approach based on equality, reconciliation, and justice. "I . . . see no other way than to begin now to speak about sharing the land that has thrust us together, and sharing it in a truly democratic way, with equal rights for each citizen," Said wrote in a 10 January 1999 essay in the New York Times titled "The One-State Solution." "There can be no reconciliation unless both peoples, two communities of suffering, resolve that their existence is a secular fact, and that it has to be dealt with as such." This solution, he pointed out in *The End of the Peace Process*, aimed neither to diminish Jewish life nor to force Palestinians to surrender their aspirations and political existence. On the contrary, it meant self-determination for both peoples.[23]

The question for Said was not how to devise a way to separate the two peoples but to see whether they might be able to live together peacefully. Azmi Bishara, the Palestinian Israeli and former member of the Knesset, talked about enlarging the concept of *citizenship* as a way of getting beyond the ethnic and religious criteria that in effect make Israel an undemocratic state for 20 percent of its population. Said built on this idea to develop a vision of a secular, democratic, nonexclusive binational state. The intellectual roots of this idea went back to the interwar period when Jewish intellectuals like Judah Magnes and Martin Buber argued and agitated for a binational state. The logic of Zionism defeated their efforts, but the binational vision had not lost its appeal, at least not for Edward Said. "The essence of that vision," he wrote, "is coexistence and sharing in ways that require an innovative, daring, and theoretical willingness to get beyond the arid stalemate of assertion, exclusivism and rejection. Once the initial acknowledgement of the Other is made, I believe the way forward becomes not only possible but attractive."[24]

Thus, after three decades of reflecting, debating, writing, and meandering around the Palestine question, Edward Said had come back to his original view. Indeed, he emerged as the most passionate and eloquent proponent of the one-state solution on either side of the Palestinian-Israeli divide. In a series of searing essays that refracted the reality of those terrible years, Said elaborated on this theme with extraordinary insight and compassion.[25]

In his final years, as illness ravaged his health and the violence in Israel-Palestine kept escalating, Said decided to channel his energies into music. In 1999, he and Daniel Barenboim, the Israeli pianist and conductor, established the West-Eastern Divan Orchestra. The two friends were united in their belief that art and music transcend political ideology. They also shared a cosmopolitan outlook and a commitment to musical education.[26] Their orchestra is made up of young Israeli and Arab musicians who meet every summer in Seville for intensive rehearsals and a concert tour. Raised in enmity, these talented young men and women set an example by their devotion to their common craft. Together they play with wonderful energy and unanimity in an orchestra that is larger than life. When looking at the orchestra, it is utterly impossible to tell the Israelis from the Arabs or Palestinians. The workshop is a brilliantly successful experiment in breaking down national stereotypes and in artistic collaboration across the battle lines. Amid the doom and gloom surrounding the Arab-Israeli conflict in the era of Yasir Arafat and Ariel Sharon, it was a beacon of hope.

Said eloquently spoke of the thinking that led to the orchestra in a lecture at London's School of Oriental and African Studies in 2003 to inaugurate the Sir Joseph Hotung Center of Law, Human Rights and Peace Building in the Middle East. "In our work and planning and discussions our main principle is that separation between peoples is not a solution for any of the problems that divide peoples. And certainly ignorance of the other provides no help whatever. Cooperation and coexistence of the kind that music lived as we have lived, performed, shared and loved it together, might be. I for one am full of optimism despite the darkening sky and the seemingly hopeless situation for the time being that encloses us all."

The orchestra was Edward Said's proudest achievement. It stood in marked contrast to the countless conferences that he had attended with Israeli moderates that produced no tangible results and sometimes ended in mutual recrimination. Music, in contrast, was an exercise in harmony. It brought welcome relief from the frustrations of a debate and a dialogue that went over and over the same ground and seemed to lead nowhere. The orchestra embodied Said's conviction that we know best what we make, and it spoke to his inclusive vision of society. It gave concrete expression to his belief that playing music together can change attitudes and shift the boundaries of the mind. But his passionate devotion to the orchestra also stemmed from the lesson that he had learned from his aunt Nabiha in his childhood: that being a Palestinian means, above all, not pontificating but doing something useful, not engaging in futile argument but rendering practical service to the community. The orchestra was the noblest service that Said could render to his beloved Palestine. It was also one of his most striking successes in engaging meaningfully with the Other.

Edward Said described the orchestra as "one of the most important things I have done in my life." He believed that the orchestra, even more than the two dozen books he had written, would be the most significant legacy of his life.[27] It is therefore a fitting epitaph for an intellectual who spent a lifetime grappling with the complexities and contradictions of the Arab-Israeli conflict yet never gave up hope for coexistence and peace. For Said—the private person, as opposed to the public intellectual—helping young men and women from societies at war with one another to rise above the political divide in order to meet and make music together was a deeply rewarding experience. It went beyond politics, beyond polemics, beyond argument, beyond words.

NOTES

1. Edward W. Said, "Afterword: The Consequences of 1948," in *The War for Palestine: Rewriting the History of 1948*, ed. Eugene L. Rogan and Avi Shlaim (Cambridge: Cambridge University Press, 2001), 206.

2. Ibid., 207; also, Edward W. Said, *Out of Place: A Memoir* (London: Granta Books, 1999), 118–21.

3. Edward W. Said, *The Politics of Dispossession: The Struggle for Palestinian Self-Determination, 1969–1994* (London: Chatto and Windus, 1994), xv.

4. "Edward Said," obituary, *Daily Telegraph*, 26 September 2003.

5. Said, *The Politics of Dispossession*, xxiv–xxv.

6. Ibid., xxv.

7. Malise Ruthven, obituary of Edward Said, *Guardian*, 26 September 2003.

8. Christopher Hitchens, "My Friend Edward," *Observer*, 28 September 2003.

9. Edward W. Said, *The Question of Palestine* (New York: Vintage Books, 1979), 119.

10. Said, *The Politics of Dispossession*, xxv.

11. Said, "Afterword," 212.

12. John Higgins, "He Spoke the Truth to Power," *Times Higher Education Supplement*, 10 October 2003.

13. Said, *The Question of Palestine*, 220.

14. Said, *The Politics of Dispossession*, xxv.

15. Ibid., xx, 145–51.

16. Christopher Hitchens, "My Friend Edward."

17. Said, *The Politics of Dispossession*, 175–99; and conversation with Mariam Said, Seville, Spain, 27 July 2004.

18. Edward Said, "The Morning After," *London Review of Books*, 21 October 1993.

19. Edward Said, *Peace and Its Discontents: Gaza-Jericho, 1993–1995* (London: Vintage, 1995), 4.

20. Ibid., 2.

21. Conversation with Mariam Said, Seville, Spain, 27 July 2004.

22. Edward W. Said, *The End of the Peace Process: Oslo and After* (London: Granta Books, 2000), 181.

23. Ibid., 318.

24. Ibid., 319.

25. Edward W. Said, *From Oslo to Iraq and the Roadmap* (London: Bloomsbury, 2004).

26. Daniel Barenboim and Edward W. Said, *Parallels and Paradoxes: Explorations in Music and Society* (London: Bloomsbury, 2002).

27. Jacqueline Rose, "Simply the Most Wondrous, Loyal, Warm-hearted Friend," *Observer*, 5 October 2003.

16

Representation and Liberation

From Orientalism to the Palestinian Crisis

Bill Ashcroft

Edward Said's *Orientalism* changed the way the world thought about the relationship between the West and its "others." Possibly no other work of the twentieth century has had the impact of this text, which has been lauded and attacked for three decades. Whether the revolution in consciousness it triggered has led to the liberation of the "Oriental" is a more contentious question. For instance, if we ask what *Orientalism* might have to do with Palestine, one of the most obvious and tragic examples of othering in contemporary times, we might conclude that analysis has not led, and perhaps cannot lead, to liberation. But Palestine was at the center of the writing of *Orientalism* because it had become, after the Arab-Israeli war of 1967, the pressing focus of Said's identity. This opus and the two works that followed it, *The Question of Palestine* (1980) and *Covering Islam* (1981), emerged directly from Said's observation that the representation of Palestine and Palestinians was in the hands of others. For him, power over representation was the key to liberation, as much as it had been the central strategy of imperial dominance. That Palestine has not yet succeeded in gaining power over its representation in the world, over the way it is seen, does not alter the fact that for Said, this demonstration of the link between knowledge and power was more comprehensive, more far-reaching and more powerful than military action. *Orientalism* is not so much an accurate and comprehensive account of Orientalism as it was practiced in nineteenth-century Europe as it is an account of the pervasive nature and continuing power of representation in the domination of the Middle East. It is, above all, an account of the "worldliness" (Said's term) of representation—of the power of *representers*. In this respect, Said's caveat about representation is worth keeping in mind: "The real issue is whether there can be a true representation of anything, or whether any and all representations, because they *are* representations, are embedded first in the language and then in the culture, institutions and political ambience of the representer. If the latter alternative is the correct one (as I believe it is), then we must be prepared to accept the fact that a representation is *eo ipso* implicated, intertwined, embedded and interwoven with a great many other things besides the 'truth,' which is itself a representation" (1978: 272). This caveat cuts through all quibbles about whether Said is too Foucauldian or not Foucauldian enough, whether he believes a "real" Orient exists or whether the misrepresentations of Orientalism can be countered by a "true" representation. It even cuts through the strong reservations we might have about Said's view of the location of Orientalism in European history.

The key feature of Said's argument is his view of the proactive and overbearing character of contemporary Orientalism. He locates the origins of Orientalism very late—in Napoleon's invasion of Egypt—and by doing so tends to view it as an active policy of domination best represented by colonial occupation. But the development of Orientalism is a lot more complex than this view suggests and, of course, goes back a lot further. European fascination with exotic Oriental cultures goes back at least to the time of the Crusades, but Orientalist accounts such as those in Parker's *Early Modern Tales of the Orient* (1999) indicate that the discourse of Orientalism coincides with the early modern expansion of Europe. The origins of a modern philological and cultural fascination with the Orient arguably stem from a 1786 address by William Jones to the Bengal Asiatic Society, in which he made a statement that was to change the face of European intellectual life. "The Sanskrit language, whatever its antiquity, is of a wonderful structure, more perfect than the Greek, more copious than the Latin, and more exquisitely refined than either, yet bearing to both of them a stronger affinity, both in the roots of verbs, and in the forms of grammar, than could possibly have been produced by accident; so strong, indeed, that no philologer could examine them all three, without believing them to have sprung from some common source, which, perhaps, no longer exists" (*Asiatic Researches* 1788, cited in Poliakov 1974: 190).

Jones's pronouncement initiated a kind of "Indomania" throughout Europe as scholars looked to Sanskrit for an origin to European languages that went even deeper than Latin and Greek. What remained in the aftermath of Indomania were the entrenchment of Orientalism and the vast expansion of philology. For the next century, European ethnologists, philologers, and historians were obsessed with the Orient and the Indo-European group of languages because these seemed to carry the roots of European civilization itself.

In Said's view, Orientalism was a way of defining and "locating" Europe's others. But as a group of related disciplines, Orientalism was, in important ways, about Europe itself and hinged on arguments about national distinctiveness and racial and linguistic origins. Thus the elaborate and detailed examinations of Oriental languages, histories, and cultures were carried out with unquestioning acceptance of

REPRESENTATION AND LIBERATION 293

the supremacy and importance of European civilization. This, of course, supports Said's main point, that although Orientalists were often devotees and passionate observers of Oriental culture, the manner of representing Oriental cultures inhabited "a common field of play defined for them, not by some inherent common subject matter alone, but by some common history, tradition, universe of discourse. Within this field, which no single scholar can create but which each scholar receives and in which he then finds a place for himself, the individual researcher makes his contribution" (1978: 272–73).

Indeed, such was the vigor of this "universe of discourse" that myth, opinion, hearsay, and prejudice generated by influential scholars quickly assumed the status of received truth. For instance, the influential French philologist and historian Ernest Renan could declare confidently, "Every person, however slightly he may be acquainted with the affairs of our time, sees clearly the actual inferiority of Mohammedan countries" (1896: 85). We can be in no doubt about Renan's audience nor the nature of the cultural assumptions it shared with him: "All those who have been in the East, or in Africa are struck by the way in which the mind of the true believer is fatally limited, by the species of iron circle that surrounds his head, rendering it absolutely closed to knowledge". (85).

We can, however, find just as many statements by European scholars that attest to the value and worth of Oriental culture and to the capacity of Orientalism to break down the East-West cultural divide. Max Müller, in his presidential address to the Ninth International Congress of Orientalists, claimed that "one of the greatest achievements of Orientalist scholarship is the proof that the separation of East and West did not exist from the beginning" (1898: vol. 1, 39). Rehearsing the most prominent obsession of Orientalism, the origin of all Indo-European languages in Sanskrit, he observed that the field "breaks down the idea of the impenetrable separation between different societies showing that they often share a common heritage" (1898: vol. 1, 59). Although we might say that this sharing is a form of cultural appropriation, it is decidedly contrary to the process of othering that appears to dominate Orientalist discourse in our post-Saidian imagination.

I offer these examples of the different ways Orientalism can be interpreted, and the different notions of its origins and trajectories, to point out that *Orientalism* itself is a representation. In this sense, the book performs the task it sets for the "Oriental" and the Palestinian in particular—to take back the power of representation from the dominant culture. Clearly, representation is not about "truth" but about power, and a contest of power is embedded in the task of reclaiming self-representation. *Orientalism* was the first of a trilogy of books that marked a burst of activity from Said at the end of the 1970s. The other two, *The Question of Palestine* and *Covering Islam*, demonstrated that Orientalism was not just a phenomenon of nineteenth-century Europe, a historical oddity, but a deeply ingrained habit of representation that continues into the present. Indeed, the essential message of the trilogy is that the function of Orientalist representation not only continues into the realm of popular culture and print capitalism, but it proceeds at a faster pace and at a more devastating scale than the largely academic enterprise of Orientalism itself.

For this reason, the impact of Orientalism is just as critical, if not more so, than it was when Said wrote his trilogy. His article "A Window on the World" in 2003 showed the way in which Orientalist thinking fed directly into the motivation for the Iraq war:

> Without a well-organised sense that the people over there were not like "us" and didn't appreciate "our" values—the very core of traditional orientalist dogma—there would have been no war. The American advisers to the Pentagon and the White House use the same clichés, the same demeaning stereotypes, the same justifications for power and violence (after all, runs the chorus, power is the only language they understand) as the scholars enlisted by the Dutch conquerors of Malaysia and Indonesia, the British armies of India, Mesopotamia, Egypt, West Africa, the French armies of Indochina and North Africa. These people have now been joined in Iraq by a whole army of private contractors and eager entrepreneurs to whom shall be confided everything from the writing of textbooks and the constitution to the refashioning of Iraqi political life and its oil industry. (Said 2003)

Orientalism continues its tenacious hold on the representational strategies that define the relationship between the West and its others. In particular, the trilogy showed how significant Orientalist thinking was for the Palestinian people. Said's own sense of being "othered" by Orientalist thought explains the passion of *Orientalism*. But *Orientalism* also remains significant for more positive reasons. Not only does it continue to expose the West's habit of demonizing its others, but it also initiates a discourse of transformation. *Orientalism* transformed both the representation and the understanding of the representation of the Middle East, and in doing so, it capitalized on a strategy that is fundamental to postcolonial societies. I propose that this process of transformation is fundamental to the engagement of postcolonial societies with imperial power. Postcolonial transformation occurs when these societies take hold of the various cultural technologies of colonial domination and use them for a particularly subtle and constructive form of resistance. The term *postcolonial* does not mean "after colonialism"—for Palestine is certainly still colonized; it means, rather, "after colonization" and invokes that continual engagement with colonial power that characterizes the agency and resistance of colonized people. The key to the success of this resistance, in all postcolonial societies, has not been opposition but the seizing of the power of self-representation (Ashcroft 2001). In this chapter, I focus on the link between Said's view of representation and the strategy of transformation, particularly in the context of the present Palestinian situation: How might a devastated, powerless, and abject Palestinian people obtain power? Given that this will never be attained by war or violence, what message does Said's analysis of representation have for his people?

If any people have been denied the opportunity for self-representation, it is the Palestinian people. But the word *denied* is an interesting one. Who or what has denied Palestinians the power of self-representation? To what extent has their poor leadership denied them this power? To what extent is such denial of power an overwhelming habit of Western thinking? These questions take us to the heart of colonial discourse and the transformative power of the postcolonial. We must concede that Palestinians are the end result of an extraordinarily overdetermined discourse of denial. The present military campaign is based on a simple refusal to accept Palestinian existence. But this plight of the Palestinians is not a matter of individual prejudices nor Zionist propaganda. The invisibility of Palestine originates in the discourse of Orientalism, which has, says Said, an "entrenched *cultural* attitude toward Palestinians deriving from age-old Western prejudices about Islam, the Arabs, and the Orient" (Said 1980: xiv), an attitude in which the Palestinian people have often concurred in their own derogation and invisibility.

In this complicity we find the real complexity of denial. For both ordinary Israelis and Palestinians are locked into a structure of representations, a binary structure of alterity that originated before the establishment of Israel. In effect, both have denied themselves. Both societies are trapped by an extraordinary polarity of monologisms with which they are either actively or passively complicit—not Islam and Judaism but the binary established by Orientalism itself: Islam and the West. Palestinian complicity has not been merely a matter of being invisible but of accepting the violent binary presented by colonialist discourse. And although Said has provided us with a remarkably astute discursive strategy with which to address this denial, his own rhetoric often displays the ease with which the binary Zionist/Palestinian construct can dominate argument. The essence of postcolonial transformation is the disruption of this binary structure of representation, a refusal to be located; in turn, transformative strategies operate by interpolating the structures and discourses of colonial power that deny recognition.

For Said, the "question" of Palestine was how to understand "the contest between an affirmation and a denial" that characterizes this structure. It is a contest that sees the "civilizing" forces of the Europeans pitted against the "uncivilized" Arabs. This view entails the shaping of history, "so that this history now *appears* to confirm the validity of the Zionist claims to Palestine, thereby denigrating Palestinian claims" (Said 1980: 8). In response to this distortion, Said defined the occupation of Palestine as a colonial occupation, a colonization that did not end with the creation of Israel but rather was intensified by it.

The peculiar character of this colonization, the notion of a redemptive mission, the fulfillment of God's promise, is one that Said regards as unique, with the possible exception of the Puritans' coming to America in the seventeenth century. "That Messianic, redemptive quality," says Said, "it's so foreign to me, so outside me, so unlike anything I have experienced, that it endlessly fascinates me" (Ashcroft 1996:

13). This redemptive occupation is the key to the erasure of Palestinians from history. The Zionist discourse that created Israel began not in the Middle East but in the capital cities of the West. The Balfour Declaration of 2 November 1917, by which Britain sought to get Jewish support for World War I, expressly guaranteed protection of the rights of Palestinians: "His Majesty's Government view with favour the establishment in Palestine of a national home for the Jewish people, and will use their best endeavours to facilitate the achievement of this object, it being clearly understood that nothing shall be done which may prejudice the civil and religious rights of existing non-Jewish communities in Palestine, or the rights and political status enjoyed by Jews in any other country" (Israel Ministry of Foreign Affairs 2008). How was this recognition of Palestinian rights so easily subverted? First, despite the purported "civil and religious rights" of Palestinians, they were accorded no rights to land. Instead a whole apparatus supporting the ideology of property swung into place, making its specific claim of sovereignty over Nature. Second, because Palestinians were landless in the mind of Britain, they were, to all intents, invisible to political discourse. The task of representing them was appropriated by those to whom Britain gave access—Jews, particularly the members of the Zionist movement. Zionists were able to deploy the classic colonialist tactic of the civilizing mission, arguing that Palestine mostly was *unoccupied* or that it was inhabited by "natives." Palestinian resistance was ignored as the real story became the Zionist terrorist struggle with Britain: "Zionists made it their claim that Britain was blocking their greater and greater penetration of Palestine" (Said 1980: 23). The Zionist slogan about Palestinian territory—"a land without people for a people without land"—entrenched the Balfour Declaration's denial not simply of the state of Palestine but of the very existence of Palestinians and served to justify the absence of land rights. This denial explains the Israelis' attitude toward refugee camps and their treatment of the Palestinian government in Gaza. We are familiar with this construction of a *terra nullius* in Australia. It emerges from a conflation of place with property that has been deeply embedded in European thought since Locke. Jewish settlers were able to establish—as did the Europeans in the Americas, Asia, Australia, and Africa—that the land was unoccupied, or that it was occupied by uncivilized people who had little or no use for the land, and thus dispossess indigenous people in order to "civilize" them. The colonization of Palestine differed from that of other colonial settler states. The project was not simply a matter of establishing a settler class for whose benefit an indigenous population could be mobilized. Rather, it displaced the Palestinians while creating a state for all Jewish people, who were granted a "kind of sovereignty over land and peoples that no other state possessed or possesses" (84). Arabs and Palestinians were not only prevented from representing themselves but deemed *incapable* of representing themselves, confirming Marx's adage "They cannot represent themselves; they must be represented," which Said cites in an epigraph to *Orientalism*. A key victory for Israel was its success in representing and explaining Oriental Arabs to the West through the Western media. As Said pointed out, the Israelis "emancipated themselves from the worst Eastern excesses, to explain the Oriental Arabs to the West, to assume responsibility for expressing what the Arabs were really like and about, never to let the Arabs appear equally with them as existing in Palestine" (26). In an uncanny reprise of Orientalist attitudes, the Israeli take was that "Arabs are Oriental, therefore less human and valuable than Europeans and Zionists; they are treacherous, unregenerate, etc." (28). This distinction arose from the idea of the historic conflict between the West and Islam. Said noted that Israel was a device for holding Islam—and later the Soviet Union, or communism—at bay. The West associated Zionism and Israel with liberalism, freedom and democracy, knowledge and light, the principles "we" understand and fight for. By contrast, in this view, Zionism's enemies were simply a twentieth-century version of the alien spirit of Oriental despotism, sensuality, ignorance, and similar forms of backwardness (29). We see then how deeply this denial of Palestine and of Palestinian self-representation is embedded and how successful and intransigent Orientalist discourse has been. It is in America that the Palestinian question is most vigorously suppressed and the Arab most often portrayed as a terrorist. As an example, Said describes how the American press came to view Menachem Begin—himself a terrorist, from the evidence of his book, *The Revolt* (1972)—as a "statesman," while all but forgetting the atrocities he had committed against the Arabs (and the British). George W. Bush once stated that Sharon, often referred to as "the butcher of Shatila," and now of Jenin, was a "man of peace." As Prince Faisal (of Saudi Arabia) retorted, "I doubt if even Ariel Sharon believes that."

The most powerful contemporary expression of this denial was the representation of the Palestinian/Arab/Islamic world by contemporary media, which Said exposed in *Covering Islam*. Despite Islam's complexities and its multiple expressions, cultural backgrounds, and sects, the Western media have covered it within an extraordinarily simpleminded and pared-down version of Orientalist discourse. The media more than any other institution has "portrayed it, characterized it, analyzed it, given instant courses on it, and consequently they have made it 'known'" (Said 1997: li). After the OPEC oil crisis of the early 1970s, Islam became a scapegoat for every part of the entire political spectrum: "For the right, Islam represents barbarism; for the left, medieval theocracy; for the center, a kind of distasteful exoticism" (lv). The contemporary Islamic Orient is especially important because of its rich oil resources and its strategic geopolitical location, and battalions of experts have been assembled to render this Islamic Orient visible to the West. More importantly, the popular media has made Islam a major item of news and a consumable commodity for the mass of the population. "Muslims and Arabs are essentially covered, discussed, and apprehended either as oil suppliers or as potential terrorists. Very little of the detail, the human density, the passion of Arab-Muslim life has entered the awareness of even those people whose profession it is to report the Islamic world" (28). The representation of Islam since September 11, 2001, has become even more brutally simplistic. Both in popular Western imagination and media representation, terrorism is virtually synonymous with Islam. The representation of Islam has always been an important part of the Palestinian question because it has been used to silence the Palestinians, the majority of whom are Islamic. Since September 11, the situation has become catastrophic. Said's claim that the Palestinians must be permitted to speak, that they must demand "permission to narrate" (1984), to break the silence, has never been more urgent. September 11—so manifestly put forth as proof positive of the demonic duplicity, suicidal fanaticism, and barbaric violence of the Islamic world—is not so much part of Osama bin Laden's fiendish and paranoid plan to bring down the United States, as he has so obligingly claimed, as it is the natural consequence of an acceptance of two hundred years of Orientalist representations. It is, in effect, a denial of the ability to represent oneself, a surrender to Orientalist discourse, and a complicit affirmation of the truth of Orientalist denial. Palestinians have now been sucked into the vortex of global terrorism by their implication in the massive justification of Orientalism represented by September 11.

The "clash of civilizations" thesis (Huntington 1996), an example of perhaps the most virulent strain of Orientalist discourse, is simply a reification into historical "truth" of the polarities established by Orientalism over the past two centuries. In Western eyes, the Palestinians have no way of separating the suicide bombings carried out by their youth, even though these attacks originate in a specific national cause, from Osama bin Laden's monumental surrender to the Orientalist myth on September 11, 2001. Suicide attacks by Palestinian youth are not only an obvious self-destruction but a massive process of self-denial, a denial of self-representation. By representing themselves as martyrs to a desperate Palestinian population and a frustrated and impotent Arab world, the suicide bombers have chosen the wrong audience.

POSTCOLONIAL TRANSFORMATION

By undertaking a postcolonial analysis and observing the strategies of colonized people in discursive resistance, we can find a way to move past Palestinian silence. How does one obtain the "permission to narrate"? How does one *seize* the permission to narrate? The question seems almost self-indulgently theoretical in the present circumstances, yet the very existence of Palestine depends on this narration. The problem hinges on the question of resistance, and one useful way to identify postcolonial strategies of resistance is to examine postcolonial literatures, which give us some of the most developed strategies of self-empowerment and self-representation. The key difference for the Palestinian people is that liberation does not lie in resistance to its actual colonizers—the Israelis. Nonetheless, their free-

dom does lie in resistance to the hegemonic discourse that propels that colonization. The place of that resistance is the critical issue.

The topic of literature and resistance is particularly interesting in the Palestinian context because "resistance" *(muqāwamah)* was first applied to Palestinian literature in 1966 by the Palestinian writer and critic Ghassan Kanafani (1987: 2). For
Kanafani, resistance literature invoked a distinction between an "occupied" people
and a people in exile. It was seen as an identifiable, and significant, accompaniment
to the movement for political, military, and social national liberation. Particularly
interesting in light of my (admittedly somewhat harsh) suggestion that the Palestinians have been complicit in the denial of self-representation is Kanafani's claim
that no research into such literatures "can be complete unless the researcher is located within the resistance movement itself inside the occupied land" (3). This invocation of critical exclusivity and insider knowledge is familiar in postcolonial criticism and raises similar questions about the capacity of the literature itself to
communicate "outside the occupied land." For whom and to whom, we might ask,
does any writer write?

This view of resistance literature emerges from the idea that only literature that
is associated with resistance movements can truly resist. But, ironically, this view
of resistance, by barricading itself behind a binary opposition, is a *refusal of the right
to speak* because it excludes any but the most limited audience. We have seen this
pattern time and again in every avenue of communication available to the Palestinians in the present conflict. The idea that "counterforce" is the best response to
the colonialist myth of force binds the colonized into the myth. The futility of counterforce is nowhere more obvious than in Palestine, where the conflict is so unequal
that its logical extension is the extermination of the Palestinian people.

Palestine may be the site of struggle, but it is not the site of victory. Just as the
state of Israel took shape in the capitals of Europe, just as the representation of Palestinians takes place in the Western media, so the site of transformation is the imperial center—in this case, the United States. And this is not just the U.S. government
but American public opinion. Such is the lesson taught by postcolonial writers, that
the secret of self-representation is to capture the audience: to appropriate English,
interpolate the dominant discourse, and transform that discourse at the site of power.
If liberation lies in self-representation, then the battlefield is nowhere near Israel:
its front lines are on American television. Just as the most powerful perpetuation of
Orientalism has been in the Western media's "coverage" of Islam, so the most strategic site for transforming the representation of the Middle East in general and the
Palestinians in particular is also the Western media.

Television, with its sound bites and its power to invest ideology in images, is only
the front line. Colonized peoples have engaged in the much deeper and more lasting strategy of influencing cultural representation on the battlefield of hegemonic
discourse. In other words, they represent themselves on the other's territory with

the other's tools. Engaging the discourse at the dominant site of representation is not simply a matter of appropriating English; it also involves learning about and understanding the imperial culture. Obtaining permission to narrate is not simply a matter of speaking but a matter of speaking in a way that may be heard. The model of postcolonial literature—appropriating the language, interpolating dominant systems of publishing and distribution, and transforming the dominant culture itself—answers the following despairing cry of Edward Said:

> What has enabled Israel to deal with us with impunity has been that we are unprotected by anybody of opinion that would deter Sharon from practising his war crimes and saying what he has done is to fight terrorism. Given the immense, diffusionary, insistent, and repetitive power of the images broadcast by CNN, for example, in which the phrase "suicide bomb" is numbingly repeated a hundred times an hour for the American consumer and tax-payer, it is the grossest negligence not to have had a team of people like Hanan Ashrawi, Leila Shahid, Ghassan Khatib, Afif Safie—to mention just a few—sitting in Washington ready to go on CNN or any of the other channels just to tell the Palestinian story, provide context and understanding, give us a moral and narrative presence with positive, rather than merely negative, value. We need a future leadership that understands this as one of the basic lessons of modern politics in an age of electronic communication. Not to have understood this is part of the tragedy of today. (Said 2002)

This observation is indisputable, but it represents a fundamental strategy of postcolonial transformation: the ability to interpolate into the dominant discourse images of a contrary reality. The Palestinians need to provide the images of their reality, replacing the representations of insanity and violence that dominate the media not just with images of humiliation and despair but also with images of a valid cultural reality, a world as valid as Okonkwo's world of Umuofia in Achebe's *Things Fall Apart*. The failure to communicate is starkly revealed by a *Time* article that discusses the prospect of Palestinian suicide bombers attacking America. The fact that such an article could appear in a respected journal shows how far the work of self-representation has to go. The extraordinarily simplistic images of Islam and Palestine in the Western press—beards, veils, bombs, and wild-eyed craziness—cannot, tragically, be countered with images of despair and humiliation, although these are true to Palestinians' reality, but with images of reason and humanity. And this step is necessary not only in the visual media but also in intellectual discourse, with Palestinian intellectuals taking hold of the discourse in the English language.

The appropriation of English is a touchy issue because many people may interpret it as a capitulation to the discourse of power. Whether using a colonial language keeps the speaker or writer colonized is an argument that has raged for many years. But literatures written in "appropriated" English demonstrate most clearly the political and cultural agency that writers can achieve by appropriating the dominant language, transforming it, and using it to reveal a cultural reality to a world audience. In the same way, the lesson of postcolonial writing is that appropriating English is not capitulation but an essential strategy of self-representation. If the task is to construct an audience out of the American public, then use of competent and persuasive English is essential.

The British Empire was able to establish cultural hegemony in its colonies particularly by disseminating English literary studies as a civilizing discourse and thereby instilling a deep knowledge of the dominant colonizing culture. This type of cultural comprehension is absent from all Arab dealings with America. In a 2002 article in *Al-Ahram Weekly*, Said repeated a refrain he had used often in discussing Arab representation:

> There is simply no use operating politically and responsibly in a world dominated by one superpower without a profound familiarity and knowledge of that superpower— America, its history, its institutions, its currents and counter-currents, its politics and culture, and, above all, a perfect working knowledge of its language. To hear our spokesmen, as well as the other Arabs, saying the most ridiculous things about America, throwing themselves on its mercy, cursing it in one breath, asking for its help in another, all in miserably inadequate fractured English, shows a state of such primitive incompetence as to make one cry. America is not monolithic. We have friends and we have possible friends. We can cultivate, mobilise and use our communities and their affiliated communities here as an integral part of our politics of liberation, just as the South Africans did, or as the Algerians did in France during their struggle for liberation. Planning, discipline, coordination. We have not at all understood the politics of non-violence. (2002)

In this passage, Said refers mainly to the need for Palestinian spokespeople to make themselves available to the U.S. media, and this need continues. The longer-term strategies of representation are to produce and disseminate cultural representations that communicate with a targeted audience. But even more important for capturing the immediate global audience is to disseminate images. Images of the massacre at Jenin taken by Palestinians would have provided a dramatic counterweight to the Israelis' refusal to grant media access. But the more lasting and effective images will be those of a Palestinian society representing its own humanity.

The site of the struggle may expand beyond Israel, but the work of communication is to deconstruct the cultural binary in which both Palestinians and Israelis are caught. This binary is built on Orientalism, initiated by Zionism, and perpetuated by the Western media. It is a struggle between affirmation and denial, between speech and silence; it is a struggle to move out of denial into self-representation. Freedom from silence involves both parties because both are to some extent colonized by an almost impenetrable discourse. "Moreover, neither have we understood the power of trying to address Israelis directly, the way the ANC [African National Congress] addressed the white South Africans, as part of a politics of inclusion and mutual respect. Coexistence is our answer to Israeli exclusivism and belligerence.

This is not conceding: it is creating solidarity, and therefore isolating the exclusivists, the racists, the fundamentalists" (2002).

Unfortunately the trap in which both Israelis and Palestinians are caught is not amenable to successful communication simply because the extremists have control on the ground. The most compelling option appears to be the one so seldom tried— a conversation between ordinary Palestinians and Israelis. But just as the most far-reaching exertion of power in the British Empire was the cultural hegemony perpetuated through the dissemination of European culture, so the most effective long-term resistance by postcolonial peoples is to transform imperial discourse. Postcolonial writing shows us that a hegemonic structure of representations can be transformed. Such a transformation is not only possible but critical, for it is the key to the material and political liberation of colonized people.

Said gives a moving conclusion to this intervention. "As Palestinians, I think we can say that we left a vision and a society that has survived every attempt to kill it. And that is something. It is for the generation of my children and yours, to go on from there, critically, rationally, with hope and forbearance" (2002). The most moving words in this passage are "And that is something." For that something is so much and yet so little. Survival is something, but in light of the longing for home, the longing for a place, the longing for peace, it is also very little. But the way home has been demonstrated so many times by colonized people who have extricated themselves from the binary trap of representation and denial. Home is not paradise. Home is not the "nonplace"—Utopia—nor is home the shimmering object in the distance. Home is the luminous possibility of the present.

WORKS CITED

Ashcroft, B. 1996. "Interview with Edward Said." *New Literatures Review* 32: 3–22.

———. 2001. *Post-Colonial Transformation.* London: Routledge.

Begin, M. 1972. *The Revolt.* Trans. Samuel Kalz. Jerusalem: Steimatzkys Agency.

Huntington, S. P. 1996. *The Clash of Civilizations and the Remaking of World Order.* New York: Simon & Schuster.

Israel Ministry of Foreign Affairs. 2008. The Balfour Declaration, 1917. www.mfa.gov.il/MFA/ Peace+Process/Guide+to+the+Peace+Process/The+Balfour+Declaration.htm (accessed 10 August 2009).

Kanafani, G. 1987. *Literature of Resistance in Occupied Palestine: 1948–1966.* Beirut: Institute for Arabic Research. In Arabic.

Müller, M. 1898. *Collected Works.* 2 vols. London: Longmans Green.

Parker, K., ed., 1999. *Early Modern Tales of the Orient.* London: Routledge.

Poliakov, L. 1974. *The Aryan Myth: A History of Racist and Nationalist Ideas in Europe.* Trans. Edmund Howard. London: Chatto & Windus.

Renan, E. 1896. *Caliban: A Philosophical Drama Continuing "The Tempest" of William Shakespeare.* Trans. Eleanor Grant Vickery. Repr. New York: AMS, 1971.

Said, E. W. 1978. *Orientalism*. New York: Vintage.

———. 1980. *The Question of Palestine*. London: Vintage.

———. 1981. *Covering Islam*. New York: Vintage.

———. 1984. "Permission to Narrate: Reconstituting the Siege of Beirut." *London Review of Books*, February 16–29, 13–17.

———. 1997. Introduction to *Covering Islam*. 2nd ed. New York: Vintage.

———. 2002. "Thinking Ahead: After Survival, What Happens?" *Al-Ahram Weekly*, April 4–10; http://weekly.ahram.org.eg/2002/580/op2.htm (accessed 21 June 2009).

———. 2003. "A Window on the World." *Guardian*, August 1.

17

Said and the Palestinian Diaspora

A Personal Reflection

Ghada Karmi

In the immediate aftermath of Edward Said's death in September 2003, I remember wondering if, while we Palestinians mourned his passing, Israelis and their supporters were celebrating the demise of one of their most successful, articulate, and effective opponents. The Israeli political establishment does not seriously fear Palestinian military resistance or Palestinian "terrorism," or the threats of militants, however much it has proclaimed that Palestinian resistance is the major problem for Israel. The battle Israel cannot afford to lose is the one for hearts and minds, the public relations contest, which it has always won hands down against a poor and ineffectual Arab opposition. Over three decades, Edward Said reversed that perception in the most important arena for Israel and its supporters: the United States and the West. He was more effective than a dozen armies and a fleet of F16s in the struggle against the Zionists. His role brings to mind a former Israeli prime minister's words in a totally opposite setting. After the Deir Yassin massacre by Zionists in April 1948 had terrified thousands of Palestinians into fleeing (including my own family), Menachem Begin, the commander of the operation, said that the massacre had been worth half a dozen battalions in the war against the Palestinian Arabs.

Most of Said's many admirers—scholars and literati, musicians and historians, political analysts and activists—were Western or non-Arab during his life. This is understandable, because the West was his milieu from adolescence onward; he wrote in English, and his achievements in diverse fields of European thought made him a worthy exponent of several Western disciplines. Indeed, Edward Said, like all intellectuals, could be said to belong to the whole of humanity. But to identify him in

304

this way is to misunderstand the Palestinian context that animated him and from which his inspiration sprang. In this sense, it is the Palestinian people who must claim him first, as one of their subtlest, cleverest, and most loyal fighters, the foremost cultural bridge that connected and explained their cause to Western sensibilities. But it is also the fact that to underestimate the importance of Palestine as an inspiration and motivational force for his talent would also yield only a partial grasp of his work and lessen our understanding of its significance.

THE PALESTINIAN CONTEXT

My friendship with Edward Said spanned twenty-seven years, during which time I found inspiration but also identification with him. We were both born in Jerusalem, and we both grew up in exile, he in the affluent Western milieu of colonial Cairo and later in America, I in England. For both of us, political awakening came with the Arab defeat in the 1967 Arab-Israeli war and led to a new career of active involvement in the politics of Palestine. When he generously endorsed my memoir, *In Search of Fatima*, in 2001, I thought that he saw in my story the same sense of unbelonging and dispossession that he felt. We first met in Libya in 1976, when he was not yet well-known, as guests at a conference on Zionism and racism sponsored by Colonel Muammar Gaddafi. We met again in New York when his major literary work, *Orientalism*, was published in 1978. Given that he came from a radically different discipline than mine, I little appreciated the importance of the book at first. The storm of controversy it aroused was remarkable and, to many of us, surprising. Without reading the book, we supported him on the most simplistic of levels: he was attacking a hegemonic West for its dominance of Arabs and the East, and that seemed only right. When I finally read the book, I began to understand its true significance, especially for Palestinians.

Like all great ideas, the central theme of *Orientalism* seemed at first simple and instantly familiar, as if we had all known it for ages. Its exposé of a paternalistic and colonialist Western scholarship toward the Orient aroused hostility and admiration in equal measure. But for Arabs, Said's book had an instinctive appeal that did not need the intellectual underpinnings of his argument because it resonated with their collective consciousness of denigration and inadequacy at Western hands. For Palestinians, Edward Said's real achievement is to have defined what I will call the will to dispossess that is at the heart of Orientalist scholarship. The Western writers who described the people of the Orient dispossessed them too, not by physical eviction, as happened in Palestine, but through an elegant and subtle erudition. For a people who are re-created through the prism of an alien scholarship, influenced by alien notions of supremacy, are robbed of their real history and true identity. And that intellectual theft is a sort of dispossession.

These ideas were not just relevant to another age. They are with us today, as he asserted, and permeate much of the currently hostile attitudes and discourse of America and the West toward Arabs and Islam. In this sense, we can see that much of his writing is properly situated in this consciousness of dispossession that has its springboard in his Palestinian origins. To understand his significance properly is to understand the recent history of Palestine. The country he was born into in 1935 had been ruled by a British colonial administration under U.N. mandate since 1922. The environment of his childhood was subsumed with colonialist notions, and the Zionist enterprise, which had begun to flourish under British patronage at that time, was also colonialist. Although the Said family was affluent and his father a wealthy Christian businessman who afforded the young Edward a Western-style education in expensive schools, the general parameters of his Arab existence were inescapably colonialist.

These influences dominated his upbringing. When the Said family left Jerusalem in 1947, it went to Cairo, where he received a private English education. His home environment was imbued with admiration for Western culture, music, opera, literature, and above all, the English language. Said noted that this appreciation of things Western induced a split in his sense of identity during adolescence from which he never recovered. In an interview with Imre Salusinszky, he said, "My background is a series of displacements and expatriations which cannot be recuperated. The sense of being between cultures has been very, very strong for me. I would say that's the single strongest strand running through my life: the fact that I'm always in and out of things, and never really of anything for long."[1]

The establishment of the state of Israel in 1948 led to the forcible expulsion and flight of three-quarters of a million Palestinians. This physical dispossession had its parallel in his spiritual dispossession and became a basic theme in his worldview. The Palestinian refugees' right to return to the homeland from which they had been evicted was a central aspect of his work. He always returned to the fundamental elements of the conflict between Israel and the Palestinians: the latter's dispossession and Israel's evasion of its responsibility for their plight. From the start of Israeli statehood, that evasion took a path of obsessive denial. To maintain its fiction of innocence, Israel set about eradicating all traces of the Palestinian presence in the land. Over five hundred villages were demolished, and new settlements sprang up in their place. The history of "Israel" that Israeli children learn at school is distorted so as to exclude the Arab presence. An intricate mythology of Israel's origins maps a Jewish continuity from biblical times to the present, only interrupted by phases of transient settlement by Romans, Ottomans, and British. If you knew no different, it would be entirely possible to believe that no Arabs had ever existed in the country but for a few wandering Bedouin tribes. By such methods, the Israelis have attempted to annihilate a whole people: their history, memory, language, and culture.

SAID AND DISPOSSESSION

All Palestinians feel this insult of a double dispossession of their bodies and their souls, with no acknowledgment of their history as a separate people or of their resulting sufferings. Edward Said felt this dismissal keenly, and many of his writings reflect this feeling in one way or another. Finding a thematic connection in his wide and apparently disparate compositions is difficult, because he wrote on a variety of subjects, ranging from intellectual history to current affairs. Abdirahman Hussein, in his intellectual biography of Edward Said, questions whether it is possible, given this range of writing, to discern a common thread.[2] Yet the themes of exile and dispossession seem to be central preoccupations, expressed mainly in his political writings and in his most important work, *Orientalism*. Said had a syncretic quality, an uncommon ability to cross intellectual boundaries and to step in and out of apparently unrelated topics—literary criticism, politics, culture, history, methodologies— in a fluid and effortless way.

This ability to inhabit the "in-between zone" echoed the experience of exile, when survival frequently depends on the capacity to merge or adapt one's own identity and behavior to an environment that may be inimical to one's original culture and experience. Said's adolescent experience in the United States, of which he writes in his memoir, *Out of Place*, forced upon him just such a situation, in which he learned to cope with remarkable intellectual and emotional agility. Yet it left its mark and led to his persistent feeling of being "between cultures." A number of commentators have related his ability to cross intellectual boundaries to this experience of exile.[3]

One might wonder why a man who never personally experienced the Nakba, the 1948 mass exodus of Palestinians from their homeland, should have been so affected by its consequences, not just in an intellectual or political sense but with great empathy and personal distress. He himself recognized that he had not been through the depredations of expulsion and camp life, that he was indeed privileged. But the event and its aftermath nonetheless had the profoundest impact on him and drove him to produce, in my view, his most lucid, passionate, and compelling prose. "Palestinian life is scattered, discontinuous, marked by the artificial and imposed arrangements of interrupted or confined space, by the dislocations and unsynchronised rhythms of disturbed time."[4]

The Zionist denial of Palestinian life and history spurred him to reverse that denial and break the artificially imposed silence decreed by Zionism but colluded with by the Western world. "Since our history is forbidden, narratives are rare; the story of origins, of home, of nation is underground. When it appears it is broken, often wayward and meandering in the extreme, always coded—mock-epics, satires, sardonic parables, absurd rituals—that make little sense to an outsider."[5]

This dual problem, the deprivation of his people of the basics of normal existence—home, roots, social continuity—and the ferocious and effective assault on these *as historical facts* by Zionists and their supporters, exercised Said for most of his life. His foremost role in Palestinian life was, inevitably, as spokesman and representative of the diaspora that was his natural constituency. "Behind every Palestinian there is a great general fact: that he once—and not so long ago—lived on a land of his own called Palestine, which is now no longer his homeland. No nuances are necessary for a Palestinian to make such a statement."[6]

ZIONISM AND DISPOSSESSION

Palestinian dispossession is in a sense like no other, for in this case, the agent of dispossession claims a moral right that supersedes that of the dispossessed people to their land. And the remarkable thing is that this idea has taken firm hold of the Western imagination. Said believed that intellectuals involved in the discourse on Orientalism, imperialism, and Zionist political philosophy helped create the doctrine that such things as pure national, racial, or cultural and religious identities actually exist and that such identities may be nobler than and superior to others. In *Orientalism*, he focuses on the Orientalist construction of an identity that misrepresents Third World peoples and derives from a supremacist view of the world that defines categories of "them" and "us." We can see in this act a ready parallel with the Zionist construction of a special Jewish people with a supreme mission that displaces the rights of a lesser people, the Palestinians, who are represented as absent or unworthy and defective. Interestingly, in this context Jonathan Raban evokes Said in a recent article about the horrors of the American occupation of Iraq. He remarks on the way in which the Iraqi people have been "Orientalized"—dehumanized and robbed of their "intractable particularity." He wonders if Iraq's American tormentors have a copy of Edward Said's book by their bedsides to ransack for ideas.[7]

It engaged Said's attention that a manifestly colonialist, discriminatory and supremacist ideology, Zionism, was able to present itself as a socialist, democratic egalitarian enterprise. What was it that ensured the credibility of this misrepresentation and its achievements? He asserted that one could not understand this distortion outside the context of European imperialism and Orientalist discourse:

> Effective political ideas like Zionism need to be examined historically in two ways: (1) genealogically in order that their provenance, their kinship and descent, their affiliation both with other ideas and with political institutions may be demonstrated; (2) as practical systems for accumulation of power, (land, ideological legitimacy), and displacement (of people, other ideas, prior legitimacy). Present political and cultural actualities make such an examination extraordinarily difficult, as much because Zionism in the post-industrial West has acquired for itself an almost unchallenged hegemony in liberal "establishment" discourse, as because in keeping with one of its central ideological characteristics Zionism has hidden, or caused to disappear, the lit-

eral historical ground of its growth, its political cost to the native inhabitants of Palestine, and its militantly oppressive discrimination between Jews and non-Jews.[8]

Thus, Zionism inserted itself into the dominant Western discourse that saw the Arabs as "natives" of lesser worth, the "non-Jewish communities" of the Balfour Declaration whose destiny was to be decided by others and whose needs could be subordinated to those of a superior race. Such a project as the Zionist colonization of Palestine would have been impossible without this discourse of power and specialness, which arose from a Eurocentric, Orientalist philosophy. Thus, Europe, with its grand culture and civilization, was assumed to be the moral, political, and aesthetic center of the world, and the rest of humanity, the "natives," occupied a lower position. The idea of empire, establishing colonies of Europeans in far-flung countries and without regard for the colonized peoples' wishes in the matter, was well established by the time Zionism appeared on the scene. Hence, Said considered the colonizing Zionist project to be part and parcel of this structure of attitudes and saw Orientalism as its indispensable component. In determining the fate of the "natives" of Palestine, colonial officials like Arthur Balfour and the Zionist leadership were in profound agreement. Thus, modern Zionism was allied from the start to the most extreme forms of European exclusivism and supremacism. This shared view enabled the building of a Jewish state in another country and at the expense of its natives in broad daylight, so to speak, with the full knowledge of its British patrons that Palestine was already home to an existing people. It is impossible to doubt that either the Zionists or the British colonial administration in Palestine did not always intend "the total reconstitution" of Palestine as a Jewish state with no room for non-Jews.

Israel developed as a social polity out of the Zionist thesis that Palestine's colonization and the displacement of the Palestinians were to be accomplished simultaneously for and by Jews. Zionism, as Said pointed out, attempted first to minimize, then to eliminate, and finally to subjugate the natives as a way of guaranteeing that Israel would not be simply the state of its citizens (which included Arabs, of course) but the state of "the whole Jewish people." The Zionists established a kind of sovereignty over land and peoples that no other state possessed or possesses. Since then, the Arab Palestinians have been trying to resist and provide an alternative for this anomaly. For all these reasons, Said was preoccupied with the question of Israel: how it was able to displace and obliterate the Palestinian presence and the fact that the Palestinians never stopped resisting their imposed fate or devising counterstrategies, of which the one-state solution was the one he most strongly advocated in his later years. Of course, he never underestimated the enormity of the task facing the Palestinians. This simple, largely agricultural people with poor education and modest political aspirations had been forced into close proximity with a formidable foe: European Jews allied to European imperialism, who were imbued with a "yearning for Jewish political and religious self-determination . . . to be exercised on the promised land."[9] From the outset, the struggle was grossly unequal, and given the phenomenal success of the Zionist project on the international stage, it continues to be so. However, Said was fond of saying that this project, which the Palestinians experienced as a total calamity, nevertheless put them on the political map. Who would ever have heard about them if their invaders had been Chadians or Ukrainians?[10] It is precisely because the protagonists were Jews with a complex history, grounded in European persecution and guilt, that the Palestinians acquired an unusual and unwelcome prominence.

SAID AND THE DIASPORA

As we have seen, Said's foremost place in the Palestinian context was as an explicator and representative of Palestinian exile—so much so that he struck many Palestinians "inside" as remote or even irrelevant to their lives. He once told me early in the 1990s that he nowhere felt more undervalued than among his own people. He was hurt that some of those under Israeli occupation accused him of Western remoteness and intellectual hauteur, and therefore of an inability to empathize with their plight. By the time of his death, however, he had been showered with praise, admiration, and gratitude by critics and friends alike, and he was acknowledged as one of Palestine's greatest sons. One can trace his "integration" into larger Palestinian society from his 1992 visit to Israel, when he returned to Jerusalem for the first time since childhood to find his family home. His connection with the people of the "inside" became decisively concretized with the signing of the Oslo Accords in 1993. Notwithstanding other objections to these accords, their most serious effect was to deepen the gulf between Palestinians inside Palestine and those outside. Worse still, the agreement drew the leadership of the Palestine Liberation Organization (PLO), which had always been a diaspora organization, into the occupied territories—that is, inside—and thereby effectively destroyed it. The diaspora was left leaderless and, with the death of Yasir Arafat in November 2004, is even more so today. In this sense, the Oslo Accords must be viewed as the most successful Israeli venture to divide the Palestinians to date.

Whereas the PLO had led the struggle for liberation since 1965 and achieved the impossible—unifying more or less the exiled, 1948 Palestinians, who are numerically the majority, under one banner—the Oslo Accords, with their exclusive emphasis on the post-1967 population and territories, managed to delete what had gone before, both the history and the people, as if they were irrelevant. The West now focuses its attention exclusively on the events, strategies, and behavior of the Palestinians under occupation, as if there were no diaspora community and no issue other than the occupation. We know, of course, that the divisive process did not stop there, for Israel has continued to fragment post-1967 Palestinian society ever since into cantons and areas permanently separated from each other. But the major rift between the two main Palestinian communities had already been effected in 1993, to the detriment of the Palestinian national cause and, no doubt, to Israel's satisfaction in its long-running battle with Palestinian nationalism. It was at this moment that Said had such a signal role. In the last decade of his life, his involvement with the Palestinians of the inside helped revive Palestinians' consciousness of themselves as a people with one cause. He did so not only through his writings and media appearances but also through projects such as the musical-training initiative for young Palestinian musicians in Ramallah that he initiated with Daniel Barenboim. His best book on the subject, *The Question of Palestine*, had been out since 1979.

In the last few years of his life, he became a prolific writer of regular columns in the Arabic press, mainly the London-based *Al-Hayat* and Cairo's *Al-Ahram Weekly*. It is easy to forget that all this activity only appeared in the mid-1990s, no doubt linked to the diagnosis of his final illness in 1992. His articles provided more than commentary on the current situation; they gave many in the Arab world a keen insight into American thinking on the Middle East and, as such, were eagerly anticipated and read by Palestinians and many other Arabs. Through these means, he introduced fresh ways of looking at events and helped shape the political debate. His writing paralleled his increasing engagement with the Palestinians in the occupied territories, which he started to visit and where he frequently delivered lectures. This last function was one of the most important he performed for Palestinians, for he provided a bridge between the "inside" and the "outside" and reconnected the various parts of this dispersed people, when the rift between them widened after 1993 and no national organization was properly functioning. His harsh criticisms of the Palestinian leadership antagonized many of his admirers and endeared him to intellectuals in Israel and the West. Right to the end, he was fearless in railing against incompetence and corruption among Palestinian leaders, most notably Arafat himself. In a private e-mail to me on September 5, 2003, three weeks before his death, he described the Arab-Israeli orchestra he had set up with Daniel Barenboim (of which more below). I had expressed reservations about Barenboim's politics, and he responded as follows:

I don't know a single Arab artist or intellectual who has done anything remotely like this. I think you should celebrate the man's courage and his extraordinary genius and the fact that, when it comes to politics, there's very little to choose between him and us. I hope this somewhat restores your enthusiasm which I fear too many years of fruitless verbal politics and political manoeuvring has depressed. We have established a foundation in Seville. Included is a complete program for Palestinian musical education, sponsored by Daniel and myself, to be run entirely by the Palestinian National Conservatory.

In this world of Abu Mazens and Abu Shitheads, surely these are shining achievements.

His archenemy, Yasir Arafat, died just one year after his own death. How interesting to ruminate on what Said would have said about that event and about the subsequent election of Abu Mazen.

THE FUTURE OF PALESTINE/ISRAEL

Said was never under any illusion that the solution to the conflict between Israelis and Palestinians was anything but elusive and seemingly impossible. For all his concern about the alliance between imperialism and Zionism, he never misread the Zionist project as simply a colonialist enterprise, which would therefore go the way of all others before it. His life and experiences in the United States, where he saw daily evidence of Zionist power and influence, precluded any such simplistic judgment. For this reason, he frequently wrote of the need to understand the other side and for all Arabs to acquaint themselves with the Holocaust in all its detail and to study Israeli society. He deprecated the lack of centers in the Arab world devoted to studying Israeli affairs and especially to studying America, Israel's greatest supporter. In his own life, he encouraged connections, even friendships, with like-minded Israelis. In his last years, he became an associate of many prominent Israelis, gave interviews to Israel's *Ha'aretz* newspaper, and became well-known to Israeli intellectuals. His association with the pianist Daniel Barenboim is one particularly fruitful example, for it culminated in a joint musical project, the West-Eastern Divan Workshop and Orchestra, with a membership of young Arabs and Jews. I attended an ecstatically received first concert by this orchestra in London in August 2003. Even so, the project did not gain everyone's approval, and some of us found a disturbing dissonance between the celebration in London of a "friendship" between Arabs and Israelis while Israelis conducted a pitiless onslaught on Palestinians back in Palestine.

Nevertheless, this kind of initiative showed the direction in which Said would most likely have gone had he lived longer. The one-state solution that he espoused was premised on the understanding that because of Palestinians' and Israelis' respective histories, neither can make the other disappear. He believed that relationships between peoples should transcend boundaries, racial exclusivity, and difference and that a new state built on tolerance, harmony, and coexistence was an infinitely better goal to fight for than one based on separateness, anger, hatred, and injustice.

"Perhaps our dream 20 years ago for a Palestinian state was realisable then," he wrote in 1999, "but today we have neither the military, nor the political nor the moral will or capacity to create a real independent state . . . Israeli dreams are equally unimplementable . . . therefore the only acceptable political logic for Palestinians is to move our struggle from the level of high-ranking negotiations to the level of the actual on-the-ground reality." He argued for coexistence and an alliance between like-minded Palestinians and Israelis to realize this goal. "I write in order to be heard by other Arabs and other Israelis, those whose vision can extend beyond the impoverishing perspectives of what partition and separation can offer."[11]

In a later article, inspired by his visit to South Africa, where the African National Congress had defeated the separation between peoples imposed by apartheid, he reiterated his belief in Israelis' and Palestinians' "common humanity": "Separation can't work in so tiny a land [as Israel/Palestine] any more than Apartheid did." So his answer was "two people in one land. Or, equality for all. Or, a common humanity asserted in a binational state."[12] The call for a one-state solution came late in Said's professional life; for many years, he supported, either actively or passively, the two-state idea. Yet his vision for this alternative solution toward the end of his life was as compelling and inspiring as if he had always espoused it. When one surveys Palestine's last remnants today, the stunning power of Israel's hold on the United States, the terminal decline of the Arab world, and the immoral complicity of the international community in this situation, can anyone still believe in the two-state solution? Can we not now see, as some of us have seen since 1948, that an Israeli state built on overwhelming power and oppression of others has no stable future? And is not the only possible and humane way out of this nightmare the creation of a common state, where those who know it as their homeland can share it in equality and amity?

NOTES

1. Imre Salusinszky, ed., *Criticism in Society* (London: Routledge, 1987), 127–28.

2. Abdirahman Hussein, *Edward Said: Criticism and Society* (London: Verso, 2002), 2.

3. See, for example, Ella Shohat, "Antinomies of Exile: Said at the Frontiers of National Narrations," in *Edward Said: A Critical Reader*, ed. Michael Sprinker (Oxford: Blackwell, 1993), 121–43.

4. Edward W. Said, *After the Last Sky: Palestinian Lives*, photographs by Jean Mohr (London: Faber and Faber, 1986), 20.

5. Ibid.

6. Edward W. Said, *The Question of Palestine* (London: Vintage, 1992), 115.

7. Jonathan Raban, "Emasculating Arabia," *Guardian*, 13 May 2004.

8. Said, *The Question of Palestine*, 57.

9. Ibid., 56–57.

10. From a speech Said gave at the Bloomsbury Theatre, London, September 1998.

11. Edward W. Said, "What Can Separation Mean?" *Al-Ahram Weekly*, 11–17 November 1999.

12. Edward W. Said, "The Only Alternative," *Al-Ahram Weekly*, 1–7 March 2001; see also Said, "The One-State Solution," *New York Times*, 10 January 1999.

18

The Question of Zionism

Continuing the Dialogue

Jacqueline Rose

"Why should the Palestinians make the effort to understand Zionism?" The question came from a young woman in the audience at one of the many memorials held for you, this one in London in November 2003 under the auspices of the *London Review of Books*. It was not your priority, responded Ilan Pappe. And Sara Roy simply and powerfully told the anecdote of how she had witnessed Palestinians flooding with joy onto the curfewed streets of the West Bank, where she was living, when the possibility of a Palestinian state was first acknowledged by Israel, while the soldiers stood by in silence and just watched. There will be understanding enough, I heard her saying, when there is justice.

They were of course both right: your preoccupation was with justice. In one of your most irate pieces about the occupation, "Sober Truths about Israel and Zionism," which you wrote for *Al-Ahram* and *Al-Hayat* in 1995, when the bitter reality of post-Oslo was becoming clearer by the day, you mince no words about the cruel asymmetry of the conflict and the peculiar injustice of the settlements—what they tell us about Israel as a nation, about Zionism as its founding idea. Once a piece of land is confiscated, it belongs to the "Land of Israel" and is officially restricted for the exclusive use of Jews. Many nations, including the United States, you allow, were founded on the confiscation of land, but no other country then designates this land for the sole use of one portion of its citizens. You are citing Israel Shahak, Holocaust survivor, founder of the Israeli League of Human Rights, "one of the small handful of Israeli Jews who tells the truth *as it is*."[1]

Earlier in the essay, you tell the anecdote of a Palestinian student at Birzeit University who, at the end of a lecture in which you were advocating a more "scientific and precise" approach on the part of the Arab world to understanding the United

States, raised his hand to say "that it was a more disturbing fact that no such pro-gramme existed in Palestine for the study of Israel" (anticipating in reverse the young woman in London).[2] Shahak is your answer. Understanding Israel means under-standing the discriminatory foundations of the nation-state: "Unless we recognise the real issue—which is the racist character of the Zionist Movement and the State of Israel and the roots of that racism in the Jewish religious law [Halacha]—we will not be able to understand our realities. And unless we can understand them, we will not be able to change them."[3]

If that was all you had to say, if you had had just that much to say, you would have already been saying, and so fully in character, so much. This is speaking truth to power—"*as it is*"—a truth rarely acknowledged in Israel's self-representation, still less to the outside world. My only question would be to that last line of Shahak's: does speaking this particular truth, which is indeed heard today both inside and outside the country, make it easier to change, or is it driving Israel, yet again on the defensive, ever more fiercely to entrench itself?

And yet, to stop there is not, I believe—and I believe you believed—to go far enough. Your view was more complex. In fact, you decried the U.N. resolution that equated Zionism with racism as politically counterproductive: "I was never happy with that resolution."[4] Significantly, given your call for scientific precision in un-derstanding, it was not *precise* enough: "Racism is too vague a term. Zionism is Zion-ism."[5] "The question of Zionism," you said in conversation with Salman Rushdie in 1986, "is the touchstone of contemporary political judgement."[6] What did you mean?

Speaking at the memorial in 2003, I cited what remains for me one of your most poignant pleas: "We cannot coexist as two communities of detached and uncom-municatingly separate suffering"—the "we" performing the link for which it ap-peals.[7] I cannot remember whether it was this quotation or my later attempt in the discussion to talk about Zionism that provoked the question of the young woman from the floor. But, for me, it is the peculiar quality and gift of your thought that you could make your denunciation of the injustice of Israel toward the Palestini-ans while also speaking—without ever softening the force of that critique—if not quite *for,* nonetheless *of* the reality of the other side: what drove Israel? how had it come to be? what makes it what it is now?

Perhaps your best-known discussion of Zionism is "Zionism from the Stand-point of Its Victims," in *The Question of Palestine* of 1979, which was your first ex-tended analysis of this history. The title unambiguously announces that your pri-ority is to raise the plight of the Palestinians, at the time more or less passed over in silence, both in the world and for themselves. Yet that objective, on which you never wavered, is already here accompanied by interconnections and diffusions of another kind. You were, after all, both a political thinker and a literary critic (the two roles passionately, intimately joined). "The task of criticism, or, to put it an-other way, the role of the critical consciousness in such cases," you write in the chapter, "is to be able to make distinctions, to produce differences where at present there are none."[8] To critique Zionism is not, you insisted then, anti-Semitic (an assertion that critics of Israel, especially post-9/11, are forced to make even more loudly today). It is, in one of your favorite formulas of Gramsci's, to make an inventory of the historical forces that have made anyone—a people—who they are. Zionism needs to be read. What is required is a critical consciousness that dissects the obdurate language of the present by delving into the buried fragments of the past, to produce differences "where at present there are none." It is not therefore a simple political identity that you are offering the Palestinians on whose behalf you speak, nor a simple version of the seemingly intractable reality to which they find themselves opposed. It is rather something more disorienting that confers and troubles identity at one and the same time (if the past is never a given nor, once uncovered, is it ever merely a gift).

For me, Gramsci's injunction always contained a psychoanalytic demand: "The consciousness of what one really is . . . is 'knowing thyself,'" although such knowledge is hardly easy, as every psychoanalyst will attest.[9] I see this as your injunction to Zionism and Palestinian nationalism alike. By the time we get to "Bases for Coexistence" in 1997, to this classic Freudian dictum, you have added another no less painful and difficult dimension: "We cannot coexist as two communities of detached and uncommunicatingly separate suffering." And then, against the grain of your own and your people's sympathies, "There is suffering and injustice enough for everyone."[10] (After this piece appeared in Al-Hayat and Al-Ahram, you received your first hate mail in the Arab press.) Not just self-reflective, nor just internally unsettling, but perhaps precisely because it is both of these, such knowledge has the power to shift the boundaries between peoples. There can be no progress in the Middle East, I hear you saying, without a shared recognition of pain.

As I reread you today on Zionism, this strained, complicated demand seems in fact a type of constant. This may be, of course, because I personally so want and need it to be (as Brecht notoriously acknowledged when asked whether his interpretation of Coriolanus was true to Shakespeare's meaning—he was both "reading in and reading into" the play). But it seems to me that—contrary to your detractors—you were always trying to do two things at once that you knew to be well-nigh impossible. As if you were requiring of all critics of Israel—whether Arab and Jewish, and without dissolving the real historical and political differences between the two peoples—to hold together in our hearts and minds the polar-opposite emotions of empathy and rage (however reluctant the first, however legitimate the second for your people might be). Today the understanding of Zionism seems an even more crucial task than when you made the question the touchstone of political judgment nearly twenty years ago. I want to place the role of the critic as you defined it in 1979 together with the plea for a shared recognition of suffering of 1997 on either side of your answer to the Palestinian student at Birzeit. What then do we see?

Zionism has been a success. You said this many times. Shocking, given the catastrophe for the Palestinians, but true—even for those such as David Grossman and Yaakov Perry, former head of Shin Bet (to mention just two), who see Israel today as in a perhaps irreversible decline, in thrall to a militarism destructive of the Palestinians and of itself. Historically, Israel has fulfilled its aims. You repeat the point in an interview with Hasan M. Jafri for the *Karachi Herald* as late as 1992: "Zionism for the Jew was a wonderful thing. They say it was their liberation movement. They say it was that which gave them sovereignty. They finally had a homeland."[11] But, as you laid it out so clearly in "Zionism from the Standpoint of Its Victims," Zionism suffers from an internal "bifurcation" or even, to push the psychoanalytic vocabulary one stage further, splitting: "between care for the Jews and an almost total disregard for the non-Jews or native Arab population."[12] Not only unjust, this splitting is self-defeating for the Israeli nation. In the eyes of the Arabs, Zionism becomes nothing other than an unfolding design "whose deeper roots in Jewish history and the terrible Jewish experience was necessarily obscured by what was taking place before their eyes."[13] Freud of course spoke of the "blindness of the seeing eye" (or, in the words of Jean-Luc Godard, "shut your eyes, and *see*"). Zionism, we could say, has done itself a major disservice. So fervently has it nourished the discrimination between Jew and non-Jew, the rationale for its dispossession of the Palestinians, that while it may have seized the earth, it has also snatched the grounds for understanding from beneath its own feet.

This is not, of course, an apology for Israel—that much must be clear. It is more that the Palestinian cause has been weakened by its failure to understand the *inner* force of what it is up against (as Lenin once famously remarked, you should always construct your enemy at its strongest point). The "internal cohesion and solidity" of Zionism have completely "eluded the understanding of Arabs."[14] As has the "intertwined terror and exultation" out of which it was born; or in other words, "what Zionism meant for the Jews."[15] It is the affective dimension, as it exerts its pressure historically, that has been blocked from view. You are analyzing a trauma—"an immensely traumatic Zionist effectiveness."[16] Terror, exultation, trauma—Zionism has the ruthlessness of the symptom (it is the symptom of its own success). Given this emphasis, your unexpected and rarely commented remarks on the "benevolent," "humanistic" impulse of Zionism toward its own people are even more striking (there is no one- or even two-dimensionality here). On the colonial nature of the venture and the cruel Orientalism of how the Arab people were treated and portrayed, you never ceased to insist. But what if the key to understanding the catastrophe for the Palestinians, of 1948 and after, were to be found in the love that the Jewish people—for historically explicable reasons—lavish on themselves?

We have entered the most stubborn and self-defeating psychic terrain, where a people can be loving and lethal, and their most exultant acts towards—and triumph over—an indigenous people expose them to the dangers they most fear. For it is not just of course that Israel's conduct has made it impossible for the Arabs to understand her, nor that Israel has been blind towards the Arabs (in fact never true), but that she sees things in the wrong place: "Everything that did stay to challenge Israel was viewed not as something *there*, but as something *outside* Israel and Zionism bent on its destruction—from the outside."[17] Israel is vulnerable because it cannot see the people who—whether in refugee camps on the borders (the putative Palestinian state), inside the country (the Israeli Arabs), or scattered all over the world (the Palestinian diaspora)—are in fact, psychically as well as politically *in its midst*.

Contrast this again, as you do repeatedly, with Israel as a nation for *all* Jewish people—this passionately inclusive, and violently excluding, embrace. Here time and place are infinite: "If every Jew in Israel represents 'the whole Jewish people'— which is a population made up not only of the Jews in Israel, but also of generations of Jews who existed in the past (of whom the present Israelis are the remnant) and those who exist in the future, as well as those who live elsewhere," then "Israel would not be simply the state of its citizens (which included Arabs of course) but the state of 'the whole Jewish people,' having a kind of sovereignty over land and peoples that no other state possessed or possesses."[18] This is in fact far worse than merely "two communities of uncommunicatingly separate suffering," which might suggest indifference or ignorance of a more straightforward kind. This is a historically embedded failure of vision—multiply determined, and with multiple, self-perpetuating effects. In these early readings, you delve into the past, telling all the parties that the main critical and political task is to understand how and why.

I realize now that my writing on Zionism is an extended footnote to your questions, an attempt to enter into the "terror and exultation" out of which Zionism was born, to grasp what you so aptly term the "immense traumatic effectiveness" of the Israeli nation-state. You mean, of course, traumatic for the Palestinians. I would add also for the Jews (exultation does not dispel fear). But I have also wanted to revive the early Jewish voices—Martin Buber, Hans Kohn, Hannah Arendt, and Ahad Haam, some of whom called themselves Zionists—who sounded the critique, uttered the warnings that have become all the more prescient today. Somewhere, I believe, Zionism had the self-knowledge for which Gramsci and, through him, you make your plea, although I know in the case of Buber and Arendt you feel they were not finally equal to their critique. Calling up these voices, torn from the pages of a mostly forgotten past, I like to think that—as well as rebuilding the legacy of my own Jewish history—I am also doing what you would have wanted, fulfilling a very personal demand from you to me.

We did not, of course, always agree. I am sure that, in the last analysis, you believed that entering the Zionist imagination might be risking one identification too far. "Are you writing an apology?" you once asked. I was preparing the Christian

Gauss seminars to be delivered in September 2003 under the title "The Question of Zion," a deliberate echo of, and my tribute to, *The Question of Palestine*. When I was writing them in the summer, you wanted to read them, but I needed to finish them first. "I might be able to help you," you said. It was July and we were sitting in your favorite London hotel with your son Wadie and his wife, Jennifer, arguing about Zionism while violins played their accompaniment to afternoon tea.

You were planning to attend the second lecture, but knowing by the time of my visit that you might not be well enough, I hurriedly e-mailed them to my neighbor here before I left so they could be sent to your personal assistant, Sandra Fahy, who was always so helpful, just in case. Then, as happens, something was wrong with the attachments, so they could not be sent when you asked for them. I arrived at your apartment clutching a rapidly photocopied version when I visited you on the Sunday four days before you died. Amongst many other things, we talked about the dreadful, deteriorating situation in Israel/Palestine—a decline that had so cruelly tracked your illness over the past decade. "I will read them this afternoon," you said at the end. You were admitted to the hospital the next day. It was, of course, the conversation I most wanted to have. I had held back in the blithe belief that our dialogue would be endless, that having defeated your illness so many, many times before, you would go on doing so forever. I will not have the gift of your response to the lectures. Which is doubtless why I have used this occasion to lift out of your work the inspiration and form of its imagining.

NOTES

This essay first appeared as "Edward Said: Continuing the Conversation," special issue, ed. W. J. T. Mitchell and Homi K. Bhabha, *Critical Inquiry* 31, no. 2 (Winter 2005); also in Jacqueline Rose, *The Last Resistance* (London: Verso, 2008).

1. Edward Said, "Sober Truths about Israel and Zionism," in *Peace and Its Discontents* (New York: Random House; London: Vintage, 1995).
2. Ibid., 126.
3. Ibid., 127.
4. Edward W. Said, "What People in the U.S. Know about Islam Is a Stupid Cliché," a 1992 interview with Hasan M. Jafri, in *Power, Politics, and Culture: Interviews with Edward W. Said*, ed. Gauri Viswanathan (London: Bloomsbury, 2004), 378–89.
5. Edward W. Said, *The Question of Palestine* (1979; repr. New York: Vintage Books, 1992), 112.
6. Edward W. Said, "A Conversation with Salman Rushdie" (1986), *The Politics of Dispossession: The Struggle for Palestinian Self-Determination, 1969–1994* (London: Random House, 1994).
7. Edward W. Said, "Bases for Coexistence" (1997), in *The End of the Peace Process: Oslo and After* (London: Granta, 2000), 208.
8. Edward W. Said, "Zionism from the Standpoint of Its Victims," in *The Question of Palestine*, 73.
9. Ibid.
10. Said, "Bases for Coexistence," 207.
11. Said, "What People in the U.S. Know about Islam," 378.

12. Said, "Zionism from the Standpoint of Its Victims," 83.
13. Ibid.
14. Ibid., 88.
15. Ibid., 60, 66.
16. Ibid., 83.
17. Ibid., 89.
18. Ibid., 104, 84.

19

Edward Said's Impact on Post-Zionist Critique in Israel

Ilan Pappe

Edward Said's general study of culture in the postcolonial era, along with his commitment to representing the Palestinian case wherever and whenever he could, informed his intellectual and public life. Something of this mixture and balance was also in his books. He will be remembered, and justly so, for *Orientalism* and *Culture and Imperialism*—twin works that shaped, nourished, and invigorated the fields of postcolonialism and cultural studies. But people in Palestine will remember more his various books on their country, the most important of which was probably *The Politics of Dispossession*. These short and lucid interventions, quite often immediate reactions to a recent crisis or juncture in the life of Palestine and the Palestinians, always placed the day's most pressing event, and Said's thoughts on it, within the march of history.[1]

Said's ability to move from a clear-sighted political position vis-à-vis the Palestine question to a theoretical insight on the interpretation of culture, while musing on his love for music and agonizing about the less pleasant chapters in his life—is beautifully demonstrated in his memoir, *Out of Place*, a rare historical document on an era in the eastern Mediterranean that is gone forever but that is vividly alive in Said's autobiography.

This intertwined interest in the world of the subalterns and in Palestine explains why Said influenced the academic scene in Israel as well. His inputs meshed well with the emergence in the 1990s of what I term elsewhere the "post-Zionist" movement and decade.[2] A movement that shook the social and human sciences in Israel, it began as a modest attempt to revisit the 1948 Zionist narrative. This "new history" of Israel, as it was called at the time, culminated in a scholarly internal Israeli deconstruction of the entire Zionist project and a severe academic critique of

Israeli policies since the creation of the state. Critical historians and sociologists focused in particular on the state's early policies toward the Palestinian minority and the Mizrahi Jews from Arab countries.

By 2000, many of these critical voices in Israel had subsided, and the academics who produced knowledge relevant to the present political predicaments reverted to eschewing the consensual interpretation of reality. For this reason, one cannot easily determine how significant or unique this chapter of Israeli history of ideas and ideologies is. It may prove to be a passing anecdote, as alas it seems now, or it may be the precursor of a more revolutionary future, if we wish to take a more optimistic view of the chances for peace and reconciliation in the torn land of Palestine.[3]

Whatever the future brings, we need to revisit those criticisms because they constitute the infrastructure for a different reality in Israel and Palestine. Taken together, they are simultaneously a critique of the past and a vision of the future. Thus, apart from stimulating a natural intellectual curiosity about them, they still carry potential that warrants reassessment.

Said's insights and writings played an instrumental role in the formulation of this local version of postcolonialist critique, especially the concrete deconstruction of the Zionist and Israeli scholarly writings that helped sustain it—such as the mainstream Israeli historiography and sociology of the Arab world at large and the Palestinians in particular. One can detect this impact in several major areas: the analysis of Israel as an "Orientalist" state, the examination of the dialectical relationship between power and academic knowledge within the local context, the introduction of the postcolonial prism into the study of the society, and the critique of the present peace process and the adoption of an alternative way forward.

THE ORIENTALIST STATE

Said's influence could be traced, albeit indirectly, as early as the first phase of the post-Zionist critique, that of the "new history" of the 1948 war. The new history corroborated the major Palestinian claims about the 1948 war, notably the claim of ethnic cleansing in that year. Some of the new historians argued that new archival material prompted their revisionist historiography. But they were clearly influenced by the comprehensive shift in attitudes toward non-Western historical perspectives, to which Said contributed more than anyone else. The legitimization process meant accepting the professional validity of the Palestinian narrative, or part of it, while exposing the ideological and polemical dimensions of Israeli historiography.[4]

After that first phase, critical energies were directed into the more contemporary history, during the early years of Israeli statehood in the 1950s. This critique deconstructed the mythological Israeli concept of a "melting-pot" Zionist society that had successfully integrated all the Jewish immigrants and indigenous Arab population into one modern nation. This modernizationist notion was debunked with the help of Said's own deconstruction of Orientalism. His work not only helped alert critics to the actual policies toward the Palestinian minority in Israel and the Jewish immigrants from Arab countries, but also to the examination of the crucial role played by local academia in sustaining and justifying these policies of discrimination and exclusion.

Said was not the exclusive influence, nor even a central one. The political developments that bred these criticisms took place over a twenty-year period that began in the early 1970s and culminated in the 1990s. Nonetheless, his input provided a coherent intellectual approach to articulate these challenges. His works helped readers translate their emotional response to the historical and contemporary evils in the Israel/Palestine conflict into an intellectual statement that questioned almost every foundational myth of the Jewish state.

The new research—as well as the intensive press and media coverage of it—was triggered by events in the 1970s. It began with the 1973 war, which inflicted the first cracks in Israel's wall of moral smugness and self-satisfaction. More importantly, in the relative calm that followed the war, tension grew between the "melting-pot" ideal of the founding fathers, on the one hand, and the tense reality within Israel's multicultural and multiethnic fabric, on the other. Social and cultural undercurrents of dissatisfaction and antagonism in Israeli society erupted in the early 1970s and swelled into a social protest movement against the evils the state inflicted on the deprived Jewish communities, mostly North African in origin. Young and vociferous activists tried to emulate African Americans' strategies of dissent and established in the early 1970s their equivalent of the Black Panther movement. The movement represented a social demand for a new and fairer distribution of the economic resources of the country and a share in the definition of its cultural identity. The protesters failed to move the Israeli Left but attracted the attention of the Right, which skillfully manipulated their protest into a mass movement that brought the right-wing leader, Menachem Begin, and his Likud party to power in 1977. The Israeli Left lost its natural constituency, but some of its supporters in the academy began identifying more closely with the causes of the deprived groups within the society throughout the years.[5]

The Mizrahi protest movement was an internal social affair, and as such, it engaged the interest of sociologists. They were not content with concrete research on the early chapters of the state's history; they were equally intrigued by the theoretical and methodological implications of the development of a social protest movement in Israel. The Mizrahi social protest movement coincided with a growing sense of national assertiveness among the Palestinians in Israel, and its case gave strength to others who felt excluded from the Zionist historical narrative and whose chronicles had been distorted in schools and university curricula.

From the late 1970s onward, academics, with the help of historical or sociological research, represented the cause of all the deprived groups as scientifically valid.

They were less successful as political agents of change in Israel: their attempt to tie together, as they did in their research, the plight of Palestinians, Mizrahi Jews, and women (as a minority group) to create a joint political front was a total political failure. Its message, however, remained a popular vision for the more hopeful members of the academic protest movement. These developments matured after the 1982 Lebanon war. The public debate about that war seemed to encourage novelists, filmmakers, playwrights, musicians, poets, artists, and journalists to jointly construct a non-Zionist interpretation of the past and contemporary realities.

The theoretical basis for the critical sociology in the 1970s and 1980s was Marxist, whereas that of the 1990s was more postcolonial in orientation. More than anything else, the Saidian critique of Orientalism in its various media appealed to Israeli academics who sought an intellectual departure point, beyond the Marxist one that had characterized the first critical wave of the 1970s. The focus moved from economic means of production and social deprivations to questions of ethnicity, race, and nation. The subject matter was the new identity of the Jews as reformulated after they had moved into Palestine as part of the colonialist era and project. The only way to define a Jew was by describing him or her as a non-Arab. Much as Said claims in *Orientalism*, the Orient helped to define Europe, and the West, as its ultimate opposite—in perception, in ideas, in personality, and in the experience. This statement by itself inspired a critical survey, mainly by Mizrahi and Palestinian scholars in Israel, of state and society attitudes in the 1950s.[6] This reformulation of identity informed the attitude toward Palestinians, wherever they were, and created the biggest problem possible for the nascent Jewish state when it prodded one million Arab Jews to immigrate because of its failure to bring enough Jews from Europe after the Holocaust. How would a Jew be defined? The particular Orientalist praxis and discourse in Israel solved the dilemma by de-Arabizing those Jews.

The Jewish immigrants from Arab countries were de-Arabized upon arrival in order to fit the Zionist dream of an ethnic Jewish state, but they were at the same time pushed to the social and geographical margins of society.[7] This confusion of identity explains the great paradox that has accompanied their lives since their arrival: although most of the right-wing electorate comes from these communities— and with it a racist and hostile attitude toward everything Arab—its members are still seeking their Arab roots in culture and tradition as the best form of protest against the Ashkenazi establishment that perpetuated their deprivation and frustration. The deconstruction of their socialization in the early years of statehood and exposure of the Israelis' exclusion of everything and everyone suspected of being "Arab" owed much to Said's remarks on the issue of victimization in his works.

But Said provided also a clue to the role played by Israeli academia in this policy of abuse and discrimination. The Orientalist paradigm needed not only policy makers but also experts. "The interchange between the academic and the more or less imaginative meanings of Orientalism is a constant one, and since the late eighteenth century there has been a considerable, quite disciplined—perhaps even regulated—traffic between the two," wrote Said in *Orientalism*.[8] The Israeli academy, sociologists and anthropologists—loyal to modernization theories and counting themselves as "experts" on Arab affairs—together with the local Orientalists, provided the scholarly scaffolding for the aggressive and coercive policies toward Palestinians and any Jews who came from Arab countries.

Not only had the Israeli academy developed an Orientalist interpretation of reality, the state as a whole adopted such a self-image. To this day, and more so after the American occupation of Iraq, the state of Israel sells itself as a deciphering agent for the West in general and the United States in particular. The state, which is in the area but not part of it, claims to understand the secrets of the "barbaric" and "enigmatic" Middle East. This self-presentation is the principal explanation for, and the mechanism for perpetuating, its alienating existence in the midst of the Arab world.

Perhaps Theodore Herzl's vision of Israel best represents the Orientalist dimension of the state: "There (in Palestine) we shall be a sector of the wall of Europe against Asia, we shall serve as the outpost of civilization against barbarism."[9]

POWER AND KNOWLEDGE

As we have seen, the challenge for critical sociologists in 1990, inspired by global and theoretical developments in the humanities, was postcolonial in nature. These scholars echoed the disenchantment among Western academics with the fallacies and illusions created by "enlightenment," "modernity," and other Western concepts signifying the triumph of science and logic over the non-Western world's "uncivilized" notions. The Israeli challengers adopted the more skeptical approach to truth and data, particularly truth and data within a national context that emanated from the elite and the court academicians serving this power structure. Israeli academia is an integral part of Western academia, so it is not surprising that historians and sociologists in Israel adopted a Western interdisciplinary, skeptical, and subjective view toward their own history. It allowed them, as academicians, to represent the Palestinian, the Mizrahi, and the feminist side of the local history, much as American scholars wished to represent the multicultural reality in U.S. society.

The critical sociologists did not simply challenge the "facts" in their predecessors' work. They also felt the need to reassess the basic paradigms these scholars employed. They pointed to a contradiction between mainstream Israeli scholars' contribution to nation building and the university's mandate to promote critical and pluralistic research. The critical sociologists were a more diverse group than the new historians. Some were more relativistic; some were more anti-Zionist. Probably for the sake of convenience, several people, including me, labeled themselves "post-Zionists."

Common to all these challenges was the underlying assumption that collective memory officially was constructed through the educational system and the media. In most articles and books, the major and opening reference was to Said's *Orientalism* and later to *Culture and Imperialism*. His insights into these issues helped these scholars expose the role the academic establishment played in the nation-building process, at the expense of freedom of thought and self-criticism. History and memory became an act of exclusion as much as tool of inclusion. Hence the new focus was very much in the footsteps of Said's voyage into the symbols and manifestations of the Orientalist discourse in European culture: official texts, museums, ceremonies, school curricula, and national emblems drew the academic community's attention to the way in which the dominant Ashkenazi group and its narrative had excised others from national memory. As Said said in his essay "Reflections on Exile," "All nationalisms have their founding fathers, their basic quasi-religious texts, their rhetoric of belonging, their historical and geographical landmarks, their official enemies and heroes."[10]

In proper Saidian manner, these works exposed the sociological, anthropological, and historiographical discourses used in research on "Arabs"—whether Israeli Palestinians, inhabitants of neighboring Arab states, or Mizrahi Jews. The act of grouping Arabs, Palestinians, and Oriental Jews as one subject matter in scholarly research in Israel was a revolution by itself. This step could take place only through the adoption of the critical paradigm of Orientalism offered by Said. In fact, for years such grouping or reification was taboo, as one of the first scholars to adopt this approach—Ella Habiba Shohat—learned when condemnation by her peers forced her to leave the Israeli academy.[11]

In a fruitful dialogue with Said, Shohat debunked the Zionist myth that Israel had saved the Arab Jews and laid open the dominant discourse in the academy that presented the Mizrahim and the Arabs in much the same way that Orientalist discourses in the West presented the Orient.[12]

In her footsteps, many scholars began to preface their critical examination of policies toward, and representations of, Mizrahi Jews and Palestinian Israelis by acknowledging a theoretical background based on Said's works. From there, the road was short to a bolder definition of Israeli society as an "Orientalist" one.[13]

Said's forays, inspired by Michel Foucault's works, into the dialectics and problematique of power and knowledge were attempted again in the 1990s by a new generation of Israelis that won the admiration of Said himself.[14] More directly, his particular interest in the memorialization of the Holocaust and the Nakba emboldened researchers to follow his call for a universalization of the Holocaust memory, both as a critique on the Zionist manipulation of that memory and as a rejection of the Holocaust-denial tendencies in the Arab and Palestinian worlds. Both Palestinian and Jewish scholars expanded his basic ideas, aired for the first time in *The Politics of Dispossession*. These ideas inspired me and others to look into the dialectical relationship and to connect both sides' memories of the Nakba and the Holocaust.[15]

As Said wrote in *The Politics of Dispossession*,

> What Israel does to the Palestinians it does against a background, not only of the long-standing Western tutelage over Palestine and Arabs ... but also against a background of an equally long-standing and equally unfaltering anti-Semitism that in this century produced the Holocaust of the European Jews. We cannot fail to connect the horrific history of anti-Semitic massacres to the establishment of Israel; nor can we fail to understand the depth, the extent and the overpowering legacy of its suffering and despair that informed the postwar Zionist movement. But it is no less appropriate for Europeans and Americans today, who support Israel because of the wrong committed against the Jews to realize that support for Israel has included, and still includes, support for the exile and dispossession of the Palestinian people.[16]

Another example of Said's direct impact was his presentation of the concept of a "historical document." On several occasions, more so orally than in writing, Said related directly to the historian's workshop on this topic. When moderating a meeting between Israeli and Palestinian historians in Paris in 1998, Said explained in a few sentences, and in a very patient voice, to the attentive public at large, and to the less attentive Israeli historians in particular, his definition of a historical document. The Israeli historians expressed their almost religious belief that their approach was both ideologically and empirically just and declared that the only reliable sources for the reconstruction of the 1948 war were in the Israeli Defense Forces archives. Said pointed out that a report by a soldier from 1948 is as much an interpretation, and quite often a manipulation, of the reality of the war as any other human recollection of it; no recollection can be the reality itself. He wanted his listeners to grasp the vitality and significance of oral history in the reconstruction of the past. A full understanding of the most horrific aspects of the Nakba—the dozens of massacres that accompanied the Israeli ethnic cleansing of Palestine in 1948—and the expellee's experience of expulsion is possible only when the investigator adopts such a historiographical position.[17]

Attendees also addressed the question of positionality at that meeting, going beyond the theoretical debate and vague deconstructive discourse. Said was at his best, because he was able to articulate what others felt but were unable to express in a meaningful manner. He wondered aloud how anyone could relate to the Nakba's essence—as the most traumatic catastrophe that befell the Palestinian people—without showing even a modicum of solidarity with or sympathy for its victims (he directed this comment particularly to Benny Morris). Showing his typical foresight, he already knew in 1998 what the world learned in 2000—that Morris was a racist historian who stumbled on the 1948 catastrophe, did not like what he found, and then sought to justify the Israeli war crimes. As Said noted, Israeli historians would not have tolerated such a treatment of Holocaust history.

POSTCOLONIALISM IN ISRAEL

In the spring of 2002, there were enough Israeli scholars of postcolonialism to put together a special issue of *Theory and Criticism* on the topic.[18] The issue's title, "The Postcolonial Gaze," was a tricky way to describe scholarship in a state that is still colonialist in many of its policies and characteristics. Indeed, some of the articles spoke more to an anticolonialist agenda than to a postcolonialist one. Thus, a brilliant and pioneering deconstruction of the Israeli Orientalist discourse can still be seen as part of a colonialist rather than a postcolonialist reality, as can any of the other works that expose with Saidian zeal colonialist scenes in the local literature, poetry, and cinema.[19]

Postcolonialism seems to be a more apt categorization when Jewish women and the Mizrahi Jews are the focus of this scholarly interest. Work on the subject includes intriguing analyses of the way the Mizrahi Jews are manipulated into adopting racist positions toward the Palestinians and everything Arab, an almost self-destructive journey.[20]

Also appropriate is the connection Said made between cultural and postcolonial studies that illuminate one of the most important devices in making the state of Israel a state of denial. In particular, he explored the possibilities for dialogue between colonizers and the colonized as part of a restorative process of reconciliation. The first step in such a peaceful dialogue—and away from the alternative of an explosive violent clash over, and because of, history—was to acknowledge past evils.[21] This seemingly elementary observation was ignored by all the powers and individuals involved in peacemaking in Palestine, whose vision of peace was total absolution for Israel for its crimes in 1948 and ever after.

Said's journeys into the juncture between cultural and postcolonial studies produced another intriguing echo in Israeli local studies. His interest, which comes to the forefront most clearly in *Culture and Imperialism,* was in locating the points of ambiguity where the oppressors and the victimizers are also oppressed and victimized. A victim can become a victimizer. This idea inspired an ambivalent Mizrahi position, which is that a social protest of Mizrahi Jews can be simultaneously supportive of, and subversive toward, the hegemonic Zionist discourse.

This rather rough dichotomy between anticolonialist and postcolonialist tendencies in the critique can be found in Said's retrospective assessment of his work (mainly in the introduction he wrote for the thirtieth-anniversary edition of *Orientalism*). He came to see the concept of Orientalism as both a concrete act of colonialist representation, anchored in a particular period, and a discursive practice, free of place or time. (The latter is indeed the direction in which postcolonialist studies developed after, and as a criticism of, Said's dichotomous approach but is not part of this analysis.)

In this area, a curious, quite parochial, yet potentially significant internal Israeli debate arose between self-appointed "Saidians" and "Bhabhaians" (supporters of Homi Bhabha's criticism of Said). On one side of the divide are post-Zionists who find Bhabha's hybrid approach to intercultural meetings sufficient for describing and analyzing the Israeli situation. For this group, Bhabha provides an alternative to the view that colonialism is an oppressive force in Israel and Palestine. As in Bhabha's general assessment, it depicts the colonialist era as a meeting ground for different cultures with varieties of interactions. On the other side of the debate is the more critical "Saidian" school, almost Fanonian in spirit, which may accept the hybrid perspective as a possible prescription for the future, as did Said in *Culture and Imperialism*, but views the past as everything but a benign meeting point of cultures.[22]

Yehuda Shenhav and Hanan Hever, who are Bhabhaians of a sort, clearly and intriguingly articulate this stance in their latest local publication, *Mizrachim in Israel*. Their impulse seems to be to extract the Mizrahi Jews from the slot of victimization; the prize, however, is an inevitable softening of their critique of Zionism. They are criticized by Sami Shalom Shitrit, who claims that Bhabha's main impulse was to allow comfortable life to those non-Western individuals, especially intellectuals, who have tired of the struggle and retreated to life under the present phase of "white racism." Shitrit's view may apply to post-Zionism today.

Although the principal problem in Israel seems to be a matter of distinction, most researchers, including those whose territory is philosophy, such as Ilan Gur-Zeev, do not seem to distinguish between Said and Bhabha and lump the post-Zionists together as "postcolonialists," whom they see as too nationalistic. However, they do not seem to place liberal Zionism in this category.[23]

For this reason, we should be thankful to Ella Shohat, who articulated better than anyone the different and conflicting implications of these stances for the local Israeli context. In *Israeli Cinema: East/West and the Politics of Representation* (1989), she distinguished between hybridity, contradiction, and ambivalence. By viewing the Eurocentric cinematic scene in Israel through the Saidian prism, she concluded that hybridity is hardly present in the Israeli cultural media that deal with the past or the present realities. However, contradiction and ambivalence seem to dominate the scene. In her essay in this volume, Shohat examines the Saidian, Bhabhaian, and other prisms' trajectory from their places of origins, so to speak, to Israel. She is not as bitter as Shitrit is, but she is equally critical of what she sees as a liberal Zionist tendency to adopt hybridity to avoid a clear-cut confrontation with the colonialist conditions in Israel. On the one hand, she accuses post-Zionists of mistranslating Said's view onto the Israeli reality; on the other, she ridicules them for trying, and failing, to bridge the general postcolonial position and Zionism. How can the term *hybridity* or indeed *postcolonial* fit the land of partitions and walls? wonders Shohat.[24]

THE PAST IN THE SERVICE OF THE PRESENT

In pure, indeed crude, ideological terms, post-Zionism was not a viable position. However, it was a fitting tool for describing a certain trend in cultural production. This trend could also be defined politically as an academic input colored by anti-Zionism, with varying degrees of conviction. As such, the academic research separated the "post-Zionist" scholars, as citizens, from their natural political habitat in Israel, the Peace Now or peace-camp milieu. Because the signifier in Israeli politics is one's position toward the areas that Israel occupied in 1967, the only thing that the Peace Now movement—the largest exparliamentary movement on the left— could offer was an agenda for Israeli withdrawal from the West Bank and the Gaza Strip. The Israeli Zionist peace movement did not challenge the mainstream positions on the essence of Zionism, the 1948 war, or the Orientalist attitude. Post-Zionist scholarship debunked the mythology not only of the state but also of the Zionist Left. Hence the post-Zionists could identify with the Saidian vision for the future of Palestine. Like Said, they treated the concrete questions of the peace process through their postcolonialist deconstruction of the present reality.

In this realm, one can find direct references to Said's singular critique of the Oslo peace process starting in 1993. Post-Zionist scholars shared Said's critique of the "new Middle East" scenario that accompanied the Oslo Accords and the pax Americana of the 1990s. Like him, they saw the process as new, softer, and nicer, clothing for the self-presentation of Israel as an Orientalist country in the area.

The major publication for the post-Zionist critique in Israel is the journal *Theory and Criticism* published by the Van-Leer Institute in Jerusalem. Since its launch in 1993, it has devoted much of its energy to connecting deconstructive theories with local case studies. From the beginning, Said's inputs influenced this journal considerably. Whether the studies it publishes focus on Zionism as colonialism, the treatment of Mizrahim or Palestinians in various historical periods, or the general questions of representation, power, and knowledge, they all in one way or another acknowledge his inspiration.

But I would like to highlight two other venues where he will be remembered as an intellectual who breathed new life into a stagnating industry of knowledge production. One is the Israeli Oriental Society. Its organ, *Ha-Mizrach Ha-Hadash* (The New East), in one of its recent issues paid tribute to the lessons that Israeli Orientalists could have, but did not, learn from his works.[25] This publication is a voice in the wilderness within the Israeli Orientalist establishment—still very much part of the security and military complex but nonetheless a novel and fresh voice.

The other venue is monthly meetings in Ramallah by a group of Israeli and Palestinian historians and sociologists who have taken encouragement from Said's conceptualization of reconciliation through the rewriting of history. The group, known today as PALISAD, the Palestine Israel Academic Dialogue, has been meeting since 1997 and is still active, although meeting under the present circumstances in Ramallah is far more difficult than in the past. The meetings are inspired by theoretical inputs—such as subjectivity, reflexivity, positionality, and contextualization—in an attempt to find bridging narratives into the past that might provide a basis for building a different future. No scholar could even have ventured such thoughts without Said's works and, no less important, without the personal connection many of the participants had with him throughout the years. Should they succeed, their achievement would be a fitting monument to his intellectual contribution.[26]

NOTES

1. Edward W. Said, *The Politics of Dispossession: The Struggle for Palestinian Self-Determination, 1969–1994* (London: Chatto and Windus, 1994).

2. Ilan Pappe, "The Post-Zionist Critique; Part 1: The Academic Debate," *Journal of Palestine Studies* 26, no. 2 (Winter 1997): 29–41.

3. Ilan Pappe, "The Post-Zionist Discourse in Israel, 1991–2001," *Holy Land Studies* 1, no. 1 (2002): 3–20.

4. This process of legitimizing non-Western perspectives was inspired by Edward W. Said, *The Question of Palestine* (New York: Vintage Books, 1980), which appeared later in Hebrew.

5. The works are summarized and analyzed in Hanan Hever, Yehouda Shenhav, and Pnina Motzafi Haller, *Mizrachim Be-Israel, Iyun Mehudash (Mizrahim in Israel: A Critical Observation into Israel's Ethnicity)* (Jerusalem: Van Leer Institute, 2002), in Hebrew.

6. The best example of this new focus is one of the first works on the subject: Yerach Gover, *Zionism: The Limits of Moral Discourse in Israeli Hebrew Fiction* (Minneapolis: University of Minnesota Press, 1994).

7. Ella Shohat, "Sepharadim in Israel: Zionism from the Standpoint of Its Jewish Victims," in *Dangerous Liaisons: Gender, Nation and Post-Colonial Perspectives*, ed. A. McClintock, A. Mufti, and E. Shohat (Minneapolis: University of Minnesota Press, 2002); and in *Social Text* 19–20: 1–35.

8. In Edward W. Said, *Orientalism* (London: Verso, 1978), 3.

9. Quoted in Paul-Mendes Flohr and Judah Rienhartz, eds., *The Jew in the Modern World: A Documentary History* (New York: Oxford University Press, 1995), 350.

10. Edward W. Said, *Reflections on Exile and Other Essays* (Cambridge, MA: Harvard University Press, 2002), 40–42.

11. Ella Shohat, *Zichronot Asurim (Forbidden Reminiscences; A Collection of Articles)* (Tel-Aviv: Keshet Ha-Mizrach, 2001), 5–11, in Hebrew.

12. Ella Shohat, "Columbus and the Arab Jews: Toward a Relational Approach to Community Identity," in *Cultural Identity and the Gravity of History: Reflections on the Work of Edward Said*, ed. K. Ansell-Pearson, B. Parry, and J. Squires (New York: Lawrence and Wishart, 1997), 88–105.

13. The most recent work on the subject pays such a tribute to Said; see Sami Shalom Shitrit, *Hamavak Hamzirachi Be-Israel; Bein Dikuy le-Shihrur, Bein Hizdahut le-alternativa (The Mizrachi Struggle in Israel: Between Oppression and Liberation, Identification and Alternative, 1948–2003)* (Tel-Aviv: Am Oved, 2004), in Hebrew.

14. Said, special preface to the Hebrew Edition of *Orientalism* (Tel Aviv: Am Oved, 2000).

15. Ilan Gur-Zeev and Ilan Pappe, "Beyond the Deconstruction of the Other's Collective Memory: Blueprints for Palestinian/Israeli Dialogue," *Theory, Culture & Society* 20, no. 1 (February 2003): 93–108.

16. Said, *The Politics of Dispossession,* 34.

17. Edward W. Said, *The End of the Peace Process: Oslo and After* (New York: Vintage Books, 2001), 273–77.

18. Yehouda Shenhav, ed., "The Postcolonial Gaze," special issue, *Theory and Criticism* 20 (Spring 2002), in Hebrew.

19. For just two examples, see Anat Rimon-Or, "From Silence to Voice: 'Death to the Arabs' in Contemporary Israeli Culture," ibid., 23–56; and Gil Eyal, "Dangerous Liaisons: The Relations between Military Intelligence," ibid., 137–64.

20. Yehouda Shenhav and Hanan Hever, introduction, "The Postcolonial Gaze," ibid., 9–22.

21. Edward W. Said, *Culture and Imperialism* (London: Vintage, 1994).

22. For an example of the Bhabhaian viewpoint, see Nir Baram, "Kishalon Hamahpecha Ha-Mizrachit" ("The Failure of the Mizrachi Revolution"), *Ma'ariv,* 24 March 2003; for an example of the Saidian view, see Sami Shalom Shitrit, "Hearot la Hevdelim Bein 'Orientalism' le 'Hiberidiyut,'" ("Notes on the Difference between Orientalism and Hybridity"), 28 March 2003, www.kedma.co.il (accessed 10 August 2009).

23. Ilan Gur-Zeev, *Moderniyut, Post-Moderniyut ve-Hinuch (Modernity, Post-Modernity and Education)* (Tel-Aviv: Ramot, 1999), in Hebrew.

24. Ella Shohat, "The 'Postcolonial' in Translation: Reading Said in Hebrew," ch. 20 of this volume.

25. This tribute was due to the appointment of a new editor, Haim Gerber, who recognized Said's importance.

26. I have coedited a book on PALISAD that will soon appear in English: Ilan Pappe and Jamil Hilal, eds., *Across the Wall: The Palestinian-Israeli Academic Dialogue* (London: I. B. Tauris, 2010).

20

The "Postcolonial" in Translation

Reading Said in Hebrew

Ella Shohat

This essay focuses on the "travel" of various debates—Orientalism, postcolonialism, postzionism—between the U.S. and Israel, between one institutional zone and another. Through a comparative history of these critical intellectual debates, I consider key moments and issues in the "translation" of Said's ideas into Hebrew. The essay considers the reception of Said's work in its contradictory dimensions, especially in liberal-leftist circles, where the desire to go beyond Said offers some ironic twists. Among the issues it examines are the nature of the "post" in the concepts of the "post-colonial" and "post-Zionism," the problem of "hybridity" and "resistance" in the land of partitions and walls, and the mediation in Israel, via the Anglo-American academy, of the "subaltern" intellectual.

Although Edward Said's ideas have traveled through many worlds, writing about his work as a "traveling theory" requires a sense of cross-border mediation and translation, as ideas are hybridized, resisted, contained, and recontextualized. Here I focus on one form of such "travel," that between the United States and Israel, a situation where the receiving space for Said's ideas is a nation-state whose very foundation engendered his exile. When Said invokes the right of return to that place—with the state possessing the power not only to authorize or deny his return but also to oversee the circulation of his texts about displacement—then the question of his "out-of-placeness" becomes even more fraught. While my hope in this publication in honor of Said would have been to tell a purely celebratory tale of Said's pervasive influence on Israeli intellectual life, the highly charged space of Zionism and Israel, and my own intricate positioning, make that task rather complicated. Beginning in the 1980s, my work initiated a conversation with Said's critique of Orientalism by examining the politics of representation in Zionist histo-riographical discourse and Israeli cultural practices.[1]

The hostile reception of that work in Israel, I think, was partly related to its as-sociation with Said's work and even to my own closeness to Said. In those pre-Oslo days, dialogue between Israelis and Palestinians was literally and legally taboo, de-clared out of bounds by the "only democracy in the Middle East." I want to clarify at the outset, then, that I write as one personally involved in the "translation" of Said's thought into Hebrew. One leftist reviewer of my work compared both Said and myself, in our supposedly naive admiration of the Western "intellectual appa-ratus," to the "miserable nigger, the victim of colonization, who licks his lips in ex-citement at the gold buttons and colorful glass beads offered by the cunning white merchant."[2] This rather amusing reproach of our "inauthenticity" as "spokesper-sons for the Third World" appeals to the old colonial trope of mimicry while pro-jecting the East/West dichotomy onto intellectuals whose biography and analysis clearly refuse that dichotomy. What interests me here, then, is the shuttling back and forth of Said's work between one site of political semantics and another. Here I consider some symptomatic moments and issues in this cross-border movement, asking when and which of Said's texts have been stamped with an entry visa to Is-rael, which were permitted to settle, and which had to be smuggled in or even forced to wander in a laissez-passer "no man's land."

POSTCOLONIAL STUDIES GOES
TO WASHINGTON (VIA TEL AVIV)

For well over a decade, "postcolonial studies" has been highly visible even beyond academe. Said's preeminence in the postcolonial field, however, seemed discon-nected from the Israel/Palestine debates, where Said's name was also prominent. The animosity generated in the wake of Said's "trilogy"—*Orientalism, The Question of Palestine,* and *Covering Islam*—reached its paroxysm when panicked critics as-signed him the hyperbolic label of "professor of terror." In the post–September 11 landscape, the Orientalist Right found the time opportune to reconquer what had earlier been "their" ivory towers. They could now enjoy a powerful observation post as self-anointed monarchs surveying these "un-American" activities. A highly vis-ible coalition of (anti-Semitic) Christian fundamentalists, neocon Zionists, and cul-turalist Orientalists united to bring academia, allegedly taken hostage by "tenured radicals," back into the warm embrace of Western values. In the June 2003 con-gressional hearings on Title VI, Stanley Kurtz of the *National Review* denounced the usual critical Middle Eastern studies scholars, Said most prominently.[3] What was most striking, however, was the new focus on a different academic discipline—postcolonial studies. Postcolonial theory, which emerged as a prestigious field of inquiry in the late 1980s and which had generally escaped the institutional backlash directed at the revisionist historians and radical multiculturalists, for the first time began to "scan" on the neocon radar.

I do not mean to imply, of course, that the neocons have suddenly become devout exegetes of postcolonial texts. These critics are not in the least conversant with the anti-colonial writings and poststructuralist theories—intellectual currents at the heart of Said's contribution—that shaped the field of inquiry that came to be called "postcolonial studies," in which *Orientalism* has constituted a key text. Said's intervention, to my mind, forms part of a larger epochal shift in academia that began in the late 1960s, at a time of the emergence of ethnic studies and women's studies programs and the academic formation of diverse critical areas of inquiry such as Marxism, Third Worldism, and feminism. During the same period, area studies programs began to bypass or reject the post–World War II vision of scholarship promoted by the U.S. Defense Department in the service of cold war geopolitics. Since the 1970s, Latin American studies had been producing an impressive corpus of work critical of neocolonial policies and imperial discourses. The writings of figures such as Fanon, Galleano, Frank, Dorfman, Schiller, and Mattelart played a crucial role, becoming a kind of lingua franca in progressive circles. In Middle Eastern studies, meanwhile, critical scholars—many of whom contributed to *Middle East Report* and the *Journal of Palestine Studies*—were politically and intellectually allied with Said's critique of Orientalism, which helped transform the field of Middle Eastern studies itself. Although the paradigm shift in Middle Eastern studies came later, it was more publicly contested, especially as a battery of well-oiled foundations and institutes began to take aim at the entire field.

In his exposé, Kurtz accuses postcolonial studies in general of "undermining America's security," yet all the scholars that he denounces from within this vast field "happen" to work on the Middle East.[4] Moreover, his claim that "postcolonial theory" forms the ruling intellectual paradigm in academic area studies (especially Middle Eastern studies)[5] is simply mistaken, for although poststructuralist methodologies are widely practiced in literature departments, they form only a minor presence in Middle Eastern studies departments. By singling out Middle Eastern studies, then, critics could target both the territory and the author, providing the missing link that turned postcolonial studies into the public enemy of the day. At last the new guardian angels could meaningfully tie together the two strands of "Said's double career," to cite a 1989 *Commentary* piece, "as literary scholar and ideologue of terrorism," whose "spilling of ink" was deemed akin to "the spilling of blood."[6] This long and winding road to postcolonial studies passes partly via Jerusalem, or better, Tel Aviv. Said's reception in Israel has varied over the years, in some ways allegorizing the shifting state of the debates about the conflict. Said's entry into media visibility during the First Intifada came in the form of virulent attacks. Israel's largest daily, *Yedi'ot Aharonot*, accused U.S.-based Palestinian professors like Said of "taking control" of the TV screen, luring naïve image-obsessed Americans to side with Palestinian views through a new *trompe l'oeil*. In a new twist on the old anti-Semitic motif of the Jewish chameleon hiding his innate outsiderness by impersonating "normal" Europeans, the critics charged Said with hiding terrorist intent behind a Western-style mask.[7] The recent attempts by campus patrollers to intimidate scholars challenging the Israeli official line can be traced to this earlier anxiety that new Palestinian "public relations techniques" might provoke a shift in American views. With a direct pipeline to the White House, then, well-endowed research institutes could now threaten to teach a lesson to straying academics.

In a verbatim Hebrew recycling of the Kurtz tirade, the *Ma'ariv* journalist Ben-Dror Yemini, who opposes the occupation, praised Campus Watch and called for a withdrawal of government subsidies for anti-Israeli academics within Israel.[8] Yemini proclaimed that the Middle East Studies Association's recognition of the "guru" Said was "one of the biggest bluffs of Middle Eastern studies" and linked it to Arab funding, further blaming Said for the "silencing of alternative voices" such as those of Fouad Ajami and Bernard Lewis.[9] Acquiring the aura of a prophet in the wake of the Second Intifada and 9/11, Lewis was said to have predicted the unfolding culture clash and thus the collapse of Said's thesis in *Orientalism*. Asked by *Ha'aretz* whether he would recommend *Orientalism* to the Hebrew student, Lewis responded, "Only if the student is interested in the pathology of American campus life"; otherwise, the "book lacks value."[10] Meanwhile, Tel Aviv University professor Shimon Shamir suggested in his review of Martin Kramer's *Ivory Towers on Sand* that Orientalists from Lewis's school had been "completely marginalized by Saidism . . . haunted by the orientalist label, treated with a mixture of condemnation and disdain." Shamir praises Kramer for addressing the "damage" caused by the Saidian "take-over" of U.S. Middle Eastern studies. He also raises the issue of whether Israeli Middle Eastern studies are guilty of the same charge made by Kramer against their U.S. counterparts but quickly reassures readers that in Israel these departments are "well anchored in scientific disciplines," without "the same militant slide toward anti-Orientalism." Shamir does, however, criticize Kramer for ignoring the positive Saidian contribution to the rejection of essentialism.[11]

Emmanuel Sivan, meanwhile, argues in his 1985 book that *Orientalism* lent credence to the "all-embracing smear of the West" and to the "glorification of the East," attributing to Said the very East-West dichotomy that he had so painstakingly disassembled.[12] Sivan further accuses Said of essentialism, even as he himself demonstrates epidermic essentialism by enlisting the Arab identity of Said's critics as proof against Said. Another scholar, Avi Bareli, dismisses the Saidian "analytical method" as offering only a "moralizing approach," whose main objective is to "catch" and categorically condemn "the crook" rather than understand "the historical processes."[13] Such critics evoke Said's name in tandem with their critique of postzionist historians and sociologists. The reception of Said's work in Israel, then, has taken place within an institutional context largely shaped by Orientalist-Zionist ideologies. As in the United States, it was not so much Said's study of French and British Orientalism of the colonial past (albeit relevant to the present) that provoked the backlash; rather it was the book's implications for a critique of Zionist discourse, especially when that discourse was mobilized to defend Israel's current policies.

WRITING SAID IN HEBREW

Israeli Orientalists had assailed *Orientalism* long before the Hebrew edition saw the light of day in August 2000, a full twenty-two years after the original English version.[14] Despite this legacy of hostility, by the time the book was published by the establishment press Am Oved, it engendered quite a few celebratory media interviews with Said.[15] The book is now being taught in various Israeli university departments, largely by self-designated leftist professors, some identifying with the label of "post-Zionism," some with "Zionism," and a few with "non-" or "anti-Zionism."[16] More recently, the translation of Said's memoir, *Out of Place*, generated both accusatory and favorable reviews.[17] Yet it remains unacknowledged that Said's *The Question of Palestine* had already been published in Hebrew in 1981, soon after its appearance in English, and that earlier that year the literary quarterly *Siman Kri'a* published Said's essay "Zionism from the Standpoint of Its Victims."[18]

Defining Said's essay as "controversial," *Siman Kri'a*'s editors, many associated with Peace Now, included within the same issue a response titled "Zionism, Its Palestinian Victim and the Western World" by the historian of Zionism Yigal Elam. While Ronald Aronson's response to the same Said essay in *Social Text*, where it was originally published in English, highlighted the Holocaust,[19] Elam privileged the putative responsibility of Palestinians themselves for their own dislocation: "The Palestinian nationalist movement made a severe mistake when it initiated violent confrontation with Zionism," because it was "not ready to pay the price of diplomatic compromise." Like many liberal Zionists in the wake of 1977, Elam acknowledges in the piece that "occupation corrupts" but denies any colonial dimension to Zionism. He concludes with a rush to defend "the West": " 'Nationalism,' 'state,' 'democracy,' 'self-definition,' 'citizenship,' 'equal rights,' 'secular culture,' 'sovereignty,'—all are rooted in a Western context . . . It is the West that supplies the only terminological context to solve the Israeli-Palestinian conflict, since even the PLO formula of a 'democratic secular state' comes out of the political philosophy of the West."[20]

This unthinking equation of the West and democracy came four decades after the advent, in the very heart of Europe, not only of the Holocaust but also of the fascism of Hitler, Mussolini, Franco, and Pétain, and just two decades after French colonialism's brutal war in Algeria. Furthermore, such historians do not take on the critique of the Eurocentric premises of Zionist discourse, which shaped Zionist practices in Palestine. In fact, the Israeli peace camp's investment in the Enlightenment narrative of the "West" is fundamental to its vision of itself, constituting at once an ontological apologia and an identity marker; consequently, this narrative has played a pivotal role in the reception of Said's work.[21]

The Question of Palestine, meanwhile, was published by the now-defunct non-profit press Mifras, some of whose associates were linked to the anti-Zionist group Matzpen.[22] Mifras published a few critical Hebrew writers[23] and translated a number of works by Arab and other Third World writers, including Ghassan Kanafani's Men in the Sun, Paulo Freire's Pedagogy of the Oppressed, Henri Curiel's On the Altar of Peace, Ali Mazrui's The African Condition, Abu Iyad's My Home My Land, and Emile Habiby's The Pessoptimist. "Despite the daily focus on the complications of the Israeli-Arab conflict," the mission statement declared, "there hardly exists in Hebrew literatures that open a window to a deep and critical understanding of Arab society and individuals." Mifras enlisted the peace-camp artist and intellectual Yigal Tumarkin to write the preface to The Question of Palestine, titled "My Dream Zionism." Yet, in defiance of the generic protocols of prefaces, which usually offer a hospitable prelude to the text in question, Tumarkin's introduction deployed the hegemonic narratives against Said. Resurrecting the Promethean making-the-desert-bloom trope, for example, he complains that Said speaks as if "swamps and malaria never existed and are merely part of the Zionist publicity machine." For Tumarkin, Said's book "is a manifesto of frustration," offering a "black and white picture" in contrast to his own "dream Zionism" where "there is light." He thus concludes, " . . . it is hard to negotiate when one positions himself as a victim of the other side. What occurred was miserable and fated, a tragedy that victimized both sides, and now we need to seek a way to understanding based on logic and not on a division between the righteous and wicked. We have to think about the future and not remain captive to the burdens of the past and its lugubrious memories."

The preface, in dissonance with Mifras's mission statement, failed to create an intertextual environment that placed Said's argument within the larger frame of anti-colonial discourse. Tumarkin's preface could not be farther from comparable prefaces within the anti-colonialist tradition, such as Sartre's passionate endorsement of Fanon, at the height of the French/Algerian war, in his preface to The Wretched of the Earth. Said's literary work, meanwhile, was not a real presence in the work of his most logical "interpretative community"—literary theorists within the emerging field of poststructuralism in Israel. A 1988 Hebrew translation of a book by the poststructuralist Christopher Norris, which praised both Orientalism and The World, the Text, and the Critic, transliterated Said's name incorrectly as "Sed,"[24] when it could have been easily rendered correctly in Hebrew, which possesses the exact equivalent letters to the Arabic. The name "Sa'eed" in its Arabic pronunciation perhaps was hard to "hear" or digest within a deconstructionist academic ambiance. In a context where the imagined inferiority of Arabic and Arabs usually goes hand in hand with the valorization of anything English, Edward Said's name condenses an oxymoronic tension. The miswriting—or better, misreading—of his last name betrays the disconnect between the worlds of anti-colonial literature and Israeli literary studies. It betokens both the desire for the new theory of deconstruction and the lack of familiarity with one of the major poststructuralist scholars, whose book *Orientalism* had been foregrounded by Norris himself as an exemplar of interweaving text and context. Thus, at a time when Said's writing was broadening the scope of literary studies in the Anglo-American academy, Israeli literary theory hardly engaged his literary scholarship.

The translated *The Question of Palestine,* by now long out of print, did not leave a visible imprint in liberal-leftist publications. Yet by the late 1990s, *Ha'aretz*'s translations of several of Said's pieces on current events eased its readers into a celebratory reception of *Orientalism.* The shift from the marginal publication of *The Question of Palestine* to the mainstream publication of *Orientalism* reflected shifting trends in Israeli academia. By legalizing Israeli-Palestinian dialogue, the Rabin-Arafat handshake had rendered such academic engagements less taboo ridden. In the following years, a small but influential group of largely postzionist academics helped make Said a legitimate intellectual interlocutor. *Orientalism*'s more recent "travel" into Israel was also facilitated by Said's prestigious status in the Anglo-American academy, just as the elite aura of the term *postcolonial* enabled its absorption into Israeli academic discourse. The time lapse between the translations, however, suggests a more complex genealogy for critical thinking in Israel and for the trajectory of Said's reception before the postzionist debate. Mifras's impressive earlier efforts to bring Said to the Hebrew reader should not be deemed irrelevant to the history of the debates. Similarly, over the past two decades, Said's "travel" into Israel has also been supported by the Alternative Information Center and its publications,[25] which explicitly articulate Zionism's relation to colonialism.[26]

By now, the impact of Said's work has been felt in various fields in critical writings about Zionist discourses and Israeli practices. Even when Said's writing is not foregrounded, its influence is felt and acknowledged in such texts as Smadar Lavie's ironic look at Israeli anthropology of the Bedouins; Ammiel Alcalay's historical reflection on Mizrahi writers as intimately embedded in Arab culture; Yerach Gover's critique of the images of Arabs in Hebrew literature and of Zionist literary assumptions; Azmi Bishara's invocation of Orientalism to address racist discourses about "educated Arabs" within Israel, in a context where Bishara's very writing in Hebrew challenges the limits of Israeli citizenship; Sami Shalom Chetrit's historical account of Mizrahi struggle within anti-Zionist paradigms; Simona Sharoni's discussion of the gendered militarism of Israeli society; Sarah Chinski's look at the Orientalist underpinning of Israeli art history; Gabriel Piterberg's examination of the Orientalist foundations of Israeli history books; Henriette Dahan-Kalev's discussion of the Mizrahi as an Orientalized "other"; Irit Rogoff's exploration of the imaging of boundaries in Israeli visual culture; Yosefa Loshitzky's invocation of Said's reading of Camus to critique similar representations of the Arab in Israeli cinema; Dan Rabinowitz's overview of Israeli anthropological texts on the Palestinians; Shoshana Madmoni's account of racist media representation of the kidnapping of Yemeni/Mizrahi babies in Israel; and Oren Yiftachel's discussion of ethnocracy in land development and Palestinian dislocation within Israel.[27]

Amnon Raz-Krakotzkin makes significant use of Said's critique of Orientalism to address the Zionist negation of Jewish exile, highlighting "religious colonial nationalism." He discusses the dialectics of messianism and redemption as constituting the Orientalist framework of Zionist nationalism, and the place of theological debate within it. He also answers those critics of *Orientalism* who faulted the book for ignoring German forms of Orientalism. In contrast, Raz-Krakotzkin looks at the Zionist shaping of Jewish History scholarship as itself emerging from German Orientalist views about Jews in modern Europe. The possibilities offered by *Orientalism* have been extended to other domains within Jewish studies, where the easy East/West dichotomy has also proven problematic in discussing Arab Jews. Ruth Tsoffar offers an anti-Orientalist reading of the interpretations and practices of the Egyptian Karaites in their San Francisco diaspora. Gil Anidjar, meanwhile, suggests that Kabbalah scholarship, especially Gershom Scholem's valorization of mysticism over rationalism, neglected to see the Kabbalah's embeddedness in the Islamic world and Arabic writing.[28]

"POSTZIONISM"—WHOSE "POST" IS IT ANYWAY?

The changing discourses of the Anglo-American academy, energized by multiculturalism and the diverse "post" fields of inquiry (postmodernism, poststructuralism, postnationalism, and postcolonialism), facilitated Said's "voyage" to Israel and made possible the marriage of still another "post" with another "ism": post-Zionism. The scholars known as postzionists did not all identify with the label, constituting a heterogeneous group vis-à-vis the concept of "Zionism."[29] Revisionist historians such as Tom Segev, Avi Shlaim, Benny Morris, and Ilan Pappe performed invaluable scholarly work by challenging the hegemonic account of the partition and of the 1948 exodus, thus provoking the rage of mainstream Zionists. The Second Intifada posed a challenge to postzionists' rather ambiguous positions on Zionism. Whereas some explicitly announced themselves to be devout Zionists (Morris), endorsing the "Barak offered-them-everything-but-I'm-disappointed-in-the-Palestinians" narrative, a few others became more radicalized, breaking away from postzionism (Pappe).

The visibility of the postzionists was in many ways a product of the Oslo Accords. That these historians could be consulted and help shape *Tekuma*—the TV history series produced for the fiftieth anniversary of the state of Israel—spoke volumes about their positioning as legitimate scholars in the public sphere. It is important to appreciate, however, the identity politics that permitted a favorable reception of postzionist scholars in and outside Israel. It seemed that Palestinian history could be better heard if mouthed by (largely Ashkenazi) Israeli men. Many of the celebratory articles about postzionism treated the work as sui generis, marginalizing the contribution of Palestinian research on the same issues. The revisionist historians, as pointed out by such scholars as Nur Masalha, Rashid Khalidi, and Joseph Massad, basically put an Israeli imprimatur on earlier arguments made by Palestinian scholars.[30] The reception of postzionism has also reflected an Israeli-centric approach to the representation of scholarship, tending to write off Palestinian scholars as subjects of intellectual history.

Said noted the "schizophrenia" informing postzionist texts. While some of these texts establish beyond any doubt that the forced exodus of Palestinians was the result of a specific transfer policy adopted and approved by Ben-Gurion, they refuse to acknowledge any Zionist plan to empty Palestine of its inhabitants.[31] "Morris's meticulous work," writes Said,

> showed that in district after district commanders had been ordered to drive out Palestinians, burn villages, systematically take over their homeland property. Yet strangely enough, by the end of the book Morris seems reluctant to draw the inevitable conclusions from his own evidence. Instead of saying outright that the Palestinians were, in fact, driven out he says that they were partially driven out by Zionist forces, and partially "left" as a result of war. It is as if he was still enough of a Zionist to believe the ideological version—that Palestinians left on their own without Israeli eviction— rather than completely to accept his own evidence, which is that Zionist policy dictated Palestinian Exodus.[32]

The bifurcated discourse that characterizes even relatively critical circles can, in my view, be traced to the very origins of Zionism. Elsewhere I have argued that Zionism as an ideology, and Israel as a nation-state, form an anomalous project, narrating Jewish nationalism as liberatory vis-à-vis Europe even as it claims to carry out the same type of "civilizing mission" that the European powers proclaimed during their thrust into "found lands." Zionist discourse itself thus embodies schizophrenic master narratives: a redemptive nationalist narrative vis-à-vis Europe and anti-Semitism, and a colonialist narrative vis-à-vis the Arab people who "happened" to reside in the place designated as the Jewish homeland. Yet, unlike colonialism, Zionism was also a response to millennial oppression, and in contradistinction to the classical colonial paradigm, had no "mother country." Metropole and colony, in this case, were the same place. Zionist discourse concerning a "return to the mother land" suggests a double relation to that land, where the "East" is simultaneously the place of Judaic origins and the locus for implementing the "West." Thus the "East," associated on the one hand with backwardness and underdevelopment, is associated on the other with oasis and solace—a return to geographical origins and reunification with the biblical past. The West, meanwhile, is also viewed ambivalently, both as the historic crime scene of anti-Semitism and as an object of desire, an authoritative norm to be emulated in the East.[33]

Within a postzionist perspective, Zionism ceases to constitute a relevant category, since the Israeli state has presumably reached a postnationalist stage. The relative legitimacy of "postzionism" has derived precisely from a sense of opting out of or bypassing the question of Zionism's relation to colonialism. Emerging in the 1990s, the term *post-Zionism* suggested a premature eagerness to claim to have "gone beyond" Zionism even while Zionist ideology exerted more power than ever, both in Jerusalem and in Washington. Echoing various critical-theoretical "posts," postzionism was also a product of a certain postmodernist euphoria, a time when "post" fields were proliferating with abandon.

The "post" in "post-Zionism" paralleled Fukuyama's rather precipitous announcement of the "end of history" or Lyotard's annunciation of "the death of metanarratives." The similarly euphoric postzionism pointed to a rather ambiguous conceptual project that promised to carry us beyond the tiresome debate over Zionism versus anti-Zionism. Yet what this "beyondness" has meant is a question unto itself—since the implied haven of the "post" remains haunted by Zionism's kinship with both the "national" and the "colonial." *Postzionism* also carries traces of the term *postcolonial*. The prefix *post* was attached to Zionism at precisely the moment that the term *postcolonial* reached the height of its aura of prestige in the Anglo-American academy. The questions I have proposed elsewhere about the spatiotemporal ambiguity of the "post-colonial" might equally be posed about the term *post-Zionism*: that is, "post" in relation to what, where, when, and whom? When exactly does the "post" in "post-Zionism" begin? And what kind of location and perspective does the term reflect?[34] And what discourse does "post-Zionism" go beyond? The "beyond" of the "post" in "post-Zionism," unlike in "post-colonialism," takes us into a more complicated realm, precisely because the parallelism between Zionism and colonialism remains sublimated. In the term *post-colonial*, it is the prefix *post* that carries an ambiguous spatiotemporality, whereas the substantive suffix *colonial*, despite debates about historical and geographical variations, remains a more or less agreed-upon signifier and frame of reference. In the term *post-Zionism*, in contrast, both the prefix *post* and the substantive suffix *Zionism* are contested. Thus the valence of what follows the prefix and the hyphen in "postcolonialism" and "post-Zionism" in many ways constitutes the distinguishing element between the two fields of inquiry.

TRAVELING POSTCOLONIAL THEORY

Postcolonial theory, then, has recently traveled via the Anglo-American academy into a certain postzionist world, where the "colonial" itself has hardly been thought through in any depth. It is in this context that one must understand a rather striking phenomenon central to the emergent postzionist-postcolonial discourse. Academic and journalistic texts have fashioned a kind of folk wisdom suggesting that Homi Bhabha has surpassed Said. Immediately after Said's death, leftist columnist Nir Baram wrote a "sober obituary": "For many years, Said's hegemony has remained dominant, unopposed, despite the unexpected biting from Homi K. Bhabha, a brilliant scholar, who unlike Said redeemed the orient from the ultimate role of the victim and the slave, understanding that the imagination is not one-way but two-way: in other words, the orient also imagines the west and imitates it. Bhabha, speaking about two creatures that move in a constantly changing dynamic space, perfected Said's frozen thesis, and led the way into a much more fascinating discourse."[35] This vision, which shows Said outclassed by the more sophisticated Bhabha, has become a kind of topos in numerous Hebrew publications. Without engaging Said's oeuvre in any depth or delving into the varied debates around postcolonial studies, the facile recital of the Bhabha-beyond-Said mantra has come to be an entrance requirement for "doing the postcolonial" in Israel, a gatekeeping exercise that only selectively draws upon dimensions of the Anglo-American postcolonial corpus.

This narrativizing of the English-language postcolonial field seems to date back to the 1994 translation of Bhabha's "The Other Question" in the postzionist journal *Teoria veBikoret* (Theory and Criticism: An Israeli Forum). The editorial preface to the translation, written by philosopher Adi Ophir and literary critic Hannan Hever, presented the Bhabha-over-Said topos as a way out of the fixity of the stereotype as presumably deployed in *Orientalism*.[36] Although the editors' efforts to bring Bhabha's text to the Hebrew reader deserve strong praise, the politics of translation and the framing of the debate raise serious questions about the journal's positioning of Said and, implicitly, of Israeli postcolonials themselves. By selecting this Bhabha piece, and by writing a preface highlighting Bhabha's transcendence of Said, the editors cast Bhabha as the subverter of Said's hegemony. Yet at the time of the translation of Bhabha's essay, the bulk of Said's work—including *Orientalism* and, for that matter, any of Said's literary and postcolonial theoretical work—was (and still is) largely untranslated. Although *Teoria veBikoret* had translated Foucault, Deleuze, de Certeau, and later Spivak,[37] the journal had not translated any of Said's articles, yet its readers were urged to go "beyond" Said. To really "go beyond" Said, however, the Hebrew reader would first have had to have "gone through" Said's major texts. I am obviously not suggesting that one should not critique Said's work; the problem is that the journal's implicit call to "go beyond" Said—or, better, its suggestion that we are all *already* beyond Said—was not accompanied by an exploration of the broad theoretical intertext and historical context that inform his work, and thus hardly does justice to the intellectual debate.

Postcolonial theory consequently was introduced to the Hebrew reader within an intellectual and political vacuum, not only in relation to the huge body of postcolonial work but more importantly in relation to anti-colonial history and writings. In Israel, the anti-colonial antecedents of postcolonial writings—for example, texts by DuBois, C. L. R. James, Cabral, Césaire, Fanon, Senghor, Retamar, and Rodinson—have never been translated into Hebrew. Albert Memmi's books on Jewish-related questions, meanwhile, were translated in the 1960s and 1970s, but his classic anti-colonialist texts were not. In his preface to the recent (1999) Hebrew translation of his 1982 *Racism*, Memmi writes, "We cannot boast of having created morality and simultaneously dominate another people. For this reason I always regretted that no Israeli publisher agreed to publish any of my writing on these issues, and especially the *Portrait of the Colonized*... I am waiting hopefully for [it] also... [to] be published in Hebrew. It will mean that the Israeli public will see itself finally as deserving to cope with the difficulties of its national existence."[38]

The "going-beyond-Said" move, in other words, comes in a historical context of little engagement with the foundational anti-colonial texts. Bhabha's essay, astonishingly, came into Hebrew existence not only before Said's *Orientalism* but also before the books of the major figure whom both Said and Bhabha assumed as a significant influence and interlocutor—Frantz Fanon. For Israeli postcolonials who discover and ventriloquize Fanon only via Bhabha, the intellectual "jump" into the "post" becomes a magic carpet flying into the land of erasure.

This silence about Said's profound and diverse contribution, the caricaturing or "fixing" of his oeuvre into a few sentences about his putative fixity, raises doubts about the postcolonial reception of Said in Hebrew. Like a few poststructuralist critics in the Anglo-American academy, these Hebrew writers seem to displace Said's deconstruction of the binarism of colonial discourse onto Said's own text, as if Said, and not colonialism and racism, were binarist. The editors and their followers, furthermore, have filtered Said's oeuvre only through Bhabha's comments on Said in one section of an essay, concerning the fixity of the stereotype, an issue now misleadingly placed at the core of the Anglo-American postcolonial field.[39] The very complex and multifaceted field of postcolonial studies—which explores such varied issues as the intersection of race and gender in anti-colonial thought, the narrated and constructed nature of the nation, the imperial substratum of texts and institutions, the tropes of Orientalist discourse, the role of the diasporic intellectual in the metropole—is reduced to a stagist narrative of Bhabhaesque mobility superseding Saidian stasis. Bhabha's dialogue with and incorporation of Said's writings in other essays such as "On Mimicry and Man," "Signs Taken for Wonder," and "Dissemination," meanwhile, went unmentioned by the editors and by the budding postcolonials seemingly eager to liberate the Hebrew reader from the Palestinian intellectual Said.[40] This rather tendentious framing of Said's vast corpus elides the common intertexts—specifically poststructuralist theory and anti-colonialist discourse—engaged by Said and Bhabha. Thus, in the name of going beyond binarism, *Teoria veBikoret* introduced its own binarism for the postcolonial field, limiting it to a brawling arena where two intellectual wrestlers, one supposedly fixed and static and the other fluid and mobile, fight it out. Their shared (albeit differently accented) poststructuralist concerns with antiessentialism and anti-Manicheanism are here pushed out of the ring.

The scholars who apparently endorse Bhabha's Derridian-Lacanian–inflected discourse, furthermore, do not actually themselves perform that discursive analysis through deconstructionist-psychoanalytical readings.[41] The current editor of *Teoria veBikoret*, the sociologist Yehouda Shenhav, for example, repeats the Bhabha-over-Said mantra, associating the latter with phrases like "dichotomous," "static," and "rigid," in contrast with Bhabha's fluidity, "third space," and "hybridity." Yet in the same text that endorses this destabilizing mode of analysis, the author, oblivious to the methodological inconsistency, also invokes the almost antithetical disciplinary grid of "social psychology,"[42] as though the highly theoretical discourses of Lacanian psychoanalysis and the basically positivist domain of social psychology could be regarded as the same thing. The endorsement of the Bhabha style of discourse seems especially curious, then, since most of the texts that claim to go beyond Said do not themselves move in the direction in which Bhabha's Lacanian discourse points. Thus one has the impression that it is not so much a question of moving into psychoanalytic-postcolonial discourse, but rather of staging a narrative in which Bhabha ends up delegitimizing Said. A more serious Hebrew account of the English debates, moreover, would have at least acknowledged, if not necessarily embraced, the diverse critiques not only of psychoanalytic theory but also of Bhabha's writings—for example, by Benita Parry, who sees his work as depoliticizing the critique of colonialism through a hyperdiscursive turn. Nor do such postcolonial Hebrew texts explore how psychoanalysis might help illuminate a contested history in which the fundamental debate, despite an undeniable psychoanalytical dimension, is shaped by the material issue of land, and in which the psychic economy of the conflict is caught up in unequal power relations "on the ground."

Other texts in this Hebrew postcolonial corpus form an amalgam of errors and imprecisions concerning intellectual and political genealogies. In *Teoria veBikoret*'s recent issue "The Postcolonial Gaze," the authors of the introductory essay, Shenav and Hever—who again reduce Said to rigid binarism—seem to suggest that Fanon, the quintessential *anti*-colonial writer, historically belongs to *post*-colonial thought.[43] They attribute to the "postcolonial" the "effort toward liberation from colonialist discursive modes" while somehow dropping from the equation the *anti*-colonial discourse that had already attempted to do precisely that. In a case of the missing "anti," the reader moves from the "colonial" to the "post-colonial" without passing through the "*anti*-colonial." (I am not proposing here a stagist understanding of history but rather a careful sequencing of debates.) In another text, Shenhav writes, in a curiously anachronistic account, that the post-colonial movement developed in the Third World in the 1960s.[44] According to the author's discursive sequencing, "The multi-cultural movement began in the post-colonial stream that developed in the Third World. . . . This movement was joined by other important struggles of the last thirty years: the feminist, the racial, the sexual, and the generational. . . . To the help of these struggles came the post modern tradition, which tried to formulate the epistemological basis of new forms of cognition."[45]

Disentangling these scrambled intellectual histories would require more effort than they deserve, but suffice it to say that neither "multiculturalism" nor "postcolonialism" began in the Third World; that the "feminist, racial, and sexual" struggles shaped postmodernism as much as postmodernism "helped" these struggles; and that there never was a postcolonial movement per se, even in the late 1980s. There was only a postcolonial theory, which emerged from diasporic "Third World" intellectuals operating in "First World" academe. Within the Israeli public arena, such authors, in other words, seem to speak confidently of oppositional intellectual history, situated in-between the "First" and "Third" Worlds, even while demonstrating a shallow understanding of that history. Said's work is thus received in a problematic intellectual environment, giving the impression of a faddish recycling of trends from the Anglo-American academe without a thoroughgoing engagement of the historical trajectories that shaped those trends.

A "POST" WITHOUT ITS PAST

In the United States, the Left had prepared the terrain for Said's *Orientalism* in 1978 by a long series of struggles around civil rights, decolonization, Third Worldism, Black Power, and anti-imperialism. In Israel, intellectuals lived these moments quite differently. With a few exceptions, such as the small Matzpen group and the left wing of the Mizrahi Black Panthers, Israeli intellectuals did not engage in the debates about decolonization–Black Power–Third Worldism. Thus, the arrival of the "postcolonial" in the Anglo-American academy in the late 1980s, unlike its subsequent arrival in Israel, formed part of a distinct trajectory. Postcolonial discourse emerged after ethnic studies had already challenged the Western canon and in the wake of substantial (albeit insufficient) institutional reforms and corrective measures like affirmative action—themselves the result of various antiracist and anti-imperialist revolts dating back to the 1960s and 1970s. While more radical U.S. students were supporting America's "own" indigenous people (as represented in the American Indian Movement, for example), Israeli students were celebrating their state's victory over "their" indigenous people, the Palestinian Arabs.

Postcolonial theory in the Anglo-American academy also emerged from the anticolonialist moment and Third Worldist perspective; that history is at least partly what makes it "post." But in Israel one finds a "post" without its past. Postzionist-postcolonial writing in Israel—and this is another reason why the analogy between the two terms is problematic—comes out of an academic context often untouched by the anti-colonialist debates. In the Third World, anti-colonial nationalism gave way to some "course corrections" and a measure of disillusionment, partially due to the return of neo-colonialism. This disillusionment with the aftermath of decolonization and with Third Worldism, which provides the affective backdrop for postcolonial theory, had no equivalent in Israel. The question of exactly when the "post" in the "post-colonial" begins had already provoked a debate in English. But to suggest moving beyond "the colonial" in a nation-state and in an academic space historically untouched by Third Worldism requires that we ask this question with even more vigor. In the first instance, anti-colonial discourse gives way to post-colonial discourse, but in the second, it is not anti-Zionist discourse that gives way to post-Zionist discourse but Zionist discourse that gives way to post-Zionist discourse. It is a case, again, of the missing "anti."

Reading Zionism through the prism of colonialism has been taboo in Israeli academe. Thus one would think that the scholarly embrace of "the postcolonial" would foreground the discussion of Zionism's relation to colonialism. But instead one sometimes finds a kind of upside-down camera obscura discourse, even when in political terms these postcolonial post-Zionist writers oppose the occupation. Hannan Hever, for example, criticizes Said for viewing the Law of Return as racist and for not recognizing that the law, like American affirmative action, was designed as positive discrimination in favor of refugees and the persecuted.[46] But this analogy is ultimately fallacious. Affirmative action in the United States aimed to compensate those the nation-state had *itself* oppressed, those on whose backs the nation-state had been created, especially Native Americans, African Americans, and Chicanos. In Israel, in contrast, the Law of Return has been offered to those taking the place of the dispossessed, those who come to constitute the nation. To ask Said to accept the Law of Return as a form of affirmative action for Jews misses the basic point: for Palestinians, the Law of Return simply continues a history of dispossession. The Law of Return–affirmative action analogy, furthermore, is made in an Israeli context where affirmative action for Palestinians and other minorities has never been institutionalized and where it has often been caricatured, including in so-called liberal-left publications, in terms borrowed from the U.S. Right, as a kind of obnoxious "political correctness." Although postzionist-postcolonials have certainly made a contribution by challenging certain Zionist orthodoxies, one wonders how post is this "post" when a term borrowed from the alternative American lexicon ("affirmative action") surfaces in Israel in the defense of the dominant ideology; when the Palestinian desire for a right of return is repressed from the discussion; and when the relevance of the critique of the "colonial" to the account of the "Law of Return," "affirmative action," and the "right of return" is circumvented. As with the term *post-colonialism,* the prefix *post-* in "post-Zionism" erases both colonial lineages and anti-colonial intellectual history with a magical stroke of the "post."

While Hebrew texts on "the postcolonial gaze" may denounce the abuses of the military occupation, they hardly articulate the links between that political stance and the Bhabhaesque theoretical model of "third space," resulting in an unthinking celebration of the "in-between" in the land of partitions and walls. Although Said's work engaged the question of flows between cultures—his notion of "traveling theory" is a case in point—most Israeli postcolonial texts reject his work for its presumed lack of "hybridity, in which "not-only-the-colonized-but-also-the-colonizer-engages-in-mimicry." Under the sign of "hybridity," Nir Baram is thus able to contrast Said, unfavorably, with Ajami, praising the latter for his "deep research into the orient itself" and for his courage in daring to criticize the politics of the Arab world. This comparison overlooks Said's criticism of the Palestinian Authority and the Arab regimes, while ignoring Ajami's binarist discourse that essentializes the clash between the West and the East.[47] It also mobilizes "fluidity" against Said, yet nominates Ajami, often viewed as an opportunist who flatters the Orientalist illusions of the Right, as the new model of sly civility.

"Hybridity," an invaluable instrument for cultural analysis—and indeed a very old trope in Latin America and the Caribbean—has been useful both in transcending the myth of racial purity central to colonial discourse and in challenging a Third Worldist discourse that projected the Nation as culturally homogenous. But "hybridity" must be seen as always already power laden. Too often "hybridity" becomes a catchall term, without any serious probing of its different modalities. In a copy-and-paste approach to a certain postcolonial discourse in English, the postcolonial in its Hebrew translation offers an undifferentiated valorization of "hybridity." How can we think through the relation between a postcolonial discourse that reads resistance into the fact of hybridities, on the one hand, and the current apartheid-like and literally fenced-in reality of Israel/Palestine, on the other? Think about, for example, the cruel hybridity imposed in construction sites of the Separation Wall, where the linguistic frontiers of Hebrew and Arabic are indeed traversed but where Palestinians are obliged to build the very wall that tears their lives apart. What is gained, then, when the asymmetries of hybridity are bracketed, or even elided and encoded as resistant?

In fact, such Hebrew texts lack a comprehensive engagement with the English-language postcolonial debate that a decade earlier probed the potentially depoliticizing effects of hybridity. Notions of "oppression" and "resistance" are too easily dismissed as binarist simplifications, whereas "collaboration" and "co-optation" happily find their way to an all-embracing space where the colonizer and the colonized perform mutual mimicry. Passing off hybridity as already "resistant" appears to sanctify the fait accompli of colonial violence. Such a "postcolonial gaze" turns a blind eye to Said's gesture of opening a conceptual space for Zionism's victimization in a context that had previously permitted the narration exclusively of Jewish victimization and Zionist redemption. Flattening Said's argument, these texts overlook other productive Saidian categories, such as the critique of "origins" in *Beginnings;* the concentration on power-knowledge "affiliations"; the notion of the "worldly" adversarial intellectual; the idea of "mutually haunting" histories; and the privileging of spatial categories in *Culture and Imperialism*—all of which are highly relevant to the engagement of Israel/Palestine. Instead, within these texts, the reference to Said's work has the sole function of a slot to go beyond, a point to be departed from and transcended. In this way, the current Israeli postcolonial narrative relegates Said, and the people he stands for, to a space I have elsewhere termed the realm of the "pre-postcolonial" within what Joseph Massad has called the "post-colonial colony."[48] By applying the term *hegemony* to Said's influential work, such authors abuse the term while ignoring the centrality of that Gramscian concept to Said's own work, all part of a rush to perform a rather hegemonic burial of Said's oppositional texts. In the context of U.S.-Israel traveling debates, then, Said occupies a paradoxical site in relation to the "postcolonial"; he represents at once a disempowered, displaced Palestinian and an empowered American intellectual. As a Palestinian, Said evokes colonized and dominated people; as an American literary scholar, he evokes the prestigious field of postcolonial theory. Said's own Janus-faced position is part and parcel of the contradictory passing of his work through diverse checkpoints in Israel. Reading Said in Hebrew condenses an oxymoronic friction between the imagined geographies of Arabic (as East) and English (as West)—in the first, he is a haunting exile from Palestine, whereas in the latter, he holds the powerful wand of academic America. That Said's final resting place is in Broummana, Lebanon, rather than either New York, where he lived for decades, or Jerusalem, where he was born, provides a suitably troubled and inconclusive allegory for the equally ruptured voyages of his ideas across national borders.

NOTES

This essay first appeared in the *Journal of Palestine Studies* 33, no. 3 (Spring 2004): 55–75; and in Ella Shohat, *Taboo Memories, Diasporic Voices* (Durham, NC: Duke University Press, 2006), 359–84.

1. My early dialogue with Said's work includes "The Trouble with Hanna," *Film Quarterly* 38, no. 2 (Winter 1984–85): 50–55 (coauthored with Richard Porton); "Sephardim in Israel: Zionism from the Standpoint of its Jewish Victims," *Social Text* 19–20 (Fall 1988): 1–35; *Israeli Cinema: East/West and the Politics of Representation* (Austin: University of Texas Press, 1989). Said's endorsement on the book cover, published in Hebrew in 1991 by the Alternative Press, Breirot, further pointed to our affiliation.

2. Yigal Bursztyn, a Tel Aviv University professor, suggested that Said and I, unlike Fanon, are products of Western academe and therefore inauthentic Third Worlders, forgetting that Fanon himself was educated in the French academy. See his "The Bad Ashkenazis Are Riding Again," *Ma'ariv,* 7 February 1992.

3. House Subcommittee on Select Education, Committee on Education and the Workforce, "Statement of Stanley Kurtz," 19 June 2003.

4. Stanley Kurtz, "Anti-Americanism in the Classroom: The Scandal of Title VI," *National Review,* 15 July 2002.

5. "Statement of Stanley Kurtz."

6. Edward Alexander, "Professor of Terror," *Commentary* 88, no. 2 (August 1989): 49–50. See also "Professor of Terror: An Exchange—Edward Alexander and Critics," *Commentary* 88, no. 6 (December 1989).

7. Arel Ginai, Tzadok Yehezkeli, and Roni Shaked, "The Media Experts," *Yedi'ot Aharonot*, 17 February 1989. For a fuller critique, see Shohat, "Antinomies of Exile," in *Edward Said: A Critical Reader*, ed. Michael Sprinker (Oxford: Blackwell, 1992), 125–28.

8. Ben-Dror Yemini, "Academia under Investigation," *Ma'ariv*, 4 July 2003. Although Yemini's article was written in Hebrew, and the *National Review* website provided a link to the article, English and Hebrew seem to reinforce each other's legitimacy. On the links between right-wing Israeli and U.S. policy, see Joel Beinin, "The Israelization of American Middle East Policy Discourse," in "Palestine in a Transnational Context," ed. Timothy Mitchell, Gyan Prakash, and Ella Shohat, special issue, *Social Text*, no. 75 (Summer 2003): 1–5.

9. Ben-Dror Yemini, "The Faculties for the Hate of Israel," *Ma'ariv*, 17 December 2002.

10. Uria Shavit, "Peace? Forget About It," *Ha'aretz*, 22 March 2001.

11. Shimon Shamir, "The Argument that the Anti-Orientalists Love to Hate," *Ha'aretz*, 12 December 2001.

12. Emmanuel Sivan, *Interpretations of Islam* (Princeton, NJ: Darwin Press, 1985), 141. For a critique of Sivan's essentialist usage of Arab identity against Said, see Barbara Harlow, "'The Palestinian Intellectual and the Liberation of the Academy," in Sprinker, *Edward Said*. Yitzhak Laor suggested with irony that these Arab critics would presumably also have something to say about Israeli Orientalism; see his "Pam-pram-pam-pam, Post-Zionism," *Ha'aretz*, 15 August 1997. Haim Gerber of the Hebrew University, meanwhile, called for his Orientalist colleagues to change their attitude toward *Orientalism* in "More on the Orientalism Debate," *Teoria veBikoret* 14 (Summer 1999).

13. Avi Bareli, "Forgetting Europe: Perspectives on the Debate about Zionism and Colonialism," in *Israeli Historical Revisionism*, ed. Anita Shapira and Derek J. Penslar (London: Frank Cass, 2003), 103.

14. Gabriel Pieterberg, who was then teaching at Be'er Sheva University, facilitated *Orientalism*'s publication by Am Oved (translated by Atalia Zilberg) with the support of the Hayeem Herzog Center for the Study of the Middle East and Diplomacy.

15. Ari Shavit, "My Right of Return," *Ha'aretz*, 8 August 2000. Edward Said, interviewed by Kobby Meidan, *Nightly Meeting*, channel 2 (Israeli TV), October 2002.

16. In the early 1990s, at the invitation of Mizrahi leftist activists and writers Sami Shalom Chetrit and Tikva Levi, I began translating the introduction and the first chapter of *Orientalism* for a Hebrew anthology of translated anti-colonial writings, but the project came to an end because of lack of funds from alternative presses and lack of interest from mainstream publishers.

17. Said's *Out of Place: A Memoir* was published by Yedi'ot Aharonot Books and Chemed Books, 2001. *Ha'aretz* (8 September 1999) translated Said's response to Justus Weiner's accusation that Said manipulated his biography ("'My Beautiful Old House' and Other Fabrications by Edward Said" in *Commentary* [September 1999]: 23–31). Dan Rabinowitz was among those writing in defense of Said; see "Politically Contested Childhood," *Ha'aretz*, 26 August 1999. (At the invitation of Rabinowitz, Said delivered the keynote address at the 1998 meeting of the Israeli Anthropological Association.) Similarly, Amnon Yuval wrote a positive review of *Orientalism* (*Ma'ariv*, 1 September 2000), and Tuvia Blumenthal did the same for Said's *The End of the Peace Process* (*Ha'aretz*, 2 December 2001), a book that has not been translated.

18. *Siman Kri'a*, a quarterly sponsored by Tel Aviv University in conjunction with the establishment press ha'Kibutz haMeuhad, translated the essay, which Said had written in 1979 for *Social Text*'s first issue; Said, "Zionism from the Standpoint of Its Victims," *Siman Kri'a*, no. 14 (June 1981).

19. Ronald Aronson, "Never Again? Zionism and the Holocaust," *Social Text* 3 (Fall 1980).

20. Yigal Elam, "Zionism, Its Palestinian Victim and the Western World," *Siman Kri'a*, no. 14 (June

1981): 367. The author puts his faith in the West's ending the conflict, but he does so on the basis of the West's "political culture" of "equilibrium." "In the Israeli side there is little sensitivity and understanding of these Western criteria; while on the Palestinian side I doubt it if there is any sensitivity and understanding at all. Even Edward Said still does not improve the picture on the Palestinian side, to judge by his article on Zionism" (368). Elam's use of the word *even* suggests that one expects more from a modern educated Arab living in the West.

21. In his review of *Orientalism*, the leftist Yoram Bronovsky invokes Athenian democracy versus Persian tyranny to criticize Said's own critical invocation of Aeschylus ("The West Is Right, Sometimes," *Ha'aretz*, 10 March 1995). Bronovsky premises his argument on the idea that democracy is a Greek inheritance and that Athens was indeed a democracy. In fact, democratic social organizing has been found in diverse African and indigenous American contexts, and Athenian democracy was based on slavery.

22. Ronit Lentin and Yahali Amit translated *The Question of Palestine* (Shelat Falestin) (Haifa: Mifras, 1981). I am grateful to Lentin for sharing with me the details of the book's Hebrew publication.

23. Among the original Hebrew books that Mifras published were Shlomo Swirski's *Campus, Society and State* (1982), Ronit Lentin's *Conversations with Palestinian Women* (1982), and Yemini's *A Political Punch* (1986), which recounts his political transformation from Right to Left.

24. Christopher Norris, *Decontructzia* (1988; repr., Tel Aviv: Sifriat Poalim, 1993), 88 (1993 ed.).

25. The Alternative Information Center publication *News from Within* dedicated its October 2003 (19, no. 8) issue to Said's memory. Said joined the board at the invitation of its then editor, Tikva Parnass.

26. The previous director of the Alternative Information Center, Michael Warshawski, wrote an anti-Zionist criticism of the postzionist historians. The current director, Moshe Behar, intervened in the *Al-Ahram Weekly* debate—in which Fawzi Mansour critiqued Said's articles (published between 9 April and 25 June 1998) in the essay "Culture and Conflict" (no. 386, 16–22 July 1998)—concerning Arab-Jews, offering an anti-Zionist reading, "Time to Meet the Mizrahim?" 15–21 October 1998.

27. The writings include Smadar Lavie, *The Poetics of Military Occupation* (Berkeley: University of California Press, 1990); Ammiel Alcalay, *After Jews and Arabs* (Minneapolis: University of Minnesota Press, 1993); Yerach Gover, *Zionism: The Limits of Moral Discourse in Israeli Hebrew Fiction* (Minneapolis: University of Minnesota Press, 1994); Azmi Bishara, "On the Question of the Palestinian Minority in Israel," *Teoria veBikoret* 3 (Winter 1993); Sami Shalom Chetrit, *The Mizrahi Struggle in Israel, 1948–2003* (Tel Aviv: Am Oved, 2004); Simona Sharoni, *Gender and the Israeli-Palestinian Conflict* (Syracuse, NY: Syracuse University Press, 1995); Sarah Chinski, "Silence of the Fish," *Teoria veBikoret* 4 (Autumn 1993); Gabriel Piterberg, "Domestic Orientalism," *British Journal of Middle Eastern Studies* 23 (1996); Henriette Dahan-Kalev, "Ethnicity in Israel," in *Modernism, Post-Modernity and Education*, ed. Ilan Gur-Ze'ev (Tel Aviv: Ramot Press, Tel Aviv University, 1999); Irit Rogoff, *Terra Infirma* (London: Routledge, 2000); Yosefa Loshitzky, *Identity Politics of the Israeli Screen* (Austin: University of Texas Press, 2001); Dan Rabinowitz, *Anthropology and the Palestinians* (Jerusalem: Institute for Israeli Arab Studies, 1998); Shoshana Madmoni, "Media Construction of the Kidnapped Babies Affair" (Ph.D. diss., University of Massachusetts, Amherst, 2003); Oren Yiftachel, "Nation-Building and the Division of Space," *Nationalism and Ethnic Politics* 4, no. 2 (1998). (At the invitation of Yiftachel, Said served on the board of the English-language Israeli journal *Hagar: International Social Science Review*.)

28. Amnon Raz-Krakotzkin, "Orientalism, Jewish Studies and Israeli Society," *Jama'a* 3 (1999); Ruth Tsoffar, *The Stains of Culture: An Ethnoreading of Karaite Bodily Rituals and Text* (forthcoming); Gil Anidjar, "Jewish Mysticism Alterable and Unalterable," *Jewish Social Studies* 3, no. 1 (1996).

29. The revisionist sociologist Uri Ram was one of the first to use the term *post-Zionism* in his introduction to his Hebrew edited volume, *Israeli Society: Critical Perspectives* (Tel Aviv: Breirot Publishers, 1993), where he proposed post-Zionism as a hope for a new social agenda. In the same volume, Gershon Shafir, whose work unusually examines the relationship between Zionism and colonialism, also invoked the term to offer a "new universalist tendency" in contrast to the "rise of neo-Zionism."

30. Nur Masalha, "Debate on the 1948 Exodus," *Journal of Palestine Studies* 21, no. 1 (Autumn 1991): 90–97; Rashid Khalidi, in Jonathan Mahler's "Uprooting the Past," *Lingua Franca* (August 1997): 32; Joseph Massad in a conversation with Benny Morris, "History on the Line: No Common Ground," *History Workshop Journal* 53, no. 1 (Spring 2002): 205–16. Although some revisionist history books refer to Arab and Palestinian sources such as memoirs, diaries, or correspondence, the centerpiece of the argument relies on the declassified Israeli state archives. Masalha suggests that Morris seems hardly aware of the growing body of Palestinian history.

31. Edward Said, "New History, Old Ideas," *Al-Ahram Weekly*, 21–27 May 1998. Nur Masalha also had asked how revisionist historians such as Morris could argue that Israel had no expulsion policy when their work rests on "carefully released partial documentation and when much of the Israeli files and documents relating to the subject are still classified and remain closed to researchers," in "Debate on the 1948 Exodus."

32. Said, "New History, Old Ideas." Said singled out Ilan Pappe as the only Israeli revisionist historian who had showed consistency at the 1998 Paris meeting with Palestinian historians such as Elias Sanbar. Such tensions, I should add, also exist vis-à-vis the question of the Mizrahim. Tom Segev's book *1949: The First Israelis* (New York: Free Press, 1986) was received positively by leftist Mizrahi activist/intellectuals in the mid-1980s, who felt vindicated that a book, based on the Israeli state archives, indeed indicated an intentional discriminatory policy, yet Segev reproached this reading of his book.

33. I have elaborated on this schizophrenic discourse in such texts as "Master Narrative/Counter Readings," in *Resisting Images: Essays on Cinema and History*, ed. Robert Sklar and Charles Musser (Philadelphia: Temple University Press, 1990); "Taboo Memories, Diasporic Visions: Columbus, Palestine and Arab-Jews," in *Performing Hybridity*, ed. May Joseph and Jennifer Fink (Minneapolis: University of Minnesota Press, 1999).

34. Ella Shohat, "Notes on the 'Post-Colonial,'" *Social Text* 31–32 (Spring 1992).

35. Nir Baram, "The Crown of the East," *Ma'ariv*, 3 October 2003.

36. Hannan Hever and Adi Ophir, "Homi K. Bhabha: Theory on a Tight Rope," *Teoria veBikoret* 5 (Autumn 1994), published by the Van Leer Institute. The translation of Bhabha's subtitle into Hebrew has an interesting and perhaps symptomatic slip. Instead of the original "Difference, Discrimination, and the Discourse of Colonialism," the Hebrew subtitle reads "Difference, Discrimination, and Post-Colonial Discourse."

37. Spivak is the only other postcolonial author to have been translated by the journal. (The essay, "Can the Subaltern Speak?" originally appeared in *Marxism and the Interpretation of Culture*, ed. Cary Nelson and Lawrence Grossberg [Urbana, IL: University of Illinois Press, 1988], 217–313.) The issue in which her essay appeared did not generate a reflexive discussion on the journal's own politics of representation—for example, the absence or the very limited presence of local critical "Third World" women (Palestinian or Mizrahi) on its board. Gramsci, another major Saidian intertext not translated by the journal, is forthcoming from Resling Press.

38. Albert Memmi's books appeared in Hebrew in the following order: *Pillar of Salt* (Tel Aviv: Am Oved, 1960), *Jews and Arabs* (Tel Aviv: Sifriat HaPoalim, 1975), *The Liberation of the Jew* (Tel Aviv: Am Oved, 1976), and *Racism* (Jerusalem: Karmel, 1999).

39. In fact, the *Teoria veBikoret* editors selected the 1990 version of Bhabha's "The Other Question" in which he states that Said's "suggestion that colonial power and discourse is possessed entirely by the colonizer" is a "historical and theoretical simplification." These words were removed in Bhabha's later version of the essay in *The Location of Culture*. *Teoria veBikoret*'s editors were aware of this later version— because they indicate that Bhabha's last paragraph in Hebrew is modified according to the later version. Yet they frame Said through the prism of the word *simplification*, which was omitted from Bhabha's later version but has nonetheless become the focal point for Israeli postcolonial studies. To compare the two versions, see Bhabha's "The Other Question," in *Out There: Marginalization and Contemporary Culture*,

ed. Russell Ferguson, Martha Gever, Trinh T. Minh-ha, and Cornel West (Cambridge, MA: MIT Press, 1990), 77; and Bhabha, *The Location of Culture* (London: Routledge, 1994), 72.

40. Bhabha's texts acknowledge the pioneering nature of Said's work, and Said endorsed Bhabha's *The Location of Culture.*

41. Among the few exceptions that systematically deploy psychoanalytic post-colonial frameworks are Raz Yosef, *Beyond Flesh: Queer Masculinities and Nationalism in Israeli Cinema* (Piscataway, NJ: Rutgers University Press, 2004), and Orly Lubin, who partially incorporates this method in *Woman Reading Woman* (Haifa: Haifa University Press, 2003).

42. For the Bhabha-over-Said argument, see Yehouda Shenhav, "Jews of Arab Countries in Israel," in *Mizrahim in Israel*, ed. Hannan Hever, Yehouda Shenhav, and Pnina Motzafi-Haller (Jerusalem: Van Leer Institute and Hakibbutz Hameuchad, 2002), 147–48; and throughout *The Arab-Jews* (Tel Aviv: Am Oved, 2003); for the "social psychology" reference, see *The Arab-Jews*, 115.

43. Shenhav and Hever's theoretical preface, *Teoria veBikoret* 20 (Spring 2002): 11.

44. Shenhav, *The Arab-Jews*, 149.

45. Yehouda Shenhav, "Precious Culture," in *The Israeli Experience*, ed. Sami Michael (Tel Aviv: Ma'ariv Book Guild, 2001), 87.

46. Hever briefly contrasts Said with Anton Shammas in an essay on *Arabesques*, "Hebrew from an Arab Pen," *Teoria veBikoret* 1 (Summer 1991): 30.

47. Baram, "The Crown of the East." He also applied this skewed version of postcolonial theory to the Mizrahi question, to which Sami Shalom Chetrit offered a critical response in "Fed Up with the Askenazized," *Ma'ariv*, 4 April 2003.

48. Joseph Massad, "The 'Post-Colonial' Colony," in *The Pre-Occupation of Post-colonial Studies*, ed. Fawzia Afzal-Khan and Kalpana Seshadri Crooks (Durham, NC: Duke University Press, 2000); on the "pre-postcolonial" and "hybridity," see Shohat, "Notes on the 'Post-Colonial.'"

21

Exile With/Out God

A Jewish Commentary in Memory of Edward Said

Marc H. Ellis

Exile is a strange place to be, and stranger still when one is affluent and secure. For Jews, exile is supposed to be at its end, especially in America and Israel. Exile is a time warp, a place we were then and often, to be remembered on specific holy days, to be invoked on spiritual and political occasions, certainly not to be lived and never to be chosen. To say that exile is ahead of us, that if we are awake, exile cannot be avoided, is to cry out in an era of empowerment and status that liberation has betrayed us or, more poignantly, that we have failed our liberation. Although perhaps all peoples fail their own liberation, few are haunted so specifically and recently by the shadows of Auschwitz as the Jews. To come so far from those fires and to descend so rapidly is a dual—albeit dismal—feat, without compare.

If there is no exile, not even the possibility of exile, then there are neither prophets nor potential prophets. The Jewish community has arrived, if by arrived we mean survived and flourished. Yet if this arrival has been achieved at the expense of others, reversing our place in the cycle of injustice and atrocity, then it has been at our expense as well.

Ethically, at least, the cost of Jewish empowerment is the loss of our moral compass, the gutting of the values and voice that howled at the injustices done to us. Losing the ethical compass is this loss and more; our hearing, once intense and critical, attuned to exposing piety and power alone or conjoined, is now limited and itself in need of aid.

Is exile, or at least its possibility, necessary to retrieve the ethical? Are there times, notably times of affluence and power, when exile must be chosen? And can a Jew choose exile in light of our history, in the contemporary period, after Auschwitz, when

Auschwitz is memorialized on the National Mall in Washington, D.C., the very center of global power?

Some years ago I read Edward Said's "Reflections on Exile." Said was an expert on literature and the relation between literary interpretation and the politics of empire. Most importantly for this discussion, he was a Palestinian of moral courage. His exile was compelled, geographic in scope and linguistic in tone, a forced exchange of East and West, Arabic and English. Said's exile began with the formation of the state of Israel, itself a response to exile, and for him, without religion or God, it was solely a secular experience of displacement and the search for place and language.[1]

As I read Said's essay, the Palestinian Authority, formed in exile and ostensibly a step toward the end of the Palestinian diaspora, was becoming a force for a second exile. Initially displaced by Jews, Palestinians hoped for a new sensibility in governance and democracy, and Said was among its leading proponents. Would the Palestinian exile fashion a people who could practice a new politics? By the mid-1990s Said realized that the Palestinian return from exile had taken a turn for the worse and that a second exile had been forced upon him and others. This, I think, was the reason for his vehement attacks on Yasser Arafat and his governing authority, the sense that an opportunity for Palestinians, but also a chance to model the end of exile for the world community, was being squandered.[2]

Reading Said's essay, I wondered about his secularity. Said was of Christian background, a confirmed agnostic, perhaps even an atheist, yet he had a rage for justice and a moral sensibility lacking in most believers. Said retained his ethical compass without God and persevered in an exile once forced and now chosen, affected by neither malice nor fear. I could relate to his understanding of exile as "irremediably secular and unbearably historical; that it is produced by human beings for other human beings; and that, like death but without death's ultimate mercy, it has torn millions of people from the nourishment of tradition, family, and geography."[3]

As a Jew, I faced a dilemma. Could we Jews have endured exile for so many years without God? And could I, in the shadow of Auschwitz, choose exile today without God? I had before me many Jews, including some Jewish Israelis who, like Said, but from a position of communal empowerment, chose exile as a secular option.

Who could blame these Jews, or Said for that matter, for refusing God? Jews survived the Constantinian face of God in Christianity through the millennia only to endure the development of a Constantinian Judaism that seeks to end Jewish exile forever. In the meantime, this emerging Constantinian Judaism created another exile that changed the trajectory of Palestinian life. Who could blame Said for his agnosticism when he, with others in the Middle East, experienced wave after wave of militant crusading Christianity and periodically reactionary Islam, ending in a settler Judaism that claims it is acting on the promises of God?

Said developed a practice of exile without God that was grounded in a thoroughly secular amalgam of suspicion and thought. Critical to this stance was an openness to crossing borders and boundaries. Said saw identity politics, so often framed in a religious sensibility, as something to fight against. An evolutionary sense of identity was crucial to Said's practice of secular reasoning. For him, religion was a mystifying factor and a dangerous one when enshrined in identity and political discourse. Worse still was religion in the public square. With Said's background and experience, one can hardly blame him for his thinly disguised disdain for religion in general.

In reading Said, I face a further question. Can I agree with his embrace of secular reason and his concern that identity and religious discourse encourage and sometimes demand mystification while remaining true to my religious self, and even deepening my religiosity? If the contemporary Jewish community has wielded its religiosity as a blunt instrument and in so doing caused Said's exile and my own; if it can point to its founding texts and commentary, not discounting its prayers over the millennia of promise and land; if it can furthermore point to a history of wandering and suffering precisely because of a lack of land and power, thus invoking God, scripture, political maturity and strategic positioning, all in the shadow of Auschwitz; how can this panoply of argumentation and appeal be left without support?

To say that one is a religious Jew today carries theological baggage raised to political stakes; the implications are frightening because the implicit, sometimes explicit, warning is that a second Auschwitz awaits the Jewish people. From this perspective, those Jews who enter exile for moral and ethical reasons court this disaster and even hasten it. Turning one's back on the promise of God *and* becoming the engine of a second destruction *become the focus* of the Jewish world, a focus once reserved for ethics and the prophetic.[4]

Reading Said, I wondered if it was possible to have this prophetic voice as a religious Jew in exile, holding forth a secular reasoning, living in the shadow of Auschwitz *and* Israel. The displacement of the Palestinian people and the damage done to them over the past decades has left a permanent scar on Jewish history. Like the Holocaust and Christianity, though on a different continent and in different circumstances, the oppression of another people cannot be forgotten or overcome through barriers and separation; only the inclusion of the victim allows a movement forward. Confession and justice are the hallmarks of this movement, the places where forgiveness can become revolutionary.

The movement forward, however, cannot be a return to innocence in the political or religious sense, or even to a God of promise and deliverance, as if the history of displacement has not occurred. A scar is left on the very texts of the community, on its hopes and prayers. Is this scarring the same as that from a time when the community was itself oppressed by others? Perhaps the Jewish community, its tradition and God, have been scarred twice in recent years by the Holocaust *and* by Israel.[5]

ON CONSTANTINIAN JUDAISM

I write this meditation after watching a television show featuring a panel discussion of James Carroll's *Constantine's Sword: The Church and the Jews: A History*.[6] Carroll's book traces the history of Catholic-Jewish relations through its darkest periods as well as through its periods of hope, especially the post–Vatican II era and its opening to Jews and to the world. The horror of Auschwitz shadows this history and calls it beyond the era of Vatican II. Carroll calls for a new Vatican council to consider a Catholic reformation that would include an expanded repudiation of anti-Jewishness and the end of explicit and implicit supercessionism.

On the dais at the televised event were Elie Wiesel, the Nobel laureate whose autobiographical *Night* is a standard of Holocaust literature; Cynthia Ozick, a Jewish novelist and commentator; and Mary Gordon, a Catholic counterpart to Ozick. The evening was carried live on television, and I tuned in after Wiesel's comments and about midway through Carroll's presentation, in which he was summarizing the conclusions of his book.

I knew of Carroll as a novelist and of his interest in the Holocaust and had read an occasional article by him on the subject and then parts of his 700+-page book. I was intrigued by the force of his delivery: considered, impassioned, direct. As in the book, but now in a verbal and concise articulation, Carroll, as a practicing Catholic, spoke of ends and beginnings, of anti-Jewishness and Auschwitz, on the one hand, and the cleansing of the Catholic tradition, on the other. He saw no middle road on the issue of the Jews: the members of the Church and its hierarchy needed to confess to the Jews, with no expectation of anything in return. The sin of anti-Jewishness was hardly an aberration in the history of the Church; rather it defined its essence. There could be no further delay of complete repentance.

The hall was packed, and when Carroll finished, the audience offered applause but also a deep and reverent silence. Ozick, who was the first to respond, was clearly moved by the presentation, and after recounting her childhood fears of Christianity, referred to Carroll's work and lecture as a prophetic moment. Mary Gordon followed Ozick and likewise congratulated Carroll for an important work that challenged the Church to its core, but she thought he was too kind to the then-sitting pope. For Gordon, John Paul II repented *and* maintained a Christian triumphalism, apologizing for the sins of some Christians while keeping the Church and its doctrines above the fray, as if the sins of anti-Jewishness were not part of Catholic text and dogma. The elevation to sainthood of Edith Stein, a Jewish convert to Christianity who later died in Auschwitz, along with the attempt to place Popes Pius IX and Pius XII, both with controversial records in relation to Jews, in a similar category, betrayed an ecumenical sleight of hand.

At the conclusion of the evening, when each participant was asked for a final comment, Ozick spoke briefly. For her, to speak of the sins of the Church and the need for a new reformation was prophetic but also somewhat facile, because the Holocaust is past. Today, she contended, the challenge is solidarity with Jews who are alive, especially in Israel, which now is "under siege." The date was January 11, 2000, the height of the Al Aqsa Intifada, which began when Ariel Sharon, later prime minister of Israel, strode the length of the Temple Mount. As had happened before, the peace process between Israelis and Palestinians broke down. But this time the violence accelerated to a new and more dangerous level, with closure of Palestinian towns and cities for weeks at a time. Soon Israeli tanks and helicopter gunships sent rockets into defenseless civilian areas.

I knew of Ozick's writing on the Israeli-Palestinian question; I had written on her hard words about Palestinians and Jewish dissenters. To say that Ozick ignores Palestinian rights and Israeli militarism is to be polite. Her ignorance of the real history of Israel and Palestine is trumped only by the arrogance of her Jewish claims and her disdain for Palestinian dignity. Her evocation of the Holocaust in her writings and again in her presentation that evening rang hollow when the other side of her complaint about Christian hatred and perversion of Jesus's message was blanketed with a determined silence about Jewish injustice and atrocity.[7]

To watch such an evening unfold is difficult enough during periods of relative quiescence in the Middle East. But the telecast was on the heels of Ehud Barak's failure and in the middle of the election campaign that brought Ariel Sharon to power. In the end, Sharon's policies differed from Barak's only on the fringes, though the rhetoric the two men used in explaining initiatives varied in tone. Netanyahu was different from Rabin in a similar way: settlements and occupation continued, and the Oslo process, seemingly so hotly contested, disguised these similarities. Like most realities in Israel, the consensus on land and security, and for that matter on "the Arabs," was joined by Israelis across the political spectrum.

Most Jews do not understand this actualization. They have little sense of the reality of Israel, nor do they understand the agreements offered—the map, as it were—of the Israeli and Palestinian future. Few Jews in America have actually met Palestinians or traveled in Palestinian areas. They haven't witnessed the checkpoints, the bypass roads and tunnels, the demolished homes and olive groves, the encircling of Palestinian villages, towns, and cities by Jewish settlements and military.

This ignorance is part of my exile and the exile of many Jews who understand and witness the map of Israel and Palestine and realize the irreversibility of the process of Jewish settlements. But more than exhibiting disregard of the Palestinians' plight per se, Jewish leaders are willfully ignorant and maintain a silence on injustice toward Palestinians, always couched in pleas for Jewish security and continual assertions of Jewish innocence in suffering *and* in empowerment.

In turn, major Jewish organizations constantly make pleas for Jewish unity in paid advertisements in leading newspapers, even as helicopter gunships circle Palestinian towns and cities that have already been closed by the Israeli military. Then come urgent e-mails and phone calls that seek to limit Jewish dissent through character assassination and innuendo. Jews who speak on behalf of the Palestinians are portrayed as traitors, self-haters, tragic figures who abandon their own people in a time of need. Is Ozick right that Israel is under siege? Does God want us to be silent at this moment to achieve a unity that legitimates oppression? Is silence a commandment that defines our Jewishness?[8]

Whereas exile is a familiar theme in Jewish history, statehood is a recent experience. That the "return" to the land in the framework of a state should precipitate an exile *is* a *novum* in Jewish history. That the space of exile is filled with Jews of Conscience who are almost all completely secular in outlook is also unprecedented. Is it a coincidence that these Jews of Conscience, who cannot avert their eyes from the actualities of history and who function within the context of historic Jewish suffering and the covenantal obligations of justice and reconciliation, cannot utter the word God? Or do they not do so because of the misuse of religion and faith in their Constantinian dispensation? One can hardly blame Jews of Conscience for fleeing Constantinian Christianity *and* Constantinian Judaism as one flees from a burning building.

Ozick's inability as a literary figure and commentator to make the connection between Jews and others who are suffering as the result of Jewish empowerment, coupled at the time with the emergence of Ariel Sharon as a mainstream politician in Israel, signals a fundamental break in Jewish history as we have known and inherited it. Thus, exile is a response, perhaps the only response, a witness, if you will, at the end of Jewish history.

Could it be that Jews of Conscience carry the covenant with them into exile and that this is the last exile in Jewish history? Will this exile take Jews so far outside of mainstream Judaism that they will have no possibility of return?

THE NEW DIASPORA

The flight from Constantinian Judaism is as old as the formation of Jewish Constantinianism is recent. The pioneer of Constantinianism, at least in the West, is Christianity, the 1,500-year association of church and state, the latter granting a religious monopoly and status, the former blessing power and empire. Jews in exile meet many Christians whose exile is longstanding, having awakened after the Holocaust to the anti-Jewishness of the Nazis and of Christian Europe. James Carroll's work details this long history and his individual journey beyond the confines of Christendom and its oppressive mentality. Liberation and feminist theologians go further and deeper than Carroll, for they see this Constantinian history continuing into the present. A critical approach to tradition is a necessity; that critique always poses further questions.

Carroll ended his remarks by suggesting that the Catholic Church needed to apologize to the Jews without expecting anything in return. Is this the case? Jews do not need to answer for their own persecution, but Jews do need to be accountable for their role in the oppression of the Palestinian people. Honesty must be met with honesty on the subject of Jewish history.

Jewish silence furthers the exile within the Jewish community. It also furthers the exile within the Christian community. For in exile, Jews and Christians of Conscience need one another to bolster the spirit and combat the aloneness of exile. Jews and Christians in dialogue with one another—from a position of power and silence on the next questions—are participants in a deal that further isolates the people in both communities who are already marginalized and dispersed.

By posing certain questions, such as questions about the anti-Jewishness of Christian history, and foreclosing others, such as the idea that Jews have sins to confess, one cheapens the confession. Ozick's remarks—that living Jews are the pressing question—is correct, yet the uncritical acceptance of an Israel "under siege" places the subversive memory of suffering under guardianship of empire. The intended confession becomes fuel for further oppression; a new pact is signed that consigns others to oblivion. For Jews and Christians of Conscience, the exile deepens.

Does God stand with the ecumenical dealers, even those who vehemently criticize historical Constantinianism while leaving the present untouched? Or does God stand with those in exile? Does the particularity of one's community define exile and the expectations of God's presence within it, or does a new particularity form that is forged in exile?

Exiles who begin to recognize that the historic communities they come from and the traditions they inherit have come to an end come to understand that they have no relational chain to appeal to. Instead, they seek out others in exile, not as distant and exotic beings merely to be acknowledged but as part of a new diaspora in the making. In this way, community is formed and values are developed; the loneliness of exile is softened and fidelity is deepened by others who are also struggling to be faithful.

A new ecumenism takes shape in the new diaspora, one that responds in light of history to contemporary questions and is open to the next questions as well. And questions abound. What will the new diaspora look like? Will the particularities that people bring to the new diaspora survive? Will this diaspora become a new particularity? Will God be named in the new diaspora? If so, will the diaspora agree on one name for God or insist on many names? What status, if any, will the Bible have in the new diaspora? Will Jews be called Jews; Christians, Christians; Muslims, Muslims? Perhaps these labels and traditions will fade in relevancy and accessibility.

These questions suggest another one: what practice or practices will develop in the new diaspora? At least in Judaism, Christianity, and Islam, the practice of faith emerges from understandings of revelation, texts, tradition, and history. Over time precepts for thinking and living have evolved, and though arguments, even wars, have been fought within and between these religions, basic understandings have evolved so that practices identifiable as Jewish, Christian, and Muslim are discernible.

What revelation, texts, tradition, and history will define the practice of the new diaspora? Will practice rely simply on a compilation of the diverse heritages of the populations that make up the community or, because of the exile, the fragments of these heritages? Each generation has different experiences, and the children of those who have fled exile are at home in the new community. What was whole and is then fragmented for the previous generation is often neither for the next; the current generation knows only one situation as its own. The question then will be whether the new diaspora, once it is no longer new, can generate its own meanings and structures, its own practice.

We cannot predict the answers to these questions. The exile has its own force, and prediction of the future should be left to the many observers of religion that fill academic life. For the religious person, exile is simply a period of intense movement that challenges the internal landscape of the person and the community. Lament is ever present; return is impossible. The gates of acceptance are closed.

Although the situation of the exile can and should be analyzed within the secular framework that Said proposed, the reality, at least for me, is more complex. Exile is a reality that can only be understood rationally. How else can we understand the reasons for our exile?

Reason can reach only so far. Most of the powerful are able to live quite well materially and psychologically with injustice; many who experience injustice can, when the tables are reversed, mete it out in equal measure. Many who disagree with communal policies simply despair of justice and go on their way with no commitments other than to their own survival. At the same time, those who move into exile are flawed, often living in and sometimes benefiting from the systems that oppress. The picture is complex. Complicity, cynicism, and compromise abound in exile as well.

Within this complexity, a postmodern approach might suggest itself. Text and commentary, interwoven and cross-referenced, a veritable playground of possibility, emerge. Yet in reading such an approach, even and especially within the Jewish framework of renewal, history is seemingly absent. Gone are the Holocaust, Israel, and the Palestinians—absences that are shocking unless one understands that the Jewish renewal movement seeks to transcend the internal Jewish civil war that continues today.

For textual critics and postmodern enthusiasts, the recovery of the Jewish tradition in dialogue with contemporary reality demands that history be deemphasized even as it is being created. One can have difficulty seeing how religious texts, especially the Talmud, which were formed in a period of Jewish life that had little material and state power to sustain it, can speak to our time. When the bind of contemporary Jewish life is so blatant, and the power of the Jewish community and Israel continues despite critique and opposition, how can we blame those who seek a way forward to chart new territory without the interference and frustration of power that will not heed the ethical imperative?[9]

Reading Said against a backdrop of postmodern Jewish thinkers is delightful; his challenge is unrelenting. For him, that challenge is always the reality of Palestine, a challenge both practical and grounded in historical fact. To the mystic flight of text and tradition, Said forces a secular reasoning on a new form of pious religiosity. His exile confronted academic mysticism, and the suffering of those in Palestine continues to confirm the duty of Jewish thinkers and practitioners.

ENDINGS/BEGINNINGS

Exile is an ending, but it is also a beginning. The place of exile is forever. Even a return to a specific geography is experienced as difference, for one's starting place is altered almost beyond recognition. Yet this alteration can bring closure, a return not to a specific location but to a landscape that is before and after exile.

This landscape takes shape within a history, culture, and religion of a people, a people among others, and as a bridge between these. Discontinuity of time and place exist; they are formative experiences for the extension of thought and sensibility. In this space, compassion and the quest for justice deepen. Continuity, or at least the illusion of continuity, is the place of empire.

Community is the realization, more the experience, of discontinuity, and therefore it is the sense that only within the brokenness of life are embrace and love possible. This fracture in the structure of life is personal and communal; it drives the perpetual choice of empire or community. At the end of the day, are we not defined by this simple choice, this direction, of journeying toward empire or journeying toward community?

Exile is the end of empire or at least the realization that empire, while triumphant in the here and now, is not the last word. Exile is less the overcoming of empire— new empires will always arise to replace those that fall. Rather exile is an alternative that is tangible in its beginnings and always incomplete. Exile is the affirmation that within empire, choices are possible that may soften its blows. Exile may bring empire closer to peace and justice than will the violence that it lives within and perpetrates. Religion has this mixture of empire and community within itself; witness the internal religious civil wars that have raged throughout history. The declaration of the end of religion may be the end of this civil war or simply another vantage point, with different language, from which to continue this struggle.

Perhaps the language of religion is a dated way of expressing this struggle and is therefore now irrelevant. Edward Said affirmed this understanding. For him, secularity was the way to penetrate the mysticism that reifies identity and politics. In this view he is joined by other Palestinians and by many Jews who prize secularity almost as a release from the bondage of religion. He also warned against romanticizing exile, even in the service of humanism, let alone religion: "Against this large, impersonal setting, exile cannot be made to serve notions of humanism. On the twentieth-century scale, exile is neither aesthetically nor humanistically comprehensible: at most the literature about exile objectifies an anguish and a predicament most people rarely experience first hand; but to think of the exile informing this literature as beneficially humanistic is to banalize its mutilations, the losses it inflicts on those who suffer them, the muteness with which it responds to any attempt to understand it as 'good for us.'"[10] One can only honor this warning.

Yet for me, this warning leads elsewhere, to an exile from God. This God can be found in the Jewish tradition, especially in the Hebrew Bible, as a covenantal God whose proffer, once given, is free of God. In other words, the covenant, once given, exists within history, suggesting a reality beyond the known while demanding a reason that can understand the world. Covenantal reason seeks to know and transform the world from empire toward community. This form of reasoning has compassion and justice at its center. With that center as the practice of reason, does it matter if the language is defined as religious? What, specifically, qualifies as religious language? And why does religious language so often have violence at its center? A corresponding question is also important: why does "religious" language so often have compassion and justice at its center?

Here, in exile, we search for another language. This language, while recognizing an end, can only suggest a beginning. Of course we cannot come to an end without a sense of a beginning, and perhaps this fact, the realization of both, defines the human. We also know that endings are themselves beginnings. The truly difficult and complex realization is that the beginning is found within the ending and it is also an extension of the ending. The fresh start occurs within the old dispensation. Breaking free of history, whether it be personal or communal, is an illusion.

Jews of Conscience remain in exile. Their end is coterminous with the end of Palestine and the exile of Palestinians, both within Palestine and outside of it. The tandem exiles grow in depth and numbers; the mutual recognition of exile is the key to a return to sanity, a return to the land, and is essential for a life after empire. We are not witnessing this type of beginning today, a beginning to which Edward Said testified so forcefully until the end of his life.

Said wrote often about the fluidity of identity, suggesting that identity has no unchanging essence, no ethnic, cultural, political, or religious core. As an exile, Said lived the new diaspora, with its fluid identities, in many ways. In fact, in a startling interview with Ari Shavit, an Israeli Jewish journalist, Said reversed the entire question of Jewish identity by claiming, as a Palestinian in exile, to be among the last of the Jews. In so doing, he also helped define what it means to be a Jew for those struggling with that identity—precisely because of the exilic condition of Palestinians like himself. When Shavit asked Said whether he was addicted to homelessness, he responded:

364   MARC H. ELLIS

I don't know if I'm addicted. But I don't own any real estate. The flat I live in is rented. I see myself as a wanderer. My position is that of a traveler, who is not interested in holding territory, who has no realm to protect.

[Theodore] Adorno says that in the twentieth century the idea of home has been superseded. I suppose part of my critique of Zionism is that it attaches too much importance to home. Saying, we need a home. And we'll do anything to get a home, even if it means making others homeless.

Why do you think I'm so interested in the binational state? Because I want a rich fabric of some sort, which no one can fully comprehend, and no one can fully own. I never understood the idea of this is my place, and you are out. I do not appreciate going back to the origin, to the pure. I believe the major political and intellectual disasters were caused by reductive movements that tried to simplify and purify.

I don't believe in all that. I wouldn't want it for myself. Even if I were a Jew. I'd fight against it. And it won't last. Take it from me, Ari. Take my word for it. I'm older than you. It won't even be remembered.[11]

Ari Shavit responded that Said sounded very Jewish. Said replied, "Of course. I'm the last Jewish intellectual. You don't know anyone else. All your other Jewish intellectuals are now suburban squires. From Amos Oz to all these people here in America. So I'm the last one. The only true follower of Adorno. Let me put it this way: I'm a Jewish-Palestinian."[12]

Perhaps Said was indeed the last Jewish intellectual or the hybrid Jewish-Palestinian he also claimed to be. The latter category may one day evolve an identity all its own, taking from both peoples and traditions and fusing them into a search for justice and reconciliation that Said himself exemplified. Yet, as usual, Said added a caveat: "Exiles feel, therefore, an urgent need to reconstitute their broken lives, usually by choosing to see themselves as part of a triumphant ideology or a restored people. The crucial thing is that a state of exile is free from this triumphant ideology—designed to reassemble an exile's broken history into a new whole—virtually unbearable, and virtually impossible in today's world."[13]

Today, with the wall now encircling the Palestinians—and, in another way, encircling Jewish life and thought as well—Said's voice is needed more than ever. As a Jew in exile, I know we have no way forward without his voice and his witness. Nor can Jews find a way forward without an embrace of the Palestinian people. Said's witness therefore continues to offer us a beacon. In an exile seemingly without end and increasing in ferocity, no Jew could ask for more at the end of Jewish history.

NOTES

1. Said's "Reflections on Exile" was originally published in *Granta* 13 (Winter 1984); it was later republished in his *Reflections on Exile and Other Essays* (Cambridge, MA: Harvard University Press, 2000), 173–86. For the details of this exile, see Said's autobiography, *Out of Place: A Memoir* (New York: Knopf, 1999). I first read Said's essay on exile to prepare a lecture in his honor at a conference in Windsor, Canada,

in 1997. That lecture was later published as "Edward Said and the Future of the Jewish People," in *Revising Culture: Reinventing Peace: The Influence of Edward Said*, ed. Naseer Aruri and Muhammed Shuraydi (New York: Interlink, 2001), 38–72. That essay led me to further reflection in *Practicing Exile: The Religious Odyssey of an American Jew* (Minneapolis: Fortress, 2002).

2. Said's voluminous writings, a virtual around-the-clock criticism of the Palestinian Authority, can only be explained as a prophetic outburst lamenting the squandering of an alternative politics that Said spent his lifetime articulating. For the first of a number of collections of such writings, see his *The End of the Peace Process: Oslo and After* (New York: Pantheon, 2000).

3. Said, *Reflections on Exile*, 174.

4. For an extended exploration of Holocaust theology and the political and theological baggage explored therein, see my *Beyond Innocence and Redemption: Confronting the Holocaust and Israeli Power* (San Francisco: Harper San Francisco, 1990), 1–55.

5. I explore these themes in *Reading the Torah Out Loud: A Journey of Lament and Hope* (Minneapolis: Fortress Press, 2007).

6. James Carroll, *Constantine's Sword: The Church and the Jews: A History* (New York: Houghton Mifflin, 2001). The televised gathering took place at the Interfaith Center of New York in New York City, January 10, 2001. A DVD of the television show is available from C-SPAN, product ID 162201–1.

7. See my take on Ozick in *O' Jerusalem: The Contested Future of the Jewish Covenant* (Minneapolis: Fortress, 1999), 85–89, 94–99.

8. For those Jews who have not been silent, see Rozne Carey and Jonathan Shainin, eds., *The Other Israel: Voices of Refusal and Dissent* (New York: New Press, 2002).

9. The shortfalls of this approach (textual reasoning) are self-evident. For example, see Peter Ochs and Nancy Levene, eds., *Textual Reasonings: Jewish Philosophy and Text Study at the End of the Twentieth Century* (Grand Rapids, MI: Eerdmans, 2003).

10. Said, *Reflections on Exile*, 174.

11. Edward W. Said, "My Right of Return," interviewed by Ari Shavit, in *Power, Politics and Culture: Interviews with Edward Said*, ed. Gauri Viswanathan (New York: Pantheon, 2001), 457–58.

12. Ibid., 458.

13. Said, *Reflections on Exile*, 177.

PART THREE

The Intellectual at a Crossroads

On wind he walks, and in wind
he knows himself. There is no ceiling for the wind,
no home for the wind. Wind is the compass
of the stranger's North.
He says: I am from there, I am from here,
but I am neither there nor here.

An eagle soaring higher and higher
bidding farewell to his height,
for dwelling on Olympus
and over heights
is tiresome.

—MAHMOUD DARWISH, *EDWARD SAID:*
A CONTRAPUNTAL READING

22

The Incalculable Loss

Conversations with Noam Chomsky

Interviewed by Adel Iskandar

Edward Said and Massachusetts Institute of Technology linguist and perennial dissenter Noam Chomsky met in the 1960s at the height of the Palestinian emancipatory struggle and became immediately and intractably connected in their recognition of the dispossession of the Palestinian people. Their sense of common purpose accented much of their writing on the Middle East, fueled by an unrelentingly lopsided political situation at the epicenter of Middle Eastern politics as well as the intersection of U.S. foreign policy with events in the region. Their treatises on the Palestinian-Israeli conflict were decidedly forged with the intention of rendering the failures of social justice and the hopelessly emaciated representations of Palestinians. Their collaboration culminated in numerous solidarity initiatives that sought to highlight the role of American foreign policy and hawkish Israeli interests in the construction of a dehumanizing narrative of Palestinian identity.[1]

In addition to sharing a concern about Palestine, Said and Chomsky found congruence in their commitment to defining a path for an exuberant culture of public intellectualism. To Said, Chomsky's evocation of this commitment was "profoundly unsettling" because it grew not out of a desire to protect territory, build his personal stature, consolidate power, or guard assets. Said too resigned himself to the inescapable reality that critical representations by intellectuals "will neither make them friends in high places nor win them official honors."[2]

In their interventions on behalf of social justice in Palestine/Israel, both thinkers became referents for their desire to interrogate U.S. and Israeli imperial ambitions in the region. Said was acutely conscious and cautious of the possibilities of co-option as an intellectual. He situated his efforts and Chomsky's as oppositional and contrapuntal to Gramsci's description of the traditional intellectual. Although the domains in which organic intellectuals could practice public criticism free of the debilitating power of institutionalization were dwindling, Said considered the American academy to be without precedent in its ability to house these efforts. He viewed this fact as an anomalous institutional contradiction that incongruously allowed his and Chomsky's work to exist.

Said expressed an affinity for Chomsky's indefatigably critical posture, describing him as "an example of independent radicalism and uncompromising severity unequalled by anyone else today."[3] He pointed out the organic nature of Chomsky's criticism: "[He] doesn't reflect theoretically on what he does, he just does it."[4] On the contrary, Said did both, thereby finding affinity in both Chomsky's responsibility and the Foucauldian self-critical deconstructive project.

The likes of Chomsky, Gore Vidal, Sartre, de Beauvoir, Fanon, and Bertrand Russell put forth an intellectual endeavor with a moral center, one that Said contrasted to the devoid highfalutin' modernist agenda of the likes of Jurgen Habermas.[5] Said and Chomsky alike saw no end to the struggle for "truth," because "there's no definitive military solution" in the battle of intellectual polemics.[6]

With the conviction of speaking truth to power, Said and Chomsky converged methodologically. However, they diverged politically on a subterranean level. Said broke from Chomsky's political engagement by interrogating his assessment of terms such as terrorism in the post-9/11 environment. Whereas Chomsky offered hegemonic "state terrorism" as a logical counterargument to the state rhetoric of "terrorism," Said remained skeptical of the deluding effect of the term. He instead pressed for a deconstruction of the language and usage of terrorism, beginning with its philological roots as a historicized semantic variable. Conversely, he opted not to give the term currency, denying its political value.[7]

Said also questioned Chomsky's view that dominating apparatus such as the state and the media are all consuming. Chomsky charged that the American media were inherently complicit with the instruments of the industrial-military-corporate system that manufactures both journalists' and audiences' consent. For Said, who saw opportunities for intervention aplenty within every repository of institutional control, this perspective was wholly insufficient, especially given Chomsky's own role.[8]

Following Said's death, a previously unexamined area of contention between them emerged. In this interview, Chomsky lays bare the dissimilarities in their views about Zionism and their visions for a binational state in Palestine/Israel. When Said started to make more regular visits to Palestine, he became acutely aware of the intractability of the status quo, the impossibility of redrawing boundaries and states, and he expressed growing disdain for the dehumanization wrought by political and cultural divisiveness.[9] Although his commitment to the one-state solution seemed to be a response to the debacle at Oslo, one need not go far in his vast humanist oeuvre to explicate his entrenched tendencies for mutualism, reconciliation, and unsettling nationalisms. What Chomsky perceived to be a political and tactical shift in Said's thinking, Said saw as the only advantageous and redemptive route toward a cultural symbiosis in Palestine/Israel.

The comments reproduced here are the most extensive ones Chomsky has offered about Said. He is at his most incisive when candidly exploring the two men's relationship, which was characterized by intellectual compatriotism and dignified friendship, along with good-faith efforts to articulate their common goals and expose their differences.

ADEL ISKANDAR (AI): *In a November 2003 presentation honoring Edward Said at Columbia University, you stated that his "death is an incalculable loss." To whom is this loss most substantial?*

NOAM CHOMSKY (NC): To begin with, it's a loss for his family and innumerable close friends, of whom I was one. So it's a personal loss. It is a tremendous loss for the Palestinians because he was far and away the most eloquent, knowledgeable, sensitive, and thoughtful spokesman for Palestinians and kept the cause alive for years and also kept it on the right course, a course that could be meaningful for Palestinian emancipation and ultimate freedom and some minimal amount of justice. And he is irreplaceable in that respect. And it's a loss for international intellectual life, in which he was a major figure and major contributor and continued to be so until the end of his life. And it's a loss for the suffering and the oppressed all over the world because he did not speak just for the Palestinians; he was committed to universal principles of justice and freedom. He was a voice of sanity and courage that supported protection for literally millions of people around the world. So the loss is really unusual.

AI: *How will losing Said affect the Palestinian struggle?*

NC: He had an impact in many dimensions. For one thing, no serious person looks at the relations between the West and the Third World the same way he or she did before the publication of his classic work *Orientalism* and other studies, which permanently shifted, I think, the way in which we think about and recognize the other. Now he wasn't the only person who was doing this, but he played a highly significant role, over and above his dedication to Palestinian rights. He did keep the Palestinian issue on the agenda despite overwhelming opposition, and that's an achievement that is lasting.

His loss now means that other people should do more. Fortunately, younger people are coming along in the Palestinian community who are doing things that weren't being done thirty years ago. In many ways, this is due to Edward's influence. So he is still here through his influence on others.

CRITICAL CONVERGENCES

AI: *In* Covering Islam, *Said reveals a side of his work that crosses over into your work in media criticism.*

NC: It is a topic that I'd been talking about and discussing, but at the same time, I was very much influenced by the way he did his critical work. We had similar values, personal friendship, mutual respect, and we followed each other's words. So obviously each of us was influenced by what the other person did.

AI: *Said further suggested, in* Culture and Resistance, *that in his engagement with the method of intellectual action, he was influenced by two polarities.*[10] *On the one hand, he was greatly affected by Foucault, and in another dimension, he developed a strong affinity to your work. Where do you situate Said?*

NC: I can't really answer that, because I never understood Foucault, so I don't understand what the two poles are. I thought Foucault had some interesting things to say about the history of ideas, but I did not understand the significance and importance of his work.

As for Said, I didn't know him personally before the late 1960s. I mean, I can see a change in his work by the late 1960s. In the time I knew him, we didn't talk that much about the past, so I can't comment on that. And as I say, I cannot really say anything about his departure from what he takes to be Foucault's stance, because I cannot understand Foucault's position. On the matter of acting to resist illegitimate authority, that should just be second nature.

AI: *Said may have seen these polarities collide in the televised debate between you and Foucault on Dutch television. Said commented that, in that encounter, Foucault "backed away and essentially admitted that he believed in no positive truths, ideas, or ideals."*[11] *Perhaps to Said the appeal of the Foucauldian critique as a method was that its call for "relentless erudition"—one that he embraced in* Orientalism *and beyond—was muted by what he saw as Foucault's betrayal of the cause of social action.*[12]

NC: I am not sure that Foucault betrayed the cause because, as far as I am aware, it was never really part of him. Again, you cannot betray something that you've never been committed to except rhetorically. In 1968, of course everybody was talking about it, but I don't take that very seriously. As far as I am aware, he was never a serious part of any struggle to combat oppression, preserve rights—apart from those that particularly interested him. He had some causes that particularly interested him, but I never thought of him, or of almost any of the Paris intellectuals, as engaged in a far-reaching way. So I don't know of any betrayal. In that debate, we actually got along fine. Foucault and I spent the day just walking through the Dutch countryside, partly for fun and partly as an experiment to see how well we would make out in a discussion, with him talking French and me talking English, and we made out fine. The technical part was overcome very easily, but we talked about all sorts of topics and our outlook on the world and so on. The formal discussion was different. There, I thought he presented himself as one of the most amoral human beings I had ever come across. As far as I could tell, he indicated that he had no moral values. I may be completely misunderstanding him. What I understood him to be saying in the formal discussion was that our moral decisions are based on our commitment to one or another system of power. That's it. There is nothing further to say. You exclude yourself from the world of moral agents. I'm sure I am misunderstanding. There has to be more to it than that, but that's what it sounded like to me.

AI: *Said describes Habermas as "appallingly solemn" and states that his actions have no moral center.*[13] *Was there a moral foundation to what you and Said did?*

NC: You're right. There certainly was. We were both very explicit about it. Neither he nor I ever concealed in the least our moral commitments. In fact, we wore them on our sleeves and had no complicated stories about how they're social constructions or whatever, and we didn't hide them in polysyllabic rhetoric. In that sense, we were very much in the same moral universe and quite openly so. With nothing concealed. Habermas is another writer I just don't feel I understand. I read his work and it's coherent, but I cannot see what he is saying that cannot be said quite simply and briefly. His point is fairly obvious. I may have a missing gene. Much of this work either seems to me pretty elementary or just obscurantism and pretentiousness, and that's probably my fault. That's just the way it looks to me.

AI: *During a 1992 interview, in a discussion of Marxist and anti-Marxist philosophers and theoreticians, Said expressed his "sympathy with Chomsky's position, a kind of anarcho-syndicalist position, which has great romantic appeal."*[14]

NC: I cannot recall that. But you have to remember that although we were very close friends, we didn't have many discussions—because of the nature of our lives. I have friends from fifty-five years ago, and we don't have time to talk. Take Israel Shahak: he was a very close friend, but we met about five times. There just isn't time. However, his comment doesn't surprise me, because I think it is consistent with the sense of justice and fairness that permeated his general approach to human affairs. But I don't recall anything specific in his writings that would point in that direction. And it's not something we discussed. I don't know if he elaborated on it anywhere. Not to my knowledge.

OF PUBLIC INTELLECTUALS

AI: *With the deteriorating current situation, and at a time when the narrative of the Palestinians is under attack, the political campaigns targeting public intellectuals, including you and Edward Said, have intensified. Some of these attacks have taken legislative forms. I am thinking specifically of the debate about Title VI funding.*[15]

NC: It comes with the turf. I don't pay that much attention to it. In any society, the commissars are going to become infuriated by those who take a critical and dissident position. In some places, like Central America, such critics may be assassinated, as in Russia in the old days. The United States is a free society, so Daniel Pipes has no power. So people like him resort to slander, vilification, and lies, but this is all normal. It used to bother Ed a lot more than it bothered me.

I don't think these campaigns do very much beyond making vulnerable people suffer, which is bad enough. They can be a nuisance, but most of the time the attackers make fools of themselves. I know that some of my friends take this situation seriously. But I think you should expect it. As far as how it might affect Edward's legacy, it won't affect it in the least. These people simply end up discrediting themselves.

AI: *Do you think that efforts to assail Said's memory alongside the general admonishment of postcolonial studies show that his contribution has been effective?*

NC: It's a sign of success. One should be proud of this. I really don't think it's important. I've been living with this type of attack, even worse, for longer than forty years. But I expect it. It comes with the turf. Anyone who takes a critical position will be denounced. Take someone like John Pilger in England. He is bitterly denounced. In fact, they even made up a word—Pilgerized—which means to tell the real truth about sacred truths. But it's used as a term of condemnation. You should expect that sort of thing.

AI: *Do you see any similarities between these attacks and those exacted against communist thinkers in the academy during the Cold War?*

NC: They're very different because the society is different. Society is simply more civilized and wouldn't tolerate some of the things people could get away with in the early 1950s. In fact, the system of repression in the U.S. is very fragile, at least for relatively privileged people, who make up a very large part of the population in a rich society. We don't have torture chambers, secret police, etcetera. The state has very little power to coerce, fortunately. So intimidation works only if you submit. The situation now is nothing like the atmosphere of the 1950s. Remember, this did not begin with Joe McCarthy; this began with Harry Truman. The Truman administration started this. It was a way to whip the country into hysteria to support a huge military budget and do what the government called "fighting the Cold War," which primarily meant controlling the ex-colonial areas and making sure that Europe and Asia stayed in line. That was a big enterprise, organizing the world. In that context, universities backed down, Hollywood backed down. Everyone was afraid. But I don't think that's going to happen now, although it could. For example, I presume, sooner or later, there will be another major terrorist attack. If so, it could help set up the environment in which the state could get away with applying coercive measures. But that would require a frightened and intimidated population. It's much harder to gain that result now than it was in the past. You can see this with the Iraq war. Take Fallujah, for instance. If Fallujah's events had happened in the 1960s, they would have been handled very simply: B-52 bombings, mass-murder operations, etcetera. You couldn't do such things this time primarily because the American population won't tolerate them. You could do them easily in the 1960s, and nobody cared. But now you cannot. Compare protests of the Iraq war with Vietnam protests. People have been asking why we don't have the kind of protests that existed during Vietnam. It's because the current situation is exactly the opposite. The Vietnam War went on for about five years before any substantial protest developed. Kennedy's military attack on South Vietnam was in 1962, and by 1966 and 1967, we started seeing some protests. By then, South Vietnam was virtually wiped out. There were probably six hundred thousand victims of chemical warfare in South Vietnam, and nobody knows because there were no protests. In Iraq, there were huge protests before the war started. This is the first time in the history of European and U.S. imperialism that mass protests took place before the war officially began. The differences reflect major changes in the population. In Iraq, the U.S. is being compelled to back down step by step. The government may not achieve its war aims. I'm sure the war aims are exactly what the people in Baghdad were thinking: get secure military bases and create a client state in the heart of the main oil-producing region of the world. It may not be able to achieve that. It's being compelled to back down step-by-step. Part of the reason is the steadfast refusal of Iraqis to go along. But it requires a background within the imperial society. If the government had the kind of support in the U.S. that it had in the 1960s, it wouldn't back down. If it had to wipe Iraq out like it did in South Vietnam, it wouldn't back down. That's why I don't think that the kind of oppression that was possible in the past is possible now. That is why I think the Title VI people are mostly making fools of themselves.

AI: *On the issue of protest, you and Edward Said are often mentioned in the same breath. What is the role of the public intellectual, and how did you and Said live that out?*

NC: Here we have to divide the question into several parts. The actual role is, with some exceptions, to serve power. The proper role is any person's role. What makes a person an intellectual? You came here in a taxi. Why isn't the taxi driver an intellectual? Why am I an intellectual? Well, I'm privileged. I have resources that he doesn't have. I have an education that he probably does not have. So it gives you opportunities to do certain things. Then comes choice. Do you want to use your privileges and resources and so on to support power and improve your own standing within powerful institutions, or do you want to use it to help people who are suffering? That is what every person ought to do. However, what privileged people tend to do is quite different. Those called public intellectuals are mostly servants of power, with a few exceptions. That is not just true of the U.S. In fact, it goes through recorded history. There were intellectuals in the Bible, the people who are called the prophets, what we would call dissident intellectuals. They gave geopolitical analyses that people in power did not like. They called on the king to be just and called on people to help the poor and the suffering, they pointed out the crimes of state, and so on. Were they treated nicely? Take a look. They were imprisoned, driven into the desert, and so on. In fact, there is a famous notion now: "hater of Israel." Where does that come from? It comes from the Bible. King Ahab, who was the epitome of evil in the Bible, called prophet Elijah to him and asked, "Why do you hate Israel?" meaning, Why do you hate me? He identified the country, society, culture with the ruling authority. The Soviet Union was the same. Dissidents were considered anti-Soviet because they condemned the policies of the state. Hating Israel, for the loyal intellectuals, means criticizing its policies. That is a totalitarian notion that comes straight out of the Bible. So it's very interesting when it is used by people who know the Bible. The concept of being anti-American is much the same, a deeply totalitarian notion. The history of intellectuals is in this vein. The mainstream intellectual tends to be strongly supportive of power and gains privilege and applause for doing that. Mild criticism is permitted, so long as he or she stays within a pretty narrow framework. There is a fringe of exceptions in most societies, and these dissident intellectuals are usually treated very badly. How badly depends on the society. In countries like the U.S. and England, where the state doesn't have much power to coerce and oppress, they are vilified, because that is the technique that is available. To go back to your question, that is why Edward and I are often lumped together.

AI: *You have pointed out that Said was in an ambivalent position in relation to the media and mainstream culture because his contribution to literary criticism was recognized and honored yet he was the constant target of vilification. Said once stated that such vilification "hasn't stopped Noam and it hasn't stopped me."*[16]

NC: It was a commonality, but it's true for almost anyone who is a dissident in society. So, for example, take our friend Israel Shahak in Israel. He was a highly respected organic chemist, but for many years (not always) he was not only vilified but they tried to throw him out of his job. Newspapers called for putting bombs in his office, and the government intervened to try to destroy the tiny civil rights organization that he was part of. In the United States, he was bitterly condemned by passionate opponents of civil liberties like Alan Dershowitz at Harvard, a professional slanderer and liar who just fabricated tales about him, and was publicly exposed, but it doesn't matter within the systems of power. I attended some of Shahak's talks here, and he was subjected to screaming and shouting. In Israel, to the Israelis' credit, in the last ten or fifteen years of his life, this treatment stopped and he was quite respected. People may not have liked what he said, but he was accepted and honored as a person. But that kind of turnaround is a bit unusual. At the same time that he was an organic chemist, he was regarded as a significant figure. You can say the same about Andre Sakharov. In Soviet mainstream circles, he was certainly highly regarded as a physicist but bitterly condemned as a political commentator. So this is standard. But there is a difference in Edward's case and mine. He wanted to be part of the respectable intellectual world, and the flood of slander and vilification was personally painful to him in ways in which it wouldn't be to somebody who doesn't care very much about those circles. It bothered him very much, but he just continued in what he thought was the right path.

AI: *Earlier you used a metaphor that placed Said in the tradition of the Hebrew prophets who risked exile and loss of prestige in the community because they spoke words against the will of the king. I find that metaphor rather telling, and one that applies to both you and Said in some respects. Said often talked about the "Chomsky condition" as a self-imposed marginalization, which you may or may not agree with, and also said that Chomsky is a solitary personality. This is something he appeared sympathetic to as an exile, not just as a Palestinian, but an intellectual in a perpetual state of in-betweenness. Would you reflect on this idea?*

NC: Arundhati Roy wrote a piece with a similar title, "The Loneliness of Noam Chomsky," at about the time that the two of us were jointly on a platform in Porto Alegre at the World Social Forum talking to an audience of maybe fifteen thousand people. Afterward we took part in a six-mile march of maybe one hundred thousand people. So it is not an obvious notion of loneliness. And, in fact, I have given talks to thousands of people; I can't accept a fraction of the invitations I receive. And I don't just give talks to people; I also participate in activities and organizations. So this is hardly loneliness. The isolation and loneliness that Edward talked about is a different type, two types actually. One is isolation from the respect of the intellectual community. So many academics choose to publish lies and slanders. So that is a kind of loneliness, but it is not of any concern to those who don't want to be part of these circles anyway. The other is just personal. I happen to be a private person. I am perfectly happy with a couple of good friends and family, but that is a personal characteristic; it's not loneliness. I don't think I'm a solitary voice if I have to spend an hour every night turning down invitations to present and speak to thousands of people, with regret. It is solitary only from the perspective of a certain elite cultural hegemony.

AI: *Which is why Said believed this loneliness is necessary. "It is better than a gregarious tolerance for the way things are," he writes in the introduction to your book* Fateful Triangle.[17] *In* The World, the Text, and the Critic, *Said identifies the intellectual tasks you once argued were necessary to wage the sociopolitical battle—"to imagine a future society that conforms to the exigencies of human nature as best we understand them; . . . [and] to analyze the nature of power and oppression in our present societies."*[18]

NC: Yes, that's a pretty good description of what he did most of his life. It's not the standard role intellectuals play, and it's honorable.

AI: *Said believed that while your position is the most admirable, it is also the least emulatable.*

NC: No, I don't think he's the person to talk about emulating. I can't think of anything I've done that he didn't do independently, often much better, so what is there to emulate?

JUSTICE IN IRAQ

AI: *Edward Said was concerned about the politics of representation. His explication of the ways in which interests intersect with portrayal is a terrain you have charted significantly over the years. In light of this concern, how would you situate Said vis-à-vis the current conflict in Iraq?*

NC: There are a few people, and Ed was one, who had a principled objection to the invasion. It came under sharp elite criticism, but on very narrow grounds rather than principled grounds. The charge was that it would be harmful for the U.S., that it wouldn't work, that there was no immediate threat, that sort of thing. But Edward wouldn't have had any of that. For example, there is an odd charade going on right now among intellectuals in England as well as here about whether the Bush administration had downgraded the threat of terror in the interest of achieving its aims in Iraq, about the revelations of Richard Clarke and so on. The only thing that is surprising about any of these discussions is that anybody takes them seriously. Of course, members of the administration downgraded the threat of terror in favor of their interests in Iraq; that's proven by the fact that they invaded Iraq. They invaded Iraq for reasons that are not allowed to be said here. They knew perfectly well that the invasion would likely increase the threat of terror; it just didn't matter. Edward was one of the few people who said this, and if he were sitting here today, would be saying this. But it's not discussable in polite circles. For example, take the Syria Accountability Act. There is a fine scholar who has written about it, Stephen Zunes, but hardly anyone else has paid attention. Syria has been highly cooperative with the United States. The Syrians don't like Islamic fundamentalists. The Syria Accountability Act, which was passed almost unanimously, is virtually a declaration of war. It cuts off the U.S. from a major source of information and support in the struggle against Al Qaeda–style terror. But it's more important to ensure that the Middle East is disciplined. In fact, if you look at the act, you will get much insight. If you look at the core criticism of Syria in it, you will find that it is based on Resolution 520, which calls for respect for the territorial integrity and sovereignty of Lebanon. People say that Syria is violating that, which is true. But nobody bothers to say that the Syrians were virtually invited in by the U.S. and Israel in 1976 to massacre Palestinians, which was considered a good thing. So they happily brought the Syrians in. But more importantly, Resolution 520 wasn't directed against Syria; it was directed against Israel. It was passed in 1982 to call on Israel to respect the territorial integrity of Lebanon, and of course Israel violated it for twenty-two years, from 1978 until 2000. Nobody mentioned sanctions against Israel. Nobody mentions that the core of the resolution against Syria is actually a resolution against Israel. This is the kind of thing that Edward would have talked about, but very few others do. And this situation goes on, case after case, after all the pretexts for war collapsed—weapons of mass destruction, ties to terror, and so on. So there is a new story: what the press calls Bush's messianic vision to bring democracy to Iraq and the Middle East. Western commentary completely fell into line with this idea, even the critics. Critics in the *New York Review of Books* or *American Prospect* say, yes, it's a liberal and generous vision, but it's overreaching and too costly, we can't do it, and so on. What's the evidence that democracy was the original goal? Do they have any evidence for it? No, no evidence. The leader said so; therefore, all news reporting presupposed it. Actually, the only major exception that I have found so far in the American press is a story in the *Washington Post* that reported a poll in Baghdad. People were asked why they thought the U.S. invaded, and almost everybody gave the obvious answer: to take control of Iraq's resources and to reorganize the Middle East to suit U.S. interest. You can't mention that idea here in the U.S. So that's the majority's view in Baghdad. How about the idea of establishing democracy? In Baghdad, one percent of respondents. To help Iraqis? Five percent. This is the kind of position Edward was invested in and for which he was at times a lone spokesman. For the most part, intellectuals simply and blindly followed what amounted to government orders. Although these orders are not enforced, people tend to fall into line. I tried to find a comment in the U.S. press noting what most people in Baghdad think, and it just isn't there, except at the margins. This silence goes on in case after case. For instance, the coverage of the Israeli-Arab conflict has been ridiculous. You simply cannot report the most elementary facts. Take the 1982 invasion of Lebanon, the worst of the five invasions. All over the Israeli press there were stories explaining what the invasion was about. High political and military echelons made it clear; the press commented. It was about the West Bank.

Israel wanted to stop the PLO's [Palestine Liberation Organization's] negotiating offers, which were an embarrassment. The Israelis couldn't fend off the PLO negotiators anymore, so they had to stop them from carrying out this embarrassing diplomatic offensive to try and settle the problem. You couldn't report this in the U.S., not a word. The story in the U.S., which was a complete fabrication, was that Israel invaded Lebanon because Katyusha rockets were falling on northern Galilee, which was complete nonsense. In fact, the first reference I've seen to what was perfectly well-known in 1982 was about a year ago [2004], when the Israel correspondent for the *New York Times*, James Bennett, embedded a line in his story saying that Israel invaded in order to stop negotiation offers. It took twenty years for a line to appear, but Edward had been talking about it, and he could reach an audience. He spoke the truth in case after case. And that is why they hate him.

AI: *When* Orientalism *came out in 1978, it was soon heralded by many as an influential text focused on perception of the other. It transformed much of the academic discourse on representation of the other, yet "othering" images persist. We still see pervasive images from Abu Ghraib prison along with the numerous atrocities committed by the empire, if you will, to subdue the other. How would Edward Said view these manifestations almost three decades after* Orientalism's *publication?*

NC: When you talk about academic discourse, you're talking about cultural studies, literary studies, not political science, not international relations, not the public intellectuals who appear in the media; they don't change in the ways you describe. His work certainly revolutionized cultural studies and the social sciences, everything from anthropology to literary criticism. It has its effects within society, but it's not going to change central properties unless it enters general consciousness and understanding. It is important for its general civilizing effect on society, but it's not going to change the propaganda function of the media and the mainstream intellectuals. This role is deeply embedded in institutionalized structures of power. In fact, if you look closely, the Abu Ghraib scandals are being handled very much like the My Lai massacre in Vietnam was. The atrocities are being blamed on "the other," not on us. It's not us nice fellows in the faculty clubs and editorial offices; it's some southern redneck who is very different from us and is uneducated and comes from a part of the world that has nothing to do with us. Just like My Lai, Abu Ghraib is not being attributed to the people who are responsible. My Lai, for example, was blamed on the uneducated, half-crazed GIs in the field who didn't know who was going to shoot them next and went wild. That's the merest fragment of the truth. The truth is that My Lai was a footnote to a big mass-murder operation that was organized by nice people just like us in air-conditioned offices. Criticism stops at the level of the soldiers on the ground.

If you look into it, which few are doing, you'll find there were orders, a framework in which the soldiers were operating, that came straight from the top. Furthermore, what were they doing? What was in the minds of these people? They were taking revenge on the "ragheads" who bombed the World Trade Center. Where did they get this idea? From the nice people who run Fox News. That's the story, but that part is being cut out. It's the other who is being blamed, and the other happens to be in U.S. uniform in this case and in My Lai, but it doesn't matter. He is still an "other," so we can attack him. The reason we can't tell the truth is that we are the ones who are responsible, not the other.

MEETING SAID AND THE PLO

AI: *Do you recall your first meeting with Edward Said?*

NC: It must have been about thirty-five years ago—in the late 1960s—but I don't remember the specific occasion. Very likely, our first meeting was in connection with the Israeli-Palestinian situation, which was very personal for both of us. In later years, we sometimes saw each other in meetings with the PLO.

AI: *Not much has been published about these meetings with Palestinian officials in New York. What was the extent of your involvement with Said during that formative period?*

NC: I have never written or even spoken much about it. Regrettably, all the other people who were involved in the meetings have died since. Now, we just have my memory to rely on. None of us talked about it much. Edward, from the 1970s, tried very hard, as did others, to influence the Palestinian leadership to undertake and pursue policies that were more constructive and conducive to achieving the rights of Palestinians. They were simply not doing that. They were following policies that couldn't have been more gratifying to hawkish Israelis and Americans. They often acted like they were paid agents of the most extremist and jingoistic elements in Israel and the United States. Another person who made these efforts was Eqbal Ahmad, who also had personal relationships with PLO leaders and was pursuing these essentially parallel arguments in his own way. The meeting in New York and other interactions were about such matters. These meetings were completely unsuccessful, I should say. The leadership simply could not comprehend the need to develop sympathy, solidarity, and support among the American population. I have had a lot to do with Third World movements over many decades, and the Palestinian leadership was the only one I have ever come across that didn't understand this. Even the North Korean leaders, in their own lunatic way, were trying to influence American opinion by sending the collected works of Kim Il-Sung and that sort of thing. It wasn't a very helpful way of doing it, but at least they understood that unless you have some degree of popular support in the U.S., you'll be smashed. That's just the way the world works. The only thing that can inhibit U.S. power and violence is domestic opinion. And the Palestinian leadership never comprehended that. If the leaders had come to the U.S. and told the truth about themselves, they would have gained enormous popular support. The truth was that they were conservative nationalists who wanted to elect their own mayors and run their societies and so on, which is a perfectly acceptable message in mainstream America. But they insisted on presenting themselves as Marxist revolutionaries carrying Kalashnikovs and leading a world revolution, which was comical. And their actions were the same. In those years (1970s), the Palestinian leaders were directing murderous, terrorist attacks against people who could have been their natural allies in Israel. Internal planning in Israel was to send the poor Arab Jews to the borders with Lebanon, and Palestinians were attacking and killing people there. Quite apart from any moral evaluation, this approach was politically imbecilic. Here was a group within Israeli society that they could have had significant interactions with, but they preferred to kill them.

Their conception of politics was that you get together with other rich people in the backroom and work out a deal. So if they could get invited to the kitchen in the White House and talk with Kissinger, that would be politics, rather than doing something that could help contribute to popular solidarity. I'll give you one concrete example to illustrate this. In the 1982 war, the murderous invasion of Lebanon wouldn't have taken place without U.S. support, including veto of Security Council resolutions calling for an end to the aggression and crimes. The events were horrifying enough, especially the bombing of Beirut, for considerable information to get into the U.S. Even Thomas Friedman reported that it's no fun being bombed by Israelis. There was an important story of an Israeli military officer, Dov Yirmiah, who was an old heroic figure in Israel, one of the founders of the Haganah, the original self-defense organization. He was greatly admired for his integrity and his courage. He was too old to be in the army, but he went with the military forces as one of the civilian authorities appointed to deal with the captured population and other matters. He was utterly appalled. His ideals were destroyed, and he couldn't stand the horrors and the atrocities. He wrote a war diary in Hebrew about his experiences—a very graphic, evocative, and compelling one. I read it in Hebrew, and I thought it would be a great idea to have it translated, and I convinced a small publisher here to translate it. It did and published it as a war diary. I asked Edward if he could persuade the PLO, which had money coming out of its ears—one of the richest Third World movements to ever exist—to help with the distribution by buying copies and distributing them to libraries, for example, so the book would be available somewhere. I was certain it was never going to be reviewed here. And the publisher didn't have any funds to advertise. He did make that request, but the PLO would do it only if the book were stamped "Published with the support of the PLO." That is typical of the PLO's failure to understand how a democratic society works. That failure was consistent and long-standing, recurring in case after case after case. Edward made major efforts to change that, and I was involved in some of them. He and I and Alex Erlich, professor of Russian history at Columbia University, met with PLO leaders, but our efforts were useless.

AI: *Retrospectively, it seems Said had significant foresight about the far-reaching negative impact of the Oslo Accords on Palestinian livelihood. Were your views compatible with Said's on the conditions of this agreement? What would Said say about the current situation?*

NC: I'll have to extrapolate. We had about the same reaction to Oslo and were both worried about it right away and spoke in almost the same terms without even talking to each other. That much is in print.

As for the present, I suspect he would react in the same way that both he and I reacted to Oslo. Objectively, the cease-fire was a total victory for the United States and Israel. In fact, it was a victory in Europe as well.

Israel and the United States had succeeded in reshaping the issue. The only thing that counts to them is Palestinian violence. Israel and the U.S. would be perfectly happy if Palestinians never raised a finger. Then they could continue their programs of integration and takeover of the West Bank, taking over the valuable land and resources, developing massive infrastructure projects that cantonize the population. And that was the goal they agreed on. There was not a single word about occupation. In their world, settlements never emerged, the Israeli development programs never emerged, the wall was not to be discussed. Just keep quiet. So that is a total victory for the U.S. and Israeli position, and rather strikingly, the victory is accepted in Europe and in fact in most of the world. This view says that the only issue is the security of Israelis, including the Israeli settlements now. Nobody wants killing anymore; everyone will be happier to see an end to the violence, yes.

CONTESTED ZIONISMS AND BINATIONALISM

AI: *In the 1990s, Said embraced and began to speak publicly of his support for the one-state solution. Were the two of you in agreement on this point? How did your visions for the peace process contrast? Did you both favor a binational solution?*

NC: That was a late view. Edward, as far as I know, never expressed that until the late 1990s.

As for me, I had been committed to that solution since childhood. During the period from 1967 and 1973, I think there was a realistic prospect. I did write and speak about it a lot. But I don't recall anyone else doing so at the time. In fact, I was vilified on both sides: Palestinians, Israelis, and, of course, American commentators went crazy. But, in that period, it was realistic. From the memoirs of top Israeli military officials, we find that proposals were coming from Israeli military intelligence that could have led in that direction. These were immediately dismissed by the higher political echelons. But from the mid-1970s, it was not feasible except as a later stage of a long-term process. At that point, the idea of a two-state settlement became the international consensus, and that is what Edward was committed to, as far as I know. I was too, though hoping that it might be a step toward closer integration. When Oslo came along, I think Edward and I saw it as essentially a sellout by the PLO from outside the territories, a case of outsider Palestinians undermining the prospects for a meaningful two-state settlement that would take into account the legitimate rights of the insiders, the Palestinians on the inside.

AI: *Do you believe that is when Edward Said embraced the idea of a one-state solution?*

NC: Take a look at his writing. As far as I am aware, the idea starts appearing in his writings a couple of years after the collapse of Oslo had become pretty apparent.

AI: *Then he became very fervent, up until his death.*

NC: That's one thing that we actually disagreed on. I was committed to it in principle from way back, in fact in the early 1940s. I thought that bringing it up in the late 1990s was a tactical and intellectual mistake. In fact, it is striking that in the late 1990s, it became a tolerable position in the mainstream. So Edward could write about it in the *New York Times,* as could Tony Judt in the *New York Review of Books,* and others elsewhere. From 1967 to the mid-1970s, when it was feasible to propose it, it literally was taboo. So what's the difference? The difference is that it was understood by the late 1990s that it was just not feasible. Suddenly it was permissible to talk about it. I am not suggesting any bad faith on anyone's part, but I think there's a misunderstanding of the situation. You can still hope for a binational settlement, but it's going to have to go through stages. In the 1967 to mid-1970s period, it could have been implemented. A federal system could have been implemented within a general peace. That's not a feasible proposal now, but it could be approached again in stages. The first stage would be a two-state solution along the lines of the Geneva Accords, at least as a basis for serious negotiations, and then you could move from there to further cooperation and integration, and so on. But talking about a single state at this point is just offering a gift to the Israeli right wing and to the United States.

I think that is why it has become a topic of legitimate discussion within the mainstream, so I did disagree with Said on that tactical matter.

AI: *In* Power, Politics, and Culture, *Said states that there are differences between you but that they are not very interesting or important.*[19]

NC: The areas of agreement were not only large but so important that we tended to keep to those, but I'm sure there were differences. I mean, for example, we never discussed it, but I'm sure I have more sympathy with the original so-called Zionist project than he did. I can understand that. I do see the conflict as a conflict of rights, and I don't think he did, at least at the level that I did.

AI: *How did your views on Zionism differ?*

NC: It grew out of a European context, but most of it was coming from Eastern Europe. That's where the immigration came from. There was political Zionism represented by Theodore Herzl and the other leading figures, but the actual settlement of the land came from an Eastern European Jewish culture that was a mixed story. This culture included elements of Russian and other Eastern European intellectual life. It was very much rooted in the Jewish ghettoes; it is a complicated mixed story. I mostly perceive things from within that framework. I was just as much opposed to political Zionism as Edward was, but there were other strands to which I was more sympathetic.

AI: *Would you elaborate on this point?*

NC: Well, I was committed since childhood to socialist binationalist tendencies in Zionism, which were opposed to a Jewish state but were in favor of building a Jewish community and cultural center and an array of socialist institutions like the cooperatives and kibbutzim, hoping that they would draw in and integrate with Palestinian society on a class basis.

Take a concrete and contentious issue. One of the elements of the Eastern European Jewish immigration into Palestine, including socialist binationalist tendencies, was the development of so-called Jewish labor. That concept essentially called for a pretty closed economy, a Jewish-based economy, with Jewish labor, Jewish production. Of course, that is discriminatory in that it discriminates against the native population. That idea is at least contentious, maybe worse. However, if you want to discuss the idea seriously, you have to ask what its sources were. And the sources were complex. To put it simply, if there was to be any immigration at all—and that goes back to another question, was there any right for there to be any immigration at all?—but if you assume for the sake of argument that there was some justification for the settlement, the establishment of a cultural center, a place where Jews have their own lives and so on, then the question of Jewish labor can be difficult. It's difficult because settlers who came perceived two choices. One was to be South African-style landowners exploiting Palestinian workers, and the other was to reverse the inverted pyramid of Jewish life as it was perceived by the leftist Jewish Zionists. In this view, normal functioning societies have a base of productive people—farmers and workers—and they form the base of the pyramid. Their productive work enables commerce, intellectuals, universities, professionals, and so on. But this latter group is the peak of the pyramid. Jewish life, many thinkers said, was inverted, there was no base. They wanted to form what they considered a normal society, which meant that there would have to be a base of a Jewish working class and a Jewish farmer's class. But that type of society is possible only if it is exclusive and exclusionary. You and I could not go to Central Africa and become part of the society and survive. We're not equipped for that. The same was true for people coming from even poorer communities in Eastern Europe. If they had tried to live the life of a Palestinian peasant, they couldn't have survived. So the choices were to create a normal society with a working-class base and to allow professionals and intellectuals to come off the surplus of the working base. To accomplish that, you almost have to have exclusionary Jewish labor, which was certainly a dilemma. But understanding the dilemma is important. It makes sense to reject the position, but only if you understand its roots and origins, which are complex.

REFLECTIONS

AI: *Looking back after having known him for so long, who is Edward Said to you?*

NC: First, he made quite a brilliant contribution to modern culture and understanding in his academic work. But he was also a courageous, honest person who insisted on telling people the truth regardless of whether they wanted to hear it. Palestinians too. He tried for years to talk some sense into the PLO leadership—a pretty hopeless enterprise—and brought me into it sometimes. So I got to see his approach firsthand. Take, for instance, the Oslo agreements: he was one of the very few people who said right away, accurately, that they would be a catastrophe for the Palestinians and he pointed out why. Palestinians didn't want to hear that. He was not preaching to the choir, but he was telling the truth to the people who had to hear it. He also received the kind of appreciation and acclaim that I think he wanted from the people whom he cared about. Even though he may not have reached certain segments of the population, people couldn't fail to recognize the importance of his contributions, regardless of how much they hated what he was doing. Some Stalinist clones condemned him with frivolous labels like "professor of terror" or whatever. But if Edward cared about that, he shouldn't have. He should have appreciated that kind of condemnation.

AI: *Did Said accomplish what he set out to do?*

NC: As far as putting and keeping the Palestinian issue on the international agenda, yes, more than anyone else. Did he achieve any measure of justice for the Palestinians? Just take a look at what is happening. The situation is as bad as it's ever been, or worse. But these are not easy things to achieve. In objective terms, Israel offers a tremendous amount to the U.S. It is a powerful state, rich, advanced; it's like an offshore military and high-technology base for the U.S. right in the most important region of the world. What do the Palestinians offer? Nothing. They don't have wealth, power, or resources, and therefore they have no value by the elementary principles of statecraft. It's a hard thing to combat. Edward tried valiantly, and he certainly succeeded in compelling people to think about it and in bringing understanding to a lot of people. The fact is that a large majority of the American public agrees with Edward. If you look at the polls in the U.S., they are astonishing. By about two to one, people in the U.S. think that the U.S. ought to cut off aid to either of the two parties, Israel and Palestine, that is not negotiating seriously for a two-state diplomatic solution. By about the same majority, the U.S. public thinks that if both parties are negotiating seriously, the U.S. should equalize aid. This idea is so remote from anything anybody can discuss that it's hard to find words for it. So public opinion, in fact, is pretty much on Edward's side on this. But in our society, public opinion is often quite divorced from policy making, not just on this issue but on many others too.

At the end of the day, Ed is sorely missed. Personally, he was a close friend and someone I admire very much.

NOTES

This interview took place in two sessions in Cambridge, Massachusetts, on June 4, 2004, and February 11, 2005.

1. These activities include several public appearances, conferences, media interviews, and collaborations or endorsements of published works, such as Said's introductions to Chomsky's *The Fateful Triangle: The United States, Israel and the Palestinians* (2000) and *Acts of Aggression: Policing "Rogue" States* (2003).

2. Noam Chomsky, *The Fateful Triangle* (Cambridge, MA: South End Press, 1983), viii.

3. Edward W. Said, *Reflections on Exile and Other Essays* (Cambridge, MA: Harvard University Press, 2000), 213.

4. Edward W. Said, "Permission to Narrate," in *The Politics of Dispossession: The Struggle for Palestinian Self-Determination, 1969–1994* (New York: Vintage, 1995), 247–68.

5. "Culture and Imperialism," in *Power, Politics and Culture: Interviews with Edward W. Said*, ed. Gauri Viswanathan (New York: Vintage, 2002), 201.

6. *Power, Politics and Culture*, 205.

7. Ibid., 203.

8. Ibid., 331.

9. Ibid., 138.

10. Edward W. Said, *Culture and Resistance: Conversations with Edward W. Said*, Interviews by David Barsamian (Cambridge, MA: South End Press, 2003), 5.

11. *Power, Politics, and Culture*, 77.

12. Ibid., p. 40.

13. Edward W. Said, *Representations of the Intellectual: The 1993 Reith Lectures* (New York: Vintage Books, 1996), xviii.

14. Ibid., 205.

15. *Power, Politics, and Culture*, 161.

16. Following Said's death, several groups with close ties to the Israel lobby within academia made a concerted effort to tarnish his legacy and his contribution to Middle Eastern studies. Various congressional hearings in 2003 were dedicated to restricting any seemingly anti-imperial discourse in the regional scholarly and curricular canon, with a particular emphasis on Said's seminal critique. These actions include a proposed bill H.R. 3077 to amend Title VI of the Higher Education Act of 1965. This legislation was developed to reprimand and punish various programs and departments by withholding funding if they were deemed to espouse an antagonistic view toward U.S. foreign policy in the Middle East or if they were critical of Israeli actions.

17. Chomsky, *Fateful Triangle*, viii.

18. Said, *World, the Text, and the Critic* (Cambridge, MA: Harvard University Press, 1983), 246.

19. *Power, Politics, and Culture*, 77.

23

"Contented Homeland Peace"

The Motif of Exile in Edward Said

Robert Spencer

He had no leisure to regret what he had lost, he was so wholly and naturally concerned for what he had failed to obtain.
—JOSEPH CONRAD, *LORD JIM*, 104

Theodor W. Adorno once described Gustav Mahler's Fourth Symphony as searching for "contented homeland peace, healed of the pain of frontiers" (Adorno 1992: 44). The phrase is also a felicitous description of the political ideal, tentatively suggested and then articulated with increasing frankness in later writings of Edward W. Said, the world-renowned critic (until his much-lamented death in 2003) of imperial arrogance, cultural misapprehension, and Israel's unremitting maltreatment of the Palestinians. As Said recognized in his *Musical Elaborations*, where he declared himself "profoundly indebted in all sorts of ways" to Adorno's work (Said 1991: 15), the pair had rather more in common than a seldom pronounced initial. I hope to show here that the aspiration that Adorno raised in a vague and even utopian fashion takes more definite shape in Said's work as a feasible political project. Notwithstanding Said's well-documented advocacy of exile as a technique of intellectual discovery and dissent, he demonstrably shared Adorno's vision of homecoming (that is, of a boundless and egalitarian polity) and rejected the practice of exile as an attractive *mode de vie* in its own right. "Marginality and homelessness," he declared, "are not, in my opinion, to be gloried in; they are to be brought to an end, so that more, and not fewer, people can enjoy the benefits of what has for centuries been denied the victims of race, class, or gender" (Said 2000a: 385). Exile, in other words, is a means not an end; it is above all a way of thinking. Exile involves a willingness to step outside the province of ideological preconceptions, sectarian loyalties, and insentient theoretical and philosophical systems. Moreover, it enables us to alert those inward-looking dogmas to the reality they obscure and to the experiences and lives, which they routinely overlook, of the persecuted, the marginalized, and the dispossessed. Exile allows us to contrast insular doctrines with the real political alternatives disclosed by open discussion, sensitive scholarship, unprejudiced cultural contact, and, above all, by a tolerant regard for the equality and diversity of human life. It involves not a cynical or complacent disengagement from the world, therefore, but a radical dissatisfaction with the needless conflicts, parochialisms, and inequalities by which the world is riven.

For Said, who was less willing than Adorno to sugarcoat this radical vision with euphemisms, a borderless homeland meant nothing less than a democratic and cosmopolitan global polity free of racial and national strife and liberated also from humanly wasteful economic exploitation. Various interpreters, sympathetic and otherwise, have sought to airbrush this ideal from Said's writings, and my purpose here is, via a close scrutiny of some of these, to place his cosmopolitan and even universalist vision at the forefront of our assessments of his impressive, not to say hugely relevant, body of work. In the academic field of postcolonial studies, for instance, which Said's *Orientalism* effectively founded, some theorists have confused the critical mind-set instilled by exile with a sort of extreme intellectual skepticism that sees the pursuit of knowledge as complicit in the pursuit of power and that dismisses universal values as a cover for imperial rule.[1] Critics like Dennis Porter (1993) and James Clifford (1988: 255–76) claim to have found an inconsistency in *Orientalism* between its humanist faith in the possibility of knowledge and the existence of common values and its methodological reliance on the antihumanist theory of Michel Foucault.[2] From a more leftist standpoint, albeit an intemperate and not very fairminded one, Aijaz Ahmad has portrayed Said as a sort of metropolitan dilettante, more interested in hovering aloofly above the fray, declining affiliations, and carping about attempts to know about or evince solidarity toward different cultures, societies, and peoples (1992: 159–219). From a quite different perspective, that of justifying the invasion and occupation of Iraq, Christopher Hitchens (2003) has argued similarly that his erstwhile collaborator slighted the possibilities of intellectual work and, specifically, denied the possibility of nonviolent communication between cultures. Faced by such mischaracterizations, we need urgently to remind ourselves that the goal of Said's thought was convergence rather than conflict, fraternity rather than frontiers, democracy rather than discord—in short, a just and reconciled international homeland rather than divisive separatism or the lawless hegemony of powerful states.

I contend that we should characterize Said's project as a dialogic or, speaking philosophically, a dialectical one. Said's work is dialectical in two senses: in its desire to sketch connections that are usually obscured by parochial points of view and in its consequent urge for reconciliation. Indeed, exile serves Said as something of a synonym for dialectical method. He argues that the responsible intelligence has a duty to set sail from the familiar views and *idées reçues* of the native realm (Said

2000a: 173–86; Said 1994b: 35–47). The exile must view the conjectures and premises of his outlook with the skeptical gaze and critical distance of the outsider, testing its tenets against the reservations of interlocutors and the possible rejoinders
of a previously unconsidered and unheeded reality. He is like the shipwrecked protagonist of Joseph Conrad's story "Amy Foster," washed up on unfamiliar shores and
abruptly "taken out of his knowledge" (Conrad 1992: 195). All of Said's work, from
Joseph Conrad and the Fiction of Autobiography (1966), his first published book, to
his final texts on the war in Iraq and the idea of lateness, was distinguished by its
awareness that personality, identity, and outlook are not set in stone but are im-
provable by exposure to novel experiences, strange encounters, and stimulating deliberations. Said's early remarks on Conrad hold true both as an encapsulation of
his approach and as a manifesto for intellectual conduct.

> Conrad's individuality resides in a continuous exposure of his sense of himself to a
> sense of what is not himself: he set himself, lumpish and problematic, against the dy-
> namic, fluid processes of life. Because of this, then, the great human appeal and dis-
> tinction of Conrad's life is the dramatic spirit of partnership, however uneasy or in-
> decorous, his life exemplifies, a partnership between himself and the external world.
> I am speaking of the full exposition of his soul to the vast panorama of existence it
> has discerned outside itself. He had the courage to risk a full confrontation with what,
> most of the time, seemed to him to be a threatening and unpleasant world. Moreover,
> the outcome of this dialectic is an experiencing of existential reality at that deepest
> level of alternative and potentiality which is the true life of the mind. (Said 1966: 9)

I wish to draw attention to that last phrase, in particular to its association of alternative and potentiality with *the true life of the mind*. By summarizing two crucial intellectual aptitudes to which the practice of exile gives rise, it captures a great
deal of what is important and salutary in Said's work. The first is the Conradian
willingness to face up to a world that is sometimes alien and minatory and by so
doing to employ the process of dialogue (of exposure to unfamiliar experiences and
points of view) to test and then refute parochial ideas and loyalties. "To be in a conversation," as Hans-Georg Gadamer, the philosopher of hermeneutics, remarks,
"means to be beyond oneself, to think with the other and to come back to oneself
as if to another" (Gadamer 1989: 110). Hence dialogue is synonymous with the
mind-broadening power of travel, of an itinerant exploration of alternative perspectives. Inseparable from the first consequence of an exilic sensibility is the second: the capacity to envision a cosmopolitan polity. If exile entails the practice of
dialogue, then the substantive ideal it entails is obviously not a carefree withdrawal
from political responsibilities. Instead, exile allows one to envision an inclusive
homeland in which all contribute equally to the common process of deliberation
and all take shelter under the legally enforceable human rights that make such participation possible. Said's proposal for a nonsectarian settlement in his native Pales-

tine is a model for such a community, underpinned by cosmopolitan solidarity and liberated from clannish fealties. Exile, then, is undertaken not for its own sake but for the sake of a cosmopolitan mentality that, in encompassing numerous experiences and points of view, begins to discern a common humanity beneath the divisive ideologies of separateness and tribal division. Exile betokens an itinerant impatience with the shelter of entrenched doctrines; it subjects insular mentalities to the myriad rejoinders of other outlooks, mind-sets, and experiences, and in so doing it strengthens the bonds of sympathy and solidarity necessary to inaugurate a just, equitable, and, to borrow Adorno's terms, contented, peaceful, and borderless homeland. A democratic global community is required to codify this cosmopolitan disposition and surmount the divisions and inequalities that capitalism and imperialism have not ceased to inflict on the ideal of human community.

WORLDLINESS

Said's universalism is thus found less in a utopian blueprint imposed on reality than in a way of thinking and criticizing that its own intrinsic momentum generates a cosmopolitan political vision. He has bequeathed less a finished system or inflexible method than an uncomplicated but profoundly enabling disposition, an exemplary commitment to the restless activity of thought that refuses to limit its range by flattering power, condoning orthodoxy, or contenting itself with parochial allegiances. His epitaph could be the final lines of the young Wordsworth's sonnet "To Toussaint l'Ouverture," which assure that fallen champion of anticolonial resistance that "thou hast great allies;/ Thy friends are exultations, agonies,/ And love, and man's unconquerable mind" (1971: 243).

That mind, as Jim Merod has written, "rejects and, ultimately, refutes the seductive persuasions of certainties that impede its own meandering path" (2000: 116). This belief in the empowering capacity of unobstructed thought illuminates all of Said's work: his philosophical disquisition on the nature of origins, his dissection of the pseudo-expertise about the non-Western world peddled in the news media, his disapproval of inward-looking theoretical standpoints, his perspicacious literary criticism and, of course, his advocacy of the Palestinian cause. The motif of exile, which is omnipresent in Said's writings, cannot be separated from what I have identified as his thought's intrepid bent because one's physical and especially *intellectual* distance is what allows one to write critically and constructively about culture and ideology and about the kinds of knowledge produced in the academy. "Exile is a model for the intellectual who is tempted, and even beset and overwhelmed, by the rewards of accommodation, yea-saying, settling in. Even if one is not an actual immigrant or expatriate, it is still possible to think as one, to imagine and investigate in spite of barriers, and always to move away from the centralizing authorities towards the margins, where you see things that are usually lost on minds that have never traveled beyond the conventional and the comfortable" (Said 1994b: 46–47).

The important point for my purposes here is that Said advocated exile as a means not an end.[3] He never followed the example of Gilles Deleuze's "nomad thought"— in which truth, physical being, and one's convictions are in a state of constant flux (Deleuze 1977)—by detaching himself from political and intellectual commitments and hymning travel as an end in itself. Moreover, nothing could be further from Said's work than Homi Bhabha's insouciant endorsement of the conditions of dispersal and homelessness.[4] He recognized that such circumstances are far more congenial for the peripatetic academic than they could ever be for the beleaguered seeker of asylum or, as Said would need no reminding, for an entire people expelled, subjugated, and punished unendingly for the sheer fact of their endurance and their still-unquenched yearning for return. We need, in other words, to distinguish Said's account of exile as a predominantly intellectual phenomenon and a source of dissidence from the kind of glib rhetoric that Michael Mann has described as "breathless transnationalism" (Mann 2001: 117), Tom Nairn has called (more unforgivingly) "departure lounge internationalism" (Nairn 2000: 148), and Andrew Smith has termed (more unforgivingly still) "the 'free-air-miles' sentiment in postcolonial theory" (Smith 2004: 245). Exile is not the same thing as intellectual license; it does not imply a sort of weightless disregard for worldly commitments. The exile, as Bruce Robbins notes, is too conscious of the manifest toll exacted by displacement and dispossession to imagine that exile is its own reward (1983: 69). For the displaced, the loss of tradition, continuity, and locality saps their individual and collective strength. In a moving commentary accompanying Jean Mohr's photographs of Palestinian lives, Said bore witness to the privation that results from losing easy contact with the conversation of sympathetic interlocutors and with the familiar reference points of a known and cherished world.

> The stability of geography and the continuity of land—these have completely disappeared from my life and the life of all Palestinians. If we are not stopped at borders, or herded into new camps, or denied reentry and residence, or barred from travel from one place to another, more of our land is taken, our lives are interfered with arbitrarily, our voices are prevented from reaching each other, our identity is confined to frightened little islands in an inhospitable environment of superior military force sanitized by the clinical jargon of pure administration. . . . Continuity for *them,* the dominant population; discontinuity for *us,* the dispossessed and dispersed. (Said 1993: 19–20)

Said's work does not confuse the agreeable wayfaring of the strong with the unenviable expatriation of the weak, or the uncommitted intellectual's frivolous wanderlust with the fate of those driven from their native soil by occupiers' rifle butts. Said considered exile a predominantly intellectual phenomenon, or else a disagreeable condition that can nonetheless, *in extremis,* be turned resourcefully to account.

In *Beginnings: Intention and Method* (1975), his dense philosophical meditation on originality, Said identified the sort of outlook that exile serves to correct. He dissects a dogma of originality that authorizes ideas and theories by situating them in a line of supposedly unbroken dynastic descent from some unchallengeable and usually divine genesis. Origins require slavish compliance. A beginning, however, is a secular departure *from* (not an obedient ratification *of* or, for that matter, a catastrophic break *with*) existing ideas and practices. Beginnings require an innovative and even subversive willingness to deviate from customary ways of thinking and acting. Origins are doctrinaire by definition: they pass themselves off as conclusive and unarguable dictates, otherworldly revelations that brook no opposition or divergence. Beginnings, in contrast, intervene creatively in meanings and institutions. "To make explicit what is usually allowed to remain implicit; to state that which, because of professional consensus, is ordinarily not stated or questioned; to begin again rather than to take up writing dutifully at a designated point and in a way ordained by tradition; above all, to write in and as an act of discovery rather than out of respectful obedience to established 'truth'—these add up to the production of knowledge, they summarize the method of beginning about which this book turns" (Said 1997a: 379).

Said expounds this method by way of an ingenious interpretation of the work of Giambattista Vico, the eighteenth-century Neapolitan philosopher of history. For Vico, the mind fashions its own world, albeit with occasionally unintended and unruly consequences: "That which did all this was mind," he asserts audaciously as he surveys human history, "for men did it with intelligence; it was not fate, for they did it by choice" (1968: 425). The world about us springs not from the incontestable edicts of scripture but from the contingent endeavors of human intellect and labor. It is not fixed or frozen, held in place by a Mosaic law of precepts and prohibitions but alive with opportunities for alteration and improvement. Its interpreters, therefore, ought to reject grand theories that endeavor in vain to encapsulate this turbulent domain with their verdicts and forecasts; they should instead fix their attention on a secular world that cannot possibly be described or evaluated except by the most meticulous sensitivity to history in all its diversity and changeableness.

Said worried that contemporary cultural theory had failed to heed these warnings. Indeed, he was convinced that theorizing takes place largely in a monastic and even provincial state of intellectual withdrawal (Hart 2000: 143–62). In "Secular Criticism," "The World, the Text, and the Critic," and "Traveling Theory" (Said 1983) and again in 1993's *Culture and Imperialism,* Said argued that theoretical systems, from the purportedly comprehensive to the most modish and apparently self-critical, are preoccupied with their own precepts rather than with the infinitely more powerful actuality of real history. The goal of criticism should be to interrogate this inwardness and escape it. "A knowledge of history, a recognition of the importance of social circumstance, an analytical capacity for making distinctions: these trouble the quasi-religious authority of being comfortably at home among one's people, supported by known powers and acceptable values, protected against the outside world" (Said 1983: 15–16).

Though he often defended the ideal of the university in the most romantic terms, Said was convinced that the academy can give rise to an introverted guild mentality in its associates, particularly those camped under the banner of postmodernism. He denounced the adherents of high theory for a fixation with textuality so extreme that they desert their duty to appraise wider society and for their similarly drastic distrust of the ideals of emancipation and enlightenment. "Cults like post-modernism, discourse analysis, New Historicism, deconstruction, neo-pragmatism transport them into the country of the blue; an astonishing sense of weightlessness with regard to the gravity of history and individual responsibility fritters away attention to public matters, and to public discourse. The result is a kind of floundering about that is most dispiriting to witness, even as the society as a whole drifts without direction or coherence" (Said 1994a: 366–67).

Attention to "public matters" rather than conformity to whatever system or method is presently in vogue in one's culture or profession is an essential part of the critic's "worldliness." The worldly critic should not, therefore, express himself in jargon; because the production and promulgation of knowledge are his aims, he will neither befuddle nor talk down to his audience but instead address a broad constituency in an intelligible but not simplistic or patronizing idiom. Said's punctilious approach to his work recalls Ernst Bloch's celebration of the similarly sharp-eyed Walter Benjamin. "A sense for the peripheral: Benjamin had what Lukács so drastically lacked: a unique gaze for the significant detail, for what lies alongside, for those fresh elements which, in thinking and in the world, arise from here, for the individual things *(Einzelsein)* which intrude in an unaccustomed and nonschematic way, things which do not fit in with the usual lot and therefore deserve particular, incisive attention" (1988: 340).

Said's often acclaimed eloquence was not so much a personal foible as an integral part of his thought. His precision of expression embodied his respect for illuminating details. Indeed, this unseasonable deference to the truth-telling capacity of language amounts to a rearguard defense of its referential role against those postmodernists for whom language is terminally inexact and whose prolix, convoluted idiom bears the scars of this rejection. Said's thought is essayistic in the best sense: discursive, informal, alert to the requirements of particular problems, and mindful of thought's obligation to its material. The essay, a form that Said celebrated in theory and employed peerlessly in practice, was thus uniquely fitted for the scrupulously precise character of his thought: "If I am to be taken seriously as saying that secular criticism deals with local and worldly situations, and that it is constitutively opposed to the production of massive, hermetic systems, then it must follow that the essay—a comparatively short, investigative, radically skeptical form—is the principal way in which to write criticism" (Said 1983: 26). This remark, with its characteristic disapproval of overbearing methods and its emphasis on specificity and intention, echoes Adorno's contention that the essay, because it is at once penetrating and self-critical, is the appropriate form for unfolding reality.

> In its relationship to scientific procedure and its philosophical grounding as method, the essay, in accordance with its idea, draws the fullest conclusions from the critique of system . . . In the realm of thought it is virtually the essay alone that has successfully raised doubts about the absolute privilege of method . . . The word *Versuch*, attempt or essay, in which thought's utopian vision of hitting the bullseye is united with the consciousness of its own fallibility and provisional character, indicates, as do most historically surviving terminologies, something about the form, something to be taken all the more seriously in that it takes place not systematically but rather as a characteristic of an intention groping its way. (Adorno 1991: 9, 16)

The essay is as distrustful of generalizations as it is sensitive to particulars. It is experimental and suggestive, a type of diligent inquiry guided not by dogma or the wish to assemble a system but by the singular qualities of objects.

The lesson we should draw from Said's advocacy of secularism and worldliness is that we ought to object to abstract systems of explanation like Orientalism not, as many of his successors in the field of postcolonial theory have assumed, because such theories are too concerned with the world outside their own sphere but because they are not concerned *enough* with that world. The reason for Said's critique of misleading scholarship about Islam and the Middle East has therefore usually been missed. The main contention of *Orientalism* is not, as that text's own idiom leads us to suspect, identical with Michel Foucault's claim that knowledge is inextricably bound up with the exercise of power. We should not be misled by that idiom into misrepresenting Said as a skeptic about the feasibility and even the desirability of instructive empirical knowledge. His critiques of scholarly misapprehension and of the sort of discourse about the world outside Europe and North America that holds sway in the news media take aim not so much at the complicity of knowledge in power as they do at the complicity of ignorance in power. For to simply map the world onto one's preconceptions is, of course, to achieve the precise opposite of wisdom. Unconscionable generalizations made without knowledge of or sympathy with their object are as noisy and as destructive but also, crucially, as ineffective as the shells of the French warship in Conrad's *Heart of Darkness*, pointlessly pounding an unknown and indomitable continent (Conrad 1995: 30–31). Catchall tags like "the East" and "the Islamic world" or, that cliché beloved of savvy-seeming television news correspondents, the fickle and unanimous temper of the "Arab Street," are less accurate designations or even harmless shorthand than ideological labels, conjectures that becloud our vision where it most needs to be enhanced. Wittingly or otherwise, they compress a dense and complex reality into an assemblage of abstract stereotypes that have the effect of painting the non-Western world as inferior, dependent, requiring and even positively beseeching the intervention and tutelage of more advanced powers.

Said's real contention in *Orientalism* is that to this day a great many of those who take it upon themselves to fathom "the East," far from being disinterested onlookers, have on the contrary connived in the oppression of its peoples. Instead of dispassionately inquiring into the circumstantial reality of other societies and ways of life, fraudulent sages have broken faith with the intellectual vocation by intensifying the kind of ignorance that breeds misapprehension, as well as fear and abuse. Despite the professed comprehensiveness of the Orientalists' categories, the so-called Orient has been not so much covered as covered up, its details and sheer variety shrouded in a thick fog of slogans and clichés. Indeed, a generalization, given the enormous variety and nuance in the object studied, cannot but be a misrepresentation. Thus scholars become complicit in the subjugation of the Orient not because of their attempt to know but because of their attempt to know it without sufficient consciousness of the dangers of parroting orthodox interpretations and of relying on the government and mainstream media for information. In doing so, they cannot have a sense of the inescapable precariousness and quixotic nature of such interpretations or the necessary discrimination and knowledge of historical context (Said 1985: 255–328).

Writers who resort to generalizations and received ideas to describe other societies succeed only in imprisoning their work behind a barricade of clichés and stereotypes. V. S. Naipaul, for instance, is no shrinking violet, but his travel writing has never set foot outside his preconceptions. Naipaul tours the globe, but his ideas, alas, do not accompany him; they stay home. In his *Among the Believers: An Islamic Journey* (1982), Naipaul tours Pakistan, Malaysia, Indonesia, and Iran without becoming any the wiser about Islam and its adherents, declaiming as he goes abusive and uninformed epithets in place of considered, knowledgeable analysis. Despite his book's portentous subtitle, it is the work of a timorous stay-at-home who never ventures far beyond the shelter of his prejudices. Naipaul sees only malcontents and ingrates, quarrelsome inhabitants of enraged but parasitic societies. "He does not learn," as Said mordantly noted, "*they* prove" (Said 2000a: 113). Naipaul's undeserved reputation for candor and "telling it like it is" actually masks a deep ignorance; he eschews well-versed inquiry in favor of fallacious and superficial reports that are both intellectually unavailing and morally unconcerned.[5] One charge that cannot be leveled at such appraisals, therefore, is that they have been too concerned with investigating the world. Rather, they have generalized from a great distance and without adequate sympathy or insight. Pontificators like Naipaul, deficient in care, respect, and sensitivity, give rise not to knowledge but to partisan systems of distortion that are bereft of either wisdom or fellow feeling.

Said's point in *Orientalism* (1985), *Covering Islam* (1997b), and *The Question of*

Palestine (1992) is that we must bear in mind the close and even causal relationship between orthodox knowledge about the rest of the world and the destructive deeds perpetrated there by corporations and states. Disregarding the lives and views of vast numbers of men and women by issuing negligent clichés that dub them profitless and unimportant (or else ignore their existence altogether) is but one short step away from enacting belligerent policies that, on the authority of such assessments, *actually* assume such people to be nugatory details, expendable pawns in a grand strategic plan. In the careless use of language, citizens and policy makers forgo the intellectual and moral effort required for worthwhile thought. They are shielded from a complex and heterogeneous reality by a thick wall of imprecise language. The real human suffering behind that wall is either unseen and unheeded or else is legitimized by the use of abstract terms to plan and prescribe outcomes, destinies, and fates. Happily, however, such terms can be challenged by sensitive interpretations or, put differently, by a dialogic alertness to the actual features of one's object of study. We should not hold forth from afar as if a complex reality can be explained away with a hunch or dissected in full with a set of largely unexamined and entirely inappropriate surmises. Said, then, was *for* rational inquiry and the pursuit of knowledge and *against* thought's habit of walling itself in with abstractions: "If it is not to be merely a form of self-validation," he wrote, "criticism must intend knowledge and, what is more, it must attempt to deal with, identify, and produce knowledge as having something to do with will and with reason" (Said 1983: 202).

To become conversant with another society, people, or culture, one's interpretations must be based on detailed scrutiny of the evidence, not on conformity to an existing system of ideas. Said modeled this approach on the aptitudes required to elucidate literary texts, which are, he shows us, sensitively analyzed and ceaselessly reinterpreted rather than subjected to some doctrinaire final assessment (Said 2000a: 201). Important works of literature contest our preconceptions. They are, he reminded Daniel Barenboim, "all about a voyage to the 'other,' and not concentrating on oneself, which is very much a minority view today. There is more of a concentration today on the affirmation of identity, on the need for roots, on the value of one's culture and one's sense of belonging. It's become quite rare to project one's self outward, to have a broader perspective" (Said and Barenboim 2004: 11).

Literature and his typically acute interpretations of it were thus the fount of Said's thought and the basis of his political vision. This approach confirms Paul Ricoeur's remark that "one of the aims of all hermeneutics is to struggle against cultural distance" (Ricoeur 1995: 159). Commencing with *Joseph Conrad and the Fiction of Autobiography,* the fruit of his doctoral studies at Harvard, Said's work displayed a remarkably consistent conviction that both personality and outlook are the products of a series of dialogic exposures to novel situations and interlocutors. This neglected monograph offers an exploration of Conrad's consciousness in the manner of the now largely forgotten Geneva School of literary criticism (whose first generation included such interesting critics as Marcel Raymond, Georges Poulet, and Albert Béguin). This unmethodical approach focuses critical attention on the exemplary consciousness of the author as it is manifested in his creative work and other written matter. The critic looks upon the work as a record of the attempt to use the confessional art of writing to elucidate an endurable relationship between the self and its world. Criticism's aim for these writers, as J. Hillis Miller has said, is to attain "consciousness of consciousness" (1966: 305). Modern subjectivity is characterized by the self-conscious mind's intense reflection on its own capacities, driven by anxiety about the perils and risks of modern life. The aftermath of this acute self-absorption is the author's desire (usually unavailing but no less impressive and even heroic for that) to negotiate a new modus operandi with the outside world whereby exile, solitude, and the fear of personal dissolution can all find a new and satisfying accommodation.

Said's book on Conrad charts the novelist's assiduous creation of a character with which to regulate the troublesome intercourse between self and world. He looks at Conrad's voluminous correspondence as a sustained elaboration and presentation of a noteworthy character and views his novels as oblique fictional enactments of the writer's extraordinary life. Conrad the letter writer's invention of a substantial personality is also the task undertaken by Conrad the author, whose tales, inspired by the events of his adventurous oceangoing career, amount to a self-conscious examination and reconstruction of his own past. Acutely conscious of the self's fragility and of his own copious and often incongruent identities (seafarer, émigré, Englishman, Pole, down-at-heel itinerant, and venerable man of letters), Conrad sought to piece together the sort of distinct, coherent personality that is endowed by an intelligible life story, in an effort to shed his discrepant selves in the figure of a true-born English gentleman. Yet this fervent Anglophile could never quite pull off that role, not just because of his Polish accent or his lugubrious self-absorption but also because of a very insistent sense of dislocation that, try as he might, he was unable to remedy. In other words, Conrad was far too complex and restless a figure to prevent his carefully formulated self-possession from being assailed and even inundated by the world's strangeness and disorder.

The uncertainty and angst that we suffer in our dealings with the outside world, but also the exhilarating sense of discovery we experience in those encounters, are for Said the perennial themes of Conrad's fiction. Not the least important reason for the feeling of dislocation and even bewilderment that is both dramatized and imparted by Conrad's oeuvre is the profound struggle he joined by choosing to write in an adopted language, one in which he occasionally sounded, despite his formidable eloquence, more like a rather melodramatic outsider than a composed native. His prose foregrounds its awkwardness and disorientation by groping, frequently in vain, for a precise expression of his intention and an adequate description of his world. Nouns in Conrad's work are frequently preceded by a surfeit of descriptive terms because, for the linguistic newcomer, the right word can never quite be found, so his prose often reads like a large gathering of adjectives attempting without success to elucidate an array of mysterious persons and events. Conrad's was the lavishly descriptive prose of an apprehensive interloper struggling to put into unfamiliar words both his outlandish experiences and the mysteries they led him to contemplate. His attempt to compose a secure personality and a settled milieu for that personality to live within are repeatedly destabilized by a nagging sense of displacement and consequent perplexity. The powerful effect of his novels and the considerable excitement and profit of reading them are attributable to this remarkable facility for using an unsuccessfully concealed deracination to evoke the difficulties and anxieties, as well as the equally profound rewards and opportunities, of a self-conscious personality. Conrad's identity was too unmanageable and his temperament too desirous of ordeals to allow him to seek extended refuge in comfortable residences and occupations. In his fiction, such accommodations cannot be found (at least without irony) and emotions and experiences can never find definitive expression.

This quality in Conrad was what influenced and even guided Said's subsequent work, to the extent that he found himself "over the years reading and writing about Conrad like a *cantus firmus,* a steady groundbass to much that I have experienced" (Said 2000a: 555). Conrad's fiction and the example of his life gave Said a modus operandi. They furnished him with examples, to which he repeatedly returned, of the audacity, inquisitiveness, and excited discomposure that drive any moral or intellectual endeavor. Conrad's life and body of work were poised between identity and its dissolution, between, as Said says in *Beginnings,* authority and its molestation (Said 1997a: 83–84). The writer's life and work evidence, therefore, not a carefully regulated accord between a self-possessed, rational being and his governable environment but a fraught, inconclusive negotiation between an individual's extremely vulnerable sense of selfhood and his conspicuously eventful life. This vulnerability gives rise to frailty and disquiet but also, in equal measure, to adventure, exploration, and wisdom.

"THE PALESTINIAN VISION"

Edifying encounters with one's world, such as those of Conrad and of his intrepid protagonists, necessitate the aptitudes that Said attributes to "worldliness." Moral and political actions, no less than scholarship, presuppose a mind-set that is both outgoing and self-conscious, at once curious about alternative perspectives and receptive to the correction of one's own. The sort of improving dialogue that is made possible by exiling oneself from received ways of thinking also constitutes the foundation of a desirable political order. That order would be democratic, egalitarian, committed to upholding the rights of all its members, and, because of its dedication to those principles, disinclined to exclude groups arbitrarily from their shelter. In this view, we discern the link between Said's method and his political vision; for the want of dialogue that gives rise to insular scholarship also hobbles the so-called peace process in the land of his birth and perpetuates the violence and inequality that disfigure that region.

Said wished to see the Palestinians assume their full rights as equal participants in dialogue, entitled to demand far more than the stingy provisions of the Oslo Accords. Since 1993 they have, he argued, been bound by a deal that takes no account of this equal standing and that seeks not to establish peace but to effect pacification. The Palestinian people are routinely treated as an inconvenient complication; they are seen not as partners in the pursuit of a just settlement but as a bothersome obstacle in the way of Israeli objectives (Said 1995a; 1995b; 2002). Time and again, Said pointed out the lopsided nature of the negotiations between the two parties, a dialogue distorted both by the disproportionate military and political clout of the Israelis and by the Palestinian leadership's acceptance of a subsidiary role.[6] Not only did one side approach the negotiations determined to exploit its strength and influence, but the other approached them not as a party convinced of the rightness of its cause but as supplicants expected and, alas, frequently willing to petition for crumbs.

Effective negotiators, Said argued, ought to reject this profitless stance and approach their disputants as articulate, proficient representatives of a just cause and of a people convinced of its own prerogative. He believed that the Palestinian struggle could be successfully concluded by genuine dialogue, rather than by the leadership's throwing itself at the mercy of discredited interlocutors or seeking, against insurmountable odds and in contravention of its democratic ideals, to overpower its adversary by force of arms. Neither mendicants nor fanatics will carry the struggle, which can—and Said would doubtless have added *should*—be won only from a position of moral strength. Said was convinced that both parties' attitudes are susceptible to moral and intellectual persuasion. In his many writings on the issue, he advised his readers forcefully and creatively to assert Palestinian rights, to stand firm against the occupation by other than apocalyptic and desperate means, to formulate secular and democratic alternatives to the failed policies of the Palestinian leadership, to mobilize international opinion, and to impress the conscience of persuadable Israelis with the Palestinian people's human and political claims. He saw hope not in belligerent, theocratic factions but in creative groups like the West-Eastern Divan Workshop (the orchestra of young Palestinian and Israeli musicians jointly founded by Said and the Israeli conductor Daniel Barenboim), in the revision of Zionist myths by Israeli historians, and in popular movements like Israeli draft resistance, the International Solidarity Movement, and the Palestinian National Initiative of Dr. Moustafa Barghouti.[7]

Partisan postures and sectional ambitions attracted Said's derision. He accused the Palestinian Authority of a loss of vision and berated it for tolerating a lack of democracy, real freedom, and due process and for neglecting the rights and aspirations of Palestinian women. All this, he contended, was a result of the Oslo Accords' deliberate substitution of strictly short-term nationalist goals for long-term social aspirations. The end of emancipation became the national flag on the sleeve of the policeman and over the headquarters of the chief's myriad security forces, rather than, as Frantz Fanon's *The Wretched of the Earth* envisaged, the liberation of consciousness, the equalization of shares, and the increasing internationalization of institutions and outlooks (Fanon 1990). Said considered Arafat's municipal aspirations and factional maneuverings to be distractions from the far more urgent task of outlining proposals for an exemplary and peaceful coexistence. Moreover, his condemnation of Zionism's unconscionable ambitions for a Greater Israel were matched by an equally uncompromising disapproval of that minority of his compatriots who had resorted to demanding the unfeasible and ultimately quite barbaric expulsion of those who had arrived since 1948. For Said, restitution for the forcibly deracinated Palestinians was emphatically not to take place at the expense of others' comparable dispossession. "The Palestinian people . . . wishes no negative form of self-determination or liberation for itself. Its bitter national experience has bred in it a respect for civil and human rights abrogated by others. The Palestinian vision therefore is predicated upon democracy and justice, upon dignity and community . . . For its part the Palestinian people wishes for no more than peace and justice, and because its unhappy fate was forced on it, there has arisen a congruent desire to end, rather than perpetuate, the anomalies of displacement, dispossession and exile" (Said et al. 2001: 292).

An exiled people cannot magically restore a native realm now extant only in the nostalgia of its former inhabitants, at least not without doing violence to others. Significantly, Said also opposed the segregation of the two peoples into partitioned zones, which would be a deprivation on a human level and, since they are now physically inseparable, impossible on a practical level. The only just objective, therefore, is a democratic, inclusive, and peaceable curtailment of exile and antagonism. The authentic "Palestinian vision" is of a new, unpartitioned state. "If we think of Palestine as having a function of both a place to be *returned to* and of an *entirely new* place, a vision partially of a restored past and of a novel future, perhaps even of a historical disaster transformed into a hope for a different future, we will understand the word's meaning better" (Said 1992: 125).

Said's alternative to partition, mutual incomprehension, and unceasing strife is a community without civil distinctions, a secular state embracing the present inhabitants of Israel and the occupied territories plus those members of the Palestinian diaspora (that is, the refugees and their descendants) who wish to return. He proposed a country that belongs to all its citizens and is not just a sectarian sanctuary for its professed titleholders, a country that constitutes a revolutionary example of reconciliation instead of a byword for internecine bloodshed.

THE GLOBAL VISION

The cosmopolitan visions generated by intellectual exile help us combat three significant dangers, in my view. The first is the resurgence of national, racial, and religious fundamentalism. In "The Clash of Definitions," Said took issue with Samuel Huntington's (1996) fanciful "clash of civilizations" thesis (a sort of nightmarish Orwellian vision of gigantic power blocs slugging it out with each other for global dominance). This ideologue's division of the globe into exclusive zones riled Said because of its utterly baseless assumption that citizens within an arbitrarily defined space are all so like- and simpleminded that they march in line behind the same banners. Regions, however, are so multiform that they defy such crude generalization. Sweeping shorthands like "the West" and the "Islamic world" close our eyes both to the laudable diversity of beliefs and practices in supposedly homogeneous camps and to the more regrettable partitions and hierarchies that characterize life in each purportedly uniform zone. Racial, confessional, class, gender, and numerous other divisions complicate Huntington's simplistic belief that we are all drones confined to our hives. Huntington is a dealer in abstractions, not a sensitive percipient; he writes not as a dispassionate student of the wider world but as a scaremongering guardian of parochial values from the threat of phantom foes and, ultimately, as a bellicose justifier of American power (Said 2000a: 569–90). The division of the world into a patchwork of discrepant regions obscures our interrelatedness, masks the power and violence that connect the world's parts, and cynically discounts the possibility of more equitable and fraternal forms of relationship. The most objectionable aspect of Huntington's idea is its complete occlusion of capitalism and its attempt to justify America's belligerent foreign policy not on the hard-to-defend grounds of imperial power but on the utterly spurious ones of civilizational survival.

The second danger that exile helps us avoid is the understandable but ultimately quite disastrous temptation to recoil from triumphalist dogmas and imperialist projects into a fretful disillusionment with the very idea of noncoercive cultural contact. Not only have belligerent neoconservatives depicted civilizations as incorrigible and irreconcilable antagonists but so have tolerant relativists who wish that cultures were inoculated against the temptations of violent interaction. But militant identity politics' vision of a diversity of unconnected and uncommunicative identities plays right into Huntington's hands and thus runs counter to Said's polemic against separation.

> Political separation is at best a makeshift measure. Partition is a legacy of imperialism, as the unhappy cases of Pakistan and India, Ireland, Cyprus, and the Balkans amply testify, and as the disasters of twentieth century Africa attest in the most tragic way. We must now begin to think in terms of coexistence, after separation, in spite of partition . . . So let us see these new partitions as the last-ditch efforts of a dying ide-

ology of separation, which has afflicted Zionism and Palestinian nationalism, both of whom have not surmounted the philosophical problem of the Other, of learning how to live with, as opposed to despite, the Other. (Said 2002: 330)

Said took issue with the transformation of diversity into a fetish. The abstract affirmation of "difference" serves only to slight the enormous potential of the idea of community. In other words, political activity should not come down to an unappealing choice between imposed uniformity and what Said called the "ideology of difference." "On the crucial issue of 'difference,' which is central to many recent theoretical and interpretive discussions, one can, however, declare oneself *for* difference (as opposed to sameness or homogenization) without at the same time being for the rigidly enforced and policed separation of populations into different groups" (Said 1995b: 80–81).

Separatist rhetoric has engendered "a critique whose premise is the need for forging connections and, more important, the existential need to find modes of knowledge, coexistence, and justice that are not based on coercive separation and unequal privilege" (Said 1995b: 83). In other words, we should press not just for the right of individuals and cultures to be different but also for their right to be the same, to enjoy the same rights and freedoms and to be treated with equal dignity and respect. To argue that diversity is desirable in all cases is manifestly absurd. Individuals and even whole communities have talents, potentials, and inclinations that are distinctive and sometimes unique; to fight for the opportunity for them to explore fully these divergent gifts is a worthy endeavor and, in Said's view, the primary objective of political action. Yet for such differences to flourish, others have to be abolished. For example, I am unlikely to be able to pursue my unfulfilled talent for playing the oboe if I have to work sixteen hours a day because I am not allowed to join a trade union or if I do not have enough to eat. We might draw two conclusions in this situation: first, that without exception, men and women should be allowed to join trade unions, and second, that the difference between those who have food and those who do not should be removed. In short, some differences should be eradicated so that those that really matter can flourish. Said's universalism, therefore, does not encourage homogeneity but seeks to lay down the conditions that must universally prevail for the general fulfillment of life's basic necessities and the pursuit of genuine difference. "We have to ensure the means of life, and the means of community," as Raymond Williams avowed. "But what will then, by these means, be lived, we cannot know or say" (1962: 321).[8]

The third objectionable idea that Said's cosmopolitan vision helps us reject is the temptation to exchange the conflict-ridden reality of our time for a precipitate celebration of the cosmopolitan ideal. Notwithstanding their best intentions, writers like Bhabha who hymn an extant cosmopolitan condition have a tendency to glide free of worldly affiliations into a sort of intercontinental latitude. Theirs is a weightless detachment from territorial boundaries and from any commitment to alleviating the plight of the vast majority of humankind that continues to live without the privileges of unlimited foreign travel or the luxury of exchanging the arduous task of political struggle for the pleasures of movement. Michael Hardt and Antonio Negri argue that a new decentered and supranational polity is being brought about by the "multitude," a planetary flow of workers moving from the poor to the rich countries: "The real heroes of the liberation of the Third World may really have been the emigrants and the flows of population that have destroyed old and new boundaries" (Hardt and Negri 2001: 362–63). For Hardt and Negri, immigration and the crossing of borders give rise to a form of cosmopolitan freedom. However, they forget something that Said emphasizes: although migration *might* be a partly salutary experience (allowing the migrant a penetrating perspective on his new locale as well as critical distance from the place he has left behind), most likely it will mean little more than penury, painful deracination, even death. The euphoric celebration of unfettered movement pays insufficient attention to the barriers that currently impede the movements of individuals and populations, the unenviable material conditions of actual migrants and forcibly relocated communities, and the vast populations condemned to the stasis of factory production, subsistence farming, and unemployment (see Abu-Manneh 2003; Brennan 2003; Parry 2004a, 2004b: 93–103). "If the new exterritoriality of the elite feels like intoxicating freedom," writes Zygmunt Bauman, "the territoriality of the rest feels less like home ground, and ever more like prison—all the more humiliating for the obtrusive sight of the others' freedom to move" (1999: 23). Just as there can be, as Adorno remarked, "no emancipation without that of society" (1974: 173) there can likewise be, as Said makes eloquently clear, no viable or legitimate cosmopolitanism that excludes the vast majority.

Much more productive and useful is a new global mentality that sees the dangers we face from the standpoint of the whole human race. These dangers include the pauperization of most of the globe's population; the emergence of virulent local, national, ethnic, and religious sentiment . . . ; the decline of literacy and the onset of a new illiteracy . . . ; the fragmentation and threatened disappearance of the grand narratives of emancipation and enlightenment. Our most precious asset in the face of such a dire transformation of tradition and of history is the emergence of a sense of community, understanding, sympathy, and hope which is the direct opposite of what in his essay Huntington has provoked . . . In what they imply, these sentiments prepare the way for a dissolution of cultural barriers as well as of the civilizational pride that prevents the kind of benign globalism already to be found, for instance, in the environmental movement, in scientific cooperation, in the universal concern for human rights, in concepts of global thought that stress community and sharing over racial, gender, or class dominance. (Said 2000a: 589–90)

"NEW IDEAS AND PROVOCATIONS"

The democratic, cosmopolitan, and universalist ideals of Said's thought offer a salutary alternative to paranoid dogmas of cultural, racial, and national self-assertion. Yet if we are to stand a realistic chance of achieving these ideals, we must combine their avowal with the most hardheaded acknowledgment of the impediments that currently forestall their realization. Peter Gowan argues that the liberal vision of globalization, in its failure to keep these obstacles in sight, is all too compatible with—indeed, is often used as rhetorical cover for—the selfish interests of powerful states. The cosmopolitan vision will not be realized while international relations and trade continue to be shaped by the United States and its subsidiaries. Indeed, the extant institutions of global governance are not brakes *on* but rather instruments *of* U.S. power. The manipulation of compliant organizations like the International Monetary Fund, the World Trade Organization, and the U.N. Security Council leads not to fair trade or respect for human rights but to belligerent and protectionist policies that perpetuate violence and inequality. We need, therefore, to add an agenda for economic and social change to the planetary ethos and international democratic institutions envisaged by the various liberal cosmopolitanisms (Gowan 2004). We should follow Fernando Coronil in contrasting globalization's ideals of equality, diversity, and liberty with the social inequity and cultural and political standardization that capitalist globalization currently engenders (Coronil 2000: 369). Held to its promise, as Immanuel Wallerstein has suggested, the laudable liberal ideal of globalization would cease to be associated solely with powerful states' self-interested reconstruction of the world and would instead allow us "to arrive hopefully at a more inclusively universalist vision of human possibility" (1997: 107). Therefore, we need a kind of "globalization-from-below," designed not to facilitate capital accumulation and thus perpetuate inequality but to protect labor rights and environmental standards and to enhance the prospects of peace and democracy (Brecher and Costello 1994; Colás 1994; Gilroy 2005).

Though Said's generous and often angry compassion for imperialism's victims was exemplary and inspiring, he seemed more comfortable reproving insularity, chauvinism, and xenophobia than combining his distaste for these things with a cogent and candid critique of the economic system that encourages them. I think he realized in his later work, particularly in the excoriating rage in *From Oslo to Iraq and the Roadmap* at the bellicose simplifications of the Bush administration and the brutal folly of Ariel Sharon, that material and strategic interests of a very fundamental kind drive American policy in the Middle East just as, at an earlier stage in history, they compelled European depredations in Africa and Asia. To avoid the precipitate optimism censured by Gowan, we should highlight Said's belated emphasis on the vast social, economic, and political obstacles that stand between his own ideals and the prospect of their realization. Alternatively, we might combine Said's emphasis on dialogue, community, and reconciliation with Adorno's re-fusal, even in his analyses of philosophical method and musical form, to let out of his sight the unrelenting actuality and maleficence of capitalism.

One gets the impression when reading Adorno that his cantankerous aversion to consolations and simplifications of any kind is connected to the interminable postponement, to which his work alerts us, of meaningful social change. He finds this sense of unfinished tasks in the intransigent and, in some cases, formally un-resolved works of great modernist composers like Mahler, Schoenberg, Berg, and even Wagner, who all trace their aptitude for incompleteness to the fractured fab-ric of Beethoven's revolutionary late style. "To the musical experience of the late Beethoven the unity of subjectivity and objectivity, the roundedness of the successful symphony, the totality arising from the motion of all particulars, in short, that which gives the works of his middle period their authenticity, must have become suspect. . . . Something in his genius, probably the deepest thing, refused to reconcile in the im-age what is unreconciled in reality" (1998: 151–52).

In Beethoven's irascible and recondite late works, the thematic resolutions of his middle period are indefinitely postponed (see Sample 1994; Paddison 1993: 233–43; Nicholsen 1997). Late style, in Adorno's account, is both an unavoidable mis-fortune in the life of the composer, who in consciousness of his own mortality ceases to impose his will on the artistic material and thus reveals its imperfect and dis-united character, and a seismic event in the history of culture, which at some point in the nineteenth century began to register in its form the antagonistic quality of a society divided into classes. The transition from Beethoven's classical to his late style reveals in aesthetic form a lack of polish, beauty, and harmony. Reprises seem forced or are ironic. Such late works are exceedingly rebarbative, truculently dismissive of youth's glib enthusiasms. They deliberately frustrate the urge for harmonious clo-sure and even the expectation of understanding. Yet their fragmentariness and their sheer bristling difficulty are useful in refusing us the sort of appeasement and con-solation furnished by more beguilingly melodious compositions and in notifying us aesthetically of the intense dissatisfaction occasioned by a similarly conflict-ridden and unreformed social order.

To be late, in Adorno's view, is therefore to observe the world with the wisdom and perhaps the disappointment but also the *indignation* of experience. Indeed, ac-cording to Said's own meditations on lateness, it is the preternatural sagacity of old age and even the unflinching consciousness of imminent death that imbue the senes-cent artist with an uncommon aptitude for facing facts, refusing the bromide of false consolation, relinquishing nostalgic dreams and precipitate visions. "Beethoven's late works remain unreconciled, uncoopted by a higher synthesis: they do not fit any scheme, and they cannot be reconciled or resolved. . . . Lateness is being at the end, fully conscious, full of memory, and also very (even preternaturally) aware of the present. Adorno, like Beethoven, becomes therefore a figure of lateness itself, an untimely, scandalous, even catastrophic commentator on the present" (Said 2006: 12, 14).

Said was such a commentator, particularly in his own late works: impatient with consoling fancies, intolerant of deceptions, and, in his own terms, preternaturally mindful of the present. In *Freud and the Non-European,* he acclaimed the developing variations of the intellectual and artistic work in progress above the finale's soothing strains: "The intellectual trajectory of the late work is intransigence and a sort of irascible transgressiveness, as if the author was expected to settle down into a harmonious composure, as befits a person at the end of his life, but preferred instead to be difficult, and to bristle with all sorts of new ideas and provocations" (2003: 29). I claim that Said's esteem for recalcitrant virtuosos and their insightful compositions evidences his increasing consciousness that his political ideal of reconciliation necessitated an unflinching acknowledgment of the present inequitable order and all its attendant chauvinisms, and that until a homeland healed of the painful frontiers of class, racial, gender, and geographical division has been inaugurated, his lifelong project, like Beethoven's fragmented and unreconciled final quartets and piano sonatas, would remain incomplete.

By emphasizing Said's attraction to revelations of incompleteness rather than premature feats of harmony, I do not mean that he was uninterested in reconciliation, because as I have been arguing, reconciliation constituted his life's work. Instead I suggest that at its best, his work was conscious that genuine reconciliation has not yet been achieved and, moreover, can only be accomplished by insisting on true democracy and equality. As he noted, the Palestinians cannot achieve their goals by making a hasty settlement with the status quo. "I am for dialogue between cultures and coexistence between people: everything I have written about and struggled for has pointed to that as the goal. But I think real principle and real justice have to be implemented before there can be true dialogue. Real dialogue is between equals not between subordinate and dominant partners" (Said 1995a: 36–37).

Unless the Palestinians decline to pursue an accommodation with a fanatically self-assured Israeli state that, armed to the teeth and indulged by the world's sole superpower, is currently highly unlikely to treat such concessions with anything other than bad faith, they could sell short what Said saw as their exemplary vision. As I write, in the first months of 2008, the "dialogue" that intermittently takes place between the two sides' representatives has recently been reconvened, with the Palestinians' leaders compelled once more to swallow the usual threats and to thrust aside their people's entitlements. The Palestinians are again and again compelled to listen to the hypocritical sermons of their occupiers, to submit uncomplainingly to yet another round of raids and random killings, and to bear without respite the unending occupation, the erection of the West Bank barrier, and their incarceration in shrinking and dismembered plots—all for the dubious privilege of sitting at Barak's or Sharon's or Olmert's groaning tables and, if they are lucky, catching some of their crumbs. The exercise is, as ever, a fraudulent and ineffectual colloquy because it takes no account of Palestinian entitlements and sufferings and imposes no obligation on Israel to recognize those things and to heed its responsibilities under international law. Until equality is contrived—until, that is, Israel stops belligerently asserting its preeminence and the Palestinian leadership ceases to rescind voluntarily rights and claims that, under any number of international covenants and resolutions, are indefeasible—then the halting dialogue of the interminable "peace process" will continue to be a cruel sham. Therefore, in drawing attention to Said's growing conviction that democracy and reconciliation can be achieved only in the company of radical democratic equality, I do not wish to suggest that these ideals be postponed. Genuine dialogue cannot wait, but if it is to realize its true potential, we must use the sense of reconciliation and solidarity that frequently illuminates the situation in Palestine and that increasingly characterizes grassroots political organization and informs the ubiquitous discourse of human rights, as a beginning and not an end, a model for the organization of society and not a substitute for or distraction from ambitious political action.

I have tried to describe the critical consciousness and intellectual deliberation engendered for Said by the experience of exile and to clarify the political ideal that such experiences imply. I have argued that exile ought not to result in a relativist dismissal of political norms, an acceptance of separation, or a premature celebration of an extant cosmopolitan condition. It should rather lead us toward Ahdaf Soueif's "common ground": that is, toward a far more internationalist and even universalist vision of human solidarity that is nevertheless acutely conscious of the obstacles that prevent us from reaching this spacious meeting point (Soueif 2004). For these reasons, Said courted exile. His was an unaccommodated voice amid a disheartening choir of consensus, complicity, and cynicism. In this context, we should recall that the critical consciousness aroused by important artists' late work is also the indispensable precondition of another very Saidian notion, that of a new beginning, a fresh start even in the midst of apparently irreversible defeats. As he makes clear in the closing moments of his memoir, *Out of Place*, uncommon alertness and farsightedness are characteristics not just of the rebel who rages against the dying of the light but also of the harbinger, who rises early to steal a march on the approaching dawn. "For me, sleep is death, as is any diminishment in awareness. . . . Sleeplessness for me is a cherished state to be desired at almost any cost; there is nothing for me as invigorating as immediately shedding the shadowy half-consciousness of a night's loss, than the early morning, reacquainting myself with or resuming what I might have lost completely a few hours earlier" (2000b: 295).

Said willingly embraced the fate of the exile, the unsleeping traveler who perseveres through the hours of darkness, but he remained forever conscious that the possibility of homecoming lurks below the horizon. He maintained an abiding fidelity to the intellectual's lonely, itinerant course but did not lose sight of the communal goal that sustained such activity. Said's benefaction is the example of an incorrigible freethinker who did not seek premature refuge in political submission, disciplinary conformity, academic nearsightedness, or intellectual orthodoxy, and who refused to swear allegiance to a circumscribed and exclusionary patria. He shared Adorno's view that "there is no longer any homeland other than a world in which no one would be cast out any more, the world of a genuinely emancipated humanity" (Adorno 1991: 85).

NOTES

I tender my thanks to the following for their invaluable comments on previous drafts of this paper: Tom Day, Neil Lazarus, Eilidh MacDonald, Benita Parry, and William Smith.

1. Timothy Brennan and Neil Lazarus persuasively distinguish the theoretical and political principles of Said's work from those of his postcolonial epigones (Brennan 2006: 93–125; Lazarus 2005).

2. Abdirahman Hussein is more convincing on what he calls the "critical misreception" of *Orientalism:* that is, its mistaken interpretation as a work of intellectual *dis*engagement (Hussein 2002: 224–35).

3. David O'Hara agrees with this point. "The problem [Said] addresses . . . is not so much how intellectuals initially free themselves from the mental hobbles of traditional values and ideas. Rather the problem is how can critical intellectuals maintain their oppositional stance without it turning into an oppositional posture habitually adopted and elaborated—refined—in the interest of perfecting their systems and methodologies . . . at the center of which appear their own idealized self-images as writers" (O'Hara 1984: 389).

4. Bhabha sings the praises of "wandering peoples who will not be contained within the *Heim* of the national culture and its unisonant discourse, but are themselves the marks of a shifting boundary that alienates the frontiers of the modern nation" (1990: 164).

5. For a compelling analysis of how in his travel writing Naipaul enlists the idiom of exile and displacement to conceal his approval of orthodox colonialist beliefs about postcolonial societies, see Nixon 1992.

6. For an account of the often duplicitous nature of Israeli negotiating tactics and of the prospects for an equitable peace, see Reinhart 2002.

7. See Said 2004: 238–44. A declaration of the Palestinian National Initiative's aims and ideals is available at www.almubadara.org (accessed 12 February 2008). On the activities of the International Solidarity Movement, see www.palsolidarity.org (accessed 12 February 2008). One historian who works assiduously to confound many of Israel's founding myths is Ilan Pappe (1992; 2007).

8. "The aim of equalizing those circumstances over which individuals have no control is to leave them free to pursue their goals: given that these goals differ, the outcome of individuals exercising their capabilities will also be different. Equality is not uniformity. The idea that it entails the suppression of individual difference is nonsense" (Callinicos 2000: 79).

WORKS CITED

Abu-Manneh, Bashir. 2003. "The Illusions of Empire." *Interventions* 5, no. 2 (2003): 159–73.
Adorno, Theodor W. 1974. *Minima Moralia: Reflections on Damaged Life.* Trans. E. F. N. Jephcott. London: New Left Books.

————. 1991. *Notes to Literature*. Vol. 1. Ed. Rolf Tiedemann. Trans. Shierry Weber Nicholsen. See especially "The Essay as Form," 3–23; and "Heine the Wound," 80–85. New York: Columbia University Press.

————. 1992. *Mahler: A Musical Physiognomy*. Trans. Edmund Jephcott. Chicago: University of Chicago Press.

————. 1998. *Beethoven: The Philosophy of Music*. Ed. Rolf Tiedemann. Trans. Edmund Jephcott. Cambridge: Polity.

Ahmad, Aijaz. 1992. *In Theory: Classes, Nations, Literatures*. London: Verso.

Bauman, Zygmunt. 1999. *Globalization: The Human Consequences*. Cambridge: Polity Press.

Bhabha, Homi K. 1990. *The Location of Culture*. London: Routledge.

Bloch, Ernst Bloch. 1988. "Recollections of Walter Benjamin." In *On Walter Benjamin: Critical Essays and Recollections*. Ed. Gary Smith, 338–45. Cambridge, MA: MIT Press.

Brecher, Jeremy, and Tim Costello, 1994. *Global Village or Global Pillage: Economic Reconstruction from the Bottom Up*. Cambridge, MA: South End Press.

Brennan, Timothy. 2003. "The Italian Ideology." In *Debating Empire*. Ed. Gopal Balakrishnan, 97–120. London: Verso.

————. 2006. *Wars of Position: The Cultural Politics of Left and Right*. New York: Columbia University Press.

Callinicos, Alex. 2000. *Equality*. Cambridge: Polity.

Clifford, James. 1988. *The Predicament of Culture: Twentieth Century Ethnography, Literature, and Art*. Cambridge, MA: Harvard University Press.

Colás, Alejandro. 1994. "Putting Cosmopolitanism into Practice: The Case of Socialist Internationalism." *Millennium* 23, no. 3: 513–34.

Conrad, Joseph. 1992. "Amy Foster." In *The Complete Short Fiction*. Vol. 1. Ed. Samuel Hynes, 181–209. London: William Pickering.

————. 1995. *Heart of Darkness*. Ed. Robert Hampson. Harmondsworth: Penguin.

————. 2000. *Lord Jim*. Harmondsworth: Penguin.

Coronil, Fernando. 2000. "Towards a Critique of Globalcentrism: Speculations on Capitalism's Nature." *Public Culture* 12, no. 2: 351–70.

Deleuze, Gilles. 1977. "Nomad Thought." In *The New Nietzsche: Contemporary Styles of Interpretation*. Ed. David B. Allison, 142–49. New York: Delta.

Fanon, Frantz. 1990. *The Wretched of the Earth*. Trans. Constance Farrington. Harmondsworth: Penguin.

Gadamer, Hans-Georg. 1989. "*Destruktion* and Deconstruction." In *Dialogue and Deconstruction: The Gadamer-Derrida Encounter*. Ed. Diane P. Michelfelder and Richard E. Palmer, 102–33. Albany: State University of New York Press.

Gilroy, Paul. 2005. "A New Cosmopolitanism." *Interventions* 7, no. 3: 287–92.

Gowan, Peter. 2004. "The New Liberal Cosmopolitanism." In *Debating Cosmopolitics*. Ed. Daniele Archibugi, 51–65. London: Verso.

Hardt, Michael, and Antonio Negri. 2001. *Empire*. Cambridge, MA: Harvard University Press.

Hart, William D. 2000. *Edward Said and the Religious Effects of Culture*. Cambridge: Cambridge University Press.

Hitchens, Christopher. 2003. "Where the Twain Should Have Met," www.theatlantic.com/doc/prem/200309/hitchens (accessed 13 March 2008).

Huntington, Samuel P. 1996. *The Clash of Civilizations and the Remaking of World Order.* New York: Simon & Schuster.

Hussein, Abdirahman A. 2002. *Edward Said: Criticism and Society.* London: Verso.

Lazarus, Neil. 2005. "Representations of the Intellectual in *Representations of the Intellectual.*" *Research in African Literatures* 36, no. 3: 112–23.

Mann, Michael. 2001. "As the Twentieth Century Ages." *New Left Review* 214: 104–214.

Merod, Jim. 2000. "The Sublime Lyrical Abstractions of Edward W. Said." In *Edward Said and the Work of the Critic.* Ed. Paul A. Bové, 114–38. Durham, NC: Duke University Press.

Miller, J. Hillis. 1966. "The Geneva School." *Critical Quarterly* 8: 305–21.

Naipaul, V. S. 1982. *Among the Believers: An Islamic Journey.* London: Andre Deutsch.

Nairn, Tom. 2000. *After Britain: New Labour and the Return of Scotland.* London: Granta.

Nicholsen, Shierry Weber. 1997. *Exact Imagination, Late Work: On Adorno's Aesthetics.* Cambridge, MA: MIT Press.

Nixon, Rob. 1992. *London Calling: V. S. Naipaul, Postcolonial Mandarin.* Oxford: Oxford University Press.

O'Hara, David. 1984. "Criticism Worldly and Unworldly: Edward W. Said and the Cult of Theory." *Boundary 2* 13, no. 1: 379–403.

Paddison, Max. 1993. *Adorno's Aesthetics of Music.* Cambridge: Cambridge University Press.

Pappe, Ilan. 1992. *The Making of the Arab-Israeli Conflict: 1947–51.* London: I. B. Tauris.

———. 2007. *The Ethnic Cleansing of Palestine.* London: Oneworld.

Parry, Benita. 2004a. "The Institutionalization of Postcolonial Studies." In *The Cambridge Companion to Postcolonial Studies.* Ed. Neil Lazarus, 66–82. Cambridge: Cambridge University Press.

———. 2004b. *Postcolonial Studies: A Materialist Critique.* London: Routledge.

Porter, Dennis. 1993. "*Orientalism* and Its Problems." In *Colonial Discourse and Postcolonial Theory.* Ed. Patrick Williams and Laura Chrisman, 150–61. London: Harvester.

Reinhart, Tanya. 2002. *Israel/Palestine: How to End the War of 1948.* New York: Seven Stories Press.

Ricoeur, Paul. 1995. "What Is a Text? Explanation and Understanding." In *Hermeneutics and the Human Sciences: Essays on Language and Interpretation.* Ed. John B. Thompson, 145–64. Cambridge University.

Robbins, Bruce. 1983. "Homelessness and Worldliness." *Diacritics* 13: 69–77.

Said, Edward W. 1966. *Joseph Conrad and the Fiction of Autobiography.* Cambridge, MA: Harvard University Press.

———. 1983. *The World, the Text, and the Critic.* London: Vintage. See especially "Secular Criticism," 1–30; "The World, the Text, and the Critic," 31–53; "Criticism between Culture and System," 178–225; and "Traveling Theory," 226–247.

———. 1985. *Orientalism.* Harmondsworth: Penguin.

———. 1991. *Musical Elaborations.* London: Vintage.

———. 1992. *The Question of Palestine.* New York: Vintage.

———. 1993. *After the Last Sky: Palestinian Lives.* Photographs by Jean Mohr. London: Vintage.

———. 1994a. *Culture and Imperialism.* London: Vintage.

———. 1994b. *Representations of the Intellectual: The 1993 Reith Lectures.* London: Vintage.

———. 1995a. *Peace and Its Discontents: Gaza-Jericho, 1993–1995.* London: Vintage.

———. 1995b. *The Politics of Dispossession: The Struggle for Palestinian Self-Determination, 1969–1994.* London: Vintage.

———. 1997a. *Beginnings: Intention and Method.* London: Granta.

———. 1997b. *Covering Islam: How the Media and the Experts Determine How We See the Rest of the World.* London: Vintage.

———. 2000a. *Reflections on Exile and Other Literary and Cultural Essays.* London: Granta. See especially "Among the Believers," 113–17; "Reflections on Exile," 173–86; "Orientalism Reconsidered," 198–215; "The Politics of Knowledge," 372–85; "Between Worlds," 554–68; and "The Clash of Definitions," 569–90.

———. 2000b. *Out of Place: A Memoir.* London: Granta.

———. 2002. *The End of the Peace Process: Oslo and After.* London: Granta.

———. 2003. *Freud and the Non-European.* London: Verso.

———. 2004. *From Oslo to Iraq and the Roadmap.* London: Bloomsbury.

———. 2007. *On Late Style: Music and Literature against the Grain.* London: Bloomsbury.

Said, Edward W., and Ibrahim Abu-Lughod, Janet L. Abu-Lughod, Muhammad Hallaj, and Elia Zureik. 2001. "A Profile of the Palestinian People." In *Blaming the Victims: Spurious Scholarship and the Palestinian Question.* Ed. Edward W. Said and Christopher Hitchens, 235–92. London: Verso.

Said, Edward W., and Daniel Barenboim. 2004. *Parallels and Paradoxes: Explorations in Music and Society.* Ed. Ara Guzelimian. London: Bloomsbury.

Sample, Colin. 1994. "Adorno on the Musical Language of Beethoven." *Musical Quarterly* 78, no. 2: 378–90.

Smith, Andrew. 2004. "Migrancy, Hybridity, and Postcolonial Literary Studies." In *The Cambridge Companion to Postcolonial Literary Studies.* Ed. Neil Lazarus, 241–61. Cambridge: Cambridge University Press.

Soueif, Ahdaf. 2004. *Mezzaterra: Fragments from the Common Ground.* London: Bloomsbury.

Vico, Giambattista. 1968. *The New Science.* Trans. Thomas Goddard Bergin and Max Harold Fisch. Ithaca, NY: Cornell University Press.

Wallerstein, Immanuel. 1997. "Eurocentrism and Its Avatars: The Dilemmas of Social Science." *New Left Review* 226: 93–107.

Williams, Raymond. 1962. *Culture and Society: 1780–1950.* Harmondsworth: Penguin.

Wordsworth, William. 1971. "To Toussaint l'Ouverture." In *Poetical Works.* Ed. Thomas Hutchinson. London: Oxford University Press.

24

A New "Copernican" Revolution

Said's Critique of Metaphysics and Theology

Abdirahman A. Hussein

The view that Edward Said is primarily a "third world" critic of Orientalism, imperialism, and Zionism has gained wide currency in the academic community and beyond. This appropriation of his writings, which has helped launch the increasingly important field of postcolonial studies, is perhaps not surprising. After all, Said over the years wrote a great deal about these related areas of knowledge and sociopolitical combat. Some of the most compelling insights in his oeuvre concern modern Euro-American imperialism—its genesis, evolution, consolidation, reversal, and recrudescence; its doctrinal audacity and epic scope; its trails of scent and lines of descent; its enormous capacity for self-fortification, self-idealization, and (in the case of contemporary America) self-occultation. *Orientalism*, his most famous book (it has been translated into thirty-six languages worldwide), is an encyclopedic, meticulously diagnostic dissection and indictment of Orientalist discourse.[1] Presumptively disinterested but—in Said's view—profoundly motivated, this hybrid field of knowledge about the Orient (especially the Arab-Islamic Near East), though having medieval wellsprings, has over the past two and a half centuries matured into a formidable, theoretically armored discipline closely entwined with imperial dogma and practice.

Said also magisterially documented the scandals of Zionism, from the moment it piggybacked itself onto European imperialism in the nineteenth century to its political and ideological triumph in the mid-twentieth century and its desperate twilight in the early twenty-first. All but stripped of its multilayered ideological disguise, this colonial venture is nowadays sustained by almost unlimited American aid (both moral and material) and the use of the most defamatory anti-Muslim, anti-Arab representations to come out of the Orientalist tradition. Finally, Said was for decades a symbol of diasporic Palestine in the West, a precarious position he occupied with dignity and fortitude until his death in September 2003. He also belongs in the ranks of a small but (I hope) growing minority of secular intellectuals who have tried to find ways of transforming the conflict between Palestinians and Israelis into a meaningful debate, advancing beyond mutual demonizations and recriminations, and, instead, envisioning the possibility of reconciliation between these two victimized communities on the basis of equality. Given the sense of urgency—even crisis—that permeates his reflections on these problems (in, for example, *Orientalism*, *The Question of Palestine*, *Covering Islam*, *Culture and Imperialism*, and *The Politics of Dispossession*), it is no wonder that the reception of his writings by multiple audiences has been largely determined by interest in (or debates about) decolonization, the North-South divide, theories of race construction, and the dialectic between cultural capital and imperial power.[2]

And yet Said's intellectual legacy extends far beyond these related areas. In fact, I would go so far as to argue that his critical practice has potentially revolutionary implications for the humanities and social sciences. A careful, comprehensive examination of his work—especially such texts as *Joseph Conrad and the Fiction of Autobiography*; *Beginnings: Intention and Method*; *The World, the Text, and the Critic*; and *Humanism and Democratic Criticism*—shows that Said is a radical humanist bent on enhancing, amplifying, and extending the best that secularism has to offer an increasingly globalized world, while also exposing modernity's scandalous secrets, its unacknowledged or deliberately suppressed barbarism.[3] Combining sociopolitical and intellectual history, philosophical reflection, and ideology critique—all of them left-handed, suspicious, often scathingly polemical—his "technique of trouble" was above all intended to initiate new intellectual habits. He asked what advanced, academic, secular criticism can—and ought to—do: what range of issues it should engage; what kinds of questions it should raise; what its relationship should be to other knowledge systems, social reality, and its own past and future; what its raison d'être is, as a form of consciousness that necessarily—by definition— gauges the gap between the grand claims often made for civilization and the actualities of history. In other words, Said's aim was to *dedomesticate* criticism. By this I mean that, on the one hand, he tried to expand vastly its proper purview beyond the academic cul-de-sac to which it has been consigned by professionalization and by a culture built largely on consent and internalized censorship. But on the other hand, he hoped to reinvest it with the kind of intellectual potency and drama that "it has sorely needed since [Matthew] Arnold covered critical writing with the mantle of cultural authority and reactionary political quietism."[4] In short, Said's various writings, including the least immediately political studies, embody an attempt to turn the corrosive power of criticism into a mechanism of radical reperception and social change.

In an earlier study, I reflected extensively on Said's place in modern intellectual traditions, examining his affinities with (or distance from) thinkers who have participated in what has come to be known as the modernity-postmodernity debate.[5] I argued that, although his critical practice unfolded in a historico-theoretical space—cleared by phenomenological hermeneutics, revisionist Marxism, post-structuralism, philology, and anti-imperialist discourse—Said was a protean scholar who cannot be easily placed in one camp or another. Rather he was at once restlessly eclectic—crossing intellectual, cultural, and historical boundaries—and highly idiosyncratic. His method of extremes, which I characterized as "a technique of trouble," involves the coactivation of agonistic dialectic and archaeology/genealogy.

In this chapter, I want to isolate and amplify a few propositions about Said's critical practice that were not foregrounded in my earlier study. Specifically, I want to outline two theses intended to show how (and why) I believe Said could teach us a great deal more than he is usually given credit for: first, I argue that Said's confrontation with metaphysics and theology should be seen as a reenactment, extension, and transformation of earlier, well-known critiques, such as those of Vico (from whom Said appropriated a great deal) and Kant (whose ideas are barely given more than a passing gloss); second, I suggest that for Said, criticism was a highly ambitious endeavor, wielded as a precise tool for diagnosis and crisis management in a flawed society.

On the first count, I argue that Said's critique is in important respects far more compelling than those of eighteenth-century thinkers, at least in part because it is intended to come to terms with the multiple sociocultural effects of modernity over the past two centuries or so; in other words, Said's reengagement of ontotheology appears to have been necessitated by his belief that, despite Kant's much-vaunted "Copernican revolution," a largely sublimated but otherwise dogmatically insistent substratum of both metaphysics and theology holds modernity hostage; this substratum is continually (re)fashioned (and in turn gives sustenance to) the dialectical interplay between the two forces he occasionally called culture and system— that is, the cultural authority derived from the humanistic and social/scientific disciplines in conjunction with sociopolitical institutions and technological power.

Thus Said's project should be understood as both a metaphilosophical and a metahistorical exercise. First, despite the presumptively "radical" nature of the dialectic, the presence of the ontotheological core, which (appropriating and expanding upon Said's characterization of the "mature" version of Orientalism)[6] I call a median category, entails the strategic and systematic fusion of conservation and expenditure, consumption and discharge, formation and transformation—all of which are primed for the unparalleled preservation and expansion of "the West," at the expense of the "non-West," as a set of identities, ideas, ideals, institutions, and practices. Second, notions that have traditionally been framed in leftist parlance as ideological illusions cannot be clearly understood (or adequately critiqued) unless one fully recognizes their subterranean connections with this metaphysical and theological residuum. This median category, thanks to its enormous capacity for elasticity, plasticity, and absorptivity, has normalized itself to such a degree that its multiple dimensions have not been adequately registered, let alone rigorously examined—not even by Marxists, who have used the notion of dialectic as a fiery historico-theoretical engine of unparalleled power and energy.

These multiple dimensions include not only the psychological, logical, epistemological, economic, and ethico-political elements at work in the dialectical sublation but also the stark contradictions created in the multipolar interplay, which have often been smoothed over right in the heart of the median category and in the resilient infrastructure created as an assertively proactive blueprint and as a huge wake of destruction, reconstruction, and consolidation. For example, the vectors that have enabled Western powers to secure economic gains, political control, scientific, and pseudoscientific knowledge, or cultural hegemony in the non-West have almost always trumped ethical concerns—if such concerns were expressed at all by mainstream thinkers and policy makers (the occasional—and sometimes vocal—protests of mavericks have almost without exception been suppressed or marginalized). The synthesizing power of the median category was—and continues to be—so powerful that even Marx, the most impassioned and insightful critic of injustice within Western society in the nineteenth century, was not immune to it: witness his condoning of British imperialism in India. Hence the knowledge systems and sociopolitical institutions that have "matured" in the wake of the Enlightenment have both been advanced and inhibited by the various movements, stases, limits, and pressure points of the category.

On the one hand, these new "categorical" intellectual and historical constructs appear to have largely or totally disengaged themselves from the presumptively dogmatic, vague, inchoate speculations of metaphysics and theology but are in fact ultimately authorized by these seemingly silent yet powerfully insistent origins. That is to say, the category is what it is, for good or ill, precisely because its religious-metaphysical source (which could be characterized as a strong undercurrent, an undissolved core, or a saturating presence—but never a depleted residuum or a receding background) is both constitutive and unacknowledged. On the other hand, as a result of that contraband cultural self-authorization, new pathologies have cropped up over the last several centuries, manifesting themselves in astonishingly asymmetrical experiences and interpretations of modernity in various historical and cultural contexts. (Consider, for example, the antithetical meanings and "values" conveyed by the terms *democracy* and *the law* to the indigenous peoples of North America and to the whites who were busily displacing them by whatever means possible). A slightly different way of phrasing this point is to say that the ideas, ideals, institutions, and practices that have shaped modern Western society (and reverberated to the non-West thanks to imperialism) have come into being by virtue of an unacknowledged, and often disastrous, synthesis of idealism and empiricism, understood as modes of intellection and (by extension) philosophical/cultural traditions. Described by Said as a form of "rationalism based on dry-as-dust traditionalism, memory, and scholastic rigidity," this synthesizing dialectic is kept on course—and in place—by a foundationalist, instrumental realism, which has ontological, epistemological, and ethico-political dimensions.[7] If Said is right, an essentially medieval, fundamentalist species of normativity courses through the knowledge systems and institutions of modernity in the West, in the process considerably diminishing—if not entirely eviscerating—the purportedly enormous emancipatory potential of secular humanism. This conceptualization, I argue, is a considerable advance on (as well as a complement of) formulations based on orthodox Marxism and related critiques of ideology, which have traditionally explained pathologies in social reality almost entirely in economistic/sociologistic terms.

But Said was also conscious of the self-inflicted limitations—the fundamentalism, apologeticism, ossification, and mimicry—that have made the world of Islam the site of both discontent and impotence. Thanks largely to his withering indictment of the Orientalist tradition, as well as the postcolonial and "worldly" criticism that his oeuvre has given rise to over the past several decades, a substantial consensus now exists, both inside and outside academia, that most of the studies of Arab-Islamic culture and religion in the West that have been presented for centuries as objective, neutral, or disinterested are profoundly contaminated by unacknowledged cultural and political motivations. But it is also my considered judgment that the response of Muslim elites to the political and intellectual challenges of Euro-Americans has been extremely disappointing. As I write, the sociopolitical scene is (and has been for decades) a vast disaster zone created by mediocre leaders who have little respect for themselves and even less for their own peoples; as a direct result of their lamentable performance generation after generation, they have lost all legitimacy in the eyes of the vast majority of their own citizens; the scholarly world is largely divided into two broad, generally antithetical camps: Islamicist scribes who mostly churn out hagiographies, braggadocios, and literalist interpretations of religious doctrine; and self-declared secularists who mostly reproduce, parrotlike, the stale commonplaces of the Enlightenment. Economically, despite its vast human and natural resources, the Arab-Islamic world is amazingly incapacitated by its own internal contradictions (contrast, for example, the lazy opulence of the oil-rich Gulf states with the degrading poverty of tens of millions in Egypt alone) and by its entrapment in the hegemonic bear hug of the West—an asymmetrical relationship that hasn't changed much for more than two centuries. Technologically, stagnation and dependence are the rule; and if the militaristic misadventures in Iraq, Afghanistan, and elsewhere are any indication of the West's current attitude toward the Islamic world, the prospects for the future are grim indeed. In short, the prolonged soul-searching that started among Muslims in 1799 when Napoleon Bonaparte landed on the shores of Egypt has produced tremendously more heat than light. Said was aware of all these problems—and his critique was inclusive of them, directly or indirectly.[8]

This point brings us to my second thesis, about Said's view of the function, scope, and technology of criticism, or critical consciousness. The compound heuristic that I described earlier as a coactivation of agonistic dialectic and archaeology/genealogy gives us a glimpse of criticism's intended role. For Said, it was an index of congenital crisis, a finely honed instrument of diagnosis, a negative meter of distance or discrepancy, a corrosive solvent of congealed dogma, and an indicator of utopian possibilities. Said's criticism is an ambitious project that calls for extraordinary discipline and presence of mind. (My reflections on these problematics will be strategically selective and schematic, because I discuss most of them in detail in *Edward Said: Criticism and Society*.)[9] In articulating Said's criticism, an examination of Kant's approach to metaphysics is in order. Because Said has never offered sustained expositions, beyond brief allusions of Kant's critical philosophy, my attempt to lump together the two thinkers here may seem a bit forced. However, the sage of Konigsberg has cast a long shadow over modern philosophy; more specifically, the entire province of what has conventionally been known as first philosophy, or metaphysics, has been largely disregarded in post-Kantian thought. Indeed, apart from a few noted exceptions (such as Heidegger and Derrida, who have tried to deflate what they consider to be metaphysical hubris through an ontologically inflected destruction and the deconstruction of the language of subjectivity), most major philosophers in both the continental and Anglo-American traditions have generally tended to assume that, after Kant's exhaustive and judicious accounting, the topic is no longer a matter of immediate concern or relevance. This assuredly was not the case for Said. Despite Said's critique having a Vichian point of departure, it would be fruitful here to set up a dialogue between him and Kant, since the affinities between them are, perhaps surprisingly, very strong.

By this I mean that both thinkers are determined to draw an airtight demarcated boundary line between, on the one hand, the grand illusions (like the Platonic forms and Descartes' clear and distinct ideas) that reason has traditionally dreamt up in its moments of extravagant flight, and on the other, the more modest but more legitimate claims of validity it can make as soon as it accepts its anthropomorphic and "earthbound" (Said's term) status. Thus, for example, when Said identifies the ultimate Ur-substance (Origin or truth in his terminology) as silent, he is in effect describing the realm of noumena, Kant's terra incognita. In both cases, originary authority—conceived as the repository of an ontological, epistemological, or divine primacy and warrant (together with an attendant uniqueness, purity, and transparency)—is pronounced as entirely beyond the compass of human experience. Both Said and Kant also acknowledge that, thanks to humanity's almost limitless desire to endow itself with larger-than-human sanction, the mind is often driven to go beyond the boundaries of experience and to pronounce judgments pertaining to supersensible realms—hence arriving at irresolvable paradoxes and conundrums. (Kant describes these as antinomies; Said does not use a single over-arching formulation, but as I have tried to show elsewhere, the agonistic dialectic and archaeology/genealogy together bring about multiple double binds.)[10] Both thinkers also conceive what each considers to be the legitimate point of departure for reason properly understood—one that disallows lapses into metaphysical illusions but earns greater legitimacy for epistemological judgments made in the circumstances of space and time. (Kant reserves that honor for the forms of intuition and the categories of understanding; Said uses the notion of beginning intention as a methodological fulcrum.) Finally, in the writings of Said and Kant, one finds a strong commitment both to a noncoercive, universalist vision of human community and to the view that the individuated self is autonomous and inviolate. Phrased differently, both argue that human equality, freedom, and dignity ought to constitute the core constellation of values necessary for the ethical community to even come into existence.[11]

Despite these broad areas of, if not total agreement, then at least strong affinities (or affiliations, as Said would probably say), there can be no doubt that irreconcilable differences separate Kant and Said—differences that have as much to do with philosophical orientations and individual temperaments as with historical and theoretical transformations over the past two centuries. The most obvious, and in some respects most crucial, divergence is in their views on history—or, more precisely, the relationship between sociohistorical reality and what we might simply call theoretical systematicity. Said's entire conception of human thought and action is infused with, though not reducible to, a radically dynamic vision of historicity, materiality, and multiplicity that is almost completely antithetical to Kant's airless architectonic. In broad terms, this idea of historical change and circumstance is traceable not only to the dialectical materialism of the Marxist tradition but also (as we shall see shortly) to the philologically inflected humanism of Vico and to Foucault's idea of discursivity. Although Said occasionally used such notions as form and structure as methodological devices, his attitude toward system building in general was largely hostile—as evinced by his repeated attacks on formalism and structuralism, for example.[12] His suspicion is grounded in the belief that such ahistorical, abstractive formulations have the tendency to freeze into self-stabilizing, functionalist totalities with little room for the energy-laden presence of human intentionality; for the saturated density, vastness, and richness of sociocultural reality; or for the powerfully motivated contests over authority and privilege that determine the pace and direction of historical change and the nature of political practice.

Said was, of course, not averse to theory as such. In fact he repeatedly deployed a battery of theoretical insights drawn from diverse tributaries of modern thought. After all, rigorous critique would be well nigh impossible without theoretical support. However, he was opposed to pure, disembodied theory as a game played by armchair philosophers and other academicians. He found it both empty and false— empty, because it is no more than an imposing shell, a mere representation of reality that passes itself off as the genuine item; false, because, to the degree that it gives theorists a sense of (explanatory, interpretive, or evaluative) power and control that is only partially theirs, it is a distortion of reality and the capacity of theory to impact that reality. Said's lifelong interest in phenomenology and (to a lesser extent) existentialism was powered by the conviction that, unlike "linguacentric" (his term) approaches (like structuralism) or transparently facile theories (like commonsense realism), these two attitudes place a high premium on the dialectical interplay between embodied human agency and the sociocultural world given to it— and hence make available a much more authentic rendering of reality. Perhaps the most important (and most unnerving) aspect of Said's thought is his conception of rationality as such: to him, reason was not a cool, neutral light democratically casting its substance to reveal the good and the beautiful; nor was it a sure-footed, punctual geist—a continual fusion of telos and logos to shepherd life ineluctably to an assigned locus of perfection; it was rather a turbulent force that (in his words) "includes rational sentiment, passion, and urgency."[13] In fact, he often radicalized the implications of his position, insisting that we should recognize both rationality's great capacity for violence, folly, and deception and its equally great potential for critical transgression, insurrection, even anarchy. In Said's thought, reason-as-intentionality is always profoundly motivated and experimental; saturated with will, myth, dream, and desire, it is irreducibly poetic.

Kant, in contrast, belongs in the ranks of a grand pantheon of philosophical system builders in the traditional sense, who saw reason as the ultimate practical and theoretical court of appeal. His ambitious synthesis aimed to rescue philosophical reasoning from the sniping skepticism and syncretic empiricism of Hume as well as the metaphysical hauteur of rationalists (like Leibniz and Wolff); but he also wanted to trump both schools by carrying out a rigorous accounting and putting an end to philosophical bickering once and for all. There is a sense, therefore, in which his conception of rational *systematicity* (if not its ethical and epistemological implications) is almost completely opposed to Said's understanding of what reason is or does.

The divergence becomes even sharper when we examine Kant's formulation of how consciousness relates to the object domain given to it: although, *pace* the rationalists, Kant thought that the senses are as indispensable to the acquisition of knowledge as the mind. His privileging of representation (and hence of form) over matter, coupled with his (not particularly convincing) claim that the thing-in-itself (or noumenal reality) is beyond the grasp of the understanding, in practical terms turned philosophical attention away from the domain of sociohistorical reality. And, unlike Said, Kant never took into consideration the palpable materiality and recalcitrance of language, which he presumably saw as a neutral medium of communication. Finally, Kant's view of historical change, though vaguely evolutionary in a generic fashion, lacks the Vichian-inspired sense of drama, multiplicity, occasionality, and interactiveness that animates Said's conception of history. Kant was, of course, a creature of his time. As the beneficiary and apotheosis of an Enlightenment project that hadn't yet given up its hubris, he was intent on establishing solid apodictic foundations for Newtonian physics and Euclidean geometry; he was also determined to demonstrate that a less metaphysically inclined, more scientific (and hence more mature) rationality than in the past could build equally sturdy foundations for ethico-political practice. The extent to which he succeeded (or did not succeed) can be gauged from the fact that practically all the philosophical movements that have come into prominence in the West over the past two centuries—including some that are decidedly anti-Kantian—are in one way or another responses to Kant's critical project.

The point of immediate relevance, though, is that, whatever Kant's idea of critique was, his crucial metatheoretical contribution—the transcendental logic—was subsequently appropriated in a way that considerably toned down the ethico-political uses of criticism because it was far more oriented to form, structure, and system than to the urgent, quotidian concerns of everyday life. Hence, Kant can without too much exaggeration be characterized as the philosophical grandfather of various species of scientism, formalism, and idealism—among them Anglo-American literary/critical formalism and analytic philosophy, as well as, of course, German idealism. And even when critique gained considerable power with the rise of Marxism, its practitioners rarely recognized, let alone tried to dismantle, the Kantian glass ceiling that severely circumscribed their intellectual freedom: most leftist thinkers, with the possible exception of Adorno and Horkheimer, did not feel compelled to revisit the metaphysical domain that Kant had opened up for criticism; instead, they opted for a quarrel (and occasional truces) with Hegel, whose philosophy was assumed to embody the ultimate metaphysical bogeyman. And, of course, much of what is known as classical Marxism is itself burdened with positivist pretensions, thereby smuggling in a scientific version of metaphysical realism through the back door while at the same time condemning idealism for being too metaphysical. However, philosophers—like Nietzsche, Heidegger, and Derrida—who did recognize the need to dismantle the conceptual armor of metaphysics at its foundations—never warmed up to ideology critique as practiced on the left. Hence, the idea of critique launched by the Kantian project split into divergent currents that were largely alienated from one another. The result has been, in my opinion, disastrous, especially for philosophy, the humanities, and the social sciences. It has also had a crippling effect on secular modernity and humanism as a whole, in ways I have been hinting at throughout this discussion. We could, therefore, conclude this brief comparison by saying that Said's critical project ultimately amounts to a strategic reversal of Kant's project, even while we acknowledge the uncanny affinities between them.

Said's project intended not only to heal the split in the heart of critique but also to recuperate the power, cogency, and comprehensiveness that this notion has lost since the eighteenth century. In this endeavor, we see Vico's importance to Said. To assess the extent of that debt, let us have a look at a passage from *Beginnings,* the most philosophical of Said's books:

> Although Vico's subject is the common law of nations, and his ambition is to find a common beginning—a genealogical project—his "topical" method is everywhere to amass evidence by correlation, complementarity, and adjacency. Although his desire is to locate a primeval beginning, a line of direct filiality, the material testimony of language and his learning restrain his desire, engaging it instead with the susceptibility of language to divination and poetry. A distant and irrecoverable origin is not yearned after fruitlessly, because the mind can reexperience its making power by forging novel connections again and again—thus *adjacency, complementarity, parallelism, and correlation as methods employed in the interests of a genealogical goal.* In what Vico called the gentile world, this does away entirely with such common hierarchies as a spirit higher than body, a meaning higher than evidence, a father who because he is older is wiser than his son, a philosopher or a logician who is more "rational" than a poet, an idea that is higher than clusters of words.[14]

The passage draws attention to several crucial aspects of Said's critique of ontotheology and to his methodology in general. Vico provided him with the historico-theoretical tools to make an important demarcation line between origin and beginning. I discuss the distinction (and nexus) between these two notions in my book, so I won't tarry with them here; we need only remind ourselves that Said identified the former with the prerogatives of divinity and metaphysics, which, in his view, have been so thoroughly eroded over the past three hundred years by the corrosive spirit of secular humanism and by the restless nomadism of modern(ist) subjectivity that they are practically exhausted and irrelevant. Origins, Said tells us, are silent, passive, inoperative; originary plenitude, often understood in terms of normative simplicity and fullness, is unavailable to the disenchanted subject of modernity. It can be accessed neither by our minds nor by our language—even if we are impelled to search for it by humanity's desire to revisit primeval sites. Beginning, in contrast, is entirely human; it inaugurates human (or in Vichian parlance, poetic and profane) history, undergoes a series of cyclical and dialectical transformations, and creates a fraternity of laterally connected nations and cultures. This transgressive, autodidactic fraternity thrives despite great odds against it because, as basic institutions (such as marriage and the burial of the dead) strengthen, the human mind acts as a monitor, ensuring that humanity's gradual physical and intellectual maturity enables us to establish stable social structures yet leaving latitude for creative freedoms. And so on and on. This Vichian distinction is crucial to an understanding of Said's assault on metaphysics and theology.

Hence in various texts, Said ultimately appeals to this distinction when he argues that effective ideas in modern history can be traced back not to some unique, unconditioned, transcendent center or source that both stands aloof from and bestows normative warrant on them but to indisputably human, appetitive "beginnings"; that—no matter how rarefied, elevated, or valorized these ideas have become over the past three centuries or so—they can never be completely cleansed of their inaugural motivations or severed from their material moorings; that, given these facts, both the ideas themselves and the institutions and practices they have brought into being (for good or ill) can—indeed have to—be reexamined, reappropriated, rejected, reversed, or otherwise revised with the full knowledge that they are not the embodiments of theological or metaphysical truths but rather secular constructions fashioned in spatiotemporal circumstances. This view supports the argument that human cultural productions and reproductions are both occasional and relational, context bound and dynamic, practical and poetic, local and universal. In short, human agency expresses itself by way of conation or desire and on the logic of adjacency, complementarity, and correlation. This is clearly as far removed as one can imagine from Kant's austere, ahistorical, abstract architectonic. But Said also intends it to be a critique of ontotheology that is every bit as sharp as (if not sharper than) Kant's.

The passage I cite above also alludes ever so slightly to another tensive distinction—this one drawn within the notion of beginning itself and in some respects of far greater import to the pressing crises of the modern world: the boundary between transitive and intransitive beginnings. The distinction turns on a series of questions that can be raised along the following lines: Can one argue that, in spite of their decided passivity and somnolence, silent origins still exercise a powerful, and largely unrecognized hold on modern agency? If so, how can we account for this strange subjection to a largely primitive state of affairs whose claims to primacy presumably were laid to rest by the Enlightenment revolt? What mechanisms are used, wittingly or otherwise—as allies, alibis, stand-ins, resurrections, and other species of Trojan horse—to effect this unseemly reversal? Can it be shown that the interplay between the dominant culture and the exponential explosion of knowledge systems indirectly serves this effective capture of modernity for atavism, tribalism, and reaction?

For example, exactly what lies behind such summational, totalizing, identitarian fictions as "the West," "the Orient," "Natives," "the Arab mind," or "Islam," which are alternately idealized or demonized depending on who is speaking about them? Can one argue that these fictions could not have been perpetuated with such ease—even promiscuity—over long periods if modern humanistic, scientific, and social scientific discourses had not been susceptible to this kind of reductiveness and compartmentalization? For example, to what extent is the disciplinary creation of such fields as linguistics, biology, anthropology, and sociology inextricably tied to hieratic, comparatist, exclusionary ideas about races, cultures, languages, and value systems? In what way are the geneses, maturations, and mutations of national literatures and of the field of comparative literature connected not only to ideas and institutions about modern (European) national identities (and hence the powerful concept of the nation-state and nationalism) but also to a valorized, essentialized, collective sense of Europe constructed around an equally valorized Grand Canon of Great Books? How has the modern discipline of history and historicity served both as a surreptitious conduit for such Eurocentrism (together with the attendant vision of national destinies and great traditions) and as a normative mechanism for objectifying, demoting, excommunicating, and often visiting great violence on non-Westerners?

To approach the matter from a slightly different angle, how do we explain the fact that modern history has stood witness to what are undoubtedly the most massive genocides humanity has ever endured, as well as the greatest expansion of imperial ideology and practice the world has ever seen? Do not such grandiose commonplaces as freedom, humanism, democracy, and rationality ultimately camouflage all kinds of crude, age-old motivations—including greed, ambition, and bigotry? The list of such questions can easily go on, but the point is that the distinction within the idea of beginning itself marks a very troubling bifurcation in the heart of secular humanism as a modern form of consciousness.

As I have tried to show elsewhere, both transitive and intransitive beginnings are products of human intentionality: unlike origins, they are laden with conative desire and willfulness.[15] However, whereas the former is "project- and problem-oriented" (Said's phrasing), pragmatic, and progressive, the latter tends to be backward looking and obsessively self-parodying. One is sensitive to historical circumstance; the other is aloof, self-subsistent; one is responsive to discontinuity, repetition, dispersal, transformation, and thus affiliative; the other resists change, encouraging continuity, exclusivity, centripetality. It is filiative through and through. In short, transitive beginnings make available the kind of inaugural freedom necessary for critical disengagement and distance, whereas intransitive beginnings make available what amounts to ideological currency.

We can reach two conclusions about the cluster of issues above: one is that the problem of metaphysics is every bit as urgent today as it was in the eighteenth century, and as a topic of *critical* attention, it belongs as much to the domain of rarefied philosophical reflections as it does to other disciplinary fields—humanistic and scientific alike. To the extent that seemingly benign or disinterested aesthetic, ethical, political, and scientific ideas lead to or encourage unicentric, filiative, restorative, and ultimately redemptive visions of reality; to the extent that definitive authority is invested not in the distinctively new, which for that reason is equipped with hind-

sight, but to an anterior cause; to the extent that normativist methods of explanation, interpretation, and valuation seek after "a spirit higher than a body, a meaning higher than evidence, a father who because he is older is wiser than his son, a
philosopher or a logician who is more 'rational' than a poet, [or] an idea that is higher
than clusters of words"; to the extent that Kant's ostentatious proclamation that he
had effectively *deposed* "the queen of all the sciences" was decidedly premature; or
worse, it may have given his philosophical heirs and other thinkers a false sense of
security in the belief that scientific and humanistic knowledge born and bred in the
wake of Kant was mature, that to be post-Kantian also meant, ipso facto, to be post-
metaphysical. This conclusion was reached despite the fact that every single, solitary discipline, discourse, or cultural construct deployed in the past two centuries
is infected with a metaphysical virus to some degree or other.

This is in effect what transpires from Said's critiques of what he considers to be
collaborative dogmas, dodges, diversions, discrepancies; as well as projections, pro-
motions, power trips; and other species of orchestrated folly, self-delusion, aggression, and mindlessness. His assaults on Orientalism, imperialism, Zionism, and religious fundamentalism operate within this scope, as do his complaints against
collusive intellectuals, critical system building, "literary refinement," and the cult
of the expert. In other words, he considered modern, post-Enlightenment ideologies to be as fundamentalist, metaphysical, and destructive as anything that preceded them; however, because the ontotheological current that feeds them is subterranean, the cultural and political elites who use and disseminate them from above
have either misrecognized its saturating presence or colluded with it secretly, systematically, and consciously. Why such commissions and omissions? One of Said's
responses is as blunt as it is damning: "because that is where the money has been."[16]
But obviously other types of rewards accrue to intellectual workers who directly or
indirectly serve the dominant culture and its instruments of power: a general sense
of distinction, the knowledge that one owns intellectual capital not available to the
rabble, the herd of common humanity; the guild mentality associated with this status, the feeling that one belongs to an exclusive club of initiates with its own rituals and paraphernalia, and the belief that the normative content of the Tradition—
what Matthew Arnold called the best thought of Europe—is worth preserving and
transmitting.

Finally, we can see at this point that classical Marxist conceptions of ideology—
for example, the claim that it is a species of false consciousness or that it embodies
class interests—alone are not adequate and, worse, may even be simplistic. Over
the years, Said indeed borrowed valuable insights from revisionist Marxist thinkers:
his reflections on history, hegemonic culture, identitarian thinking, critical consciousness, and the late style are permeated by Lukácsian, Adornian, Gramscian,
and Williamsian ideas. And, of course, Said's own appropriation of dialectical sublation, which I have described as agonistic, is largely traceable to Western Marx-

ism. However, because Said took equally valuable insights from scholars outside the Marxist tradition, including liberals and conservatives, in order to make sense of, resist, and expose the insidious metaphysical and theological thought forms that have in his view blighted modernity, we should not be surprised that he thought we should look for critical tools much sharper than those made available by the Marxist tradition of ideology critique. This explains why Said reserved the place of honor for Vico, an early eighteenth-century maverick whose influence on Enlightenment and post-Enlightenment thought has been at best minimal.

Said tells us—and this brings us to my second conclusion—that Vico is fully aware of the temptation to embrace nice, comforting ideas about origination and filiation—for example, "a primeval beginning [and] a line of direct filiality"—but consciously resists that desire, opting instead for oblique, lateral techniques of investigation in his study of language, the mind, and history: "Thus *adjacency, complementarity, parallelism,* and *correlation* [are] *employed* [by Vico] *in the interests of a genealogical goal.*" Said used precisely such indirect methods in practically all of his writing, powering his "technique of trouble" by activating together agonistic dialectic and archaeo/genealogy. The specific metacritical devices he used over the years—meditation, affiliation, and contrapuntality, for example—are appropriations and radicalizations of these Vichian assumptions, with the important rider that (as I have pointed out) Said buttressed them with an entire constellation of heuristics taken from phenomenology and existentialism, structuralism and poststructuralism, literary modernism, anti-imperialist discourse, and antisystematic thought in general—even as he diverged from aspects of these methodologies. Perhaps the most important non-Vichian influence on Said was another maverick thinker of our own times: Michel Foucault. Said had this to say about him in *The World, the Text, and the Critic:* "It is now certain that Foucault's greatest intellectual contribution is to an understanding of how the will to exercise dominant control in society and history has also discovered a way to clothe, disguise, rarefy, and wrap itself systematically in the language of truth, discipline, rationality, utilitarian value, and knowledge."[17] Foucault's twinning of power and knowledge in the structure and texture of modern discourses is the clearest, most compelling crystallization of a thesis that Said stated early on in his career and elaborated in various studies: in the context of modernity, the will to truth and the will to mastery are almost as absolutely inseparable as they are almost equally invisible. And, of course, Foucault's analytics are as unconventional as Vico's and Said's.

It is this antidynastic, antilinear, and ultimately spatial logic that ratifies Said's argument that secular criticism ought to be used as a powerfully demystifying force, not as an undercover ally of ideology and system. In his writings, critical consciousness is worldly in the multiple senses of that word: it is both local and global, historical and theoretical, spatial and temporal; it "travels" (Said's phrasing)—that is, it is restless, unhoused, in exile—with the understanding that the entire world is its home; it is aware of the interconnectedness of all cultures without embracing an empty form of universalism; it recognizes the diversity and multiplicity of hu- man cultural forms without endorsing the celebratory, often frivolous, and ulti- mately divisive gestures of postmodernism and multiculturalism. It is a latecomer on the intellectual scene—and is therefore mindful of its parasitic, tentative status— but it is neither haunted by nostalgia nor dogged by a spirit of defeat, disinheri- tance, or inferiority. It is never sentimental, self-excusing, or self-indulgent; it is also, however, profoundly infused with the most cherished ideals of humanity—justice, compassion, freedom, equality, charity, and love. This is the domain of critique, the domain of the oppositional intellectual par excellence—that rare breed of scholar- activist who embodies erudition, independence, rigor, resilience, and moral courage in equal measure, a breed whose almost total disappearance from the contempo- rary sociocultural scene Said bewailed in various studies. In short, criticism—what the critic professes and deploys—is a sharp, multibladed tool of demystification that helps turn history, knowledge, and current sociocultural practices upside down and inside out.

As a practicing *oppositional* intellectual Said used this technique in two com- plementary ways: on the one hand, his critical practice was interdisciplinary and multidimensional. He often engaged a broad range of discursive topics—say, hu- man intentionality as an overarching appetite (philosophy); historical understand- ing in the context of modernity (historiography); literature as an institutional and cultural agency (literary/cultural studies); or Orientalism as a discursive objectifi- cation of the Orient (philology; critique of race theory, empire, and anthropology). However, instead of conducting these inquiries in isolation from one another (in the name of a presumed thematic or disciplinary integrity), he tended to map out their *affiliations*—their dialectical collations, cohabitations, tensions, confrontations, and the like—and especially their effects in the world. That is to say, he saw them as actively contested sociocultural force fields in which ideas and ideals are never self-subsistent but work in concert with—or in opposition to—aspects of political and civil society. For him, criticism was a form of historically and theoretically in- formed intellectual energy that dissolves ossified dogmas, dismantles artificial walls, overcomes tyrannical hierarchies, and opens up new horizons for investiga- tion. Alternatively, the knowledge furnished about this defamiliarized force field is decidedly uncanny, often unnervingly so. Although it is never entirely pessimistic, it is seldom comforting or conformist. On the contrary, it is provocatively eccen- tric and transgressive. And it is never easily consumable or digestible: for example, seemingly normal aspects of social reality may come to be seen as pathological through and through, and a high premium is placed on tension, paradox, opposi- tion, discrepancy, distanciation, and dissensus—rather than clarity, coherence, catholicity, consensus, or synthesis. Finally, it is neither explanatory nor hermeneu- tical in the conventional senses of these terms. Rather, it subsumes and goes far beyond them both, calling for a kind of insurrectionary activism that is rarely encountered in academia these days. In other words, Said's critical practice, whose ambitious range stretched from metaphysics to journalism, was a deliberately, even intransigently, heightened form of awareness about ourselves and the world we live in—an awareness that involved maximum diagnostic rigor, reflection, and passion.

I would like to conclude with a passage about humanism in Said's posthumously published book *Humanism and Democratic Criticism*:

> Humanism, I think, is the means, perhaps the consciousness we have for providing that kind of finally antinomian or oppositional analysis between the space of words and their various origins and deployments in physical and social place, from text to actualized site of either appropriation or resistance, to transmission, to reading and interpretation, from private to public, from silence to explication and utterance, and back again, as we encounter our own silence and mortality—all of it occurring in the world, on the ground of daily life and history and hopes, and the search for knowledge and justice, and then perhaps also for liberation.[18]

NOTES

An earlier version of this article appeared as part of "Edward Said and After: Toward a New Humanism," a collection published by *Cultural Critique*, no. 67 (Fall 2007): 88–106. I thank the editors of the journal, as well as the University of Minnesota Press, for granting permission for its inclusion in this volume.

1. Edward W. Said, *Orientalism* (New York: Vintage Books, 1978).

2. Ibid. Edward W. Said, *The Question of Palestine* (1979; New York: Vintage Books, 1992); *Covering Islam: How the Media and the Experts Determine How We See the Rest of the World*, rev. ed. (New York: Vintage Books, 1997); *Culture and Imperialism* (New York: Alfred A. Knopf, 1993); *The Politics of Dispossession: The Struggle for Palestinian Self-Determination, 1969–1994* (New York: Pantheon Books, 1994).

3. Edward W. Said, *Joseph Conrad and the Fiction of Autobiography* (Cambridge, MA: Harvard University Press, 1966); *Beginnings: Intention and Method* (New York: Basic Books, 1975); *The World, the Text, and the Critic* (Cambridge, MA: Harvard University Press, 1983); *Humanism and Democratic Criticism* (New York: Columbia University Press, 2004).

4. Said, *The World, the Text, and the Critic*, 28.

5. Abdirahman A. Hussein, *Edward Said: Criticism and Society* (London: Verso, 2002), 8–90.

6. On Said's "mature" version of Orientalism, see *Orientalism*, 58–59.

7. Said, *Beginnings*, 40.

8. See, for example, Said, "Al-tamanu', Wal-tajathub, Wal-ta'ruf," *Mawaqif*, March 1972.

9. See Hussein, *Edward Said*, 92–97; also, Said, *Beginnings*, 1–78.

10. See Hussein, *Edward Said*, 4–8.

11. Said reflects on the metaphysical and theological issues, especially their relationship to epistemological and ethical aspects of normativity, in *Beginnings*. But he engages these problematics indirectly in most of his other texts. Kant's most sustained examination of metaphysics, especially with respect to epistemology and ethics, takes place in the first and second critiques. See Emmanuel Kant, *Critique of Pure Reason*, trans. Mary J. Gregor (Cambridge: Cambridge University Press, 1996); and *Critique of Practical Reason*, trans. Paul Guyer and Allen W. Wood (Cambridge: Cambridge University Press, 1998).

12. These critiques appear mostly in *Beginnings* and *The World, the Text, and the Critic;* also see my exposition of these critiques in *Edward Said.*

13. Said, *Beginnings,* 40.

14. Ibid., 352.

15. See Hussein, *Edward Said,* 72–96.

16. Said, *The World, the Text, and the Critic,* 173.

17. Ibid., 216.

18. Said, *Humanism and Democratic Criticism,* 83.

25

Edward Said and the Possibilities of Humanism

R. Radhakrishnan

I felt posthumous when I bought Edward Said's *Humanism and Democratic Criticism* at a Chennai bookstore run by a close friend of mine. For the first time I was "buying" Said as a no-longer-alive author. Whatever grief or melancholy I felt was immediately expelled when I saw the cover of this first edition of the book, which showed a hefty book lying on its side with a small ticket protruding from the top, bookmark style, bearing the words "Admit All"; at once, everything felt fine and restored again. The long-lasting significance of Said, his work, and the things he stood for seemed for a moment to have triumphed over the fact of his death. That cover sums up Said's political, aesthetic, and existential ethic with grace and sophistication. The semiotics of the image of the ticket are complex and multilayered. The mere existence of the ticket suggests that entry is limited, but the "All" stamped on it instantly deconstructs this idea of restriction. And the use of the ticket as a bookmark, jauntily jutting out from the ponderous-appearing book calls into question the ticket's nature and sublimates it to a higher and inclusive authority, the "All." But the textual interplay that Edward would have appreciated is between the mystical idea that the "All" can gain admittance through some transcendent or ahistorical process and the reality of the disciplinary and institutional intermediary, the power in charge of the "Admit." The "All" becomes "worldly" only through an act of transgressive representation. The authority of the ticket that admits some and not others is maintained under erasure to tell us that admittance is being won and secured in the name of all. Moreover, the "Admit" points to that threshold where the real enters in the form of representation; in this sense, admittance includes the possibility of legitimation along with the permission to represent. Finally, the imperative mood of the sentence, with its implicit subject, suggests a kind of reflexivity.

431

After all, who is the authority giving permission to "admit all," and do these words constitute a command, an imperative, a request, an appeal, or an exhortation? This "speaker" is humanity, inviting itself, in a nondenominational, nonparochial and nonsectarian manner, into the world of secular humanism. The exhortation as permission is an immanent critique of a world structured in dominance, where some are admitted so that others may be excluded.

To Edward Said, this book, necessary and precious as it was, was also a special point of entry into the worldliness of the world. In this chapter, I explore the manner in which Said inhabited the space that he loved to call "secular humanism." Powerful and persuasive as Said's use of these terms was, his spin on them was quite personal and even idiosyncratic. I point this out not to question the precision of his usage but to argue that Said, precisely by inflecting received terms in a certain pragmatic way, was able to re-create them as essential tools in the service of worldliness. With and after the publication of *Orientalism,* and with his public lecture "Secular, Oppositional Humanism," at the 1982 summer session of the School of Criticism and Theory at Northwestern University, Said made a clear choice. No more would he pursue the immanent complexity of erudition for the sake of erudition or the fetishization of specialist discourses in the name of their internal organization and adequacy; particularly, no more would he engage in convoluted debates about the dialectical, or otherwise, nature of the relationship between theory and practice. He would thenceforth not call himself a theorist or an exemplary practitioner of any ism, or any epistemological school. He would rather call himself a "critic," in the old-fashioned sense of the term: one who is informed and inspired by "critical consciousness." We all know how high theorists diagnosed Said's recantation of his early theoretical and somewhat poststructuralist trajectories: ruefully, seeing his decision as a kind of recidivism brought about by too keen a passion for the political. Others nodded their heads and welcomed Said back into their conservative "humanist" fold, happy not to have lost so brilliant a one to the life-denying deconstructionists and Foucauldians. In an acute and telling way, Said's "worldly turn" (in contrast to the "linguistic turn" brought about by structuralism) raises a crucial question about what is radical and what is conservative.

There are two main axes along which one could determine which is which: the truth/content axis or the method/form axis. A critic who stands for values that are revolutionary, transformative, and in dire avant-garde transgression of the norm could be deemed as radical along the truth/content axis. This radical bent would take the form of a macropolitical ideological confrontation with the status quo. However, a critic could also be recognized as radical by virtue of his methodology or specialized ways of knowing, or of asking questions that set him apart from and ahead of all the canonical practitioners of the field. A New Historicist, a Foucauldian discourse analyst, or a Derridean deconstructionist could be considered a micropolitical radical, irrespective of the outcome of his or her specialist practices. But Said completely upsets this neat scheme. Having gone through the radical micrological regimen, and having produced *Beginnings* (an exemplary work of the specialist, even as it opens up other possibilities), he breaks from that regime precisely because he considers its formal and theoretical virtuosity an alibi and a camouflage for something else: for quietism, critical inertia, and a vicious narcissistic complacency. He then reclaims some of the old humanist "conservatives," such as Leo Spitzer, Eric Auerbach, and Matthew Arnold as though they were the radical ones. Needless to say, here too Said's use of these thinkers is idiosyncratic and quite tendentious. His particular readings of these theorists make them worldly, oppositional, and conducive to his own project of secular humanism. Said's work finds high theory suspect precisely because, in an "always already" mode, it credited itself with radicalism. Within high theory, one cannot be an agential critic; one can at best be an exemplar of a mode of thinking that in some a priori, immaculate, and transhistorical and transempirical way claims to be the embodiment of radicality. In seeing the need to go against the current of such orthodoxy, Said reclaims the humanist legacy that allows him space for individual critical creativity, intentionality, and intervention.[1]

The question that came up, sometimes rigorously and at other times disingenuously, right after Said's "relapse into humanism" was, After such knowledge, could there be a going back? Having been so profoundly influenced by poststructuralism, and in particular by the thought of Foucault, could Said "go back" to the humanism that had been so thoroughly problematized, in theory, by Foucault and others? Some critics were even angry and resentful enough to ask, in effect, Who does Said think he is to dramatically divest from the epistemological practices that have made him what he is and suddenly celebrate his freedom from specialist discourses in the name of a maverick nature and free critical consciousness working toward worldliness? A slightly different tack is best represented by a statement from Stanley Fish at a plenary session at the Modern Language Association convention: "I am not a Palestinian-American. I am not Edward Said, and I don't have a politics." We need to unpack the assumptions behind these criticisms and accusations carefully. What does it mean to be influenced by a particular epistemology or a school of thought, and how does one evaluate the legitimacy or the statute of limitations of any school of thought within the history of ideas? Is there a developmental, an evolutionary, or a revolutionary logic to the history of ideas that prevents previously repudiated and disproved paradigms from enjoying another inning in human history? For example, one would not, in any serious sense, want to believe in a phlogiston theory of combustion or the music of the Ptolemaic spheres or a geocentric universe (though the Pope's recent pardon of Galileo for his heresy is hilarious), nor would one want to hold on to the theory that the world was created in seven days. These ideas have been definitively superannuated, and one cannot entertain these positions as cognitively viable postures. One could perhaps accommodate them in one's heart or soul for other reasons: poetic, personal, or redemptive. And one, of course, can believe in placebos, or as John Lennon once said, "Whatever gets you through the night," but this posture would be one of belief, which has a different structure from that of truth claims.

Here I take the risk of speaking for Said in a way in which he refused to represent himself. In doing so, I am guilty of trying to create a coherent connection between his political choices and the epistemological underpinnings of these choices. As we have seen, with *Orientalism* Said radically redefined his accountability as scholar-critic-intellectual. I think he would have agreed with Nietzsche that history is to be done in the name of the present and that the purpose of historicizing is not to fetishize the past or to be interpellated by it.[2] We also know that for Said, macropolitical traces meant a lot more than those created by professionalization. Thus Said would honor his commitment to being an Arab or a Palestinian American but not to being a card-carrying member of something called poststructuralism or Marxism. He would not characterize the professional realm as "worldly." On the contrary, he strongly maintained that when the domain of the profession arrogates a world unto itself, such a world is a fiefdom rather than a world.[3] But he would by no means, in the name of the political, abandon his nuanced enjoyment of music, literature, narrative, and the world of philosophical, cultural, and aesthetic abstraction. The only difference is that he would access them now with his "critical consciousness," a term that he often used to connect humanism with the secular.

So, let us hear Said on humanism:

> I should stress again that I am treating this subject not in order to produce a history of humanism, nor an exploration of all its possible meanings, and certainly not a thoroughgoing examination of its metaphysical relationship to a prior Being in the manner of Heidegger's "Letter on Humanism." What concerns me is humanism as a useable praxis for intellectuals and academics who want to know what they are doing, what they are committed to as scholars, and who want also to connect these principles to the world in which they live as citizens. This necessarily involves a good deal of contemporary history, some sociopolitical generalization, and above all a sharpened awareness of why humanism is important to this society at this time, more than ten years after the end of the Cold War, as the global economy is going through major transformations, and a new cultural landscape seems to be emerging, almost beyond the precedents of our experiences to date.[4]

Much is going on in this seemingly simple passage. First, Said deprofessionalizes, deacademizes, and laicizes the term *secularism*. He expresses more kinship with a nontechnical nonhumanities person on the street than with a philosopher to whom humanism is actually "humanism." He lists for himself and for the reader the things he is not doing with the term: he is engaging with it selectively, strategically, and opportunistically. All that is fine and unproblematic. But the reference to Heidegger and his implication that he has a true understanding of the meaning of Heidegger's "letter" does pose a problem. If Said agrees, and I think he does, that a metaphysical connection exists between humanism and a "prior Being," then secularism is automatically not a form of humanism. Indeed, humanism is ahistorical, primordial, and essentialist. Why then is Said not bothered about this conceptual dissidence? Is it not worthy of concern? Or is it worthy of concern only for nitpickers and academic philosophers? Has Said, by virtue of disclosing his reasons for engaging with humanism, succeeded in delimiting and sanitizing it for his purposes? If humanism is theoretically and epistemologically not secular, how is Said so confident that his practical instrumentalization of it will somehow exorcize the metaphysics in humanism? Just when he thinks he is utilizing humanism, is he perhaps "being had" by humanism? I do not suggest that Said was not aware of these questions; my point is that he agrees to find satisfaction in what I call the understanding that "humanism is what humanism does." Questions like, is existentialism a form of humanism? and is Marxism a form of humanism? would have made urgent sense to him earlier in his development, but not any more.

The moving aspect of his invocation of humanism is that it is in the context of contemporary human tragedy, suffering, injustice, and peril. He posits humanism as an omnihistorical state of being human that responds to worldly situations in the name of freedom and justice. Knowing that the term *humanism* and its indeterminacy have been appropriated in several mutually exclusive ways, he is keen on recuperating it in the name of a multilateral and secular humanity that is unfortunately structured in dominance. He then says something that is part confident affirmation and part self-reflexive interrogation: "And also, as scholars and teachers we believe we are right to call what we do 'humanistic' and what we teach 'the humanities.' Are these still serviceable phrases, and if so in what way? How then may we view humanism as an activity in light of its past and of its probable future?" A little later in the essay, he makes his intentions crystal clear: "I believed then, and still believe, that it is possible to be critical of humanism in the name of humanism and that, schooled in its abuses by the experience of Eurocentrism and empire, one could fashion a different kind of humanism that was cosmopolitan and text-and-language bound in ways that absorbed the great lessons of the past from, say, Eric Auerbach to Leo Spitzer and more recently from Richard Poirier, and still remain attuned to the emergent voices and currents of the present, many of them exilic, extraterritorial, and unhoused, as well as uniquely American."[5]

Humanism to Edward Said was a *longue durée*, and any reports of an epistemological break from humanism are irresponsible and apocryphal. In a strange way, in this insistence, Said resembles Jacques Derrida, who would aver that one cannot step outside the pages of the book called logocentrism. What, then, could constitute a break in the history of humanism? What kind of counterexample of "humanist terror" would persuade Said that the time had come to break from humanism?[6] The answer is nothing would. Said was resolute that an ideal and desirable humanism could be reimagined despite the many horrors perpetrated in its name. There is a good humanism and a bad humanism, depending on how it is accessed and in-strumentalized. When Said maintained that it is possible to critique humanism in the name of humanism, he was operating as a supreme deconstructionist. There is no *hors-texte* to humanism, or to secularism for that matter. Eurocentrism, the white man's burden, patriarchy, and a whole series of manmade calamities are deplorable parts of humanist history, yet, Said saw a way to reengage "innocently" with humanism and claim it in the name of its better half. Like Fredric Jameson, who main-tained that Marxism is the ultimate horizon that subsumed every other struggle and political practice, Said used humanism as an inclusive umbrella rubric to cover universal history.[7] Said felt compelled to connect the thinkers of the distant and re-cent past with contemporary practitioners such as Poirier within the transcenden-tal affiliation to humanism. This stance resembles Frantz Fanon's call for a new hu-manism based not only on the deconstruction of the colonizer-colonized binary but on the deconstruction of binarity as such: "The Negro is not, any more than the white man."[8] Said used the term to capture the near and the far, the local and the remote, the past and the present; and in the present, the hegemonic and the subal-tern, the canonical and the emergent. In his thinking, humanism thus works to con-serve the best moments and episodes in history; and it also works across the asym-metry between the ex-colonizer and the ex-colonized and between metropolitan and subjugated peripheral knowledges. Sure enough, Said spoke and wrote on nu-merous occasions and with great eloquence to enable a politics across this symmetry and beyond the mutually reductive game between the politics of blame and the pol-itics of guilt. His need to believe in humanism was so intense that often he credited fairly platitudinous statements with rare profundity: "A superb sentence by Leo Spitzer, as brilliant a reader of texts as this century has produced and who spent his last years as an American humanist of European origin and training, is singularly apt. 'The Humanist,' he says, 'believes in the power of the human mind of investi-gating the human mind.' Note that Spitzer does not say the European mind, or only the western canon. He talks about the human mind *tout court*."[9]

I confess that if Said had not presented Spitzer's sentence in this way, I would have read it in the Spitzer *oeuvre* and gone on without comment. Said was appar-ently so disgusted and nauseated by the self-serving proliferation of specialist dis-course and jargon that he was prepared to settle for a few transparent hortatory declamations. Elsewhere, almost à la Matthew Arnold and his "touch stone" criti-cism, Said extols simple declaratory sentences as though simplicity qua simplicity were a guarantor of deep sense. Though I am no scholar of Spitzer, I offer a differ-ent reading of that sentence. First, aside from what Spitzer's intention might have been, the fact that the "European" remains unmarked as a sign of the universal in an utterance that comes from the heart of Eurocentric humanist discourse is not surprising. But more importantly, has not every manifesto of freedom, such as "All men are created equal," functioned on the basis of blindness, whereby the "all" does not include the all but functions and is defined by a procedural norm that is violated by its own content? And have not Foucault and Derrida had the singular insight that any emancipatory statement, including the ones to come, speaks in ideological but not real plenitude? In a similar vein, Said considered what to me is a normal and nonexceptional statement by Walter Benjamin, his memorable aphorism about barbarism and civilization, to be extreme and not representative. Equally revealing in the above quote is the superb way in which he connects Spitzer's capacity for rare insight with his training and ability as a reader of texts. Here, the cultural-literary-aesthetic realm all comes together with worldliness. Said is also careful to point out that Spitzer, despite his non-jargon-laden simplicity, is as perspicacious and insightful as any contemporary reader trained in a whole range of hermeneutic, structuralist, and poststructuralist practices. How can we forget that "textuality" and "reading" were the two key concepts that secured the elitist superiority of poststructuralism: Derrida, de Man, and Barthes on the text and so on? Let us also remember his essay "Criticism between Culture and System," where he begins to develop, by way of his critical readings of Foucault and Derrida, a different relationship between what I call "the worldliness of the text and the textuality of the world," and "the language of Being and the being of Language," à la Heidegger.[10] Said, whether or not one agrees with his evaluation of Spitzer's interpretive prowess, succeeds brilliantly in valorizing the cultural in the political and vice versa.

If I may slide into an anecdotal mode, I had the singular good fortune of being a student of Said's at the 1982 summer session of the School of Criticism and Theory at Northwestern University. At the time, I was a finishing doctoral student from the State University of New York at Binghamton and a student of the ever-fiery and ever-engaged intellectual William V. Spanos. During the summer course, I had the thrilling opportunity, though I was nervous as hell, of presenting a talk in avid support of Michel Foucault, and this presentation took place after all of us students had discussed, with Said's guidance, the celebrated discussion between Chomsky and Foucault on Dutch TV.[11] Despite my solidarity with Said's worldly project, I disagreed then, as I do now, with Said's reading of Foucault. I argued in class that Foucault's genealogical analysis that refused to anchor justice and freedom in something called reason, and his insistence that the history of the making of reason has been unreasonable, had much more potential for "emancipation" for freedom and justice than Chomsky's neo-Kantian position. I remember with great gratitude the solicitous manner with which Said challenged my stance, offering serious questions, objections, and criticisms. Perhaps I was not and am not a good student of Said's, or maybe I failed to learn something crucial from his reasoning, but to this day, despite my other published criticisms of Foucault, I remain convinced that Foucault's commentary on "freedom" and "justice" is more far-reaching than Chomsky's, precisely because he refuses the coincidence of politics with epistemology and thereby opens up possibilities of a perennial revolution by way of the history of the present and its dire injustices and inequalities.[12]

I find it ironic and even poignant that Said's project had so much in common with Foucault's: despite their deep modal differences, the two men shared the desire to produce noncoercive forms of truth. I also have difficulty understanding how and why Said found the Chomskian blend of political anarchism and epistemological a priorism more appealing and persuasive than the Foucauldian blend of relentless archaeology and interventionary genealogy. My guess, at the risk of veering into pop psychology, is that Said found in Foucault a mirror image of his own predicaments and contradictions—a grid that he wanted to move away from. Chomsky, in contrast, offered him both the solace of perennial oppositionality and a way to anchor politics firmly in epistemology. In the passage above, I am not sure exactly what Said's critical attitude is toward foundationalism and antifoundationalism. Is he arguing for an epistemological foundationalism, of whatever kind or provenance? Or is he saying that Lyotard's manner of critiquing foundationalism is precious and pretentious? Or is he suggesting that it has become fashionable to use antifoundationalism as a glib "foundation" for an indeterminate radicalism? What would Said's foundation be? One might argue that an oppositional secularism is both antifundamentalist and antifoundationalist. Said's confident claim that "freedom" and "justice" are evacuated from the scheme of things once the human becomes "human," reminds me of the earlier debate about morality and religion. "If God is dead, anything is possible." Was Said's resistance to epistemological antifoundationalism an isomorphic version of the argument that morality has nothing to stand on once religion is defunct? I do not think so, because Said's own memorable advocacy of secularism and his virtuosic relativization of Beginning to heterogeneous and contingent "beginnings" make it abundantly clear that he had no need for transhistorical or primordial inaugurations. In this respect, as a literary reader and interpreter of texts, Said had more in common with the Derrida who called for a decentered play that put the very center in play than with Chomsky's linguistics and transformational grammar. The problem is that unlike, say, Partha Chatterjee, Said did not differentiate between secularism as a political vision and secularism as an epistemological blueprint. Unlike a number of South Asian cultural critics who find themselves "double-conscious" on the matter of secularism, Said was entirely happy with secularism and its embeddedness in the good humanism.

Given these views, how valid is Said's claim that the fight against injustice and oppression cannot be based on a theoretical or ideological antihumanism? Does Foucauldian genealogy not allow the human subject to gain an ethico-political foothold for projects of worldly change? Here I disagree with Said quite entirely, and I hold that his reading of Foucault is in error. Unlike Said, I do not see Foucauldian genealogy precipitating an ascesis of the ethico-political human subject. Foucault's legitimation of his projects takes a different path from that of Chomsky and Said. His critical attitude to what I call the category of "in the name of" is as follows. Foucault does not grant a separation between the historicity of emancipatory projects and the historicity of the principles "in the name of which" these projects are undertaken. As a meticulous genealogist, he will not concede to freedom and liberty the status of the a priori. Human nature, to Foucault, is undecided and undecidable, and yet, choices need to be made strategically and contingently. If the very history of the production of reason is an unreasonable history, then any project undertaken in the name of reason should be both reasonable and unreasonable (in Dostoevsky's sense of the term in his *Notes from the Underground*). The invocation of reason has to be double coded. It is an antifoundationalist project only because it realizes first, that one cannot separate reason from reasons of State and polemical reason, and second, that the only temporality when reason can be invoked in its innocent plenitude is during a dystopic regime that is fully coextensive with the body of reason: a regime in which all forms of alterity have already been taken care of.

The essential difference between Foucault and Said is that Foucault refuses to give belief and faith any epistemological credence or basis, whereas Said takes that leap.[13] And yet, I believe that Said and Foucault are much more akin than they appear to be in Said's self-understanding. Consider, for example, Said's attitude to nationalism. Did Said believe that nationalism is a valid and legitimate affiliation? No. Was he himself a nationalist? No. Given a choice between cosmopolitan identity and a Palestinian national identity, which would he claim? Clearly, the former. Yet, rightly and magnificently so, Said fought, campaigned, "threw stones," and was vilified as "the professor of terror" precisely because he was an indefatigable advocate of Palestinian national rights. In an uneven world structured in dominance, there really was no contradiction between Said's political espousal of the Palestinian nationalist cause and his intellectual-theoretical repudiation of the claims of nationalism. If so, was Said not practicing the same kind of politics that he found suspect: an antifoundationalist politics that fights in the name of a certain principle whose legitimacy is not absolute but immanent with the terrain of contestation? How then did Said defend his political support of a particular nationalism in the context of his general rejection of nationalism? The fact that he did makes him unique and credible as an intellectual. Precisely because as a critic-intellectual he embraced the worldly task of living and making choices in a symptomatic world of contradiction, he commands our admiration and emulation. Rather than pose as a totalizing theorist who would act only in the name of the purity of a methodology, Said was prepared to think-tinker his way through the dilemmas and crises of historical existence. What he did not do, however, was provide a theoretical justification for breaking the impasse of aporias and dilemmas by the exercise of a political and worldly will.

Said's repudiation of the claims of antihumanism (would calling it posthuman-ism make a difference to Said? perhaps not) was based on a disagreement that was both affective and cognitive. In other words, he disagreed with both the sensibility and the thought of poststructuralist antihumanists. Here is how he described the emergence and popularity of antihumanism in academia.

It must be remembered that antihumanism took hold on the United States intellec-tual scene partly because of widespread revulsion with the Vietnam War. Part of the revulsion was the emergence of a resistance movement to racism, imperialism gen-erally, and the dry-as-dust humanities that had for years represented an unpolitical, unworldly, and oblivious (sometimes even manipulative) attitude to the present, all the while adamantly extolling the virtues of the past, the untouchability of the canon, and the superiority of "how we used to do it"—superiority, that is, to the disquieting appearance on the intellectual and academic sense of such things as women's, ethnic, gay, cultural, and postcolonial studies and, above all I believe, a loss of interest in the vitiation of the core idea of the humanities. The certainty of the great literary texts was now threatened not only by popular culture but also by the heterogeneity of up-start or insurgent philosophy, politics, linguistics, psychoanalysis, and anthropology. All these factors may have done a great deal to discredit the ideology, if not the com-mitted practice, of humanism.

But it is worth insisting, in this as well as other cases, that attacking the abuses of something is not the same thing as dismissing or entirely destroying that thing. So, in my opinion, it has been the abuse of humanism that discredits some of humanism's practitioners without discrediting humanism itself.[14]

This passage invites serious commentary and critical reflection. Let me start at the end. Said expresses an a priori conviction that humanism needs to be salvaged from both its detractors and its own aberrations. He is also convinced that these aberrations are not an essential part of humanism. The abuses of humanism have a different etiology from that of the proper and celebrated uses of humanism. Are these valid intellectual assumptions, or are they necessary articles of faith? If the same humanism authored both colonialism and anticolonialism, both the domi-nance of the master and the insurrection of the slave, where within this binary struc-turation is the true nature of humanism to be found and preserved? If the true free-dom of the slave is to go beyond his or her desire to occupy the position of the master, can such a freedom be accommodated within the binary logic of humanism? When abuses occur, who is accountable: the system, the proponent of the discourse, or the individuals who could have but did not make the difference? Is humanism an ideology that interpellates its subject, or is it a transideological commonsensical phi-losophy that functions freely without interpellation? I claim that racism and colo-nialism and anti-Semitism and patriarchy have all been versions of humanism, al-though one might add that these isms are chapters in the long and unending book called "The Historical Progress of Humanism through Civilization and Barbarism."

If one accepts Walter Benjamin's dictum, can we consider the barbaric side to be less representative of human nature than the civilizational dimension?

Who, then, is the intended addressee of humanism, and how do we decide this issue? I frame the question in terms of an "address" and an "addressee" to invoke the significant earlier moment when Sartre, in his preface to Frantz Fanon's impassioned *The Wretched of the Earth*, pronounced that even though Fanon was addressing Africa, Europe should listen, and be courageous enough to be transformed by the ethico-political authority of Fanon's discourse.[15] Said would claim that he too, like the world at large, was the addressee not only of "Western" humanism but of any body of thought produced anywhere in the world: Confucianism, Buddhism, Vedantic thought, Islam. Said brilliantly recognized that no philosophy is produced with solipsistic reference just to its provenance and that the concrete universality produced by any system of thought is intended as a negotiating participant in the production of a relational human universality. In his rigorous efforts to avoid macropolitical universals, Foucault in fact opted out completely from having a say about universality. We can find yet another stark difference between Said and Foucault. I suggest that of the two, Foucault was the provincial Eurocentric intellectual, whereas Said was a multilateral, multivalent, multicultural, cosmopolitan intellectual. Said was the "border intellectual" whose work moved among, across, athwart multiple boundaries and sovereignties, whereas Foucault, despite his archaeological erudition and genealogical intensity, remained a prisoner to the Eurocentric episteme. The Saidian possibility of existing simultaneously in multiple worlds, of experiencing windows as mirrors and mirrors as windows, of perennially transcribing any inside space as a space of the outside, and of dwelling in "many betweens" as homes and as locations was not even thinkable for Foucault. To Said, these liminal possibilities were not just the fancy fabrications of theorizing, they were experiential verities. At the risk of stating the point too strongly, I would say the chronotopes in which Said lived and thought were far more avant-garde than the location of Foucault's theory, however magnificent and groundbreaking. In other words, Foucault, the indefatigable critic of representation, ended up in a desiccated and an attenuated macropolitical universe, whereas Said, whose theoretical belief in representation may sound retrogressive compared to Foucault's, saw his work achieve multiple representations across borders and territories.

In Foucault's discourse, the human subject interpellates humanism without being able to develop an attitude toward the interpellation. On the contrary, in Said's rhetoric, humanism is a way of doing things, whatever one may be doing. Foucault's focus is on humanism, but Said's is on the humanist. The significance of the task is not exhausted either by the might of the interpellation or by the disciplinary or modal immanence of the activity itself. There is room for critically transcending the terms of the interpellation and for putting the interpellation (which is procedural in nature) to work one way rather than another. In Said's work, humanism is an ethico-political imperative of the second order that gives a certain secular and worldly shape and direction to whatever one is doing. A person can be a practicing humanist engineer, a humanist interpreter of texts, a humanist economist, a humanist educator, a humanist government administrator. Every individual has the option of practicing his or her trade or profession in a humanist, ahumanist, antihumanist, or nonhumanist way. This reconfiguration of the term is brilliant because now the value of humanism is not inherent in disciplinarity or in the specialized discourse of the profession. Humanism is an ethico-political stance that tells the intellectual from "without" the domain of professional specialization how to handle and use and direct the discourse. Said essentially "amateurizes" humanism and thereby endows it with a worldliness that is often foreclosed without compunction in the immanence of "wall-to-wall discourses." Of course, in rendering humanism an orientation, he runs the risk of a certain simplemindedness, as is evident from this quotation from *Humanism and Democratic Criticism*: "Change is human history, and human history as made by human action and understood accordingly is the very ground of the humanities."[16] Remarkably, even after an avalanche of specialist isms, discourses, and methodologies, Said finds Giambattista Vico's articulation of the secular to be quite revolutionary, yet Vico simply said that "the historical world is made by men and women, and not by god." This statement is not earthshaking, particularly in our times. Nonetheless, to Said it was a crucial retrieval: first, because it keeps theodicy out, and second, because it also challenges the occlusion of the human by the "human."

Said's strategy here was relationally critical. He sought to intervene in professionalism by way of humanism. He interwove two objectives to form an inclusive worldly project: the task of decelebrating professionalism and the work of affirming humanism. Affirming humanism was the main project, but this affirmation requires the critique of professionalism. Here, for example, Said extols the virtues of simplicity:

> Unfortunately, Adorno's poetic insights and dialectical genius are in very short supply even among those who try to emulate his style: as Sartre said in another context, Valery was a petit bourgeois, but not every petit bourgeois is a Valery. Not every coiner of rebarbative language is Adorno.
>
> The risks of specialized jargon for the humanities, inside and outside the university, are obvious: they simply substitute one prepackaged idiom for another. Why not assume instead that the role of the humanistic exposition is to make the demystifications and questionings so central to our enterprise *as transparent and efficient as possible?* Why turn "bad writing" into an issue at all, except as a way of falling into the trap of focusing uselessly on how something is said rather than the more important issue of what is said? There are too many available models of intelligible language all around us whose basic graspability and efficiency goes the whole range from difficult to comparatively simple, between the language of, say, Henry James and that of W. E. B.

DuBois. There is no need to employ preposterously outré and repellent idioms as a way of showing independence and originality. Humanism should be a form of disclosure, not of secrecy or religious illumination. Expertise as a distancing device has gotten out of control, especially in some academic forms of expression, to the extent that they have become antidemocratic and even anti-intellectual. At the heart of what I have been calling the movement of resistance in humanism—the first part of this being reception and reading—is critique, and critique is always restlessly self-clarifying in search of freedom, enlightenment, more agency, and certainly not their opposites.[17]

One can respond to the multiple arguments and positions taking shape in this passage in several ways. As the devil's advocate, one could exclaim, "Not every coiner of simple and transparent language is Edward Said." This position raises an enormous question about the exemplarity, emulability, and representativeness of literary style. Is it easier to write like Hemingway than to write like Virginia Woolf? Is it easier to philosophize à la Jacques Derrida, or like Bertrand Russell? The answers must account for the conditions under which certain thoughts, ideas, and sensibility take shape and condense into a style: no room exists for facile form-content dichotomy. One could write like Hemingway but be simpleminded and perceptually impoverished; and one could write like Virginia Woolf yet be guilty of logorrhea and muddleheadedness. But, of course, the literary world has not seen too many Hemingways or Woolfs. In the heat of his polemic, Said overlooks the fact that style is the felicitous coming together of the form of the content and the content of the form. To dismiss difficulty and complexity because of the greater importance of what is being said and the lesser importance of how it is being said does not work as an argument. What, then, about literature as a genre, or poetry, which Valéry compared to a dance (with prose like walking), in which the way of writing is its fundamental ethic? Clearly, Said would not go the Sartre way in making easy distinctions between prose and poetry, or between *literature engagé* and aesthetic literature. Said also overlooks the fact that there are ways and ways of problematizing common sense and of quarreling with language. A number of philosophers and writers have taken the trouble to imagine new contents through new forms and have sought to derail and problematize transparency (Heidegger comes to mind, and John Cage in composition) to avoid easy orthodoxies and to point out the ponderous constructedness of so-called transparency. Again, not every long-haired dropout is a radical, and not every stuttering, catatonic musical composer is a John Cage. The quarrel with language as such is not always a radical revolution, nor is it always a version of formal narcissism.

In Said's discourse, the humanist subject/individual does the talking. Foucault as a posthumanist thinker was quite happy to accept the model of perennial epistemological self-styling, as well as the model of "aimless" epistemological wandering in the name of the history of the present. It is not clear, as one reads Foucault, if he believed that such a theoretical and epistemological engagement with the present was already a political model or would beget a compatible political model. In Said's case, "home" and "the humanist subject" resonated differently. Said lived between home and not home, and his thoughts were those of a subject who straddled politics and epistemology. Though comfortable as an exile, Said understood the need and the significance of home on a political level. As an intellectual exile, he would not glorify political exile as a desirable state for anyone or any people, Palestinians and others. Even as he privileged exile as an intellectual perspective, he sought justice for a people demanding home and advocated their right to speak, narrate, tell their own stories, represent their points of view. I suggest, then, that to Said, the value of "home" was the value of a resistance and an antagonism rather than a "thing in itself." Only because the world is structured in dominance and several peoples have been dispossessed of home through colonization and occupation does "home" continue to be a terrain where battles are fought. The Israeli-Palestinian is a particularly tragic case in point: a people decimated by the Holocaust, a people in search of a home they can call their own don't find it unconscionable that in the process of "homing themselves," they are ruthlessly "un-homing" another people. Said makes this point eloquently in his essay "Zionism from the Point of View of Its Victims."[18] He asks why people in search of their own home find it quite acceptable to trounce someone else's home and keep building settlements on someone else's land. He ponders whether there is something fundamentally wrong and unethical about "home-centric" thinking. Is there something intrinsic to the model, cognitively and epistemologically, that makes the home a fortress with moats and drawbridges—the moats filled with crocodiles, tanks, and armies to keep the "other" out? Said makes a distinction between the political need for home and the ethical attitude toward home. Thus he finds it possible and coherent to argue for a home in the mode of political resistance and redress while problematizing the notion of home as such.

This double attitude to "home" and to "what is one's own" marks the brilliant originality of Said's thinking. To avail of Walter Mignolo's phrase, Said's tireless efforts to build bridges between "the places where one lives" and "the places where one thinks" are what make him so special and so indispensable under our present conditions of world-historical existence.[19] For example, in a lecture on Freud vis-à-vis the non-European, Said found the freedom both to make Freud his own *and* to historicize Freud in relationship to Eurocentrism. "In any event, I believe," he said, "it is true to say that Freud's was a Eurocentric view of culture—and why should it not be? His world had not yet been touched by the globalization, or rapid travel, or decolonization, that were to make many formerly unknown or repressed cultures available to metropolitan Europe."[20] This is a quintessentially generous Saidian evaluation that leaves room for contrapuntal play and negotiation. Yet it is not generous at the expense of historical or theoretical rigor. Said does not exonerate Freud or his discourse for the sake of being forgiving and magnanimous: he signals both a quarrel and an understanding here. He raises a question about intentionality and accountability. Of course, Freud was Eurocentric by way of his discourse. Given his times, and this is true for all human endeavors that are conditioned by historical circumstances, Freud cannot be criminalized as an individual. He was Eurocentric, yes, but that was not all that he was. Someone's thought can be centric in one sense and still be valuable in other ways and for other reasons. By contrast, Said's evaluation of Foucault (who could have been more aware of certain historical happenings but chose not to for whatever reason) is a lot stricter, based on historical circumstantiality. "The most striking of his blind spots was, for example, his insouciance about the discrepancies between his basically limited French evidence and his ostensibly universal conclusions. Moreover, he showed no real interest in the relationships his work had with feminist or postcolonial writers facing problems of exclusion, confinement, and domination. Indeed, his Eurocentrism was almost total, as if 'history' itself took place only among a group of French and German thinkers."[21]

The origins of a theory never really mattered to Said. He saw no need to create a counterhumanism that was non-Occidental or anti-Occidental. He was much happier producing contrapuntal readings within the musical text called humanism. Humanism to him, intentionally at least, was just humanism, not Western humanism. This attitude seems both deferential to the West, because it seems to exculpate the West a little too easily, and transgressively transformative, because it takes humanism away from its putative Occidental provenance, in the name of all humanity. Is this Said's deconstructive and metamorphic reading of humanism, or has such a possibility always been inherent in Western humanism? Said did not offer the human subject either a "true" or an "ideal" humanism. His was a contrapuntal and secular humanism that would not allow the truth of humanism to shine as a predetermined and transhistorical essence or understand itself as the unfolding of a specific teleology available only to a few special subjects, and in a few chosen narratives. He sought to pit humanism against itself, deconstructively and contrapuntally, so that it might "self-correct" in response to principles of a secular and "bounded rationality." His agenda was to open humanism up to its own potential, to let hitherto "subjugated knowledges" transform humanism in the name of all humanity, and to decolonize humanism as a Eurocentric fetish. The Said who defended humanism multilaterally and the Said who tirelessly demonstrated the interimbricatedness of different histories were one and the same. What is deceptive is the singularity of the term *humanism* that is symptomatic of the colonial-modernist will to produce the normative-dominant one out of the many through processes of cleansing, "sublating," and reformed representation. Said was interested in the multeity of humanism: its internally heterogeneous interrelatedness. Said's rhetoric renders humanism accountable to its Eurocentric past, and only when it accepts such accountability can humanism begin to measure up to the "human." Unlike Chinua

Achebe, who does not identify with the West except by way of the execrable accident of colonialism, Said was a happy and voluntary citizen of Western thought and literature. In this sense, he was a native son of the West and had no problem taking the West to task for its racism and colonialism. Not unlike Foucault and Derrida and Sartre and Adorno, he could therefore be a magnificent and powerful insider-antagonist. Said believed unequivocally that the complicity between culture and imperialism had to be shown up with the utmost rigor and in utter accountability. But he argued that such a project, by definition, has to be contrapuntal. It has to acknowledge the potential for good and the harm done and to recognize the constitutive relationship between the two. Precisely because he "owned" the West as culture, scholarship, and erudition, Said not only had a stake in the West and its future unraveling but also had confidence that he could read the West against itself, change its course, and use its considerable resources selectively and righteously. He engaged in the important task of translating the West to itself, despite itself.

The singularly fascinating aspect of Said's work to me is that the sense of closure and conviction it offers on one level—that of the political and the didactic—is immediately made to seem contingent and vulnerable on another level: at the level of thought concretized as style. In this light, I conclude this chapter with a quotation from Said's *Freud and the Non-European*, a book whose very title is contrapuntal. Here, Said comments on the late works of Beethoven and Freud, fascinated by the fact that even though these works were composed toward the very end of their authors' lives, they exhibit an unruliness and a lively and rebellious rejection of closure. Said could well have been writing about himself.

> In Beethoven's case and in Freud's, as I hope to show, the intellectual trajectory conveyed by the late work is intransigence and a sort of irascible transgressiveness, as if the author was expected to settle down into a harmonious composure, as befits a person at the end of his life, but preferred instead to be difficult, and to bristle with all sorts of new ideas and provocations . . . Freud and Beethoven present material that is of pressing concern to them with scant regard for satisfying, much less placating, the reader's need for closure. Other books by Freud were written with a didactic or pedagogic aim in mind: *Moses and Monotheism* is not. Reading the treatise, we feel that Freud wishes us to understand that there are other issues at stake here—other, more pressing problems to expose than the ones whose solution might be comforting, or provide a sort of resting-place.[22]

NOTES

A longer version of this chapter appeared as chapter 2, "Edward Said and the Politics of Secular Humanism" in R. Radhakrishnan, *History, the Human, and the World Between* (Durham, NC: Duke University Press, 2008), 115–82.

1. See Edward W. Said, *The World, the Text, and the Critic* (Cambridge, MA: Harvard University Press, 1982), where he revisits "intentionality" as an essential component of "worldliness."

2. Friedrich Nietzsche made this point in his impassioned tract *The Use and Abuse of History*, trans. Adrian Collins (Indianapolis: Bobbs-Merrill, 1949).

3. Among the many critics who have worked on the theme of professionalism, I would like to single out Stanley Fish, Bruce Robbins, and Gerald Graff.

4. Edward W. Said, *Humanism and Democratic Criticism* (New York: Columbia University Press, 2004), 7.

5. Ibid., 7, 10–11.

6. For an eloquent and politically responsible treatment of the relationship between humanism and terror, see Maurice Merleau-Ponty, *Humanism and Terror*, trans. John O'Neill (Boston: Beacon Press, 1969).

7. Fredric Jameson employs the term *humanism* usefully in *The Political Unconscious: Narrative as a Socially Symbolic Act* (New York: Cornell University Press, 1981).

8. See Frantz Fanon, *Black Skins, White Masks* (New York: Grove Press, 2008).

9. Said, *Humanism and Democratic Criticism*, 26.

10. See Said, "Criticism between Culture and System," in *The World, the Text, and the Critic*, 178–225.

11. The debate transcript is available in *The Chomsky-Foucault Debate: On Human Nature* (New York: New Press, 2006).

12. For my disagreement with Foucault on the nature of intellectuality, see "Toward an Effective Intellectual: Foucault or Gramsci?" in *Diasporic Mediations: Between Home and Location* (Minneapolis: University of Minnesota Press, 1996), 27–61.

13. For more on the nature of belief in the context of secularism, see "Critical Secularism: A Reintroduction for Perilous Times," the introduction by editor Amir Mufti, in a special issue, *boundary 2* 31, no. 2 (Summer 2004): 1–9. See also William Connolly, *Why I Am Not a Secularist* (Minneapolis: University of Minnesota Press, 1999); Rustom Bharucha, *In the Name of the Secular: Contemporary Cultural Activism in India* (Oxford: Oxford University Press, 1998); the works of Partha Chatterjee and Ashis Nandy; Talal Asad, *Formations of the Secular: Christianity, Islam, Modernity* (Stanford, CA: Stanford University Press, 2003); and chapter 5 in R. Radhakrishnan, *Theory in an Uneven World* (Oxford: Blackwell, 2003), 122–90.

14. Said, *Humanism and Democratic Criticism*, 12–13.

15. See Jean-Paul Sartre's ringing preface to Frantz Fanon's *The Wretched of the Earth*, trans. Constance Farrington (New York: Grove Press, 1963).

16. Said, *Humanism and Democratic Criticism*, 10.

17. Ibid., 72–73.

18. See Edward W. Said, "Zionism from the Point of View of Its Victims," *Social Text*, no. 1 (Winter 1979): 7–58.

19. See Walter Mignolo, *Local Histories/Global Designs: Coloniality, Subaltern Knowledges, and Border Thinking* (Princeton, NJ: Princeton University Press, 2000).

20. Edward W. Said, *Freud and the Non-European* (London: Verso, 2003), 16.

21. Edward W. Said, "Michel Foucault: 1927–1984," in *Reflections on Exile and Other Essays* (Cambridge, MA: Harvard University Press, 2003), 187–97.

22. Said, *Freud and the Non-European*, 29–30.

26

The Language of the Unrequited

Memory, Aspiration, and Antagonism in
the Utopian Imagination of Edward Said

Asha Varadharajan

The figure of Edward W. Said, for all his reiteration of a sensibility "not quite right and out of place" (Said 2000b: 295), has come to be indelibly, and not unjustly, synonymous with a heroic humanism. Convinced that "every great civilization is made up of endless traffic with others" (Said 1999: 291), Said made this generous and contrapuntal vision of global history singularly his own. A keen eye for overlapping territories and intertwined histories, the dream of mutuality and the hope of reconciliation, the defiance of power in the name of truth, and the scrupulous mapping, Cardinal Newman-like, of the relative disposition of things have become hallmarks of the synthetic imagination that inspired Said's inventive and prolific intellectual career. Yet, as his readers and interlocutors are never allowed to forget, Said's faith in "human existential integrity" is the paradoxical consequence of his keen comprehension of the brutal conflicts at the heart of contemporary existence (Said 2002a: 410). Said's recovery of a "critical model for humanism with a heroic ideal at its core" is, therefore, a radically subversive rather than recuperative enterprise (Said 1999: 286). It is a counterintuitive and unseemly fable of survival snatched from the jaws of extinction; an inscription of the anomaly, the exception, the excentric, and the minority at the heart of the universal; an affective and visceral response to the vicissitudes of displacement; and an homage to those moments when the contingent and the untimely disrupt the fatality of history.

Said's *Humanism and Democratic Criticism*, which was published posthumously in 2004, has, not surprisingly, been received as a manifesto of sorts for a life that embraced the secular, the humane, and the universal. In the book, Said rather unapologetically identifies his resurrection of philology and his defense of humanism with the practice of criticism in the cause of (democratic) freedom. This book is, in many ways, a rushed and peremptory, even occasionally unremarkable, work, without the nuanced precision and eloquence of *Representations of the Intellectual* (1994), for example—reflecting, perhaps, the urgency of Said's exhortation to "reconsider, reexamine, and reformulate the relevance of humanism" in unconscionable times (6).

Said's recapitulation of arguments that he made with more patience and elaboration over the years hinges on his insistence that humanism is nothing more than the irrefutable conviction that "change is human history" and that the "historical impact" of "human agency and labor" cannot be underestimated by even the most plausible antifoundationalist theories of human intention and action (10). The "untidiness" (Victor Li's apt term) of Said's brand of humanism (Said's own words are "incomplete, insufficient, . . . disputable") does not vitiate its value or necessity; indeed, the "critical investigation of values, history, and freedom" must, he contends, once again become the mandate of the humanities (12, 14).

In Said's view (2004b), the discipline of the humanities was distressingly powerless to affect anyone or anything (14), and his aim, in the essays in *Humanism and Democratic Criticism*, is to reject the "carping and narrow" "elite formation" of humanism for one whose force will dwell in its "democratic, secular, and open character" (22). Said's ire is directed against the complacency of those who treat humanism as either "unadulterated" or "uncomplicatedly redemptive"; instead, he invokes the compassionate understanding of history "in all its suffering *and* accomplishment" as the sine qua non of humanist sensibility (23, 22, emphasis mine). Said's antiquated insistence on a "catholicity of vision" is of a piece with his seemingly newfangled commitment to the "challenges of the emergent, the insurgent, the unrequited, and the unexplored" (27, 26). If history is never "marmoreally finished in itself," humanism cannot but divide its attention between "codified certainties" and "countercurrents" (26, 28).

Said's fidelity, however, is less to an obsolete notion of fair play, to holding in animated and scrupulous suspension the "clash of civilizations," or even to hoping that cultures and peoples might one day engage in "a compelling dialogue" as a prelude to the "practice of participatory citizenship," than to a certain insurrectionary spirit that he strenuously distinguishes from the "bellicose . . . unanimity" that taints custodians of the eternal verities (28, 22, 25). Although Said's emphasis on "self-understanding and self-realization" seems to envision historical becoming as a rational unfolding, his description (adapting Raymond Williams's formulation) of contemporary (American) intellectual and political culture as a "seething discordance of unresolved notations" hints at a belligerent and iconoclastic rather than a serene and contemplative humanism (26, 28). Said's lucid attempts to rescue humanism from both abuse and veneration could all too readily be dismissed as "misty-eyed pieties," but this tart phrase suggests that Said thinks otherwise (3).

In his presidential address to the Modern Language Association (MLA) in 1999,

Said had already begun to represent humanism as more than a sop to reigning pieties. He described the practice of humanism as "determined effort and risk," as emphatically *not* an act of conformism, consolidation, or "amiable respect," and as the expression of the stubborn belief that the "struggle is not yet, is never, over" (290). Here Said privileged the heroic critical spirit, indomitable in its resistance to the "thrall of Eurocentrism" or the "powers that be," "immersing [itself] in the element of history" in order to recover "the topics of mind from the turbulent actualities of human life" (291, 290). Despite the critic's commitment to the disclosure of what lies forgotten or buried and, therefore, to truths that might raze rather than lay the foundations of society, Said emphasized the "rational processes of judgment and criticism" and the critic's role as the agent of order and intelligibility, albeit of a potentially radical alternative to "imperial knowledges and [the] will to rule" (290, 291). This emphasis on the critical subject of humanism, I suggest, is in contradistinction to the one that emerges in *Humanism and Democratic Criticism,* where Said focuses, instead, on the *effect* of humanist critical practice.

If Said (2004b), with R. P. Blackmur, imagines humanism as a "technique of trouble" (77), it seems odd that his pronouncements (at least in the liberal academy) have been met with little serious (rather than merely intemperate) rebuke or dissent. If Said's take on the "implacable dynamic of place and displacement" produces no more than a *frisson* of sympathy or regret (82), his endorsement of "lost causes" no more than admiration for his romantic intransigence or distant solidarity for the suffering of Palestinians (33), and his "stubborn, and secular" criticism no more than the self-congratulation of comparably "worldly" critics (49), then we might conclude that Said's writings inspire and inform but do not deracinate in the profound manner that his frequent use of words like "insurgent," "discordant," and "unsettling" suggests. Said's writings have, of course, provoked widespread debate and generated excellent criticism, but where, precisely, does their power to *disturb* lie? In other words, how does one assume the mantle of "Saidian humanism" (Emily Apter's phrase [2004]) without letting the practice of criticism dwindle into unexceptional bromides about the quest for knowledge, justice, and liberation (Said 2004b: 83) or into interminable musings on the antinomian struggle between intellectual detachment and political belonging? My claim is that the promise and enchantment of Said's writings lie elsewhere than in the obvious struggles they delineate.

My focus on the more enigmatic and elusive moments of his corpus is not simply perverse or idiosyncratic; I want to consider the possibility that Said's logic, like that of Erich Auerbach, avoids a "relentless sequential movement" and follows, instead, the guidance of burgeoning motifs that develop a logic and movement of their own (Said 2004b: 116). This approach will, I believe, not only restore vitality to writings that are becoming merely familiar but also transfer critical scrutiny to the legacy of Said's thought, adumbrate its utopian imagination, and clarify his critical example. I want, in short, to indicate what remains once the temptation to hagiography passes and the squabbles over this or that inconsistency or contradiction in his oeuvre subside.

An intriguing moment in Said's 1999 presidential address to the MLA illuminates a generally neglected aspect of the heroic ideal at the core of Said's brand of humanism and can help us articulate how Said's critical imagination insinuates itself into contemporary consciousness in what I hope are less predictable terms. I allude here to Said's curiously prolonged attention to Freud's "manually and heroically produced text[s]" (287). Said was fascinated by the saturated significance of "the lone black American fountain pen" on display at the Freud exhibition in Vienna (287). This "humbly recumbent pen" becomes the occasion for Said's musings on "the sheer unremitting scriptual effort and its physical realization" manifested in Freud's manuscripts (287). I suggest that Said's gesture beyond politics toward an enduring human dignity and an endearing human vulnerability not only authorizes a reading of his texts as the "solid material expression of his *intellectual* will" (287, emphasis mine), but functions as implicit permission to intuit a consistency of style and *affect* that "furnish[es] [them with] texture, surface, and character" (288). (I am applying Said's comments on Freud to his own work.) This intuition, I argue, returns us to rather than transcends politics.

Said's writing constitutes a sort of cultural and critical patrimony to contemporary critical consciousness. This unremarkable observation acquires the character of a paradox when one is compelled to consider the power and poignancy with which Said turns rootlessness into the condition and effect of thought. We can benefit from revisiting the unique affect of his writings—more than their method, discourse, politics, or even vision—if only because this shift in emphasis might reveal both the magical potency and painful allure of accents of loss and hope. My contention, to put it baldly, is that the affective qualities of Said's writing and perception will survive the memory of its contents.[1] In the meditation that follows, I identify exhortation, quiet intransigence, irony, and impossibility as the defining features of Said's existential (and critical) metamorphoses.

The movement of Said's thought acquires both the density of history and the substance of individuality despite its chronic restlessness and its apparent refusal to find solace in the certainties of place, nation, idiom, and sentiment. The experience of loss and dispossession, dislocation and disorientation, precipitous disturbance and lonely contemplation becomes the measure of the truth he tells. The inspiration and disillusion that Palestine signified were the source of both Said's blindness and his insight. In his work, Palestine represents the incomprehensible violence of history that blots out all else, even as it provides "a different set of lenses" through which to reveal all else (Said 2002d: xxxv). In a telling passage (one of many in his work), Said writes enigmatically of "how perspective in the Nietzschean sense is less a matter of choice than of necessity" (xxxv), attesting, thereby, to the manner in which a "scrupulous subjectivity" invests historical events and philosophical categories with shape, meaning, and desire (Said 2002e: 184). By the same token, subjectivity painstakingly acquires both scruple and perspective only because it has been blinded and shattered by the force of historical events and the fraud of the triumphalist categories that define them.

The paradoxes of a voice and vision refracted from the experience of displacement and predisposed to empathize with the "losers in the social contest" are well worth exploring because the turbulences and mutilations of exile produce prose of such consummate serenity and poise (Said 2002d: xxix). In other words, even though Said admires the manner in which Joseph Conrad's writing "wears its author's existential unsettlement on its surface," his own compositions, while no stranger to anger, resentment, pathos, or trembling uncertainty, let unsettlement infect their vision, not their syntax (xxii). Perhaps this dissonance between structure and meaning, voice and affect, illustrates with wrenching precision how life haunts writing and writing evades life, and asseverates that the (f)act of writing, for Said, was both an homage to the pleasures of exile and a cry against its invidious and destructive force.

If Said's career can be read as the usurpation and reclamation of the "permission to narrate" (the title of a 1984 essay), a defiance of the injunction to silence imposed on a people deprived of land and identity, the artful seamlessness of his prose challenges the conditions that it expresses. In other words, the sense that his writings articulate is instructively at odds with the sensibility that fashioned and enunciated it. Said's works more often than not give me the impression of an unwavering attention and persuasive insistence rather than grim satisfaction in winning bouts with epistemological and moral foes. Despite Said's gleeful indulgence in the riposte or withering dismissal, I find his writing to be somber without being sentimental. He comes across as a critic who conceives of his intellectual *dharma* as atonement for the identity "inside which so many have stood and suffered and later, perhaps, even triumphed" (Said 2004a: 54).

I will have more to say about the lineaments of such an intellectual regimen; for the moment, however, I turn my attention to how Said transforms psychic trauma into a political parable and makes philosophical contemplation into a moral lament (see Rose 2003: 67; I have used Jacqueline Rose's insight to slightly different effect). Just as Freud's pen is the "palpable physical coefficient" to his work (Said 1999: 287), Said's words function as the "solid material expression" of his victory over silence and mortality, the encounter with which he makes the condition of humanist endeavor (see Said 2004c: 82). This fugitive inclusion of existential obstacles to the pursuit of his personal dream of humanism sets the stage for the invention of historical consciousness and the assertion of political opposition—themselves the unlikely fruits of the encounter with silence and mortality.

In the concluding section of "The Return to Philology" in *Humanism and Dem-*

ocratic Criticism, Said offers a compelling articulation of a longtime feature of his thought: its attention to the spatial, rather than only temporal, dimension of human history. This time, Said explains his quixotic abandonment of the temporal or diachronic in favor of the spatial and synchronous as the only responsible form of millenarian humanism. In this explication, the temporal reappears in the guise of movement across frontiers and in the pendulum swings between displacement and enforced settlement. He reports that our age spews up "migrants, pilgrims, and castaways" with astonishing regularity even as it continues to imbue places with phantasms of belonging (82). Human mobility, therefore, cannot be understood without acute attention to the words and images that transform places, quite literally, into figments of the imagination. The simultaneous mobility of populations and metaphors produces the urgent need for an altogether different "humanistic attention" to the insidious manner in which the domain of the temporal modulates itself into the intricate relationships between physical and social space (82). In other words, human history is less a record of imprints than a quest for vanishing traces of habitation, memory, bodies, and structures. Said demands a rethinking of the dimension of temporality because the phenomenon of migration has fundamentally altered the "ground of daily life and history" (83); that is, the movement across space becomes the measure of temporal repetition and historical change.

Said's observations here are of a piece with those in his powerful commentary on the impossibility of extricating memory from geography in "Invention, Memory, and Place" (2000a). In considering the role of invention in constructing memory and producing narratives of identity and nationalism, Said undertakes a tour of the burgeoning scholarship in the "study of human space" (175). His focus on the "art of memory" naturally centers on the "inventive reordering and redeploying" of memory and geography in the interests of conquest and domination (180–81). Said rewrites Palestinian history as a territorial and "rhetorical dispute" in which Palestinians suffer not only eviction and displacement but even more cruelly, surrender their "right to a remembered presence and, with that presence, the right to possess and reclaim a collective historical reality" (182, 184). Said's conclusion is uncompromising: the guardians of collective memory have been transformed into its assassins because the decimation wrought by the Holocaust justifies the continuing assault on Palestinian memory and existence. Instead of allowing overlapping and mutually replenishing narratives, the sacralized Zionist tale banishes Palestine from the frame. In this deadlock, ironically enough, "history, geography, and political actuality" leave Israel and Palestine no choice but to envisage a "sustained reconciliation" rather than mutual extermination (191).

Said's emphasis in this essay, as it is in the bulk of his writing on Palestine, is on the *politics* of memory, its ruthless manipulation to produce a "community of blood," in every sense of the phrase (191). Collective memory, then, becomes a malignant force rather than a benign aesthetic of invention and imagination, and Said wants to insist on the distinction between the deployment of memory and its material-ization as narrative. The scholarship that Said chooses to explicate in this essay, there-fore, serves a corrective function rather than simply providing an alternative per-spective. I am reminded of his words to Jacqueline Rose in his 1996 interview, "Returning to Ourselves": "I've been suspicious, for as long as it's been around, of deconstruction: people who say, well, it all depends on how you look. I believe in facts and very often the facts get abused, or left out, or embroidered or hidden or for-gotten" (Said 2002f: 420). Said recognizes that the task of Palestinians and of Jew-ish historians who continue to write against the grain is not to restore balance in a skewed universe; for them, plucking memory from oblivion can only result in an "other" narrative with its own peculiar and unyielding integrity. In other words, Palestinian history in the prevailing circumstances does not qualify, nuance, or even fill in the gaps in Zionist memory; its tale, quite simply, is different.

Mustapha Marrouchi would describe this feature of Said's thought as "tact—in choosing when to record, and when to invent" (2001: 89); I would like, instead, to insist on the risk Said takes (implicitly perhaps) in "Invention, Memory, and Place" (2000a) in attributing invention to Zionism and giving credit for recording or doc-umentation to those who challenge the dehumanization and ossification inherent in that invention (190). The dream of reconciliation, which was, for Said, the only possible political solution to the Palestinian predicament as well as the only way for Zionists to acknowledge responsibility for the past, is not to be confused with a literal and metaphorical ceding of ground; rather, Said urges the far more ardu-ous course, that "these two communities confront each's experience in the light of the other" (192).

Said's solution is predicated on an impossibility: he acknowledges that "the in-flamed atmosphere of military occupation and injustice" (2000a: 192) precludes the possibility that either side will have the capacity to think "beyond identity" (2002c: 431). Neither a "potent humanism" (Apter's characterization on the back cover of Paul Bové's *Edward Said and the Work of the Critic*) nor conscientious political ac-tion serves Said's purposes in this essay, but his faith in "lost causes" did not waver thereafter; he continued, and *Humanism and Democratic Criticism* is no exception, to charge "emancipatory humanism" with delineating the "ethics of coexistence" (Emily Apter's phrases [2004: 35]). The temptation is to interpret Said's refusal to countenance anything else as a naïve, even foolhardy stance, but it is the beginning of an elaboration of the "humanistic attention" he unreservedly endorses in his lat-est work. When one probes this possibility further, humanism appears to be less the noble contrary of political action than its goad; that is, the messy compromises in the world of politics are the consequence of ignoring logical and cultural flaws in political processes, failing to appeal to conscience rather than consciousness, and denying the value of historical understanding. Significantly, Said catalogues these failures as *pragmatic* obstacles in the peace process rather than as features of an im-

possible idealism and impotent empathy that are remote from the implacable violence of territorial negotiations. His assertion of the salience of facts, in this context, is unquestionably and precisely *humane*, because facts are the only available
antidotes to the destiny of Palestinians, to "being left out of the progress of history"
(419). If humanism is to be more than an ideal to which the world no longer aspires, according to Said, it must reconstitute itself as a political *morality*, as " 'the
fusing of the moral will with the grasping of evidence' " (420, my emphasis).

This fusion continues to smack of a reluctant yoking together, but Said's position becomes somewhat clearer if one envisages his analyses less as examples of a
consistent (contrapuntal) methodology than as a rich palimpsest of allegory and
history, psychic identifications or states of being and political actualities, the literal
and the metaphorical, memory and invention, dreams and rights, exile and return.
I prefer the epithet *palimpsestic* to *contrapuntal* because the former allows the relations among the constituent elements to remain partially obscured and irrevoca-
bly contingent, whereas the latter's emphasis on counterpoint and "simultaneous
awareness" is more likely to hold putative oppositions in strenuous suspension or
in anticipated concord.[2] The difficulty and excitement of Said's mode of reflection
in *Power, Politics, and Culture* is the brilliant way in which he sustains the distinctions among the moral, the political, and the epistemological, or between the lived
and the metaphorical, while refusing to be intimidated or disheartened when these
categories slide unceremoniously into each other.

I have had occasion elsewhere to challenge the antidialectical character of Said's
concepts, his reluctance to *think* contradiction, but I believe Said's engagement with
the question of Palestine as "one of the most interesting twentieth-century experiences of dispossession, exile, migration" forces him to pursue a more courageous
(and therefore more troublesome) option (Said 2002c: 429).[3] When Israelis are in-
sulated from the very facts that made their society possible, and Palestinians dream
of restoring themselves to themselves but are either denied the right to return or
find return inconceivable (428–29), irony and contradiction become both banal and
horrifying. Critical scrupulousness, then, becomes a matter of refusing to be cowed
by contradiction and of affirming, instead, the revolutionary potential of *simultaneity*, of overlapping rather than singular histories or nationalities, of the "pathologies of power" (Eqbal Ahmad's phrase) and the potential for noncoercive community (429), and, finally, of "elusive and inconstant life" and "the false and killing
certainties of . . . conventional human arrangements" (430; Said and Rose, respectively). This dwelling in simultaneity, however, is a gesture of transcendence; that
is, thinking together inevitably entails thinking beyond the ruins of history, the loss
of memory, and the limits of identity.

Said's humanism remains on solid ground for much of *Power, Politics, and Culture*, alive to the cruelty and chicanery in the world and yet unwilling to trade hope
for despair, but by this time in his writing, cracks are beginning to appear in the in-

domitable façade and not only because Said concedes, in the concluding pages of "Returning to Ourselves," that he has begun to "[feel] the impress or weight of mortality" (430). The interview with Rose leaves unanswered a particularly troubling question about "the non-rational, unconscious, almost pathological dimension of political processes," revealing that the humanist in Said cannot afford to surrender history to pathology or will to desire (426). Said's incomparable complexity of vision and argument falters here because human blindness or cruelty and political violence must be susceptible to rational explanation rather than merely symptomatic, just as the ideological manipulation of historical memory must be subject to critical exposure rather than accepted as irrevocable and traumatic loss. Said is moved to respond in terms of the *irrational* (as opposed to nonrational) attitudes of Israelis and Palestinians alike and to transfer the discussion from the unconscious dimension of political processes to the rational and moral plane of individual human consciousness and collective conscience. He is immediately comfortable with proposing strategic alternatives while relinquishing the psychic (insubstantial) mode of being in favor of literal, concrete, lived existence. Yet his final words in the interview are about death as an escape from the stranglehold of identity and, intriguingly, about forgetting.

I believe this faint allusion to the intangible and the imponderable sheds unexpected light on Said's humanism as a pyrrhic encounter with silence and mortality as well as an enigmatic paean to forgetting. "Invention, Memory, and Place" and "Returning to Ourselves" are ruminations in which memory and geography intertwine, as Marrouchi (2001) has said, to "reveal the struggle to *relocate* the past" and to "[translate] unhappiness at exile into anxiety about time" (89, 108, italics in original).[4] The chiasmic transmutation of time into space in both these works reveals that the logic of temporality (the movement in time) continues to elude Said, who unabashedly maps the spatial dimension (movement across spaces and between frontiers) instead. Said justifies this move because Palestinian exile embodies a people dispossessed *of* history. Time, in other words, is on the side of Israel. But Said knows only too well that Palestinians must "seize and understand [themselves] and [their] history," and he thus proceeds to "speak [the Palestinian] case" against the distortions of Zionism and to suture the gaps of Palestinian memory (Said 2002c: 427, 429). Paradoxically, however, the survival of Said's historical imagination depends on the demise of "the empiricist illusion" (Said 2004b: 82) and on ". . . the conversion of the discrete particular into a world-historical process" (Said 1979: 259).[5]

A seemingly insignificant section in "The Return to Philology" (if the absence of critical comment on it is to be taken at face value) confirms my surmise even as it justifies juxtaposing *Humanism and Democratic Criticism* with *Freud and the Non-European* as intrepid quests for the "essential principle of what is lived and *seen on the ground*" (Said 2004c: 82, italics in original). Rather than accept the fusion of the moral will with the grasping of evidence, Said rejects the empiricist illusion and embraces the genealogical impulse. Said and the Palestinian community are no longer willing to let their undocumented, illegitimate, and refugee status bear mute witness to the injustice of the past. Said elevates the historical dispossession of the Palestinians into the essential principle rather than the material embodiment of what is lived and seen on the ground. Their grief, in short, bears the mark of the universal rather than functioning as one instance among many of the doom of exile. This originary displacement is the force that inaugurates universal history; in order to explain this ingenious supposition, Said returns to the keeper of the chronicles of Occidental memory, Sigmund Freud.

We must look at *Freud and the Non-European* in tandem with "On Lost Causes," where Said explains what it means for the Palestinians to "live through their own extinction" and wonders whether nobility can be extracted from failure (2002b: 545, 541). He concludes with a moving reformulation and assumption of resignation (in Adorno's sense) as a means of "blunting the anguish and despondency of the lost cause." "From this perspective," Said asks, can "any lost cause ever really be lost?" (553). I dwell on this essay because it highlights the counterintuitive and untimely character of Said's thought; not only does writing annihilate extinction and resignation constitute hope, but lost causes contain within them the momentum of historical necessity. If Said counters official historical imagination with the extinct and the untimely in "On Lost Causes," his incursion into the annals of collective memory might be interpreted as a certain tactical anachronism. In *Freud and the Non-European,* Said "dramatize[s] the latencies in a prior figure or form that suddenly illuminate the present" (2004a: 25). He returns to Sigmund Freud's *Moses and Monotheism,* a text seemingly inhospitable to dispossessed Palestinians, in order to actualize their history and reanimate their cause. In *Reflections on Exile,* he indicates that "since almost by definition exile and memory go together," his genealogical quest can be interpreted as an exercise in excavation and invention in the name of an alternative mythology and an altered destiny (Said 2002d: xxxv).

Said's enterprise here is not simply a rather stale desire to treat "Palestine" as the forgotten or the repressed in the manner of a chic civilization and its discontents, or even to launch a tame contrapuntal attempt to treat "Palestine" as the "simultaneous dimension" that would give Freud's investigation of the origins of Judaism a "plurality of vision" (2002d: 186). In a daring departure from his usual effort to make ideas travel—to chart the waning or acquisition of their force in novel contexts—Said makes his encounter with Freud confrontational, marching the "antinomian force" of those texts "which brush up unstintingly against historical constraints" with an intolerable compulsion of his own to find in the figure of Moses the constitutive fissure of the "unreconstructed non-Jewish Egyptian" (2004a: 27, 42).

If I may ponder the implications of thinking identity as "a troubling, disabling, destabilizing secular wound" a bit longer, both intellectual vocation and historical possibility become fundamentally at stake for Said in the project of delineating a "politics of diaspora" for "besieged identities." Said's assertion that identity cannot "imagine itself without that radical originary break or flaw which will not be repressed" may perhaps ring all too familiar to everyone but neophytes in the world of critical discourse, but what we might miss in this formulation is the sleight-of-hand that turns history not into the return of the repressed but into the force that, as Said says, inexorably "represses the flaw" that must be noted if identity is to be imagined. Said demands that the utopian imagination write this uncertain history, of the before rather than the after, undeterred by irresolution and impossibility (54, 55).

In his elegant disquisition on Said's memoir, *Out of Place*, Marrouchi characterizes the work as an "act of reinvention, a disobedient labor of remembrance," a calculated vengeance against the indecipherability of history, and a poignant surrender to the lure of anamnesis (92). Although one can certainly read *Freud and the Non-European* in these terms, I cling to the possibility that Said's peregrination through the past not only serves to "arrest the present" (see Said 2002c: 494) but, in its agonistic fantasy of the non-Jewish Egyptian as the limit inscribed within any imagined community, it also performs an astonishing act of forgetting, erasing the historical past in order to beget the imagined future. The journey is the contingency that erupts in the fatality of history, and the traveler is the inhabitant of nowhere committed to shattering every pretension to place, identity, and community. The historical persistence, and the enchantment, of the foundational fantasy is broken, but Said is careful to indicate that the repressed history of the Palestinians does not preexist its rememoration—thus *Freud and the Non-European*.

Palestinian history that preexists Israeli settlement is exhaustively documented in films such as *The Land Speaks Arabic* (2008), but the archival footage, interviews with Palestinians who remember life before Israeli occupation, conversations with Zionists, and historical research still require reconstruction that makes sense of the evidence and infuses events with narrative logic and historical causation. While *The Land Speaks Arabic* is a remarkable example of fusing the moral will with the grasping of evidence, Said would still see it as an act of rememoration rather than of recovery. Restoring Palestinians to themselves is never simply a question of the return of the repressed; it requires memory *and* imagination.

Said's touching moment of vulnerability at the end of "Returning to Ourselves," when he speaks of the need to forget, reveals itself as a knowing gesture. He bides his time, hoping that the act of forgetting will become the ground of an ethical relation to difference and the mark of a heretical politics. His appreciative essay on Jacqueline Rose's *States of Fantasy* preceded "Returning to Ourselves" by only a year; taken together they constitute, with *Freud and the Non-European*, Said's attempt to evaluate psychoanalysis as an agent in historical revision and political change. His reading of Freud acknowledges the accuracy of Rose's assessment of the constitutive role of fantasy in the making of states and nations. Rose is concerned to explain the fragmentation and historical alienation of identity consequent upon the force of traumatic repetition, but she gives this traumatic repetition a twist by reading it in light of Israel's dispossession of Palestine. This dispossession functions as the symptomatic engendering of the conditions of its own existence and marking of boundaries (see Said 2002c: 496).

She believes that *Freud and the Non-European* idealizes a tragic condition and discounts the force of trauma, but I want to defend the "groundless optimism" on display in Said's re-membering of Freud. (I have deliberately taken this phrase out of context. It appears in Said 2002c: 527–54.) Only because (and not despite the fact that) the history on whose behalf he speaks is irredeemable and would not exist if sociality were somehow extricable from violence can Said dream of the healing power of wounds, of the human born on the terrain of its obscene negation.

If "humanist reading" that relies merely on its "direct confrontation with reality" is inadequate for Said's purposes, *Freud and the Non-European* breaks with the "empiricist illusion" in the name of harnessing the "vernacular energies" of humanism to dissent from "social and cultural fate" (Said 2004a: 82; Richard Poirier quoted by Said, 29). Whereas the emergent and the insurgent obey, readily enough, the laws of historical repetition and causality (today's canon is composed of yesterday's insurgents) and the unexplored may be dependent for its articulation on its logical contradiction (mapped terrain), the unrequited, by definition, flout the laws of the history that cannot sustain them. The fundamental revisions and subtle alterations that Saidian humanism undergoes in its career enable it to speak the language of the unrequited and to write history as the narrative and (failed) resolution of the "aspiration and antagonism" driving these changes (59). This strain in Said's reinvention of humanism is the element that fashions his corpus as an "*unsettling* adventure in difference" (55, emphasis mine).

NOTES

I first experimented with the ideas in this essay in "Indigent Dwelling, Itinerant Thought," which appeared in "Edward Said: Tributes," a special issue of *Politics and Culture: An International Review of Books*, ed. Amitava Kumar and Michael Ryan, no. 1 (2004); http://aspen.conncoll.edu/politicsandculture/page .cfm?key=302 (accessed 1 July 2009). I am grateful to Amitava Kumar for inviting me to contribute to that issue. The essay owes its current (considerably revised) form to the acute insight and generous encouragement of Adel Iskandar, the enterprising research of Sam McKegney, and the practical assistance of Sylvia Söderlind. I wish to acknowledge the financial support of the Social Sciences and Humanities Research Council of Canada.

1. In his interview with Jacqueline Rose, "Returning to Ourselves" (Said 2002f: 419), Said speaks of his hope (borrowing from Adorno) that his words will be remembered exactly as he wrote them. My point here is that such fidelity and exactitude are impossible unless one attends equally to how words resonate and what they signify.

2. See Armstrong 2003 for a lucid discussion of the perils of counterpoint and the (ethical) plea-

sures of play. See also Gourgouris 2004 for an unusually compelling articulation of Said's contrapuntal method as a "complex orchestration" within which constituent elements "might be privileged provisionally and always in distinctive relation" (63). Gourgouris would disagree with Armstrong because he believes that contrapuntal reading, and by extension secular criticism, is exemplary in its performativity (Armstrong's "play") and indistinguishable from "mobility, mutability, displacement, nonidentity, transgression, transformation" (69). My definition of the virtues of palimpsestic thinking complements Gourgouris's outright affirmation of contestation, entwinement, and coincidence in Said's secular transgressions; however, I continue to believe, unlike Gourgouris, that the contrapuntal method must be distinguished from dialectics and that one can do so without detriment to either. Said certainly found dialectics inadequate to explain what Gourgouris describes as "an antagonistic entwinement between two ongoing complicitous histories" (75). (Neither antagonism nor complicity is necessarily dialectical even if the two might be reciprocal or mutually reinforcing, for example.) Moreover, Said's emphasis on fusion suggests that he often perceived at least no logical contradiction between personal homelessness and political community (74), between the literal and the metaphorical, between life and writing, or between self and history.

3. See my *Exotic Parodies* (1995). See also Hussein 2002 for a meticulous account of Said's dialectical affinities.

4. Marrouchi's subject is Said's memoir, *Out of Place*, but he would not disagree that much of his critique could apply to Said's work as a whole. I find Marrouchi's encapsulation of some complicated maneuvers in Said's arguments particularly succinct in this instance.

5. Emily Apter (2004) cites this observation of Said's in the interests of tracing the lineaments of critical secularism as humanism's mandate (45). She describes Said's move as an attempt to salvage humanism *tout court* rather than only from its complicity with Orientalism. Although I do not disagree with Apter's idea, my aim is to elaborate on the manner in which Said's transformation of humanism in the interests of the Palestinian cause also entailed a movement from the grasping of evidence to the construction of what Apter discerns earlier in her argument as an "allegorical typology [which] may be applied . . . to the analysis of global humanity" (43). Said's modest claim that Palestinian exile constitutes *one* of the significant experiences of the twentieth century rapidly acquires, in Said's late work, a certain paradigmatic value, and he comes to valorize the condition of statelessness rather than an existential homelessness as an ethical mode of being. Put simply, Apter turns her insight into the many guises of Saidian humanism into the definition of critical secularism, whereas my effort is to determine how a humanism based on the study of space became, by the end of Said's career, a reinvention of the logic of temporality and a revelation of the unconscious of history.

WORKS CITED

Ahmad, Eqbal. 2000. *Confronting Empire: Interviews with David Barsamian.* Cambridge, MA: South End Press.

Apter, Emily. 2004. "Saidian Humanism." *boundary 2* 31, no. 2: 35–53.

Armstrong, Paul B. 2003. " 'Begin Out of Place': Edward W. Said and the Contradictions of Cultural Differences." *Modern Language Quarterly* 64, no. 1 (March): 97–121.

Bové, Paul. 2000. *Edward Said and the Work of the Critic: Speaking Truth to Power.* Durham, NC: Duke University Press.

Freud, Sigmund. 1967. *Moses and Monotheism.* New York: Vintage.

Gourgouris, Stathis. 2004. "Transformation, Not Transcendence." *boundary 2* 31, no. 2 (Summer): 55–79.

Hussein, Abdirahman A. 2002. *Edward Said: Criticism and Society.* London: Verso.

Li, Victor. 2004. "Edward Said's Untidiness." *Postcolonial Text* 1, no. 1, http://postcolonial.org/index.php/pct/article/view/309/106 (accessed 30 June 2009).

Marrouchi, Mustapha. 2001. "Exile Runes." *College Literature* 28, no. 3 (Fall): 88–128.

Rose, Jacqueline. 1998. *States of Fantasy.* New York: Oxford University Press.

———. 2003. "Response to Edward Said." In Said, *Freud and the Non-European,* 63–80. New York: Verso.

Said, Edward W. 1979. *Orientalism.* New York: Vintage.

———. 1984. "Permission to Narrate—Edward Said Writes about the Story of the Palestinians." *London Review of Books,* 16–19 February, 13–17.

———. 1996. *Representations of the Intellectual.* New York: Vintage.

———. 1999. "Humanism and Heroism," MLA Presidential Address. *PMLA* 115, no. 3 (2000): 285–91.

———. 2000a. "Invention, Memory, and Place." *Critical Inquiry* 26, no. 2 (Winter): 175–92.

———. 2000b. *Out of Place: A Memoir.* New York: Vintage.

———. 2002a. "The Anglo-Arab Encounter: On Ahdaf Soueif." In *Reflections on Exile and Other Essays,* 405–10.

———. 2002b. "On Lost Causes." In *Reflections on Exile and Other Essays,* 527–53.

———. 2002c. *Power, Politics, and Culture.* New York: Vintage.

———. 2002d. Introduction, *Reflections on Exile and Other Essays.*

———. 2002e. "Reflections on Exile." In *Reflections on Exile and Other Essays,* 173–86.

———. 2002f. "Returning to Ourselves." Interviewed by Jacqueline Rose. In Said, *Power, Politics, and Culture,* 419–31.

———. 2004a. *Freud and the Non-European.* New York: Verso.

———. 2004b. *Humanism and Democratic Criticism.* New York: Palgrave Macmillan.

———. 2004c. "The Return to Philology." In *Humanism and Democratic Criticism,* 57–84.

Varadharajan, Asha. 1995. *Exotic Parodies: Subjectivity in Adorno, Said, and Spivak.* Minneapolis: University of Minnesota Press.

27

Between Humanism and Late Style

Lecia Rosenthal

The new is the longing for the new, not the new itself: That is what everything new suffers from.

—THEODOR ADORNO, *AESTHETIC THEORY*[1]

"A KIND OF HEROISM"

As far as criticism goes, there are, according to Edward Said, two ways of thinking about the future. The first is oriented intrinsically, positing futurity within the boundaries of an already existing tradition. This mode is essentially conservative, its vision of the future self-confirming and dedicated to reproducing its own continuity. "Such critical activities set not only discrete and finite goals that can be accomplished within one or two works of criticism, but also larger goals that may include the production of many more works of that particular type and the transformation of idle readers into active believers in, practitioners of, a certain kind of criticism."[1] Thus this mode of criticism projects the future as an extension of the already thought, a repetition of the past and its achieved conclusions. Rigidly "systematic and doctrinal," it produces disciples and resists change.[2] Appropriating the unknown into an already settled horizon of the known, this mode of criticism negates the radical potential of futurity and thus, according to Said, has no future at all.

For readers of Said's work, it will come as no surprise that he is quite critical of this first approach. While he acknowledges that it is "dialectically interwoven" with the second mode of criticism, it is clear that, however necessary the former may be, Said uses it primarily to establish the limitations and blind spots he wants the second to overcome. In this second, alternative mode, the future extends beyond one that would remain its "own." Recognizing and indeed insisting upon the possibility of criticism's "extrinsic" effects, this mode eschews disciples and resists codification. Perhaps most crucially, in its openness to an encounter with the "external" world (the outline of the extrinsic, and indeed that which would render it as such, is necessarily incomplete and shifting, but Said does allude to a range of contextual-historical formations ignored by criticism in its first mode; these include nonacademic institutions, mass culture, and the "claims of feminism, of Europe's others, of subaltern cultures, of theoretical currents running counter to the rule of affirmatively dominant pragmatism and empiricism"), this mode of criticism resists the becoming-obsolete of criticism itself. For Said, such marginalization implies not simply the threat of relative silence, obscurity, and irrelevance, or a kind of historical senescence of the intellectual's social power, but rather the already prevalent *domestication* of a criticism all too easily managed by "the institutions of a mass society whose aim is nothing less than a political quiescence."[3]

How does Said argue for the latter model of intellectual practice? Indeed, can there be a model for that which remains open to the future as undomesticated, undecided, and radically unsystematizable alterity? Said's argument in "The Future of Criticism" points a tension that persists throughout his work as it reflects upon and elaborates various models, ideals, and possible futures of critical practice. Extrapolating from the two modes of futurity outlined above, this tension can be described as a vacillation between affirmative normativity and critique of totality; between the possibility of prescriptive completion and an emphasis on resistance and the open-ended; between an approach to the new as dialectical expansion of the already thought and as radical irruption of the unassimilated, the incommensurable, and perhaps even the unthinkable. In Said's late works, this tension will become one, if not more than one, between humanism and late style.

From the outset, I hope to be clear (clarity, as readers of Said's early, middle, *and* late works will recall, is a measure of a critic's self-restraint) that I am not proposing to locate any strict or static division between Said's work on late style and his call for a return (if a return it is) to the values of humanist practice.[4] Rather, I am interested in the ways in which Said's late works, which include both the work on humanism (particularly as put forward in *Humanism and Democratic Criticism*) and the reflections on late style (in the essays and fragments collected posthumously in *On Late Style*, as well as in *Freud and the Non-European*), intersect each other at the nodal point of "lateness," a strange and uncertain term that Said defines, by way of Adorno, as "the idea of surviving beyond what is acceptable and normal; in addition, lateness includes the idea that one cannot really go beyond lateness at all, not transcending or lifting oneself out of lateness but rather deepening that lateness."[5] If lateness, then, articulates the impossibility of "going beyond," marking the limit of any dialectical overcoming and expansion, might it have something to say about the limits of humanism?

Humanism and Democratic Criticism makes some extraordinary claims for comprehending and achieving (not to mention reviving) the "essence of humanism." As in the two modes of criticism outlined in "The Future of Criticism," the book vacillates between an openness to the historically and epistemologically "new," and an insistent (Said would say "intransigent") rhetoric, indeed a rhetoric of insistence that aims to prescribe and lay claim to a future outcome. Thus, after arguing for an open-ended understanding of history, or that field of production and knowledge that remains "still unresolved, still being made, still open to the presence and the challenges of the emergent, the insurgent, the unrequited, and the unexplored," Said continues, "Not to see that the essence of humanism is to understand human history as a continuous process of self-understanding and self-realization, not just for us, as white, male, European, and American, but for everyone, is to see nothing at all."[6] Opposing an affirmative model of progressive insight ("a continuous process of self-understanding and self-realization") over and against a position of absolute blindness ("to see nothing at all"), Said defends his defense of a humanist universal, a mode of intellectual and critical practice for which there can and will be no "others."

Humanism and Democratic Criticism's defense of the values of humanism (or, as Said will often say, his "belief in" such values) is certainly not without precedent in his work. As early as Beginnings, Said offers a detailed critique of antihumanism as part of his discussion of structuralism. Said takes issue with the "linguistic reduction of man" and structuralism's emphasis on a totalized world in which "intention has been . . . totally domesticated by system."[7] As part of the book's focus on the problem of beginnings, Said criticizes the antihumanist critique of intentionality and the rational, autonomous subject, arguing that the structuralists fail to account for the emergence of new forms of meaning, such that they "gravely underestimat[e] the rational potency of the beginning, which to them is an embarrassment for systematic thought" (320). This "embarrassment," Said argues, functions implicitly and utterly such that for structuralism the system is an all-encompassing and self-expanding vortex, a productive enclosure that enables and accounts for even the critic's own efforts to describe an ordered universe of signs. "Like science, structuralism is meta-linguistic—language studying language, linguistic consciousness appropriating linguistic competence and performance" (326). The tenuous status of the prefix "meta-" is suggestive of what for Said is the paradoxical and unresolved tension within structuralism between an originary linguicity and a critique of origins; between a metaphysics of Man and a critical language that depends on the language and concepts of metaphysics to make its arguments; between a critic who has access to an understanding of structure even as he argues that structure itself produces his thought.

If "in the structuralist universe the problem of belief is never relevant, since belief entails a hierarchy of meanings. For structuralism there are only significations, and they are either adequate or inadequate for their signifying intentions," in Said's universe the rhetoric of belief reemerges with positive significance.[8] Thus, despite the preference in Beginnings for Foucault's work, by the time Said writes Orientalism, he will argue, "Yet unlike Michel Foucault, to whose work I am greatly indebted,

I do believe in the determining imprint of individual writers upon the otherwise anonymous collective body of texts constituting a discursive formation like Orientalism."[9] This "belief" in the generating, indeed "determining" power and effects of an author's "imprint" will lead Said to leave structuralism behind, as it were, as he turns to Adorno for an alternative model for theorizing the possibility—and limits—of resistance.

As we have seen, "The Future of Criticism" argues for a criticism characterized by radical resistance to standardization. Such resistance would imply a persistent extraterritoriality, a "kind" of criticism that has neither definite genre nor representative figure. Yet, this type of criticism, insofar as it is a "type," does have an exemplary form: the essay; and a paradigmatic practitioner: Adorno. Adorno, Said argues, "cannot be paraphrased nor, in a sense, can he be transmitted: the notion of an Adorno *fils* is quite laughable. . . . insofar as its [the mode of criticism Said associates with Adorno's name] future effects are concerned, they are what can be called oppositional and secular" (168). Of course, here and elsewhere, Said does "paraphrase" Adorno, whose work becomes, just at the moment of "The Future of Criticism," integral (if not through "transmission" as genetic or privileged inheritance, then through reading) to Said's understanding of the aesthetic within history, criticism within the world.[10]

Among Said's privileged terms for theorizing this nondeterministic "withinness" are categories such as worldliness, the oppositional and the secular (as in the passage above), traveling theory, exile, contrapuntal criticism, affiliation, amateurism, rational intentionality, and perhaps most importantly, humanism. Risking generality, one can say that each of these terms enables Said to address the relationships between text and context, work and setting, aesthetic and history. For the most part, Said will follow an Adornian insistence on the dialectical yet *unreconcilable* relationship between each of these paired terms. In discussions of this tension, Said will often return to the notion of "paradox," as in the following discussion of "style": "Any style involves first of all the artist's connection to his or her own time, or historical period, society, and antecedents; the aesthetic work, for all its irreducible individuality, is nevertheless a part—or, paradoxically, not a part—of the era in which it was produced and appeared. This is not simply a matter of sociological or political synchrony but more interestingly has to do with rhetorical or formal style."[11] I will return to this definition of style below.

Despite his emphasis on paradox, however, Said will repeatedly insist that he is interested in something "more" than what he sees as the ultimately unproductive, profitless, arid terrain of "those varieties of deconstructive Derridean readings that end (as they began) in undecidability and uncertainty."[12] For Said the point (and, undoubtedly, part of the point is that there *be* a point) remains that criticism should be a matter of taking sides, not simply against one kind of criticism or for another but, more crucially, for an affirmative understanding of what criticism and culture can and indeed should do. His argument continues: "To reveal the wavering and vacillation in all writing is useful up to a point, just as it may here and there be useful to show, with Foucault, that knowledge in the end serves power. But both alternatives defer for too long a declaration that the actuality of reading is, fundamentally, an act of perhaps modest human emancipation and enlightenment that changes and enhances one's knowledge for purposes other than reductiveness, cynicism, or fruitless standing aside. . . . Otherwise, why bother at all?"[13] The answer to "why bother" for Said is, again and again, connected to emancipation and affirmative futurity.

Just as Said criticizes deconstruction for lacking a sufficiently immediate or obvious use-value, he criticizes, through his notion of "worldliness," that part of cultural studies that has produced reductive historicisms. Thus the "more," the productive value of "worldliness" is a remedial project of "restoration," of resituating the work within an expansive, even infinitely "worldly" totality. "*Worldliness* is therefore the restoration [Said has been arguing against provincializing readings, especially vis à vis works of non-European literature, where critics might be tempted to frame such works through the reductive "category of national allegory"] to such works and interpretations of their place in the global setting, a restoration that can only be accomplished by an appreciation not of some tiny, defensively constituted corner of the world, but of the large, many-windowed house of human culture as a whole."[14] The very possibility of situating a work within the "whole" of human culture suggests the level of mastery and near-omniscience Said demands. (It is in this vein that Auerbach functions as an exemplary and "heroic" figure for Said.) Despite being "many-windowed," the figure of the "house of human culture as a whole" posits a critical scope and practice without frontier. At the same time, this image confers an implacable demand; the limit of totality, the enclosure of the whole of the world, will always lie beyond—beyond another horizon, beyond reach, beyond what has already been said or done.

Said's emphasis is indeed on something beyond, something more, something other—beyond, more than, and other to the limits of the already decided. In *Freud and the Non-European*, he will elaborate upon the "contrapuntal" as both an effect of and an approach to "those figures whose writing travels across temporal, cultural and ideological boundaries in unforeseen ways to emerge as part of a new ensemble *along with* later history and subsequent art."[15] The "unforeseen" and the "new" thus emerge not only because of a particular method, but also because the works themselves—and in particular those works that he will discuss under the heading of "lateness"—survive beyond any context and filiation to demand renewed attention.[16] It is in the allowance for and insistence upon such surplus and crossings that the refrain of the new as the emancipatory finds its foothold in Said's work. As his discussion of worldliness in "The Politics of Knowledge" continues, the accent turns to the problem of provincializing and deterministic readings. Said calls for something "other than" what they have to offer. Thus,

> It seems to me absolutely essential that we engage with cultural works in this unprovincial, interested manner while maintaining a strong sense of the contest for forms and values which any decent cultural work embodies, realizes, and contains. A great deal of recent theoretical speculation has proposed that works of literature are completely determined as such by their situation, and that readers themselves are totally determined in their responses by their respective cultural situations, to a point where no value, no reading, no interpretation can be anything other than the merest reflection of some immediate interest. All readings and all writing are reduced to an assumed historical emanation. (383)

Other than reductive contextualizations, Said will propose a great deal more, "to read a text in its fullest and most integrative context [which] commits the reader to positions that are educative, humane, and engaged, positions that depend on training and taste and not simply on a technologized professionalism, or on the tiresome playfulness of 'postmodern' criticism, with its repeated disclaimers of anything but local games and pastiches. Despite Lyotard and his acolytes, we are still in the era of large narratives, of horrendous cultural clashes, and of appallingly destructive war."[17]

Humanism and Democratic Criticism is to a large extent a reprise of such arguments. This is not to say that it does not contain any new material, but rather to suggest that it is part of an ongoing, and in many ways continuous, elaboration of a "Saidian" lexicon, style, and system. Through an accrued textuality and repeated invocation, terms such as "worldliness" become a part of that system in its "intransigence" and "mobility." Thus, for example, when Said speaks of his use of "worldliness," it is a matter of retrospective consolidation, a return to the past in the present through a rhetoric of self-citation. "The key word here is 'worldly,' a notion I have always used to denote the real historical world from whose circumstances none of us can in fact ever be separated, not even in theory. . . . Worldliness—by which I mean at a more precise cultural level that all texts and all representations were *in* the world [the past tense here suggests historical *as opposed to* literary time] and subject to its numerous heterogeneous realities."[18]

As an alternative to Lyotard's critique of the master-narrative, Said offers a unifying, if not yet complete, narrative of humanism as emancipatory discourse and ideal, no longer limited to or undermined by the biases of the Eurocentric but expanded globally to overcome them. If structuralism fails on account of its tendential oversystematization and adherence to totalizing formalizations, we are justified in asking how Said's late defense of humanism will offer an alternative. "Is it possible to do something to the concept, which otherwise tendentially locks us into sameness, in order to use it as a mode of access to difference and the new?"[19] For Said in *Humanism and Democratic Criticism,* humanism is a concept, a practice, a set of texts, and even a thing ("it is worth insisting, in this as well as other cases, that attacking the abuses of something is not the same thing as dismissing or entirely destroying the thing" [13]). Above all humanism is a "belief" (20, 42). Said insists that it is not a form of religious enlightenment ("Humanism should be a form of disclosure, not of secrecy or religious illumination" [73]). Nonetheless, humanism is a "mission," a "particular kind of faith," an "inner faith" (49, 64–65). It is possible to speak of "the spirit of the original humanism" (21) and "in the name of humanism" (21, 10). Humanism is a "kind of heroism" practiced and emulated by those who are willing to submit to its "shattering experience" (67).

It would be mere stupidity to suggest that Said is blindly reproducing faith in a discredited god.[20] Said's reasons for defending humanism outwit such reductive nonsense and cynical bad faith. Indeed he circles the ranks of the merely "smug" by posing the following question: "When will we stop allowing ourselves to think of humanism as a form of smugness and not as an unsettling adventure in difference, in alternative traditions, in texts that need a new deciphering within a much wider context than has hitherto been given them?"[21] The answer to this question is, of course, both unknown (as a specific moment, date, or event in the future) and rhetorically presumed (the cessation of a certain type of thinking is already underway in the speaker's ability to articulate a set of goals and values, and to do so within an inclusive mode of address, an entreaty made to "ourselves"). The impatient demand of this question bristles into an ambivalent critique of any humanism for which "identity itself" remains at the "core." Though unequivocally critical of such residual investiture, along with the "politics of identity" and "nationalistically grounded system of education" that accompany its agenda, Said remains invested in a recentering of humanism as a kind of "core" theory, a deciphered, post-Eurocentric, and indeed post-postmodern theory of intellectual practice that will carry "us," as a worldly and politically interdependent "whole," into the future.[22]

What interests me here is the connection Said draws between belief in humanism's global future and a return to a certain "*modernist* theory." Witnessing the hostile takeover of the academy by postmodernism, which threatens an "aggressive" and "depoliticized" wager against "a collective human history as grasped in some of the global patterns of dependence and interdependence," Said offers a critical alternative, posed as another question, "Would it be possible to introduce a *modernist* theory and practice of reading and interpreting the part to the whole in such a way as neither to deny the specificity of the individual experience in and of an aesthetic work nor to rule out of the validity of a projected, putative, or implied sense of the whole?"[23] Within the series of lecture-essays that make up *Humanism and Democratic Criticism* as a whole, the answer to the question, Said signals, is to be found in "The Return to Philology," the chapter in which Said introduces the possibility of a reenergized ideal, if not the entirely "shattering experience," of "humanistic heroism" (68). Reemphasizing the link between humanism and modernism, here through a reference to Blackmur and the notion of modernism as "a technique of trouble," Said leaves open the question of how modernism might provide, justify, or rejuvenate a "theory" of humanism's value.[24]

I want to suggest that one way of reading, if not answering, the question Said has posed above (might it be "possible to introduce a *modernist* theory . . . ?") can be broached through "A Note on Modernism," where Said argues for a reading of modernist poetics as "a response to the external pressures on culture from the *imperium*."[25] The "formal patterns" of modernism, including those of "self-consciousness, discontinuity, self-referentiality, and corrosive irony," rather than autonomous developments driven by artistic genius alone (along the lines of what is sometimes called modernism's "romantic ideology" or what becomes, for the later Lukács, modernism's ideological "negation of outward reality"), are, for Said, indissociably affiliated with a wider context in which "empire as a fact of national destiny" was no longer self-evident, and in which Europe began to see its hegemony as "vulnerable." Said argues that modernism "responds" to such shifts with a new "encyclopedic form" marked by three aspects, each of which I find relevant to Said's proposed "theory" of humanism.[26] First, Said finds "a circularity of structure, inclusive and open at the same time." Here, I understand Said to mean a narrative and epistemological inconclusiveness that is seductive ("inclusive") rather than merely *outré* (among the examples Said gives are Joyce's *Ulysses* and Conrad's *Heart of Darkness*). Second, "a novelty based almost entirely on the reformulation of old, even outdated fragments drawn self-consciously from disparate locations, sources, cultures," a common enough characterization of modernism, but one that, in the context of Said's later argument, suggests the importance of an expansive citational reach, one that would "borrow" its authority not from merely one tradition, genre, or past, but rather from a more hybrid and exilic textuality (one thinks here of Said's repeated invocation of the essay as the strongest form of criticism). In this aspect, modernism is a model of a kind of writing for which no category of "identity," whether formal, cultural, or racial, remains either solidly familiar or entirely alien. As the exemplary instance of this unsettling practice of admixture, Said invokes "Joyce's fusing of the *Odyssey* with the Wandering Jew, advertising and Virgil (or Dante)." Third, Said describes "the irony of a form that draws attention to itself as substituting art and its creations for the once-possible synthesis of the world empires. When you can no longer assume that Britannia will rule the waves forever, you have to reconceive reality as something that can be held together by you the artist, in history rather than in geography."[27]

If the future of humanism is to be found in a "*modernist* theory," it is fair to read the idea of such a theory along the three lines Said has outlined. The last of these, that of an aesthetic resolution to worldly disintegration, returns in Said's late work, perhaps *without* the "pervasive irony" that defines modernism for Said in "A Note on Modernism." Thus, the intellectual's responsibility is to resist the sundering of "part" and "whole," where by such oppositions Said implies, as I read him, not only the singularity of the aesthetic as distinct from the "rest" and the "whole" of the world (wherein one could read a range of problematics, including the privileging of one tradition over others; the separation of text from worldly conditions; a refusal to allow for the "partial" autonomy of the aesthetic precisely in relation to totality). Said also suggests here that humanism, as mediator of the dialectic between part and whole, might function to reconcile intellectual practice to an increasingly disintegrated sense of responsibility within and to that mangled "whole" Said calls the whole of the world.

Yet this is not the whole of the story. Within his call for a modernist humanism that would recognize the whole of the world, Said is certainly cognizant of the impossibility and undesirability of a naïve return to an idealism in which master-narratives would necessarily come at the price of false reconciliations and coercively manufactured flights of transcendence (this despite his inclination to have done with Lyotard).[28] He argues that "at a time when the national and international horizon is undergoing massive transformations and reconfigurations," it is up to humanism not simply to hold its ground under duress, but, in doing so, to acknowledge that its "task is constitutively an unending one, and it should not aspire to conclusion of the sort that has the corollary and, in my estimate deleterious, effect of securing one an identity to be fought over, defended, and argued, while a great deal about our world that is interesting and worth venturing into simply gets left aside."[29] Against the violence of identity, a humanism without boundaries, is an ideal that comes with a force of its own. *Humanism and Democratic Criticism*, as I hope to demonstrate in what follows, can be read as a question of force, the force and the question of the work of late style.

THE WORK OF LATE STYLE

Lateness, as elaborated by both Adorno and Said, is irreducibly bound up with difficulty. For Adorno an aesthetics of lateness is marked in part by its resistance to appropriation and methodological standardization. If, as Said argues in "Adorno as Lateness Itself" of Adorno's critical style more broadly, "Adorno is impossible to assimilate into any system" (278), late style becomes one name for this impossibility, pointing toward the very problem of identifying an author or artist's style as such. As Adorno puts it in "Late Work without Late Style," where he reads Beethoven's *Missa Solemnis* as a "late work": "Be careful of over-easy answers."[30] For Said, this resistance to precipitous syntheses and dialectical resolutions (of the tension, for example, between a "late work" and the oeuvre from which it has departed) characterizes not only the late Beethoven, but also Adorno's style *tout court*; notwithstanding the risk of an "easy" essentialization, along with that of betraying the very anti-identitarian principles of late style, Said concludes that Adorno's ongoing refusal of the comforts of closure makes him into a figure of "lateness itself" (272).

Said's interest in late style can be traced back at least as far as *Musical Elaborations*, where late style is an emergent part of the book's stated concerns, many of which draw on Adorno's *Philosophy of Modern Music*.[31] These include "the problematic of music's autonomy" and the tendency within cultural criticism toward totalizing universals and "inevitabilism," which Said links to a "Eurocentric or imperial" worldview.[32] In *Musical Elaborations*, Said is interested in those

> rare number of works making (or trying to make) their claims entirely *as music*, free of many of the harassing, intrusive, and socially tyrannical pressures that have limited musicians to their customary social role as upholders of things *as they are*. . . . works [that express] a very eccentric kind of transgression, that is, music being reclaimed by uncommon, and perhaps even excessive, displays of technique whose net effect is not only to render the music socially superfluous and useless—to *discharge* it completely— but to recuperate the craft entirely of the musician as an act of freedom. (71)

Such concerns will later be expanded under the heading of late style. Immediately following the passage quoted above, Said goes on to make a brief argument about the "radical amorality" of *Così fan tutte*, preparing the way for what would become *On Late Style*'s third chapter, "*Così fan tutte* at the Limits." Similarly, *Musical Elaborations* includes a short discussion (and, in a sense, defense) of Strauss's late works that will inform chapter 2 of *On Late Style*, "Return to the Eighteenth Century."

Just after he gave the lectures that were to become *Musical Elaborations*, Said published "On Jean Genet's Late Works."[33] The essay transposes the category of late style from music to literature, reading Genet as a figure of "negative identity" (32), "fierce antinomianism" (37), and "intransigent paradox" (39). In *The Screens* and *Prisoner of Love*, Said finds "the extreme radicality of Genet's anti-identitarian logic" (36), a resistance to domestication and sentimentality that revolves around the tension between, on the one hand, Genet's "frankly partisan mode," or his commitment to, and love for, the fighters of lost causes (specifically the Algerian and Palestinian resistance), and, on the other, the often eroticized motifs of betrayal, disruption, and transgression that make Genet "like that other great modern dissolver of identity, Adorno" (39). Notwithstanding the incommensurable and inassimilable singularity of these two heroic figures, Said does compare them, finding in their work not the either-or but the both-and of "resistance and hopelessness together" (39). As for Genet, Said concludes, "In no other late-twentieth-century writer are the dangers of catastrophe and the lyrical delicacy of affective response to them sustained together as grandly and fearlessly" (42), a description that hints towards a late style sublime.[34]

In *Musical Elaborations*, Said takes from Proust the phrase "*air de la chanson*"

and uses it to name "a writer's distinct sound not only as a distinctive imprint, something like a signature or stamp of particular possession, but also as a special theme,
personal obsession, or recurrent motif in the work of an artist that gives all of his
work its own recognizable identity." Said will call this mark of distinction "the music of music" and will associate it in particular with the late work of Beethoven,
Bruckner, and Richard Strauss (93). Later, in his reading of Freud's *Moses and
Monotheism* as a work of late style, Said will reintroduce the motif of "obsession,"
not as a mark of identity but as its dissolution.

Like the category of style itself, the category of late style confronts the tension
between an emphasis on particularity (style as individuating mark) and the conditions that would enable any such *stylization* (the style of style) to function. This tension can be restated as that which inheres between the singularity and generalizability of style, or the way in which style, precisely as unique idiomaticity, becomes
legible and recognizable to a wider audience. If the possibility of style as a unique
or signatory mark depends upon the possibility of its being read and categorized
as such (such that one might speak of a "Saidian" or an "Adornian" style), it also includes the possibility of its appropriation, imitation, co-optation. It is in the tension between this double possibility—style as unique, even disturbingly transfigu-
rative event and style as domesticated repetition—that Adorno locates the history,
and ultimately the failure, of the "New Music."[35] If, as Adorno, and Said after him,
will insist, late style is to be privileged precisely to the extent that it resists domestication (and for Said, then comes to represent a model for such resistance), upon
what character—what style, what lateness—does this critical privilege rest?

In *The World, the Text, and the Critic,* Said defines style,

> in the simplest and least honorific sense of that very complex phenomenon. Once again
> I shall arbitrarily exclude a whole series of interesting complexities in order to insist
> on style as, from the standpoint of producer and receiver, the recognizable, repeat-
> able, preservable sign of an author who reckons with an audience. Even if the audi-
> ence is as restricted as oneself and as wide as the whole world, the author's style is par-
> tially a phenomenon of repetition and reception. But what makes style receivable as
> the signature of its author's manner is a collection of features variously called idiolect,
> voice, or irreducible individuality. (33)

The notion of idiolect is one way of thinking about the "paradox" of style, or its
double position between invention and citation. Idiolect, as Jakobson has argued,
implies "a single individual's way of speaking at a given time," a joining of *langue*
and *parole* in such a uniquely circumscribed way as to suggest a linguistic world
comprised of a single speaker. Thus Jakobson concludes, for cases other than apha-
sia, the very idea of "idiolect proves to be a somewhat perverse fiction."[36] Similarly,
an understanding of style as idiolect, or, as Said argues in *Beginnings,* style as "the
relatively pure sign of, the relatively pure activity of, a writer's presence at a specified

moment in history" (257), is a fiction, if not necessarily a "perverse" one, then certainly one that finds its mark in deviation and difference.

Unlike the notion of style as such, or style as unifying "fiction" that designates the "sign of an author" as fullness and presence of "voice," late style for Adorno is a category of negativity. As a critical and stylistic term, late style implies the paradox of an authorial signature present in its withdrawal, or, as Adorno argues of the *Missa*, it "lacks all unmistakably Beethovenian characteristics. He has, as it were, eliminated himself."[37] The notion of lateness as a comparative dissonance between late work and past works brings the totality of an oeuvre into question, giving the late work a critical priority precisely in its departure from precedent styles and achievements. Hence Adorno's argument that the third-period Beethoven represents a retrospective critique of the "bourgeois spirit" successfully embodied in the second-period works. "The key to the very late Beethoven probably lies in the fact that in this music the idea of totality as something already achieved had become unbearable to his critical genius."[38] Biographically and historically, to live after or beyond an achieved totality would imply the "unbearable" superfluity of the insignificant remnant, a mute and unproductive leftover living without a future.

Lacking the "unmistakably" authorial, torn from the oeuvre and context as exceptional departure, the late work is marked by fragmentation, alienation, and dissonance. For Adorno, late style is both an immanent part of the work itself *and* a critical reading and evaluative categorization of the work. The opening of "Late Style in Beethoven" demonstrates less a theory than an effortful, highly figurative description of late style. It is as if Adorno is striving to reproduce in his own language the very qualities he attributes to his object. Thus the essay begins with a negative analogy to an aesthetic experience (in the sense of sensual apprehension) of that natural condition known as "ripeness," or the visual perception and the taste of fruit at "maturity": "The maturity of the late works of significant artists does not resemble the kind one finds in fruit. They are, for the most part, not round, but furrowed, even ravaged. Devoid of sweetness, bitter and spiny, they do not surrender themselves to mere delectation. They lack all the harmony that the classicist esthetic is in the habit of demanding from works of art, and they show more traces of history than of growth. The usual view explains this with the argument that they are products of an uninhibited subjectivity" (102–3).

Adorno makes several distinctions here. First, artists who are discussed under the heading of "late style" are necessarily and already "significant." At the same time, late style is marked by a resistance to tastefulness, in the sense that it is not an experience of "delectation." This resistance is also a matter of a "lack"—of harmony as understood by the "classicist esthetic" and of "growth" understood as a developmental peak ("maturity" as "ripeness"). Finally, and perhaps most importantly, late style is, contrary to the "usual view," not an expression of another kind of fullness, that of subjective expression.

The critique of a reduction of late style to "psychological origins" (103) is the most significant and difficult part of Adorno's argument in "Late Style in Beethoven." Rejecting that kind of biographical reading through which "late works are relegated to the outer reaches of art, in the vicinity of document" (103), Adorno's argument is not so much antihistorical as antipsychological. In some ways, Adorno's critique of the "subjectivist methodology" ("For the first commandment of every 'subjectivist' methodology is to brook no conventions, and to recast those that are unavoidable in terms dictated by the expressive impulse" [104]), prefigures, in its own efforts to "recast" form against the subjectivist grain, the more widely invoked (if only by title) arguments of Roland Barthes's "The Death of the Author."[39] The "formal law" of late works, Adorno argues, "is, at the least, incapable of being subsumed under the concept of expression" (104), a formulation that leaves us in the negative register, an emphasis on what the late work, along with the interpretive approach to it, is *not*.

The negativity of the "formal law" might be said to have a "positive" inflection, though not necessarily a fullness of content or what would amount to a method. This inflection, which constitutes the "style" of late style, emerges on several levels. The first is that of a return to a reading of the late Beethoven that would "brook" a focus on "conventions," or a mode of "technical analysis" rather than a reversion to lateness as "psychologically motivated" by conditions known as "biography and fate" (103–5). Still, the argument for a focus on form goes further than a mere formalism or science of stylistics. As a "formal law," late style teeters at the brink of "metaphysics." "By declaring mortal subjectivity to be the substance of the late work, it [the "psychological interpretation"] hopes to be able to perceive death in unbroken form in the work of art. This is the deceptive crown of its metaphysics" (105). At the same time, the late work *does* function as "witness" to "subjectivity" at its limit, and indeed *as* a limit—the limit of self-expression understood as unbounded freedom, the limit of achieving any appropriate or adequate form for the completion of the life-work or the overcoming of finitude. Adorno continues,

> The power of subjectivity in the late works of art is the irascible gesture with which it takes leave of the works themselves. It breaks their bonds, not in order to express itself, but in order, expressionless, to cast off the appearance of art. Of the works themselves it leaves only fragments behind, and communicates itself, like a cipher, only through the blank spaces from which it has disengaged itself. Touched by death, the hand of the master sets free the masses of material that he used to form; its tears and fissures, witnesses to the finite powerlessness of the I confronted with Being, are its final work. (105)

There is so much that is *odd* about Adorno's argument. It takes the form of a "not this, but this" argument, where the latter appears not as a clear alternative, but a truth that speaks "like a cipher."

Adorno produces a reading—a theory—of late style governed by a "formal law," one that emphasizes fragmentation over completion, rupture over continuity, dissonance over harmony. At the same time, this "law" links problems of style and form to a truth-content that, ultimately, does find "expression" in the work, albeit negatively, jarringly, and obliquely. In this essay, Adorno's rendering of this truth itself takes several forms, all of them extremely enigmatic, as difficult to decipher as the late works under discussion. Above, for example, one might say that Adorno reads the late work as an allegory of a negative metaphysics, finding in the form of Beethoven's late style (its "tears and fissures") an act of "witnessing" to a metaphysics of subjection, of the powerlessness and finite before its own condition, a condition from which it is also necessarily alienated ("the finite powerlessness of the I confronted with Being"). And yet such "powerlessness," the masculinized impotence of the creator subjected to a condition of finitude, is not all. It is certainly not defeat, not withdrawal or negativity *as* defeat. When Adorno speaks of the "explosive force of subjectivity in the late work" (105), there is no reason to conclude, finally and after all, that lateness means loss of mastery, power, or, alternatively, restraint. Indeed, it might be the case that lateness doesn't *mean* at all.

It is indeed the case that Adorno's formulations in this essay, as it spins out a dense yet filigreed rereading of late style, resist paraphrase. As we have seen, Said has argued this of Adorno's work more generally. To the extent that this is the case, to say that "The Late Style in Beethoven" is itself a late work, or a work of late style, becomes problematic, as it withholds from us a coherent and generalizable theory. Categorizing it as such betrays the very resistance to domestication embodied in its "idiolect," that most intransigent, nontraveling language, the fiction of a singular style.

And yet, if not a theory, the essay opens onto reading; indeed in its resistance to method, it compels us to work all the more to make reading pay off. Perhaps this is the "point" of late style, its refusal to come to a point, to end well, to withdraw easily, without resistance, before our efforts to pin it down. In this regard, the ending of Adorno's essay, the most explosively unresolved moment of the work, a climax that hardly brings resolution, demands our attention. The essay's last sentence reads, "In the history of art late works are the catastrophes" (107). As readers of Adorno's work will recall, "catastrophe" gathers force in his oeuvre, particularly in his postwar writings, where he will provocatively theorize the "European catastrophe," and more broadly, the problem of culture and art "after the world catastrophe," according to the logic of that most perverse of dialectics, the "dialectic of enlightenment."[40] In "Late Style in Beethoven," however, the figure of catastrophe, of the downward spin of lateness, is far more enigmatic.

If, inevitably, late style carries quasi-biographical connotations related to the finitude of the authorial, that is to say of human life, one might say that for Adorno this finitude is the late work's "catastrophic" condition, an aesthetically embodied "wound" lodged within life as it anticipates an ungraspable ending, an event that it cannot survive or live to represent. This, of course, is my inflection, but it is also one that will help me to read Said's late work, *Freud and the Non-European,* where Said interprets Freud's text so as to define the secular itself as a wound.

It is nearly impossible to read Adorno as framing any event, including the "catastrophic" event he calls late style, nonhistorically. As Rose Subotnik has argued, Adorno understands Beethoven's late style as a mode of "double negation," a leaving-behind of the synthesis achieved in the middle period and a refusal to accord with the "external disintegration of human integrity, to the enslaving dehumanizing compartmentalization (for example, into individual and social identities) forced upon man by society."[41] Thus Adorno's argument that the "formal law" of the late work "is revealed precisely in the thought of death" (105) is unhinged from the metaphysical frame of human finitude confronting its "own" limits. In this reading, one that is more evident in Adorno's other writings on Beethoven, death is subsumed within the larger problem of an exhausted yet defiant aesthetic that no longer has the space to take flight from the limits imposed upon it, as it were, externally, from an "outside" that the artwork can neither make its own nor fully exteriorize.[42]

In "Adorno as Lateness Itself," Said, following Subotnik, situates Adorno's arguments on late style within an historical narrative, such that "Beethoven's late-style works constitute an event in the history of modern culture: a moment when the artist who is fully in command of his medium nevertheless abandons communication with the bourgeois order of which he is a part and achieves a contradictory, alienated relationship with it" (268). The rupturing force of this event depends upon and produces a resistance to schematization—at the level of Adorno's comments and in Beethoven's work. Therefore, the "paradoxical" style of Adorno *and* Beethoven's lateness, wherein

> you cannot say what connects the parts other than by invoking "the figure they create together." Neither can you minimize the differences between the parts, and, it would appear, you cannot actually *name* the unity, or give it a specific identity, which would then reduce its catastrophic force. Thus the power of Beethoven's late style is negative, or rather, it *is* negativity: where one would expect serenity and maturity, one finds bristling, difficult and unyielding—perhaps even inhuman—challenge.... Beethoven's late compositions are about, are in fact "lost totality," and therefore catastrophic. (271–72)[43]

Whereas in *Humanism and Democratic Criticism,* Said seeks to hold together the ideals of humanism so as to harness them against a trend of intellectual quietism, the work of late style is a "force" that remains insistently negative, refusing the consolations of a new upward turn. Disintegrative, difficult, and unyielding, it negates attempts to resolve contradiction, create reconciliation, synthesize the parts. And while its force may not be quite "catastrophic," humanism may have a certain bearing upon the work of late style, as well as upon Said's interest in what he insists *must* be the "constructive" bent of Adorno's theory. For all its "intransigence" and "negativity," late style, were it to only be a "repeated *no* or *this will not do*," would remain "totally uninteresting and repetitive. There must be a *constructive* element above all, which animates the procedure."[44] This insistence on establishing an affirmative moment in Adorno's work, and in late style in particular, is far from unjustified by Adorno's writing, where he concludes that the "musical demythologization" articulated in Beethoven's late works (as well as in his own criticism) includes a horizon of hope: "in this process of musical demythologization, in the abandonment of the illusion of harmony, there is an expression of hope. In Beethoven's late style this hope flourished very close to the margin of renunciation, and yet is not renunciation. And I would like to think that this difference between resignation and renunciation is the whole secret of these pieces."[45]

The "secret" of late style, then, is precisely to be found in its element of hope, that "cipher" of the late work in which renunciation and leave-taking express more than acts of empty negation. *Humanism and Democratic Criticism* names its purpose and wants to make itself heard as clearly as possible; it can hardly be read as guarding a "secret" hope. Nonetheless, its late style is to be found, perhaps, in taking its intransigence seriously. Formulaic it is, but we are left with the dialectic of an open-ended yet prescriptive futurity: a negation of the negation of humanism, the positing of a synthesis—that "*modernist* theory" of wholeness—yet one that, Said insists, remains open to, and is itself predicated upon, the possibility of the "shattering force of the new."[46]

"MORE" OF LATE STYLE, OR THE FUTURE OF A WOUND

After *Musical Elaborations* and his essay on Genet, it is with the publication of "Adorno as Lateness Itself" that Said consolidates his reflections on the significance of late style as a critical term.[47] In this essay, Said extends and reformulates lateness as a critical term, one that emphasizes a work's dissonance in at least two ways. First, like Adorno, Said does not frame the late work's discordant elements through an explanatory or diagnostic psychological narrative; whatever connection lateness might have to experience and the life of its creator, that experience is itself refracted rather than reflected in the work, a distinction that finds its most extreme articulation in the approach to death. This approach, to the extent that it can be read as such (as approach, it does not lead "back" to an intending subject made whole and reconfirmed in its autonomous priority but rather suggests the encroachment of a finitude unassimilable by the subject or to any notion of mastery), takes place within the work as style.

For Said, style, even without the specificity of its *late* iteration, already indicates a tension between text and context, work and history, originality and repetition. As Said argues, "Any style involves first of all the artist's connection to his or her own

time, or historical period, society, and antecedents; the aesthetic work, for all its irreducible individuality, is nevertheless a part—or, paradoxically, not a part—of the
era in which it was produced and appeared. This is not simply a matter of sociological or political synchrony but more interestingly has to do with rhetorical or
formal style."[48]

What, then, is "more interesting" about privileging of style over synchrony? Com-
pacted into the opposition between "rhetorical or formal style" and "sociological
or political synchrony" are a set of arguments Said made throughout his career,
through categories such as we have seen above (worldliness, for example) about situating a text within history without reducing it to what Adorno would call "mere
document." Like worldliness, style names the "paradoxical" way a text both belongs
to and departs from its time. This is the second way in which Said draws upon
Adorno's emphasis on the dissonance of the late work.

In "Adorno as Lateness Itself," rather than an understanding of style as the mark
of the frivolous, whimsical, or merely literary, Said uses it to name a problem that
demands and yields "more interest." At stake in Said's take on late style is a way of
theorizing an aesthetic in which "the conclusiveness of death" (265) is neither
negated through a cyclical temporality nor dialectically uplifted as redemption. For
Said, such would be an aesthetic of "ending *and* surviving" (267), where "survival"
implies neither symbolic immortality nor a negation of death, but a kind of historical superannuation, a condition of remaining "after" the end of "what is acceptable
and normal," or a mode of becoming-posthumous (and perhaps, as we saw above,
"inhuman") in the present. "For Adorno *lateness* includes the idea of surviving beyond what is acceptable and normal; in addition, lateness includes the idea that one
cannot really go beyond lateness at all, not transcending or lifting oneself out of
lateness but rather deepening the lateness, as in his book *The Philosophy of Modern
Music*, Adorno says Schoenberg essentially prolonged the irreconcilabilities, nega-
tions, immobilities of the late Beethoven" (272).

As opposed to a "going beyond," lateness returns again and again to a problem
that has resisted mastery and remained as the excess of any one enclosure. Said offers
another paradox: "There is a paradox: how essentially unrepeatable, uniquely articulated aesthetic works written not at the beginning but at the end of a career can
nevertheless have an influence on what comes after them. And how does that influence enter and inform the work of the critic whose whole enterprise stubbornly
prizes its own intransigence and untimeliness?" (276). It is just this description of
the late work that Said will return to in his reading of *Moses and Monotheism* as a
"contrapuntal" work.

Freud and the Non-European is Said's late rereading of Freud's *Moses and Monotheism* from a "cosmopolitan" point of view.[49] Said first associates the cosmopolitan with
an "interpretive option" (52), a way of reading Freud's Moses against the grain of
identity and nationalism. In the place of any essential continuity with Jewishness,

Said insists upon an "irremediably diasporic, unhoused character," one that does not "belong" to any one person (Freud), group (the Jews), or national narrative (Zionism), but rather is characteristic of a general, if often poorly understood, condition. From "interpretive option," the cosmopolitan shifts to a kind of "consciousness":

> In our age of vast population transfers, or refugees, exiles, expatriates and immigrants, it [Said here refers to "Freud's uneasy relationship with the orthodoxy of his own community"] can also be identified in the diasporic, wandering, unresolved, cosmopolitan consciousness of someone who is both inside and outside his or her community. This is now a relatively widespread phenomenon, even though an understanding of what that condition means is far from common. Freud's meditations and insistence on the non-European from a Jewish point of view [Said's reading of Freud's text vacillates between reinscribing and displacing the notion of a "Jewish point of view"] provide, I think, an admirable sketch of what it entails, by way of refusing to resolve identity into some of the nationalist or religious herds in which so many people want so desperately to run. (53)

Said's polemical approach to Freud's text centers around a rereading of the figure of Freud's Moses, which I won't attempt to render here in its detail. Suffice it to say that his argument attempts to situate the late Freud within the explosive context of Europe in the 1930s, and from there to connect that historical moment to a "deliberately antinomian"(32) Freud who produces a text of late style, one in which the composite figure of Moses will carry the burden of the *idea* of an unresolved identity, a split origin lodged between the European present and a "non-European past." This burden is not attributable to a psychological condition that would be, in some unique way, Freud's or Freudian, but rather, for Said, is the effect of a "deliberately provocative" act in which "Freud mobilized the non-European past in order to undermine any doctrinal attempt that might be made to put Jewish identity on a sound foundational basis, whether religious or secular" (44–45).

Certainly Said's text itself is deliberately provocative. He mobilizes his reading of Freud's text quite explicitly in order to use it for a critique of "Israeli legislation," which he argues, "countervenes, represses, and even cancels Freud's carefully maintained opening out of Jewish identity towards its non-Jewish background" (44). *Freud and the Non-European* uses the category of late style as a critical departure, if not justification, for such a deliberately provocative reading of Freud's text.

Freud and the Non-European repeats many of the arguments Said has already made about late style—the late style work "suggests not resolution and reconciliation . . . but, rather, more complexity and a willingness to let irreconcilable elements of the work remain as they are: episodic, fragmentary, unfinished (i.e. unpolished)" (28). The "late work is "alienating" and pays "scant regard for satisfying, much less placating, the reader's need for closure" (30). The late work, Said insists, refuses to provide "comforting" solutions to the questions it poses and the problems it might create (30). What interests me here is the characterization of late style as an "obsessive" return to problems that have not been resolved. "Like Beethoven's late works, Freud's *Spätwerk* is obsessed with returning not just to the problem of Moses's identity—which, of course, is at the very core of the treatise—but to the very elements of identity itself, as if that issue so crucial to psychoanalysis, the very heart of the science, could be returned to in the way that Beethoven's late work returns to such basics as tonality and rhythm" (29).

It would seem that late style has become a somewhat stabilized category available for reliable, if also provocative, redeployment. And despite his prior insistence on Freud's text as a "deliberate" act, Said now suggests that Freud is not entirely in control, that he is compelled, obsessionally, to return to a set of unresolved problems. Between deliberate act and obsessive return, Freud's text, Said goes on to conclude, is the site of an open "wound."

> Identity cannot be thought or worked through itself alone; it cannot constitute or even imagine itself without that radical originary break or flaw which will not be repressed, because Moses was Egyptian, and therefore always outside the identity inside which so many have stood, and suffered—and later, perhaps, even triumphed. The strength of this thought is, I believe, that it can be articulated in and speak to other besieged identities as well—not through dispensing palliatives such as tolerance and compassion but, rather, by attending to it as a troubling, disabling, destabilizing secular wound—the essence of the cosmopolitan, from which there can be no recovery, no state of resolved or Stoic calm, and no utopian reconciliation even within itself. (54)

What I find so fascinating here is the rethinking of what Said once called the "salutary intransigence" of a certain kind of criticism.[50] If late style is "intransigent," the "more" of its interest comes not from being insistent on an affirmative futurity, but from the uncertain effects and impossible return of a "troubling, disabling, destabilizing secular wound . . . from which there can be no recovery." This state of inevitable return alongside impossible recovery becomes, as Said concludes his argument, a set of questions wholly bound up with the uncertain language and complex temporality of trauma.[51] The "experience" of the wound, Said argues, is a "necessary psychological experience, Freud says, but the problem is that he doesn't give any indication of how long it must be tolerated or whether, properly speaking, it has a real history—history being always that which comes after and, all too often, either overrides or represses the flaw. The questions Freud therefore leaves us with are: can so utterly indecisive and so deeply undetermined a history ever *be* written? In what language, and with what sort of vocabulary?" (55).

Without answering these questions, Said suggests that the "wound" lodged within Freud's late style is a festering, and therefore productive and compelling, site of reading and critique. It is from the wound at the origin, a founding schism, that the possibility of a new history, a new story, a new language for the writing of identity might emerge. This claim, tenuous, troubling, and problematic as it may be, is Said's most important and interesting discussion of the work of late style.

CODA: IN-CONSOLATION

In *Beginnings*, Said put forward a theory of the four "phases" or "stages" of the writer's career, each phase associated with a particular opposition or problematic. Focusing in particular on the "modern writer," Said concludes his narrative schema with the writer in his fourth and final phase. Whereas in the third phase, the writer had successfully negotiated the opposition between "innovation and repetition," in the fourth phase he will more likely fail. As he "begins to view himself as nearing the end of his career, tempted with the idea of going on, yet often able to recognize that his writing has reached its conclusion . . . a failing impulse produces suitable matching work with frequent references to an antipoetic old age" (260). With references to the late works of Shakespeare, Hopkins, Yeats, Conrad, T. S. Eliot, and Gide, Said concludes that the final phase is often one of sterility and exhaustion in which the writer makes "recourse to a recapitulatory, essential image." An act of merely commemorative self-citation, "this image is really a vehicle for the author's superannuated 'voice,' with all the fruits of senescence added to it, sometimes embarrassingly" (261).

There is something satisfying about the fact that Said would later revise this fourfold model, interrupting it just before the depressing inevitability of a period of unproductive retrospection, one in which "senescence" can only mean decline. The model in its threefold form changes the terms of tension, rewriting the very notion of ending. *On Late Style* begins with the more traditional structure of a life, a story, and a set of problematics divided into beginning, middle, and end. But instead of outlining a third period in which conflict is resolved into propitious synthesis, the category of late style rewrites the nearing-to-end as a period of tension, impasse, and irreconcilability. Rather than merely collapsing the fourth category from the prior model, with its emphasis on failure, or senescence as the end of style's ability to restylize itself, into what has now become the period and work of late style, Said has shifted the discussion to a wider set of concerns. Superannuation, the becoming-remainder of work and style, now articulates the aporetic position of the survivor. And while the chronological, finite time of an individual author's life is never left behind, death itself has become historically and politically charged. "Genet's last works," Said argues in "On Jean Genet's Late Works," are "saturated with images of death, especially *Un* [sic] *Captif,* part of whose melancholy for the reader is the knowledge that Genet was dying as he wrote it and that so many of the Palestinians he saw, knew, and wrote about were also to die" (41). Thus Said approaches Genet's late style by problematizing the notion of a "natural death," that most bizarre and contradictory of concepts (what could resist naturalization more than that which can only be thought, never experienced, only reflected upon and symbolized, by another, from the distance of the survivor?), not only in his reading of Genet's insistence on placing death in the context of "the ceaseless social turbulence and revolutionary disruption that are central to his interest" (41).[52] Late style as a critical category is, in part, a question of reading death as a threat not only to life but also to narrative and meaning.

Above, I suggested the ways in which one might read *Humanism and Democratic Criticism* along the lines of late style, as positing an unbending, if also quite coherent and even exhortative, textual and human effort to resist the trends of the times as Said sees them. Still, there is a tension between Said's fascination with late style, or what he calls in *On Late Style* its accents of "daring and startling newness" (135), and his attempt to retrieve humanism from the academic dustbin, and, perhaps more significantly, from the important and enduring legacies wrought by humanism's many critics, none of whom Said engages in his late work (Marx, Heidegger, Althusser, Lyotard, to name only a few). With Auerbach, Said attempts "to rescue sense and meanings from the fragments of modernity," a project that marks the peculiar modernism of Said's humanism.[53] As "rescue" work, this project promises a quasi-messianic ideal, an ongoing scholarly future for which "there was never a misinterpretation that could not be revised, improved, or overturned. There was never a history that could not to some degree be recovered and compassionately understood in all its suffering and accomplishment."[54]

It would be a mistake to privilege late style as a master category by which one could evaluate or synthesize Said's work. Indeed, there are reasons to be skeptical about the generalization of the term as it "travels" from Euripides to Strauss, making stops along the way to include Mozart, Genet, Gould, Britten, Freud, Lampedusa, Visconti, Cavafy, and Hopkins, not to mention those writers included in passing (Proust, Beckett, Yeats, Ibsen), and, of course, Beethoven, Adorno, and Said himself. If, as *On Late Style* wants us to conclude, "the prerogative of late style" is that "it has the power to render disenchantment and pleasure without resolving the contradiction between them" (148), it would seem to be the case that any work of literature worth reading would necessarily take and offer this prerogative. Indeed, as "prerogative," late style is ultimately less of an immanent aspect of the work itself, or even of its style, than a critical category whose deployment, as style, weapon, or defense, lies with the critic.

By way of conclusion, I want to suggest that Said's late style, to the extent that there is one, can be read in the tension between the concluding remarks of *Humanism and Democratic Criticism* and those of *Freud and the Non-European*. This tension lies both within and between each. It is the tension between possibility and impossibility; the consolations of belief and the acknowledgment of a finitude of means, including those of time, knowledge, and reason; intransigence as unyielding hope and as withdrawal or resignation. Thus, of the yet-to-be-written history proleptically inscribed in the "secular wound" of Freud's text, Said asks in *Freud and the Non-European,* "Can it aspire to the condition of a politics of diaspora life? . . . I myself believe so" (55). And "I conclude with the thought that the intellectual's provisional home is the domain of an exigent, resistant, intransigent art into which, alas, one can neither retreat nor search for solutions. But only in that precarious exilic realm can one first truly grasp the difficulty of what cannot be grasped and then go forth anyway."[55] The echoes to Beckett are noted.[56]

NOTES

This essay first appeared in *Cultural Critique* 67 (2007): 107–40. I would like to thank Matthew Abraham and Andrew Rubin, the editors of the journal's special issue "Edward Said and After: Toward a New Humanism." For his gracious support and generous comments, I am grateful to Joseph Massad.

1. Edward Said, "The Future of Criticism," in *Reflections on Exile and Other Essays* (Cambridge: Harvard University Press, 2002), 166.

2. Ibid., 170.

3. Ibid., 169, 171.

4. From *The World, the Text, and the Critic* onward, Said becomes increasingly "impatient" with what he calls the "*outré* jargon" of certain theorists and worse, of their disciples. See, for instance, "Traveling Theory," in *The World, the Text, and the Critic* (Cambridge, MA: Harvard University Press, 1983), 228. Reserving the prerogative to decide between the merely difficult and the productively challenging, Said will dismiss, by proper name and by category, deconstruction (Derrida), psychoanalysis (Lacan), poststructuralism (Foucault, to whom he is indebted nonetheless), and postmodernism (Lyotard). In part, Said's critique is a matter of style. See, for example, *Humanism and Democratic Criticism* (New York: Columbia University Press, 2004), where Said mentions recent debates over "bad writing" (with an ambivalent nod to Judith Butler, whose important essay "The Values of Difficulty," Said allusively acknowledges only to dismiss). Adorno's critique of predigested language notwithstanding, Said concludes, "Not every coiner of rebarbative language is an Adorno" (72).

5. Edward Said, "Adorno as Lateness Itself," in *Apocalypse Theory and the Ends of the World*, ed. Malcolm Bull (Oxford: Blackwell, 1995), 272.

6. Said, *Humanism and Democratic Criticism*, 26.

7. Edward Said, *Beginnings: Intention and Method* (New York: Columbia University Press, 1985), 319.

8. Ibid.

9. Edward Said, *Orientalism* (New York: Vintage, 1979), 23. In *Beginnings*, Said argues at several points for the exceptionality of Foucault's structuralism. Unlike Lévi-Strauss, Foucault, Said argues, is interested in a project of liberation, one in which the critic would, through his intellectual labor, enable and encourage intervention into the "tyranny" of structural inevitability "by laying bare its workings" (289).

10. "The Future of Criticism" was first published in 1984. It was at this time, just after the publication of *The World, the Text, and the Critic* (which appeared in 1983 and in which Said makes no reference to Adorno), that Adorno began to appear as a crucial figure for Said. Despite the "laughable" idea of an "Adorno *fils*," Said would later remark, in an interview that has become somewhat legendary, that he was the "only true follower of Adorno" ("My Right of Return," in *Power, Politics, and Culture: Interviews with Edward Said*, ed. Gauri Viswanathan [New York: Random House, 2001], 458). One suspects that the critical irony of this claim is given far less attention than it deserves, perhaps because it appears in connection with another exquisitely provocative, and perhaps more controversial, moment of hyperbole: "I'm the last Jewish intellectual. . . . I'm a Jewish Palestinian" (458).

11. Edward Said, "Glimpses of Late Style," in *On Late Style: Music and Literature Against the Grain* (New York: Pantheon, 2006), 134.

12. Said, *Humanism and Democratic Criticism*, 66. In "Criticism Between Culture and System," Said, while critical of Derrida's "manner of muddling traditional thought beyond the possibility of usefulness," maintains an investment in reading Derrida (*The World, the Text, and the Critic*, 203).

13. Said, *Humanism and Democratic Criticism*, 66–67.

14. Said, "The Politics of Knowledge" in *Reflections on Exile and Other Essays*, 382.

15. Said, *Freud and the Non-European* (London: Verso, 2003), 24.

16. For the crucial significance of Said's distinction between "filiation" and "affiliation," as well as between the related categories of origin and beginning, see chapter 1 in this volume, Joseph Massad's "Affiliating with Edward Said." In particular, Massad's argument that [I've edited the following quote to reflect its final wording in Massad's chapter] while Said "was filiatively connected to Palestine through the accident of birth, he later sought to affiliate with it—to begin again from a new point" (34) suggests a related tension wherein late style, for Adorno and Said, traces an antinomy between objectively imposed limits and willful critique.

17. Said, "The Politics of Knowledge," 383. Said's cursory dismissal of Lyotard is unfortunate. While it is true that Lyotard's account (inevitably, a narrative) about the decline of narrative does challenge the legitimacy and future of a collective humanist inheritance, it is not as nihilistic as Said makes it out to be. See in particular Lyotard, *The Postmodern Condition*, trans. Geoff Bennington and Brian Massumi (Minneapolis: University of Minnesota Press, 1984), 66–67.

18. Said, *Humanism and Democratic Criticism*, 48–49.

19. Fredric Jameson, *Late Marxism: Adorno, or, The Persistence of the Dialectic* (London: Verso, 1992), 17.

20. In *Freud and the Non-European*, Said inveighs against those among his critics he finds guilty of "stupidity" (23). In a somewhat similar gesture, Adorno uses the term "musical stupidity" to describe an "inane tendency" toward the formulaic within music. See Theodor Adorno, *Beethoven: The Philosophy of Music*, ed. Rolf Tiedemann, trans. Edmund Jephcott (Stanford, CA: Stanford University Press, 1998), 58–59, 71. As Avital Ronell has shown, one of the problems of vanquishing stupidity is that knowledge has a hard time exteriorizing it, least of all "in any simple way." Ronell, *Stupidity* (Urbana: University of Illinois Press, 2002), 5.

21. Said, *Humanism and Democratic Criticism*, 55.

22. Ibid.

23. Ibid., 55–56.

24. Rereading Said's essay "The Horizon of R. P. Blackmur" (in *Reflections on Exile and Other Essays*), I am struck by how much the piece, no doubt in retrospect, suggests a reading of Blackmur's work along the lines of the "troubled technique" of late style. Blackmur, who "occupies a position of intransigent honor," is a writer whose work "at its center cradles the paradox that whatever criticism urges or delivers must not, indeed cannot, be replicated, reproduced, re-used as a lesson learned and then applied" (247). Like Beethoven for Adorno, Blackmur for Said has a "third" period whose style, like Beethoven's late style as Adorno understands it, is precisely a critique of the survival of "the tradition of European bourgeois humanism" through institutional legitimation (258–59). Aside from whatever interest it may hold for a genealogy of the development of an idea within Said's work, the identification of late style (as named category, implicit critical interest, incipient or explicit motif, etc.) runs the risk of *generalizing* the term *beyond interest*. Taking into account the inanity of making late style into a code to be found, more or less encrypted, here or there in Said's oeuvre, one could argue that the problems posed by late style are working on Said from the very beginning, at least as early as *Beginnings*, where he proposes a narrative schematization of the four phases of a writer's career.

25. Edward Said, "A Note on Modernism," in *Culture and Imperialism* (New York: Vintage, 1994), 188.

26. Georg Lukács, "The Ideology of Modernism," trans. John Mander and Necke Mander, in *Realism in Our Time: Literature and the Class Struggle* (New York: Harper and Row, 1962), 25. Lukács's cri-

tique of modernism differs significantly from Said's more affirmative discussion. For Lukács, modernism, in its writing of and emphasis on psychological interiority, is a reification of pathology and a denial of any possibility for the thinking of objective totality. "Man is reduced to a sequence of unrelated experiential fragments; he is as inexplicable to others as to himself. . . . Lack of objectivity in the description of the outer world finds its complement in the reduction of reality to a nightmare. . . . [Modernism] leads straight to a glorification of the abnormal and to an undisguised anti-humanism" (26, 31, 32). For Said's view, see his "A Note on Modernism," 189.

27. Said, "A Note on Modernism," 189–90.

28. For a discussion of the secular politics of Said's modernism, see Stathis Gourgouris, "Transformation, Not Transcendence," *boundary 2* 31, no. 2 (2004): 55–79.

29. Said, *Humanism and Democratic Criticism*, 77.

30. Adorno, *Beethoven*, 139.

31. See Theodor Adorno, *Philosophy of Modern Music*, trans. Anne G. Mitchell and Wesley V. Blomster (New York: Continuum, 2004). For Said's early interest in Adorno and late style, see Said, *Musical Elaborations* (New York: Columbia University Press, 1991), where "late style" appears as an explicit concern in the first chapter, "Performance as an Extreme Occasion" (1–34). If it is fair to say that Said takes the term from Adorno, and more specifically that his reading and elaboration of it has its impetus in Adorno's essay "Late Style in Beethoven," it is somewhat misleading to say that "the term is Adorno's" (see Michael Wood's introduction to *On Late Style*, xiii), if only because such a statement seems to indicate that Adorno coined or conceived of the term. Adorno, particularly in "The Late Style of Beethoven," takes on what he calls "the usual view" (*Beethoven*, 103) of late style, thus indicating the term's prior history. For a discussion of this history, see Karen Painter, "On Creativity and Lateness," in *Late Thoughts: Reflections on Artists and Composers at Work*, ed. Karen Painter and Thomas Crow (Los Angeles: Getty Research Institute, 2006), 1–11. Parts of Adorno's essay "Late Style in Beethoven," trans. Susan Gillespie, in *Raritan* 13, no. 1 (1993): 102–7, reappear in *Philosophy of New Modern Music*, 119–20. See also "The Late Style (I), in *Beethoven*, 123–37. For the German publication of 1937, see "Spätstil Beethovens," in *Moments Musicaux* (Frankfurt am Main: Suhrkamp Verlag, 1964): 13–17, also in *Gesammelte Schriften* vol. 17 (Frankfurt: Suhrkamp, 1982), 13–17. My citations of "Late Style in Beethoven" refer to the Gillespie translation in *Raritan*.

32. Said, *Musical Elaborations*, 48, 51. In his critique of the tendency toward the all-encompassing and the inevitable, Said makes an interesting argument about the centrality of the "European avalanche" to cultural criticism. "What is especially important is that not *all* cultural or political endeavors were engulfed by the European avalanche, which while it did bring disasters to millions was neither the only aspect of history to have mattered nor the only one that should be returned to by specialized scholars and general intellectuals for counsel and instruction" (*Musical Elaborations*, 54). This "not all" provides a crucial component of Said's continued investment in humanism. I don't have room to expand upon the place Adorno plays in Said's argument here, but suffice it to say that Said implicitly associates him with a double limitation, both that of a Eurocentrism so focused on what Adorno will call the "European catastrophe" (Adorno, "The Aging of the New Music," trans. Susan H. Gillespie, in *Essays on Music*, ed. Richard Leppert [Berkeley: University of California Press, 2002], 199) that it is blind to the "rest" of the world, and that of a "pessimistic" systematic critical model that closes off the possibility of "transgression" (Said, *Musical Elaborations*, 55). Clearly, this is a different approach to Adorno than the one Said typically offers. Still, it is useful to note that Said, however invested he remains in Adorno's negative dialectics as a model of secular criticism in all its "intransigence," does, from time to time, criticize Adorno's "fascination with the techniques of domination" (Said, "Criticism and the Art of Politics," in *Power, Politics, and Culture*, 137). This "fascination" is one Said invokes repeatedly in his critique of structuralism, and more specifically of Foucault.

33. "On Jean Genet's Late Works" was first published in *Grand Street* 36, no. 9 (1990): 27–42. With

slight but significant revisions, it is included in *On Late Style* as chapter 4, "On Jean Genet." Subsequent references are to the original version of the essay.

34. Faced with the threat of overwhelming loss and the danger of extinction, late style, not unlike the sublime, finds its tenuous power through negative identification with a prior and extant failure (typically of the imagination, language, or other mode of "presentation"). For Said, who does not make the connection to the sublime, the danger and promise of failure emerges from a historical accumulation of defeat and defeatism, as in his essay "On Lost Causes," in *Reflections on Exile*, which links late style to the affirmative reappropriation of failure.

35. Adorno's argument in "The Aging of the New Music" that the initial "critical impulse" of the new music wanes under the "total rationalization of music" (181, 191) pertains to my reading of Said's late style as it vacillates between an emphasis on singularity and generalizability, a vacillation that has a corollary in the tension between criticism as event and criticism as prescriptive normativity.

36. Roman Jakobson, "Two Aspects of Language and Two Types of Aphasic Disturbance," in *Language in Literature*, ed. Krystyna Pomorska and Stephen Rudy (Cambridge, MA: Harvard University Press, 1996), 104.

37. Adorno, *Beethoven*, 139.

38. Ibid., 14.

39. There are indeed quite a few similarities between the two essays. Yet Barthes's "countertheological" reading of literature ("The Death of the Author," in *The Rustle of Language*, trans. Richard Howard [Berkeley: University of California Press, 1989], 54), despite its argument that "writing is the destruction of every origin" (49), including those putative origins of affective expression, psychological plenitude, and authorial signature, is more interested in privileging—liberating—the reader as agent of interpretation, if not of meaning, whereas Adorno stops short of making any such recuperative, or, as Said might say, "salutary," restoration. Moreover, the two essays differ in their approach to the problem of death "in" the work, or death as a limit to the closures of expressive totality. Whereas Barthes will argue that it is only and precisely to the extent that "the voice loses its origin, the author enters into his own death, [that] writing begins" (49), Adorno's emphasis on the "formal law" of late style, as I argue above, remains invested in a dialectic in which death-as-limit returns as "catastrophe."

40. Adorno, "The Aging of the New Music," 199, 181.

41. Rose Rosengard Subotnik, "Adorno's Diagnosis of Beethoven's Late Style: Early Symptom of a Fatal Condition," *Journal of the American Musicological Society* 29, no. 2 (1976): 254.

42. See, for example, Adorno's argument in *Beethoven*, where individual death in its "insignificance" is linked to the unfreedom of the subject within the dialectic. "The ideas set down here need to be related to the Hegelian notion of bad individuality, the conception that only the universal is substantial. The purpose of the *fractured* quality of the late Beethoven would then be to express the fact that such substantiality of the universal represents *alienation*, violence, privation—that is, it does not raise the individual to a higher level. Beethoven becomes 'inorganic,' fractured, at the point where Hegel becomes ideological. . . . In other words, the late style is the self-awareness of the insignificance of the individual, existent. Herein lies the relationship of the late style to *death*" (161).

43. Again, one might note here a connection between late style and the sublime, particularly in the tension between "power" and "lost totality." For the relationship between the sublime, totality, and modernism, see Lyotard, "Answering the Question: What Is Postmodernism?" in *The Postmodern Condition*, 71–84.

44. Said, *On Late Style*, 18.

45. Adorno, *Beethoven*, 193.

46. Said, *On Late Style*, 17.

47. One might be tempted to connect Said's interest in late style to his illness. Given his own references to it (*On Late Style*, 6), and given the fact that *On Late Style* bears the mark of the posthumous,

that is to say of death, this connection is somewhat inevitable. Yet it is also worthwhile to note that Said began his work on late style prior to being diagnosed with cancer in 1992 (I am grateful to Andrew Rubin for providing information about Said's diagnosis). One has no way of knowing how much Said's ongoing work on late style was motivated by his experience of illness. And, as Adorno's essay will suggest, there is no reason to presume that illness is a necessary or privileged condition for a thinking of lateness. "Adorno as Lateness Itself" was given as a lecture in October 1993 and first published in the volume *Apocalypse Theory and the Ends of the World*, edited by Malcolm Bull (1995). In the fall of 1995, Said taught "Last Works / Late Style," at Columbia University, a graduate seminar in which I participated, where he continued to reflect upon the "lateness" of certain artists, Genet included. Some of the material from "Adorno as Lateness Itself" reappears in revised form in the posthumously published "Thoughts on Late Style" (*London Review of Books*, 2004) and, again amended, in *On Late Style* (primarily in chapter 1, "Timeliness and Lateness," and chapter 7, "Glimpses of Late Style").

48. Said, "Glimpses of Late Style," 134.

49. Said, *Freud and the Non-European* (London: Verso, 2003), 52.

50. Said, "The Future of Criticism," 169.

51. For a discussion of the question of trauma in Said's text, see Jacqueline Rose's "Response to Edward Said," in Said, *Freud and the Non-European*. Included at the end of the text, Rose's response becomes a kind of paratextual, alternative conclusion to Said's reading of Freud, one that problematizes the "sanguine" hope that, in the future, the rewriting of trauma might dislodge the violent certitudes of origins and identity (75–77). Interestingly, Adorno makes several references to the "violence" of Beethoven's negation of the impossibility of negation, or "the Promethean, voluntarist, Fichtean element . . . its untruth: the manipulation of transcendence, the *coercion*, the violence" (*Beethoven*, 78). One might read the tension between Rose's less hopeful reading and Said's perhaps more "sanguine" anticipatory futurity alongside Adorno's ambivalent take on a passage from Marx's *Eighteenth Brumaire* (see *Beethoven*, 79, 190).

52. Admittedly, this is a somewhat naïve way of problematizing a well-trod, though certainly far from resolved, issue. To cite merely one text from the many fields—philosophy, anthropology, history, sociology, linguistics, psychoanalysis, literature, biology, medicine, and certainly there are others—that have engaged in the question of the "nature" of death, Freud's *Beyond the Pleasure Principle* (trans. James Strachey [New York: Norton, 1961]) comes to mind. The text, and its famously unsuccessful attempt to locate that ever-receding "beyond" of the pleasure principle, along with its unresolved effort to determine the outline and nature of the instincts, reaches one of its many knotted crescendos when Freud concludes, "What we are left with is the fact that the organism wishes to die only in its own fashion" (47). After this tautological restatement of the "fact" of the death-drive's desire as species-ontology, Freud goes on to invoke, and then to problematize, the notion of "natural death" (47, 53).

53. Said, *Humanism and Democratic Criticism*, 115.

54. Ibid., 22.

55. Ibid., 144.

56. "I can't go on, you must go on, I'll go on, you must say words, as long as there are any . . . I'll never know, in the silence you don't know, you must go on, I can't go on, I'll go on" (Samuel Beckett, *The Unnamable* [New York: Knopf, 1997], 476).

WORKS CITED

Adorno, Theodor W. *Aesthetic Theory*. Trans. and ed. Robert Hullot-Kentor. Minneapolis: University of Minnesota Press, 1997.

———. "The Aging of the New Music." Trans. Susan H. Gillespie. In *Essays on Music*, 181–202. Ed. Richard Leppert. Berkeley: University of California Press, 2002.

————. *Beethoven: The Philosophy of Music.* Ed. Rolf Tiedemann. Trans. Edmund Jephcott. Stanford, CA: Stanford University Press, 1998.

————. "Late Style in Beethoven." Trans. Susan Gillespie. *Raritan* 13, no. 1 (1993): 102–7.

————. "Late Work without Late Style." In *Beethoven: The Philosophy of Music*, 138–53. Ed. Rolf Tiedemann. Trans. Edmund Jephcott. Stanford, CA: Stanford University Press, 1998.

————. *Philosophy of Modern Music.* Trans. Anne G. Mitchell and Wesley V. Blomster. New York: Continuum, 2004.

Barthes, Roland. "The Death of the Author." In *The Rustle of Language*, 49–55. Trans. Richard Howard. Berkeley: University of California Press, 1989.

Beckett, Samuel. *The Unnamable.* New York: Knopf, 1997.

Bull, Malcolm, ed. *Apocalypse Theory and the Ends of the World.* Oxford: Blackwell, 1995.

Freud, Sigmund. *Beyond the Pleasure Principle.* Trans. James Strachey. New York: Norton, 1961.

Gourgouris, Stathis. "Transformation, Not Transcendence." *boundary 2* 31, no. 2 (2004): 55–79.

Jakobson, Roman. "Two Aspects of Language and Two Types of Aphasic Disturbance." In *Language in Literature*, 95–114. Ed. Krystyna Pomorska and Stephen Rudy. Cambridge, MA: Harvard University Press, 1996.

Jameson, Fredric. *Late Marxism: Adorno, or, The Persistence of the Dialectic.* London: Verso, 1992.

Lukács, Georg. "The Ideology of Modernism." In *Realism in Our Time: Literature and the Class Struggle*, 17–46. Trans. John and Necke Mander. New York: Harper and Row, 1962.

Lyotard, Jean-Francois. *The Postmodern Condition.* Trans. Geoff Bennington and Brian Massumi. Minneapolis: University of Minnesota Press, 1984.

Painter, Karen. "On Creativity and Lateness." In *Late Thoughts: Reflections on Artists and Composers at Work*, 1–11. Ed. Karen Painter and Thomas Crow. Los Angeles: Getty Research Institute, 2006.

Ronell, Avital. *Stupidity.* Urbana: University of Illinois Press, 2002.

Rose, Jacqueline. "Response to Edward Said." In Edward Said, *Freud and the Non-European*, 65–79. London: Verso, 2003.

Said, Edward. "Adorno as Lateness Itself." In *Apocalypse Theory and the Ends of the World*, 264–80. Ed. Malcolm Bull. Oxford: Blackwell, 1995.

————. *Beginnings: Intention and Method.* New York: Columbia University Press, 1985.

————. "Criticism and the Art of Politics." Interview with Jennifer Wicke and Michael Sprinker (1992). In *Power, Politics, and Culture: Interviews with Edward Said*, 118–63. Ed. Gauri Viswanathan. New York: Vintage, 2002.

————. "Criticism Between Culture and System." In *The World, the Text, and the Critic*, 178–225. Cambridge, MA: Harvard University Press, 1983.

————. *Freud and the Non-European.* London: Verso, 2003.

————. "The Future of Criticism." In *Reflections on Exile and Other Essays*, 165–72. Cambridge, MA: Harvard University Press, 2002.

————. "Glimpses of Late Style." In *On Late Style: Music and Literature Against the Grain.* New York: Pantheon, 2006.

————. "The Horizon of R. P. Blackmur." In *Reflections on Exile and Other Essays*, 246–67. Cambridge, MA: Harvard University Press, 2002.

————. *Humanism and Democratic Criticism.* New York: Columbia University Press, 2004.

————. *Musical Elaborations.* New York: Columbia University Press, 1991.

————. "My Right of Return." In *Power, Politics, and Culture: Interviews with Edward Said*, 443–58. Ed. Gauri Viswanathan. New York: Random House, 2001. Original interview with Ari Shavit, *Ha'aretz Magazine*, Tel Aviv, 2000.

————. "A Note on Modernism." In *Culture and Imperialism*, 186–90. New York: Vintage, 1994.

————. "On Jean Genet's Late Works." *Grand Street* 36, no. 9 (1990): 27–42.

————. *On Late Style: Music and Literature Against the Grain.* New York: Pantheon, 2006.

————. "On Lost Causes." In *Reflections on Exile and Other Essays*, 527–53. Cambridge, MA: Harvard University Press, 2002.

————. *Orientalism.* New York: Vintage, 1979.

————. "The Politics of Knowledge." In *Reflections on Exile and Other Essays*, 372–85. Cambridge, MA: Harvard University Press, 2002.

————. *Reflections on Exile and Other Essays.* Cambridge, MA: Harvard University Press, 2002.

————. "The Return to Philology." In *Humanism and Democratic Criticism*, 57–84. New York: Columbia University Press, 2004.

————. "Thoughts on Late Style." *London Review of Books* 26, no. 15 (2004).

————. "Traveling Theory." In *The World, the Text, and the Critic*, 226–47. Cambridge, MA: Harvard University Press, 1983.

————. *The World, the Text, and the Critic.* Cambridge, MA: Harvard University Press, 1983.

Subotnik, Rose Rosengard. "Adorno's Diagnosis of Beethoven's Late Style: Early Symptom of a Fatal Condition." *Journal of the American Musicological Society* 29, no. 2 (1976): 242–75.

Wood, Michael. Introduction to *On Late Style: Music and Literature Against the Grain*, xi–xix. New York: Pantheon, 2006.

28

Secular Divination

Edward Said's Humanism

W. J. T. Mitchell

Humanism . . . generates its own opposite.
—EDWARD SAID, *BEGINNINGS*

Any continuation of the conversation with Edward Said would have to include the question of humanism and its many discontents. Humanism for Said was always a dialectical concept, generating oppositions it could neither absorb nor avoid. The very word used to cause in him mixed feelings of reverence and revulsion, an admiration for the great monuments of civilization that constitute the archive of humanism and a disgust at the underside of suffering and oppression that, as Benjamin insisted, make them monuments to barbarism as well. Said's last book, *Humanism and Democratic Criticism* is, among other things, his attempt to trace the evolution of his own thinking from his training as an academic humanist in the philological tradition of Auerbach and Spitzer, through the antihumanist period of French theory in the U.S. academy since the sixties, to the present moment of posthumanism, when humanism looks to many like a dead issue, not even requiring or generating an interesting opposition anymore (unless the "posthuman" is to be understood as a dialectical moment of humanism rather than some irrevocable cancellation of it).[1] Said was perhaps uniquely situated to trace this process because he, among all the academic intellectuals of the sixties and seventies generation, seemed to simultaneously absorb and resist the arrival of antihumanism in the form of what is loosely called "French theory." Said's engagement with Foucault in *Beginnings* and *Orientalism* was persistent and deep, leading James Clifford to question whether it was possible for Said to continue to profess allegiance to humanism, with its assumptions of subjective agency and will, while embracing the antihumanist tendencies of structuralism and poststructuralism.

Said's answer to Clifford is, quite simply, yes: "It is possible to be critical of humanism in the name of humanism," and perhaps even more emphatically, it is *necessary* to be critical of humanism in order to be worthy of the name.[2] Humanism shows a double face as, on the one hand, the capacious learning, the extended intelligence (what Bourdieu, quoted by Said, calls the "collective intellectual") that provides the materials and archives for human self-knowledge, but which left to itself, has produced a stuffy, sterile antiquarianism, a sentimental piety about the human as an empty slogan, a development which has in turn produced the various shallow antihumanisms and posthumanisms as a reaction to it. Said wanted to reclaim and revivify humanism for our time, to link the work of academics with the precedent of Auerbach (on the side of learning) but also with criticism and the precedents of Fanon and Trilling—the moment of choice, decision, taking of sides, judgment. Without criticism, humanism remains a sterile fever for the archive as a dynastic treasure and an end in itself. Without humanism, criticism is nothing but empty quibbling and opinion.

So where does this leave the issue of democracy? This, I think, is precisely the space, both real and utopian, in which humanism and criticism make their connection. Said knows very well that "democracy" is (like the niggling, fussy irrelevance of criticism and the musty tomes of the humanists) a hollow term, too often used as a cover for imperialist adventures (we are, after all, currently trying to bring democracy to Iraq by military force). The language of democracy, of equality, of power sharing, of justice, of secular self-governance must not be co-opted by ideologues who use it as a cover for imperialism, but must be reclaimed and reinfused with practical meaning for human relationships. And a democracy is, if anything, a place where power grows out of arguments, knowledge, language, persuasion, and reason—in short, out of the resources made available by humanism and criticism. "Democratic criticism," then, means the right to dissent and the obligation to dissent, to break one's silence and passivity and to "speak the truth to power" without fear of censorship or violence. Humanism is what gives the critic something to say. Criticism is what gives the humanist a motive, occasion, and obligation to say something. And democracy is the space in which knowledge and judgment, learning and dissent, come together. It is the space that allows for this convergence, whether in the sphere of politics and society or in the smaller world of academic discussion, right down to the democratic classroom. It is also the space *created by* this convergence, the (relatively) noncoercive, or at least nonviolent realm of the free play of ideas and imagination which is never perfectly realized, but always approached as the goal of discourse.

Said's great enemies, then, are never merely political, but intellectual, cultural, and academic. They are: the tendency to obfuscation and mystification; the cult of expertise, whether in academic jargon or in the prattlings of the policy wonks; the countercult of false "transparency" in the oversimplified sound bites of the punditocracy; the simplistic binarisms of the "clash of civilizations" thesis; the "axis of evil"; and the reductionism of mass media "information." Complexity without mystification, dialectics without the disabling equivocation of "ambivalence" or deconstructive "undecidability," recognition of the baffling limits of human knowledge without obscurantism or quietism a recognition of the situatedness and contingency of every utterance without a surrender to relativism and without a sacrifice of abiding principles.[3] Sooner pass a camel through the eye of the needle than come up to the unbelievably demanding standards Said set for intellectual expression. No wonder that the transcendent standard above all this is a term that (so far as I can recall) he never invokes in *Humanism and Democratic Criticism* but that informs all his work: and that is *virtuosity,* an agile, improvisational sense of balance, coupled with a dogged and tireless preparation for the next moment of struggle.

I do not know how *Humanism and Democratic Criticism* will be remembered and compared with his other great works. My favorites are still *Beginnings, Orientalism,* and *After the Last Sky,* his marvelous collaboration with the Swiss photographer Jean Mohr in an effort to "represent" the Palestinians to themselves and to the world. But this book strikes me as a distillation of what Said called his "late style," informal, freely ruminative, personal, and tirelessly engaged with the modification of his thinking as it encountered the new circumstances of the post-9/11 world. It is a performance of exactly the convergence of the humanistic with the critical and the democratic that his title promises. Critical of humanism and humanists, humane in the motivations of its criticism, and relentlessly critical of the world's most powerful democracy, its delusions and its promises, it is a worthy testament, a kind of farewell letter to Edward's devoted, diverse, and always contentious following.

In Edward's own spirit, then, I would like to raise a question that has always nagged me throughout his work: his division of the secular from the sacred. This distinction is absolutely foundational for Said, and in some versions of it I see a problem that remains unresolved. Here is this formulation in *Humanism and Democratic Criticism:* "The core of humanism is the secular notion that the historical world is made by men and women, and not by God, and that it can be understood rationally according to the principle formulated by Vico in *New Science,* that we can really know only what we make or, to put it differently, we can know things according to the way they were made."[4]

Vico's scientific humanism, as formulated by Said, contains the implicit suggestion that we *cannot* know things that we have not made. This leads then to the notion that religious knowledge, sacred knowledge, is really a kind of ignorance, or at least an unscientific and even inhuman form of knowledge. This would presumably be the case whether religious knowledge expressed itself by a kind of confession of ignorance and uncertainty or conversely, by an assertion of dogma based in faith. Either way, "sacred knowledge" is a kind of oxymoron and has no claim to share in the progressive, open, dialogical, and (ultimately) democratic ethos that Said associates with humanism.

There is a further implication in Viconian humanism, and that is the question of the scientific knowledge of nature. If the Viconian postulate is taken at face value, human beings should not be able to have rational knowledge of nature, because they did not create it. Only human nature, specifically human history, is open to rational understanding. "The world of civil society has certainly been made by men, and . . . its principles are therefore to be found within the modifications of our own human mind. Whoever reflects on this cannot but marvel that the philosophers should have bent all their energies to the study of the world of nature, which, since God made it, He alone knows; and that they should have neglected the study of the world of nations, or civil world, which, since men had made it, men could come to know."[5]

The natural and supernatural realms are both closed to rational inquiry of the sort distinctive to humanism. This seems like an obvious problem, especially on the side of the natural sciences, which are generally taken to be accessible to rational, open, empirical, and even democratically progressive forms of knowledge. Humanistic knowledge is generally taken to be a poor relation of natural science when it comes to precision and certainty. If anything, natural science is a kind of model for what secular humanism might aspire to. Said admits as much when he praises Darwin's "lifelong attention to the earthworm revealed [in] its capacity for expressing nature's variability and design without necessarily seeing the whole of either one or the other," and thus, in Adam Phillips's words (quoted by Said), "replacing 'a creation myth with a secular maintenance myth.'"[6]

One can hear the resonance of Said's distinction between "origin myths" and "beginnings" echoing in this passage. Beginnings are provisional, historically situated actions, decisions, and choices, not reified, timeless moments that precede human agency. They do not have the absoluteness or certainty of creation ex nihilo but are provisional origins that could turn out to be dead ends, or the start of something big. Beginnings are also connected immediately with acts of continuation (or of turning, swerving aside) and not with some predestined fate or necessity. As such, they perfectly negotiate the dilemma of agency versus external determination that James Clifford criticized in Said's Foucauldian work, where he seemed not to have worked out the relation between his humanistic emphasis on freedom and agency and Foucault's antihumanistic determinism.[7] Is not a "secular maintenance myth," epitomized by the blind labors of the earthworm, exactly a figure of the refusal to choose between these false alternatives, and is not Darwin himself implicitly a kind of earthworm in his patient, tireless work, in which the lowest and the highest forms of knowledge must be combined?

I am not primarily concerned here with pointing up the obvious problem in Vico's epistemology that this example illustrates. The notion that we can have rational knowledge only of what we have made is clearly wrong, but the sphere of natural science is not really the focus of Said's insistence on the secular character of humanism. (Also, to be precise about Vico, his view was that scientific knowledge actually *is* a human creation, insofar as experimental research must imitate the processes of nature and reproduce them under artificial conditions that make them accessible to knowledge; in that sense, natural science *is* a form of knowledge of human productions. What we "know" in natural science is not nature in any direct sense but a second nature fabricated in the laboratory.)

But it is the domain of religion, which Said so often characterizes in terms of fairly reductive stereotypes: dogmatic, fanatical, irrational, intolerant, and obsessed with mystery, obfuscation, and human helplessness in the presence of the inscrutable divine (or demonic) design. "Religious enthusiasm is perhaps the most dangerous of threats to the humanistic enterprise, since it is patently anti-secular and antidemocratic in nature."[8] If natural science turns human beings into objects buffeted by impersonal, nonhuman forces, religion does the same thing, only with the added problem of mystery, irrationality, and dogma, accompanied by authoritarian institutions and radically undemocratic, coercive practices. At least the forces of nature can be understood and to some extent controlled by human agency; the divine, in Said's lexicon, seems to be exactly that sphere of the uncontrollable and inexplicable that, at the same time, has an immense power over human thought and action. Religion for Said is an expression of the alienated capacities of the human imagination, a system of ideological deception and coercive authority.

I bring this up as an issue because it strikes me as a limitation in Said's thinking that he often transcended in practice, but (so far as I know) never at the level of theoretical reflection. It leads me to the point where I think of Said's work as intersecting most directly with my own, and yet where I often felt the greatest distance between our ways of thinking. This "point" is not really any single issue, but it does revolve around questions of religion and mystery, on the one hand, and problems of mass culture, media, and (for lack of a better word) "images," "imagination," and "the visual," on the other, as Edward's self-confessed "blind spot," the domain of visual art that so frequently left him baffled or panicky. Said's aesthetic polestars were music and literature, two great orders of art that to him were much more than mere cultural ornaments or diversions, but exemplars of human possibility in its most ambitious moments. Literature, of course, for Said included not only the usual suspects of fiction, poetry, and dramatic writing but the nonfiction prose, the "critical" writing, and the philological learning that lay behind it. Philology for Said was the "love of words," quite literally, a love that treated words not as mere instruments for polemic or analysis but as living presences that animate discourse with passion, eloquence, and exactly that form of self-knowledge and self-criticism that makes humanism worthy of its name. He rejected the divisions between "writers" and "intellectuals" or "critics" and tried to fuse the vocations of all three—creativity, learning, and judgment— in the role of that rarest of creatures in American culture, the "public intellectual."

As for music, my sense is that this is where Said's identity as a formalist, an aesthete, and a high modernist intellectual is most firmly located. His role as a talented amateur musician perfectly exemplified his refusal of specialization, on the one hand, while his writing on music in the tradition of Adorno carried him well beyond any taint of amateurism into the virtuosic company of the Barenboims and the Glenn Goulds. Beyond this, music had for him a kind of analogical significance in his insistence on translating the abstruse turnings of dialectical reasonings into a style of "contrapuntal" critical writing, a prose that continually played multiple countermelodies against the main line of his thought, qualifying, intersecting, correcting, and elaborating in surprising new forms. Above all is his sense of what Wordsworth called "the still sad music of humanity," never more movingly expressed than in his sense of the final unity of the two peoples most separated by savage violence in the contemporary world, the Israelis and the Palestinians, whose intertwined, contrapuntal relationship he compared to a "tragic symphony."[9]

What, then, of the visual arts? I interviewed Said on this subject for a special issue of *boundary 2* in 2001 and encountered a strange, unusual diffidence in his approach to the subject.[10] After noting his "highly developed vocabulary" for talking about "the auditory and the verbal," he confessed himself to be "tongue-tied" with the visual arts: "Just to think about the visual arts generally sends me into a panic."[11] Of course, this turned out to be only a momentary perplexity, and Said quickly regained his balance, talking with considerable eloquence about a range of visual art works from masters of painting such as El Greco, Goya, and Picasso to his childhood memories of the wax museum of Egyptian history in Cairo and the anatomical representations of human diseases in the Agriculture Museum of Giza. The consistent form this eloquence took, however, was a registering of the "haunted" and "frightening" character of the religious images, the "terrified fascination" that the medical images produced, and (most centrally) the deformed bodies of El Greco, Francis Bacon, and Goya, with their lurid colors and scenes of monstrous disfiguration. Of all the artists we discussed, Edward felt the most affinity for Goya, whose combination of detached irony, passionate involvement, and "a kind of gentleness amidst all the violence" (33) impressed him like no other paintings.[12]

I would like to suggest a link, however speculative and impressionistic, between Said's "panic" with images and visual representations, with what Lacan (whom I am pretty sure Edward mainly disliked) would have called "the Imaginary," and with one of the most characteristic gestures of Said's writing: that is the moment of "bafflement" or mystification of coming to the limits of his thought and recognizing that encounter in his own discourse. This is, of course, a familiar rhetorical trope (perhaps a form of *occupatio*, the saying of what cannot or will not be said), but it is also a deeply ethical gesture, a kind of deferral of authority and a public confession of uncertainty.

I want to see this as Said's gesture toward the limits of his thought and link them to his deep involvement with similar issues in Vico. For Vico, the image, the imaginary (whether visual or verbal, picture or metaphor), is the expressive mode of primitive man immersed in the realm of fantasy, idols, animism, personification, and vivid poetic figures. It is the language of religion and myth—not, however, the language of *revealed* religion ("the Hebrew religion was founded by the true God on the prohibition of divination on which all the gentile nations arose").[13] Judaism, like other religions of the book, is grounded on a prohibition of idols, images, and divination. Vico is talking about pagan religions of icons, fetishes, not the religions of the book. The interesting twist is that Vico's concept of the secular rests on, and grows out of, the mythologies of the gentiles, not out of revealed religion. More precisely, the history of civil society, of the "gentiles" and nations, is the *subject* of Vico's "new science," while its epistemological foundations lie outside that subject, in the unquestioned (and tactfully unexamined) dogmas of "true" (i.e. revealed) religion. Vico's notion of a secular history is framed inside a providential yet tragic cycle: men begin as bestial savages, develop gods out of their projected fantasies based in fear of nature, and grow toward gradual refinement, to civilization, and finally, to decadence produced by skepticism. The clearest expression of this is when Vico says that revealed religion of the Jews was grounded on "the prohibition of divination," which is fundamentally the second commandment, the prohibition on graven images.[14] But this means that the distinction between the sacred and secular is not quite so clean as it might seem: it is actually more like the difference between direct access to the divine word and divination of sacred images. But this requires a modification in Vico's sense of where human knowledge can attain most clarity. For the sacred images that are created by men, the idols that mystify them, are precisely what eludes their understanding. "Divination" of idols or other symbols is, from the point of view of revealed religion, nothing but magical, superstitious ritual, the false attribution of intentions and desires to inanimate objects and images. Insofar as secular knowledge is to be distinguished from revealed religion, then, it is much *less* certain about its claims, necessarily provisional and hypothetical. It is, in fact, grounded in divination rather than revelation, and the genealogy of the secular goes deeper than the Enlightenment, reaching back into pagan origins. Divination might be seen, paradoxically, as a distinctly *secular* hermeneutics, in contrast to the sacred hermeneutic tradition grounded in the Bible. Divination is associated with the interpretation of human and natural objects—auguries based in the material body and its states, prophecies based in the formal alignments of stars or the behavior of animals, or diagnoses based in the analysis of dreams, and (most notably) in graven images and works of art.

The strange lineage of the sacred/secular distinction in Vico, then, is I think one explanation for Said's frequent recourse to the language of uncertainty, paradox, irresolution, and what he calls "bafflement" in his writings. Bafflement is associated with unresolved contradictions; mysterious, labyrinthine forms; the "magic" of words; the encounter with what Leo Spitzer called "the inward life center" of the work of art. And of course there is Said's almost structural distaste for religion and myth, as opposed to his secular or "rational civil theology," the phrase that Vico uses to describe his own position.[15] Like Vico, Said wants to see all these myths and images as human productions, therefore accessible to rational understanding, because man-made in the first place. But to inhabit a regime of these images is precisely to be beset by the irrational, by the mysterious forces of the alienated productions of the human imagination—the "tyrannical feedback system" that Said found diagnosed and (he hoped) resisted in the work of Foucault.[16] Suppose Vico's deeper lesson was that human beings finally cannot sustain a knowledge/power relation to their own creations, but find themselves caught up as victims in the terrible systems (social, economic, and political) that they have wrought. This is the strange, melancholy lesson of the *Scienza Nuova*. Vico's tragic narrative tells us that man only emerges briefly (during the age of man) from the age of gods and heroes before sinking back into savagery with the rise of skepticism and the resurgence of superstition. This narrative helps clarify why Said was so antagonistic to deconstruction, posthumanism, and antifoundationalism and why refined, technical academic discourse was so grating on his ears. It was part of his resistance to decadence and decline, his insistence on the intellectual's responsibility to lost causes and unfashionable ideas (humanism, criticism) and his wariness about hollow ideals (democracy) used in the service of domination.

Vico's "rational civil theology" is the best name for Edward Said's religion of reading and writing, humanism and democratic criticism. It is, however, a rationality that collides routinely with the irrational products of the human imagination—the cultural, social, and political creations that should be intelligible because they are human creations but which continually elude that understanding, whether they are the heroic products of artistic volition or alienated structures such as the unconscious, colonialism, or capital. Early in his career, Edward rejected the "uncanny" criticism of Hillis Miller and the Yale school because he thought it gave in too easily and reveled in the irrational, indecidable character of arts and letters. But it is clear that his own brand of canny, secular criticism is devised precisely as a form of resistance to an uncanny element in the objects of study—the productions of the human mind. Part of his canniness was to recognize itself as a kind of interpretive "lost cause" which would continually founder on the object of its study. Let us call it by the name of "secular divination," an oxymoron that Vico and Said would have understood. Like all the other lost causes that Said pursued, this one gave his writing that bracing sense of clarity, resolute determination, and tragic pathos that was the distinctive feature of his style, both early and late.

NOTES

This chapter first appeared in *Critical Inquiry*'s special issue "Edward Said: Continuing the Conversation," coedited by Mitchell and Homi Bhabha, vol. 31, no. 2 (Winter 2005): 365–529; and was subsequently reissued as a chapter in the book version of the special issue published by the University of Chicago Press in 2006.

1. Edward W. Said, *Humanism and Democratic Criticism* (New York: Columbia University Press, 2004). This paper was first composed for a colloquium at Columbia on the occasion of the publication of this book, April 27, 2004.

2. Ibid., 10.

3. On dialectics without equivocation, see ibid., 66.

4. Ibid., 11.

5. Giambattista Vico, "New Science," in *The Rise of Modern Mythology, 1680–1860*, ed. Burton Feldman and Robert D. Richardson (Bloomington: Indiana University Press, 1972), 57.

6. Said, *Humanism and Democratic Criticism*, 140–41.

7. James Clifford, "On Orientalism," in *The Predicament of Culture* (Cambridge, MA: Harvard University Press, 1988), 255–76. See also Akeel Bilgrami's excellent preface to Said, *Humanism and Democratic Criticism*, xii.

8. Said, *Humanism and Democratic Criticism*, 51.

9. Edward W. Said, "My Right of Return," in *Power, Politics, and Culture: Interviews with Edward Said*, ed. Gauri Viswanathan (New York: Pantheon, 2001), 447.

10. The interview, "The Panic of the Visual," is reprinted in *Edward Said and the Work of the Critic: Speaking Truth to Power*, ed. Paul Bové (Durham, NC: Duke University Press, 2000), 31–50.

11. Ibid., 31.

12. Ibid., 33.

13. Vico, "New Science," 56.

14. For the link between the prohibition on divination and the second commandment, see Moshe Halbertal and Avishai Margalit, *Idolatry* (Cambridge, MA: Harvard University Press, 1992), 105–6.

15. Vico summarizes his brand of humanism with this phrase. See Feldman and Richardson, *The Rise of Modern Mythology*, 54.

16. Edward W. Said, *Beginnings: Intention and Method* (New York: Columbia University Press, 1985), 288.

29

Countercurrents and Tensions in Said's Critical Practice

Benita Parry

So many questions have been asked of Said's work in bad faith that many who have learned from and leaned on his thinking may now be inhibited from asking any at all. Such reticence would be untrue to Said's insistence that the labor of criticism must include attention to "countercurrents, ironies and even contradictions," an imperative he heeded in his generous appreciations of others.[1] I want then to consider some theoretical matters relating to an erudite, innovative, nonconformist and mutable body of writing in which Said, during his "middle period," knowingly brought politics to his academic projects. Although in a late interview Said accepted, indeed affirmed, the irreconcilability of his two lives as a literary critic and an engaged public figure, at this time his writings were notable for making visible "the actual affiliations that exist between the world of ideas and scholarship on the one hand, and the world of brute politics, corporate and state power, and military force on the other."[2] This nexus shapes these middle-period essays, which can swoop with acrobatic elegance from—for example—the interlocution of sound and silence in music to the silences installed by the official record and broken by historians of the working class and the colonized: "There is no sound," he wrote in 1997, "no articulation that is adequate to what injustice and power inflict on the poor, the disadvantaged, and the disinherited. But these are approximations to it, not representations of it, which have the effect of punctuating discourse with disenchantment and demystifications."[3]

In alluding, as I will do, to Said's early, middle, and late periods, I am aware that some critics insist that his work, despite changes in technique and subjects of address, manifests a methodological consistency and constancy.[4] However, by observing variations in both the objects of Said's critical affections and the conceptual categories he brought to their pursuit, I am not proposing a series of absolute breaks between theoretical positions, nor am I attempting to establish a progression/ regression in the percipience and ingenuity of his criticism. Rather I suggest a cir- cuitous process of inclinations moving between normative literary critical concerns, the integration of aesthetics and politics—where the social and ideological were in- trinsic and not just context to considerations of rhetoric, narrative, and form—and the location of these categories as coextensive but distinctive spheres. Thus in his last years Said urged a mode of criticism requiring "complete historical under- standing of the situation—socio-political, spiritual, etc.," together with "an appre- ciation of the aesthetical element, which can't be reduced simply to an ideological or superstructural phenomenon, but which has its own integrity [that] cannot be reconciled with the world from which it came."[5] In adding, "there has to be a way of dealing with a work that in a certain sense escapes its historical determinism," Said reminds the reader that his own philological practice joined historical aware- ness to the close study of and respect for the singularity of any piece of writing with which he engaged.[6] Moreover, because Said considered the author to be an agent of and in the text, he—against prevailing trends and in emulation of Auerbach— articulated his own meetings with the unique mind and inventions of the histori- cally situated individual writer.

From the outset of his career Said was immersed in the hermeneutics of com- parative literary studies and wedded to the idea that "the critical act is first of all an act of comprehension . . . a phenomenon of consciousness," a notion much later ex- panded as "a humanistic activity" encompassing "erudition and sympathy" and a sensitivity to inner tensions.[7] What seems to have altered between the appearance of Said's first book, *Conrad and the Fiction of Autobiography* (1966), and *Culture and Imperialism* (1993) was his own critical consciousness; in those intervening years he appeared to acquire an intellectual compass, prompted by the punishments visited on the Palestinian people but extending to all situations of repression and injustice.[8] "My position," Said wrote during the 1980s, is "that texts are worldly . . . a part of the social world, human life, and of course the historical moment in which they are located and interpreted . . . The realities of power and authority—as well as the resistances offered by men, women and social movements, to institutions au- thorities and orthodoxies—are the realities that make texts possible, that deliver them to their readers, that solicit the attention of criticism."[9]

This position distanced him from the New Criticism already in place within the academy and from the poststructuralism threatening its predominance, inspiring a generation of disaffected young scholars to cross the disciplinary boundaries of history, political theory, anthropology and literary criticism in order to examine the uses of representation in the installation and exercise of domination.

With growing disappointment in the isolation of contemporary theory, Said showed increased openness to the thinking of Marxists of various persuasions—

Gramsci, Lukács, Adorno, Fanon, and Raymond Williams. By the time he wrote *Culture and Imperialism* (1993), which extended his existing interest in colonialist texts to examine evidence of the agency, resistance, and liberation struggles of oppressed peoples, Said had made known his irritation with "cults like post-modernism, discourse analysis, New Historicism [and] deconstruction" for giving intellectuals "an astonishing sense of weightlessness with regard to the gravity of history."[10] Speaking yet more explicitly after the publication of the study, he said, "All the literary analysis, explications, and commentary that I have in this book I see as under—'under' in the sense of commanded by, or patronized by. Or under the influence of some fairly gross historical realities, which for me are basically two: on the one hand, the reality of the colonized and, on the other, the reality of the colonizer."[11] Such a declaration, which would have been out of place in his early work and displaced in his last writings by the force of countercurrents, could surely have been made only in Said's "middle period."

The spectrum of Said's theoretical dispositions registers both an individual journey across a rapidly changing intellectual landscape, in whose transformation he was a major participant, and an inimitable instance of "traveling theory."[12] What is singular about Said's criticism, to which he brought a breadth of learning, an untrammeled imagination, and a penchant for representing personal experiences as signs of collective social identities and existential conditions, is that from the selective deployment of existing theoretical modes, he formed uniquely eclectic and virtuoso critical practices that in his lateness were liberated from the constraints of "method." He celebrated this freedom in closing the Introduction to the fiftieth-anniversary edition of Auerbach's *Mimesis* with a bravura and self-reflexive defiance of "theory" and even of the protocols of literary criticism. Auerbach, he wrote,

> offers no system, no short cut to what he puts before us as a history of the representation of reality in Western literature. From a contemporary standpoint there is something impossibly naïve, if not outrageous, that hotly contested terms like "Western," "reality," and "representation"—each of which has recently brought forth literally acres of disputatious prose amongst critics and philosophers—are left to stand on their own, unadorned and unqualified. It is as if Auerbach was intent on exposing his personal explorations, and perforce, his fallibility to the perhaps scornful eye of critics who might deride his subjectivity.[13]

I will illustrate what I see as the variable tendencies in Said's critical practice by referring to his commentaries on *Heart of Darkness* and *Nostromo*, two "colonial" novels by a writer whom he repeatedly credited as a major presence in his intellectual life. These works indicate diverse understandings of the immanence of empirical reality and the imprint of social forces in literature. Describing his 1966 study on Conrad as attempting "a phenomenological exploration of Conrad's consciousness" in interaction with his immediate social world, Said focused on "the *idiom*" in which Conrad rendered this experience of existential reality and the exigencies of his personal situation, at the center of which was a notion of truth as shadowy, as "the negation of intellectual differentiation ... a dark, sinister and fugitive shadow with no image."[14] Because Said privileges authorial intention over unintentional revelation, and the ontological over the historical, he sees Conrad as continually examining "the encounter between abstraction and concreteness, darkness and illumination," which permits him to read the darkness of *Heart of Darkness* as an image of truth.[15] He offers a differently inflected reception of the same text in *Culture and Imperialism* (1993), perceiving narrative form, trope, and language as inseparable from their historical roots and political resonances and attributing the darkness disparaged by Conrad, Marlow, and Kurtz to a non-European world "*resisting* imperialism" by withholding its own meanings from the invaders: "One must connect the structures of a narrative to the ideas, concepts and experiences from which it draws support. Conrad's Africans ... come from a huge library of *Africanism* ... as well as from Conrad's personal experiences. What we have in *Heart of Darkness* ... is a politicized, ideologically saturated Africa ... far from *Heart of Darkness* and its image of Africa being 'only' literature, the work is extraordinarily caught up in, is indeed an organic part of, the 'scramble for Africa' that was contemporary with Conrad's composition."[16]

In an interview during the last year of his life, Said's persistent sensitivity to imponderables and mysteries was to the fore. He reiterated the novel's political dimensions and contemporary relevance (pointing to Conrad's encyclopedic description of the world of empire, his portrait of a continent, his "relentlessly open-ended, aggressively critical inquiry into the mechanisms and presuppositions and situatedness and abuses of imperialism"). But these perceptions coexist in his comments with a pronounced regard for the writer's "metaphysical radicalism," his responsiveness to the primordial, his confrontation with intangibles, and the way he was able to connect the historical world with what he saw and understood "impressionistically but in a sense more profoundly, as part of some conjunction between nature, the human mind, and more abstract forces like 'will' and the 'unconscious.'"[17]

Variations in perception are also registered in Said's analyses of *Nostromo*. In his 1975 study *Beginnings: Intention and Method,* he warns against readings that "overemphasize its political dimension," and argues that "instead of mimetically authoring a new world *Nostromo* turns back to its beginnings as a novel, to the fictional, illusory assumption of reality; in thus overturning the confident edifice that novels normally construct *Nostromo* reveals itself to be no more than a record of novelistic self-reflection."[18] Subsequently Said was to discover that the novel's edifice was built of historical and political materials, whereas in a late commentary, when his criticism leaned toward an interest in "the meta-poetic work ... that turns on questions of the medium itself," he joined his acknowledgment of *Nostromo* as "the great novel of empire and imperial arrogance" to an appraisal of its autonomy:

"But the other fact about the book, which I think is more interesting, is an aesthetic fact that stands against contemporary history in an Adornian way ... what Conrad is attempting in *Nostromo* is a structure of such monumental solidity that it has an integrity of its own quite without reference to the outside world. Though this is only a speculation, I think that halfway through the book it's as if Conrad loses interest in the real world and becomes fascinated with the workings of his method and his own writing."[19]

Said is appreciative of the novel's having "an integrity quite of its own," but in the same interview he also says that works about "withdrawal from the world into an aesthetic project" must necessarily register the failure of this project; and elsewhere he stresses the need for "elucidating relationships between books and the world they belonged to."[20] This statement suggests that he was also concerned with literature's autonomy and its worldliness but did not need to repeat the dialectical reversal effected by Adorno: "There is no material content, no formal category of artistic creation, however mysteriously transmitted and itself unaware of the process, which did not originate in the empirical reality from which it breaks free."[21] If there appear to be intimations of sympathy with artistic disengagement, these are offset by acknowledgment of art's genesis in the base zone; indeed, in his role as an embattled public intellectual Said did not cease to pour out essays, articles, books, and addresses analyzing, exposing, and protesting Israel's messianic colonialism and America's violent imperial interventions.[22] Yet whereas these intercessions confirm belief in the necessity of agency, opposition, and political action (see "On Lost Causes" in *Reflections on Exile* and "Traveling with Conrad," for example), they are coextensive with his last critical meditations, where the will to confront, struggle against, and overcome the fissures and oppressions within the world is accompanied by an inconsolable but not demoralized intellectual pessimism, matching that of Adorno, who had become another major presence in Said's intellectual life and whose thoughts on "late style" had a profound influence on Said's own articulations of "lateness."[23]

. . .

In this journey, the route and destination of his interpretation of Adorno's theories were determined by Said's own purposes and preferences.[24] These, I suggest, were contingent on a deliberated disengagement from Marxism: as he wrote in the early 1980s, "Criticism modified in advance by labels like 'Marxism' or 'liberalism' is in my view an oxymoron ... the dictum, 'solidarity before criticism' means the end of criticism ... I have been more influenced by Marxists than by Marxism or any other *ism*."[25] Although a formal resistance to recognizing Marxism as inherently and inescapably *critical* was countermanded in practice at this time by Said's explications of key Marxist concepts (such as totality and dialectical thinking) in the work of Lukács, Goldmann, and Raymond Williams, this judicious detachment did not persist.[26] In subsequently dismissing "the dialectic between opposed factors" in the theories of Hegel and Marx as routinely resulting "in synthesis, resolution, transcendence, or *Aufhebung*," Said conflated the mechanistic form favored by Stalinism with other versions and misattributed closure to *Aufhebung*—a concept where negation and preservation, denial and affirmation remain bound together, hence denoting not concord and completion but the dynamics of further, endless, and always irreconcilable contradiction.[27]

Ironically the work that has focused my attempts to think about the overt avoidance of dialectics in Said's intellectual project is one whose premises I find unconvincing. The thesis of Abdirahman Hussein's learned but formulaic book *Edward Said: Criticism and Society* follows Said in dismissing dialectics as the "relatively smooth, predictable and straightforward sublation à la Hegel and Marx" and commends Said for activating a confrontation between "agonistic dialectic and archaeology/genealogy." Such moments, Hussein maintains, dramatize a conflictual "either/or transaction" instantiating "a multiplicity of disjunctions, torsions, and oppositions"; the agonism of this dialectic is to be understood not just existentially but in "logical, epistemological, historical and ethico-political terms."[28] Hussein's negligent disposal of Marxist dialectics is matched by an endorsement of Said's methodology that rests on an incoherent alignment of concepts: the agonistic and transactional are distinct from the conflictual, whereas either/or is a static construct, indicating a choice between unchanging categories rather than a dialectical interaction effecting the dynamic alteration of both. However instrumental Hussein's account of Said's critical practice may be, it does throw light on Said's circumvention of dialectics, a practice more appropriately characterized as "a ceaseless generation and dissolution of intellectual categories."[29]

Convinced that Marxism belonged with "the German idealist tradition of synthesizing the antithetical," Said was able to disregard the caveat of Adorno's "negative dialectics," which, to cite Fredric Jameson, has no choice but "to affirm the notion and value of an ultimate synthesis, while negating its possibility and reality in every concrete case that comes before it."[30] Indifferent to the strategy of "dialectical reversals," Said could claim Adorno as an unequivocal defendant of the rights of the aesthetic by dispensing with Adorno's understanding that the historicity of an art work is a presence that is cancelled and restored.[31] "It is precisely as artifacts, as products of social labour that they [works of art] . . . communicate with the empirical experience that they reject and from which they draw their content. Art negates the categorical determinations stamped on the empirical world and yet harbours what is empirically in its own substance. If art opposes the empirical through the element of form—and the mediation of form and content is not to be grasped without their differentiation—the mediation is to be sought in the recognition of aesthetic form as sedimented content."[32]

Because of Said's reductive construction of dialectics, he necessarily refrained from naming Adorno's thinking as dialectical, even while pressing an association with Adorno's practice and delivering glosses attuned to his thought processes. Said understood that the cataclysmic vision disseminating Adorno's interpretations of Beethoven's third period emanated from a perception of "the fractured" objective landscape of a degenerated bourgeois revolution, whose earlier spirit and highest achievement Beethoven had once incarnated and against which the last compositions came to stand: "In the history of art late works are the catastrophes."[33] Elaborating on this point, Said wrote that for Adorno Beethoven's late style constituted "a moment when the artist who is fully in command of his medium nevertheless abandons communication with the bourgeois order of which he is a part and achieves a contradictory, alienated relationship with it . . . Thus late-style Beethoven presides over music's rejection of the new bourgeois order."[34] So too Said fully grasped the implications of Adorno's "rule of thumb that in the contemporary world cultural forms that appear most distant from society—for example the lyric, and dodecaphonic music—are the best places to see the imprint as well as the distortions of society upon the subject."[35]

Indeed, Adornian insights entered Said's own reading of Lampedusa's *The Leopard*, where he represents the Prince's consciousness of "death, decay and decrepitude" as inseparable from "social disintegration, the failure of revolution" and "a sterile and unchanging [Italian] South." However, observations of the historical infusions into the individual experience of decline are moderated by Said's empathetic attention to the Prince's personal pessimism of both intellect and will, his unrepentantly individualist dismissal of "whatever is melioristic, whatever promises development and real change," his refusal of "the supposed serenity or maturity" of old age, his rejection of redemption.[36] In these comments are echoes of an element that Said considered quintessential to the proper articulations of the "provocations, intransigence, contradictions and mystifyingly unsatisfactory conclusions" of "late style." Where Adorno held that the degradations of the social world compel artists to inscribe disappointment in the very form of their late work, Said attributed the characteristics of late style to the imprint of existential experience: "The phenomenon of late style is something I have been studying for some time, since it concerns the way in which writers confront mortality in their last works, and how a separate, individualistically inflected late style . . . emerges accordingly. A striking difference is to be observed between two types of late work: those . . . in which resolution and reconciliation occur, and those . . . in which all the contradictions and unresolved antinomies of life are left standing, untouched by any sort of autumnal mellowness."[37]

Lateness, he wrote apropos Adorno and self-reflexively, "is being at the end, fully conscious, full of memory, and also very (even preternaturally) aware of the present"; and he sees Adorno "as lateness itself . . . as scandalous, even catastrophic commentator on the present . . . One has the impression reading Adorno that what he looked for in style was the evidence he found in late Beethoven of sustained tension, unaccommodated stubbornness, lateness and newness next to each other by virtue of an 'inexorable clamp that holds together what no less powerfully strives to break apart.'"[38]

Because critical interpretations of Adorno are so dissimilar, Said cannot be faulted for disposing of Adorno's thinking in the interest of elaborating his own apprehension of late style; however, when he seeks to detach Adorno from Marxism by disputing Jameson's location of his lateness within Marxist thought, more appears to be at stake: "My reading of Adorno, with his reflections about music at its centre, sees him as injecting Marxism with a vaccine so powerful as to dissolve its agitational force almost completely. Not only do the notions of advance and culmination in Marxism crumble under his rigorous negative scorn, but so too does anything which suggests movement at all."[39]

Whatever else we can infer from this cryptic passage in an essay of 1995—is he criticizing Adorno for draining Marxism of its "agitational force" and its commitment to "movement," or is he approving Adorno's "negative scorn"?—the use of words relating to immunization against disease suggests to me recoil from an analytic system that to him practiced a smooth and straightforward progression in thought processes and predicted inevitable progress toward a desirable end state of harmony in the real world.[40] Although the tensions within Said's later writings, with their condensation of incommensurable stances, make them the most resistant to generalizing propositions, one cannot overlook his frequent articulations of hostility to notions of reconciliation, organic wholeness, and happy ends, already apparent earlier in his disdain for "the revolutionary optimism" of Lukács's "Marxist faith" that culminates in a "revolutionary vision of 'totality.'"[41] Yet this repudiation of concordance is incompatible with Said's subsequent appreciation of Auerbach and his peers for choosing "to overcome bellicosity and what we now call 'the clash of civilizations' with a welcoming, hospitable attitude of humanistic knowledge designed to realign warring cultures in a relationship of mutuality and reciprocity."[42] In turn, the disparagement of utopian aspirations revokes a previous and repeated attestation of the harmonic universalism envisioned by Césaire in the climatic moment of *Cahier d'un retour*: "no race possesses the monopoly of beauty, of intelligence, of force, and there is a place for all at the rendez-vous of victory."[43]

· · ·

The culminating moment of Said's "middle period" was the publication of *Culture and Imperialism*. Advancing "a contrapuntal perspective" on the overlapping histories of oppressor and oppressed, the book reveals its impossibility; proceeding from optimistic premises, the study registers their frustration. Because of a fondness for contrapuntalism as a signifier of the unexpected and arresting juxtaposition of incongruent concepts and disparate categories, Said heard in Adorno's work not a contest between incommensurables but "a contrapuntal voice intertwined with fascism, bourgeois mass society, and communism, inexplicable without them, always critical and ironic about them."[44] In the term *contrapuntal*, Said substitutes a more neutral and inert notion for the turbulent energies of contradiction conceived in a dialectic process, which as Lukács wrote, is "more than the interaction of *otherwise unchanging objects*."[45] Of Said's methodology Asha Varadharajan has maintained that "the antidialectical nature of Said's arguments as well as [of] his predilection for contrapuntal analysis" explains his "comfortable residence in contradictions that complement rather than destroy each."[46] This assessment of Said's "static" positioning of poles rather than their reciprocal or dialectical mediation is confirmed in Said's comments in 2003 that Palestinian and Israeli claims were a "clash of oppositions . . . sustained by history and reality—as opposites. So the genius of the situation is that there might be some mode of sustainment—not in a state of extremism and impossibly aggressive opposition. But rather in some state, however irreconcilable the elements, of maintained coexistence, without minimizing the extremes and antagonisms involved. . . . It points to a musical metaphor of one sort or another—the contrapuntal for example—rather than a grand Hegelian solution of synthesis."[47] Since this musical phrase rather than dialectics indicates the combination of two or more independent themes into a single texture, can it do the work of thinking about antagonistic, indeed warring, social processes? It is the benign term *contrapuntal*, not Said's *practice*, that allowed Paul Bové to assert in his 1993 review of *Culture and Imperialism* that Said "takes up Auerbach's defense of a culture in which humanity, fully marked by historical and experiential difference, nonetheless forms itself in reconciliation . . . Reconciliation is a creative effort, a narrativization of overlapping experiences."[48] This verdict runs counter to the irreconcilable conflicts Said encounters and confronts in the book, which render a contrapuntal methodology nugatory. If Said set out to "think through and interpret together experiences that are discrepant" and to understand the interdependence of colonizer and colonized, then these affirmations are repeatedly interrupted by observations of inequality, coercion, and contest, of the "fundamental ontological distinctions," the absolute discrepancy in power, the withholding of mutuality, the codification of difference. For running like a fissure through the "imperialist ensemble," Said writes, "is the principle of domination and resistance based on the division between the West and the rest of the world." The contradictions in recommending contrapuntal readings of colonialism become apparent when Said concurs with those scholars writing from within the once-colonized worlds, who have described colonial control as "almost total" and "in devastating continuous conflict" with the colonized: "To tell the narrative of how a continuity is established between Europe and its peripheral colonies is therefore impossible, whether from the European or the colonial side." And countermanding the many gestures to hope inscribed in *Culture and Imperialism*, Said in the last section of the book makes this melancholy remark: "History . . . teaches us that domination breeds resistance, and that the violence inherent in the imperialist contest—for all its occasional profit and pleasure—is an impoverishment for both sides."[49] In these words he undoes the facile notion of complicity between colonizer and colonized that has become a commonplace in postcolonial studies.

For all the criticism *Culture and Imperialism* has generated from critics appreciative of his work, it remains—in its engaged scholarship and resolute materialism—a landmark anticolonial book written on the fringes of but outside that tradition of thought that has done most to explain modern empire as integral to capitalism's beginnings and global entrenchment.[50] Said's was the long view of "imperialism" as "the practice, the theory and the attitude of a dominating centre ruling a distant territory," and because his interest was in the formation of ideologies underwriting a European hegemony, the study is not concerned with differentiating between mercantile-plantation colonialism, which stimulated the accumulation of capital in Europe, and the subsequent industrial-military interventions of metropolitan nation-states in overseas territories, an era known to historians and political scientists as "imperialism" and austerely described by Rosa Luxemburg as "the political expression of the accumulation of capital in its competitive struggle for what remains still open of the non-capitalist environment."[51] Said wrote with passionate intensity about imperial aggression without referring to the analysis of Lenin or Luxemburg; he distinguished between anticolonial nationalism and liberation movements without alluding to the communist orientation of the latter or the class interests of either; and he placed economic and political machinery and territorial aggrandizement at the center of modern empire without specifying capitalism's world system. At the same time he cited adherents of the Marxist critique such as Aimé Césaire, Fanon, C. L. R. James, Eqbal Ahmad, Amilcar Cabral, and Walter Rodney with respect, embracing them as comrades in the struggle against colonialism.

When faced with the historical realities of a violent colonialism, Said wrote against the grain of the "contrapuntal perspective" he had proposed; toward the end, he replaced the notion of the interdependence of disjunctive concepts or experiences or aspirations with one of stationary coexistence. Of Freud's *Moses and Monotheism* he wrote in 2003: "Everything about the treatise suggests not resolution and reconciliation . . . but, rather more complexity and a willingness to let irreconcilable elements of the work remain as they are: episodic, fragmentary, unfinished."[52] And in an interview in the year of his death, he said, "I draw the distinction between late works that are about reconciliation, about the final work . . . where the artist has this vision of wholeness, of putting everything together, of reconciling conflict . . . versus another late style, which is the one I'm interested in, which is the opposite: where everything gets torn apart and instead of reconciliation there's a kind of nihilism and a kind of tension that is quite unique."[53]

In affirming discontent and dissonance, disobedience and insubordination, in this passage, Said reiterates his position as a nonconformist and a dissident. Is he here exercising a critical consciousness that spurns imaginary solutions to real conflicts and refuses the solace of utopian expectations? Or is this declaration an abnegating gesture, which in a dialectical reversal becomes affirmative by intimating incompletion not as a sign of failure but of futurity, of history as having no ending? For we are left with the awareness that the allusive expressions of disappointment were concurrent with writings and speeches that overtly excoriated the actions driven by an imperial worldview, protested the inflictions endured by the dispossessed, and testified to a conviction in political engagement. Adorno had declared that "in the history of art, late works are the catastrophes"; and of Adorno Said had self-reflexively written, "Lateness is being at the end, fully conscious, full of memory, and also very (even preternaturally) aware of the present." Like Adorno, Said was a mandarin exiled from his milieu by the untimeliness of his own elite tastes and by contempt for the hegemonic ethos. Perhaps, then, Said was taking on the role he had assigned to Adorno of a "scandalous, even catastrophic commentator on the present."[54] If so, we can hear his own late utterances not as the voice of retreat from persistent and unresolved contradictions but as that of righteous indignation at a disgraceful world.

NOTES

My thanks to Tim Brennan, Laura Chrisman, Priya Gopal, and Neil Lazarus for their questions, not all of which I have been able to answer.

1. Edward W. Said, introduction to Eric Auerbach's *Mimesis*, in *Humanism and Democratic Criticism* (New York: Columbia University Press, 2004), 96.

2. Edward W. Said, "Opponents, Audiences, Constituencies, and Community," in *Reflections on Exile and Other Literary and Cultural Essays* (2000; repr., London: Granta Books, 2001), 119.

3. Edward W. Said, "From Silence to Sound and Back Again," in *Reflections on Exile*, 526.

4. See especially Abdirahman Hussein, *Edward Said: Criticism and Society* (London: Verso, 2002). A more nuanced position on the consistency of Said's work is taken by Tim Brennan, who while allowing that there were changes of view and different emphases over time, considers that in *Beginnings* Said "staked out all the motifs, including the political outlooks, of subsequent decades" (personal correspondence).

5. Edward W. Said, "Traveling with Conrad: An Interview with Edward Said," conducted by Peter Mallios on 28 February 2003, in *Conrad in the Twenty-First Century*, ed. Carola Kaplan, Peter Mallios, and Andrea White (London: Routledge, 2005), 300. One critic attentive to this shift toward aesthetics is Tim Lawrence, "Edward Said, Late Style and the Aesthetic of Exile," *Third Text*, Spring 1997, 15–24.

6. Said, "Traveling with Conrad," 300.

7. Edward W. Said, *Conrad and the Fiction of Autobiography* (Cambridge, MA: Harvard University Press, 1966), 7; Said, introduction to *Mimesis*, 92.

8. See Edward W. Said, "Between Worlds," in *Reflections on Exile*, 560.

9. Edward W. Said, "Secular Criticism," in *The World, the Text, and the Critic* (1982; repr., London: Faber, 1984), 3, 4, 5 (page numbers from the 1982 edition).

10. Edward W. Said, *Culture and Imperialism* (New York: Vintage, 1994), 303.

11. Edward W. Said, "Culture and Imperialism," interview by Joseph A. Buttigieg and Paul A. Bové, in *boundary 2*, 1993, in *Power, Politics, and Culture: Interviews with Edward W. Said*, ed. Gauri Viswa-

nathan (New York: Pantheon Books, 2001), 192–93. Scorning accommodation and contemptuous of the generation of artists and intellectuals who had volunteered to serve in the cold war, and whose heirs today are apologists for the violent foreign policies of the United States, Said urged, "There is a special duty to address the constituted and authorized powers of one's own society." He further observed that a political world "animated by considerations of power and interest writ large . . . as Marx so fatefully said, take the intellectual from relatively discrete questions of interpretation to much more significant ones of social change and transformation." *Representations of the Intellectual: The 1993 Reith Lectures* (London: Vintage, 1994), 72, 82.

   12. See Edward W. Said, "Traveling Theory," in *The World, the Text, and the Critic* (1982), and "Traveling Theory Reconsidered" (2000), in *Reflections on Exile*, 436–52.

   13. Said, introduction to *Mimesis*, 117.

   14. Said, *Conrad and the Fiction of Autobiography*, 7, 12, 137, 138.

   15. Ibid., 147.

   16. Ibid., 33, 79, 80.

   17. Said, "Traveling with Conrad," 288.

   18. Edward W. Said, *Beginnings: Intention and Method* (New York: Columbia University Press, 1985), 134, 137.

   19. On Said's evolving view of the historical and political foundations of the novel, see *Culture and Imperialism*. Quotes are from Said, "Traveling with Conrad," 285, 293.

   20. Said, "Traveling with Conrad," 286; Said, introduction to *Mimesis*, 87.

   21. Theodor Adorno, "Adorno on Brecht," in *Aesthetics and Politics*, by Theodor Adorno, Walter Benjamin, Ernst Bloch, Bertolt Brecht, and Georg Lukács (London: New Left Books, 1977), 190: "Works of art that react against empirical reality obey the forces of that reality, which reject intellectual creations and throw them back on themselves." See also Adorno, "Cultural Criticism and Society," in *Prisms*, trans. Samuel Weber and Sherry Weber (Cambridge, MA: MIT Press, 1967): "They [art and philosophy] have always stood in relation to the actual live-process of society from which they distinguished themselves" (23).

   22. Edward W. Said, "The Public Role of Writers and Intellectuals" (2001), in *Humanism and Democratic Criticism*, 119–44.

   23. Edward W. Said, "On Lost Causes," in *Reflections on Exile*, 527–53; Said, "Traveling with Conrad," 290, 291.

   24. In "The Adorno Files," Andrew Rubin cites Said's address, "An Unresolved Paradox," in the MLA *Newsletter*, Summer 1999: "Would it be more appropriate to teach and read *The Tempest* as a play mainly about modern colonialism . . . or as a late play of reconciliation and departure with Shakespeare's oeuvre?" Rubin remarks, "What some might find unexpected about Said's affiliation with Adorno is that Said has emphasized precisely those aspects of Adorno's writing that are in fact most critical of certain forms of political commitment." In *Adorno: A Critical Reader*, ed. Nigel C. Gibson and Andrew Rubin (Oxford: Blackwell 2002), 185, 186.

   25. Said, "Secular Criticism," 28. More than a decade ago Michael Sprinker referred to Said's slighting of Marxism "as a coherent—if not unproblematically unified—system of thought and action," at the core of which is the notion and analysis of the capitalist *system*. Thus Sprinker notes that although Said made selective use of Marxist concepts and paradigms, he did so without foregrounding" the unity and consistency in thought that their political and methodological commitments impose." See Sprinker, "The National Question: Said, Ahmad, Jameson," *Public Culture* 6, no. 1 (1993–94). On Said and Marxism, see also Tim Brennan, "Places of Mind, Occupied Lands: Edward Said and Philology," in *Edward Said: A Critical Reader*, ed. Michael Sprinker (Oxford: Blackwell, 1992), 74–95.

   26. For Said's explication of Marxist ideas in these writers, see "Traveling Theory," 230–42.

   27. Quote from Said, "Traveling Theory Reconsidered," 438. Summary dismissals of dialectics may

send some readers to or back to contemporary Marxist exegeses of the concept. See Roy Bhaskar, "Dialectics," in *A Dictionary of Marxist Thought*, ed. Tom Bottomore (Oxford: Blackwell, 1991). Laurence Harris, V. G. Kiernan, and Ralph Miliband: "Any Marxian dialectic will be objectively conditioned, absolutely finitist and prospectively open (i.e. unfinished) . . . Marxist critical dialectics may perhaps best be understood as an empirically open-ended, materially conditioned and historically circumscribed, dialectical phenomenology" (146, 147).

28. Hussein, *Edward Said*, 4–5.

29. Frederic Jameson, *Marxism and Form: Twentieth-Century Dialectical Theories of Literature* (Princeton, NJ: Princeton University Press, 1971), 336. See also Jameson's *A Singular Modernity: Essays on the Ontology of the Present* (London: Verso, 2002), where he describes dialectics as "a conceptual coordination of incommensurables," which comes into being "as an attempt to hold the[se] . . . contradictory features of structural analogy and the radical differences in dynamic and in historical causality together within the framework of a single thought or language" (64, 65).

30. Said, "Between Worlds," 565; Jameson, *Marxism and Form*, 56.

31. The following passage from *Prisms* provides an example of Adorno's style: "A successful work . . . is not one that resolves objective contradictions in a spurious harmony, but one which expresses the idea of harmony negatively by embodying the contradictions, pure and uncompromised, in its innermost structure" (32).

32. Theodor Adorno, *Aesthetic Theory*, ed. Gretel Adorno and Rolf Tiedemann, trans. and ed. Robert Hullot-Kentor (London: Athlone Press, 1997), 5.

33. Theodor Adorno, "Late Style in Beethoven" (1937), *Raritan* 13 (1993): 107.

34. Edward W. Said, "Adorno as Lateness Itself," in *Apocalypse Theory and the Ends of the World*, ed. Malcolm Bull (Oxford: Blackwell, 1995), 268, 272. See also Martin Jay: "The particular 'catastrophe' in which Adorno was interested was the *Missa Solemnis*, which was unintelligible to most of [Beethoven's] first listeners. By returning to the seemingly archaic form of the religious mass, the composer, still himself a secular humanist, registered the failure of the bourgeois emancipation from its pre-enlightenment past. By disappointing the expectations of his audience, he registered the growing alienation of the artist from his public . . . Perhaps most significant of all, by abandoning the sonata form with its developing variation in favour of more static contrapuntal forms, he called into question the bourgeois subject's achievement of genuine autonomy." *Adorno* (Cambridge, MA: Harvard University Press, 1984), 144.

35. Edward W. Said, "The Future of Criticism" (1984), in *Reflections on Exile*, 166.

36. Edward W. Said, "Thoughts on Late Style," *London Review of Books* 26, no. 15 (5 August 2004): 5–6.

37. Said, "On Lost Causes," 540–41.

38. Said, "Adorno as Lateness Itself," 275.

39. Ibid., 272, 273. For Fredric Jameson, "No other Marxist theoretician has ever staged this relationship between the universal and the particular, the system and the detail, with this kind of single-minded yet wide-ranging attention . . . Adorno's life work stands or falls with the concept of 'totality,'" the instance being the economic system of late capitalism. *Late Marxism: Adorno, or the Persistence of the Dialectic* (London: Verso, 1990), 9.

40. This attribution of a triumphal route toward a unity within which opposition and antithesis are instantly resolved conforms neither with Lukács's concept of a totality or system that "does not reduce its various elements to an undifferentiated uniformity" nor with a dialectical process that takes place between the real and the theoretical: "When a totality is known they [the contradictions of capitalism] will not be transcended and *cease* to be contradictions . . . When theory (as the knowledge of the whole) opens up the way to resolving these contradictions it does so by revealing the real tendencies of social evolution. For these are destined to effect real resolution of the contradictions that have emerged in the course of history." See Georg Lukács, *History and Class Consciousness: Studies in Marxist Dialectics*, trans.

Rodney Livingstone (London: 1922; repr. London: Merlin Press, 1971), 10. Steven Best's analysis of the poststructuralist critique of totality sees this concept "as a contextualizing act which situates seemingly isolated phenomena within their larger relational context and draws connections [or mediations] between the different aspects of a whole." Best, "Jameson, Totality and the Poststructuralist Critique of Totality," in *Postmodernism/Jameson/Critique*, ed. Douglas Kellner (Washington, DC: Maisonneuve Press, 1989), 344. The notion of reciprocal interactions between uneven, autonomous instances within an open, untotalizable dialectical, dynamic, irredeemably heterogeneous and open-ended constellation is common in Marxist thought. As Henri Lefebvre proposed, it may be possible for these expressions "to be integrated into an open totality, perpetually in the process of being transcended." See *Dialectical Materialism*, trans. John Sturrock (1940; repr., London: Jonathan Cape, 1968), 111.

41. Said, "Traveling Theory Reconsidered," 437.

42. Said, introduction to *Mimesis*, 93.

43. For citations of these lines, see, for example, "Representing the Colonized" in *Culture and Imperialism*, 314; and "The Politics of Knowledge" (1991) in *Reflections on Exile*, 379.

44. Said, "Adorno as Lateness Itself," 278.

45. Lukács, *History and Class Consciousness*, 13 (italics in original). Of the *Missa Solemnis*, Adorno wrote, "The formal organization of the whole work is not that of a process developing through its own impetus—it is not dialectical—but seeks accomplishment by a balance of the individual sections, of the movements, through contrapuntal enclosure." In "Alienated Masterpiece: The *Missa Solemnis*" (1959), *Telos* 28 (Summer 1976): 113–24, quote on 117. See also "The Actuality of Philosophy" (1931): "The interpretation of given reality and its abolition are connected to each other, not . . . in the sense that reality is negated in the concept, but that out of the construction of a configuration of reality the demand for its real change always follows promptly. The change-causing gesture of the riddle process—not its resolution as such—provides the image of resolutions to which materialist praxis alone has access. Materialism has named this relationship with a name that is philosophically certified: dialectic. Only dialectically, it seems to me, is philosophic interpretation possible." Cited in Martin Jay, *Marxism and Totality: The Adventures of a Concept from Lukács to Habermas* (Berkeley: University of California Press, 1984), 258.

46. Asha Varadharajan, *Exotic Parodies: Subjectivity in Adorno, Said and Spivak* (Minneapolis: University of Minnesota Press, 1995), 135.

47. Said, "Traveling with Conrad," 301.

48. Paul Bové, "Hope and Reconciliation," *boundary 2* 20, no. 2 (1993): 274.

49. Said, *Culture and Imperialism*, 36, 129, 195, 60, 308, 348.

50. The disconnection of colonialism from capitalism in Said's work may have given comfort to postcolonial critics who wanted to represent empire as a cultural event or a discursive construct. So too Said's poignant meditations on the loss and satisfaction of exile have been appropriated for both a sanguine representation of the diasporic condition that appears unaware of its own elitism and a mindless celebration of nomadism that occludes the experiences and aspirations of those—the majority of the world's populations—who cannot and would not choose displacement.

51. Rosa Luxemburg, *The Accumulation of Capital*, trans. Agnes Schwarzschild (1913; repr., London: Routledge and Kegan Paul, 1951), 446.

52. Edward W. Said, *Freud and the Non-European* (London: Verso, 2003), 28.

53. Said, "Traveling with Conrad," 285.

54. Edward W. Said, *On Late Style: Music and Literature against the Grain* (New York: Vintage, 2007), 14.

CONTRIBUTORS

BILL ASHCROFT is professor of English at the University of New South Wales, Australia, and chair of the English department at the University of Hong Kong. His book *The Empire Writes Back*, coauthored with Gareth Griffiths and Helen Tiffin, was the first text to examine systematically the field now known as postcolonial studies. His publications include *The Postcolonial Studies Reader* (1995), *The Gimbals of Unease: The Poetry of Francis Webb* (1997), *Key Concepts in Post-colonial Studies* (1998), *Edward Said: The Paradox of Identity* (1999), *Edward Said* (2001), *Post-colonial Transformation* (2001), *On Post-colonial Futures* (2001), and *Caliban's Voice* (2008).

BEN CONISBEE BAER is assistant professor of comparative literature at Princeton University. He works on Bengali literature and other literatures of South Asia, modernism, Marxism, and postcolonial criticism. He is completing the forthcoming book *Vanguard and Voice: Modernism and the Colonial World, 1920s–1940s*. He is also translating from Bengali Tarashankar Bandopadhyay's 1947 classic novel *Hansuli Banker Upakatha* (The Tale of Hansuli Turn), forthcoming from Columbia University Press in 2010.

DANIEL BARENBOIM made his debut as a pianist in Vienna and Rome in 1952 and completed his first gramophone recordings in 1954 at the age of twelve. In 1991, he succeeded Sir Georg Solti as music director of the Chicago Symphony Orchestra. Barenboim has been the longtime music director of the *Staatsoper Unter den Linden* (Berlin State Opera) and the Berlin Staatskapelle. Today he is considered one of the preeminent musicians and conductors of the late twentieth and early twenty-first centuries. Barenboim and Edward Said met in the early 1990s and collaborated on musical events to further their shared vision of peaceful coexistence in the Middle East. This collaboration inspired Barenboim's first concert on the West Bank, a piano recital at the Palestinian Birzeit University in February 1999. Said and Barenboim later founded the West-Eastern Divan Workshop and Orchestra and through the Barenboim-Said Foundation, Barenboim continues to organize and promote music and cooperation through projects targeted at young Arab and Israeli musicians. Barenboim and Edward Said jointly received Spain's prestigious Prince of Asturias Concord Prize for their work in founding the West-Eastern Divan Workshop. Barenboim is the author of *A Life in Music*, and with Edward Said, *Parallels and Paradoxes: Explorations in Music and Society*, a series of conversations between the two authors. In January 2005, Barenboim delivered the first Edward Said Lecture at Columbia University, and in 2006, he was the first musician to deliver the prestigious BBC Reith Lectures.

TIMOTHY BRENNAN is professor of comparative literature and English at the University of Minnesota. His essays on literature, cultural politics, American intellectuals, and colonialism have appeared in numerous publications, including the *Nation*, the *Times Literary Supplement*, *New Left Review*, *Critical Inquiry*, and the *London Review of Books*. His recent books include *Wars of Position: The Cultural Politics of Left and Right* (2006) and *Secular Devotion: Afro-Latin Music and Imperial Jazz* (2008).

NOAM CHOMSKY is Institute Professor and professor of linguistics (emeritus) in the Department of Linguistics and Philosophy at the Massachusetts Institute of Technology, where he has taught since 1955. He has written and lectured widely on linguistics, philosophy, intellectual history, contemporary issues, international affairs, and U.S. foreign policy. One of the most influential thinkers of the last half century, Chomsky has received honorary degrees from twenty-two universities worldwide and is the recipient of many awards, including the Distinguished Scientific Contribution Award (American Psychological Association), the Kyoto Prize in Basic Sciences, the Helmholtz Medal, and the Dorothy Eldridge Peacemaker Award. He has written more than fifty books, including: *Cartesian Linguistics; Language and Mind; Peace in the Middle East?; Reflections on Language; The Political Economy of Human Rights*, Vols. 1 and 2; *Rules and Representations; Fateful Triangle; On Power and Ideology; Language and Problems of Knowledge; Manufacturing Consent; Necessary Illusions; The New Military Humanism; Rogue States; Failed States; 9–11; Understanding Power, Failed States, Hegemony or Survival; Perilous Power;* and *Interventions*.

NICHOLAS B. DIRKS is professor of anthropology and history and vice president for arts and sciences at Columbia University, where he specializes in South Asian history, historical anthropology, and British imperial history. His publications include *The Hollow Crown: Ethnohistory of an Indian Kingdom* (1993); as editor, *Colonialism and Culture* (1992); as editor, *In Near Ruins: Cultural Theory at the End of the Century* (1998); "Is Vice Versa? Historical Anthropologies and Anthropological Histories" (1996); "Colonial Histories and Native Informants: Biography of an Archive" (1993); and "Castes of Mind" (1992). *Castes of Mind: Colonialism and the Making of Modern India* was published in 2001. His most recent book is *The Scandal of Empire: India and the Creation of Imperial Britain* (2006).

MARC H. ELLIS is University Professor of Jewish studies and director of the Center of Jewish Studies at Baylor University in Texas. He has lectured and traveled extensively throughout the world and is the author of more than twenty books. His *Toward a Jewish Theology of Liberation* (2004) is now in its third edition. Among his other books are *Unholy Alliance: Religion and Atrocity in Our Time* (1997) and *Out of the Ashes: The Search for Jewish Identity in the Twenty-First Century* (2003). Most recently, he authored *Reading the Torah Out Loud: A Journey of Lament and Hope* (2007) and *Judaism Does Not Equal Israel* (2009).

ROKUS DE GROOT is a musicologist and composer. He conducts research on music of the twentieth and twenty-first centuries, especially on the systematics of composition, interactions between cultural traditions, and (re)conceptualizations of past and present religious and spiritual ideas. He holds the chair of musicology at the University of Amsterdam, after occupying a personal chair, Music in the Netherlands since 1600, at the University of Utrecht (1994–2000). He obtained his master's degree at the University of Amsterdam (with Frank Ll. Harrison and Ton de Leeuw) and his doctorate at the University of Utrecht (with Paul Op de Coul and Jos Kunst). Recently he composed dance music theater in which singers, musicians, and dancers from India, the Middle East, Europe, and the United States cooperate, such as *Song of Songs: The Love of Mirabai* (New Delhi 2005), and *Layla and Majnun: A Composition about the Night* (Amsterdam 2006). He maintains a musicology website at www.musicology.nl.

SABRY HAFEZ is research professor of modern Arabic and comparative literature at the School of Oriental and African Studies, University of London, and the editor of the bilingual cultural monthly *Al-Kalimah* (www.al-kalimah.com). He is the author of *The Genesis of Arabic Narrative Discourse: A Study in the Sociology of Modern Arabic Literature* (1993) and *The Quest for Identities: The Development of the Modern Arabic Short Story* (2007), as well as twenty other books in Arabic. He is the editor of numerous books and essays on Arabic language, literature, identity, and politics, including the multivolume *Longman Anthology of World Literature* (2004), and *Den Arabiske Verden Forteller* (1997).

ABDIRAHMAN A. HUSSEIN is the author of *Edward Said: Criticism & Society* (2002), a comprehensive, unified study of Edward Said's entire oeuvre, from his early writings on Conrad to his later works. In this analysis, Hussein places Said's work in the broader context of contemporary critical theory. He is currently writing a book expanding the purview of Said's "worldly" critique to mainstream Enlightenment thought and to modern Islam.

ARDI IMSEIS, barrister at law of Osgoode Hall, is field legal officer for the U.N. Relief and Works Agency for Palestine Refugees in the Near East, working in the West Bank Field Office in Jerusalem, Occupied Palestinian Territory. He is also editor in chief of the *Palestine Yearbook of International Law*. Imseis has taught public international law at Birzeit University and has lectured on international refugee law at Bethlehem University. His work has been published in numerous law reviews and journals, including the *American Journal of International Law*, the *Harvard International Law Journal*, the *Berkeley Journal of International Law*, and the *Oxford Journal of Legal Studies*. Imseis is a former Human Rights Fellow and Harlan Fiske Stone Scholar at the Columbia University School of Law and Canada Doctoral Fellow of the Social Sciences and Humanities Research Council.

ADEL ISKANDAR is a media scholar interested in postcolonial theory, international communication, and Arab diaspora. He has taught at the American University in Washington, D.C., and the University of Texas at Austin. Iskandar has lectured extensively worldwide, serving as a Visiting Fellow and master class teacher at the Center for Cultural Research at the University of Western Sydney and Visiting Scholar at Georgetown University. He is author and coauthor of several studies of media in the Arab world, including *Al-Jazeera: The Story of the Network That Is Rattling Governments and Redefining Modern Journalism* (with

Mohammed el-Nawawy, 2003). Iskandar teaches in the Center for Contemporary Arab Studies at Georgetown University.

GHADA KARMI is Research Fellow at the Institute of Arab and Islamic Studies, University of Exeter, England. She is a Palestinian, born in Jerusalem. Her books include *Jerusalem Today: What Future for the Peace Process?* (1996), *The Palestinian Exodus 1948–1998* (edited with Eugene Cotran), *In Search of Fatima: A Palestinian Story* (2002), and her most recent work, *Married to Another Man: Israel's Dilemma in Palestine* (2007).

KATHERINE CALLEN KING is professor of comparative literature and classics at the University of California, Los Angeles, and also teaches for the Women's Studies Program. Her two published books, *Achilles: Paradigms of the War Hero from Homer to the Middle Ages* and *Homer* (edited), reflect her scholarly interest in why and how a writer manipulates important cultural texts for ideological purposes. She has published many articles on both ancient and modern subjects and is currently working on two major projects: *Imaginary Women*, a cross-cultural analysis of female cultural archetypes; and *An Introduction to Ancient Epic*.

JOSEPH MASSAD is associate professor of modern Arab politics and intellectual history at Columbia University. He is author of *Colonial Effects: The Making of National Identity in Jordan* (2001), *The Persistence of the Palestinian Question* (2006), and *Desiring Arabs* (2007), the winner of the 2008 Lionel Trilling Award.

W. J. T. MITCHELL is professor of English and art history at the University of Chicago. He is editor of the interdisciplinary journal *Critical Inquiry*. A scholar and theorist of media, visual art, and literature, Mitchell focuses on the emergent fields of visual culture and iconology. His publications include *What Do Pictures Want?* (2005), *Picture Theory* (1994), *Art and the Public Sphere* (1993), *Landscape and Power* (1992), *Iconology* (1987), *The Language of Images* (1980), *On Narrative* (1981), and *The Politics of Interpretation* (1984).

LAURA NADER is professor of anthropology at the University of California, Berkeley. Her areas of interest include comparative ethnography of law and dispute resolution, conflict, comparative family organization, the anthropology of professional mind-sets, and the ethnology of the Middle East, Mexico, Latin America, and the contemporary United States. Nader has edited and published numerous essays and books on the anthropology of law, including *Law in Culture and Society* (1969), *The Disputing Process: Law in Ten Societies* (1978), *Harmony Ideology: Justice and Control in a Mountain Zapotec Village* (1990), *The Life of the Law: Anthropological Projects* (2002), *Energy Choices in a Democratic Society* (1980), and *Naked Science: Anthropological Inquiry into Boundaries, Power, and Knowledge* (1996).

DENISE DECAIRES NARAIN is a senior lecturer in English at the University of Sussex, where she teaches courses on postcolonial literature with an emphasis on Caribbean writers. She has also taught at the University of the West Indies and at the Open University. DeCaires Narain has published widely on Caribbean women's writing, including *Caribbean Women's Poetry: Making Style* and a forthcoming book on Olive Senior. She is currently pursuing a project on the figure of the servant in postcolonial women's writing.

ILAN PAPPE is professor of history at the University of Exeter and codirector of the Exeter Centre for Ethno-Political Studies. He is the author of, among others, *The Making of the Arab-*

Israeli Conflict (1992), *The Israel/Palestine Question* (1999), *A History of Modern Palestine* (2006), *The Modern Middle East* (2005), and *The Ethnic Cleansing of Palestine* (2006).

BENITA PARRY is professor of postcolonial studies in the English and Comparative Literature Department, University of Warwick, England. Parry has written on the literature of empire, colonial discourse, South African writing, liberation theory, and the trauma of modernity in the Third World (Fanon, Tayeb Salih). Her publications include *Delusions and Discoveries: India in the British Imagination* (1972, 1998), *Conrad and Imperialism* (1984), and *Postcolonial Studies: A Materialist Critique* (2004), on tendencies and directions in the postcolonial discussion. Parry is now participating in a collective project on the aesthetics of peripheral modernisms.

R. RADHAKRISHNAN is professor of English, Asian American studies, and comparative literature at the University of California, Irvine. He is the author of *Diasporic Mediations: Between Home and Location* (1996), *Theory in an Uneven World* (2003), *Between Identity and Location: The Cultural Politics of Theory* (2007), and *History, the Human, and the World Between* (2008) and has edited *Theory as Variation* (2006) and with Susan Koshy, *Transnational South Asians: The Making of a Neo-Diaspora* (2008); with Kailash Baral, *Theory after Derrida: Essays in Cultural Praxis* (2009). He is currently completing *Edward Said: A Contrapuntal Introduction* (forthcoming in 2010) and a collection of essays titled *When Is the Political?* He is also the author of a volume of poems in Tamil and a translator of contemporary Tamil fiction into English.

JAHAN RAMAZANI is Edgar F. Shannon Professor of English and department chair at the University of Virginia. He is the author of *Yeats and the Poetry of Death: Elegy, Self-Elegy, and the Sublime* (1990), *Poetry of Mourning: The Modern Elegy from Hardy to Heaney* (1994), *The Hybrid Muse: Postcolonial Poetry in English* (2001), and *A Transnational Poetics* (2009). He coedited the third edition of *The Norton Anthology of Modern and Contemporary Poetry* (2003) and the eighth edition of *The Twentieth Century and After*, of *The Norton Anthology of English Literature* (2006).

JACQUELINE ROSE is professor of English at Queen Mary, University of London. A founding signatory of Independent Jewish Voices in England, her most recent publications are *The Last Resistance* (2007), *The Question of Zion* (2005), *On Not Being Able to Sleep: Psychoanalysis in the Modern World* (2003), and the novel *Albertine* (2001). In 2002, she was writer and presenter of the Channel 4 British Television documentary *Dangerous Liaisons: Israel and USA*. She was also the respondent to Edward Said's *Freud and the Non-European*, published in 2003.

LECIA ROSENTHAL is assistant professor in the Department of English at Tufts University, where she teaches courses on modernism, psychoanalysis, and literary and critical theory. Her book *Mourning Modernism: Literature, Catastrophe, and the Politics of Consolation* is forthcoming from Fordham University Press.

HAKEM RUSTOM is completing a doctorate in social anthropology at the London School of Economics. His work focuses on the social history of Anatolian Armenians in republican Turkey and their migration to France since the 1970s.

AVI SHLAIM is a Fellow of St. Antony's College and professor of international relations at the University of Oxford. He held a British Academy Research Professorship in 2003–6 and

518   CONTRIBUTORS

was elected Fellow of the British Academy in 2006. His books include *Collusion across the Jordan: King Abdullah, the Zionist Movement, and the Partition of Palestine* (1988), *The Politics of Partition* (1990 and 1998), *War and Peace in the Middle East: A Concise History* (1995), *The Iron Wall: Israel and the Arab World* (2000), and *Lion of Jordan: The Life of King Hussein in War and Peace* (2007).

ELLA HABIBA SHOHAT teaches cultural studies and Middle Eastern studies at New York University. She has lectured and published extensively on issues of race, gender, Eurocentrism, Orientalism, postcolonialism, transnationalism, and diaspora, often transcending disciplinary and geographical boundaries. A substantial part of her work has examined theses issues in relation to the question of Arab Jews. Her books include *Taboo Memories, Diasporic Voices* (2006), *Israeli Cinema: East/West and the Politics of Representation* (1989), and *Talking Visions: Multicultural Feminism in a Transnational Age* (1998). With Robert Stam, she has coauthored *Unthinking Eurocentrism*, which won the Katherine Singer Kovacs Prize in 1994, and *Flagging Patriotism: Crises of Narcissism and Anti-Americanism* (2007); currently the coauthors are in the final stages of writing *The Culture Wars in Translation*. Her book *Le Sionisme vu par ses victimes juives: les juifs orientaux en Israel,* recently published by La fabrique editions (Paris), includes a new preface to a piece originally published as the opening essay of a special issue of *Social Text,* "Colonial Discourse," in 1988. Shohat has served on the editorial boards of several journals, including *Critique, Meridians,* and *Social Text,* for which she coedited a special issue dedicated to the memory of Edward Said.

ROBERT SPENCER is lecturer in postcolonial literature and culture at the University of Manchester. He has published articles in numerous journals and edited collections on subjects such as African fiction, postcolonial theory, the philosophy of modernism, and the work of Edward Said. He is currently working on a book on the relevance of cosmopolitan ideas to debates within postcolonial theory and literary criticism.

GAYATRI CHAKRAVORTY SPIVAK is the Avalon Foundation Professor in the Humanities and the director of the Center for Comparative Literature and Society at Columbia University. Her work focuses on the intersections of feminism, Marxism, deconstruction, and globalization. Spivak's numerous books include *Myself Must I Remake: The Life and Poetry of W. B. Yeats* (1974), *Of Grammatology* (a translation, with critical introduction, of Jacques Derrida's *De la grammatologie,* 1976), *In Other Worlds: Essays in Cultural Politics* (1987), *Selected Subaltern Studies* (ed., 1988), *The Post-Colonial Critic: Interviews, Strategies, Dialogues* (1990), *Thinking Academic Freedom in Gendered Post-Coloniality* (1993), *Outside in the Teaching Machine* (1993), *The Spivak Reader* (1995), *A Critique of Postcolonial Reason: Towards a History of the Vanishing Present* (1999), *Death of a Discipline* (2003), *Other Asias* (2005), and *Red Thread* (forthcoming). She is the author of such notable articles as "Subaltern Studies: Deconstructing Historiography" (1985), "Three Women's Texts and a Critique of Imperialism" (1985), "Can the Subaltern Speak?" (1988), "The Politics of Translation" (1992), "Righting Wrongs" (2003), "Ethics and Politics in Tagore, Coetzee, and Certain Scenes of Teaching" (2004), and "Translating into English" (2005).

ANASTASIA VALASSOPOULOS has been teaching world literatures at the University of Manchester since 2004. Her main area of research is the postcolonial literature and culture of the Middle East and North Africa. Her most recent publication is *Contemporary Arab Women*

Writers for the Routledge Research in Postcolonial Literatures series. She has also published articles on Tunisian film; Arab women writers such as Nawal el-Saadawi, Ahdaf Soueif and Hanan Al-Shaykh; and Arab popular culture, music, the graphic novel and Middle Eastern feminism. She is currently editing three special issues ("Arab Feminisms" for *Feminist Theory*, "Arab Cultural Studies" for the *Journal of Cultural Research*, and with coeditor Robert Spencer, "Responses to the War on Terror" for the *Journal of Postcolonial Writing*). She teaches widely in the field of postcolonial fiction and film.

ASHA VARADHARAJAN is associate professor of English at Queen's University in Canada. She is the author of *Exotic Parodies: Subjectivity in Adorno, Said, and Spivak* (1995). Her most recent publications include "The Unsettling Legacy of Harold Bloom's *Anxiety of Influence*" in *Modern Language Quarterly* (December 2008), "Afterword: 'The Phenomenology of Violence' and the 'Politics of Becoming'" in *Comparative Studies of South Asia, Africa, and the Middle East* (2008), and "'On the Morality of Thinking': Or Why Still Adorno" in *Adorno and the Need in Thinking*, ed. Donald Burke, Colin J. Campbell, Kathy Kiloh, Michael K. Palamarek, and Jonathan Short (University of Toronto Press, 2007). She is currently at work on two book-length manuscripts, *Violence and Civility in the New World Order* and *Enchantment and Deracination: The Lure of Foreignness in Contemporary Cinema*, and her essays on Nick Hornby, Eric Idle, and Hanif Kureishi appear in the *Dictionary of Literary Biography* (Bruccoli Clark Layman, 2009). Her writing and research encompass the biopolitics of citizenship, the globalization of culture, the conjunction of religion and violence, and the politics of representation in media and visual cultures.

MICHAEL WOOD is the Charles Barnwell Straut Professor of English and professor of comparative literature at Princeton University. He is the recipient of many fellowships and honors, including a National Endowment for the Humanities Fellowship, and is an ongoing Fellow of the New York Institute for the Humanities. He serves on the editorial board of *Kenyon Review*. Wood's works include books on Stendhal, Garcia Marquez, Nabokov, Kafka, and films. He is also a widely published essayist, with articles on film and literature in *Harper's*, the *London Review of Books*, the *New York Review of Books*, the *New York Times Book Review*, the *New Republic*, and others. His most recent book is *Literature and the Taste of Knowledge*. He edited Edward Said's final manuscript, *On Late Style* (2006).

INDEX

AAUG (Association of Arab American University Graduates), 177, 189n30
Abdel-Malik, Anwar, 89
"Abecedarium culturae" (Said), 56
Abu Ghraib, 380–81
Abu-Lughod, Ibrahim, 74, 171, 177, 188–89n30, 256
Abu-Lughod, Janet, 177
Abu Mazen, 311, 312
academe. *See* education; intellectuals
Achebe, Chinua, 10, 163, 300, 445–46
Adawiya, Ahmad, 196
Adonis, 178, 189n36, 190n56, 194
Adorno, Theodor W., 14, 159, 171, 176–77, 459n1, 511n31; *Aesthetic Theory*, 462; barbarism in European culture, 29; and capitalism, 407; catastrophe, 475–77, 485n32, 509, 511n34; contrapuntal voice, 506–7; dialectics, 177, 442, 503–7, 512n45; dissolver of identity, 471; on emancipation, 405; essay, 396; Eurocentrism, 214, 485n32; Hegelian tradition, 107, 116, 225n63; on home, 7, 364, 389, 390, 392, 410; lateness, 11, 201, 407–8, 463, 470–78, 484–87, 503, 505–6; "Late Style in Beethoven," 474–78, 485n31, 505–6; Lukács radicalized by, 44; Marxism, 506, 511n39; metaphysics, 422; music, 176, 201–5, 214, 220–22, 389, 407, 471–78, 484–87, 505–6, 512n45; *Philosophy of Modern Music*, 471, 478; politics, 177, 389, 510n24; on popular culture, 197; rebarbative language, 442, 483n4; resignation, 457; resistance, 465; Said as only true follower of, 6, 364, 483n10; Said performing, 44; on tradition, 97
"Adorno as Lateness Itself" (Said), 470–71, 476–78, 487n47, 505–6
AEI (American Enterprise Institute), 73
aesthetics, 9–10, 205, 494; Arab popular culture, 191–92, 200; and hybridity, 214; Lukács's *Aesthetik*, 113; music, 206, 211–13; and politics, 10–11, 159, 191–92, 200, 206. *See also* art
Aesthetic Theory (Adorno), 462
affiliation, 23–46, 428; cross-cultural, 164; dangerous, 104; filiation and, 23, 33–34, 38, 123, 484n16; othered women, 121–41; Palestine, 24, 33–34, 38, 147, 281; performance as, 44; politics and scholarship, 499
affirmative action, U.S., 347
al-Afghani, Jamal al-Din, 171
Afghanistan, sacrifice of innocent civilians, 28
Africa: decolonization, 164; France and Algeria, 337, 338; Jewish communities, 323. *See also* South Africa
African Americans, strategies of dissent, 323
African National Congress (ANC), 34, 268, 301, 313
After the Last Sky (Said), 13, 14, 159, 492; Mohr photos, 35–37, 39, 492; Palestinian subaltern, 56–57

colonialism *(continued)*
337, 339, 341, 347, 414. *See also* decolonization; imperialism; postcolonialism
Columbia University, 55, 58, 59, 242; comparative literature, 103, 108, 117n3, 234, 281;
November 2003 presentation honoring Said,
370; Said's "Last Works/Late Style" seminar,
487n47
Commentary, 335
The Commitments (Doyle), 163
communism, 43, 374, 508. *See also* Marxism
comparative analysis, 77–84
comparative literature, 280, 281; Columbia
University, 103, 108, 117n3, 234, 281;
hermeneutics, 10, 175–76, 398, 500; Lyon,
108; Said's studies, 9–10, 60–70, 93, 98,
102–20, 142, 144, 159–69, 175, 233, 281;
Sorbonne, 108; Zurich, 108. *See also* literary
criticism
*Comparative Literature in the Age of Multi-
culturalism* (Bernheimer), 109–10
completion, 61–62, 407
Conrad, Joseph, 9, 10, 60–63, 68, 97, 452; "Amy
Foster," 391; displacement, 175–76, 400;
Heart of Darkness, 10, 258–59, 396, 469,
501–2; *Joseph Conrad and the Fiction of Autobiography* (Said), 188n23, 391, 398–400,
415, 500, 501–2; *Lord Jim,* 66, 389; *Nostromo,*
501, 502–3; Said's doctoral thesis, 60, 175,
188n23; theory, 66
*Constantine's Sword: The Church and the Jews:
A History* (Carroll), 357
Constantinianism, 355, 357–60
contradiction, 63–64, 507, 511nn29,31,40
contrapuntal. *See* counterpoint
Cook, Captain, 92
"Copernican" Revolution, 416; Said as new,
414–30
Coronil, Fernando, 406
"*Così fan tutte* at the Limits" (Said), 471
cosmopolitanism: Saidian, 6, 11, 174, 391–92,
403–6, 439, 478–79. *See also* worldliness
"Counternarratives, Recoveries, Refusals"
(Marrouchi), 200

counterpoint, 11, 30, 466, 495, 506–8; Beethoven, 511n34; colonial, 39, 92, 507; *Culture
and Imperialism* (Said), 30, 506–7; defined,
209; dialectical, 495, 506–7; emancipation
and, 12; feminist, 122–23, 127; Freire, 21n76;
home, 123; humanism and, 445, 455; identity,

76; lack of, 208–9; literary, 105; *Moses and
Monotheism,* 478; and palimpsestic thinking,
455, 460n2; political, 6, 10, 229–46, 455;
responsibility, 210–11, 217; between traditions, 215–17
The Country without a Post Office (Ali), 166
Covering Islam (Said), 15, 178, 334, 415; Chomsky
and, 370–77; main point, 397–98; representation, 291, 293–94, 297
crimes: war, 257, 300, 328. *See also* terrorism
critical sociology, 324–25
criticism, 415–29, 443, 494, 499–512; Arab, 180–
83; Arab popular culture, 191–203; critical
consciousness, 24, 315–16, 409, 419, 427–
28, 432–34, 451, 500, 509; cultural, 97, 178,
181–83, 214, 380, 471, 485n32; dedomestica-
tion of, 415; democratic, 491, 492; domestication of, 463; essay form, 395–96; existential and phenomenological, 176; future of,
462–66; Kant, 419–23; media, 370–71;
music, 211–14, 471; *al-Naqd al-Tahqafi,*
181–82; New, 104, 107, 175, 176, 500; and
rational knowledge, 63, 398; before solidarity, 7, 11, 24, 150, 157nn66,67, 503;
"speaking truth to power," 23, 255–68, 491;
and theory, 180–81, 394–95; "uncanny," 62.
See also literary criticism; secular criticism
"Criticism between Culture and System" (Said),
437
Cromer, Lord, 145, 148, 153, 155n16, 157n60
The Crusades through Arab Eyes (Maalouf), 76,
77
Culler, Jonathon, 128
Cultural Anthropology, 96
cultural criticism, 97, 178, 181–83, 214, 380,
471, 485n32. *See also* literary criticism
"Cultural Politics" (Said), 191–92, 194, 199
cultural relativism, 125
culture concept, 95–97
Culture and Imperialism (Said), 14–15, 72,
97–99, 121, 321, 329, 415, 500; affiliations,
123; American self-deception, 167; Arab
intellectuals and, 181–82; Barenboim on,
233; Bové review, 507; colonizer/colonized,
15, 328, 501, 507–8; Conrad, 502; counterpoint, 30, 506–7; and decolonization, 160–61,
165; deconstruction, 58; history, 501; Israeli
challengers and, 326; limited engagement
with "native"/"local" cultures, 122; nativism,
122, 124; "A Note on Modernism," 469–70;
oppressors and victimizers/oppressed and

nomadic: celebration of, 59n4; Guattari's notion, 5; in music; 199, 207, 219; ontological, 6
nomadism: of exiled intellectual, 16; Saidian, 5–7, 17, 18n17, 59n4
nomadology, Deleuze and Guattari, 58, 59n4
Norris, Christopher, 338–39
Northwestern University, School of Criticism and Theory, 432, 437
Nostromo (Conrad), 501, 502–3
"A Note on Modernism" (Said), 469–70
Notes from the Underground (Dostoevsky), 439
novel, European, 68, 98
Nu'aimah, Mikha'il, 173

Obeyesekere, Gananath, 92–93
Occidentalism, 26, 27, 78–79, 111, 145–46
October 1973 War, 31, 177, 189n33, 323
oil: crisis/embargo (1970s), 31, 297; politics of states rich in, 34, 184, 189n36
Okigbo, Christopher, 163, 164
"The One-State Solution" (Said), 287
"On Jean Genet's Late Work" (Said), 471, 477, 481–82
On Late Style (Said), 463, 481, 482; "*Così fan tutte* at the Limits," 471; "On Jean Genet," 486n33; and popular culture, 201; post-humously published, 4, 186, 486–87n47; "Return to the Eighteenth Century," 471; stylistics of criticism, 11; Wood introduction, 4, 186
"On Repetition" (Said), 60, 73n3
operas, Da Ponte, 45–46
Ophir, Adi, 343
Orientalism, 86–101, 184–85, 333–34, 414; anti-Semitic, 30–35, 39, 327; *Arabian Nights*, 130–31; and decolonization, 160–61; dispossession, 305–6, 307; double gaze, 78–79; European, 25–28, 32–37, 93, 160, 291–98, 309, 324; failing to identify with human experience, 154n12; feminism and, 123–24, 125; German, 340; imperialism linked to, 80, 123, 309; India, 54, 91; Iraq, 294, 308, 325; toward Islam, 54, 74, 295, 297–98; Israeli, 322–26, 330, 337; al-Jabarti and, 76–77; of Lévinas, 55; "mature" version, 416; Ninth International Congress of Orientalists, 293; "orientalizing the Orient," 87, 94; origins, 292; otherness created by, 14, 54–55, 86–87, 98, 124, 126, 179, 292–94, 380–81; toward Palestinians, 30–37, 253, 295–99, 301–2, 324–25, 327; Right, 334; and servants, 126–29,

131; "social-science" approach, 142; Soueif's *The Map of Love*, 143, 153; from standpoint of victims, 21n75; travels, 25–28; Western projection, 25, 30–31, 160, 305, 324
Orientalism (Said), 3, 15, 25–30, 54, 56, 60, 77, 123, 253–54, 280, 291–98, 370, 414, 415, 434, 492; anthropology and, 86–101; and Arab culture, 28, 30, 126, 177–78, 180; Arabic translation, 178, 189n36; Barenboim and, 233, 234; Canadian students and, 2–3; and colonialism, 14–15, 86–101, 123, 292, 309; comparative literature, 110–15; "critical misreception," 410n2; current academic work and, 198; and decolonization, 160–61; and Foucault, 390, 396, 464–65, 490; Gerome's *The Snake Charmer* on the cover, 2; Gramsci influence, 93, 176; Hebrew reading, 338–40, 343; hope for unity, 145; introduction for thirtieth-anniversary edition of, 328–29; Islamist response to, 145–46, 178–79; Israeli challengers and, 326; Karmi and, 305; lasting impact, 201; main contention, 396–98; othering persisting afterward, 380–81; on Palestinian, 30–37, 253; and postcolonial studies, 9, 54, 60, 88, 89, 93, 97, 98, 178, 280, 321, 335–36, 390; published (1978), 3, 26, 28, 56, 60, 86, 93, 112, 145, 177–78; response to war, 107–9, 177; Shalaby copies, 2; signs of othering, 126; Soueif's *The Map of Love* and, 144–46; supremacist identity construction, 308; traditionalist response to, 178–79; traveling, 25–28; and women, 123–24, 125; on writers' imprints, 142
"Orientalism Reconsidered" (Said), 89
origins, beginnings distinguished from, 29–30, 33–34, 65, 394, 423–25, 493
Oslo Accords (1993)/Declaration of Principles on Interim Self-Governing Arrangements (DOP), 4, 261–68, 271; Arafat/PLO, 34, 147, 231, 235, 261, 265–68, 285–86, 287, 310, 384; Chomsky critique, 384; *From Oslo to Iraq and the Road Map* (Said), 262, 265, 266–67, 275–76n59, 406–7; Hatoum's art and, 39; Israel, 261–62, 275–76n59, 286–87, 383; Israeli leaders, 358; new beginnings, 33–34; Oslo II (1995), 286; post-Zionism and, 340–41; Said-Barenboim relationship, 230, 237; Said critique, 39, 147, 231, 285–87, 330, 383, 384, 386, 401, 402; and Said's commitment to the one-state/binational solution, 34, 271, 283, 286–87, 370, 384;

liberation from dogma of, 180–81, 432–33, 501; literary, 66–69, 107, 109–10, 115–17, 176, 188n28, 338–39; origins of, 445; simplification, 352n39. *See also* "traveling theory"

Theory and Criticism/Teoria veBikoret, 328, 330, 343–45, 352n37

Theory of Literature (Wellek and Warren), 106

Things Fall Apart (Achebe), 300

third space, 348

Third World, 84; Europe as creation of, 25, 97–98; hybridity and, 348; intellectuals' inauthenticity as spokespersons for, 334; liberation heroes, 405; postcolonial studies, 346; Said as, 414; U.S. public support, 381–82; women, 352n37. *See also* Orientalism; subalterns

Thomas, Nicholas, 96–97

Thompson, E. P., 110

A Thousand Plateaus (Deleuze and Guattari), 58

Through Arab Eyes, radio CKDU-FM, 3

time: alternative concept of, 214–15, 218–19; and Arab-Israeli conflict, 237–38. *See also* temporality

Time magazine, 300

Time and the Other (Fabian), 89

Title VI, U.S., 334, 373–74, 375, 388n16

Tocqueville, Alexis de, 247–48

Toscanini, Arturo, 44

totality, 463, 470, 486n39, 511n40; Foucault, 113; limit of, 466; lost, 486n43; Lukács, 113–14, 485n26, 506, 511n40; Marxist, 503, 506, 511–12nn39,40; music, 46, 214, 224, 407, 473, 476; public intellectualism, 79; Williams, 113; worldly, 466

Totality and Infinity (Lévinas), 55

"To Toussaint l'Ouverture" (Wordsworth), 392

Toughan, Ahmed, 1

Toward the Decolonization of African Literature, 164

tradition: Adorno on, 97; counterpoint between traditions, 215–17; countertradition, 212–15, 218; difference and, 217; gender and, 133–35; repressive, 8. *See also* countertradition

traditionalists, response to *Orientalism* (Said), 178–79

transformation, postcolonial, 294, 295, 298–302

transgression: music, 198–99, 207, 211, 219–21, 222–23nn28,29, 224n49, 226n81, 408; popular culture, 198–99

translation: *Culture and Imperialism* (Said), 189n36; *Orientalism* (Said), 178, 189n36,

343; Orientalist texts into Arabic, 146; *The Question of Palestine* (Said), 337, 338, 339, 351n22; Said for Arafat, 281, 284–85; Said in Israel and U.S., 333–53; Soueif's *The Map of Love* and, 152, 153

transnationalism, 104–5, 162–66

"traveling theory," 27–28, 42, 179–81, 333–34, 427–28, 501; degraded, 25; between Israel and U.S., 333–53; Orientalism, 25–28; postcolonial, 342–46, 348. *See also* displacement; translation

"Traveling Theory" (Said), 113, 180, 394

"Traveling Theory Reconsidered" (Said), 27, 44, 180

Trilling, Lionel, 67, 491

TriQuarterly, 56

Trotskyism, intellectuals and, 43

Truman, Harry, 374

truth: Israeli challengers and, 325; noncoercive forms, 438; representation and, 26, 84, 94–95, 292, 293; theory and, 66; truth/content axis, 432–33. *See also* "speaking truth to power"

Tsoffar, Ruth, 340

Tumarkin, Yigal, 338

al-Tunisi, Khayr al-Din, 179

Turgenev, Ivan, 153, 157n69

Turkey: Auerbach's wartime exile, 110; women, 81–84

Ummayad caliphs, 183

United Nations: Lebanon invasion (1982), 382; Palestine, 252, 261, 270, 271, 277n67, 280, 306; Security Council, 270, 406; Zionism equated with racism, 315

United States: affirmative action, 347; antihumanism, 490; Arab community, 172–74; civilization concepts, 28, 403; Clinton, 262–63, 285; cosmopolitan vision and, 406; Defense Department vision of scholarship, 335; as "dominant outside force," 121–22; immigration of European critical masters to, 104, 107; imperialism, 260–63, 369, 375, 414; indigenous people, 346; intellectuals, 73, 119n28, 334–53, 369–70, 510n11; language about Israel, 41; Left preparing way for *Orientalism,* 346; literary theory, 176, 188n28, 339; Marxism timid in, 113; media complicit with industrial-military-corporate system, 370–71; media representation of Muslims/Arabs, 13–14, 281–82, 297–301;

TEXT
10/12.5 Minion Pro

DISPLAY
Minion Pro (Open Type)

COMPOSITOR
Integrated Composition Systems

INDEXER
Barbara Roos

PRINTER AND BINDER
Maple-Vail Book Manufacturing Group